SECOND EDITION

Programming C#

Jesse Liberty

O'REILLY®

Beijing · Cambridge · Farnham · Köln · Paris · Sebastopol · Taipei · Tokyo

Programming C#, Second Edition
by Jesse Liberty

Published by O'Reilly & Associates, Inc., 1005 Gravenstein Highway North, Sebastopol, CA 95472.

O'Reilly & Associates books may be purchased for educational, business, or sales promotional use. Online editions are also available for most titles (*safari.oreilly.com*). For more information, contact our corporate/institutional sales department: (800) 998-9938 or *corporate@oreilly.com*.

Editor:	Valerie Quercia
Contributing Writer:	Brian Jepson
Production Editor:	Mary Brady
Cover Designer:	Ellie Volckhausen
Interior Designer:	David Futato

Printing History:

July 2001:	First Edition.
February 2002:	Second Edition.

Programming C#

Table of Contents

Part II.   Programming with C#

Part III.   The CLR and the .NET Framework

Preface

Every 10 years or so a new approach to programming hits like a tsunami. In the early 1980s, the new technologies were Unix, which could be run on a desktop, and a powerful new language called C, developed by AT&T. The early 90s brought Windows and C++. Each of these developments represented a sea change in the way you approached programming. Now, .NET and C# are the next wave, and this book is intended to help you ride it.

Microsoft has 'bet the company' on .NET. When a company of their size and influence spends billions of dollars and reorganizes its entire corporate structure to support a new platform, it is reasonable for programmers to take notice. It turns out that .NET represents a major change in the way you'll think about programming. It is, in short, a new development platform designed to facilitate object-oriented Internet development. The programming language of choice for this object-oriented Internet-centric platform is C#, which builds on the lessons learned from C (high performance), C++ (object-oriented structure), Java (garbage collected, high security), and Visual Basic (rapid development) to create a new language ideally suited for developing component-based n-tier distributed web applications.

About This Book

This book is a tutorial, both on C# and on writing .NET applications with C#. If you are already proficient in a programming language, you may be able to skim a number of the early chapters, but be sure to read through Chapter 1, which provides an overview of the language and the .NET platform. If you are new to programming, you'll want to read the book as the King of Hearts instructed the White Rabbit: "Begin at the beginning, and go on till you come to the end: then stop."*

---

* *Alice's Adventures in Wonderland* by Lewis Carroll.

How the Book Is Organized

Part I focuses on the details of the language. Part II details how to write .NET programs, and Part III describes how to use C# with the .NET Common Language Runtime library.

Part 1, The C# Language

Chapter 1, *C# and the .NET Framework*, introduces you to the C# language and the .NET platform.

Chapter 2, *Getting Started: "Hello World"* demonstrates a simple program to provide a context for what follows, and introduces you to the Visual Studio IDE and a number of C# language concepts.

Chapter 3, *C# Language Fundamentals*, presents the basics of the language, from built-in datatypes to keywords.

Classes define new types and allow the programmer to extend the language so that you can better model the problem you're trying to solve. Chapter 4, *Classes and Objects*, explains the components that form the heart and soul of C#.

Classes can be complex representations and abstractions of things in the real world. Chapter 5, *Inheritance and Polymorphism*, discusses how classes relate and interact.

Chapter 6, *Operator Overloading*, teaches you how to add operators to your user-defined types.

Chapter 7 and Chapter 8 introduce *Structs* and *Interfaces*, respectively, both close cousins to classes. Structs are lightweight objects that are more restricted than classes, and that make fewer demands on the operating system and on memory. Interfaces are contracts; they describe how a class will work so that other programmers can interact with your objects in well-defined ways.

Object-oriented programs often create a great many objects. It is often convenient to group these objects and manipulate them together, and C# provides extensive support for collections. Chapter 9, *Arrays, Indexers, and Collections*, explores the collection classes provided by the Framework Class Library and how to create your own collection types as well.

Chapter 10 discusses how you can use C# to manipulate text *Strings and Regular Expressions*. Most Windows and web programs interact with the user, and strings play a vital role in the user interface.

Chapter 11, *Handling Exceptions*, explains how to deal with exceptions, which provide an object-oriented mechanism for handling life's little emergencies.

Both Windows and web applications are event-driven. In C#, events are first-class members of the language. Chapter 12, *Delegates and Events*, focuses on how events are managed, and how *delegates* (object-oriented type-safe callback mechanisms) are used to support event handling.

Part II, Programming with C#

This section and the next will be of interest to all readers, no matter how much experience you may already have with other programming languages. These sections explore the details of the .NET platform.

Part II details how to write .NET programs: both desktop applications with Windows Forms and web applications with Web Forms. In addition, Part II describes database interactivity and how to create web services.

On top of this infrastructure sits a high-level abstraction of the operating system, designed to facilitate object-oriented software development. This top tier includes ASP.NET and Windows Forms. ASP.NET includes both Web Forms, for rapid development of web applications, and web services, for creating web objects with no user interface.

C# provides a Rapid Application Development (RAD) model similar to that previously available only in Visual Basic. Chapter 13, *Building Windows Applications*, describes how to use this RAD model to create professional-quality Windows programs using the Windows Forms development environment.

Whether intended for the Web or for the desktop, most applications depend on the manipulation and management of large amounts of data. Chapter 14, *Accessing Data with ADO.NET*, explains the ADO.NET layer of the .NET Framework and explains how to interact with Microsoft SQL Server and other data providers.

Chapter 15 combines the RAD techniques demonstrated in Chapter 13 with the data techniques from Chapter 14 to demonstrate *Building Web Applications with Web Forms*.

Not all applications have a user interface. Chapter 16 focuses on the second half of ASP.NET technology: *Web Services*. A *web service* is a distributed application that provides functionality via standard web protocols, most commonly XML and HTTP.

Part III, The CLR and the .NET Framework

A runtime is an environment in which programs are executed. The *Common Language Runtime* (CLR) is the heart of .NET. It includes a data-typing system which is enforced throughout the platform and which is common to all languages developed for .NET. The CLR is responsible for processes such as memory management and reference counting of objects.

Another key feature of the .NET CLR is *garbage collection*. Unlike with traditional C/C++ programming, in C# the developer is not responsible for destroying objects. Endless hours spent searching for memory leaks are a thing of the past; the CLR cleans up after you when your objects are no longer in use. The CLR's garbage collector checks the heap for unreferenced objects and frees the memory used by these objects.

The .NET platform and class library extends upward into the middle-level platform, where you find an infrastructure of supporting classes, including types for interprocess communication, XML, threading, I/O, security, diagnostics, and so on. The middle tier also includes the data-access components collectively referred to as ADO. NET, which are discussed in Chapter 14.

Part III of this book discusses the relationship of C# to the Common Language Runtime and the Framework Class Library.

Chapter 17, *Assemblies and Versioning*, distinguishes between private and public assemblies and describes how assemblies are created and managed. In .NET, an *assembly* is a collection of files that appears to the user to be a single DLL or executable. An assembly is the basic unit of reuse, versioning, security, and deployment.

.NET assemblies include extensive metadata about classes, methods, properties, events, and so forth. This metadata is compiled into the program and retrieved programmatically through reflection. Chapter 18, *Attributes and Reflection*, explores how to add metadata to your code, how to create custom attributes, and how to access this metadata through reflection. It goes on to discuss dynamic invocation, in which methods are invoked with late (runtime) binding, and ends with a demonstration of *reflection emit*, an advanced technique for building self-modifying code.

The .NET Framework was designed to support web-based and distributed applications. Components created in C# may reside within other processes on the same machine or on other machines across the network or across the Internet. *Marshaling* is the technique of interacting with objects that aren't really there, while *remoting* comprises techniques for communicating with such objects. Chapter 19, *Marshaling and Remoting*, elaborates.

The Framework Class Library provides extensive support for asynchronous I/O and other classes that make explicit manipulation of threads unnecessary. However, C# does provide extensive support for *Threads and Synchronization*, discussed in Chapter 20.

Chapter 21 discusses *Streams*, a mechanism not only for interacting with the user but also for retrieving data across the Internet. This chapter includes full coverage of C# support for *serialization*: the ability to write an object graph to disk and read it back again.

Chapter 22, *Programming .NET and COM*, explores interoperability—the ability to interact with COM components created outside the managed environment of the .NET Framework. It is possible to call components from C# applications into COM and to call components from COM into C#. Chapter 22 describes how this is done.

The book concludes with an appendix of *C# Keywords*.

Who This Book Is For

Programming C#, Second Edition was written for programmers who want to develop applications for the .NET platform. No doubt, many of you already have experience in C++, Java, or Visual Basic (VB). Other readers may have experience with other programming languages, and some readers may have no specific programming experience but perhaps have been working with HTML and other web technologies. This book is written for all of you, though if you have no programming experience at all, you may find some of it tough going.

C# Versus Visual Basic .NET

The premise of the .NET Framework is that all languages are created equal. To paraphrase George Orwell, however, some languages are more equal than others. C# is an excellent language for .NET development. You will find it is an extremely versatile, robust and well-designed language. It is also currently the language most often used in articles and tutorials about .NET programming.

It is likely that many VB programmers will choose to learn C#, rather than upgrading their skills to VB.NET. This would not be surprising because the transition from VB6 to VB.NET is, arguably, nearly as difficult as from VB6 to C#—and, whether it's fair or not, historically, C-family programmers have had higher earning potential than VB programmers. As a practical matter, VB programmers have never gotten the respect or compensation they deserve, and C# offers a wonderful chance to make a potentially lucrative transition.

In any case, if you do have VB experience, welcome! This book was designed with you in mind too, and I've tried to make the conversion easy.

C# Versus Java

Java Programmers may look at C# with a mixture of trepidation, glee, and resentment. It has been suggested that C# is somehow a "rip-off" of Java. I won't comment on the religious war between Microsoft and the "anyone but Microsoft" crowd except to acknowledge that C# certainly learned a great deal from Java. But then Java learned a great deal from C++, which owed its syntax to C, which in turn was built on lessons learned in other languages. We all stand on the shoulders of giants.

C# offers an easy transition for Java programmers; the syntax is very similar and the semantics are familiar and comfortable. Java programmers will probably want to focus on the differences between Java and C# in order to use the C# language effectively. I've tried to provide a series of markers along the way (see the notes to Java programmers within the chapters).

C# Versus C++

While it is possible to program in .NET with C++, it isn't easy or natural. Frankly, having worked for ten years as a C++ programmer and written a dozen books on the subject, I'd rather have my teeth drilled than work with managed C++. Perhaps it is just that C# is so much friendlier. In any case, once I saw C#, I never looked back.

Be careful, though; there are a number of small traps along the way, and I've been careful to mark these with flashing lights and yellow cones. You'll find notes for C++ programmers throughout the book.

Conventions Used in This Book

The following font conventions are used in this book:

Italic is used for:

- Pathnames, filenames, and program names.
- Internet addresses, such as domain names and URLs.
- New terms where they are defined.

`Constant Width` is used for:

- Command lines and options that should be typed verbatim.
- Names and keywords in program examples, including method names, variable names, and class names.

`Constant Width Italic` is used for replaceable items, such as variables or optional elements, within syntax lines or code.

`Constant Width Bold` is used for emphasis within program code.

Pay special attention to notes set apart from the text with the following icons:

This is a tip. It contains useful supplementary information about the topic at hand.

This is a warning. It helps you solve and avoid annoying problems.

Support

As part of my responsibilities as author, I provide ongoing support for my books through my web site:

http://www.LibertyAssociates.com

You can also obtain the source code for all of the examples in *Programming C#* at my site You will find access to a book-support discussion group with a section set aside for questions about C#. Before you post a question, however, please check the FAQ (Frequently Asked Questions) and the errata file. If you check these files and still have a question, then please go ahead and post to the discussion center.

The most effective way to get help is to ask a very precise question or even to create a very small program that illustrates your area of concern or confusion. You may also want to check the various newsgroups and discussion centers on the Internet. Microsoft offers a wide array of newsgroups, and Developmentor (*http://www. develop.com*) has a wonderful .NET email discussion list, as does Charles Carroll at *http://www.asplists.com*.

We'd Like to Hear from You

We have tested and verified the information in this book to the best of our ability, but you may find that features have changed (or even that we have made mistakes!). Please let us know about any errors you find, as well as your suggestions for future editions, by writing to:

O'Reilly & Associates, Inc.
005 Gravenstein Highway North
Sebastopol, CA 95472
(800) 998-9938 (in the United States or Canada)
(707) 829-0515 (international or local)
(707) 829-0104 (fax)

We have a web page for the book, where we list examples and any plans for future editions. You can access this information at:

http://www.oreilly.com/catalog/progcsharp2

To comment or ask technical questions about this book, send email to:

bookquestions@oreilly.com

For more information about our books, conferences, Resource Centers, and the O'Reilly Network, see our web site at:

http://www.oreilly.com

For more information about this book and others, as well as additional technical articles and discussion on the C# and the .NET Framework, see the O'Reilly & Associates web site:

http://www.oreilly.com

and the O'Reilly .NET DevCenter:

http://www.oreillynet.com/dotnet/

Acknowledgments

To ensure that *Programming C#* is accurate, complete and targeted at the needs and interests of professional programmers, I enlisted the help of some of the brightest programmers I know, including Donald Xie, Dan Hurwitz, Seth Weiss, Sue Lynch, Cliff Gerald, and Tom Petr. Jim Culbert not only reviewed the book and made extensive suggestions, but continually pointed me back at the practical needs of working programmers. Jim's contributions to this book cannot be overstated.

Mike Woodring of Developmentor taught me more about the CLR in a week than I could have learned on my own in six months. A number of folks at Microsoft and O'Reilly helped me wrestle with the twin beasts of C# and .NET, including (but not limited to) Eric Gunnerson, Rob Howard, Piet Obermeyer, Jonathan Hawkins, Peter Drayton, Brad Merrill, and Ben Albahari. Susan Warren may be one of the most amazing programmers I've ever met; her help and guidance is deeply appreciated.

John Osborn signed me to O'Reilly, for which I will forever be in his debt. Valerie Quercia, Brian McDonald, Jeff Holcomb, Claire Cloutier, and Tatiana Diaz helped make this book better than what I'd written. Rob Romano created a number of the illustrations and improved the others. Tim O'Reilly provided support and resources, and I'm grateful.

Many readers have written to point out typos and minor errors in the first edition. Their effort is very much appreciated, with special thanks to Sol Bick, Brian Cassel, Steve Charbonneau, Randy Eastwood, Andy Gaskall, Bob Kline, Jason Mauss, Mark Phillips, Christian Rodriguez, David Solum, Erwing Steininger, Steve Thomson, Greg Torrance, and Ted Volk. We've worked hard to fix all of these errors in this second edition. We've scoured the book to ensure that no new errors were added, and that all of the code compiles and runs properly with the latest release edition of Visual Studio .NET. That said, if you do find errors, please check the errata on my web site (*http://www.LibertyAssociates.com*) and if your error is new, please send me email at *jliberty@libertyassociates.com*.

Finally, a special thank you to Brian Jepson, who is responsible both for the enhanced quality of the second edition and for its timeliness. He has gone above and beyond in this effort and I very much appreciate it.

PART I

The C# Language

CHAPTER 1

C# and the .NET Framework

The goal of C# is to provide a simple, safe, modern, object-oriented, Internet-centric, high-performance language for .NET development. C# is a new language, but it draws on the lessons learned over the past three decades. In much the way that you can see in young children the features and personalities of their parents and grandparents, you can easily see in C# the influence of Java, C++, Visual Basic (VB), and other languages.

The focus of this book is the C# language and its use as a tool for programming on the .NET platform. In my primers on C++,* I advocate learning the language first, without regard to Windows or Unix programming. With C# that approach would be pointless. You learn C# specifically to create .NET applications; pretending otherwise would miss the point of the language. Thus, this book does not consider C# in a vacuum but places the language firmly in the context of Microsoft's .NET platform and in the development of desktop and Internet applications.

This chapter introduces both the C# language and the .NET platform, including the .NET Framework.

The .NET Platform

When Microsoft announced C# in July 2000, its unveiling was part of a much larger event: the announcement of the .NET platform. The .NET platform is, in essence, a new development framework that provides a fresh application programming interface (API) to the services and APIs of classic Windows operating systems (especially the Windows 2000 family), while bringing together a number of disparate technologies that emerged from Microsoft during the late 1990s. Among the latter are COM+ component services, the ASP web development framework, a commitment to XML and object-oriented design, support for new web services protocols such as SOAP, WSDL, and UDDI, and a focus on the Internet, all integrated within the DNA architecture.

---

* See *Sams Teach Yourself C++ in 21 Days,* also by Jesse Liberty.

Microsoft says it is devoting 80% of its research and development budget to .NET and its associated technologies. The results of this commitment to date are impressive. For one thing, the scope of .NET is huge. The platform consists of four separate product groups:

- A set of languages, including C# and Visual Basic .NET; a set of development tools, including Visual Studio .NET; a comprehensive class library for building web services and web and Windows applications; as well as the *Common Language Runtime* (CLR) to execute objects built within this framework.

- A set of .NET Enterprise Servers, formerly known as SQL Server 2000, Exchange 2000, BizTalk 2000, and so on, that provide specialized functionality for relational data storage, email, B2B commerce, etc.

- An offering of commercial web services, called .NET My Services; for a fee, developers can use these services in building applications that require knowledge of user identity, etc.

- New .NET-enabled non-PC devices, from cell phones to game boxes.

The .NET Framework

Microsoft .NET supports not only language independence, but also language integration. This means that you can inherit from classes, catch exceptions, and take advantage of polymorphism across different languages. The .NET Framework makes this possible with a specification called the *Common Type System* (CTS) that all .NET components must obey. For example, everything in .NET is an object of a specific class that derives from the root class called System.Object. The CTS supports the general concept of classes, interfaces, delegates (which support callbacks), reference types, and value types.

Additionally, .NET includes a *Common Language Specification* (CLS), which provides a series of basic rules that are required for language integration. The CLS determines the minimum requirements for being a .NET language. Compilers that conform to the CLS create objects that can interoperate with one another. The entire Framework Class Library (FCL) can be used by any language that conforms to the CLS.

The .NET Framework sits on top of the operating system, which can be any flavor of Windows,[*] and consists of a number of components. Currently, the .NET Framework consists of:

- Four official languages: C#, VB.NET, Managed C++, and JScript .NET

- The Common Language Runtime (CLR), an object-oriented platform for Windows and web development that all these languages share

---

[*] Because of the architecture of the CLR, the operating system can be potentially any variety of Unix or another operating system altogether.

- A number of related class libraries, collectively known as the Framework Class Library (FCL).

Figure 1-1 breaks down the .NET Framework into its system architectural components.

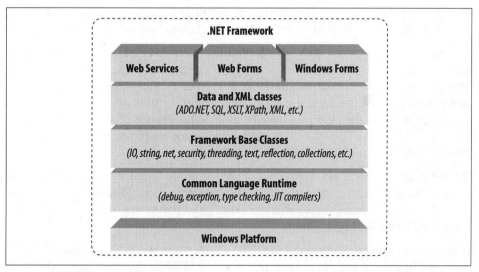

Figure 1-1. NET Framework architecture

The most important component of the .NET Framework is the CLR, which provides the environment in which programs are executed. The CLR includes a virtual machine, analogous in many ways to the Java virtual machine. At a high level, the CLR activates objects, performs security checks on them, lays them out in memory, executes them, and garbage-collects them. (The Common Type System is also part of the CLR.)

In Figure 1-1, the layer on top of the CLR is a set of framework base classes, followed by an additional layer of data and XML classes, plus another layer of classes intended for web services, Web Forms, and Windows Forms. Collectively, these classes are known as the Framework Class Library (FCL), one of the largest class libraries in history and one that provides an object-oriented API to all the functionality that the .NET platform encapsulates. With more than 4,000 classes, the FCL facilitates rapid development of desktop, client/server, and other web services and applications.

The set of framework base classes, the lowest level of the FCL, is similar to the set of classes in Java. These classes support rudimentary input and output, string manipulation, security management, network communication, thread management, text manipulation, reflection and collections functionality, etc.

Above this level is a tier of classes that extend the base classes to support data management and XML manipulation. The data classes support persistent management of data that is maintained on backend databases. These classes include the Structured Query Language (SQL) classes to let you manipulate persistent data stores through a standard SQL interface. Additionally, a set of classes called ADO.NET allows you to manipulate persistent data. The .NET Framework also supports a number of classes to let you manipulate XML data and perform XML searching and translations.

Extending the framework base classes and the data and XML classes is a tier of classes geared toward building applications using three different technologies: Web Services, Web Forms, and Windows Forms. Web services include a number of classes that support the development of lightweight distributed components, which will work even in the face of firewalls and NAT software. Because web services employ standard HTTP and SOAP as underlying communications protocols, these components support plug-and-play across cyberspace.

Web Forms and Windows Forms allow you to apply Rapid Application Development techniques to building web and Windows applications. Simply drag and drop controls onto your form, double-click a control, and write the code to respond to the associated event.

For a more detailed description of the .NET Framework, see *.NET Framework Essentials*, by Thuan Thai and Hoag Lam (published by O'Reilly & Associates, 2001).

Compilation and the MSIL

In .NET, programs are not compiled into executable files; they are compiled into *Microsoft Intermediate Language* (MSIL) files, which the CLR then executes. The MSIL (often shortened to IL) files that C# produces are *identical* to the IL files that other .NET languages produce; the platform is language-agnostic. A key fact about the CLR is that it is *common*; the same runtime supports development in C# as well as in VB.NET.

C# code is compiled into IL when you build your project. The IL is saved in a file on disk. When you run your program, the IL is compiled again, using the *Just In Time* (JIT) compiler (a process often called *JIT'ing*). The result is machine code, executed by the machine's processor.

The standard JIT compiler runs *on demand*. When a method is called, the JIT compiler analyzes the IL and produces highly efficient machine code, which runs very fast. The JIT compiler is smart enough to recognize when the code has already been compiled, so as the application runs, compilation happens only as needed. As .NET applications run, they tend to become faster and faster, as the already compiled code is reused.

The CLS means that all .NET languages produce very similar IL code. As a result, objects created in one language can be accessed and derived from another. Thus it is possible to create a base class in VB.NET and derive from it in C#.

The C# Language

The C# language is disarmingly simple, with only about 80 keywords and a dozen built-in datatypes, but C# is highly expressive when it comes to implementing modern programming concepts. C# includes all the support for structured, component-based, object-oriented programming that one expects of a modern language built on the shoulders of C++ and Java.

The C# language was developed by a small team led by two distinguished Microsoft engineers, Anders Hejlsberg and Scott Wiltamuth. Hejlsberg is also known for creating Turbo Pascal, a popular language for PC programming, and for leading the team that designed Borland Delphi, one of the first successful integrated development environments for client/server programming.

At the heart of any object-oriented language is its support for defining and working with classes. Classes define new types, allowing you to extend the language to better model the problem you are trying to solve. C# contains keywords for declaring new classes and their methods and properties, and for implementing encapsulation, inheritance, and polymorphism, the three pillars of object-oriented programming.

In C# everything pertaining to a class declaration is found in the declaration itself. C# class definitions do not require separate header files or Interface Definition Language (IDL) files. Moreover, C# supports a new XML style of inline documentation that greatly simplifies the creation of online and print reference documentation for an application.

C# also supports *interfaces*, a means of making a contract with a class for services that the interface stipulates. In C#, a class can inherit from only a single parent, but a class can implement multiple interfaces. When it implements an interface, a C# class in effect promises to provide the functionality the interface specifies.

C# also provides support for *structs*, a concept whose meaning has changed significantly from C++. In C#, a struct is a restricted, lightweight type that, when instantiated, makes fewer demands on the operating system and on memory than a conventional class does. A struct can't inherit from a class or be inherited from, but a struct can implement an interface.

C# provides component-oriented features, such as properties, events, and declarative constructs (called *attributes*). Component-oriented programming is supported by the CLR's support for storing metadata with the code for the class. The metadata describes the class, including its methods and properties, as well as its security needs and other attributes, such as whether it can be serialized; the code contains the logic necessary to carry out its functions. A compiled class is thus a self-contained unit; therefore, a hosting environment that knows how to read a class' metadata and code needs no other information to make use of it. Using C# and the CLR, it is possible to add custom metadata to a class by creating custom attributes. Likewise, it is possible to read class metadata using CLR types that support reflection.

An *assembly* is a collection of files that appear to the programmer to be a single dynamic link library (DLL) or executable (EXE). In .NET, an assembly is the basic unit of reuse, versioning, security, and deployment. The CLR provides a number of classes for manipulating assemblies.

A final note about C# is that it also provides support for directly accessing memory using C++ style pointers and keywords for bracketing such operations as unsafe, and for warning the CLR garbage collector not to collect objects referenced by pointers until they are released.

CHAPTER 2

Getting Started: "Hello World"

It is a time-honored tradition to start a programming book with a "Hello World" program. In this chapter, we create, compile, and run a simple "Hello World" program written in C#. The analysis of this brief program will introduce key features of the C# language.

Example 2-1 illustrates the fundamental elements of a very elementary C# program.

Example 2-1. A simple "Hello World" program in C#

```
class HelloWorld
{
    static void Main( )
    {
        // Use the system console object
        System.Console.WriteLine("Hello World");
    }
}
```

Compiling and running HelloWorld displays the words "Hello World" at the console. Let's take a closer look at this simple program.

Classes, Objects, and Types

The essence of object-oriented programming is the creation of new types. A *type* represents a thing. Sometimes the thing is abstract, such as a data table or a thread; sometimes it is more tangible, such as a button in a window. A type defines the thing's general properties and behaviors.

If your program uses three instances of a button type in a window—say, an OK, a Cancel, and a Help button—each instance will share certain properties and behaviors. Each, for example, will have a size (though it might differ from that of its companions), a position (though again, it will almost certainly differ in its position from the others), and a text label (e.g., "OK", "Cancel," and "Help"). Likewise, all three buttons will have common behaviors, such as the ability to be drawn, activated, pressed, and so forth. Thus, the details might differ among the individual buttons, but they are all of the same type.

As in many object-oriented programming languages, in C# a type is defined by a *class*, while the individual instances of that class are known as *objects*. Later chapters explain that there are other types in C# besides classes, including enums, structs, and delegates, but for now the focus is on classes.

The "Hello World" program declares a single type: the HelloWorld class. To define a C# type, you declare it as a class using the class keyword, give it a name—in this case, HelloWorld—and then define its properties and behaviors. The property and behavior definitions of a C# class must be enclosed by open and closed braces ({}).

 C++ programmers take note: there is no semicolon after the closing brace.

Methods

A class has both properties and behaviors. Behaviors are defined with member methods; properties are discussed in Chapter 3.

A *method* is a *function* owned by your class. In fact, member methods are sometimes called *member functions*. The member methods define what your class can do or how it behaves. Typically, methods are given action names, such as WriteLine( ) or AddNumbers( ). In the case shown here, however, the class method has a special name, Main( ), which doesn't describe an action but does designate to the Common Language Runtime (CLR) that this is the main, or first method, for your class.

Unlike C++, Main is capitalized in C# and can return int or void.

The CLR calls Main( ) when your program starts. Main( ) is the entry point for your program, and every C# program must have a Main( ) method.[*]

Method declarations are a contract between the creator of the method and the consumer (user) of the method. It is likely that the creator and consumer of the method will be the same programmer, but this does not have to be so; it is possible that one member of a development team will create the method and another programmer will use it.

---

[*] It is technically possible to have multiple Main( ) methods in C#; in that case you use the /main command-line switch to tell C# which class contains the Main( ) method that should serve as the entry point to the program.

To declare a method, you specify a return value type followed by a name. Method declarations also require parentheses, whether the method accepts parameters or not. For example:

```
int myMethod(int size );
```

declares a method named myMethod that takes one parameter: an integer which will be referred to within the method as *size*. My method returns an integer value. The return value type tells the consumer of the method what kind of data the method will return when it finishes running.

Some methods do not return a value at all; these are said to return *void*, which is specified by the void keyword. For example:

```
void myVoidMethod( );
```

declares a method that returns void and takes no parameters. In C# you must always declare a return type or void.

Comments

A C# program can also contain comments. Take a look at the first line after the opening brace:

```
// Use the system console object
```

The text begins with two forward slash marks (//). These designate a *comment*. A comment is a note to the programmer and does not affect how the program runs. C# supports three types of comments.

The first type, just shown, indicates that all text to the right of the comment mark is to be considered a comment, until the end of that line. This is known as a *C++ style comment*.

The second type of comment, known as a *C-Style comment*, begins with an open comment mark (/*) and ends with a closed comment mark (*/). This allows comments to span more than one line without having to have // characters at the beginning of each comment line, as shown in Example 2-2.

Example 2-2. Illustrating multiline comments

```
class Hello
{
    static void Main( )
    {
        /* Use the system console object
           as explained in the text in chapter 2 */
        System.Console.WriteLine("Hello World");
    }
}
```

It is possible to nest C++ style comments within C-style comments. For this reason, it is common to use C++ style comments whenever possible, and to reserve the C-style comments for "commenting-out" blocks of code.

The third and final type of comment that C# supports is used to associate external XML-based documentation with your code, and is illustrated in Chapter 13.

Console Applications

"Hello World" is an example of a *console* program. A console application has no user interface (UI); there are no list boxes, buttons, windows, and so forth. Text input and output is handled through the standard console (typically a command or DOS window on your PC). Sticking to console applications for now helps simplify the early examples in this book, and keeps the focus on the language itself. In later chapters, we'll turn our attention to Windows and web applications, and at that time we'll focus on the Visual Studio .NET UI design tools.

All that the Main( ) method does in this simple example is write the text "Hello World" to the monitor. The monitor is managed by an object named Console. This Console object has a method WriteLine( ) that takes a *string* (a set of characters) and writes it to the standard output. When you run this program, a command or DOS screen will pop up on your computer monitor and display the words "Hello World."

You invoke a method with the dot operator (.). Thus, to call the Console object's WriteLine( )method, you write Console.WriteLine(...), filling in the string to be printed.

Namespaces

Console is only one of a tremendous number of useful types that are part of the .NET Framework Class Library (FCL). Each class has a name, and thus the FCL contains thousands of names, such as ArrayList, Hashtable, FileDialog, DataException, EventArgs, and so on. There are hundreds, thousands, even tens of thousands of names.

This presents a problem. No developer can possibly memorize all the names that the .NET Framework uses, and sooner or later you are likely to create an object and give it a name that has already been used. What will happen if you develop your own Hashtable class, only to discover that it conflicts with the Hashtable class that .NET provides? Remember, each class in C# must have a unique name.

You certainly could rename your Hashtable class mySpecialHashtable, for example, but that is a losing battle. New Hashtable types are likely to be developed, and distinguishing between their type names and yours would be a nightmare.

The solution to this problem is to create a *namespace*. A namespace restricts a name's scope, making it meaningful only within the defined namespace.

Assume that I tell you that Jim is an engineer. The word "engineer" is used for many things in English, and can cause confusion. Does he design buildings? Write software? Run a train?

In English I might clarify by saying "he's a scientist," or "he's a train engineer." A C# programmer could tell you that Jim is a science.engineer rather than a train. engineer. The namespace (in this case, science or train) restricts the scope of the word that follows. It creates a "space" in which that name is meaningful.

Further, it might happen that Jim is not just any kind of science.engineer. Perhaps Jim graduated from MIT with a degree in software engineering, not civil engineering (are civil engineers especially polite?). Thus, the object that is Jim might be defined more specifically as a science.software.engineer. This classification implies that the namespace software is meaningful within the namespace science, and that engineer in this context is meaningful within the namespace software. If later you learn that Charlotte is a transportation.train.engineer, you will not be confused as to what kind of engineer she is. The two uses of engineer can coexist, each within its own namespace.

Similarly, if it turns out that .NET has a Hashtable class within its System. Collections namespace, and that I have also created a Hashtable class within a ProgCSharp.DataStructures namespace, there is no conflict because each exists in its own namespace.

In Example 2-1, the Console object's name is restricted to the System namespace by using the code:

```
System.Console.WriteLine( );
```

The Dot Operator (.)

In Example 2-1, the dot operator (.) is used both to access a method (and data) in a class (in this case, the method WriteLine( )), and to restrict the class name to a specific namespace (in this case, to locate Console within the System namespace). This works well because in both cases we are "drilling down" to find the exact thing we want. The top level is the System namespace (which contains all the System objects that the Framework provides); the Console type exists within that namespace, and the WriteLine( ) method is a member function of the Console type.

In many cases, namespaces are divided into subspaces. For example, the System namespace contains a number of subnamespaces such as Configuration, Collections, Data, and so forth, while the Collections namespace itself is divided into multiple subnamespaces.

Namespaces can help you organize and compartmentalize your types. When you write a complex C# program, you might want to create your own namespace hierarchy, and there is no limit to how deep this hierarchy can be. The goal of namespaces is to help you divide and conquer the complexity of your object hierarchy.

The using Keyword

Rather than writing the word System before Console, you could specify that you will be using types from the System namespace by writing the statement:

```
using System;
```

at the top of the listing, as shown in Example 2-3.

Example 2-3. The using keyword

```
using System;
class Hello
{
    static void Main( )
    {
        //Console from the System namespace
        Console.WriteLine("Hello World");
    }
}
```

Notice the using System statement is placed before the HelloWorld class definition.

Although you can designate that you are using the System namespace, unlike with some languages you cannot designate that you are using the System.Console object. Example 2-4 will not compile.

Example 2-4. Code that does not compile (not legal C#)

```
using System.Console;
class Hello
{
    static void Main( )
    {
        //Console from the System namespace
        WriteLine("Hello World");
    }
}
```

This generates the compile error:

```
error CS0138: A using namespace directive can only be applied to namespaces; 'System.
Console' is a class not a namespace
```

The using keyword can save a great deal of typing, but it can undermine the advantages of namespaces by polluting the namespace with many undifferentiated names. A common solution is to use the using keyword with the built-in namespaces and with your own corporate namespaces, but perhaps not with third-party components.

Case Sensitivity

C# is case-sensitive, which means that writeLine is not the same as WriteLine, which in turn is not the same as WRITELINE. Unfortunately, unlike in Visual Basic (VB), the

C# development environment will not fix your case mistakes; if you write the same word twice with different cases, you might introduce a tricky-to-find bug into your program.

To prevent such a time-wasting and energy-depleting mistake, you should develop conventions for naming your variables, functions, constants, and so forth. The convention in this book is to name variables with camel notation (e.g., someVariableName), and to name functions, constants, and properties with Pascal notation (e.g., SomeFunction).

 The only difference between camel and Pascal notation is that in Pascal notation, names begin with an uppercase letter.

The static Keyword

The Main( ) method shown in Example 2-1 has one more designation. Just before the return type declaration void (which, you will remember, indicates that the method does not return a value) you'll find the keyword static:

```
static void Main( )
```

The static keyword indicates that you can invoke Main( ) without first creating an object of type Hello. This somewhat complex issue will be considered in much greater detail in subsequent chapters. One of the problems with learning a new computer language is you must use some of the advanced features before you fully understand them. For now, you can treat the declaration of the Main( ) method as tantamount to magic.

Developing "Hello World"

There are at least two ways to enter, compile, and run the programs in this book: use the Visual Studio .NET Integrated Development Environment (IDE), or use a text editor and a command-line compiler (along with some additional command-line tools to be introduced later).

Although you *can* develop software outside Visual Studio .NET, the IDE provides enormous advantages. These include indentation support, Intellisense word completion, color coding, and integration with the help files. Most important, the IDE includes a powerful debugger and a wealth of other tools.

Although this book tacitly assumes that you'll be using Visual Studio .NET, the tutorials focus more on the language and the platform than on the tools. You can copy all the examples into a text editor such as Windows Notepad or Emacs, save them as text files, and compile them with the C# command-line compiler that is distributed with the .NET Framework SDK. Note that some examples in later chapters use Visual Studio .NET tools for creating Windows Forms and Web Forms, but even these you can write by hand in Notepad if you are determined to do things the hard way.

Editing "Hello World"

To create the "Hello World" program in the IDE, select Visual Studio .NET from your Start menu or a desktop icon, and then choose File → New → Project from the menu toolbar. This will invoke the New Project window (if you are using Visual Studio for the first time, the New Project window might appear without further prompting). Figure 2-1 shows the New Project window.

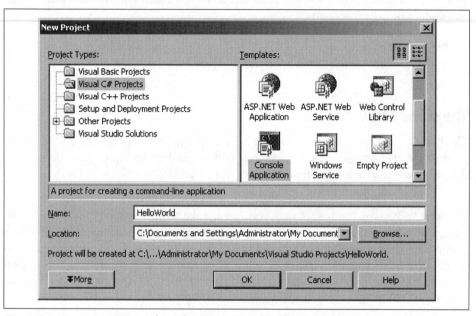

Figure 2-1. Creating a C# console application in Visual Studio .NET

To open your application, select Visual C# Projects in the Project Type window and select Console Application in the Templates window. You can now enter a name for the project and select a directory in which to store your files. Click OK, and a new window will appear in which you can enter the code in Example 2-1, as shown in Figure 2-2.

Notice that Visual Studio .NET creates a namespace based on the project name you've provided (HelloWorld), and adds a using System statement because nearly every program you write will need types from the System namespace.

Visual Studio .NET creates a class named Class1, which you are free to rename. When you rename the class, be sure to rename the file as well (*Class1.cs*). To reproduce Example 2-1, for instance, change the name of Class1 to HelloWorld, and rename the *Class1.cs* file (listed in the Solution Explorer window) to *HelloWorld.cs*.

Finally, Visual Studio .NET creates a program skeleton, complete with a TODO comment to get you started. To reproduce Example 2-1, remove the arguments (string[] args) and comments from the Main( ) method. Then copy the following two lines into the body of Main( ):

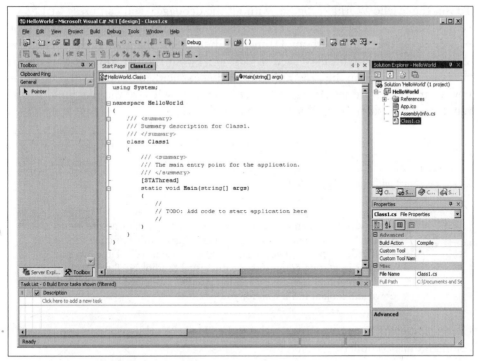

Figure 2-2. The editor opened to your new project

```
// Use the system console object
System.Console.WriteLine("Hello World");
```

If you are not using Visual Studio .NET, open Notepad, type in the code from Example 2-1, and save the file as a text file named *Hello.cs*.

Compiling and Running "Hello World"

There are many ways to compile and run the "Hello World" program from within Visual Studio .NET. Typically you can accomplish every task by choosing commands from the Visual Studio .NET menu toolbar, by using buttons, and, in many cases, by using key-combination shortcuts.

For example, to compile the "Hello World" program, press Ctrl-Shift-B or choose Build → Build Solution. As an alternative, you can click the Build button on the Build button bar (you may need to right-click on the toolbar to add the Build button bar). The Build button icon is shown in Figure 2-3.

Figure 2-3. Build button icon

To run the "Hello World" program without the debugger, you can press Ctrl-F5 on your keyboard, choose Debug → Start Without Debugging from the IDE menu toolbar, or press the Start Without Debugging button on the IDE Build toolbar, as shown in Figure 2-4 (you may need to customize your toolbar to make this button available). You can run the program without first explicitly building it; depending on how your options are set (Tools → Options) the IDE will save the file, build it, and run it, possibly asking you for permission at each step.

Figure 2-4. Start without debugging button

 I strongly recommend that you spend some time exploring the Visual Studio .NET development environment. This is your principal tool as a .NET developer, and you want to learn to use it well. Time invested up front in getting comfortable with Visual Studio .NET will pay for itself many times over in the coming months. Go ahead, put the book down and look at it. I'll wait for you.

Use the following steps to compile and run the "Hello World" program using the C# command-line compiler:

1. Save Example 2-1 as the file *hello.cs*.

2. Open a command window (Start → Run and type in cmd).

3. From the command line, enter:

    ```
    csc /debug hello.cs
    ```

   This step will build the executable (EXE) file. If the program contains errors, the compiler will report them in the command window. The /debug command-line switch inserts symbols in the code so you can run the EXE under a debugger or see line numbers in stack traces. (You'll get a stack trace if your program generates an error that you do not handle.)

4. To run the program, enter:

    ```
    Hello
    ```

   You should see the venerable words "Hello World" appear in your command window.

Using the Visual Studio .NET-Debugger

Arguably, the single most important tool in any development environment is the debugger. The Visual Studio debugger is very powerful, and it will be well worth

Just In Time Compilation

Compiling *Hello.cs* using *csc* creates an executable (EXE) file. Keep in mind, however, that the *.exe* file contains op-codes written in Microsoft Intermediate Language (MSIL), which is introduced in Chapter 1.

Interestingly, if you had written this application in VB.NET or any other language compliant with the .NET Common Language Specification, you would have compiled it into the same MSIL. By design, Intermediate Language (IL) code created from different languages is virtually indistinguishable; this is the point of having a common language specification in the first place.

In addition to producing the IL code (which is similar in spirit to Java's byte-code), the compiler creates a read-only segment of the *.exe* file in which it inserts a standard Win32 executable header. The compiler designates an entry point within the read-only segment; the operating system loader jumps to that entry point when you run the program, just as it would for any Windows program.

The operating system cannot execute the IL code, however, and that entry point does nothing but jump to the .NET Just In Time (JIT) compiler (also introduced in Chapter 1). The JIT produces native CPU instructions, as you might find in a normal *.exe*. The key feature of a JIT compiler, however, is that functions are compiled only as they are used, Just In Time for execution.

whatever time you put into learning how to use it well. That said, the fundamentals of debugging are very simple. The three key skills are:

- How to set a breakpoint and how to run to that breakpoint
- How to step into and over method calls
- How to examine and modify the value of variables, member data, and so forth

This chapter does not reiterate the entire debugger documentation, but these skills are so fundamental that it does provide a crash (pardon the expression) course.

The debugger can accomplish the same thing in many ways—typically via menu choices, buttons, and so forth. The simplest way to set a breakpoint is to click in the lefthand margin. The IDE will mark your breakpoint with a red dot, as shown in Figure 2-5.

```
for (int i = 0;i < 3; i++)
{
    winArray[i].DrawWindow();
}
}
```

Figure 2-5. A breakpoint

Discussing the debugger requires code examples. The code shown here is from Chapter 5, and you are not expected to understand how it works yet (though if you program in C++ or Java, you'll probably understand the gist of it).

To run the debugger you can choose Debug->Start or just press F5. The program will compile and run to the breakpoint, at which time it will stop and a yellow arrow will indicate the next statement for execution, as in Figure 2-6.

```
        for (int i = 0;i < 3; i++)
        {
            winArray[i].DrawWindow();
        }
    }
```

Figure 2-6. The breakpoint hit

After you've hit your breakpoint it is easy to examine the values of various objects. For example, you can find the value of the variable i just by putting the cursor over it and waiting a moment, as shown in Figure 2-7.

```
    for (int i = 0;i < 3; i++)
    {
            i = 0
        winArray[i].DrawWindow();
    }
```

Figure 2-7. Showing a value

The debugger IDE also provides a number of very useful windows, such as a Locals window that displays the values of all the local variables (see Figure 2-8).

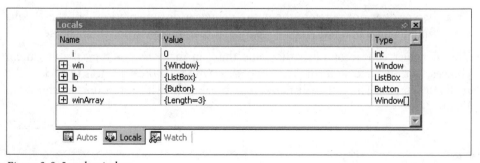

Figure 2-8. Locals window

Intrinsic types such as integers simply show their value (see i earlier), but objects show their type and have a plus (+) sign. You can expand these objects to see their internal data, as shown in Figure 2-9. You'll learn more about objects and their internal data in upcoming chapters.

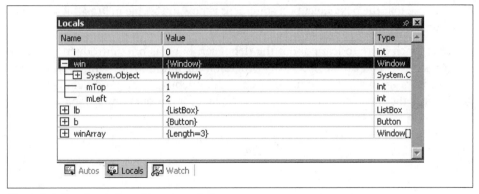

Figure 2-9. Locals window object expanded

You can step into the next method by pressing F11. Doing so steps into the DrawWindow( ) method of the WindowClass, as shown in Figure 2-10.

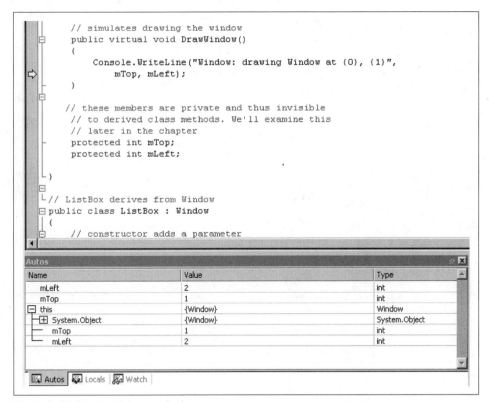

Figure 2-10. Stepping into a method

You can see that the next execution statement is now WriteLine in DrawWindow( ). The autos window has updated to show the current state of the objects.

There is much more to learn about the debugger, but this brief introduction should get you started. You can answer many programming questions by writing short demonstration programs and examining them in the debugger. A good debugger is, in some ways, the single most powerful teaching tool for a programming language.

CHAPTER 3

C# Language Fundamentals

Chapter 2 demonstrates a very simple C# program. Nonetheless, there is sufficient complexity in creating even that little program that some of the pertinent details had to be skipped over. The current chapter illuminates these details by delving more deeply into the syntax and structure of the C# language itself.

This chapter discusses the type system in C#, drawing a distinction between built-in types (int, bool, etc.) versus user-defined types (types you create as classes and interfaces). The chapter also covers programming fundamentals such as how to create and use variables and constants. It then goes on to introduce enumerations, strings, identifiers, expressions, and statements.

The second part of the chapter explains and demonstrates the use of branching, using the if, switch, while, do...while, for, and foreach statements. Also discussed are operators, including the assignment, logical, relational, and mathematical operators. This is followed by an introduction to namespaces and a short tutorial on the C# precompiler.

Although C# is principally concerned with the creation and manipulation of objects, it is best to start with the fundamental building blocks: the elements from which objects are created. These include the built-in types that are an intrinsic part of the C# language as well as the syntactic elements of C#.

Types

C# is a strongly typed language. In a strongly typed language you must declare the type of each object you create (e.g., integers, floats, strings, windows, buttons, etc.) and the compiler will help you prevent bugs by enforcing that only data of the right type is assigned to those objects. The type of an object signals to the compiler the size of that object (e.g., int indicates an object of 4 bytes) and its capabilities (e.g., buttons can be drawn, pressed, and so forth).

Like C++ and Java, C# divides types into two sets: *intrinsic* (built-in) types that the language offers and *user-defined* types that the programmer defines.

C# also divides the set of types into two other categories: *value* types and *reference* types.[*] The principal difference between value and reference types is the manner in which their values are stored in memory. A value type holds its actual value in memory allocated on the stack (or it is allocated as part of a larger reference type object). The address of a reference type variable sits on the stack, but the actual object is stored on the heap.

If you have a very large object, putting it on the heap has many advantages. Chapter 4 discusses the various advantages and disadvantages of working with reference types; the current chapter focuses on the intrinsic value types available in C#.

C# also supports C++ style *pointer* types, but these are rarely used, and only when working with unmanaged code. Unmanaged code is created outside of the .NET platform, such as COM objects. Working with COM objects is discussed in Chapter 22.

Working with Built-in Types

The C# language offers the usual cornucopia of intrinsic (built-in) types one expects in a modern language, each of which maps to an underlying type supported by the .NET Common Language Specification (CLS). Mapping the C# primitive types to the underlying .NET type ensures that objects created in C# can be used interchangeably with objects created in any other language compliant with the .NET CLS, such as VB.NET.

Each type has a specific and unchanging size. Unlike with C++, a C# int is always 4 bytes because it maps to an Int32 in the .NET CLS. Table 3-1 lists the built-in value types offered by C#.

Table 3-1. C# built-in value types

Type	Size (in bytes)	.NET type	Description
byte	1	Byte	Unsigned (values 0–255).
char	2	Char	Unicode characters.
bool	1	Boolean	true or false.
sbyte	1	SByte	Signed (values –128 to 127).
short	2	Int16	Signed (short) (values –32,768 to 32,767).
ushort	2	UInt16	Unsigned (short) (values 0 to 65,535).
int	4	Int32	Signed integer values between –2,147,483,648 and 2,147,483,647.
uint	4	UInt32	Unsigned integer values between 0 and 4,294,967,295.

---

[*] All the intrinsic types are value types except for Object (discussed in Chapter 5) and String (discussed in Chapter 10). All user-defined types are reference types except for structs (discussed in Chapter 7).

Table 3-1. C# built-in value types (continued)

Type	Size (in bytes)	.NET type	Description
float	4	Single	Floating point number. Holds the values from approximately +/–1.5 * 10^{-45} to approximate +/–3.4 * 10^{38} with 7 significant figures.
double	8	Double	Double-precision floating point; holds the values from approximately +/–5.0 * 10^{-324} to approximate +/–1.8 * 10^{308} with 15–16 significant figures.
decimal	12	Decimal	Fixed-precision up to 28 digits and the position of the decimal point. This is typically used in financial calculations. Requires the suffix "m" or "M."
long	8	Int64	Signed integers ranging from –9,223,372,036,854,775,808 to 9,223,372,036,854,775,807.
ulong	8	UInt64	Unsigned integers ranging from 0 to 0xffffffffffffffff.

 C and C++ programmers take note: Boolean variables can only have the values true or false. Integer values do not equate to Boolean values in C# and there is no implicit conversion.

In addition to these primitive types, C# has two other value types: enum (considered later in this chapter) and struct (see Chapter 4). Chapter 4 also discusses other subtleties of value types, such as forcing value types to act as reference types through a process known as *boxing*, and that value types do not "inherit."

The Stack and the Heap

A *stack* is a data structure used to store items on a last-in first-out basis (like a stack of dishes at the buffet line in a restaurant). *The* stack refers to an area of memory supported by the processor, on which the local variables are stored.

In C#, value types (e.g., integers) are allocated on the stack—an area of memory is set aside for their value, and this area is referred to by the name of the variable.

Reference types (e.g., objects) are allocated on the heap. When an object is allocated on the heap its address is returned, and that address is assigned to a reference.

The garbage collector destroys objects on the stack sometime after the stack frame they are declared within ends. Typically a stack frame is defined by a function. Thus, if you declare a local variable within a function (as explained later in this chapter) the object will be marked for garbage collection after the function ends.

Objects on the heap are garbage collected sometime after the final reference to them is destroyed.

Choosing a built-in type

Typically you decide which size integer to use (short, int, or long) based on the magnitude of the value you want to store. For example, a ushort can only hold values from 0 through 65,535, while a uint can hold values from 0 through 4,294,967,295.

That said, memory is fairly cheap, and programmer time is increasingly expensive; most of the time you'll simply declare your variables to be of type int, unless there is a good reason to do otherwise.

The signed types are the numeric types of choice of most programmers unless the programmer has a good reason to use an unsigned value.

Although you might be tempted to use an unsigned short to double the positive values of a signed short (moving the maximum positive value from 32,767 up to 65,535), it is easier and preferable to use a signed integer (with a maximum value of 2,147,483,647).

It is better to use an unsigned variable when the fact that the value must be positive is an inherent characteristic of the data. For example, if you had a variable to hold a person's age, you would use an unsigned int because an age cannot be negative.

Float, double, and decimal offer varying degrees of size and precision. For most small fractional numbers, float is fine. Note that the compiler assumes that any number with a decimal point is a double unless you tell it otherwise. To assign a literal float, follow the number with the letter f. (Assigning values to literals is discussed in detail later in this chapter.)

```
float someFloat = 57f;
```

The char type represents a Unicode character. char literals can be simple, Unicode, or escape characters enclosed by single quote marks. For example, A is a simple character while \u0041 is a Unicode character. Escape characters are special two-character tokens in which the first character is a backslash. For example, \t is a horizontal tab. The common escape characters are shown in Table 3-2.

Table 3-2. Common escape characters

Char	Meaning
\'	Single quote
\"	Double quote
\\	Backslash
\0	Null
\a	Alert
\b	Backspace
\f	Form feed
\n	Newline

Table 3-2. Common escape characters (continued)

Char	Meaning
\r	Carriage return
\t	Horizontal tab
\v	Vertical tab

Converting built-in types

Objects of one type can be converted into objects of another type either implicitly or explicitly. Implicit conversions happen automatically; the compiler takes care of it for you. Explicit conversions happen when you "cast" a value to a different type. The semantics of an explicit conversion are "Hey! Compiler! I know what I'm doing." This is sometimes called "hitting it with the big hammer" and can be very useful or very painful, depending on whether your thumb is in the way of the nail.

Implicit conversions happen automatically and are guaranteed not to lose information. For example, you can implicitly cast from a short int (2 bytes) to an int (4 bytes). No matter what value is in the short, it is not lost when converting to an int:

```
short x = 5;
int y = x; // implicit conversion
```

If you convert the other way, however, you certainly can lose information. If the value in the int is greater than 32,767, it will be truncated in the conversion. The compiler will not perform an implicit conversion from int to short:

```
short x;
int y = 500;
x = y;  // won't compile
```

You must explicitly convert using the cast operator:

```
short x;
int y = 500;
x = (short) y;  // OK
```

All of the intrinsic types define their own conversion rules. At times it is convenient to define conversion rules for your user-defined types, as discussed in Chapter 5.

Variables and Constants

A variable is a storage location with a type. In the preceding examples, both *x* and *y* are variables. Variables can have values assigned to them, and those values can be changed programmatically.

Create a variable by declaring its type and then giving it a name. You can initialize the variable when you declare it, and you can assign a new value to that variable at any time, changing the value held in the variable. This is illustrated in Example 3-1.

WriteLine( )

The .NET Framework provides a useful method for writing output to the screen. The details of this method, System.Console.WriteLine( ), will become clearer as we progress through the book, but the fundamentals are straightforward. Call the method as shown in Example 3-1, passing in a string that you want printed to the console (the screen) and, optionally, parameters that will be substituted. In the following example:

```
System.Console.WriteLine("After assignment, myInt: {0}", myInt);
```

the string "After assignment, myInt:" is printed as is, followed by the value in the variable myInt. The location of the *substitution parameter* {0} specifies where the value of the first output variable, myInt, will be displayed—in this case at the end of the string. We see a great deal more about WriteLine( ) in coming chapters.

Example 3-1. Initializing and assigning a value to a variable

```
class Values
{
    static void Main( )
    {
        int myInt = 7;
        System.Console.WriteLine("Initialized, myInt: {0}",
            myInt);
        myInt = 5;
        System.Console.WriteLine("After assignment, myInt: {0}",
            myInt);
    }
}
```

Output:
```
Initialized, myInt: 7
After assignment, myInt: 5
```

Here we initialize the variable myInt to the value 7, display that value, reassign the variable with the value 5, and display it again.

Definite Assignment

C# requires definite assignment; that is, variables must be initialized or assigned to, before they are used. To test this rule, change the line that initializes myInt in Example 3-1 to:

```
int myInt;
```

and save the revised program shown in Example 3-2.

Example 3-2. Using an uninitialized variable

```
class Values
{
```

Example 3-2. Using an uninitialized variable (continued)

```
static void Main( )
{
   int myInt;
   System.Console.WriteLine
   ("Uninitialized, myInt: {0}",myInt);
   myInt = 5;
   System.Console.WriteLine("Assigned, myInt: {0}", myInt);
}
}
```

When you try to compile this listing, the C# compiler will display the following error message:

```
3.1.cs(6,55): error CS0165: Use of unassigned local
variable 'myInt'
```

It is not legal to use an uninitialized variable in C#. Example 3-2 is not legal.

So, does this mean you must initialize every variable in a program? In fact, no. You don't actually need to initialize a variable, but you must assign a value to it before you attempt to use it. Example 3-3 illustrates a correct program.

Example 3-3. Assigning without initializing

```
class Values
{
   static void Main( )
   {
      int myInt;
      myInt = 7;
      System.Console.WriteLine("Assigned, myInt: {0}", myInt);
      myInt = 5;
      System.Console.WriteLine("Reassigned, myInt: {0}", myInt);
   }
}
```

Constants

A *constant* is a variable whose value cannot be changed. Variables are a powerful tool, but there are times when you want to manipulate a defined value, one whose value you want to ensure remains constant. For example, you might need to work with the Fahrenheit freezing and boiling points of water in a program simulating a chemistry experiment. Your program will be clearer if you name the variables that store the values FreezingPoint and BoilingPoint, but you do not want to permit their values to be reassigned. How do you prevent reassignment? The answer is to use a constant.

Constants come in three flavors: *literals*, *symbolic constants*, and *enumerations*. In this assignment:

```
x = 32;
```

the value 32 is a literal constant. The value of 32 is always 32. You can't assign a new value to 32; you can't make 32 represent the value 99 no matter how you might try.

Symbolic constants assign a name to a constant value. You declare a symbolic constant using the const keyword and the following syntax:

```
const type identifier = value;
```

A constant must be initialized when it is declared, and once initialized it cannot be altered. For example:

```
const int FreezingPoint = 32;
```

In this declaration, 32 is a literal constant and FreezingPoint is a symbolic constant of type int. Example 3-4 illustrates the use of symbolic constants.

Example 3-4. Using symbolic constants

```
class Values
{
   static void Main( )
   {
      const int FreezingPoint = 32;   // degrees Farenheit
      const int BoilingPoint = 212;

      System.Console.WriteLine("Freezing point of water: {0}",
           FreezingPoint );
      System.Console.WriteLine("Boiling point of water: {0}",
           BoilingPoint );
      //BoilingPoint = 21;

   }
}
```

Example 3-4 creates two symbolic integer constants: FreezingPoint and BoilingPoint. As a matter of style, constant names are written in Pascal notation, but this is certainly not required by the language.

These constants serve the same purpose of always using the *literal* values 32 and 212 for the freezing and boiling points of water in expressions that require them, but because these constants have names they convey far more meaning. Also, if you decide to switch this program to Celsius, you can reinitialize these constants at compile time, to 0 and 100, respectively; all the rest of the code ought to continue to work.

To prove to yourself that the constant cannot be reassigned, try uncommenting the last line of the program (shown in bold). When you recompile you should receive this error:

```
error CS0131: The left-hand side of an assignment must be
a variable, property or indexer
```

Enumerations

Enumerations provide a powerful alternative to constants. An enumeration is a distinct value type, consisting of a set of named constants (called the *enumerator list*).

In Example 3-4, you created two related constants:

```
const int FreezingPoint = 32;
const int BoilingPoint = 212;
```

You might wish to add a number of other useful constants as well to this list, such as:

```
const int LightJacketWeather = 60;
const int SwimmingWeather = 72;
const int WickedCold = 0;
```

This process is somewhat cumbersome, and there is no logical connection among these various constants. C# provides the *enumeration* to solve these problems:

```
enum Temperatures
{
    WickedCold = 0,
    FreezingPoint = 32,
    LightJacketWeather = 60,
    SwimmingWeather = 72,
    BoilingPoint = 212,
}
```

Every enumeration has an underlying type, which can be any integral type (integer, short, long, etc.) except for char. The technical definition of an enumeration is:

```
[attributes] [modifiers] enum identifier
    [:base-type] {enumerator-list};
```

The optional attributes and modifiers are considered later in this book. For now, let's focus on the rest of this declaration. An enumeration begins with the keyword enum, which is generally followed by an identifier, such as:

```
enum Temperatures
```

The base type is the underlying type for the enumeration. If you leave out this optional value (and often you will) it defaults to int, but you are free to use any of the integral types (e.g., ushort, long) except for char. For example, the following fragment declares an enumeration of unsigned integers (uint):

```
enum ServingSizes :uint
{
    Small = 1,
    Regular = 2,
    Large = 3
}
```

Notice that an enum declaration ends with the enumerator list. The enumerator list contains the constant assignments for the enumeration, each separated by a comma.

Example 3-5 rewrites Example 3-4 to use an enumeration.

Example 3-5. Using enumerations to simplify your code

```
class Values
{

    enum Temperatures
    {
        WickedCold = 0,
        FreezingPoint = 32,
        LightJacketWeather = 60,
        SwimmingWeather = 72,
        BoilingPoint = 212,
    }

    static void Main( )
    {

        System.Console.WriteLine("Freezing point of water: {0}",
            (int) Temperatures.FreezingPoint );
        System.Console.WriteLine("Boiling point of water: {0}",
            (int) Temperatures.BoilingPoint );

    }
}
```

As you can see, an enum must be qualified by its enumtype (e.g., Temperatures. WickedCold). By default, an enumeration value is displayed using its symbolic name (such as BoilingPoint or FreezingPoint). When you want to display the value of an enumerated constant, you must cast the constant to its underlying type (int). The integer value is passed to WriteLine, and that value is displayed.

Each constant in an enumeration corresponds to a numerical value—in this case, an integer. If you don't specifically set it otherwise, the enumeration begins at 0 and each subsequent value counts up from the previous.

If you create the following enumeration:

```
enum SomeValues
{
    First,
    Second,
    Third = 20,
    Fourth
}
```

the value of First will be 0, Second will be 1, Third will be 20, and Fourth will be 21.

Enums are formal types; therefore an explicit conversion is required to convert between an enum type and an integral type.

 C++ programmers take note: C#'s use of enums is subtly different from C++, which restricts assignment to an enum type from an integer but allows an enum to be promoted to an integer for assignment of an enum to an integer.

Strings

It is nearly impossible to write a C# program without creating strings. A string object holds a string of characters.

You declare a string variable using the `string` keyword much as you would create an instance of any object:

```
string myString;
```

A string literal is created by placing double quotes around a string of letters:

```
"Hello World"
```

It is common to initialize a string variable with a string literal:

```
string myString = "Hello World";
```

Strings are covered in much greater detail in Chapter 10.

Identifiers

Identifiers are names that programmers choose for their types, methods, variables, constants, objects, and so forth. An identifier must begin with a letter or an underscore.

The Microsoft naming conventions suggest using *camel notation* (initial lowercase such as `someName`) for variable names and *Pascal notation* (initial uppercase such as `SomeOtherName`) for method names and most other identifiers.

Microsoft no longer recommends using Hungarian notation (e.g., `iSomeInteger`) or underscores (e.g., `SOME_VALUE`).

Identifiers cannot clash with keywords. Thus, you cannot create a variable named `int` or `class`. In addition, identifiers are case-sensitive, so C# treats `myVariable` and `MyVariable` as two different variable names.

Expressions

Statements that evaluate to a value are called *expressions*. You may be surprised how many statements do evaluate to a value. For example, an assignment such as:

```
myVariable = 57;
```

is an expression; it evaluates to the value assigned, which, in this case, is 57.

Note that the preceding statement assigns the value 57 to the variable `myVariable`. The assignment operator (=) does not test equality; rather it causes whatever is on the right side (57) to be assigned to whatever is on the left side (`myVariable`). All of the C# operators (including assignment and equality) are discussed later in this chapter (see "Operators").

Because `myVariable` = 57 is an expression that evaluates to 57, it can be used as part of another assignment operator, such as:

```
mySecondVariable = myVariable = 57;
```

What happens in this statement is that the literal value 57 is assigned to the variable `myVariable`. The value of that assignment (57) is then assigned to the second variable, `mySecondVariable`. Thus, the value 57 is assigned to both variables. You can thus initialize any number of variables to the same value with one statement:

```
a = b = c = d = e = 20;
```

Whitespace

In the C# language, spaces, tabs, and newlines are considered to be "whitespace" (so named because you see only the white of the underlying "page"). Extra whitespace is generally ignored in C# statements. Thus, you can write:

```
myVariable = 5;
```

or:

```
myVariable        =                    5;
```

and the compiler will treat the two statements as identical.

The exception to this rule is that whitespace within strings is not ignored. If you write:

```
Console.WriteLine("Hello World")
```

each space between "Hello" and "World" is treated as another character in the string.

Most of the time the use of whitespace is intuitive. The key is to use whitespace to make the program more readable to the programmer; the compiler is indifferent.

However, there are instances in which the use of whitespace is quite significant. Although the expression:

```
int x = 5;
```

is the same as:

```
int x=5;
```

it is not the same as:

```
intx=5;
```

The compiler knows that the whitespace on either side of the assignment operator is extra, but the whitespace between the type declaration `int` and the variable name `x` is *not* extra, and is required. This is not surprising; the whitespace allows the compiler

---

to parse the keyword int rather than some unknown term intx. You are free to add as much or as little whitespace between int and x as you care to, but there must be at least one whitespace character (typically a space or tab).

 Visual Basic programmers take note: in C# the end-of-line has no special significance; statements are ended with semicolons, not newline characters. There is no line-continuation character because none is needed.

Statements

In C# a complete program instruction is called a *statement*. Programs consist of sequences of C# statements. Each statement must end with a semicolon (;). For example:

```
int x;     // a statement
x = 23;    // another statement
int y = x; // yet another statement
```

C# statements are evaluated in order. The compiler starts at the beginning of a statement list and makes its way to the bottom. This would be entirely straightforward, and terribly limiting, were it not for branching. There are two types of branches in a C# program: *unconditional branching* and *conditional branching*.

Program flow is also affected by looping and iteration statements, which are signaled by the keywords for, while, do, in, and foreach. Iteration is discussed later in this chapter. For now, let's consider some of the more basic methods of conditional and unconditional branching.

Unconditional Branching Statements

An unconditional branch is created in one of two ways. The first way is by invoking a method. When the compiler encounters the name of a method, it stops execution in the current method and branches to the newly "called" method. When that method returns a value, execution picks up in the original method on the line just below the method call. Example 3-6 illustrates.

Example 3-6. Calling a method

```
using System;
class Functions
{
    static void Main()
    {
        Console.WriteLine("In Main! Calling SomeMethod()...");
        SomeMethod();
        Console.WriteLine("Back in Main().");
```

Example 3-6. Calling a method (continued)

```
    }
    static void SomeMethod()
    {
        Console.WriteLine("Greetings from SomeMethod!");
    }
}
```

Output:
```
In Main! Calling SomeMethod()...
Greetings from SomeMethod!
Back in Main().
```

Program flow begins in Main() and proceeds until SomeMethod() is invoked (invoking a method is sometimes referred to as "calling" the method). At that point program flow branches to the method. When the method completes, program flow resumes at the next line after the call to that method.

The second way to create an unconditional branch is with one of the unconditional branch keywords: goto, break, continue, return, or throw. Additional information about the first four jump statements is provided later in this chapter, in the sections titled "Switch statements: an alternative to nested ifs," "The goto statement," and "The continue and break statements." The final statement, throw, is discussed in Chapter 11.

Conditional Branching Statements

A conditional branch is created by a conditional statement, which is signaled by keywords such as if, else, or switch. A conditional branch occurs only if the condition expression evaluates true.

If...else statements

If...else statements branch based on a condition. The condition is an expression, tested in the head of the if statement. If the condition evaluates true, the statement (or block of statements) in the body of the if statement is executed.

If statements may contain an optional else statement. The else statement is executed only if the expression in the head of the if statement evaluates false:

```
if (expression)
    statement1
[else
    statement2]
```

This is the kind of description of the if statement you are likely to find in your compiler documentation. It shows you that the if statement takes a Boolean *expression* (an expression that evaluates true or false) in parentheses, and executes statement1 if the expression evaluates true. Note that statement1 can actually be a block of statements within braces.

You can also see that the else statement is optional, as it is enclosed in square brackets. Although this gives you the syntax of an if statement, an illustration will make its use clear. Example 3-7 illustrates.

Example 3-7. If ... else statements

```
using System;
class Values
{
    static void Main( )
    {
        int valueOne = 10;
        int valueTwo = 20;

        if ( valueOne > valueTwo )
        {
            Console.WriteLine(
              "ValueOne: {0} larger than ValueTwo: {1}",
                    valueOne, valueTwo);
        }
        else
        {
            Console.WriteLine(
              "ValueTwo: {0} larger than ValueOne: {1}",
                    valueTwo,valueOne);
        }

        valueOne = 30; // set valueOne higher

        if ( valueOne > valueTwo )
        {
            valueTwo = valueOne++;
            Console.WriteLine("\nSetting valueTwo to valueOne value, ");
            Console.WriteLine("and incrementing ValueOne.\n");
                Console.WriteLine("ValueOne: {0}  ValueTwo: {1}",
                    valueOne, valueTwo);
        }
        else
        {
            valueOne = valueTwo;
            Console.WriteLine("Setting them equal. ");
                Console.WriteLine("ValueOne: {0}  ValueTwo: {1}",
                    valueOne, valueTwo);
        }
    }
}
```

In Example 3-7, the first if statement tests whether valueOne is greater than valueTwo. The relational operators such as greater than (>), less than (<), and equal to (==) are fairly intuitive to use.

The test of whether valueOne is greater than valueTwo evaluates false (because valueOne is 10 and valueTwo is 20, so valueOne is *not* greater than valueTwo). The else statement is invoked, printing the statement:

```
ValueTwo: 20 is larger than ValueOne: 10
```

The second if statement evaluates true and all the statements in the if block are evaluated, causing two lines to print:

```
Setting valueTwo to valueOne value,
and incrementing ValueOne.

ValueOne: 31   ValueTwo: 30
```

Statement Blocks

You can substitute a statement block anyplace that C# expects a statement. A *statement block* is a set of statements surrounded by braces.

Thus, where you might write:

```
if (someCondition)
    someStatement;
```

you can instead write:

```
if(someCondition)
{
    statementOne;
    statementTwo;
    statementThree;
}
```

Nested if statements

It is possible, and not uncommon, to nest if statements to handle complex conditions. For example, suppose you need to write a program to evaluate the temperature, and specifically to return the following types of information:

- If the temperature is 32 degrees or lower, the program should warn you about ice on the road.
- If the temperature is exactly 32 degrees, the program should tell you that there may be ice patches.
- If the temperature is higher than 32 degrees, the program should assure you that there is no ice.

There are many good ways to write this program. Example 3-8 illustrates one approach, using nested if statements.

Example 3-8. Nested if statements

```
using System;
class Values
{
    static void Main( )
    {
        int temp = 32;

        if (temp <= 32)
        {
            Console.WriteLine("Warning! Ice on road!");
            if (temp == 32)
            {
                Console.WriteLine(
                "Temp exactly freezing, beware of water.");
            }
            else
            {
                Console.WriteLine("Watch for black ice! Temp: {0}", temp);
            }
        }

    }
}
```

The logic of Example 3-8 is that it tests whether the temperature is less than or equal to 32. If so, it prints a warning:

```
if (temp <= 32)
{
    Console.WriteLine("Warning! Ice on road!");
```

The program then checks whether the temp is equal to 32 degrees. If so, it prints one message; if not, the temp must be less than 32 and the program prints the second message. Notice that this second if statement is nested within the first if, so the logic of the else is "since it has been established that the temp is less than or equal to 32, and it isn't equal to 32, it must be less than 32."

Switch statements: an alternative to nested ifs

Nested if statements are hard to read, hard to get right, and hard to debug. When you have a complex set of choices to make, the switch statement is a more powerful alternative. The logic of a switch statement is "pick a matching value and act accordingly."

```
switch (expression)
{
    case constant-expression:
        statement
        jump-statement
    [default: statement]
}
```

All Operators Are Not Created Equal

A closer examination of the second if statement in Example 3-8 reveals a common potential problem. This if statement tests whether the temperature is equal to 32:

```
if (temp == 32)
```

In C and C++, there is an inherent danger in this kind of statement. It's not uncommon for novice programmers to use the assignment operator rather than the equals operator, instead creating the statement:

```
if (temp = 32)
```

This mistake would be difficult to notice, and the result would be that 32 was assigned to temp, and 32 would be returned as the value of the assignment statement. Because any nonzero value evaluates to true in C and C++, the if statement would return true. The side effect would be that temp would be assigned a value of 32 whether or not it originally had that value. This is a common bug that could easily be overlooked—if the developers of C# had not anticipated it!

C# solves this problem by requiring that if statements accept only Boolean values. The 32 returned by the assignment is not Boolean (it is an integer) and, in C#, there is no automatic conversion from 32 to true. Thus, this bug would be caught at compile time, which is a very good thing, and a significant improvement over C++—at the small cost of not allowing implicit conversions from integers to Booleans!

As you can see, like an if statement, the expression is put in parentheses in the head of the switch statement. Each case statement then requires a constant expression; that is, a literal or symbolic constant or an enumeration.

If a case is matched, the statement (or block of statements) associated with that case is executed. This must be followed by a jump statement. Typically, the jump statement is break, which transfers execution out of the switch. An alternative is a goto statement, typically used to jump into another case, as illustrated in Example 3-9.

Example 3-9. The switch statement

```
using System;

class Values
{
    static void Main( )
    {
        const int Democrat = 0;
        const int LiberalRepublican = 1;
        const int Republican = 2;
        const int Libertarian = 3;
        const int NewLeft = 4;
```

Example 3-9. The switch statement (continued)

```
    const int Progressive = 5;

    int myChoice = Libertarian;

    switch (myChoice)
    {
        case Democrat:
            Console.WriteLine("You voted Democratic.\n");
            break;
        case LiberalRepublican:   // fall through
            //Console.WriteLine(
                //"Liberal Republicans vote Republican\n");
        case Republican:
            Console.WriteLine("You voted Republican.\n");
            break;
        case NewLeft:
            Console.WriteLine("NewLeft is now Progressive");
            goto case Progressive;
        case Progressive:
            Console.WriteLine("You voted Progressive.\n");
            break;
        case Libertarian:
            Console.WriteLine("Libertarians are voting Republican");
            goto case Republican;
        default:
            Console.WriteLine("You did not pick a valid choice.\n");
            break;
    }

    Console.WriteLine("Thank you for voting.");

    }
}
```

In this whimsical example, we create constants for various political parties. We then assign one value (Libertarian) to the variable myChoice and switch on that value. If myChoice is equal to Democrat, we print out a statement. Notice that this case ends with break. Break is a jump statement that takes us out of the switch statement and down to the first line after the switch, on which we print "Thank you for voting."

The value LiberalRepublican has no statement under it, and it "falls through" to the next statement: Republican. If the value is LiberalRepublican or Republican, the Republican statements execute. You can only "fall through" in this way if there is no body within the statement. If you uncomment the WriteLine under Liberal-Republican, this program will not compile.

C and C++ programmers take note: you cannot fall through to the next case if the case statement is not empty. Thus, you can write the following:

```
case 1: // fall through ok
case 2:
```

In this example, case 1 is empty. You cannot, however, write the following:

```
case 1:
    TakeSomeAction( );
        // fall through not OK
case 2:
```

Here case 1 has a statement in it, and you cannot fall through. If you want case 1 to fall through to case 2, you must explicitly use goto:

```
case 1:
    TakeSomeAction( );
    goto case 2; // explicit fall through
case 2:
```

If you do need a statement but you then want to execute another case, you can use the goto statement, as shown in the NewLeft case:

```
goto case Progressive;
```

It is not required that the goto take you to the case immediately following. In the next instance, the Libertarian choice also has a goto, but this time it jumps all the way back up to the Republican case. Because our value was set to Libertarian, this is just what occurs. We print out the Libertarian statement, go to the Republican case, print that statement, and then hit the break, taking us out of the switch and down to the final statement. The output for all of this is:

```
Libertarians are voting Republican
You voted Republican.

Thank you for voting.
```

Note the default case, excerpted from Example 3-9:

```
default:
    Console.WriteLine(
      "You did not pick a valid choice.\n");
```

If none of the cases matches, the default case will be invoked, warning the user of the mistake.

Switch on string statements

In the previous example, the switch value was an integral constant. C# offers the ability to switch on a string, allowing you to write:

```
case "Libertarian":
```

If the strings match, the case statement is entered.

Iteration Statements

C# provides an extensive suite of iteration statements, including for, while and do... while loops, as well as foreach loops (new to the C family but familiar to VB programmers). In addition, C# supports the goto, break, continue, and return jump statements.

The goto statement

The goto statement is the seed from which all other iteration statements have been germinated. Unfortunately, it is a semolina seed, producer of spaghetti code and endless confusion. Most experienced programmers properly shun the goto statement, but in the interest of completeness, here's how you use it:

1. Create a label.

2. goto that label.

The label is an identifier followed by a colon. The goto command is typically tied to a condition, as illustrated in Example 3-10.

Example 3-10. Using goto

```
using System;
public class Tester
 {

    public static int Main()
    {
      int i = 0;
      repeat:              // the label
      Console.WriteLine("i: {0}",i);
      i++;
      if (i < 10)
         goto repeat;  // the dastardly deed
         return 0;
    }
}
```

If you were to try to draw the flow of control in a program that makes extensive use of goto statements, the resulting morass of intersecting and overlapping lines looks like a plate of spaghetti; hence the term "spaghetti code." It was this phenomenon that led to the creation of alternatives, such as the while loop. Many programmers feel that using goto in anything other than a trivial example creates confusion and difficult-to-maintain code.

The while loop

The semantics of the while loop are "while this condition is true, do this work."

The syntax is:

```
while (expression) statement
```

As usual, an expression is any statement that returns a value. While statements require an expression that evaluates to a Boolean (true/false) value, and that statement can, of course, be a block of statements. Example 3-11 updates Example 3-10, using a while loop.

Example 3-11. Using a while loop

```
using System;
public class Tester
{

    public static int Main( )
    {
     int i = 0;
     while (i < 10)
     {
        Console.WriteLine("i: {0}",i);
        i++;
     }
        return 0;
    }
}
```

The code in Example 3-11 produces results identical to the code in Example 3-10, but the logic is a bit clearer. The while statement is nicely self-contained, and it reads like an English sentence: "while i is less than 10, print this message and increment i."

Notice that the while loop tests the value of i before entering the loop. This ensures that the loop will not run if the condition tested is false; thus if i is initialized to 11, the loop will never run.

The do ... while loop

There are times when a while loop might not serve your purpose. In certain situations, you might want to reverse the semantics from "run while this is true" to the subtly different "do this while this condition remains true." In other words, take the action, and then, after the action is completed, check the condition. For this you will use the do...while loop.

```
do statement while expression
```

An expression is any statement that returns a value. An example of the do...while loop is shown in Example 3-12.

Example 3-12. The do...while loop

```
using System;
public class Tester
```

Example 3-12. The do…while loop (continued)

```
{
    public static int Main( )
    {
        int i = 11;
        do
        {
            Console.WriteLine("i: {0}",i);
            i++;
        } while (i < 10);
        return 0;
    }
}
```

Here i is initialized to 11 and the while test fails, but only after the body of the loop has run once.

The for loop

A careful examination of the while loop in Example 3-11 reveals a pattern often seen in iterative statements: initialize a variable (i = 0), test the variable (i < 10), execute a series of statements, and increment the variable (i++). The for loop allows you to combine all these steps in a single loop statement:

```
for ([initializers]; [expression]; [iterators]) statement
```

The for loop is illustrated in Example 3-13.

Example 3-13. The for loop

```
using System;
public class Tester
{
    public static int Main( )
    {
        for (int i=0;i<100;i++)
        {
            Console.Write("{0} ", i);

            if (i%10 == 0)
            {
                Console.WriteLine("\t{0}", i);
            }
        }
        return 0;
    }
}
```

Output:
```
0        0
1 2 3 4 5 6 7 8 9 10      10
11 12 13 14 15 16 17 18 19 20      20
```

Example 3-13. The for loop (continued)

```
21 22 23 24 25 26 27 28 29 30    30
31 32 33 34 35 36 37 38 39 40    40
41 42 43 44 45 46 47 48 49 50    50
51 52 53 54 55 56 57 58 59 60    60
61 62 63 64 65 66 67 68 69 70    70
71 72 73 74 75 76 77 78 79 80    80
81 82 83 84 85 86 87 88 89 90    90
91 92 93 94 95 96 97 98 99
```

This for loop makes use of the modulus operator described later in this chapter. The value of i is printed until i is a multiple of 10.

```
if (i%10 == 0)
```

A tab is then printed, followed by the value. Thus the tens (20, 30, 40, etc.) are called out on the right side of the output.

The individual values are printed using Console.Write, which is much like WriteLine but which does not enter a newline character, allowing the subsequent writes to occur on the same line.

A few quick points to notice: in a for loop the condition is tested before the statements are executed. Thus, in the example, i is initialized to zero, then it is tested to see if it is less than 100. Because i < 100 returns true, the statements within the for loop are executed. After the execution, i is incremented (i++).

Note that the variable i is scoped to within the for loop (that is, the variable i is visible only within the for loop). Example 3-14 will not compile.

Example 3-14. Scope of variables declared in a for loop

```
using System;
public class Tester
{

    public static int Main( )
    {
        for (int i=0; i<100; i++)
        {
            Console.Write("{0} ", i);

            if ( i%10 == 0 )
            {
                Console.WriteLine("\t{0}", i);
            }
        }
        Console.WriteLine("\n Final value of i: {0}", i);
        return 0;
    }
}
```

The line shown in bold fails, as the variable i is not available outside the scope of the for loop itself.

The foreach statement

The foreach statement is new to the C family of languages; it is used for looping through the elements of an array or a collection. Discussion of this incredibly useful statement is deferred until Chapter 9.

The continue and break statements

There are times when you would like to restart a loop without executing the remaining statements in the loop. The continue statement causes the loop to return to the top and continue executing.

The obverse side of that coin is the ability to break out of a loop and immediately end all further work within the loop. For this purpose the break statement exists.

Break and continue create multiple exit points and make for hard-to-understand, and thus hard-to-maintain, code. Use them with some care.

Example 3-15 illustrates the mechanics of continue and break. This code, suggested to me by one of my technical reviewers, Donald Xie, is intended to create a traffic signal processing system. The signals are simulated by entering numerals and uppercase characters from the keyboard, using Console.ReadLine, which reads a line of text from the keyboard.

The algorithm is simple: receipt of a 0 (zero) means normal conditions, and no further action is required except to log the event. (In this case, the program simply writes a message to the console; a real application might enter a timestamped record in a database.) On receipt of an Abort signal (here simulated with an uppercase "A"), the problem is logged and the process is ended. Finally, for any other event, an alarm is raised, perhaps notifying the police. (Note that this sample does not actually notify the police, though it does print out a harrowing message to the console.) If the signal is "X," the alarm is raised but the while loop is also terminated.

Example 3-15. Using continue and break

```csharp
using System;
public class Tester
{
   public static int Main()
   {
      string signal = "0";       // initialize to neutral
      while (signal != "X")      // X indicates stop
      {
         Console.Write("Enter a signal: ");
         signal = Console.ReadLine();

         // do some work here, no matter what signal you
         // receive
         Console.WriteLine("Received: {0}", signal);

         if (signal == "A")
         {
            // faulty - abort signal processing
            // Log the problem and abort.
            Console.WriteLine("Fault! Abort\n");
            break;
         }

         if (signal == "0")
         {
            // normal traffic condition
            // log and continue on
            Console.WriteLine("All is well.\n");
            continue;
         }

         // Problem. Take action and then log the problem
         // and then continue on
         Console.WriteLine("{0} -- raise alarm!\n",
            signal);
      }
      return 0;
   }
}
```

Example 3-15. Using continue and break (continued)

Output:
```
Enter a signal: 0
Received: 0
All is well.

Enter a signal: B
Received: B
B -- raise alarm!

Enter a signal: A
Received: A
Fault! Abort

Press any key to continue
```

The point of this exercise is that when the A signal is received, the action in the if statement is taken and then the program *breaks* out of the loop, without raising the alarm. When the signal is 0, it is also undesirable to raise the alarm, so the program *continues* from the top of the loop.

Operators

An *operator* is a symbol that causes C# to take an action. The C# primitive types (e.g., int) support a number of operators such as assignment, increment, and so forth. Their use is highly intuitive, with the possible exception of the assignment operator (=) and the equality operator (==), which are often confused.

The Assignment Operator (=)

The section titled "Expressions," earlier in this chapter, demonstrates the use of the assignment operator. This symbol causes the operand on the left side of the operator to have its value changed to whatever is on the right side of the operator.

Mathematical Operators

C# uses five mathematical operators, four for standard calculations and a fifth to return the remainder in integer division. The following sections consider the use of these operators.

Simple arithmetical operators (+, -, *, /)

C# offers operators for simple arithmetic: the addition (+), subtraction (-), multiplication (*), and division (/) operators work as you might expect, with the possible exception of integer division.

When you divide two integers, C# divides like a child in fourth grade: it throws away any fractional remainder. Thus, dividing 17 by 4 will return the value 4 (17/4 = 4, with a remainder of 1). C# provides a special operator (modulus (%), which is described in the next section) to retrieve the remainder.

Note, however, that C# does return fractional answers when you divide floats, doubles, and decimals.

The modulus operator (%) to return remainders

To find the remainder in integer division, use the modulus operator (%). For example, the statement 17%4 returns 1 (the remainder after integer division).

The modulus operator turns out to be more useful than you might at first imagine. When you perform modulus n on a number that is a multiple of *n*, the result is zero. Thus 80%10 = 0 because 80 is an even multiple of 10. This fact allows you to set up loops in which you take an action every *n*th time through the loop, by testing a counter to see if %n is equal to zero. This strategy comes in handy in the use of the for loop, as described earlier in this chapter. The effects of division on integers, floats, doubles, and decimals is illustrated in Example 3-16.

Example 3-16. Division and modulus

```
using System;
class Values
{
    static void Main( )
    {
        int i1, i2;
        float f1, f2;
        double d1, d2;
        decimal dec1, dec2;

        i1 = 17;
        i2 = 4;
        f1 = 17f;
        f2 = 4f;
        d1 = 17;
        d2 = 4;
        dec1 = 17;
        dec2 = 4;
        Console.WriteLine("Integer:\t{0}\nfloat:\t\t{1}",
            i1/i2, f1/f2);
        Console.WriteLine("double:\t\t{0}\ndecimal:\t{1}",
            d1/d2, dec1/dec2);
        Console.WriteLine("\nModulus:\t{0}", i1%i2);

    }
}
```

Output:
```
Integer:        4
```

Example 3-16. Division and modulus (continued)

```
float:        4.25
double:       4.25
decimal:      4.25

Modulus:      1
```

Now consider this line from Example 3-16:

```
Console.WriteLine("Integer:\t{0}\nfloat:\t\t{1}\n",
    i1/i2, f1/f2);
```

It begins with a call to `Console.Writeline`, passing in this partial string:

```
"Integer:\t{0}\n
```

This will print the characters `Integer:`, followed by a tab (`\t`), followed by the first parameter (`{0}`), followed by a newline character (`\n`). The next string snippet:

```
float:\t\t{1}\n
```

is very similar. It prints `float:`, followed by two tabs (to ensure alignment), the contents of the second parameter (`{1}`), and then another newline. Notice the subsequent line, as well:

```
Console.WriteLine("\nModulus:\t{0}", i1%i2);
```

This time the string begins with a newline character, which causes a line to be skipped just before the string `Modulus:` is printed. You can see this effect in the output.

Increment and Decrement Operators

A common requirement is to add a value to a variable, subtract a value from a variable, or otherwise change the mathematical value, and then to assign that new value back to the same variable. You might even want to assign the result to another variable altogether. The following two sections discuss these cases respectively.

Calculate and reassign operators

Suppose you want to increment the `mySalary` variable by 5000. You can do this by writing:

```
mySalary = mySalary + 5000;
```

The addition happens before the assignment, and it is perfectly legal to assign the result back to the original variable. Thus, after this operation completes, `mySalary` will have been incremented by 5000. You can perform this kind of assignment with any mathematical operator:

```
mySalary = mySalary * 5000;
mySalary = mySalary - 5000;
```

and so forth.

The need to increment and decrement variables is so common that C# includes special operators for self-assignment. Among these operators are +=, -=, *=, /=, and %=, which, respectively, combine addition, subtraction, multiplication, division, and modulus with self-assignment. Thus, you can alternatively write the previous examples as:

```
mySalary += 5000;
mySalary *= 5000;
mySalary -= 5000;
```

The effect of this is to increment mySalary by 5000, multiply mySalary by 5000, and subtract 5000 from the mySalary variable, respectively.

Because incrementing and decrementing by 1 is a very common need, C# (like C and C++ before it) also provides two special operators. To increment by 1, use the ++ operator, and to decrement by 1, use the -- operator.

Thus, if you want to increment the variable myAge by 1 you can write:

```
myAge++;
```

The prefix and postfix operators

To complicate matters further, you might want to increment a variable and assign the results to a second variable:

```
firstValue = secondValue++;
```

The question arises: do you want to assign before you increment the value or after? In other words, if secondValue starts out with the value 10, do you want to end with both firstValue and secondValue equal to 11, or do you want firstValue to be equal to 10 (the original value) and secondValue to be equal to 11?

C# (again, like C and C++) offer two flavors of the increment and decrement operators: prefix and postfix. Thus you can write:

```
firstValue = secondValue++;  // postfix
```

which will assign first, and then increment (firstValue=10, secondValue=11). You can also write:

```
firstValue = ++secondValue;  // prefix
```

which will increment first, and then assign (firstValue=11, secondValue=11).

It is important to understand the different effects of prefix and postfix, as illustrated in Example 3-17.

Example 3-17. Illustrating prefix versus postfix increment

```
using System;
class Values
{
    static void Main( )
```

Example 3-17. Illustrating prefix versus postfix increment (continued)

```
    {
        int valueOne = 10;
        int valueTwo;
        valueTwo = valueOne++;
        Console.WriteLine("After postfix: {0}, {1}", valueOne,
        valueTwo);
        valueOne = 20;
        valueTwo = ++valueOne;
        Console.WriteLine("After prefix: {0}, {1}", valueOne,
        valueTwo);
    }
}
```

Output:
```
After postfix: 11, 10
After prefix: 21, 21
```

Relational Operators

Relational operators are used to compare two values, and then return a Boolean (true or false). The greater-than operator (>), for example, returns true if the value on the left of the operator is greater than the value on the right. Thus, 5 > 2 returns the value true, while 2 > 5 returns the value false.

The relational operators for C# are shown in Table 3-3. This table assumes two variables: bigValue and smallValue, in which bigValue has been assigned the value 100 and smallValue the value 50.

Table 3-3. C# relational operators (assumes bigValue = 100 and smallValue = 50)

Name	Operator	Given this statement:	The expression evaluates to:
Equals	==	bigValue == 100	true
		bigValue == 80	false
Not equals	!=	bigValue != 100	false
		bigValue != 80	true
Greater than	>	bigValue > smallValue	true
Greater than or equals	>=	bigValue >= smallValue	true
		smallValue >= bigValue	false
Less than	<	bigValue < smallValue	false
Less than or equals	<=	smallValue <= bigValue	true
		bigValue <= smallValue	false

Each of these relational operators acts as you might expect. However, take note of the equals operator (==), which is created by typing two equal signs (=) in a row (i.e., without any space between them); the C# compiler treats the pair as a single operator.

The C# equality operator (==) tests for equality between the objects on either side of the operator. This operator evaluates to a Boolean value (true or false). Thus, the statement:

```
myX == 5;
```

evaluates to true if and only if myX is a variable whose value is 5.

 It is not uncommon to confuse the assignment operator (=) with the equals operator (==). The latter has two equal signs, the former only one.

Use of Logical Operators with Conditionals

If statements (discussed earlier in this chapter) test whether a condition is true. Often you will want to test whether two conditions are both true, or whether only one is true, or none is true. C# provides a set of logical operators for this, as shown in Table 3-4. This table assumes two variables, x and y, in which x has the value 5 and y the value 7.

Table 3-4. C# logical operators (assumes x = 5, y = 7)

Name	Operator	Given this statement	The expression evaluates to	Logic
and	&&	(x == 3) && (y == 7)	false	Both must be true
or	||	(x == 3) || (y == 7)	true	Either or both must be true
not	!	! (x == 3)	true	Expression must be false

The and operator tests whether two statements are both true. The first line in Table 3-4 includes an example that illustrates the use of the and operator:

```
(x == 3) && (y == 7)
```

The entire expression evaluates false because one side (x == 3) is false.

With the or operator, either or both sides must be true; the expression is false only if both sides are false. So, in the case of the example in Table 3-4:

```
(x == 3) || (y == 7)
```

the entire expression evaluates true because one side (y==7) is true.

With a not operator, the statement is true if the expression is false, and vice versa. So, in the accompanying example:

```
! (x == 3)
```

the entire expression is true because the tested expression (x==3) is false. (The logic is "it is true that it is not true that x is equal to 3.")

Short-Circuit Evaluation

Consider the following code snippet:

```
int x = 8;
if ((x == 8) || (y == 12))
```

The if statement here is a bit complicated. The entire if statement is in parentheses, as are all if statements in C#. Thus, everything within the outer set of parentheses must evaluate true for the if statement to be true.

Within the outer parentheses are two expressions (x==8) and (y==12), which are separated by an or operator (||). Because x is 8, the first term (x==8) evaluates true. There is no need to evaluate the second term (y==12). It doesn't matter whether y is 12, the entire expression will be true. Similarly, consider this snippet:

```
int x = 8;
if ((x == 5) && (y == 12))
```

Again, there is no need to evaluate the second term. Because the first term is false, the and must fail. (Remember, for an and statement to evaluate true, both tested expressions must evaluate true.)

In cases such as these, the C# compiler will short-circuit the evaluation; the second test will never be performed.

Operator Precedence

The compiler must know the order in which to evaluate a series of operators. For example, if I write:

```
myVariable = 5 + 7 * 3;
```

there are three operators for the compiler to evaluate (=, +, and *). It could, for example, operate left to right, which would assign the value 5 to myVariable, then add 7 to the 5 (12) and multiply by 3 (36)—but of course then it would throw that 36 away. This is clearly not what is intended.

The rules of precedence tell the compiler which operators to evaluate first. As is the case in algebra, multiplication has higher precedence than addition, so 5+7*3 is equal to 26 rather than 36. Both addition and multiplication have higher precedence than assignment, so the compiler will do the math, and then assign the result (26) to myVariable only after the math is completed.

In C#, parentheses are also used to change the order of precedence much as they are in algebra. Thus, you can change the result by writing:

```
myVariable = (5+7) * 3;
```

Grouping the elements of the assignment in this way causes the compiler to add 5+7, multiply the result by 3, and then assign that value (36) to myVariable. Table 3-5 summarizes operator precedence in C#.

Table 3-5. Operator precedence

Category	Operators
Primary	(x) x.y x->y f(x) a[x] x++ x-- new typeof sizeof checked unchecked stackalloc
Unary	+ - ! ~ ++x --x (T)x *x &x
Multiplicative	* / %
Additive	+ -
Shift	<< >>
Relational	< > <= >= is as
Equality	== !=
Logical AND	&
Logical XOR	^
Logical OR	|
Conditional AND	&&
Conditional OR	||
Conditional	?:
Assignment	= *= /= %= += -= <<= >>= &= ^= |=

In some complex equations you might need to nest your parentheses to ensure the proper order of operations. Let's assume I want to know how many seconds my family wastes each morning. It turns out that the adults spend 20 minutes over coffee each morning and 10 minutes reading the newspaper. The children waste 30 minutes dawdling and 10 minutes arguing.

Here's my algorithm:

```
(((minDrinkingCoffee  + minReadingNewspaper )* numAdults ) +
((minDawdling + minArguing) * numChildren)) * secondsPerMinute.
```

Although this works, it is hard to read and hard to get right. It's much easier to use interim variables:

```
wastedByEachAdult = minDrinkingCoffee  +  minReadingNewspaper;
wastedByAllAdults =  wastedByEachAdult * numAdults;
wastedByEachKid =  minDawdling  + minArguing;
wastedByAllKids =  wastedByEachKid * numChildren;
wastedByFamily = wastedByAllAdults + wastedByAllKids;
totalSeconds =  wastedByFamily * 60;
```

The latter example uses many more interim variables, but it is far easier to read, understand, and (most important) debug. As you step through this program in your debugger, you can see the interim values and make sure they are correct.

The Ternary Operator

Although most operators require one term (e.g., myValue++) or two terms (e.g., a+b), there is one operator that has three: the ternary operator (?:).

```
cond-expr ? expr1 : expr2
```

This operator evaluates a *conditional* expression (an expression that returns a value of type bool), and then invokes either expression1 if the value returned from the conditional expression is true, or expression2 if the value returned is false. The logic is "if this is true, do the first; otherwise do the second." Example 3-18 illustrates.

Example 3-18. The ternary operator

```csharp
using System;
class Values
{
    static void Main( )
    {
        int valueOne = 10;
        int valueTwo = 20;

        int maxValue = valueOne > valueTwo ?  valueOne : valueTwo;

        Console.WriteLine("ValueOne: {0}, valueTwo: {1}, maxValue: {2}",
            valueOne, valueTwo, maxValue);

    }
}
```

Output:
```
ValueOne: 10, valueTwo: 20, maxValue: 20
```

In Example 3-18, the ternary operator is being used to test whether valueOne is greater than valueTwo. If so, the value of valueOne is assigned to the integer variable maxValue; otherwise the value of valueTwo is assigned to maxValue.

Namespaces

Chapter 2 discusses the reasons for introducing namespaces into the C# language (e.g., avoiding name collisions when using libraries from multiple vendors). In addition to using the namespaces provided by the .NET Framework or other vendors, you are free to create your own. You do this by using the namespace keyword, followed by the name you wish to create. Enclose the objects for that namespace within braces, as illustrated in Example 3-19.

Example 3-19. Creating namespaces

```csharp
namespace Programming_C_Sharp
{
```

Example 3-19. Creating namespaces (continued)

```
using System;
public class Tester
{

    public static int Main( )
    {
        for (int i=0;i<10;i++)
        {
            Console.WriteLine("i: {0}",i);
        }
        return 0;
    }
}
}
```

Example 3-19 creates a namespace called Programming_C_Sharp, and also specifies a Tester class, which lives within that namespace. You can alternatively choose to nest your namespaces, as needed, by declaring one within another. You might do so to segment your code, creating objects within a nested namespace whose names are protected from the outer namespace, as illustrated in Example 3-20.

Example 3-20. Nesting namespaces

```
namespace Programming_C_Sharp
{
    namespace Programming_C_Sharp_Test
    {
        using System;
        public class Tester
        {

            public static int Main( )
            {
                for (int i=0;i<10;i++)
                {
                    Console.WriteLine("i: {0}",i);
                }
                return 0;
            }
        }
    }
}
```

The Tester object now declared within the Programming_C_Sharp_Test namespace is:

```
Programming_C_Sharp.Programming_C_Sharp_Test.Tester
```

This name would not conflict with another Tester object in any other namespace, including the outer namespace Programming_C_Sharp.

Preprocessor Directives

In the examples you've seen so far, you've compiled your entire program whenever you compiled any of it. At times, however, you might want to compile only parts of your program—for example, depending on whether you are debugging or building your production code.

Before your code is compiled, another program called the preprocessor runs and prepares your program for the compiler. The preprocessor examines your code for special preprocessor directives, all of which begin with the pound sign (#). These directives allow you to define identifiers and then test for their existence.

Defining Identifiers

#define DEBUG defines a preprocessor identifier, DEBUG. Although other preprocessor directives can come anywhere in your code, identifiers must be defined before any other code, including using statements.

You can test whether DEBUG has been defined with the #if statement. Thus, you can write:

```
#define DEBUG

//... some normal code - not affected by preprocessor

#if DEBUG
   // code to include if debugging
#else
   // code to include if not debugging
#endif

//... some normal code - not affected by preprocessor
```

When the preprocessor runs, it sees the #define statement and records the identifier DEBUG. The preprocessor skips over your normal C# code and then finds the #if - #else - #endif block.

The #if statement tests for the identifier DEBUG, which does exist, and so the code between #if and #else is compiled into your program—but the code between #else and #endif is *not* compiled. That code does not appear in your assembly at all; it is as if it were left out of your source code.

Had the #if statement failed—that is, if you had tested for an identifier that did not exist—the code between #if and #else would not be compiled, but the code between #else and #endif would be compiled.

 Any code not surrounded by #if - #endif is not affected by the preprocessor and is compiled into your program.

Undefining Identifiers

Undefine an identifier with #undef. The preprocessor works its way through the code from top to bottom, so the identifier is defined from the #define statement until the #undef statement, or until the program ends. Thus if you write:

```
#define DEBUG

#if DEBUG
    // this code will be compiled
#endif

#undef DEBUG

#if DEBUG
    // this code will not be compiled
#endif
```

the first #if will succeed (DEBUG is defined), but the second will fail (DEBUG has been undefined).

#if, #elif, #else, and #endif

There is no switch statement for the preprocessor, but the #elif and #else directives provide great flexibility. The #elif directive allows the else-if logic of "if DEBUG then action one, else if TEST then action two, else action three":

```
#if DEBUG
    // compile this code if debug is defined
#elif TEST
    // compile this code if debug is not defined
    // but TEST is defined
#else
    // compile this code if neither DEBUG nor TEST
    // is defined
#endif
```

In this example the preprocessor first tests to see if the identifier DEBUG is defined. If it is, the code between #if and #elif will be compiled, and the rest of the code until #endif, will not be compiled.

If (and only if) DEBUG is not defined, the preprocessor next checks to see if TEST is defined. Note that the preprocessor will not check for TEST unless DEBUG is not defined. If TEST is defined, the code between the #elif and the #else directives will be compiled. If it turns out that neither DEBUG nor TEST is defined, the code between the #else and the #endif statements will be compiled.

#region

The #region preprocessor directive marks an area of text with a comment. The principal use of this preprocessor directive is to allow tools such as Visual Studio .NET to mark off areas of code and collapse them in the editor with only the region's comment showing.

For example, when you create a Windows application (covered in Chapter 13), Visual Studio .NET creates a region for code generated by the designer. When the region is expanded it looks like Figure 3-1. (Note: I've added the rectangle and highlighting to make it easier to find the region.)

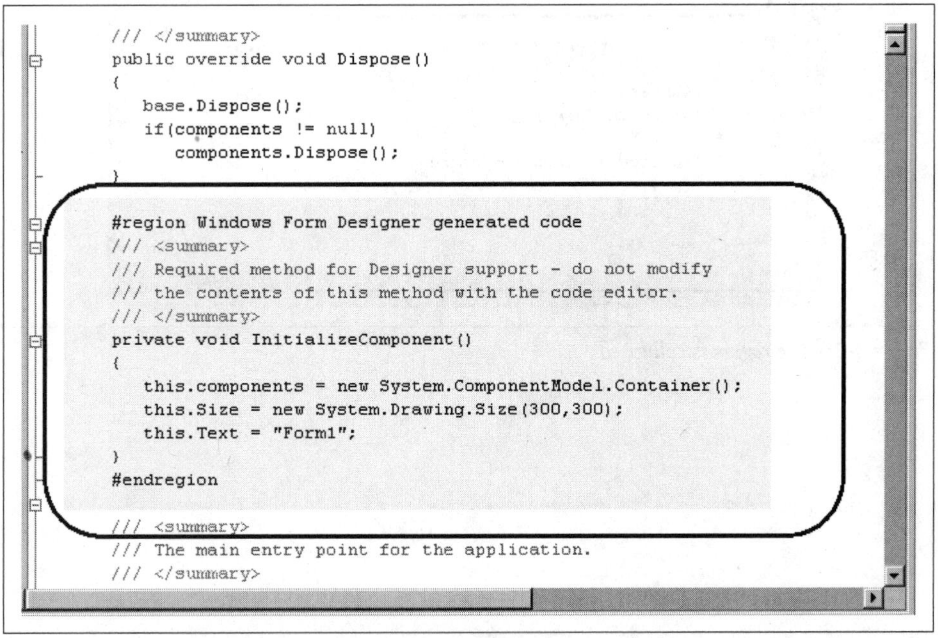

```
/// </summary>
public override void Dispose()
{
    base.Dispose();
    if(components != null)
        components.Dispose();
}

#region Windows Form Designer generated code
/// <summary>
/// Required method for Designer support - do not modify
/// the contents of this method with the code editor.
/// </summary>
private void InitializeComponent()
{
    this.components = new System.ComponentModel.Container();
    this.Size = new System.Drawing.Size(300,300);
    this.Text = "Form1";
}
#endregion

/// <summary>
/// The main entry point for the application.
/// </summary>
```

Figure 3-1. Expanding the Visual Studio .NET code region

You can see the region marked by the #region and #endregion preprocessor directives. When the region is collapsed, however, all you see is the region comment (Windows Form Designer generated code), as shown in Figure 3-2.

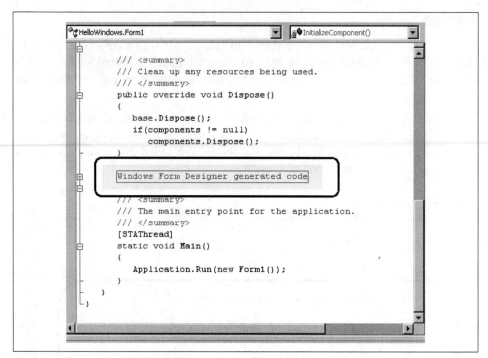

Figure 3-2. Code region is collapsed

CHAPTER 4

Classes and Objects

Chapter 3 discusses the myriad primitive types built into the C# language, such as int, long, and char. The heart and soul of C#, however, is the ability to create new, complex, programmer-defined types that map cleanly to the objects that make up the problem you are trying to solve.

It is this ability to create new types that characterizes an object-oriented language. Specify new types in C# by declaring and defining classes. You can also define types with interfaces, as you will see in Chapter 8. Instances of a class are called *objects*. Objects are created in memory when your program executes.

The difference between a class and an object is the same as the difference between the concept of a Dog and the particular dog who is sitting at your feet as you read this. You can't play fetch with the definition of a Dog, only with an instance.

A Dog class describes what dogs are like: they have weight, height, eye color, hair color, disposition, and so forth. They also have actions they can take, such as eat, walk, bark, and sleep. A particular dog (such as my dog Milo) has a specific weight (62 pounds), height (22 inches), eye color (black), hair color (yellow), disposition (angelic), and so forth. He is capable of all the actions of any dog (though if you knew him you might imagine that eating is the only method he implements).

The huge advantage of classes in object-oriented programming is that they encapsulate the characteristics and capabilities of an entity in a single, self-contained and self-sustaining *unit of code*. When you want to sort the contents of an instance of a Windows list box control, for example, tell the list box to sort itself. How it does so is of no concern; *that* it does so is all you need to know. Encapsulation, along with polymorphism and inheritance, is one of three cardinal principles of object-oriented programming.

An old programming joke asks, how many object-oriented programmers does it take to change a light bulb? Answer: none, you just tell the light bulb to change itself. (Alternate answer: none, Microsoft has changed the standard to darkness.)

This chapter explains the C# language features that are used to specify new classes. The elements of a class—its behaviors and properties—are known collectively as its *class members.* This chapter will show how methods are used to define the behaviors of the class, and how the state of the class is maintained in member variables (often called *fields*). In addition, this chapter introduces *properties*, which act like methods to the creator of the class but look like fields to clients of the class.

Defining Classes

To define a new type or class, first declare it, and then define its methods and fields. Declare a class using the class keyword. The complete syntax is as follows:

```
[attributes] [access-modifiers] class identifier [:base-class]
{class-body}
```

Attributes are covered in Chapter 18; access modifiers are discussed in the next section. (Typically, your classes will use the keyword public as an access modifier.) The identifier is the name of the class that you provide. The optional *base-class* is discussed in Chapter 5. The member definitions that make up the *class-body* are enclosed by open and closed curly braces ({}).

 C++ programmers take note: a C# class definition does *not* end with a semicolon, though if you add one, the program will still compile.

In C#, everything happens within a class. For instance, some of the examples in Chapter 3 make use of a class named Tester:

```
public class Tester
{

        public static int Main( )
        {
         /...
        }
}
```

So far, we've not *instantiated* any instances of that class; that is, we haven't created any Tester objects. What is the difference between a class and an instance of that class? To answer that question, start with the distinction between the *type* int and a *variable* of type int. Thus, while you would write:

```
int myInteger = 5;
```

you would not write:

```
int = 5;
```

You can't assign a value to a type; instead, you assign the value to an object of that type (in this case, a variable of type int).

When you declare a new class, you define the properties of all objects of that class, as well as their behaviors. For example, if you are creating a windowing environment, you might want to create screen widgets, more commonly known as controls in Windows programming, to simplify user interaction with your application. One control of interest might be a list box, which is very useful for presenting a list of choices to the user and enabling the user to select from the list.

List boxes have a variety of characteristics—for example, height, width, location, and text color. Programmers have also come to expect certain behaviors of list boxes: they can be opened, closed, sorted, and so on.

Object-oriented programming allows you to create a new type, ListBox, which encapsulates these characteristics and capabilities. Such a class might have member variables named height, width, location, and text_color, and member methods named sort( ), add( ), remove( ), etc.

You can't assign data to the ListBox type. Instead you must first create an object of that type, as in the following code snippet:

```
ListBox myListBox;
```

Once you create an instance of ListBox, you can assign data to its fields.

Now consider a class to keep track of and display the time of day. The internal state of the class must be able to represent the current year, month, date, hour, minute, and second. You probably would also like the class to display the time in a variety of formats. You might implement such a class by defining a single method and six variables, as shown in Example 4-1.

Example 4-1. Simple Time class

```
using System;

public class Time
{
    // public methods
    public void DisplayCurrentTime( )
    {
        Console.WriteLine(
            "stub for DisplayCurrentTime");
    }

    // private variables
    int Year;
    int Month;
    int Date;
    int Hour;
    int Minute;
    int Second;
```

Example 4-1. Simple Time class (continued)

```
    }

    public class Tester
    {
        static void Main()
        {
            Time t = new Time();
            t.DisplayCurrentTime();
        }

    }
```

The only method declared within the Time class definition is the method DisplayCurrentTime(). The body of the method is defined within the class definition itself. Unlike other languages (such as C++), C# does not require that methods be declared before they are defined, nor does the language support placing its declarations into one file and code into another. (C# has no header files.) All C# methods are defined inline as shown in Example 4-1 with DisplayCurrentTime().

The DisplayCurrentTime() method is defined to return void; that is, it will not return a value to a method that invokes it. For now, the body of this method has been "stubbed out."

The Time class definition ends with the declaration of a number of member variables: Year, Month, Date, Hour, Minute, and Second.

After the closing brace, a second class, Tester, is defined. Tester contains our now familiar Main() method. In Main(), an instance of Time is created and its address is assigned to object t. Because t is an instance of Time, Main() can make use of the DisplayCurrentTime() method available with objects of that type and call it to display the time:

```
    t.DisplayCurrentTime();
```

Access Modifiers

An access modifier determines which class methods—including methods of other classes—can see and use a member variable or method within a class. Table 4-1 summarizes the C# access modifiers.

Table 4-1. Access modifiers

Access Modifier	Restrictions
public	No restrictions. Members marked public are visible to any method of any class.
private	The members in class A that are marked private are accessible only to methods of class A.
protected	The members in class A that are marked protected are accessible to methods of class A and also to methods of classes *derived from* class A.

Table 4-1. Access modifiers (continued)

Access Modifier	Restrictions
internal	The members in class A that are marked internal are accessible to methods of any class in A's assembly.
protected internal	The members in class A that are marked protected internal are accessible to methods of class A, to methods of classes *derived from* class A, and also to any class in A's assembly. This is effectively protected OR internal (There is no concept of protected AND internal.)

It is generally desirable to designate the member variables of a class as private. This means that only member methods of that class can access their value. Because private is the default accessibility level, you do not need to make it explicit, but I recommend that you do so. Thus, in Example 4-1, the declarations of member variables should have been written as follows:

```
// private variables
private int Year;
private int Month;
private int Date;
private int Hour;
private int Minute;
private int Second;
```

Class Tester and method DisplayCurrentTime( ) are both declared public so that any other class can make use of them.

It is good programming practice to explicitly set the accessibility of all methods and members of your class. Although you can rely on the fact that class members are declared private by default, making their access explicit indicates a conscious decision and is self-documenting.

Method Arguments

Methods can take any number of parameters.[*] The parameter list follows the method name and is encased in parentheses, with each parameter preceded by its type. For example, the following declaration defines a method named MyMethod, which returns void (that is, which returns no value at all) and which takes two parameters: an int and a button:

```
void MyMethod (int firstParam, button secondParam)
{
  // ...
}
```

---

[*] The terms "argument" and "parameter" are often used interchangeably, though some programmers insist on differentiating between the argument declaration and the parameters passed in when the method is invoked.

Within the body of the method, the parameters act as local variables, as if you had declared them in the body of the method and initialized them with the values passed in. Example 4-2 illustrates how you pass values into a method—in this case, values of type int and float.

Example 4-2. Passing values into SomeMethod( )

```
using System;

public class MyClass
{
    public void SomeMethod(int firstParam, float secondParam)
    {
        Console.WriteLine(
            "Here are the parameters received: {0}, {1}",
            firstParam, secondParam);
    }

}

public class Tester
{
    static void Main( )
    {
        int howManyPeople = 5;
        float pi = 3.14f;
        MyClass mc = new MyClass( );
        mc.SomeMethod(howManyPeople, pi);
    }

}
```

The method SomeMethod( ) takes an int and a float and displays them using Console. WriteLine( ). The parameters, which are named firstParam and secondParam, are treated as local variables within SomeMethod( ).

In the calling method (Main), two local variables (howManyPeople and pi) are created and initialized. These variables are passed as the parameters to SomeMethod( ). The compiler maps howManyPeople to firstParam and pi to secondParam, based on their relative positions in the parameter list.

Creating Objects

In Chapter 3, a distinction is drawn between value types and reference types. The primitive C# types (int, char, etc.) are value types, and are created on the stack. Objects, however, are reference types, and are created on the heap, using the keyword new, as in the following:

```
Time t = new Time( );
```

t does not actually contain the value for the Time object; it contains the address of that (unnamed) object that is created on the heap. t itself is just a reference to that object.

Constructors

In Example 4-1, notice that the statement that creates the Time object looks as though it is invoking a method:

```
Time t = new Time( );
```

In fact, a method *is* invoked whenever you instantiate an object. This method is called a *constructor*, and you must either define one as part of your class definition or let the Common Language Runtime (CLR) provide one on your behalf. The job of a constructor is to create the object specified by a class and to put it into a *valid* state. Before the constructor runs, the object is undifferentiated memory; after the constructor completes, the memory holds a valid instance of the class type.

The Time class of Example 4-1 does not define a constructor. If a constructor is not declared, the compiler provides one for you. The default constructor creates the object but takes no other action. Member variables are initialized to innocuous values (integers to 0, strings to the empty string, etc.). Table 4-2 lists the default values assigned to primitive types.

Table 4-2. Primitive types and their default values

Type	Default Value
numeric (int, long, etc.)	0
bool	false
char	'\0' (null)
enum	0
reference	null

Typically, you'll want to define your own constructor and provide it with arguments so that the constructor can set the initial state for your object. In Example 4-1, assume that you want to pass in the current year, month, date, and so forth, so that the object is created with meaningful data.

To define a constructor, declare a method whose name is the same as the class in which it is declared. Constructors have no return type and are typically declared public. If there are arguments to pass, define an argument list just as you would for any other method. Example 4-3 declares a constructor for the Time class that accepts a single argument, an object of type DateTime.

Example 4-3. Declaring a constructor

```
public class Time
{
    // public accessor methods
    public void DisplayCurrentTime( )
    {
        System.Console.WriteLine("{0}/{1}/{2} {3}:{4}:{5}",
            Month, Date, Year, Hour, Minute, Second);
    }

    // constructor
    public Time(System.DateTime dt)
    {

        Year = dt.Year;
        Month = dt.Month;
        Date = dt.Day;
        Hour = dt.Hour;
        Minute = dt.Minute;
        Second = dt.Second;
    }

    // private member variables
    int Year;
    int Month;
    int Date;
    int Hour;
    int Minute;
    int Second;

}

public class Tester
{
    static void Main( )
    {
        System.DateTime currentTime = System.DateTime.Now;
        Time t = new Time(currentTime);
        t.DisplayCurrentTime( );
    }

}
```

Output:
11/16/2005 16:21:40

In this example, the constructor takes a DateTime object and initializes all the member variables based on values in that object. When the constructor finishes, the Time object exists and the values have been initialized. When DisplayCurrentTime( ) is called in Main( ), the values are displayed.

Try commenting out one of the assignments and running the program again. You'll find that the member variable is initialized by the compiler to 0. Integer member variables are set to 0 if you don't otherwise assign them. Remember, value types (e.g., integers) cannot be *uninitialized*; if you don't tell the constructor what to do, it will try for something innocuous.

In Example 4-3, the DateTime object is created in the Main( ) method of Tester. This object, supplied by the System library, offers a number of public values—Year, Month, Day, Hour, Minute, and Second—that correspond directly to the private member variables of our Time object. In addition, the DateTime object offers a static member method, Now, which returns a reference to an instance of a DateTime object initialized with the current time.

Examine the highlighted line in Main( ), where the DateTime object is created by calling the static method Now( ). Now( ) creates a DateTime object on the heap and returns a reference to it.

That reference is assigned to currentTime, which is declared to be a reference to a DateTime object. Then currentTime is passed as a parameter to the Time constructor. The Time constructor parameter, dt, is also a reference to a DateTime object; in fact dt now refers to the same DateTime object as currentTime does. Thus, the Time constructor has access to the public member variables of the DateTime object that was created in Tester.Main( ).

The reason that the DateTime object referred to in the Time constructor is the same object referred to in Main( ) is that objects are *reference* types. Thus, when you pass one as a parameter it is passed *by reference*—that is, the pointer is passed and no copy of the object is made.

Initializers

It is possible to initialize the values of member variables in an *initializer*, instead of having to do so in every constructor. Create an initializer by assigning an initial value to a class member:

```
private int Second  = 30;  // initializer
```

Assume that the semantics of our Time object are such that no matter what time is set, the seconds are always initialized to 30. We might rewrite our Time class to use an initializer so that no matter which constructor is called, the value of Second is always initialized, either explicitly by the constructor or implicitly by the initializer, as shown in Example 4-4.

Example 4-4. Using an initializer

```
public class Time
{
   // public accessor methods
```

Example 4-4. Using an initializer (continued)

```
    public void DisplayCurrentTime( )
    {
        System.DateTime now = System.DateTime.Now;
            System.Console.WriteLine(
            "\nDebug\t: {0}/{1}/{2} {3}:{4}:{5}",
            now.Month, now.Day , now.Year, now.Hour,
                now.Minute, now.Second);

        System.Console.WriteLine("Time\t: {0}/{1}/{2} {3}:{4}:{5}",
            Month, Date, Year, Hour, Minute, Second);
    }


    // constructors
    public Time(System.DateTime dt)
    {

        Year =      dt.Year;
        Month =     dt.Month;
        Date =      dt.Day;
        Hour =      dt.Hour;
        Minute =    dt.Minute;
        Second =    dt.Second;    //explicit assignment
    }

    public Time(int Year, int Month, int Date,
            int Hour, int Minute)
    {
        this.Year =     Year;
        this.Month =    Month;
        this.Date =     Date;
        this.Hour =     Hour;
        this.Minute =   Minute;
    }

    // private member variables
    private int Year;
    private int Month;
    private int Date;
    private int Hour;
    private int Minute;
    private int Second  = 30;  // initializer
}

public class Tester
{
    static void Main( )
    {
        System.DateTime currentTime = System.DateTime.Now;
        Time t = new Time(currentTime);
        t.DisplayCurrentTime( );
```

Example 4-4. Using an initializer (continued)

```
        Time t2 = new Time(2005,11,18,11,45);
        t2.DisplayCurrentTime( );

    }
}
```

Output:
```
Debug    : 11/27/2005 7:52:54
Time     : 11/27/2005 7:52:54

Debug    : 11/27/2005 7:52:54
Time     : 11/18/2005 11:45:30
```

If you do not provide a specific initializer, the constructor will initialize each integer member variable to zero (0). In the case shown, however, the Second member is initialized to 30:

```
    private int Second  = 30;  // initializer
```

If a value is not passed in for Second, its value will be set to 30 when t2 is created:

```
    Time t2 = new Time(2005,11,18,11,45);
    t2.DisplayCurrentTime( );
```

However, if a value is assigned to Second, as is done in the constructor (which takes a DateTime object, shown in bold), that value overrides the initialized value.

The first time through the program we call the constructor that takes a DateTime object, and the seconds are initialized to 54. The second time through we explicitly set the time to 11:45 (not setting the seconds) and the initializer takes over.

If the program did not have an initializer and did not otherwise assign a value to Second, the value would be initialized by the compiler to zero.

Copy Constructors

A *copy constructor* creates a new object by copying variables from an existing object of the same type. For example, you might want to pass a Time object to a Time constructor so that the new Time object has the same values as the old one.

C# does not provide a copy constructor, so if you want one you must provide it yourself. Such a constructor copies the elements from the original object into the new one:

```
    public Time(Time existingTimeObject)
    {
        Year = existingTimeObject.Year;
        Month = existingTimeObject.Month;
        Date = existingTimeObject.Date;
        Hour = existingTimeObject.Hour;
        Minute = existingTimeObject.Minute;
        Second = existingTimeObject.Second;
    }
```

A copy constructor is invoked by instantiating an object of type Time and passing it the name of the Time object to be copied:

```
Time t3 = new Time(t2);
```

Here an existingTimeObject (t2) is passed as a parameter to the copy constructor which will create a new Time object (t3).

The this Keyword

The keyword this refers to the current instance of an object. The this reference (sometimes referred to as a *this pointer*[*]) is a hidden pointer to every nonstatic method of a class. Each method can refer to the other methods and variables of that object by way of the this reference.

There are three ways in which the this reference is typically used. The first way is to qualify instance members otherwise hidden by parameters, as in the following:

```
public void SomeMethod (int hour)
{
    this.hour = hour;
}
```

In this example, SomeMethod( ) takes a parameter (hour) with the same name as a member variable of the class. The this reference is used to resolve the name ambiguity. While this.hour refers to the member variable, hour refers to the parameter.

The argument in favor of this style is that you pick the right variable name and then use it both for the parameter and for the member variable. The counter argument is that using the same name for both the parameter and the member variable can be confusing.

The second use of the this reference is to pass the current object as a parameter to another method. For instance, the following code:

```
public void FirstMethod(OtherClass otherObject)
{
    otherObject.SecondMethod(this);
}
```

establishes two classes, one with the method FirstMethod( ); the second is OtherClass, with its method SecondMethod( ). Inside FirstMethod, we'd like to invoke SecondMethod, passing in the current object for further processing.

The third use of this is with indexers, covered in Chapter 9.

---

[*] A pointer is a variable that holds the address of an object in memory. C# does not use pointers with managed objects.

Using Static Members

The properties and methods of a class can be either *instance members* or *static members*. Instance members are associated with instances of a type, while static members are considered to be part of the class. You access a static member through the name of the class in which it is declared. For example, suppose you have a class named Button and have instantiated objects of that class named btnUpdate and btnDelete. Suppose as well that the Button class has a static method SomeMethod( ). To access the static method you write:

```
Button.SomeMethod( );
```

rather than writing:

```
btnUpdate.SomeMethod( );
```

In C# it is not legal to access a static method or member variable through an instance, and trying to do so will generate a compiler error (C++ programmers, take note).

Some languages distinguish between class methods and other (global) methods that are available outside the context of any class. In C# there are no global methods, only class methods, but you can achieve an analogous result by defining static methods within your class.

Static methods act more or less like global methods, in that you can invoke them without actually having an instance of the object at hand. The advantage of static methods over global, however, is that the name is scoped to the class in which it occurs, and thus you do not clutter up the global namespace with myriad function names. This can help manage highly complex programs, and the name of the class acts very much like a namespace for the static methods within it.

 Resist the temptation to create a single class in your program in which you stash all your miscellaneous methods. It is possible but not desirable and undermines the encapsulation of an object-oriented design.

Invoking Static Methods

The Main( ) method is static. Static methods are said to operate on the class, rather than on an instance of the class. They do not have a this reference, as there is no instance to point to.

Static methods cannot directly access nonstatic members. For Main( ) to call a nonstatic method, it must instantiate an object. Consider Example 4-2, reproduced here for your convenience.

```
using System;

public class MyClass
```

```
{
    public void SomeMethod(int firstParam, float secondParam)
    {
        Console.WriteLine(
            "Here are the parameters received: {0}, {1}",
            firstParam, secondParam);
    }

}

public class Tester
{
    static void Main( )
    {
        int howManyPeople = 5;
        float pi = 3.14f;
        MyClass mc = new MyClass( );
        mc.SomeMethod(howManyPeople, pi);
    }

}
```

SomeMethod( ) is a nonstatic method of MyClass. For Main( ) to access this method, it must first instantiate an object of type MyClass and then invoke the method through that object.

Using Static Constructors

If your class declares a static constructor, you will be guaranteed that the static constructor will run before any instance of your class is created.

 You are not able to control exactly when a static constructor will run, but you do know that it will be after the start of your program and before the first instance is created. Because of this you cannot assume (or determine) whether an instance is being created.

For example, you might add the following static constructor to Time:

```
static Time( )
{
    Name = "Time";
}
```

Notice that there is no access modifier (e.g., public) before the static constructor. Access modifiers are not allowed on static constructors. In addition, because this is a static member method, you cannot access nonstatic member variables, and so Name must be declared a static member variable:

```
private static string Name;
```

The final change is to add a line to DisplayCurrentTime( ), as in the following:

```
public void DisplayCurrentTime( )
{
    System.Console.WriteLine("Name: {0}", Name);
    System.Console.WriteLine("{0}/{1}/{2} {3}:{4}:{5}",
        Month, Date, Year, Hour, Minute, Second);
}
```

When all these changes are made, the output is:

```
Name: Time
11/27/2005 7:52:54
Name: Time
11/18/2005 11:45:30
```

(Your output will vary depending on the date and time you run this code.)

Although this code works, it is not necessary to create a static constructor to accomplish this goal. You could, instead, use an initializer:

```
private static string Name = "Time";
```

which accomplishes the same thing. Static constructors are useful, however, for setup work that cannot be accomplished with an initializer and that needs to be done only once.

For example, assume you have an unmanaged bit of code in a legacy dll. You want to provide a class wrapper for this code. You can call load library in your static constructor and initialize the jump table in the static constructor. Handling legacy code and interoperating with unmanaged code is discussed in Chapter 22.

Using Private Constructors

In C# there are no global methods or constants. You might find yourself creating small utility classes that exist only to hold static members. Setting aside whether this is a good design or not, if you create such a class you will not want any instances created. You can prevent any instances from being created by creating a default constructor (one with no parameters), which does nothing, and which is marked private. With no public constructors, it will not be possible to create an instance of your class.[*]

Using Static Fields

A common use of static member variables is to keep track of the number of instances that currently exist for your class. Example 4-5 illustrates.

---

[*] You can create a public static method that calls the constructor and creates an instance of your class. Typically you might use this idiom to ensure that only one instance of your class ever exists. This is known as the Singleton design pattern, as described in the seminal work *Design Patterns* by Gamma, et al. (Addison Wesley, 1995).

Example 4-5. Using static fields for instance counting

```
using System;

public class Cat
{

    public Cat( )
    {
        instances++;
    }

    public static void HowManyCats( )
    {
        Console.WriteLine("{0} cats adopted",
            instances);
    }
    private static int instances = 0;
}

public class Tester
{
    static void Main( )
    {
        Cat.HowManyCats( );
        Cat frisky = new Cat( );
        Cat.HowManyCats( );
        Cat whiskers = new Cat( );
        Cat.HowManyCats( );

    }

}
```

Output:
```
0 cats adopted
1 cats adopted
2 cats adopted
```

The Cat class has been stripped to its absolute essentials. A static member variable called instances is created and initialized to zero. Note that the static member is considered part of the class, not a member of an instance, and so it cannot be initialized by the compiler on creation of an instance. Thus, an explicit initializer is *required* for static member variables. When additional instances of Cats are created (in a constructor), the count is incremented.

Destroying Objects

Since C# provides garbage collection, you never need to explicitly destroy your objects. However, if your object controls unmanaged resources, you will need to explicitly free those resources when you are done with them. Implicit control over unmanaged resources is provided by a *destructor*, which will be called by the garbage collector when your object is destroyed.

The destructor should only release resources that your object holds on to, and should not reference other objects. Note that if you have only managed references you do not need to and should not implement a destructor; you want this only for handling unmanaged resources. Because there is some cost to having a destructor, you ought to implement this only on methods that require it (that is, methods that consume valuable unmanaged resources).

Never call an object's destructor directly. The garbage collector will call it for you.

The C# Destructor

C#'s destructor looks, syntactically, much like a C++ destructor, but it behaves quite differently. Declare a C# destructor with a tilde as follows:

```
~MyClass(){}
```

In C#, however, this syntax is simply a shortcut for declaring a Finalize( ) method that chains up to its base class. Thus, when you write:

```
~MyClass()
{
    // do work here
}
```

the C# compiler translates it to:

```
protected override void Finalize()
{
```

```
    try
    {
        // do work here.
    }
    finally
    {
        base.Finalize();
    }
}
```

Destructors Versus Dispose

It is not legal to call a destructor explicitly. Your destructor will be called by the garbage collector. If you do handle precious unmanaged resources (such as file handles) that you want to close and dispose of as quickly as possible, you ought to implement the IDisposable interface. (You will learn more about interfaces in Chapter 8.) The IDisposable interface requires its implementers to define one method, named Dispose( ), to perform whatever cleanup you consider to be crucial. The availability of Dispose( ) is a way for your clients to say "don't wait for the destructor to be called, do it right now."

If you provide a Dispose( ) method, you should stop the garbage collector from calling your object's destructor. To do so, call the static method GC.SuppressFinalize( ), passing in the this pointer for your object. Your destructor can then call your Dispose( ) method. Thus, you might write:

```
using System;
class Testing : IDisposable
{
  bool is_disposed = false;
  protected virtual void Dispose(bool disposing)
  {
    if (!is_disposed) // only dispose once!
    {
      if (disposing)
      {
        Console.WriteLine("Not in destructor, OK to reference other objects");
      }
      // perform cleanup for this object
      Console.WriteLine("Disposing...");
    }
    this.is_disposed = true;
  }

  public void Dispose()
  {
    Dispose(true);
    // tell the GC not to finalize
    GC.SuppressFinalize(this);
  }
```

```
    ~Testing( )
    {
      Dispose(false);
      Console.WriteLine("In destructor.");
    }
  }
```

Implementing the Close Method

For some objects, you'd rather have your clients call the Close( ) method. (For example, Close makes more sense than Dispose( ) for file objects.) You can implement this by creating a private Dispose( ) method and a public Close( ) method and having your Close( ) method invoke Dispose( ).

The using Statement

Because you cannot be certain that your user will call Dispose( ) reliably, and because finalization is nondeterministic (i.e., you can't control when the GC will run), C# provides a using statement that ensures that Dispose( ) will be called at the earliest possible time. The idiom is to declare that objects you are using and then to create a scope for these objects with curly braces. When the close brace is reached, the Dispose( ) method will be called on the object automatically, as illustrated in Example 4-6.

Example 4-6. The using construct

```
using System.Drawing;
class Tester
{
    public static void Main( )
    {
        using (Font theFont = new Font("Arial", 10.0f))
        {
            // use theFont

        }   // compiler will call Dispose on theFont

        Font anotherFont = new Font("Courier",12.0f);

        using (anotherFont)
        {
            // use anotherFont

        }  // compiler calls Dispose on anotherFont

    }

}
```

In the first part of this example, the Font object is created within the using statement. When the using statement ends, Dispose( ) is called on the Font object.

In the second part of the example, a Font object is created outside of the using statement. When we decide to use that font, we put it inside the using statement; when that statement ends, Dispose( ) is called once again.

The using statement also protects you against unanticipated exceptions. No matter how control leaves the using statement, Dispose( ) is called. It is as if there were an implicit *try-catch-finally* block. (See the section titled "Exception Objects" in Chapter 11 for details.)

Passing Parameters

By default, value types are passed into methods by value (see the section "Method Arguments," earlier in this chapter). This means that when a value object is passed to a method, a temporary copy of the object is created within that method. Once the method completes, the copy is discarded. Although passing by value is the normal case, there are times when you will want to pass value objects by reference. C# provides the ref parameter modifier for passing value objects into a method by reference and the out modifier for those cases in which you want to pass in a ref variable without first initializing it. C# also supports the params modifier, which allows a method to accept a variable number of parameters. The params keyword is discussed in Chapter 9.

Passing by Reference

Methods can return only a single value (though that value can be a collection of values). Let's return to the Time class and add a GetTime( ) method, which returns the hour, minutes, and seconds.

Because we cannot return three values, perhaps we can pass in three parameters, let the method modify the parameters, and examine the result in the calling method. Example 4-7 shows a first attempt at this.

Example 4-7. Returning values in parameters

```
public class Time
{
    // public accessor methods
    public void DisplayCurrentTime( )
    {
        System.Console.WriteLine("{0}/{1}/{2} {3}:{4}:{5}",
            Month, Date, Year, Hour, Minute, Second);
    }

    public int GetHour( )
    {
```

Example 4-7. Returning values in parameters (continued)

```
      return Hour;
  }

     public void GetTime(int h, int m, int s)
     {
         h = Hour;
         m = Minute;
         s = Second;
     }

  // constructor
  public Time(System.DateTime dt)
  {

     Year = dt.Year;
     Month = dt.Month;
     Date = dt.Day;
     Hour = dt.Hour;
     Minute = dt.Minute;
     Second = dt.Second;
  }

  // private member variables
  private int Year;
  private int Month;
  private int Date;
  private int Hour;
  private int Minute;
  private int Second;

}

public class Tester
{
   static void Main( )
   {
      System.DateTime currentTime = System.DateTime.Now;
      Time t = new Time(currentTime);
      t.DisplayCurrentTime( );

      int theHour = 0;
      int theMinute = 0;
      int theSecond = 0;
      t.GetTime(theHour, theMinute, theSecond);
      System.Console.WriteLine("Current time: {0}:{1}:{2}",
              theHour, theMinute, theSecond);

   }

}
```

Example 4-7. Returning values in parameters (continued)

Output:
```
11/17/2005 13:41:18
Current time: 0:0:0
```

Notice that the "Current time" in the output is 0:0:0. Clearly, this first attempt did not work. The problem is with the parameters. We pass in three integer parameters to GetTime( ), and we modify the parameters in GetTime( ), but when the values are accessed back in Main( ), they are unchanged. This is because integers are value types, and so are passed by value; a copy is made in GetTime( ). What we need is to pass these values by reference.

Two small changes are required. First, change the parameters of the GetTime method to indicate that the parameters are ref (reference) parameters:

```
public void GetTime(ref int h, ref int m, ref int s)
{
    h = Hour;
    m = Minute;
    s = Second;
}
```

Second, modify the call to GetTime( ) to pass the arguments as references as well:

```
t.GetTime(ref theHour, ref theMinute, ref theSecond);
```

If you leave out the second step of marking the arguments with the keyword ref, the compiler will complain that the argument cannot be converted from an int to a ref int.

The results now show the correct time. By declaring these parameters to be ref parameters, you instruct the compiler to pass them by reference. Instead of a copy being made, the parameter in GetTime( ) is a reference to the same variable (theHour) that is created in Main( ). When you change these values in GetTime( ), the change is reflected in Main( ).

Keep in mind that ref parameters are references to the actual original value—it is as if you said "here, work on this one." Conversely, value parameters are copies—it is as if you said "here, work on one *just like* this."

Passing Out Parameters with Definite Assignment

C# imposes *definite assignment*, which requires that all variables be assigned a value before they are used. In Example 4-7, if you don't initialize theHour, theMinute, and theSecond before you pass them as parameters to GetTime( ), the compiler will complain. Yet the initialization that is done merely sets their values to 0 before they are passed to the method:

```
int theHour = 0;
int theMinute = 0;
int theSecond = 0;
t.GetTime( ref theHour, ref theMinute, ref theSecond);
```

It seems silly to initialize these values because you immediately pass them by reference into GetTime where they'll be changed, but if you don't, the following compiler errors are reported:

```
Use of unassigned local variable 'theHour'
Use of unassigned local variable 'theMinute'
Use of unassigned local variable 'theSecond'
```

C# provides the out parameter modifier for this situation. The out modifier removes the requirement that a reference parameter be initialized. The parameters to GetTime( ), for example, provide no information to the method; they are simply a mechanism for getting information out of it. Thus, by marking all three as out parameters, you eliminate the need to initialize them outside the method. Within the called method, the out parameters must be assigned a value before the method returns. Here are the altered parameter declarations for GetTime( ):

```
public void GetTime(out int h, out int m, out int s)
{
    h = Hour;
    m = Minute;
    s = Second;
}
```

and here is the new invocation of the method in Main( ):

```
t.GetTime( out theHour, out theMinute, out theSecond);
```

To summarize, value types are passed into methods by value. Ref parameters are used to pass value types into a method by reference. This allows you to retrieve their modified value in the calling method. Out parameters are used only to return information from a method. Example 4-8 rewrites Example 4-7 to use all three.

Example 4-8. Using in, out, and ref parameters

```
public class Time
{
    // public accessor methods
    public void DisplayCurrentTime( )
    {
        System.Console.WriteLine("{0}/{1}/{2} {3}:{4}:{5}",
            Month, Date, Year, Hour, Minute, Second);
    }

    public int GetHour( )
    {
        return Hour;
    }

    public void SetTime(int hr, out int min, ref int sec)
    {
        // if the passed in time is >= 30
        // increment the minute and set second to 0
        // otherwise leave both alone
```

Example 4-8. Using in, out, and ref parameters (continued)

```
            if (sec >= 30)
            {
                Minute++;
                Second = 0;
            }
            Hour = hr; // set to value passed in

            // pass the minute and second back out
            min = Minute;
            sec = Second;
        }

    // constructor
    public Time(System.DateTime dt)
    {

        Year = dt.Year;
        Month = dt.Month;
        Date = dt.Day;
        Hour = dt.Hour;
        Minute = dt.Minute;
        Second = dt.Second;
    }

    // private member variables
    private int Year;
    private int Month;
    private int Date;
    private int Hour;
    private int Minute;
    private int Second;

}

public class Tester
{
    static void Main( )
    {
        System.DateTime currentTime = System.DateTime.Now;
        Time t = new Time(currentTime);
        t.DisplayCurrentTime( );

        int theHour = 3;
        int theMinute;
        int theSecond = 20;

        t.SetTime(theHour, out theMinute, ref theSecond);
        System.Console.WriteLine(
            "the Minute is now: {0} and {1} seconds",
                theMinute, theSecond);

        theSecond = 40;
        t.SetTime(theHour, out theMinute, ref theSecond);
```

Example 4-8. Using in, out, and ref parameters (continued)

```
        System.Console.WriteLine("the Minute is now: " +
            "{0} and {1} seconds",
                theMinute, theSecond);

    }

}
```

Output:
```
11/17/2005 14:6:24
the Minute is now: 6 and 24 seconds
the Minute is now: 7 and 0 seconds
```

SetTime is a bit contrived, but it illustrates the three types of parameters. theHour is passed in as a value parameter; its entire job is to set the member variable Hour, and no value is returned using this parameter.

The ref parameter theSecond is used to set a value in the method. If theSecond is greater than or equal to 30, the member variable Second is reset to 0 and the member variable Minute is incremented.

Finally, theMinute is passed into the method only to return the value of the member variable Minute, and thus is marked as an out parameter.

It makes perfect sense that theHour and theSecond must be initialized; their values are needed and used. It is not necessary to initialize theMinute, as it is an out parameter that exists only to return a value. What at first appeared to be arbitrary and capricious rules now makes sense; values are only required to be initialized when their initial value is meaningful.

Overloading Methods and Constructors

Often you'll want to have more than one function with the same name. The most common example of this is to have more than one constructor. In the examples shown so far, the constructor has taken a single parameter: a DateTime object. It would be convenient to be able to set new Time objects to an arbitrary time by passing in year, month, date, hour, minute, and second values. It would be even more convenient if some clients could use one constructor, and other clients could use the other constructor. Function overloading provides for exactly these contingencies.

The *signature* of a method is defined by its name and its parameter list. Two methods differ in their signatures if they have different names or different parameter lists. Parameter lists can differ by having different numbers or types of parameters. For example, in the following code the first method differs from the second in the number of parameters, and the second differs from the third in the types of parameters:

```
    void myMethod(int p1);
    void myMethod(int p1, int p2);
    void myMethod(int p1, string s1);
```

A class can have any number of methods, as long as each one's signature differs from that of all the others.

Example 4-9 illustrates our Time class with two constructors, one which takes a DateTime object, and the other which takes six integers.

Example 4-9. Overloading the constructor

```
public class Time
{
    // public accessor methods
    public void DisplayCurrentTime( )
    {
        System.Console.WriteLine("{0}/{1}/{2} {3}:{4}:{5}",
            Month, Date, Year, Hour, Minute, Second);
    }


    // constructors
    public Time(System.DateTime dt)
    {
        Year =      dt.Year;
        Month =     dt.Month;
        Date =      dt.Day;
        Hour =      dt.Hour;
        Minute =    dt.Minute;
        Second =    dt.Second;
    }

    public Time(int Year, int Month, int Date,
        int Hour, int Minute, int Second)
    {
        this.Year =     Year;
        this.Month =    Month;
        this.Date =     Date;
        this.Hour =     Hour;
        this.Minute =   Minute;
        this.Second =   Second;
    }

    // private member variables
    private int Year;
    private int Month;
    private int Date;
    private int Hour;
    private int Minute;
    private int Second;

}

public class Tester
{
    static void Main( )
```

Example 4-9. Overloading the constructor (continued)

```
    {
        System.DateTime currentTime = System.DateTime.Now;

        Time t = new Time(currentTime);
        t.DisplayCurrentTime( );

        Time t2 = new Time(2005,11,18,11,03,30);
        t2.DisplayCurrentTime( );

    }

}
```

As you can see, the Time class in Example 4-9 has two constructors. If a function's signature consisted only of the function name, the compiler would not know which constructors to call when constructing t1 and t2. However, because the signature includes the function argument types, the compiler is able to match the constructor call for t1 with the constructor whose signature requires a DateTime object. Likewise, the compiler is able to associate the t2 constructor call with the constructor method whose signature specifies six integer arguments.

When you overload a method, you must change the signature (i.e., the name, number, or type of the parameters). You are free, as well, to change the return type, but this is optional. Changing only the return type does not overload the method, and creating two methods with the same signature but differing return types will generate a compile error. This is illustrated in Example 4-10:

Example 4-10. Varying the return type on overloaded methods

```
public class Tester
{
    private int Triple(int val)
    {
        return 3 * val;
    }

    private long Triple (long val)
    {
        return 3 * val;
    }

    public void Test( )
    {
        int x = 5;
        int y = Triple(x);
        System.Console.WriteLine("x: {0}  y: {1}", x, y);

        long lx = 10;
        long ly = Triple(lx);
        System.Console.WriteLine("lx: {0}  ly: {1}", lx, ly);
```

Example 4-10. Varying the return type on overloaded methods (continued)

```
    }
    static void Main( )
    {
        Tester t = new Tester( );
        t.Test( );
    }
}
```

In this example, the Tester class overloads the Triple( ) method, one to take an integer, the other to take a long. The return type for the two Triple( ) methods varies. Although this is not required, it is very convenient in this case.

Encapsulating Data with Properties

Properties allow clients to access class state as if they were accessing member fields directly, while actually implementing that access through a class method.

This is ideal. The client wants direct access to the state of the object and does not want to work with methods. The class designer, however, wants to hide the internal state of his class in class members, and provide indirect access through a method.

By decoupling the class state from the method that accesses that state, the designer is free to change the internal state of the object as needed. When the Time class is first created, the Hour value might be stored as a member variable. When the class is redesigned, the Hour value might be computed, or retrieved from a database. If the client had direct access to the original Hour member variable, the change to computing the value would break the client. By decoupling and forcing the client to go through a method (or property), the Time class can change how it manages its internal state without breaking client code.

Properties meet both goals: they provide a simple interface to the client, appearing to be a member variable. They are implemented as methods, however, providing the data hiding required by good object-oriented design, as illustrated in Example 4-11.

Example 4-11. Using a property

```
public class Time
{
    // public accessor methods
    public void DisplayCurrentTime( )
    {

        System.Console.WriteLine(
            "Time\t: {0}/{1}/{2} {3}:{4}:{5}",
            month, date, year, hour, minute, second);
    }
```

Example 4-11. Using a property (continued)

```csharp
// constructors
public Time(System.DateTime dt)
{
    year =      dt.Year;
    month =     dt.Month;
    date =      dt.Day;
    hour =      dt.Hour;
    minute =    dt.Minute;
    second =    dt.Second;
}

// create a property
public int Hour
{
    get
    {
        return hour;
    }

    set
    {
        hour = value;
    }
}

// private member variables
private int year;
private int month;
private int date;
private int hour;
private int minute;
private int second;
}

public class Tester
{
    static void Main( )
    {
        System.DateTime currentTime = System.DateTime.Now;
        Time t = new Time(currentTime);
        t.DisplayCurrentTime( );

        int theHour = t.Hour;
        System.Console.WriteLine("\nRetrieved the hour: {0}\n",
            theHour);
        theHour++;
        t.Hour = theHour;
        System.Console.WriteLine("Updated the hour: {0}\n", theHour);
    }
}
```

To declare a property, write the property type and name followed by a pair of braces. Within the braces you may declare get and set accessors. Neither of these has explicit parameters, though the set( ) method has an implicit parameter value as shown next.

In Example 4-11, Hour is a property. Its declaration creates two accessors: get and set.

```
public int Hour
{
    get
    {
        return hour;
    }

    set
    {
        hour = value;
    }
}
```

Each accessor has an accessor-body that does the work of retrieving and setting the property value. The property value might be stored in a database (in which case the accessor-body would do whatever work is needed to interact with the database), or it might just be stored in a private member variable:

```
private int hour;
```

The get Accessor

The body of the get accessor is similar to a class method that returns an object of the type of the property. In the example, the accessor for Hour is similar to a method that returns an int. It returns the value of the private member variable in which the value of the property has been stored:

```
get
{
    return hour;
}
```

In this example, a local int member variable is returned, but you could just as easily retrieve an integer value from a database, or compute it on the fly.

Whenever you reference the property (other than to assign to it), the get accessor is invoked to read the value of the property:

```
Time t = new Time(currentTime);
int theHour = t.Hour;
```

In this example, the value of the Time object's Hour property is retrieved, invoking the get accessor to extract the property, which is then assigned to a local variable.

The set Accessor

The set accessor sets the value of a property and is similar to a method that returns void. When you define a set accessor you must use the value keyword to represent the argument whose value is passed to and stored by the property.

```
set
{
    hour = value;
}
```

Here, again, a private member variable is used to store the value of the property, but the set accessor could write to a database or update other member variables as needed.

When you assign a value to the property the set accessor is automatically invoked, and the implicit parameter value is set to the value you assign:

```
theHour++;
t.Hour = theHour;
```

The advantage of this approach is that the client can interact with the properties directly, without sacrificing the data hiding and encapsulation sacrosanct in good object-oriented design.

Readonly Fields

You might want to create a version of the Time class that is responsible for providing public static values representing the current time and date. Example 4-12 illustrates a simple approach to this problem.

Example 4-12. Using static public constants

```
public class RightNow
{
    static RightNow( )
    {
        System.DateTime dt = System.DateTime.Now;
        Year =      dt.Year;
        Month =     dt.Month;
        Date =      dt.Day;
        Hour =      dt.Hour;
        Minute =    dt.Minute;
        Second =    dt.Second;
    }

    // public member variables
    public static int Year;
    public static int Month;
    public static int Date;
    public static int Hour;
```

Example 4-12. Using static public constants (continued)

```
   public static int Minute;
   public static int Second;
}

public class Tester
{
   static void Main( )
   {
      System.Console.WriteLine ("This year: {0}",
            RightNow.Year.ToString( ));
      RightNow.Year = 2006;
      System.Console.WriteLine ("This year: {0}",
            RightNow.Year.ToString( ));
   }
}
```

Output:
```
This year: 2005
This year: 2006
```

This works well enough, until someone comes along and changes one of these values. As the example shows, the RightNow.Year value can be changed, for example, to 2003. This is clearly not what we'd like.

We'd like to mark the static values as constant, but that is not possible because we don't initialize them until the static constructor is executed. C# provides the keyword readonly for exactly this purpose. If you change the class member variable declarations as follows:

```
   public static readonly int Year;
   public static readonly int Month;
   public static readonly int Date;
   public static readonly int Hour;
   public static readonly int Minute;
   public static readonly int Second;
```

then comment out the reassignment in Main( ):

```
   // RightNow.Year = 2006; // error!
```

the program will compile and run as intended.

CHAPTER 5

Inheritance and Polymorphism

The previous chapter demonstrates how to create new types by declaring classes. The current chapter explores the relationship among objects in the real world and how to model these relationships in your code. This chapter focuses on *specialization*, which is implemented in C# through *inheritance*. This chapter also explains how instances of more specialized classes can be treated as if they were instances of more general classes, a process known as *polymorphism*. This chapter ends with a consideration of *sealed* classes, which cannot be specialized, as well as *abstract* classes, which exist only to be specialized, and a discussion of the root of all classes, the class Object.

Specialization and Generalization

Classes and their instances (objects) do not exist in a vacuum but rather in a network of interdependencies and relationships, just as we, as social animals, live in a world of relationships and categories.

The *is-a* relationship is one of *specialization*. When we say that a Dog *is-a* mammal, we mean that the dog is a specialized kind of mammal. It has all the characteristics of any mammal (it bears live young, nurses with milk, has hair), but it specializes these characteristics to the familiar characteristics of *canine domesticus*. A Cat is also a mammal. As such we expect it to share certain characteristics with the dog that are generalized in Mammal, but to differ in those characteristics that are specialized in Cat.

The specialization and generalization relationships are both reciprocal and hierarchical. They are reciprocal because specialization is the obverse side of the coin from generalization. Thus, Dog and Cat specialize Mammal, and Mammal generalizes from Dog and Cat.

These relationships are hierarchical because they create a relationship tree, with specialized types branching off from more generalized types. As you move up the hierarchy you achieve greater *generalization*. You move up toward Mammal to generalize that Dogs and Cats and Horses all bear live young. As you move down the hierarchy you specialize. Thus, the Cat specializes Mammal in having claws (a characteristic) and purring (a behavior).

Similarly, when you say that ListBox and Button *are* windows, you indicate that there are characteristics and behaviors of Windows that you expect to find in both of these types. In other words, Window generalizes the shared characteristics of both ListBox and Button, while each specializes its own particular characteristics and behaviors.

About the Unified Modeling Language

The Unified Modeling Language (UML) is a standardized "language" for describing a system or business. The part of the UML that is useful for the purposes of this chapter is the set of diagrams used to document the relationships among classes.

In the UML, classes are represented as boxes. The name of the class appears at the top of the box, and (optionally) methods and members can be listed in the sections within the box.

In the UML, you model these relationships as shown in Figure 5-1. Note that the arrow points from the more specialized class up to the more general class.

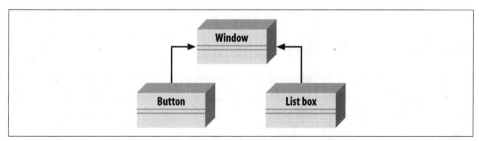

Figure 5-1. An is-a relationship

It is common to note that two classes share functionality, and then to factor out these commonalities into a shared base class. This provides you with greater reuse of common code and easier-to-maintain code.

For example, suppose you started out creating a series of objects as illustrated in Figure 5-2.

After working with RadioButtons, CheckBoxes, and Command buttons for a while, you realize that they share certain characteristics and behaviors that are more specialized than Window but more general than any of the three. You might factor these common traits and behaviors into a common base class, Button, and rearrange your inheritance hierarchy as shown in Figure 5-3. This is an example of how generalization is used in object-oriented development.

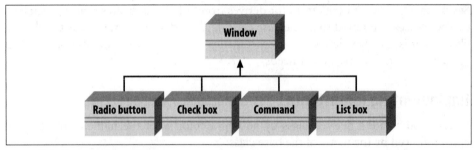

Figure 5-2. Deriving from Window

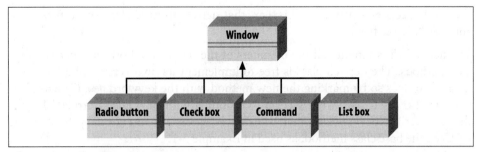

Figure 5-3. A more factored hierarchy

This UML diagram depicts the relationship between the factored classes and shows that both ListBox and Button derive from Window, and that Button is in turn specialized into CheckBox and Command. Finally, RadioButton derives from CheckBox. You can thus say that RadioButton is a CheckBox, which in turn is a Button, and that Buttons are Windows.

This is not the only, or even necessarily the best, organization for these objects, but it is a reasonable starting point for understanding how these types (classes) relate to one another.

> Actually, although this might reflect how some widget hierarchies are organized, I am very skeptical of any system in which the model does not reflect how I perceive reality. When I find myself saying that a RadioButton is a CheckBox, I have to think long and hard about whether that makes sense. I suppose a RadioButton *is* a kind of checkbox. It is a checkbox that supports the idiom of mutually exclusive choices. That said, it is a bit of a stretch and might be a sign of a shaky design.

Inheritance

In C#, the specialization relationship is typically implemented using inheritance. This is not the only way to implement specialization, but it is the most common and most natural way to implement this relationship.

Saying that ListBox inherits from (or derives from) Window indicates that it specializes Window. Window is referred to as the *base* class, and ListBox is referred to as the *derived* class. That is, ListBox derives its characteristics and behaviors from Window and then specializes to its own particular needs.

Implementing Inheritance

In C#, you create a derived class by adding a colon after the name of the derived class, followed by the name of the base class:

```
public class ListBox : Window
```

This code declares a new class, ListBox, that derives from Window. You can read the colon as "derives from."

The derived class inherits all the members of the base class, both member variables and methods. The derived class is free to implement its own version of a base class method. It does so by marking the new method with the keyword new. (The new keyword is also discussed in the section "Versioning with new and override," later in this chapter.) This indicates that the derived class has intentionally hidden and replaced the base class method, as used in Example 5-1.

Example 5-1. Using a derived class

```
using System;

public class Window
{
   // constructor takes two integers to
   // fix location on the console
   public Window(int top, int left)
   {
      this.top = top;
      this.left = left;
   }

   // simulates drawing the window
   public void DrawWindow( )
   {
      Console.WriteLine("Drawing Window at {0}, {1}",
         top, left);
   }

   // these members are private and thus invisible
   // to derived class methods; we'll examine this
   // later in the chapter
   private int top;
   private int left;
}

// ListBox derives from Window
```

Example 5-1. Using a derived class (continued)

```csharp
public class ListBox : Window
{
    // constructor adds a parameter
    public ListBox(
        int top,
        int left,
        string theContents):
        base(top, left)  // call base constructor
    {
        mListBoxContents = theContents;
    }

    // a new version (note keyword) because in the
    // derived method we change the behavior
    public new void DrawWindow()
    {
        base.DrawWindow();  // invoke the base method
        Console.WriteLine ("Writing string to the listbox: {0}",
            mListBoxContents);
    }
    private string mListBoxContents;  // new member variable
}

public class Tester
{
    public static void Main()
    {
        // create a base instance
        Window w = new Window(5,10);
        w.DrawWindow();

        // create a derived instance
        ListBox lb = new ListBox(20,30,"Hello world");
        lb.DrawWindow();
    }
}
```

Output:
```
Drawing Window at 5, 10
Drawing Window at 20, 30
Writing string to the listbox: Hello world
```

Example 5-1 starts with the declaration of the base class Window. This class implements a constructor and a simple DrawWindow method. There are two private member variables, top and left.

Calling Base Class Constructors

In Example 5-1, the new class ListBox derives from Window and has its own constructor, which takes three parameters. The ListBox constructor invokes the constructor of its parent by placing a colon (:) after the parameter list and then invoking the base class with the keyword base:

```
public ListBox(
    int theTop,
    int theLeft,
    string theContents):
    base(theTop, theLeft)  // call base constructor
```

Because classes cannot inherit constructors, a derived class must implement its own constructor and can only make use of the constructor of its base class by calling it explicitly.

Also notice in Example 5-1 that ListBox implements a new version of DrawWindow( ):

```
public new void DrawWindow( )
```

The keyword new indicates that the programmer is intentionally creating a new version of this method in the derived class.

If the base class has an accessible default constructor, the derived constructor is not required to invoke the base constructor explicitly; instead, the default constructor is called implicitly. However, if the base class does not have a default constructor, every derived constructor *must* explicitly invoke one of the base class constructors using the base keyword.

 As discussed in Chapter 4, if you do not declare a constructor of any kind, the compiler will create a default constructor for you. Whether you write it yourself or you use the one provided "by default" by the compiler, a default constructor is one that takes no parameters. Note, however, that once you do create a constructor of any kind (with or without parameters) the compiler does *not* create a default constructor for you.

Calling Base Class Methods

In Example 5-1, the DrawWindow( ) method of ListBox hides and replaces the base class method. When you call DrawWindow( ) on an object of type ListBox, it is ListBox.DrawWindow( ) that will be invoked, not Window.DrawWindow( ). Note, however, that ListBox.DrawWindow( ) can invoke the DrawWindow( ) method of its base class with the code:

```
base.DrawWindow( );  // invoke the base method
```

(The keyword base identifies the base class for the current object.)

Controlling Access

The visibility of a class and its members can be restricted through the use of access modifiers, such as public, private, protected, internal, and protected internal. (See Chapter 4 for a discussion of access modifiers.)

As you've seen, `public` allows a member to be accessed by the member methods of other classes, while `private` indicates that the member is visible only to member methods of its own class. The `protected` keyword extends visibility to methods of derived classes, while `internal` extends visibility to methods of any class in the same *assembly.*

The `internal protected` keyword pair allows access to members of the same assembly (internal) *or* derived classes (protected). You can think of this designation as `internal` *or* `protected`.

Classes as well as their members can be designated with any of these accessibility levels. If a class member has a different access designation than the class, the more restricted access applies. Thus, if you define a class, `myClass`, as follows:

```
public class myClass
{
    // ...
    protected int myValue;
}
```

the accessibility for `myValue` is protected even though the class itself is public. A *public class* is one that is visible to any other class that wishes to interact with it. Occasionally, classes are created that exist only to help other classes in an assembly, and these classes might be marked `internal` rather than `public`.

Polymorphism

There are two powerful aspects to inheritance. One is code reuse. When you create a `ListBox` class, you're able to reuse some of the logic in the base (`Window`) class.

What is arguably more powerful, however, is the second aspect of inheritance: *polymorphism*. *Poly* means many and *morph* means form. Thus, polymorphism refers to being able to use many forms of a type without regard to the details.

When the phone company sends your phone a ring signal, it does not know what type of phone is on the other end of the line. You might have an old-fashioned Western Electric phone that energizes a motor to ring a bell, or you might have an electronic phone that plays digital music.

As far as the phone company is concerned, it knows only about the "base type" phone and expects that any "instance" of this type knows how to ring. When the phone company tells your phone to *ring*, it simply expects the phone to "do the right thing." Thus, the phone company treats your phone polymorphically.

---

* An assembly (discussed in Chapter 1), is the unit of sharing and reuse in the Common Language Runtime (a logical DLL). Typically, an assembly is a collection of physical files, held in a single directory, which includes all the resources (bitmaps, *.gif* files, etc.) required for an executable, along with the Intermediate Language (IL) and metadata for that program.

Creating Polymorphic Types

Because a ListBox *is-a* Window and a Button *is-a* Window, we expect to be able to use either of these types in situations that call for a Window. For example, a form might want to keep a collection of all the instances of Window it manages so that when the form is opened, it can tell each of its Windows to draw itself. For this operation, the form does not want to know which elements are list boxes and which are buttons; it just wants to tick through its collection and tell each to "draw." In short, the form wants to treat all its Window objects polymorphically.

Creating Polymorphic Methods

To create a method that supports polymorphism, you need only mark it as virtual in its base class. For example, to indicate that the method DrawWindow( ) of class Window in Example 5-1 is polymorphic, simply add the keyword virtual to its declaration, as follows:

```
public virtual void DrawWindow( )
```

Now each derived class is free to implement its own version of DrawWindow( ). To do so, simply override the base class virtual method by using the keyword override in the derived class method definition, and then add the new code for that overridden method.

In the following excerpt from Example 5-2 (which appears later in this section), ListBox derives from Window and implements its own version of DrawWindow( ):

```
public override void DrawWindow( )
{
    base.DrawWindow( );  // invoke the base method
    Console.WriteLine ("Writing string to the listbox: {0}",
        listBoxContents);
}
```

The keyword override tells the compiler that this class has intentionally overridden how DrawWindow( ) works. Similarly, you'll override this method in another class, Button, also derived from Window.

In the body of Example 5-2, you'll first create three objects, a Window, a ListBox, and a Button. You'll then call DrawWindow( ) on each:

```
Window win = new Window(1,2);
ListBox lb = new ListBox(3,4,"Stand alone list box");
Button b = new Button(5,6);
win.DrawWindow( );
lb.DrawWindow( );
b.DrawWindow( );
```

This works much as you might expect. The correct DrawWindow( ) object is called for each. So far, nothing polymorphic has been done. The real magic starts when you create an array of Window objects. Because a ListBox *is-a* Window, you are free to place a `ListBox` into a `Window` array. You can also place a `Button` into an array of `Window` objects because a `Button` is also a `Window`:

```
Window[] winArray = new Window[3];
winArray[0] = new Window(1,2);
winArray[1] = new ListBox(3,4,"List box in array");
winArray[2] = new Button(5,6);
```

What happens when you call `DrawWindow( )` on each of these objects?

```
for (int i = 0;i < 3; i++)
{
    winArray[i].DrawWindow( );
}
```

All the compiler knows is that it has three `Window` objects and that you've called `DrawWindow( )` on each. If you had not marked `DrawWindow` as virtual, `Window`'s `DrawWindow( )` method would be called three times. However, because you did mark `DrawWindow( )` as virtual and because the derived classes override that method, when you call `DrawWindow( )` on the array, the compiler determines the runtime type of the actual objects (a `Window`, a `ListBox` and a `Button`) and calls the right method on each. This is the essence of polymorphism. The complete code for this example is shown in Example 5-2.

 This listing uses an array, which is a collection of objects of the same type. Access the members of the array with the index operator:

```
// set the value of the element
// at offset 5
MyArray[5] = 7;
```

The first element in any array is at index 0. The use of the array in this example should be fairly intuitive. Arrays are explained in detail in Chapter 9.

Example 5-2. Using virtual methods

```
using System;

public class Window
{
   // constructor takes two integers to
   // fix location on the console
   public Window(int top, int left)
   {
      this.top = top;
      this.left = left;
   }

   // simulates drawing the window
   public virtual void DrawWindow( )
   {
      Console.WriteLine("Window: drawing Window at {0}, {1}",
```

Example 5-2. Using virtual methods (continued)

```
            top, left);
    }


    // these members are protected and thus visible
    // to derived class methods. We'll examine this
    // later in the chapter
    protected int top;
    protected int left;


}

// ListBox derives from Window
public class ListBox : Window
{
    // constructor adds a parameter
    public ListBox(
        int top,
        int left,
        string contents):
        base(top, left)  // call base constructor
    {

        listBoxContents = contents;
    }

    // an overridden version (note keyword) because in the
    // derived method we change the behavior
    public override void DrawWindow( )
    {
        base.DrawWindow( );  // invoke the base method
        Console.WriteLine ("Writing string to the listbox: {0}",
            listBoxContents);
    }

    private string listBoxContents;  // new member variable
}

public class Button : Window
{
    public Button(
        int top,
        int left):
        base(top, left)
    {
    }

    // an overridden version (note keyword) because in the
    // derived method we change the behavior
    public override void DrawWindow( )
    {
        Console.WriteLine("Drawing a button at {0}, {1}\n",
            top, left);
```

Example 5-2. Using virtual methods (continued)

```
    }
}

public class Tester
{
    static void Main( )
    {
        Window win = new Window(1,2);
        ListBox lb = new ListBox(3,4,"Stand alone list box");
        Button b = new Button(5,6);
        win.DrawWindow( );
        lb.DrawWindow( );
        b.DrawWindow( );

        Window[] winArray = new Window[3];
        winArray[0] = new Window(1,2);
        winArray[1] = new ListBox(3,4,"List box in array");
        winArray[2] = new Button(5,6);

        for (int i = 0;i < 3; i++)
        {
            winArray[i].DrawWindow( );
        }
    }
}
```

Output:
```
Window: drawing Window at 1, 2
Window: drawing Window at 3, 4
Writing string to the listbox: Stand alone list box
Drawing a button at 5, 6

Window: drawing Window at 1, 2
Window: drawing Window at 3, 4
Writing string to the listbox: List box in array
Drawing a button at 5, 6
```

Note that throughout this example, we've marked the new overridden methods with the keyword override:

public override void DrawWindow( )

The compiler now knows to use the overridden method when treating these objects polymorphically. The compiler is responsible for tracking the real type of the object and for handling the "late binding" so that it is ListBox.DrawWindow( ) that is called when the Window reference really points to a ListBox object.

C++ programmers take note: you must explicitly mark the declaration of any method that overrides a virtual method with the keyword override.

Versioning with the new and override Keywords

In C#, the programmer's decision to override a virtual method is made explicit with the override keyword. This helps you release new versions of your code; changes to the base class will not break existing code in the derived classes. The requirement to use the keyword override helps prevent that problem.

Here's how: assume for a moment that the Window base class of the previous example was written by Company A. Suppose also that the ListBox and RadioButton classes were written by programmers from Company B using a purchased copy of the Company A Window class as a base. The programmers in Company B have little or no control over the design of the Window class, including future changes that Company A might choose to make.

Now suppose that one of the programmers for Company B decides to add a Sort() method to ListBox:

```
public class ListBox : Window
{
    public virtual void Sort() {...}
}
```

This presents no problems until Company A, the author of Window, releases Version 2 of its Window class, and it turns out that the programmers in Company A have also added a Sort() method to their public class Window:

```
public class Window
{
    // ...
    public virtual void Sort() {...}
}
```

In other object-oriented languages (such as C++), the new virtual Sort() method in Window would now act as a base method for the virtual Sort() method in ListBox. The compiler would call the Sort() method in ListBox when you intend to call the Sort() in Window. In Java, if the Sort() in Window has a different return type, the class loader would consider the Sort() in ListBox to be an invalid override and would fail to load.

C# prevents this confusion. In C#, a virtual function is always considered to be the root of virtual dispatch; that is, once C# finds a virtual method, it looks no further up the inheritance hierarchy. If a new virtual Sort() function is introduced into Window, the runtime behavior of ListBox is unchanged.

When ListBox is compiled again, however, the compiler generates a warning:

```
...\class1.cs(54,24): warning CS0114: 'ListBox.Sort()' hides
inherited member 'Window.Sort()'.
To make the current member override that implementation,
add the override keyword. Otherwise add the new keyword.
```

To remove the warning, the programmer must indicate what he intends. He can mark the ListBox Sort( ) method new, to indicate that it is *not* an override of the virtual method in Window:

```
public class ListBox : Window
{
    public new virtual void Sort() {...}
```

This action removes the warning. If, on the other hand, the programmer does want to override the method in Window, he need only use the override keyword to make that intention explicit:

```
public class ListBox : Window
{
    public override void Sort() {...}
```

To avoid this warning, it might be tempting to add the keyword new to all your virtual methods. This is a bad idea. When new appears in the code, it ought to document the versioning of code. It points a potential client to the base class to see what it is that you are not overriding. Using new scattershot undermines this documentation. Further, the warning exists to help identify a real issue.

Abstract Classes

Every subclass of Window *should* implement its own DrawWindow( ) method—but nothing requires that it do so. To require subclasses to implement a method of their base, you need to designate that method as *abstract*.

An abstract method has no implementation. It creates a method name and signature that must be implemented in all derived classes. Furthermore, making one or more methods of any class abstract has the side effect of making the class abstract.

Abstract classes establish a base for derived classes, but it is not legal to instantiate an object of an abstract class. Once you declare a method to be abstract, you prohibit the creation of any instances of that class.

Thus, if you were to designate DrawWindow( ) as abstract in the Window class, you could derive from Window, but you could not create any Window objects. Each derived class would have to implement DrawWindow( ). If the derived class failed to implement the abstract method, that class would also be abstract, and again no instances would be possible.

Designating a method as abstract is accomplished by placing the keyword abstract at the beginning of the method definition, as follows:

```
abstract public void DrawWindow();
```

(Because the method can have no implementation, there are no braces; only a semicolon.)

If one or more methods are abstract, the class definition must also be marked abstract, as in the following:

```
abstract public class Window
```

Example 5-3 illustrates the creation of an abstract Window class and an abstract DrawWindow( ) method.

Example 5-3. Using an abstract method and class

```
using System;

abstract public class Window
{
   // constructor takes two integers to
   // fix location on the console
   public Window(int top, int left)
   {
      this.top = top;
      this.left = left;
   }

   // simulates drawing the window
   // notice: no implementation
   abstract public void DrawWindow( );

   protected int top;
   protected int left;

}

// ListBox derives from Window
public class ListBox : Window
{
   // constructor adds a parameter
   public ListBox(
      int top,
      int left,               /
      string contents):
      base(top, left)  // call base constructor
   {

      listBoxContents = contents;
   }

   // an overridden version implementing the
   // abstract method
   public override void DrawWindow( )
   {

      Console.WriteLine ("Writing string to the listbox: {0}",
         listBoxContents);
   }
```

Example 5-3. Using an abstract method and class (continued)

```
    private string listBoxContents;  // new member variable
}

public class Button : Window
{
    public Button(
        int top,
        int left):
        base(top, left)
    {
    }

    // implement the abstract method
    public override void DrawWindow( )
    {
        Console.WriteLine("Drawing a button at {0}, {1}\n",
            top, left);
    }

}

public class Tester
{
    static void Main( )
    {
        Window[] winArray = new Window[3];
        winArray[0] = new ListBox(1,2,"First List Box");
        winArray[1] = new ListBox(3,4,"Second List Box");
        winArray[2] = new Button(5,6);

        for (int i = 0;i < 3; i++)
        {
            winArray[i].DrawWindow( );
        }
    }
}
```

In Example 5-3, the Window class has been declared abstract and therefore cannot be instantiated. If you replace the first array member:

```
    winArray[0] = new ListBox(1,2,"First List Box");
```

with this code:

```
    winArray[0] = new Window(1,2);
```

the program will generate the following error:

```
Cannot create an instance of the abstract class or interface 'Window'
```

You can instantiate the ListBox and Button objects because these classes override the abstract method, thus making the classes *concrete* (i.e., not abstract).

Limitations of Abstract

Although designating DrawWindow( ) as abstract does force all the derived classes to implement the method, this is a very limited solution to the problem. If we derived a class from ListBox (e.g., DropDownListBox), nothing forces that derived class to implement its own DrawWindow( ) method.

 C++ programmers take note: in C# it is not possible for Window. DrawWindow( ) to provide an implementation, so we cannot take advantage of the common DrawWindow( ) routines that might otherwise be shared by the derived classes.

Finally, abstract classes should not just be an implementation trick; they should represent the idea of an abstraction that establishes a "contract" for all derived classes. In other words, abstract classes describe the public methods of the classes that will implement the abstraction.

The idea of an abstract Window class ought to lay out the common characteristics and behaviors of all Windows, even if we never intend to instantiate the abstraction Window itself.

The idea of an abstract class is implied in the word "abstract." It serves to implement the abstraction "Window" that will be manifest in the various concrete instances of Window, such as browser window, frame, button, list box, drop-down, and so forth. The abstract class establishes what a Window is, even though we never intend to create a "Window" per se. An alternative to using abstract is to define an interface, as described in Chapter 8.

Sealed Class

The obverse side of the design coin from abstract is *sealed*. Although an abstract class is intended to be derived from and to provide a template for its subclasses to follow, a sealed class does not allow classes to derive from it at all. Placed before the class declaration, the sealed keyword precludes derivation. Classes are most often marked sealed to prevent accidental inheritance.

If the declaration of Window in Example 5-3 is changed from abstract to sealed (eliminating the abstract keyword from the DrawWindow( ) declaration as well), the program will fail to compile. If you try to build this project, the compiler will return the following error message:

```
'ListBox' cannot inherit from sealed class 'Window'
```

among many other complaints (such as that you cannot create a new protected member in a sealed class).

The Root of all Classes: Object

All C# classes, of any type, are treated as if they ultimately derive from System. Object. Interestingly, this includes value types!

A base class is the immediate "parent" of a derived class. A derived class can be the base to further derived classes, creating an inheritance "tree" or hierarchy. A root class is the topmost class in an inheritance hierarchy. In C#, the root class is Object. The nomenclature is a bit confusing until you imagine an upside-down tree, with the root on top and the derived classes below. Thus, the base class is considered to be "above" the derived class.

Object provides a number of methods that subclasses can and do override. These include Equals() to determine if two objects are the same, GetType(), which returns the type of the object (discussed in Chapter 18), and ToString(), which returns a string to represent the current object (discussed in Chapter 10). Table 5-1 summarizes the methods of Object.

Table 5-1. The methods of Object

Method	What it does
Equals()	Evaluates whether two objects are equivalent.
GetHashCode()	Allows objects to provide their own hash function for use in collections (see Chapter 9).
GetType()	Provides access to the type object (see Chapter 18).
ToString()	Provides a string representation of the object.
Finalize()	Cleans up nonmemory resources; implemented by a destructor (see Chapter 4).
MemberwiseClone()	Creates copies of the object; should never be implemented by your type.
ReferenceEquals()	Evaluates whether two objects refer to the same instance.

Example 5-4 illustrates the use of the ToString() method inherited from Object, as well as the fact that primitive datatypes such as int can be treated as if they inherit from Object.

Example 5-4. Inheriting from Object

```
using System;

public class SomeClass
{
   public SomeClass(int val)
   {
      value = val;
   }

   public override string ToString()
   {
      return value.ToString();
   }
```

Example 5-4. Inheriting from Object (continued)

```
    private int value;
}


public class Tester
{
    static void Main( )
    {
        int i = 5;
        Console.WriteLine("The value of i is: {0}", i.ToString( ));

        SomeClass s = new SomeClass(7);
        Console.WriteLine("The value of s is {0}", s.ToString( ));
    }
}
```

Output:
```
The value of i is: 5
The value of s is 7
```

The documentation for `Object.ToString( )` reveals its signature:

```
    public virtual string ToString( );
```

It is a public virtual method that returns a string and that takes no parameters. All the built-in types, such as int, derive from Object and so can invoke Object's methods.

Example 5-4 overrides the virtual function for SomeClass, which is the usual case, so that the class' ToString( ) method will return a meaningful value. If you comment out the overridden function, the base method will be invoked, which will change the output to:

```
    The value of s is SomeClass
```

Thus, the default behavior is to return a string with the name of the class itself.

Classes do not need to explicitly declare that they derive from Object; the inheritance is implicit.

Boxing and Unboxing Types

Boxing and *unboxing* are the processes that enable value types (e.g., integers) to be treated as reference types (objects). The value is "boxed" inside an Object, and subsequently "unboxed" back to a value type. It is this process that allowed us to call the ToString( ) method on the integer in Example 5-4.

Boxing Is Implicit

Boxing is an implicit conversion of a value type to the type Object. Boxing a value allocates an instance of Object and copies the value into the new object instance, as shown in Figure 5-4.

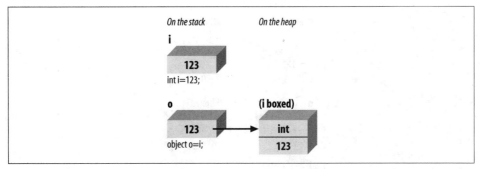

Figure 5-4. Boxing reference types

Boxing is implicit when you provide a value type where a reference is expected and the value is implicitly boxed. For example, if you assign a primitive type such as an integer to a variable of type Object (which is legal because int derives from Object), the value is boxed, as shown here:

```
using System;
class Boxing
{
    public static void Main( )
    {
        int i = 123;
        Console.WriteLine("The object value = {0}", i);
    }
}
```

Console.WriteLine( ) expects an object, not an integer. To accommodate the method, the integer type is automatically boxed by the CLR, and ToString( ) is called on the resulting object. This feature allows you to create methods that take an object as a parameter; no matter what is passed in (reference or value type) the method will work.

Unboxing Must Be Explicit

To return the boxed object back to a value type, you must explicitly unbox it. You should accomplish this in two steps:

1. Make sure the object instance is a boxed value of the given value type.

2. Copy the value from the instance to the value-type variable.

Figure 5-5 illustrates unboxing.

For the unboxing to succeed, the object being unboxed must be a reference to an object that was created by boxing a value of the given type. Boxing and unboxing are illustrated in Example 5-5.

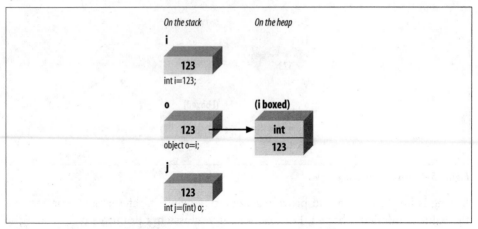

Figure 5-5. Boxing and then unboxing

Example 5-5. Boxing and unboxing

```
using System;
public class UnboxingTest
{
    public static void Main( )
    {
        int i = 123;

        //Boxing
        object o = i;

        // unboxing (must be explict)
        int j = (int) o;
        Console.WriteLine("j: {0}", j);
    }
}
```

Example 5-5 creates an integer i and implicitly boxes it when it is assigned to the object o. The value is then explicitly unboxed and assigned to a new int whose value is displayed.

Typically, you will wrap an unbox operation in a try block, as explained in Chapter 11. If the object being unboxed is null or a reference to an object of a different type, an InvalidCastException is thrown.

Nesting Classes

Classes have members, and it is entirely possible for the member of a class to be another user-defined type. Thus, a Button class might have a member of type Location, and a Location class might contain members of type Point. Finally, Point might contain members of type int.

At times, the contained class might exist only to serve the outer class, and there might be no reason for it to be otherwise visible. (In short, the contained class acts as a helper class.) You can define the helper class within the definition of the outer class. The contained, inner class is called a *nested* class, and the class that contains it is called, simply, the *outer* class.

Nested classes have the advantage of access to all the members of the outer class. A method of a nested class can access private members of the outer class.

In addition, the nested class can be hidden from all other classes—that is, it can be private to the outer class.

Finally, a nested class that is public is accessed within the scope of the outer class. If Outer is the outer class, and Nested is the (public) inner class, refer to Nested as Outer.Nested, with the outer class acting (more or less) as a namespace or scope.

 Java programmers take note: nested classes are roughly equivalent to static inner classes; there is no C# equivalent to Java's nonstatic inner classes.

Example 5-6 features a nested class of Fraction named FractionArtist. The job of FractionArtist is to render the fraction on the console. In this example, the rendering is handled by a pair of simple WriteLine( ) statements.

Example 5-6. Using a nested class

```
using System;
using System.Text;

public class Fraction
{
    public Fraction(int numerator, int denominator)
    {
        this.numerator=numerator;
        this.denominator=denominator;
    }

    public override string ToString( )
    {
        return String.Format("{0}/{1}",
            numerator, denominator);
    }

    internal class FractionArtist
    {
        public void Draw(Fraction f)
        {
            Console.WriteLine("Drawing the numerator: {0}",
                f.numerator);
            Console.WriteLine("Drawing the denominator: {0}",
```

Example 5-6. Using a nested class (continued)

```
                    f.denominator);
        }
    }
    private int numerator;
    private int denominator;
}


public class Tester
{
    static void Main( )
    {
        Fraction f1 = new Fraction(3,4);
        Console.WriteLine("f1: {0}", f1.ToString( ));

        Fraction.FractionArtist fa = new Fraction.FractionArtist( );
        fa.Draw(f1);
    }
}
```

The nested class is shown in bold. The FractionArtist class provides only a single member, the Draw( ) method. What is particularly interesting is that Draw( ) has access to the private data members f.numerator and f.denominator, to which it would not have had access if it were not a nested class.

Notice in Main( ) that to declare an instance of this nested class, you must specify the type name of the outer class:

```
    Fraction.FractionArtist fa = new Fraction.FractionArtist( );
```

FractionArtist is scoped to within the Fraction class.

CHAPTER 6

Operator Overloading

It is a design goal of C# that user-defined classes have all the functionality of built-in types. For example, suppose you have defined a type to represent fractions. Ensuring that this class has all the functionality of the built-in types means that you must be able to perform arithmetic on instances of your fractions (e.g., add two fractions, multiply, etc.) and convert fractions to and from built-in types such as integer (int). You could, of course, implement methods for each of these operations and invoke them by writing statements such as:

```
Fraction theSum = firstFraction.Add(secondFraction);
```

Although this will work, it is ugly and not how the built-in types are used. It would be much better to write:

```
Fraction theSum = firstFraction + secondFraction;
```

Statements like this are intuitive and consistent with how built-in types, such as int, are added.

In this chapter you will learn techniques for adding standard operators to your user-defined types. You will also learn how to add conversion operators so that your user-defined types can be implicitly and explicitly converted to other types.

Using the operator Keyword

In C#, operators are static methods whose return values represent the result of an operation and whose parameters are the operands. When you create an operator for a class you say you have "overloaded" that operator, much as you might overload any member method. Thus, to overload the addition operator (+) you would write:

```
public static Fraction operator+(Fraction lhs, Fraction rhs)
```

It is my convention to name the parameters lhs and rhs. The parameter name lhs stands for "lefthand side" and reminds me that the first parameter represents the left-hand side of the operation. Similarly, rhs stands for "righthand side."

The C# syntax for overloading an operator is to write the word operator followed by the operator to overload. The operator keyword is a method modifier. Thus, to overload the addition operator (+), write operator+.

When you write:

```
Fraction theSum = firstFraction + secondFraction;
```

the overloaded + operator is invoked, with the first Fraction passed as the first argument, and the second Fraction passed as the second argument. When the compiler sees the expression:

```
firstFraction + secondFraction
```

it translates that expression into:

```
Fraction.operator+(firstFraction, secondFraction)
```

The result is that a new Fraction is returned, which in this case is assigned to the Fraction object named theSum.

 C++ *programmers take note:* it is not possible to create nonstatic operators, and thus binary operators must take two operands.

Supporting Other .NET Languages

C# provides the ability to overload operators for your classes, even though this is not, strictly speaking, in the Common Language Specification (CLS). Other .NET languages, such as VB.NET, might not support operator overloading, and it is important to ensure that your class supports the alternative methods that these other languages might call to create the same effect.

Thus, if you overload the addition operator (+), you might also want to provide an add( ) method that does the same work. Operator overloading ought to be a syntactic shortcut, not the only path for your objects to accomplish a given task.

Creating Useful Operators

Operator overloading can make your code more intuitive and enable it to act more like the built-in types. It can also make your code unmanageable, complex, and obtuse if you break the common idiom for the use of operators. Resist the temptation to use operators in new and idiosyncratic ways.

For example, although it might be tempting to overload the increment operator (++) on an employee class to invoke a method incrementing the employee's pay level, this can create tremendous confusion for clients of your class. It is best to use operator overloading sparingly, and only when its meaning is clear and consistent with how the built-in classes operate.

Logical Pairs

It is quite common to overload the equals operator (==) to test whether two objects are equal (however equality might be defined for your object). C# insists that if you overload the equals operator, you must also overload the not-equals operator (!=). Similarly, the less-than (<) and greater-than (>) operators must be paired, as must the less-than or equals (<=) and greater-than or equals (>=) operators.

The Equals Operator

If you overload the equals operator (==), it is recommended that you also override the virtual Equals( ) method provided by object and route its functionality back to the equals operator. This allows your class to be polymorphic and provides compatibility with other .NET languages that do not overload operators (but do support method overloading). The FCL classes will not use the overloaded operators but will expect your classes to implement the underlying methods. Thus, for example, ArrayList expects you to implement Equals( ).

The object class implements the Equals( ) method with this signature:

```
public override bool Equals(object o)
```

By overriding this method, you allow your Fraction class to act polymorphically with all other objects. Inside the body of Equals( ), you will need to ensure that you are comparing with another Fraction, and if so you can pass the implementation along to the equals operator definition that you've written.

```
public override bool Equals(object o)
{
    if (! (o is Fraction) )
    {
        return false;
    }
    return this == (Fraction) o;
}
```

The is operator is used to check whether the runtime type of an object is compatible with the operand (in this case, Fraction). Thus o is Fraction will evaluate true if o is in fact a type compatible with Fraction.

Conversion Operators

C# converts int to long implicitly, and allows you to convert long to int explicitly. The conversion from int to long is *implicit* because you know that any int will fit into the memory representation of a long. The reverse operation, from long to int, must be *explicit* (using a cast) because it is possible to lose information in the conversion:

```
int myInt = 5;
long myLong;
```

```
myLong = myInt;         // implicit
myInt = (int) myLong;   // explicit
```

You must have the same functionality for your fractions. Given an int, you can support an implicit conversion to a fraction because any whole value is equal to that value over 1 (e.g., 15==15/1).

Given a fraction, you might want to provide an explicit conversion back to an integer, understanding that some value might be lost. Thus, you might convert 9/4 to the integer value 2.

The keyword implicit is used when the conversion is guaranteed to succeed and no information will be lost; otherwise explicit is used.

Example 6-1 illustrates how you might implement implicit and explicit conversions, and some of the operators of the Fraction class. (Although I've used Console. WriteLine to print messages illustrating which method we're entering, the better way to pursue this kind of trace is with the debugger. You can place a breakpoint on each of the test statements, and then step into the code, watching the invocation of the constructors as they occur.) When you compile this example, it will generate some warnings because GetHashCode( ) is not implemented (see Chapter 9).

Example 6-1. Defining conversions and operators for the fraction class operators

```csharp
using System;

public class Fraction
{
    public Fraction(int numerator, int denominator)
    {
        Console.WriteLine("In Fraction Constructor(int, int)");
        this.numerator=numerator;
        this.denominator=denominator;
    }

    public Fraction(int wholeNumber)
    {
        Console.WriteLine("In Fraction Constructor(int)");
        numerator = wholeNumber;
        denominator = 1;
    }

    public static implicit operator Fraction(int theInt)
    {
        System.Console.WriteLine("In implicit conversion to Fraction");
        return new Fraction(theInt);
    }

    public static explicit operator int(Fraction theFraction)
    {
        System.Console.WriteLine("In explicit conversion to int");
        return theFraction.numerator /
```

```
        theFraction.denominator;
}

public static bool operator==(Fraction lhs, Fraction rhs)
{
    Console.WriteLine("In operator ==");
    if (lhs.denominator == rhs.denominator &&
        lhs.numerator == rhs.numerator)
    {
        return true;
    }
    // code here to handle unlike fractions
    return false;
}

public static bool operator !=(Fraction lhs, Fraction rhs)
{
    Console.WriteLine("In operator !=");

    return !(lhs==rhs);
}

public override bool Equals(object o)
{
    Console.WriteLine("In method Equals");
    if (! (o is Fraction) )
    {
        return false;
    }
    return this == (Fraction) o;
}

public static Fraction operator+(Fraction lhs, Fraction rhs)
{
    Console.WriteLine("In operator+");
    if (lhs.denominator == rhs.denominator)
    {
        return new Fraction(lhs.numerator+rhs.numerator,
            lhs.denominator);
    }

    // simplistic solution for unlike fractions
    // 1/2 + 3/4 == (1*4) + (3*2) / (2*4) == 10/8
    int firstProduct = lhs.numerator * rhs.denominator;
    int secondProduct = rhs.numerator * lhs.denominator;
    return new Fraction(
        firstProduct + secondProduct,
        lhs.denominator * rhs.denominator
    );

}
```

```
    public override string ToString( )
    {
        String s = numerator.ToString( ) + "/" +
            denominator.ToString( );
        return s;
    }

    private int numerator;
    private int denominator;
}


public class Tester
{
    static void Main( )
    {
        Fraction f1 = new Fraction(3,4);
        Console.WriteLine("f1: {0}", f1.ToString( ));

        Fraction f2 = new Fraction(2,4);
        Console.WriteLine("f2: {0}", f2.ToString( ));

        Fraction f3 = f1 + f2;
        Console.WriteLine("f1 + f2 = f3: {0}", f3.ToString( ));

        Fraction f4 = f3 + 5;
        Console.WriteLine("f3 + 5 = f4: {0}", f4.ToString( ));

        Fraction f5 = new Fraction(2,4);
        if (f5 == f2)
        {
            Console.WriteLine("F5: {0} == F2: {1}",
                f5.ToString( ),
                f2.ToString( ));
        }

    }
}
```

The Fraction class begins with two constructors. One takes a numerator and denominator, the other takes a whole number. The constructors are followed by the declaration of two conversion operators. The first conversion operator changes an integer into a Fraction:

```
    public static implicit operator Fraction(int theInt)
    {
        return new Fraction(theInt);
    }
```

This conversion is marked implicit because any whole number (int) can be converted to a Fraction by setting the numerator to the int and the denominator to 1. Delegate this responsibility to the constructor that takes an int.

The second conversion operator is for the explicit conversion of Fractions into integers:

```
public static explicit operator int(Fraction theFraction)
{
    return theFraction.numerator /
        theFraction.denominator;
}
```

Because this example uses integer division, it will truncate the value. Thus, if the fraction is 15/16, the resulting integer value will be 1. A more sophisticated conversion operator might accomplish rounding.

The conversion operators are followed by the equals operator (==) and the not equals operator (!=). Remember that if you implement one of these equals operators, you must implement the other.

You have defined value equality for a Fraction such that the numerators and denominators must match. For this exercise, 3/4 and 6/8 are not considered equal. Again, a more sophisticated implementation would reduce these fractions and notice the equality.

Include an override of the object class' Equals( ) method so that your Fraction objects can be treated polymorphically with any other object. Your implementation is to delegate the evaluation of equality to the equality operator.

A Fraction class would, no doubt, implement all the arithmetic operators (addition, subtraction, multiplication, division). To keep the illustration simple, implement only addition, and even here you simplify greatly. Check to see if the denominators are the same; if so, add the following numerators:

```
public static Fraction operator+(Fraction lhs, Fraction rhs)
{
    if (lhs.denominator == rhs.denominator)
    {
        return new Fraction(lhs.numerator+rhs.numerator,
            lhs.denominator);
    }
```

If the denominators are not the same, cross multiply:

```
int firstProduct = lhs.numerator * rhs.denominator;
int secondProduct = rhs.numerator * lhs.denominator;
return new Fraction(
    firstProduct + secondProduct,
    lhs.denominator * rhs.denominator
```

This code is best understood with an example. If you were adding 1/2 and 3/4, you can multiply the first numerator (1) by the second denominator (4) and store the result (4) in firstProduct. You can also multiply the second numerator (3) by the first denominator (2) and store that result (6) in secondProduct. You add these products (6+4) to a sum of 10, which is the numerator for the answer. You then multiply the two denominators (2*4) to generate the new denominator (8). The resulting fraction (10/8) is the correct answer.[*]

Finally, to enable debugging of the new Fraction class, the code is written so that Fraction is able to return its value as a string in the format numerator/denominator:

```
public override string ToString( )
{
    String s = numerator.ToString( ) + "/" +
        denominator.ToString( );
    return s;
}
```

Create a new string object by calling the ToString( ) method on numerator. Since numerator is an int, and ints are value types, the call to the ToString() method causes the compiler to implicitly box the integer (creating an object) and calls ToString( ) on that object, returning a string representation of the numerator. Concatenate the string "/" and then concatenate the string that results from calling ToString( ) on the denominator.

With your Fraction class in hand, you're ready to test. Your first tests create simple fractions, 3/4 and 2/4:

```
Fraction f1 = new Fraction(3,4);
Console.WriteLine("f1: {0}", f1.ToString( ));

Fraction f2 = new Fraction(2,4);
Console.WriteLine("f2: {0}", f2.ToString( ));
```

The output from this is what you would expect—the invocation of the constructors and the value printed in WriteLine:

```
In Fraction Constructor(int, int)
f1: 3/4
In Fraction Constructor(int, int)
f2: 2/4
```

The next line in Main( ) invokes the static operator+. The purpose of this operator is to add two fractions and return the sum in a new fraction:

```
Fraction f3 = f1 + f2;
Console.WriteLine("f1 + f2 = f3: {0}", f3.ToString( ));
```

Examining the output reveals how operator+ works:

```
In operator+
In Fraction Constructor(int, int)
f1 + f2 = f3: 5/4
```

The operator+ is invoked, and then the constructor for f3, taking the two int values representing the numerator and denominator of the resulting new fraction.

---

[*] To recap: 1/2=4/8, 3/4=6/8, 4/8+6/8=10/8. The example does not reduce the fraction, to keep it simple.

The next test in Main( ) adds an int to the Fraction f3 and assigns the resulting value to a new Fraction, f4:

```
Fraction f4 = f3 + 5;
Console.WriteLine("f3 + 5: {0}", f4.ToString( ));
```

The output shows the steps for the various conversions:

```
In implicit conversion to Fraction
In Fraction Constructor(int)
In operator+
In Fraction Constructor(int, int)
f3 + 5 =  f4: 25/4
```

Notice that the implicit conversion operator was invoked to convert 5 to a fraction. In the return statement from the implicit conversion operator, the Fraction constructor was called, creating the fraction 5/1. This new fraction was then passed along with Fraction f3 to operator+, and the sum was passed to the constructor for f4.

In our final test, a new fraction (f5) is created. Test whether it is equal to f2. If so, print their values:

```
Fraction f5 = new Fraction(2,4);
if (f5 == f2)
{
    Console.WriteLine("F5: {0} == F2: {1}",
        f5.ToString( ),
        f2.ToString( ));
}
```

The output shows the creation of f5, and then the invocation of the overloaded equals operator:

```
In Fraction Constructor(int, int)
In operator ==
F5: 2/4 == F2: 2/4
```

CHAPTER 7
Structs

A *struct* is a simple user-defined type, a lightweight alternative to classes. Structs are similar to classes in that they may contain constructors, properties, methods, fields, operators, nested types and indexers (see Chapter 9).

There are also significant differences between classes and structs. For instance, structs don't support inheritance or destructors. More important, although a class is a reference type, a struct is a value type. (See Chapter 3 for more information about classes and types.) Thus, structs are useful for representing objects that do not require reference semantics.

The consensus view is that you ought to use structs only for types that are small, simple, and similar in their behavior and characteristics to built-in types.

Structs are somewhat more efficient in their use of memory in arrays (see Chapter 9). However, they can be less efficient when used in collections. Collections expect references, and structs must be boxed. There is overhead in boxing and unboxing, and classes might be more efficient in large collections.

In this chapter, you will learn how to define and work with structs and how to use constructors to initialize their values.

Defining Structs

The syntax for declaring a struct is almost identical to that for a class:

```
[attributes] [access-modifiers] struct identifier [:interface-list]
{ struct-members }
```

Example 7-1 illustrates the definition of a struct. Location represents a point on a two-dimensional surface. Notice that the struct Location is declared exactly as a class would be, except for the use of the keyword struct. Also notice that the Location constructor takes two integers and assigns their value to the instance members, x and y. The x and y coordinates of Location are declared as properties.

Example 7-1. Creating a struct

```
using System;

public struct Location
{
    public Location(int xCoordinate, int yCoordinate)
    {
        xVal = xCoordinate;
        yVal = yCoordinate;
    }

    public int x
    {
        get
        {
            return xVal;
        }
        set
        {
            xVal = value;
        }
    }

    public int y
    {
        get
        {
            return yVal;
        }
        set
        {
            yVal = value;
        }
    }

    public override string ToString()
    {
        return (String.Format("{0}, {1}", xVal,yVal));
    }

    private int xVal;
    private int yVal;
}

public class Tester
{
    public void myFunc(Location loc)
    {
        loc.x = 50;
        loc.y = 100;
        Console.WriteLine("Loc1 location: {0}", loc);
    }
    static void Main()
```

Example 7-1. Creating a struct (continued)

```
    {
        Location loc1 = new Location(200,300);
        Console.WriteLine("Loc1 location: {0}", loc1);
        Tester t = new Tester( );
        t.myFunc(loc1);
        Console.WriteLine("Loc1 location: {0}", loc1);
    }
}
```
Output
```
Loc1 location: 200, 300
In MyFunc loc: 50, 100
Loc1 location: 200, 300
```

Unlike classes, structs do not support inheritance. They implicitly derive from object (as do all types in C#, including the built-in types) but cannot inherit from any other class or struct. Structs are also implicitly *sealed* (that is, no class or struct can derive from a struct). Like classes, however, structs can implement multiple interfaces. Additional differences include the following:

No destructor or custom default constructor

Structs cannot have destructors, nor can they have a custom parameterless (default) constructor. If you do not supply a constructor, your struct will in effect be provided with a default constructor that will zero all the data members or set them to default values appropriate to their type (see Table 4-2). If you supply any constructor, you must initialize all the fields in the struct.

No initialization

You cannot initialize an instance field in a struct. Thus, it is illegal to write:

```
private int xVal = 50;
private int yVal = 100;
```

though that would have been fine had this been a class.

Structs are designed to be simple and lightweight. While private member data promotes data hiding and encapsulation, some programmers feel it is overkill for structs. They make the member data public, thus simplifying the implementation of the struct. Other programmers feel that properties provide a clean and simple interface, and that good programming practice demands data hiding even with simple lightweight objects. Whichever you choose is a matter of design philosophy; the language supports either approach.

Creating Structs

Create an instance of a struct by using the new keyword in an assignment statement, just as you would for a class. In Example 7-1, the Tester class creates an instance of Location as follows:

```
Location loc1 = new Location(200,300);
```

Here the new instance is named loc1 and is passed two values, 200 and 300.

Structs as Value Types

The definition of the Tester class in Example 7-1 includes a Location object (loc1) created with the values 200 and 300. This line of code calls the Location constructor:

```
Location loc1 = new Location(200,300);
```

Then WriteLine( ) is called:

```
Console.WriteLine("Loc1 location: {0}", loc1);
```

WriteLine( ) is expecting an object, but, of course, Location is a struct (a value type). The compiler automatically boxes the struct (as it would any value type), and it is the boxed object that is passed to WriteLine( ). ToString( ) is called on the boxed object, and because the struct (implicitly) inherits from object, it is able to respond polymorphically, overriding the method just as any other object might:

```
Loc1 location: 200, 300
```

Structs are value objects, however, and when passed to a function, they are passed by value—as seen in the next line of code—in which the loc1 object is passed to the myFunc( ) method:

```
t.myFunc(loc1);
```

In myFunc new values are assigned to x and y, and these new values are printed out:

```
Loc1 location: 50, 100
```

When you return to the calling function (Main( )) and call WriteLine( ) again, the values are unchanged:

```
Loc1 location: 200, 300
```

The struct was passed as a value object, and a copy was made in myFunc. Try this experiment: change the declaration to class:

```
public class Location
```

and run the test again. Here is the output:

```
Loc1 location: 200, 300
In MyFunc loc: 50, 100
Loc1 location: 50, 100
```

This time the Location object has reference semantics. Thus, when the values are changed in myFunc( ), they are changed on the actual object back in Main( ).

Calling the Default Constructor

As mentioned earlier, if you do not create a constructor, an implicit default constructor is called by the compiler. We can see this if we comment out the constructor:

```
/* public Location(int xCoordinate, int yCoordinate)
   {
       xVal = xCoordinate;
```

```
        yVal = yCoordinate;
    }
*/
```

and replace the first line in `Main( )` with one that creates an instance of `Location` without passing values:

```
// Location loc1 = new Location(200,300);
   Location loc1 = new Location( );
```

Because there is now no constructor at all, the implicit default constructor is called. The output looks like this:

```
Loc1 location: 0, 0
In MyFunc loc: 50, 100
Loc1 location: 0, 0
```

The default constructor has initialized the member variables to zero.

C++ *programmers take note:* in C#, the `new` keyword does not always create objects on the heap. Classes are created on the heap, and structs are created on the stack. Also, when `new` is omitted (as you will see in the next section), a constructor is never called. Because C# requires definite assignment, you must explicitly initialize all the member variables before using the struct.

Creating Structs Without new

Because `loc1` is a struct (not a class), it is created on the stack. Thus, in Example 7-1, when the `new` operator is called:

```
Location loc1 = new Location(200,300);
```

the resulting `Location` object is created on the stack.

The `new` operator calls the `Location` constructor. However, unlike with a class, it is possible to create a struct without using `new` at all. This is consistent with how built-in type variables (such as `int`) are defined, and is illustrated in Example 7-2.

A caveat: I am demonstrating how to create a struct without using `new` because it differentiates C# from C++, and also differentiates how C# treats classes versus structs. That said, however, creating structs without the keyword `new` brings little advantage and can create programs that are harder to understand, more error prone, and more difficult to maintain! Proceed at your own risk.

Example 7-2. Creating a struct without using new

```
using System;

public struct Location
{
    public Location(int xCoordinate, int yCoordinate)
```

Example 7-2. Creating a struct without using new (continued)

```
    {
        xVal = xCoordinate;
        yVal = yCoordinate;
    }
      public int x
    {
        get
        {
            return xVal;
        }
        set
        {
            xVal = value;
        }
    }

    public int y
    {
        get
        {
            return yVal;
        }
        set
        {
            yVal = value;
        }
    }

    public override string ToString( )
    {
        return (String.Format("{0}, {1}", xVal,yVal));
    }

    public int xVal;
    public int yVal;
}

public class Tester
{
    static void Main( )
    {
        Location loc1;          // no call to the constructor
        loc1.xVal = 75;         // initialize the members
        loc1.yVal = 225;
        Console.WriteLine(loc1);
    }
}
```

In Example 7-2 you initialize the local variables directly, before calling a method of loc1 and before passing the object to WriteLine( ):

```
    loc1.xVal = 75;
    loc1.yVal = 225;
```

If you were to comment out one of the assignments and recompile:

```
static void Main( )
{
    Location loc1;
    loc1.xVal = 75;
 //    loc1.yVal = 225;
    Console.WriteLine(loc1);
}
```

you would get a compiler error:

```
Use of unassigned local variable 'loc1'
```

Once you assign all the values, you can access the values through the properties x and y:

```
static void Main( )
{
    Location loc1;
    loc1.xVal = 75;          // assign member variable
    loc1.yVal = 225;         // assign member variable
    loc1.x = 300;            // use property
    loc1.y = 400;            // use property
    Console.WriteLine(loc1);
}
```

Be careful about using properties. Although these allow you to support encapsulation by making the actual values private, the properties themselves are actually member methods, and you cannot call a member method until you initialize all the member variables.

CHAPTER 8

Interfaces

An *interface* is a contract that guarantees to a client how a class or struct will behave. When a class implements an interface, it tells any potential client "I guarantee I'll support the methods, properties, events, and indexers of the named interface." (See Chapter 4 for information about methods and properties; see Chapter 12 for info about events, and see Chapter 9 for coverage of indexers.)

An interface offers an alternative to an abstract class for creating contracts among classes and their clients. These contracts are made manifest using the interface keyword, which declares a reference type that encapsulates the contract.

Syntactically, an interface is like a class that has only abstract methods. An abstract class serves as the base class for a family of derived classes, while interfaces are meant to be mixed in with other inheritance trees.

When a class implements an interface, it must implement all the methods of that interface; in effect the class says "I agree to fulfill the contract defined by this interface."

Inheriting from an abstract class implements the *is-a* relationship, introduced in Chapter 5. Implementing an interface defines a different relationship that we've not seen until now: the *implements* relationship. These two relationships are subtly different. A car *is a* vehicle, but it might *implement* the CanBeBoughtWithABigLoan capability (as can a house, for example).

Mix Ins

In Somerville, Massachusetts, there was, at one time, an ice cream parlor where you could have candies and other goodies "mixed in" with your chosen ice cream flavor. This seemed like a good metaphor to some of the object-oriented pioneers from nearby MIT who were working on the fortuitously named SCOOPS programming language. They appropriated the term "mix in" for classes that mixed in additional capabilities. These mix-in or capability classes served much the same role as interfaces do in C#.

In this chapter, you will learn how to create, implement, and use interfaces. You'll learn how to implement multiple interfaces and how to combine and extend interfaces, as well as how to test whether a class has implemented an interface.

Implementing an Interface

The syntax for defining an interface is as follows:

```
[attributes] [access-modifier] interface interface-name [:base-list] {interface-body}
```

Don't worry about attributes for now; they're covered in Chapter 18.

Access modifiers, including `public`, `private`, `protected`, `internal`, and `protected internal`, are discussed in Chapter 4.

The `interface` keyword is followed by the name of the interface. It is common (but not required) to begin the name of your interface with a capital I (thus, `IStorable`, `ICloneable`, `IClaudius`, etc.).

The *base-list* lists the interfaces that this interface extends (as described in the section "Implementing More Than One Interface," later in this chapter).

The *interface-body* is the implementation of the interface, as described next.

Suppose you wish to create an interface that describes the methods and properties a class needs to be stored to and retrieved from a database or other storage such as a file. You decide to call this interface `IStorable`.

In this interface you might specify two methods: `Read( )` and `Write( )`, which appear in the interface-body:

```
interface IStorable
{
    void Read( );
    void Write(object);
}
```

The purpose of an interface is to define the capabilities that you want to have available in a class.

For example, you might create a class, `Document`. It turns out that `Document` types can be stored in a database, so you decide to have `Document` implement the `IStorable` interface.

To do so, use the same syntax as if the new `Document` class were inheriting from `IStorable`—a colon (:), followed by the interface name:

```
public class Document : IStorable
{
    public void Read( ) {...}
    public void Write(object obj) {...}
    // ...
}
```

It is now your responsibility, as the author of the Document class, to provide a meaningful implementation of the IStorable methods. Having designated Document as implementing IStorable, you must implement all the IStorable methods, or you will generate an error when you compile. This is illustrated in Example 8-1, in which the Document class implements the IStorable interface.

Example 8-1. Using a simple interface

```
using System;

// declare the interface
interface IStorable
{
    // no access modifiers, methods are public
    // no implementation
    void Read();
    void Write(object obj);
    int Status { get; set; }

}

// create a class which implements the IStorable interface
public class Document : IStorable
{
    public Document(string s)
    {
        Console.WriteLine("Creating document with: {0}", s);
    }

    // implement the Read method
    public void Read()
    {
        Console.WriteLine(
            "Implementing the Read Method for IStorable");
    }

    // implement the Write method
    public void Write(object o)
    {
        Console.WriteLine(
            "Implementing the Write Method for IStorable");
    }
    // implement the property
    public int Status
    {
        get
        {
            return status;
        }

        set
        {
            status = value;
```

Example 8-1. Using a simple interface (continued)

```
        }
    }

    // store the value for the property
    private int status = 0;
}

// Take our interface out for a spin
public class Tester
{

    static void Main( )
    {
        // access the methods in the Document object
        Document doc = new Document("Test Document");
        doc.Status = -1;
        doc.Read( );
        Console.WriteLine("Document Status: {0}", doc.Status);
    }
}
```

Output:
```
Creating document with: Test Document
Implementing the Read Method for IStorable
Document Status: -1
```

Example 8-1 defines a simple interface, IStorable, with two methods, Read( ) and Write( ), and a property, Status, of type integer. Notice that the property declaration does not provide an implementation for get( ) and set( ), but simply designates that there *is* a get( ) and a set( ):

```
    int Status { get; set; }
```

Notice also that the IStorable method declarations do not include access modifiers (e.g., public, protected, internal, private). In fact, providing an access modifier generates a compile error. Interface methods are implicitly public because an interface is a contract meant to be used by other classes. You cannot create an instance of an interface; instead you instantiate a class that implements the interface.

The class implementing the interface must fulfill the contract exactly and completely. Document must provide both a Read( ) and a Write( ) method and the Status property. *How* it fulfills these requirements, however, is entirely up to the Document class. Although IStorable dictates that Document must have a Status property, it does not know or care whether Document stores the actual status as a member variable or looks it up in a database. The details are up to the implementing class.

Implementing More Than One Interface

Classes can implement more than one interface. For example, if your Document class can be stored and it also can be compressed, you might choose to implement both the IStorable and ICompressible interfaces. To do so, change the declaration (in the base-list) to indicate that both interfaces are implemented, separating the two interfaces with commas:

```
public class Document : IStorable, ICompressible
```

Having done this, the Document class must also implement the methods specified by the ICompressible interface (which is declared in Example 8-2):

```
public void Compress()
{
    Console.WriteLine("Implementing the Compress Method");
}

public void Decompress()
{
    Console.WriteLine("Implementing the Decompress Method");
}
```

Extending Interfaces

It is possible to extend an existing interface to add new methods or members, or to modify how existing members work. For example, you might extend ICompressible with a new interface, ILoggedCompressible, which extends the original interface with methods to keep track of the bytes saved:

```
interface ILoggedCompressible : ICompressible
{
    void LogSavedBytes();
}
```

Classes are now free to implement either ICompressible or ILoggedCompressible, depending on whether they need the additional functionality. If a class does implement ILoggedCompressible, it must implement all the methods of both ILogged-Compressible and ICompressible. Objects of that type can be cast either to ILoggedCompressible or to ICompressible.

Combining Interfaces

Similarly, you can create new interfaces by combining existing interfaces, and, optionally, adding new methods or properties. For example, you might decide to create IStorableCompressible. This interface would combine the methods of each of the other two interfaces, but would also add a new method to store the original size of the precompressed item:

```
interface IStorableCompressible : IStoreable, ILoggedCompressible
{
    void LogOriginalSize();
}
```

Example 8-2 illustrates extending and combining interfaces.

Example 8-2. Extending and combining interfaces

```csharp
using System;

interface IStorable
{
    void Read();
    void Write(object obj);
    int Status { get; set; }

}

// here's the new interface
interface ICompressible
{
    void Compress();
    void Decompress();
}

// Extend the interface
interface ILoggedCompressible : ICompressible
{
    void LogSavedBytes();
}

// Combine Interfaces
interface IStorableCompressible : IStorable, ILoggedCompressible
{
    void LogOriginalSize();
}

// yet another interface
interface IEncryptable
{
    void Encrypt();
    void Decrypt();
}

public class Document : IStorableCompressible, IEncryptable
{
    // the document constructor
    public Document(string s)
    {
        Console.WriteLine("Creating document with: {0}", s);

    }

    // implement IStorable
    public void Read()
    {
        Console.WriteLine(
            "Implementing the Read Method for IStorable");
    }

    public void Write(object o)
```

Example 8-2. Extending and combining interfaces (continued)

```
{
   Console.WriteLine(
      "Implementing the Write Method for IStorable");
}

public int Status
{
   get
   {
      return status;
   }

   set
   {
      status = value;
   }
}

// implement ICompressible
public void Compress()
{
   Console.WriteLine("Implementing Compress");
}

public void Decompress()
{
   Console.WriteLine("Implementing Decompress");
}

// implement ILoggedCompressible
public void LogSavedBytes()
{
   Console.WriteLine("Implementing LogSavedBytes");
}

// implement IStorableCompressible
public void LogOriginalSize()
{
   Console.WriteLine("Implementing LogOriginalSize");
}

// implement IEncryptable
public void Encrypt()
{
   Console.WriteLine("Implementing Encrypt");

}

public void Decrypt()
{
   Console.WriteLine("Implementing Decrypt");
```

Example 8-2. Extending and combining interfaces (continued)

```
    }

    // hold the data for IStorable's Status property
    private int status = 0;
}

public class Tester
{

    static void Main( )
    {
        // create a document object
        Document doc = new Document("Test Document");

        // cast the document to the various interfaces
        IStorable isDoc = doc as IStorable;
        if (isDoc != null)
        {
            isDoc.Read( );
        }
        else
            Console.WriteLine("IStorable not supported");

        ICompressible icDoc = doc as ICompressible;
        if (icDoc != null)
        {
            icDoc.Compress( );
        }
        else
            Console.WriteLine("Compressible not supported");

        ILoggedCompressible ilcDoc = doc as ILoggedCompressible;
        if (ilcDoc != null)
        {
            ilcDoc.LogSavedBytes( );
            ilcDoc.Compress( );
            // ilcDoc.Read( );
        }
        else
            Console.WriteLine("LoggedCompressible not supported");

        IStorableCompressible isc = doc as IStorableCompressible;
        if (isc != null)
        {
            isc.LogOriginalSize( );   // IStorableCompressible
            isc.LogSavedBytes( );     // ILoggedCompressible
            isc.Compress( );          // ICompressible
            isc.Read( );              // IStorable

        }
        else
        {
            Console.WriteLine("StorableCompressible not supported");
```

Example 8-2. Extending and combining interfaces (continued)

```
    }

    IEncryptable ie = doc as IEncryptable;
    if (ie != null)
    {
        ie.Encrypt();
    }
    else
        Console.WriteLine("Encryptable not supported");
    }
}
```

Output:
```
Creating document with: Test Document
Implementing the Read Method for IStorable
Implementing Compress
Implementing LogSavedBytes
Implementing Compress
Implementing LogOriginalSize
Implementing LogSavedBytes
Implementing Compress
Implementing the Read Method for IStorable
Implementing Encrypt
```

Example 8-2 starts by implementing the IStorable interface and the ICompressible interface. The latter is extended to ILoggedCompressible and then the two are combined into IStorableCompressible. Finally, the example adds a new interface, IEncryptable.

The Tester program creates a new Document object and then casts it to the various interfaces. When the object is cast to ILoggedCompressible, you can use the interface to call methods on Icompressible because ILoggedCompressible extends (and thus subsumes) the methods from the base interface:

```
ILoggedCompressible ilcDoc = doc as ILoggedCompressible;
if (ilcDoc != null)
{
    ilcDoc.LogSavedBytes();
    ilcDoc.Compress();
    // ilcDoc.Read();
}
```

You cannot call Read( ), however, because that is a method of IStorable, an unrelated interface. And if you uncomment out the call to Read( ), you will receive a compiler error.

If you cast to IStorableCompressible (which combines the extended interface with the Storable interface), you can then call methods of IStorableCompressible, Icompressible, and IStorable:

```
IStorableCompressible isc = doc as IStorableCompressible
if (isc != null)
```

```
{
    isc.LogOriginalSize();   // IStorableCompressible
    isc.LogSavedBytes();     // ILoggedCompressible
    isc.Compress();          // ICompressible
    isc.Read();              // IStorable
}
```

Accessing Interface Methods

You can access the members of the IStorable interface as if they were members of the Document class:

```
Document doc = new Document("Test Document");
doc.status = -1;
doc.Read();
```

You can also create an instance of the interface by casting the document to the interface type, and then use that interface to access the methods:

```
IStorable isDoc = (IStorable) doc;
isDoc.status = 0;
isDoc.Read();
```

In this case, in Main( ) you *know* that Document is in fact an IStorable, so you can take advantage of that knowledge.

As stated earlier, you cannot instantiate an interface directly. That is, you cannot say:

```
IStorable isDoc = new IStorable();
```

You can, however, create an instance of the implementing class, as in the following:

```
Document doc = new Document("Test Document");
```

You can then create an instance of the interface by casting the implementing object to the interface *type*, which in this case is IStorable:

```
IStorable isDoc = (IStorable) doc;
```

You can combine these steps by writing:

```
IStorable isDoc =
    (IStorable) new Document("Test Document");
```

In general, it is a better design decision to access the interface methods through an interface reference. Thus, it is better to use isDoc.Read( ), than doc.Read( ), in the previous example. Access through an interface allows you to treat the interface polymorphically. In other words, you can have two or more classes implement the interface, and then by accessing these classes only through the interface, you can ignore their real runtime type and treat them interchangeably. See Chapter 5 for more information about polymorphism.

Casting to an Interface

In many cases, you don't know in advance that an object supports a particular interface. Given a collection of objects, you might not know whether a particular object supports IStorable or ICompressible or both. You *can* just cast to the interfaces:

```
Document doc = new Document("Test Document");

IStorable isDoc = (IStorable) doc;
isDoc.Read( );

ICompressible icDoc = (ICompressible) doc;
icDoc.Compress( );
```

If it turns out that Document implements only the IStorable interface:

```
public class Document : IStorable
```

the cast to ICompressible would still compile because ICompressible is a valid interface. However, because of the illegal cast, when the program is run an exception will be thrown:

```
An exception of type System.InvalidCastException was thrown.
```

Exceptions are covered in detail in Chapter 11.

The is Operator

You would like to be able to ask the object if it supports the interface, in order to then invoke the appropriate methods. In C# there are two ways to accomplish this. The first method is to use the is operator. The form of the is operator is:

```
expression is type
```

The is operator evaluates true if the expression (which must be a reference type) can be safely cast to *type* without throwing an exception. Example 8-3 illustrates the use of the is operator to test whether a Document implements the IStorable and ICompressible interfaces.

Example 8-3. Using the is operator

```
using System;

interface IStorable
{
   void Read( );
   void Write(object obj);
   int Status { get; set; }

}

// here's the new interface
interface ICompressible
{
```

Example 8-3. Using the is operator (continued)

```
      void Compress( );
      void Decompress( );
}

// Document implements IStorable
public class Document : IStorable
{
    public Document(string s)
    {
        Console.WriteLine(
           "Creating document with: {0}", s);

    }

    // IStorable.Read
    public void Read( )
    {
        Console.WriteLine(
           "Implementing the Read Method for IStorable");
    }

    // IStorable.Write
    public void Write(object o)
    {
        Console.WriteLine(
           "Implementing the Write Method for IStorable");
    }

    // IStorable.Status
    public int Status
    {
        get
        {
            return status;
        }

        set
        {
            status = value;
        }
    }

    private int status = 0;
}

public class Tester
{

    static void Main( )
    {
        Document doc = new Document("Test Document");
```

Example 8-3. Using the is operator (continued)

```
      // only cast if it is safe
      if (doc is IStorable)
      {
         IStorable isDoc = (IStorable) doc;
         isDoc.Read( );
      }

      // this test will fail
      if (doc is ICompressible)
      {
         ICompressible icDoc = (ICompressible) doc;
         icDoc.Compress( );
      }
   }
}
```

Example 8-3 differs from Example 8-2 in that Document no longer implements the ICompressible interface. Main( ) now determines whether the cast is legal (sometimes referred to as safe) by evaluating the following if clause:

```
if (doc is IStorable)
```

This is clean and nearly self-documenting. The if statement tells you that the cast will happen only if the object is of the right interface type.

Unfortunately, this use of the is operator turns out to be inefficient. To understand why, you need to dip into the MSIL code that this generates. Here is a small excerpt (note that the line numbers are in hexadecimal notation):

```
IL_0023:  isinst      ICompressible
IL_0028:  brfalse.s   IL_0039
IL_002a:  ldloc.0
IL_002b:  castclass   ICompressible
IL_0030:  stloc.2
IL_0031:  ldloc.2
IL_0032:  callvirt    instance void ICompressible::Compress( )
```

What is most important here is the test for ICompressible on line 23. The keyword isinst is the MSIL code for the is operator. It tests to see if the object (doc) is in fact of the right type. Having passed this test we continue on to line 2b, in which castclass is called. Unfortunately, castclass also tests the type of the object. In effect, the test is done twice. A more efficient solution is to use the as operator.

The as Operator

The as operator combines the is and cast operations by testing first to see whether a cast is valid (i.e., whether an is test would return true) and then completing the cast when it is. If the cast is not valid (i.e., if an is test would return false), the as operator returns null.

The keyword null represents a null reference—one that does not refer to any object.

Using the as operator eliminates the need to handle cast exceptions. At the same time you avoid the overhead of checking the cast twice. For these reasons, it is optimal to cast interfaces using as.

The form of the as operator is:

expression as *type*

The following code adapts the test code from Example 8-3, using the as operator and testing for null:

```
static void Main( )
{
    Document doc = new Document("Test Document");
    IStorable isDoc = doc as IStorable;
    if (isDoc != null)
        isDoc.Read( );
    else
        Console.WriteLine("IStorable not supported");

    ICompressible icDoc = doc as ICompressible;
    if (icDoc != null)
        icDoc.Compress( );
    else
        Console.WriteLine("Compressible not supported");
}
```

A quick look at the comparable MSIL code shows that the following version is in fact more efficient:

```
IL_0023:  isinst      ICompressible
IL_0028:  stloc.2
IL_0029:  ldloc.2
IL_002a:  brfalse.s  IL_0034
IL_002c:  ldloc.2
IL_002d:  callvirt    instance void ICompressible::Compress( )
```

The is Operator Versus the as Operator

If your design pattern is to test the object to see if it is of the type you need, and if so you will immediately cast it, the as operator is more efficient. At times, however, you might want to test the type of an operator but not cast it immediately. Perhaps you want to test it but not cast it at all; you simply want to add it to a list if it fulfills the right interface. In that case, the is operator will be a better choice.

Interface Versus Abstract Class

Interfaces are very similar to abstract classes. In fact, you could change the declaration of IStorable to be an abstract class:

```
abstract class Storable
{
  abstract public void Read();
  abstract public void Write();
}
```

Document could now inherit from Storable, and there would not be much difference from using the interface.

Suppose, however, that you purchase a List class from a third-party vendor whose capabilities you wish to combine with those specified by Storable? In C++ you could create a StorableList class and inherit from both List and Storable. But in C# you're stuck; you can't inherit from both the Storable abstract class and also the List class because C# does not allow multiple inheritance with classes.

However, C# does allow you to implement any number of interfaces and derive from one base class. Thus, by making Storable an interface, you can inherit from the List class and also from IStorable, as StorableList does in the following example:

```
public class StorableList : List, IStorable
{
  // List methods here ...
  public void Read() {...}
  public void Write(object obj) {...}
  // ...
}
```

Overriding Interface Implementations

An implementing class is free to mark any or all of the methods that implement the interface as virtual. Derived classes can override or provide new implementations. For example, a Document class might implement the IStorable interface and mark the Read() and Write() methods as virtual. The Document might Read() and Write() its contents to a File type. The developer might later derive new types from Document, such as a Note or EmailMessage type, and he might decide that Note will read and write to a database rather than to a file.

Example 8-4 strips down the complexity of Example 8-3 and illustrates overriding an interface implementation. The Read() method is marked as virtual and implemented by Document. Read() is then overridden in a Note type that derives from Document.

Example 8-4. Overriding an interface implementation

```csharp
using System;

interface IStorable
{
   void Read();
   void Write();
}

// Simplify Document to implement only IStorable
public class Document : IStorable
{
   // the document constructor
   public Document(string s)
   {
      Console.WriteLine(
         "Creating document with: {0}", s);

   }

   // Make read virtual
   public virtual void Read()
   {
      Console.WriteLine(
         "Document Read Method for IStorable");
   }

   // NB: Not virtual!
   public void Write()
   {
      Console.WriteLine(
         "Document Write Method for IStorable");
   }

}

// Derive from Document
public class Note : Document
{
   public Note(string s):
      base(s)
   {
      Console.WriteLine(
         "Creating note with: {0}", s);
   }

   // override the Read method
   public override void Read()
   {
      Console.WriteLine(
         "Overriding the Read method for Note!");
   }
```

Example 8-4. Overriding an interface implementation (continued)

```
    // implement my own Write method
    public new void Write( )
    {
        Console.WriteLine(
            "Implementing the Write method for Note!");
    }
}
public class Tester
{

    static void Main( )
    {
        // create a document object
        Document theNote = new Note("Test Note");
        IStorable isNote = theNote as IStorable;
        if (isNote != null)
        {
            isNote.Read( );
            isNote.Write( );
        }

        Console.WriteLine("\n");

        // direct call to the methods
        theNote.Read( );
        theNote.Write( );

        Console.WriteLine("\n");

        // create a note object
        Note note2 = new Note("Second Test");
        IStorable isNote2 = note2 as IStorable;
        if (isNote != null)
        {
            isNote2.Read( );
            isNote2.Write( );
        }

        Console.WriteLine("\n");

        // directly call the methods
        note2.Read( );
        note2.Write( );
    }
}
```
Output
```
Creating document with: Test Note
Creating note with: Test Note
Overriding the Read method for Note!
Document Write Method for IStorable

Overriding the Read method for Note!
```

Example 8-4. Overriding an interface implementation (continued)

```
Document Write Method for IStorable

Creating document with: Second Test
Creating note with: Second Test
Overriding the Read method for Note!
Document Write Method for IStorable

Overriding the Read method for Note!
Implementing the Write method for Note!
```

In this example, Document implements a simplified IStorable interface (simplified to make the example clearer):

```
interface IStorable
{
    void Read( );
    void Write( );
}
```

The designer of Document has opted to make the Read( ) method virtual but not to make the Write( ) method virtual:

```
public virtual void Read( )
```

In a real-world application, you would almost certainly mark both as virtual, but I've differentiated them to demonstrate that the developer is free to pick and choose which methods are made virtual.

The new class Note derives from Document:

```
public class Note : Document
```

It is not necessary for Note to override Read( ), but it is free to do so and has in fact done so here:

```
public override void Read( )
```

In Tester, the Read and Write methods are called in four ways:

1. Through the base class reference to a derived object
2. Through an interface created from the base class reference to the derived object
3. Through a derived object
4. Through an interface created from the derived object

To accomplish the first two calls, a Document (base class) reference is created, and the address of a new Note (derived) object created on the heap is assigned to the Document reference:

```
Document theNote = new Note("Test Note");
```

An interface reference is created and the as operator is used to cast the Document to the IStorable reference:

```
IStorable isNote = theNote as IStorable;
```

You then invoke the Read( ) and Write( ) methods through that interface. The output reveals that the Read( ) method is responded to polymorphically and the Write( ) method is not, just as we would expect:

```
Overriding the Read method for Note!
Document Write Method for IStorable
```

The Read( ) and Write( ) methods are then called directly on the object itself:

```
theNote.Read( );
theNote.Write( );
```

and once again you see the polymorphic implementation has worked:

```
Overriding the Read method for Note!
Document Write Method for IStorable
```

In both cases, the Read( ) method of Note is called and the Write( ) method of Document is called.

To prove to yourself that this is a result of the overriding method, next create a second Note object, this time assigning its address to a reference to a Note. This will be used to illustrate the final cases (i.e., a call through a derived object and a call through an interface created from the derived object):

```
Note note2 = new Note("Second Test");
```

Once again, when you cast to a reference, the overridden Read( ) method is called. When, however, methods are called directly on the Note object:

```
note2.Read( );
note2.Write( );
```

the output reflects that you've called a Note and not an overridden Document:

```
Overriding the Read method for Note!
Implementing the Write method for Note!
```

Explicit Interface Implementation

In the implementation shown so far, the implementing class (in this case, Document) creates a member method with the same signature and return type as the method detailed in the interface. It is not necessary to explicitly state that this is an implementation of an interface; this is understood by the compiler implicitly.

What happens, however, if the class implements two interfaces, each of which has a method with the same signature? Example 8-5 creates two interfaces: IStorable and ITalk. The latter implements a Read( ) method that reads a book aloud. Unfortunately, this conflicts with the Read( ) method in IStorable.

Because both IStorable and ITalk have a Read( ) method, the implementing Document class must use *explicit implementation* for at least one of the methods. With explicit implementation, the implementing class (Document) explicitly identifies the interface for the method:

```
void ITalk.Read( )
```

This resolves the conflict, but it does create a series of interesting side effects.

First, there is no need to use explicit implementation with the other method of Talk:

```
public void Talk( )
```

Because there is no conflict, this can be declared as usual.

More importantly, the explicit implementation method cannot have an access modifier:

```
void ITalk.Read( )
```

This method is implicitly public.

In fact, a method declared through explicit implementation cannot be declared with the abstract, virtual, override, or new modifiers.

Most important, you cannot access the explicitly implemented method through the object itself. When you write:

```
theDoc.Read( );
```

the compiler assumes you mean the implicitly implemented interface for IStorable. The only way to access an explicitly implemented interface is through a cast to an interface:

```
ITalk itDoc = theDoc as ITalk;
if (itDoc != null)
{
    itDoc.Read( );
}
```

Explicit implementation is demonstrated in Example 8-5.

Example 8-5. Explicit implementation

```
using System;

interface IStorable
{
    void Read( );
    void Write( );
}

interface ITalk
{
    void Talk( );
    void Read( );
}

// Modify Document to implement IStorable and ITalk
```

Example 8-5. Explicit implementation (continued)

```csharp
public class Document : IStorable, ITalk
{
    // the document constructor
    public Document(string s)
    {
        Console.WriteLine("Creating document with: {0}", s);

    }

    // Make read virtual
    public virtual void Read()
    {
        Console.WriteLine("Implementing IStorable.Read");
    }

    public void Write()
    {
        Console.WriteLine("Implementing IStorable.Write");

    }

    void ITalk.Read()
    {
        Console.WriteLine("Implementing ITalk.Read");
    }

    public void Talk()
    {
        Console.WriteLine("Implementing ITalk.Talk");
    }

}

public class Tester
{
    static void Main()
    {
        // create a document object
        Document theDoc = new Document("Test Document");
        IStorable isDoc = theDoc as IStorable;
        if (isDoc != null)
        {
            isDoc.Read();
        }

        ITalk itDoc = theDoc as ITalk;
        if (itDoc != null)
        {
            itDoc.Read();
        }
```

Example 8-5. Explicit implementation (continued)

```
        theDoc.Read( );
        theDoc.Talk( );

    }

}
```

Output:
```
Creating document with: Test Document
Implementing IStorable.Read
Implementing ITalk.Read

Implementing IStorable.Read
Implementing ITalk.Talk
```

Selectively Exposing Interface Methods

A class designer can take advantage of the fact that when an interface is implemented through explicit implementation, the interface is not visible to clients of the implementing class except through casting.

Suppose the semantics of your Document object dictate that it implement the IStorable interface, but you do not want the Read( ) and Write( ) methods to be part of the public interface of your Document. You can use explicit implementation to ensure that they are not available except through casting. This allows you to preserve the semantics of your Document class while still having it implement IStorable. If your client wants an object that implements the IStorable interface, it can make an explicit cast, but when using your document *as a Document*, the semantics will not include Read( ) and Write( ).

In fact, you can select which methods to make visible through explicit implementation so that you can expose some implementing methods as part of Document but not others. In Example 8-5, the Document object exposes the Talk( ) method as a method of Document, but the Talk.Read( ) method can be obtained only through a cast. Even if IStorable did not have a Read method, you might choose to make Read( ) explicitly implemented so that you do not expose Read( ) as a method of Document.

Note that because explicit interface implementation prevents the use of the virtual keyword, a derived class would be forced to reimplement the method. Thus, if Note derived from Document, it would be forced to reimplement Talk.Read( ) because the Document implementation of Talk.Read( ) could not be virtual.

Member Hiding

It is possible for an interface member to become hidden. For example, suppose you have an interface IBase that has a property P:

```
interface IBase
{
```

```
    int P { get; set; }
}
```

Suppose you derive from that interface a new interface, IDerived, which hides the property P with a new method P( ):

```
interface IDerived : IBase
{
    new int P();
}
```

Setting aside whether this is a good idea, you have now hidden the property P in the base interface. An implementation of this derived interface will require at least one explicit interface member. You can use explicit implementation for *either* the base property or the derived method, or you can use explicit implementation for both. Thus, any of the following three versions would be legal:

```
class myClass : IDerived
{
    // explicit implementation for the base property
    int IBase.P { get {...} }

    // implicit implementation of the derived method
    public int P() {...}
}

class myClass : IDerived
{
    // implicit implementation for the base property
    public int P { get {...} }

    // explicit implementation of the derived method
    int IDerived.P() {...}
}

class myClass : IDerived
{
    // explicit implementation for the base property
    int IBase.P { get {...} }

    // explicit implementation of the derived method
    int IDerived.P() {...}
}
```

Accessing Sealed Classes and Value Types

Generally, it is preferable to access the methods of an interface through an interface cast. The exception is with value types (e.g., structs) or with sealed classes. In that case, it is preferable to invoke the interface method through the object.

When you implement an interface in a struct, you are implementing it in a value type. When you cast to an interface reference, there is an implicit boxing of the object. Unfortunately, when you use that interface to modify the object, it is the boxed object, not the original value object, that is modified. Further, if you change the value type, the boxed type will remain unchanged. Example 8-6 creates a struct that implements IStorable and illustrates the impact of implicit boxing when you cast the struct to an interface reference.

Example 8-6. References on value types

```
using System;

// declare a simple interface
interface IStorable
{
   void Read( );
   int Status { get;set;}

}

// Implement through a struct
public struct myStruct : IStorable
{

   public void Read( )
   {
      Console.WriteLine(
         "Implementing IStorable.Read");
   }

   public int Status
   {
      get
      {
         return status;
      }
      set
      {
         status = value;
      }
   }

   private int status;
}

public class Tester
{

   static void Main( )
   {
      // create a myStruct object
      myStruct theStruct = new myStruct( );
      theStruct.Status = -1;  // initialize
      Console.WriteLine(
         "theStruct.Status: {0}", theStruct.Status);
```

Example 8-6. References on value types (continued)

```
        // Change the value
        theStruct.Status = 2;
        Console.WriteLine("Changed object.");
        Console.WriteLine(
            "theStruct.Status: {0}", theStruct.Status);

        // cast to an IStorable
        // implicit box to a reference type
        IStorable isTemp = (IStorable) theStruct;

        // set the value through the interface reference
        isTemp.Status = 4;
        Console.WriteLine("Changed interface.");
        Console.WriteLine("theStruct.Status: {0}, isTemp: {1}",
            theStruct.Status, isTemp.Status);

        // Change the value again
        theStruct.Status = 6;
        Console.WriteLine("Changed object.");
        Console.WriteLine("theStruct.Status: {0}, isTemp: {1}",
            theStruct.Status, isTemp.Status);
    }
}
```

Output:
```
theStruct.Status: -1
Changed object.
theStruct.Status: 2
Changed interface.
theStruct.Status: 2, isTemp: 4
Changed object.
theStruct.Status: 6, isTemp: 4
```

In Example 8-6, the IStorable interface has a method (Read) and a property (Status).

This interface is implemented by the struct named myStruct:

```
public struct myStruct : IStorable
```

The interesting code is in Tester. Start by creating an instance of the structure and initializing its property to -1. The status value is then printed:

```
myStruct theStruct = new myStruct();
theStruct.status = -1;  // initialize
Console.WriteLine(
    "theStruct.Status: {0}", theStruct.status);
```

The output from this shows that the status was set properly:

```
theStruct.Status: -1
```

Next access the property to change the status, again through the value object itself:

```
// Change the value
theStruct.status = 2;
```

```
Console.WriteLine("Changed object.");
Console.WriteLine(
    "theStruct.Status: {0}", theStruct.status);
```

The output shows the change:

```
Changed object.
theStruct.Status: 2
```

No surprises so far. At this point, create a reference to the IStorable interface. This causes an implicit boxing of the value object theStruct. Then use that interface to change the status value to 4:

```
// cast to an IStorable
// implicit box to a reference type
IStorable isTemp = (IStorable) theStruct;

// set the value through the interface reference
isTemp.status = 4;
Console.WriteLine("Changed interface.");
Console.WriteLine("theStruct.Status: {0}, isTemp: {1}",
    theStruct.status, isTemp.status);
```

Here the output can be a bit surprising:

```
Changed interface.
theStruct.Status: 2, isTemp: 4
```

Aha! The object to which the interface reference points has been changed to a status value of 4, but the struct value object is unchanged. Even more interesting, when you access the method through the object itself:

```
// Change the value again
theStruct.status = 6;
Console.WriteLine("Changed object.");
Console.WriteLine("theStruct.Status: {0}, isTemp: {1}",
    theStruct.status, isTemp.status);
```

the output reveals that the value object has been changed, but the boxed reference value for the interface reference has not:

```
Changed object.
theStruct.Status: 6, isTemp: 4
```

A quick look at the MSIL code (Example 8-7) reveals what is going on under the hood:

Example 8-7. MSIL code resulting from Example 8-6

```
.method private hidebysig static void  Main( ) cil managed
{
  .entrypoint
  // Code size       187 (0xbb)
  .maxstack  4
  .locals init ([0] valuetype myStruct theStruct,
          [1] class IStorable isTemp)
```

Example 8-7. MSIL code resulting from Example 8-6 (continued)

```
IL_0000:  ldloca.s   theStruct
IL_0002:  initobj    myStruct
IL_0008:  ldloca.s   theStruct
IL_000a:  ldc.i4.m1
IL_000b:  call       instance void myStruct::set_Status(int32)
IL_0010:  ldstr      "theStruct.Status: {0}"
IL_0015:  ldloca.s   theStruct
IL_0017:  call       instance int32 myStruct::get_Status( )
IL_001c:  box        [mscorlib]System.Int32
IL_0021:  call       void [mscorlib]System.Console::WriteLine(string,
                                                                     object)

IL_0026:  ldloca.s   theStruct
IL_0028:  ldc.i4.2
IL_0029:  call       instance void myStruct::set_Status(int32)
IL_002e:  ldstr      "Changed object."
IL_0033:  call       void [mscorlib]System.Console::WriteLine(string)
IL_0038:  ldstr      "theStruct.Status: {0}"
IL_003d:  ldloca.s   theStruct
IL_003f:  call       instance int32 myStruct::get_Status( )
IL_0044:  box        [mscorlib]System.Int32
IL_0049:  call       void [mscorlib]System.Console::WriteLine(string,
                                                                     object)

IL_004e:  ldloc.0
IL_004f:  box        myStruct
IL_0054:  stloc.1
IL_0055:  ldloc.1
IL_0056:  ldc.i4.4
IL_0057:  callvirt   instance void IStorable::set_Status(int32)
IL_005c:  ldstr      "Changed interface."
IL_0061:  call       void [mscorlib]System.Console::WriteLine(string)
IL_0066:  ldstr      "theStruct.Status: {0}, isTemp: {1}"
IL_006b:  ldloca.s   theStruct
IL_006d:  call       instance int32 myStruct::get_Status( )
IL_0072:  box        [mscorlib]System.Int32
IL_0077:  ldloc.1
IL_0078:  callvirt   instance int32 IStorable::get_Status( )
IL_007d:  box        [mscorlib]System.Int32
IL_0082:  call       void [mscorlib]System.Console::WriteLine(string,
                                                                     object,
                                                                     object)

IL_0087:  ldloca.s   theStruct
IL_0089:  ldc.i4.6
IL_008a:  call       instance void myStruct::set_Status(int32)
IL_008f:  ldstr      "Changed object."
IL_0094:  call       void [mscorlib]System.Console::WriteLine(string)
IL_0099:  ldstr      "theStruct.Status: {0}, isTemp: {1}"
IL_009e:  ldloca.s   theStruct
IL_00a0:  call       instance int32 myStruct::get_Status( )
IL_00a5:  box        [mscorlib]System.Int32
IL_00aa:  ldloc.1
IL_00ab:  callvirt   instance int32 IStorable::get_Status( )
IL_00b0:  box        [mscorlib]System.Int32
```

Example 8-7. MSIL code resulting from Example 8-6 (continued)

```
IL_00b5:  call        void [mscorlib]System.Console::WriteLine(string,
                                                                object,
                                                                object)
IL_00ba:  ret
} // end of method Tester::Main
```

On line IL:000b, set_Status( ) was called on the value object. We see the second call on line IL_0017. Notice that the calls to WriteLine( ) cause boxing of the integer value status so that the GetString( ) method can be called.

The key line is IL_004f (highlighted) where the struct itself is boxed. It is that boxing that creates a reference type for the interface reference. Notice on line IL_0057 that this time IStorable::set_Status is called rather than myStruct::set_Status.

The design guideline is if you are implementing an interface with a value type, be sure to access the interface members through the object rather than through an interface reference.

CHAPTER 9

Arrays, Indexers, and Collections

The .NET Framework provides a rich suite of collection classes, including `Array`, `ArrayList`, `NameValueCollection`, `StringCollection`, `Queue`, `Stack`, and `BitArray`.

The simplest collection is the `Array`, the only collection type for which C# provides built-in support. In this chapter you will learn to work with single, multidimensional, and jagged arrays. You will also be introduced to indexers, a bit of C# syntactic sugar that makes it easier to access class properties, as though the class were indexed like an array.

The .NET Framework provides a number of interfaces, such as `IEnumerable` and `ICollection`, whose implementation provides you with standard ways to interact with collections. In this chapter you will see how to work with the most essential of these. The chapter concludes with a tour of commonly used .NET collections, including `ArrayList`, `Hashtable`, `Queue`, and `Stack`.

Arrays

An *array* is an indexed collection of objects, all of the same type. C# arrays are somewhat different from arrays in C++ and other languages, because they are objects. This provides them with useful methods and properties.

C# provides native syntax for the declaration of `Array` objects. What is actually created, however, is an object of type `System.Array`. Arrays in C# thus provide you with the best of both worlds: easy-to-use C-style syntax underpinned with an actual class definition so that instances of an array have access to the methods and properties of `System.Array`. These appear in Table 9-1.

Table 9-1. System.Array methods and properties

Method or property	Description
BinarySearch()	Overloaded public static method that searches a one-dimensional sorted array.
Clear()	Public static method that sets a range of elements in the array either to zero or to a null reference.

Table 9-1. System.Array methods and properties (continued)

Method or property	Description
Copy( )	Overloaded public static method that copies a section of one array to another array.
CreateInstance( )	Overloaded public static method that instantiates a new instance of an array.
IndexOf( )	Overloaded public static method that returns the index (offset) of the first instance of a value in a one-dimensional array.
LastIndexOf( )	Overloaded public static method that returns the index of the last instance of a value in a one-dimensional array.
Reverse( )	Overloaded public static method that reverses the order of the elements in a one-dimensional array.
Sort( )	Overloaded public static method that sorts the values in a one-dimensional array.
IsFixedSize	Public property that returns a value indicating whether the array has a fixed size.
IsReadOnly	Public property that returns a Boolean value indicating whether the array is read-only.
IsSynchronized	Public property that returns a Boolean value indicating whether the array is thread-safe.
Length	Public property that returns the length of the array.
Rank	Public property that returns the number of dimensions of the array.
SyncRoot	Public property that returns an object that can be used to synchronize access to the array.
GetEnumerator( )	Public method that returns an IEnumerator.
GetLength( )	Public method that returns the length of the specified dimension in the array.
GetLowerBound( )	Public method that returns the lower boundary of the specified dimension of the array.
GetUpperBound( )	Public method that returns the upper boundary of the specified dimension of the array.
Initialize( )	Initializes all values in a value type array by calling the default constructor for each value.
SetValue( )	Overloaded public method that sets the specified array elements to a value.

Declaring Arrays

Declare a C# array with the following syntax:

```
type[] array-name;
```

For example:

```
int[] myIntArray;
```

The square brackets ([]) tell the C# compiler that you are declaring an array, and the type specifies the type of the elements it will contain. In the previous example, myIntArray is an array of integers.

Instantiate an array using the new keyword. For example:

```
myIntArray = new int[5];
```

This declaration sets aside memory for an array holding five integers.

 Visual Basic programmers take note: the first element is always 0; there is no way to set the upper or lower bounds, and you cannot change the size (redim) of the array.

It is important to distinguish between the array itself (which is a collection of elements) and the elements of the array. myIntArray is the array; its elements are the five integers it holds. C# arrays are reference types, created on the heap. Thus, myIntArray is allocated on the heap. The elements of an array are allocated based on their type. Integers are value types, and so the elements in myIntArray will be value types, *not* boxed integers. An array of reference types will contain nothing but references to the elements, which are themselves created on the heap.

Understanding Default Values

When you create an array of value types each element initially contains the default value for the type stored in the array (see Table 4-2). The declaration:

```
myIntArray = new int[5];
```

creates an array of five integers, each of whose value is set to 0, which is the default value for integer types.

Unlike with arrays of value types, the reference types in an array are not initialized to their default value. Instead, they are initialized to null. If you attempt to access an element in an array of reference types before you have specifically initialized them, you will generate an exception.

Assume you have created a Button class. Declare an array of Button objects with the following statement:

```
Button[] myButtonArray;
```

and instantiate the actual array like this:

```
myButtonArray = new Button[3];
```

You can shorten this to:

```
Button[] myButtonArray = new Button[3];
```

Unlike with the earlier integer example, this statement does not create an array with references to three Button objects. Instead, this creates the array myButtonArray with three null references. To use this array, you must first construct and assign the Button objects for each reference in the array. You can construct the objects in a loop that adds them one by one to the array.

Accessing Array Elements

Access the elements of an array using the index operator ([]). Arrays are zero-based, which means that the index of the first element is always zero—in this case, myArray[0].

As explained previously, arrays are objects, and thus have properties. One of the more useful of these is Length, which tells you how many objects are in an array.

Array objects can be indexed from 0 to Length-1. That is, if there are five elements in an array, their indices are 0,1,2,3,4.

Example 9-1 illustrates the array concepts covered so far. In this example a class named Tester creates an array of Employees and an array of integers, populates the Employee array, and then prints the values of both.

Example 9-1. Working with an array

```
namespace Programming_CSharp
{
    using System;

    // a simple class to store in the array
    public class Employee
    {
        // a simple class to store in the array
        public Employee(int empID)
        {
            this.empID = empID;
        }
        public override string ToString( )
        {
            return empID.ToString( );
        }
        private int empID;
    }
    public class Tester
    {
        static void Main( )
        {
            int[] intArray;
            Employee[] empArray;
            intArray = new int[5];
            empArray = new Employee[3];

            // populate the array
            for (int i = 0;i<empArray.Length;i++)
            {
                empArray[i] = new Employee(i+5);
            }

            for (int i = 0;i<intArray.Length;i++)
            {
                Console.WriteLine(intArray[i].ToString( ));
            }

            for (int i = 0;i<empArray.Length;i++)
            {
                Console.WriteLine(empArray[i].ToString( ));
            }
        }
    }
}
```

Example 9-1. Working with an array (continued)

```
}
```

Output:
```
0
0
0
0
0
5
6
7
```

The example starts with the definition of an `Employee` class that implements a constructor that takes a single integer parameter. The `ToString( )` method inherited from `Object` is overridden to print the value of the `Employee` object's employee ID.

The test method declares and then instantiates a pair of arrays. The integer array is automatically filled with integers whose value is set to zero. The `Employee` array contents must be constructed by hand.

Finally, the contents of the arrays are printed to ensure that they are filled as intended. The five integers print their value first, followed by the three `Employee` objects.

The foreach Statement

The foreach looping statement is new to the C family of languages, though it is already well known to VB programmers. The foreach statement allows you to iterate through all the items in an array or other collection, examining each item in turn. The syntax for the foreach statement is:

```
foreach (type identifier in expression) statement
```

Thus, you might update Example 9-1 to replace the for statements that iterate over the contents of the array with foreach statements, as shown in Example 9-2.

Example 9-2. Using foreach

```
namespace Programming_CSharp
{
    using System;

    // a simple class to store in the array
    public class Employee
    {
        // a simple class to store in the array
        public Employee(int empID)
        {
            this.empID = empID;
        }
        public override string ToString( )
```

Example 9-2. Using foreach (continued)

```
    {
        return empID.ToString( );
    }
    private int empID;
}
public class Tester
{
    static void Main( )
    {
        int[] intArray;
        Employee[] empArray;
        intArray = new int[5];
        empArray = new Employee[3];

        // populate the array
        for (int i = 0;i<empArray.Length;i++)
        {
            empArray[i] = new Employee(i+5);
        }

        foreach (int i in intArray)
        {
            Console.WriteLine(i.ToString( ));
        }

        foreach (Employee e in empArray)
        {
            Console.WriteLine(e.ToString( ));
        }
    }
}
}
```

The output for Example 9-2 is identical to Example 9-1. However, rather than creating a for statement that measures the size of the array and uses a temporary counting variable as an index into the array as in the following, we try another approach:

```
for (int i = 0; i < empArray.Length; i++)
{
    Console.WriteLine(empArray[i].ToString( ));
}
```

We iterate over the array with the foreach loop, which automatically extracts the next item from within the array and assigns it to the temporary object you've created in the head of the statement.

```
foreach (Employee e in empArray)
{
    Console.WriteLine(e.ToString( ));
}
```

The object extracted from the array is of the appropriate type; thus, you may call any public method on that object.

Initializing Array Elements

It is possible to initialize the contents of an array at the time it is instantiated by providing a list of values delimited by curly brackets ({}). C# provides a longer and a shorter syntax:

```
int[] myIntArray = new int[5] { 2, 4, 6, 8, 10 }
int[] myIntArray = { 2, 4, 6, 8, 10 }
```

There is no practical difference between these two statements, and most programmers will use the shorter syntax because we are, by nature, lazy. We are so lazy we'll work all day to save a few minutes doing a task—which isn't so crazy if we're going to do that task hundreds of times!

The params Keyword

You can create a method that displays any number of integers to the console by passing in an array of integers and then iterating over the array with a foreach loop. The params keyword allows you to pass in a variable number of parameters without necessarily explicitly creating the array.

In the next example, you create a method, DisplayVals( ), which takes a variable number of integer arguments:

```
public void DisplayVals(params int[] intVals)
```

The method itself can treat the array as if an integer array were explicitly created and passed in as a parameter. You are free to iterate over the array as you would over any other array of integers:

```
foreach (int i in intVals)
{
    Console.WriteLine("DisplayVals {0}",i);
}
```

The calling method, however, need not explicitly create an array; it can simply pass in integers, and the compiler will assemble the parameters into an array for the DisplayVals( ) method:

```
t.DisplayVals(5,6,7,8);
```

You are free to pass in an array if you prefer:

```
int [] explicitArray = new int[5] {1,2,3,4,5};
t.DisplayVals(explicitArray);
```

Example 9-3 provides the complete source code illustrating the params keyword.

Example 9-3. Using the params keyword

```
namespace Programming_CSharp
{
    using System;
```

Example 9-3. Using the params keyword (continued)

```
public class Tester
{
    static void Main()
    {
        Tester t = new Tester();
        t.DisplayVals(5,6,7,8);
        int [] explicitArray = new int[5] {1,2,3,4,5};
        t.DisplayVals(explicitArray);
    }

    public void DisplayVals(params int[] intVals)
    {
        foreach (int i in intVals)
        {
            Console.WriteLine("DisplayVals {0}",i);
        }
    }
}
```
Output:
```
DisplayVals 5
DisplayVals 6
DisplayVals 7
DisplayVals 8
DisplayVals 1
DisplayVals 2
DisplayVals 3
DisplayVals 4
DisplayVals 5
```

Multidimensional Arrays

Arrays can be thought of as long rows of slots into which values can be placed. Once you have a picture of a row of slots, imagine 10 rows, one on top of another. This is the classic two-dimensional array of rows and columns. The rows run across the array and the columns run up and down the array.

A third dimension is possible, but somewhat harder to imagine. Make your arrays three-dimensional, with new rows stacked atop the old two-dimensional array. OK, now imagine four dimensions. Now imagine 10.

Those of you who are not string-theory physicists have probably given up, as have I. Multidimensional arrays are useful, however, even if you can't quite picture what they would look like.

C# supports two types of multidimensional arrays: rectangular and jagged. In a rectangular array, every row is the same length. A jagged array, however, is an array of arrays, each of which can be a different length.

Rectangular arrays

A *rectangular array* is an array of two (or more) dimensions. In the classic two-dimensional array, the first dimension is the number of rows and the second dimension is the number of columns.

To declare a two-dimensional array, use the following syntax:

```
type [,] array-name
```

For example, to declare and instantiate a two-dimensional rectangular array named myRectangularArray that contains two rows and three columns of integers, you would write:

```
int [,] myRectangularArray = new int[2,3];
```

Example 9-4 declares, instantiates, initializes, and prints the contents of a two-dimensional array. In this example, a for loop is used to initialize the elements of the array.

Example 9-4. Rectangular arrays

```
namespace Programming_CSharp
{
   using System;

   public class Tester
   {
      static void Main( )
      {
         const int rows = 4;
         const int columns = 3;

         // declare a 4x3 integer array
         int[,] rectangularArray = new int[rows, columns];

         // populate the array
         for (int i = 0;i < rows;i++)
         {
            for (int j = 0;j<columns;j++)
            {
               rectangularArray[i,j] = i+j;
            }
         }

         // report the contents of the array
         for (int i = 0;i < rows;i++)
         {
            for (int j = 0;j<columns;j++)
            {
               Console.WriteLine("rectangularArray[{0},{1}] = {2}",
                  i,j,rectangularArray[i,j]);
            }
         }
```

Example 9-4. Rectangular arrays (continued)

```
        }
    }
}
```

Output:
```
rectangularArray[0,0] = 0
rectangularArray[0,1] = 1
rectangularArray[0,2] = 2
rectangularArray[1,0] = 1
rectangularArray[1,1] = 2
rectangularArray[1,2] = 3
rectangularArray[2,0] = 2
rectangularArray[2,1] = 3
rectangularArray[2,2] = 4
rectangularArray[3,0] = 3
rectangularArray[3,1] = 4
rectangularArray[3,2] = 5
```

In this example, you declare a pair of constant values:

```
const int rows = 4;
const int columns = 3;
```

which are then used to dimension the array:

```
int[,] rectangularArray = new int[rows, columns];
```

Notice the syntax. The brackets in the int[,] declaration indicate that the type is an array of integers, and the comma indicates the array has two dimensions (two commas would indicate three dimensions, and so on). The actual instantiation of rectangularArray with new int[rows, columns] sets the size of each dimension. Here the declaration and instantiation have been combined.

The program fills the rectangle with a pair of for loops, iterating through each column in each row. Thus, the first element filled is rectangularArray[0,0], followed by rectangularArray[0,1], and rectangularArray[0,2]. Once this is done, the program moves on to the next rows: rectangularArray[1,0], rectangularArray[1,1], rectangularArray[1,2], and so forth, until all the columns in all the rows are filled.

Just as you can initialize a one-dimensional array using bracketed lists of values, you can initialize a two-dimensional array using similar syntax. Example 9-5 declares a two-dimensional array (rectangularArray), initializes its elements using bracketed lists of values, and then prints out the contents.

Example 9-5. Initializing a multidimensional array

```
namespace Programming_CSharp
{
    using System;

    public class Tester
```

Example 9-5. Initializing a multidimensional array (continued)

```
{
    static void Main( )
    {
        const int rows = 4;
        const int columns = 3;

        // imply a 4x3 array
        int[,] rectangularArray =
            {
                {0,1,2}, {3,4,5}, {6,7,8}, {9,10,11}
            };

        for (int i = 0;i < rows;i++)
        {
            for (int j = 0;j<columns;j++)
            {
                Console.WriteLine("rectangularArray[{0},{1}] = {2}",
                    i,j,rectangularArray[i,j]);
            }
        }
    }
}
```

Output:
```
rectangularArrayrectangularArray[0,0] = 0
rectangularArrayrectangularArray[0,1] = 1
rectangularArrayrectangularArray[0,2] = 2
rectangularArrayrectangularArray[1,0] = 3
rectangularArrayrectangularArray[1,1] = 4
rectangularArrayrectangularArray[1,2] = 5
rectangularArrayrectangularArray[2,0] = 6
rectangularArrayrectangularArray[2,1] = 7
rectangularArrayrectangularArray[2,2] = 8
rectangularArrayrectangularArray[3,0] = 9
rectangularArrayrectangularArray[3,1] = 10
rectangularArrayrectangularArray[3,2] = 11
```

The preceding example is very similar to Example 9-4, but this time you *imply* the exact dimensions of the array by how you initialize it:

```
int[,] rectangularArrayrectangularArray =
{
    {0,1,2}, {3,4,5}, {6,7,8}, {9,10,11}
};
```

Assigning values in four bracketed lists, each consisting of three elements, implies a 4×3 array.

Had you written this as:

```
int[,] rectangularArrayrectangularArray =
{
```

```
    {0,1,2,3}, {4,5,6,7}, {8,9,10,11}
};
```

you would instead have implied a 3×4 array.

You can see that the C# compiler understands the implications of your clustering, as it is able to access the objects with the appropriate offsets, as illustrated in the output.

You might guess that this is a 12-element array, and that you can just as easily access an element at rectangularArray[0,3] as at rectangularArray[1,0], but if you try you will run right into an exception:

```
Exception occurred: System.IndexOutOfRangeException:
Index was outside the bounds of the array.
at Programming_CSharp.Tester.Main( ) in
csharp\programming csharp\listing0703.cs:line 23
```

C# arrays are smart and they keep track of their bounds. When you imply a 4×3 array, you must treat it as such.

Jagged arrays

A *jagged array* is an array of arrays. It is called "jagged" because each of the rows need not be the same size as all the others, and thus a graphical representation of the array would not be square.

When you create a jagged array, you declare the number of rows in your array. Each row will hold an array, which can be of any length. These arrays must each be declared. You can then fill in the values for the elements in these "inner" arrays.

In a jagged array, each dimension is a one-dimensional array. To declare a jagged array, use the following syntax, where the number of brackets indicates the number of dimensions of the array:

```
type [] []...
```

For example, you would declare a two-dimensional jagged array of integers named myJaggedArray as follows:

```
int [] [] myJaggedArray;
```

Access the fifth element of the third array by writing myJaggedArray[2][4].

Example 9-6 creates a jagged array named myJaggedArray, initializes its elements, and then prints their content. To save space, the program takes advantage of the fact that integer array elements are automatically initialized to zero, and it initializes the values of only some of the elements.

Example 9-6. Working with a jagged array

```
namespace Programming_CSharp
{
    using System;
```

Example 9-6. Working with a jagged array (continued)

```
public class Tester
{
    static void Main( )
    {
        const int rows = 4;

        // declare the jagged array as 4 rows high
        int[][] jaggedArray = new int[rows][];

        // the first row has 5 elements
        jaggedArray[0] = new int[5];

        // a row with 2 elements
        jaggedArray[1] = new int[2];

        // a row with 3 elements
        jaggedArray[2] = new int[3];

        // the last row has 5 elements
        jaggedArray[3] = new int[5];

        // Fill some (but not all) elements of the rows
        jaggedArray[0][3] = 15;
        jaggedArray[1][1] = 12;
        jaggedArray[2][1] = 9;
        jaggedArray[2][2] = 99;
        jaggedArray[3][0] = 10;
        jaggedArray[3][1] = 11;
        jaggedArray[3][2] = 12;
        jaggedArray[3][3] = 13;
        jaggedArray[3][4] = 14;

        for (int i = 0;i < 5; i++)
        {
            Console.WriteLine("jaggedArray[0][{0}] = {1}",
                i,jaggedArray[0][i]);
        }

        for (int i = 0;i < 2; i++)
        {
            Console.WriteLine("jaggedArray[1][{0}] = {1}",
                i,jaggedArray[1][i]);
        }

        for (int i = 0;i < 3; i++)
        {
            Console.WriteLine("jaggedArray[2][{0}] = {1}",
                i,jaggedArray[2][i]);
        }
        for (int i = 0;i < 5; i++)
        {
            Console.WriteLine("jaggedArray[3][{0}] = {1}",
```

Example 9-6. Working with a jagged array (continued)

```
                i,jaggedArray[3][i]);
        }
      }
    }
}
```

Output:
```
jaggedArray[0][0] = 0
jaggedArray[0][1] = 0
jaggedArray[0][2] = 0
jaggedArray[0][3] = 15
jaggedArray[0][4] = 0
jaggedArray[1][0] = 0
jaggedArray[1][1] = 12
jaggedArray[2][0] = 0
jaggedArray[2][1] = 9
jaggedArray[2][2] = 99
jaggedArray[3][0] = 10
jaggedArray[3][1] = 11
jaggedArray[3][2] = 12
jaggedArray[3][3] = 13
jaggedArray[3][4] = 14
```

In this example, a jagged array is created with four rows:

```
int[][] jaggedArray = new int[rows][];
```

Notice that the second dimension is not specified. This is set by creating a new array for each row. Each of these arrays can have a different size:

```
// the first row has 5 elements
jaggedArray[0] = new int[5];

// a row with 2 elements
jaggedArray[1] = new int[2];

// a row with 3 elements
jaggedArray[2] = new int[3];

// the last row has 5 elements
jaggedArray[3] = new int[5];
```

Once an array is specified for each row, you need only populate the various members of each array and then print out their contents to ensure that all went as expected.

Notice that when you accessed the members of the rectangular array, you put the indexes all within one set of square brackets:

```
rectangularArrayrectangularArray[i,j]
```

while with a jagged array you need a pair of brackets:

```
jaggedArray[3][i]
```

You can keep this straight by thinking of the first as a single array of more than one dimension and the jagged array as an array of arrays.

Array Conversions

Conversion is possible between arrays if their dimensions are equal and if a conversion is possible between the element types. An implicit conversion can occur if the elements can be implicitly converted; otherwise an explicit conversion is required.

If an array contains references to reference objects, a conversion is possible to an array of base elements. Example 9-7 illustrates the conversion of an array of user-defined Employee types to an array of objects.

Example 9-7. Converting arrays

```
namespace Programming_CSharp
{
    using System;

    // create an object we can
    // store in the array
    public class Employee
    {
        // a simple class to store in the array
        public Employee(int empID)
        {
            this.empID = empID;
        }
        public override  string ToString( )
        {
            return empID.ToString( );
        }
        private int empID;
    }

    public class Tester
    {
        // this method takes an array of objects
        // we'll pass in an array of Employees
        // and then an array of strings
        // the conversion is implicit since both Employee
        // and string derive (ultimately) from object
        public static void PrintArray(object[] theArray)
        {
            Console.WriteLine("Contents of the Array {0}",
                theArray.ToString( ));

            // walk through the array and print
            // the values.
            foreach (object obj in theArray)
            {
                Console.WriteLine("Value: {0}", obj);
```

Example 9-7. Converting arrays (continued)

```
      }
   }

   static void Main()
   {
      // make an array of Employee objects
      Employee[] myEmployeeArray = new Employee[3];

      // initialize each Employee's value
      for (int i = 0;i < 3;i++)
      {
         myEmployeeArray[i] = new Employee(i+5);
      }

      // display the values
      PrintArray(myEmployeeArray);

      // create an array of two strings
      string[] array =
         {
            "hello", "world"
         };

      // print the value of the strings
      PrintArray(array);
   }
   }
}
```

Output:
```
Contents of the Array Programming_CSharp.Employee[]
Value: 5
Value: 6
Value: 7
Contents of the Array System.String[]
Value: hello
Value: world
```

Example 9-7 begins by creating a simple Employee class, as seen earlier in the chapter. The Tester class now contains a new static method PrintArray( ), which takes as a parameter a one-dimensional array of Objects:

```
public static void PrintArray(object[] theArray)
```

Object is the implicit base class of every object in the .NET Framework,. and so is the implicit base class of both String and Employee.

The PrintArray( ) method takes two actions. First, it calls the ToString( ) method on the array itself:

```
Console.WriteLine("Contents of the Array {0}",
   theArray.ToString( ));
```

System.Array overrides the ToString( ) method to your advantage, printing an identifying name of the array:

```
Contents of the Array Programming_CSharp. Employee []
Contents of the Array System.String[]
```

PrintArray( ) then goes on to call ToString( ) on each element in the array it receives as a parameter. Because ToString( ) is a virtual method in the base class Object, it is guaranteed to be available in every derived class. You have overridden this method appropriately in Employee so the code works properly. Calling ToString( ) on a String object might not be necessary, but it is harmless and it allows you to treat these objects polymorphically.

System.Array

The Array class has a number of useful methods that extend the capabilities of arrays and make them smarter than arrays seen in other languages (see Table 9-1 earlier in this chapter). Two useful static methods of Array are Sort( ) and Reverse( ). These are fully supported for the built-in C# types such as string. Making them work with your own classes is a bit trickier, as you must implement the IComparable interface (see "Implementing IComparable" later in this chapter). Example 9-8 demonstrates the use of these two methods to manipulate String objects.

Example 9-8. Using Array.Sort and Array.Reverse

```csharp
namespace Programming_CSharp
{
    using System;

    public class Tester
    {
        public static void PrintMyArray(object[] theArray)
        {

            foreach (object obj in theArray)
            {
                Console.WriteLine("Value: {0}", obj);
            }
            Console.WriteLine("\n");
        }

        static void Main()
        {
            String[] myArray =
            {
                "Who", "is", "John", "Galt"
            };

            PrintMyArray(myArray);
            Array.Reverse(myArray);
            PrintMyArray(myArray);
```

Example 9-8. Using Array.Sort and Array.Reverse (continued)

```
        String[] myOtherArray =
        {
            "We", "Hold", "These", "Truths",
            "To", "Be", "Self", "Evident",
        };

        PrintMyArray(myOtherArray);
        Array.Sort(myOtherArray);
        PrintMyArray(myOtherArray);

    }
  }
}
```

Output:
```
Value: Who
Value: is
Value: John
Value: Galt

Value: Galt
Value: John
Value: is
Value: Who

Value: We
Value: Hold
Value: These
Value: Truths
Value: To
Value: Be
Value: Self
Value: Evident

Value: Be
Value: Evident
Value: Hold
Value: Self
Value: These
Value: To
Value: Truths
Value: We
```

The example begins by creating `myArray`, an array of strings with the words:

```
"Who", "is", "John", "Galt"
```

This array is printed, and then passed to the `Array.Reverse()` method, where it is printed again to see that the array itself has been reversed:

```
Value: Galt
Value: John
Value: is
Value: Who
```

Similarly, the example creates a second array, myOtherArray, containing the words:

```
"We", "Hold", "These", "Truths",
"To", "Be", "Self", "Evident",
```

This is passed to the Array.Sort( ) method. Then Array.Sort( ) happily sorts them alphabetically:

```
Value: Be
Value: Evident
Value: Hold
Value: Self
Value: These
Value: To
Value: Truths
Value: We
```

Indexers

There are times when it is desirable to access a collection within a class as though the class itself were an array. For example, suppose you create a list box control named myListBox that contains a list of strings stored in a one-dimensional array, a private member variable named myStrings. A list box control contains member properties and methods in addition to its array of strings. However, it would be convenient to be able to access the list box array with an index, just as if the list box were an array. For example, such a property would permit statements like the following:

```
string theFirstString = myListBox[0];
string theLastString = myListBox[Length-1];
```

An *indexer* is a C# construct that allows you to access collections contained by a class using the familiar [ ] syntax of arrays. An indexer is a special kind of property and includes get( ) and set( ) methods to specify its behavior.

You declare an indexer property within a class using the following syntax:

```
type this [type argument]{get; set;}
```

The return type determines the type of object that will be returned by the indexer, while the type argument specifies what kind of argument will be used to index into the collection that contains the target objects. Although it is common to use integers as index values, you can index a collection on other types as well, including strings. You can even provide an indexer with multiple parameters to create a multidimensional array!

The this keyword is a reference to the object in which the indexer appears. As with a normal property, you also must define get( ) and set( ) methods, which determine how the requested object is retrieved from or assigned to its collection.

Example 9-9 declares a list box control (ListBoxTest), which contains a simple array (myStrings) and a simple indexer for accessing its contents.

C++ programmers take note: the indexer serves much the same purpose as overloading the C++ index operator ([ ]). The index operator cannot be overloaded in C#, which provides the indexer in its place.

Example 9-9. Using a simple indexer

```
namespace Programming_CSharp
{
    using System;

    // a simplified ListBox control
    public class ListBoxTest
    {
        // initialize the list box with strings
        public ListBoxTest(params string[] initialStrings)
        {
            // allocate space for the strings
            strings = new String[256];

            // copy the strings passed in to the constructor
            foreach (string s in initialStrings)
            {
                strings[ctr++] = s;
            }
        }

        // add a single string to the end of the list box
        public void Add(string theString)
        {
            if (ctr >= strings.Length)
            {
                // handle bad index
            }
            else
                strings[ctr++] = theString;
        }

        // allow array-like access
        public string this[int index]
        {
            get
            {
                if (index < 0 || index >= strings.Length)
                {
                    // handle bad index
                }
                return strings[index];
            }
            set
            {
                // add only through the add method
                if (index >= ctr )
```

Example 9-9. Using a simple indexer (continued)

```
            {
                // handle error
            }
            else
                strings[index] = value;
        }
    }

    // publish how many strings you hold
    public int GetNumEntries()
    {
        return ctr;
    }

    private string[] strings;
    private int ctr = 0;
}

public class Tester
{
    static void Main()
    {
        // create a new list box and initialize
        ListBoxTest lbt =
            new ListBoxTest("Hello", "World");

        // add a few strings
        lbt.Add("Who");
        lbt.Add("Is");
        lbt.Add("John");
        lbt.Add("Galt");

        // test the access
        string subst = "Universe";
        lbt[1] = subst;

        // access all the strings
        for (int i = 0;i<lbt.GetNumEntries();i++)
        {
            Console.WriteLine("lbt[{0}]: {1}",i,lbt[i]);
        }
    }
}
```

Output:
```
lbt[0]: Hello
lbt[1]: Universe
lbt[2]: Who
lbt[3]: Is
lbt[4]: John
lbt[5]: Galt
```

To keep Example 9-9 simple, strip the list box control down to the few features we care about. The listing ignores everything having to do with being a user control and focuses only on the list of strings the list box maintains and methods for manipulating them. In a real application, of course, these are a small fraction of the total methods of a list box, whose principal job is to display the strings and enable user choice.

The first thing to notice is the two private members:

```
private string[] strings;
private int ctr = 0;
```

In this program, the list box maintains a simple array of strings: strings. Again, in a real list box you might use a more complex and dynamic container, such as a hash table (described later in this chapter). The member variable ctr will keep track of how many strings have been added to this array.

Initialize the array in the constructor with the statement:

```
strings = new String[256];
```

The remainder of the constructor adds the parameters to the array. Again, for simplicity, simply add new strings to the array in the order received.

 Because you cannot know how many strings will be added, use the keyword params, as described earlier in this chapter.

The Add( ) method of ListBoxTest does nothing more than append a new string to the internal array.

The key method of ListBoxTest, however, is the indexer. An indexer is unnamed, so use the this keyword:

```
public string this[int index]
```

The syntax of the indexer is very similar to that for properties. There is either a get( ) method, a set( ) method, or both. In the case shown, the get( ) method endeavors to implement rudimentary bounds checking, and assuming the index requested is acceptable, it returns the value requested:

```
get
{
    if (index < 0 || index >= strings.Length)
    {
        // handle bad index
    }
    return strings[index];
}
```

The set( ) method checks to make sure that the index you are setting already has a value in the list box. If not, it treats the set as an error (new elements can only be added using Add with this approach). The set accessor takes advantage of the implicit parameter value that represents whatever is assigned using the index operator:

```
set
{
if (index >= ctr )
 {
     // handle error
 }
 else
     strings[index] = value;
}
```

Thus, if you write:

```
lbt[5] = "Hello World"
```

the compiler will call the indexer set( ) method on your object and pass in the string Hello World as an implicit parameter named value.

Indexers and Assignment

In Example 9-9, you cannot assign to an index that does not have a value. Thus, if you write:

```
lbt[10] = "wow!";
```

you would trigger the error handler in the set( ) method, which would note that the index you've passed in (10) is larger than the counter (6).

Of course, you can use the set( ) method for assignment; you simply have to handle the indexes you receive. To do so, you might change the set( ) method to check the Length of the buffer rather than the current value of counter. If a value was entered for an index that did not yet have a value, you would update ctr:

```
set
{
    // add only through the add method
    if (index >= strings.Length )
    {
        // handle error
    }
    else
    {
        strings[index] = value;
        if (ctr < index+1)
            ctr = index+1;
    }
}
```

This allows you to create a "sparse" array in which you can assign to offset 10 without ever having assigned to offset 9. Thus, if you now write:

```
lbt[10] = "wow!";
```

the output would be:

```
lbt[0]: Hello
lbt[1]: Universe
lbt[2]: Who
lbt[3]: Is
lbt[4]: John
lbt[5]: Galt
lbt[6]:
lbt[7]:
lbt[8]:
lbt[9]:
lbt[10]: wow!
```

In Main( ), you create an instance of the ListBoxTest class named lbt and pass in two strings as parameters:

```
ListBoxTest lbt = new ListBoxTest("Hello", "World");
```

Then call Add( ) to add four more strings:

```
// add a few strings
lbt.Add("Who");
lbt.Add("Is");
lbt.Add("John");
lbt.Add("Galt");
```

Before examining the values, modify the second value (at index 1):

```
string subst = "Universe";
lbt[1] = subst;
```

Finally, display each value in a loop:

```
for (int i = 0;i<lbt.GetNumEntries();i++)
{
    Console.WriteLine("lbt[{0}]: {1}",i,lbt[i]);
}
```

Indexing on Other Values

C# does not require that you always use an integer value as the index to a collection. When you create a custom collection class and create your indexer, you are free to create indexers that index on strings and other types. In fact, the index value can be overloaded so that a given collection can be indexed, for example, by an integer value or by a string value, depending on the needs of the client.

In the case of our list box, we might want to be able to index into the list box based on a string. Example 9-10 illustrates a string index. The indexer calls findString( ), which is a helper method that returns a record based on the value of the string provided. Notice that the overloaded indexer and the indexer from Example 9-9 are able to coexist.

Example 9-10. Overloading an index

```
namespace Programming_CSharp
{
   using System;

   // a simplified ListBox control
   public class ListBoxTest
   {
      // initialize the list box with strings
      public ListBoxTest(params string[] initialStrings)
      {
         // allocate space for the strings
         strings = new String[256];

         // copy the strings passed in to the constructor
         foreach (string s in initialStrings)
         {
            strings[ctr++] = s;
         }
      }

      // add a single string to the end of the list box
      public void Add(string theString)
      {
         strings[ctr] = theString;
         ctr++;
      }

      // allow array-like access
      public string this[int index]
      {
         get
         {
            if (index < 0 || index >= strings.Length)
            {
               // handle bad index
            }
            return strings[index];
         }
         set
         {
            strings[index] = value;
         }
      }

      private int findString(string searchString)
      {
         for (int i = 0;i<strings.Length;i++)
         {
            if (strings[i].StartsWith(searchString))
            {
               return i;
            }
```

Example 9-10. Overloading an index (continued)

```
        }
        return -1;
    }
    // index on string
    public string this[string index]
    {
        get
        {
            if (index.Length == 0)
            {
                // handle bad index
            }

            return this[findString(index)];
        }
        set
        {
            strings[findString(index)] = value;
        }
    }


    // publish how many strings you hold
    public int GetNumEntries( )
    {
        return ctr;
    }

    private string[] strings;
    private int ctr = 0;
}

public class Tester
{
    static void Main( )
    {
        // create a new list box and initialize
        ListBoxTest lbt =
            new ListBoxTest("Hello", "World");

        // add a few strings
        lbt.Add("Who");
        lbt.Add("Is");
        lbt.Add("John");
        lbt.Add("Galt");

        // test the access
        string subst = "Universe";
        lbt[1] = subst;
        lbt["Hel"] = "GoodBye";
        // lbt["xyz"] = "oops";
```

Example 9-10. Overloading an index (continued)

```
        // access all the strings
        for (int i = 0;i<lbt.GetNumEntries();i++)
        {
           Console.WriteLine("lbt[{0}]: {1}",i,lbt[i]);
        }        // end for
    }            // end main
  }              // end tester
}                // end namespace
```

Output:
```
lbt[0]: GoodBye
lbt[1]: Universe
lbt[2]: Who
lbt[3]: Is
lbt[4]: John
lbt[5]: Galt
```

Example 9-10 is identical to Example 9-9 except for the addition of an overloaded indexer, which can match a string, and the method `findString`, created to support that index.

The `findString` method simply iterates through the strings held in `myStrings` until it finds a string that starts with the target string we use in the index. If found, it returns the index of that string; otherwise it returns the value –1.

We see in `Main()` that the user passes in a string segment to the index, just as was done with an integer:

```
lbt["Hel"] = "GoodBye";
```

This calls the overloaded index, which does some rudimentary error checking (in this case, making sure the string passed in has at least one letter) and then passes the value (Hel) to `findString`. It gets back an index and uses that index to index into `myStrings`:

```
return this[findString(index)];
```

The set value works in the same way:

```
myStrings[findString(index)] = value;
```

 The careful reader will note that if the string does not match, a value of –1 is returned, which is then used as an index into `myStrings`. This action then generates an exception (`System.NullReferenceException`), as you can see by uncommenting the following line in `Main`:

```
lbt["xyz"] = "oops";
```

The proper handling of not finding a string is, as they say, left as an exercise for the reader. You might consider displaying an error message or otherwise allowing the user to recover from the error.

Collection Interfaces

The .NET Framework provides standard interfaces for enumerating, comparing, and creating collections. The key collection interfaces are listed in Table 9-2.

Table 9-2. Collection interfaces

Interface	Purpose
IEnumerable	Enumerates through a collection using a foreach statement.
ICollection	Implemented by all collections to provide the CopyTo( ) method as well as the Count, IsSynchronized, and SyncRoot properties.
IComparer	Compares two objects held in a collection so that the collection can be sorted.
IList	Used by array-indexable collections.
IDictionary	Used for key/value-based collections such as Hashtable and SortedList.
IDictionaryEnumerator	Allows enumeration with foreach of a collection that supports IDictionary.

The IEnumerable Interface

You can support the foreach statement in ListBoxTest by implementing the IEnumerable interface. IEnumerable has only one method, GetEnumerator( ), whose job is to return a specialized implementation of IEnumerator. Thus, the semantics of an Enumerable class are that it can provide an Enumerator:

```
public IEnumerator GetEnumerator( )
{
    return (IEnumerator) new ListBoxEnumerator(this);
}
```

The Enumerator must implement the IEnumerator methods and properties. These can be implemented either directly by the container class (in this case, ListBoxTest) or by a separate class. The latter approach is generally preferred because it encapsulates this responsibility in the Enumerator class rather than cluttering up the container.

Because the Enumerator class is specific to the container class (that is, because ListBoxEnumerator must know a lot about ListBoxTest) you will make it a private implementation, contained within ListBoxTest.

Notice that the method passes the current ListBoxTest object (this) to the enumerator, which will allow the enumerator to enumerate this particular ListBoxTest object.

The class to implement the Enumerator is implemented here as ListBoxEnumerator, which is a private class defined *within* ListBoxTest. Its work is fairly straightforward. It must implement the public instance property Current and two public instance methods, MoveNext( ) and Reset( ).

The ListBoxTest to be enumerated is passed in as an argument to the constructor, where it is assigned to the member variable lbt. The constructor also sets the member variable index to –1, indicating that you have not yet begun to enumerate the object:

```
public ListBoxEnumerator(ListBoxTest lbt)
{
    this.lbt = lbt;
    index = -1;
}
```

The MoveNext( ) method increments the index and then checks to ensure that you've not run past the end of the object you're enumerating. If you have, the program returns false; otherwise it returns true:

```
public bool MoveNext( )
{
    index++;
    if (index >= lbt.strings.Length)
        return false;
    else
        return true;
}
```

The IEnumerator method Reset( ) does nothing but reset the index to –1.

The property Current is implemented to return the current string. This is an arbitrary decision; in other classes Current will have whatever meaning the designer decides is appropriate. However defined, every enumerator must be able to return the current member, as accessing the current member is what enumerators are for:

```
public object Current
{
    get
    {
        return(lbt[index]);
    }
}
```

That's all there is to it: the call to foreach fetches the enumerator and uses it to enumerate over the array. Because foreach will display every string—whether or not you've added a meaningful value—change the initialization of strings to 8 to keep the display manageable, as shown in Example 9-11.

Example 9-11. Making a ListBox an enumerable class

```
namespace Programming_CSharp
{
    using System;
    using System.Collections;

    // a simplified ListBox control
    public class ListBoxTest : IEnumerable
    {
        // private implementation of ListBoxEnumerator
        private class ListBoxEnumerator : IEnumerator
```

Example 9-11. Making a ListBox an enumerable class (continued)

```
    {
        // public within the private implementation
        // thus, private within ListBoxTest
        public ListBoxEnumerator(ListBoxTest lbt)
        {
            this.lbt = lbt;
            index = -1;
        }

        // Increment the index and make sure the
        // value is valid
        public bool MoveNext( )
        {
            index++;
            if (index >= lbt.strings.Length)
                return false;
            else
                return true;
        }

        public void Reset( )
        {
            index = -1;
        }

        // Current property defined as the
        // last string added to the listbox
        public object Current
        {
            get
            {
                return(lbt[index]);
            }
        }

        private ListBoxTest lbt;
        private int index;
    }

    // Enumerable classes can return an enumerator
    public IEnumerator GetEnumerator( )
    {
        return (IEnumerator) new ListBoxEnumerator(this);
    }

    // initialize the list box with strings
    public ListBoxTest(params string[] initialStrings)
    {
        // allocate space for the strings
        strings = new String[8];
```

Example 9-11. Making a ListBox an enumerable class (continued)

```
        // copy the strings passed in to the constructor
        foreach (string s in initialStrings)
        {
            strings[ctr++] = s;
        }
    }

    // add a single string to the end of the list box
    public void Add(string theString)
    {
        strings[ctr] = theString;
        ctr++;
    }

    // allow array-like access
    public string this[int index]
    {
        get
        {
            if (index < 0 || index >= strings.Length)
            {
                // handle bad index
            }
            return strings[index];
        }
        set
        {
            strings[index] = value;
        }
    }

    // publish how many strings you hold
    public int GetNumEntries()
    {
        return ctr;
    }

    private string[] strings;
    private int ctr = 0;
}

public class Tester
{
    static void Main()
    {
        // create a new list box and initialize
        ListBoxTest lbt =
            new ListBoxTest("Hello", "World");

        // add a few strings
```

Example 9-11. Making a ListBox an enumerable class (continued)

```
        lbt.Add("Who");
        lbt.Add("Is");
        lbt.Add("John");
        lbt.Add("Galt");

        // test the access
        string subst = "Universe";
        lbt[1] = subst;

        // access all the strings
        foreach (string s in lbt)
        {
            Console.WriteLine("Value: {0}", s);
        }
    }
  }
}
```

Output:
```
Value: Hello
Value: Universe
Value: Who
Value: Is
Value: John
Value: Galt
Value:
Value:
```

The program begins in Main( ), creating a new ListBoxTest object and passing two strings to the constructor. When the object is created, an array of Strings is created with enough room for eight strings. Four more strings are added using the Add method, and the second string is updated, just as in the previous example.

The big change in this version of the program is that a foreach loop is called, retrieving each string in the list box. The foreach loop automatically uses the IEnumerable interface, invoking GetEnumerator( ). This gets back the ListBoxEnumerator whose constructor is called, thus initializing the index to –1.

The foreach loop then invokes MoveNext( ), which immediately increments the index to 0 and returns true. The foreach then uses the Current property to get back the current string. The Current property invokes the list box's indexer, getting back the string stored at index 0. This string is assigned to the variable s defined in the foreach loop and that string is displayed on the console. The foreach loop repeats these steps (MoveNext( ), Current, display) until all the strings in the list box have been displayed.

The ICollection Interface

Another key interface for arrays, and for all the collections provided by the .NET Framework, is ICollection. ICollection provides four properties: Count,

IsSynchronized, and SyncRoot. ICollection provides one public method as well, CopyTo( ). We look at the CopyTo( ) method later in this chapter. The property used most often is Count, which returns the number of elements in the collection:

```
For (int i = 0;i<myIntArray.Count;i++)
{
    //...
}
```

Here you are using the Count property of myIntArray to determine how many objects are in it so that you can print their values.

The IComparer and IComparable Interfaces

The IComparer interface provides the Compare( ) method, by which any two items in a collection can be ordered. You can implement IComparer in helper classes that you pass to overloaded methods such as Array.Sort(Array a, IComparer c). The IComparable interface is similar, but it defines Compare( ) on the object to be compared rather than on a helper class.

The Compare( ) method is typically implemented by calling the CompareTo method of one of the objects. CompareTo is a method of all objects that implement IComparable. If you want to create classes that can be sorted within a collection, you will need to implement IComparable.

The .NET Framework provides a Comparer class that implements IComparer and provides a default case-sensitive implementation. You'll see how to create your own implementations of IComparer and IComparable in the next section on ArrayLists.

Array Lists

The classic problem with the Array type is its fixed size. If you do not know in advance how many objects an array will hold, you run the risk of declaring either too small an array (and running out of room) or too large an array (and wasting memory).

Your program might be asking the user for input, or gathering input from a web site. As it finds objects (strings, books, values, etc.), you will add them to the array, but you have no idea how many objects you'll collect in any given session. The classic fixed-size array is not a good choice, as you can't predict how large an array you'll need.

The ArrayList class is an array whose size is dynamically increased as required. ArrayLists provide a number of useful methods and properties for their manipulation. Some of the most important are shown in Table 9-3.

Table 9-3. *ArrayList methods and properties*

Method or property	Purpose
Adapter( )	Public static method that creates an ArrayList wrapper for an IList object.
FixedSize( )	Overloaded public static method that returns a list object as a wrapper. The list is of fixed size; elements can be modified but not added or removed.
ReadOnly( )	Overloaded public static method that returns a list class as a wrapper, allowing read-only access.
Repeat( )	Public static method that returns an ArrayList whose elements are copies of the specified value.
Synchronized( )	Overloaded public static method that returns a list wrapper that is thread-safe.
Capacity	Property to get or set the number of elements the ArrayList can contain.
Count	Property to get the number of elements currently in the array.
IsFixedSize	Property to get to find out if the ArrayList is of fixed size.
IsReadOnly	Property to get to find out if the ArrayList is read-only.
IsSynchronized	Property to get to find out if the ArrayList is thread-safe.
Item( )	Gets or sets the element at the specified index. This is the indexer for the ArrayList class.
SyncRoot	Public property that returns an object that can be used to synchronize access to the ArrayList.
Add( )	Public method to add an object to the ArrayList.
AddRange( )	Public method that adds the elements of an ICollection to the end of the ArrayList.
BinarySearch( )	Overloaded public method that uses a binary search to locate a specific element in a sorted ArrayList.
Clear( )	Removes all elements from the ArrayList.
Clone( )	Creates a shallow copy.
Contains( )	Determines if an element is in the ArrayList.
CopyTo( )	Overloaded public method that copies an ArrayList to a one-dimensional array.
GetEnumerator( )	Overloaded public method that returns an enumerator to iterate an ArrayList.
GetRange( )	Copies a range of elements to a new ArrayList.
IndexOf( )	Overloaded public method that returns the index of the first occurrence of a value.
Insert( )	Inserts an element into ArrayList.
InsertRange( )	Inserts the elements of a collection into the ArrayList.
LastIndexOf( )	Overloaded public method that returns the index of the last occurrence of a value in the ArrayList.
Remove( )	Removes the first occurrence of a specific object.
RemoveAt( )	Removes the element at the specified index.
RemoveRange( )	Removes a range of elements.
Reverse( )	Reverses the order of elements in the ArrayList.
SetRange( )	Copies the elements of a collection over a range of elements in the ArrayList.
Sort( )	Sorts the ArrayList.

Table 9-3. ArrayList methods and properties (continued)

Method or property	Purpose
ToArray( )	Copies the elements of the ArrayList to a new array.
TrimToSize( )	Sets the capacity to the actual number of elements in the ArrayList.

When you create an ArrayList, you do not define how many objects it will contain. Add to the ArrayList using the Add( ) method, and the list takes care of its own internal bookkeeping, as illustrated in Example 9-12.

Example 9-12. Working with an ArrayList

```
namespace Programming_CSharp
{
    using System;
    using System.Collections;

    // a simple class to store in the array
    public class Employee
    {
        public Employee(int empID)
        {
            this.empID = empID;
        }
        public override  string ToString( )
        {
            return empID.ToString( );
        }
        public int EmpID
        {
            get
            {
                return empID;
            }
            set
            {
                empID = value;
            }
        }

        private int empID;
    }
    public class Tester
    {
        static void Main( )
        {
            ArrayList empArray = new ArrayList( );
            ArrayList intArray = new ArrayList( );

            // populate the array
            for (int i = 0;i<5;i++)
            {
```

Example 9-12. Working with an ArrayList (continued)

```
        empArray.Add(new Employee(i+100));
        intArray.Add(i*5);
    }

    // print all the contents
    for (int i = 0;i<intArray.Count;i++)
    {
        Console.Write("{0} ", intArray[i].ToString());
    }

    Console.WriteLine("\n");

    // print all the contents of the Employee array
    for (int i = 0;i<empArray.Count;i++)
    {
        Console.Write("{0} ", empArray[i].ToString());
    }

    Console.WriteLine("\n");
    Console.WriteLine("empArray.Capacity: {0}",
        empArray.Capacity);
        }
    }
}
```

Output:
```
0 5 10 15 20
100 101 102 103 104
empArray.Capacity: 16
```

With an Array class, you define how many objects the array will hold. If you try to add more than that, the Array class will throw an exception. With an ArrayList, you do not declare how many objects the ArrayList will hold. The ArrayList has a property, Capacity, which is the number of elements the ArrayList is capable of storing:

```
public int Capcity {virtual get; virtual set; }
```

The default capacity is 16. When you add the 17th element, the capacity is automatically doubled to 32. If you change the for loop to:

```
for (int i = 0;i<17;i++)
```

the output looks like this:

```
0 5 10 15 20 25 30 35 40 45 50 55 60 65 70 75 80
5 6 7 8 9 10 11 12 13 14 15 16 17 18 19 20 21
empArray.Capacity: 32
```

You can manually set the capacity to any number equal to or greater than the count. If you set it to a number less than the count, the program will throw an exception of type ArgumentOutOfRangeException.

Implementing IComparable

Like all collections, the ArrayList implements the Sort( ) method, which allows you to sort any objects that implement IComparable. In the next example, you'll modify the Employee object to implement IComparable:

```
public class Employee : IComparable
```

To implement the IComparable interface, the Employee object must provide a CompareTo( ) method:

```
public int CompareTo(Object rhs)
{
    Employee r = (Employee) rhs;
    return this.empID.CompareTo(r.empID);
}
```

The CompareTo( ) method takes an object as a parameter; the Employee object must compare itself to this object and return −1 if it is smaller than the object, 1 if it is greater than the object, and 0 if it is equal to the object. It is up to Employee to determine what smaller than, greater than, and equal to mean. For example, cast the object to an Employee and then delegate the comparison to the empId member. The empId member is an int and uses the default CompareTo( ) method for integer types, which will do an integer comparison of the two values.

 Because int derives from object, it has methods, including the method CompareTo( ). Thus int is an object to which you may delegate the responsibility of comparison.

You are now ready to sort the array list of employees, empList. To see if the sort is working, you'll need to add integers and Employee instances to their respective arrays with random values. To create the random values, you'll instantiate an object of class Random; to generate the random values you'll call the Next( ) method on the Random object, which returns a pseudorandom number. The Next( ) method is overloaded; one version allows you to pass in an integer that represents the largest random number you want. In this case, you'll pass in the value 10 to generate a random number between 0 and 10:

```
Random r = new Random( );
r.Next(10);
```

Example 9-13 creates an integer array and an Employee array, populates them both with random numbers, and prints their values. It then sorts both arrays and prints the new values.

Example 9-13. Sorting an integer and an employee array

```
namespace Programming_CSharp
{
    using System;
```

Example 9-13. Sorting an integer and an employee array (continued)

```csharp
using System.Collections;

// a simple class to store in the array
public class Employee : IComparable
{
    public Employee(int empID)
    {
        this.empID = empID;
    }

    public override  string ToString( )
    {
        return empID.ToString( );
    }

     // Comparer delegates back to Employee
    // Employee uses the integer's default
    // CompareTo method
    public int CompareTo(Object rhs)
    {
        Employee r = (Employee) rhs;
        return this.empID.CompareTo(r.empID);
    }

    private int empID;
}
public class Tester
{
    static void Main( )
    {
        ArrayList empArray = new ArrayList( );
        ArrayList intArray = new ArrayList( );

        // generate random numbers for
        // both the integers and the
        // employee id's
        Random r = new Random( );

        // populate the array
        for (int i = 0;i<5;i++)
        {
            // add a random employee id
            empArray.Add(new Employee(r.Next(10)+100));

            // add a random integer
            intArray.Add(r.Next(10));
        }

        // display all the contents of the int array
        for (int i = 0;i<intArray.Count;i++)
        {
```

Example 9-13. Sorting an integer and an employee array (continued)

```
            Console.Write("{0} ", intArray[i].ToString());
        }
        Console.WriteLine("\n");

        // display all the contents of the Employee array
        for (int i = 0;i<empArray.Count;i++)
        {
            Console.Write("{0} ", empArray[i].ToString());
        }
        Console.WriteLine("\n");

        // sort and display the int array
        intArray.Sort();
        for (int i = 0;i<intArray.Count;i++)
        {
            Console.Write("{0} ", intArray[i].ToString());
        }
        Console.WriteLine("\n");

        // sort and display the employee array
        //Employee.EmployeeComparer c = Employee.GetComparer();
        //empArray.Sort(c);
        empArray.Sort();

        // display all the contents of the Employee array
        for (int i = 0;i<empArray.Count;i++)
        {
            Console.Write("{0} ", empArray[i].ToString());
        }
        Console.WriteLine("\n");

    }
  }
}
```

Output:
```
8  5  7  3  3
105  103  102  104  106
3  3  5  7  8
102  103  104  105  106
```

The output shows that the integer array and Employee array were generated with random numbers. When sorted, the display shows the values have been ordered properly.

Implementing IComparer

When you call Sort() on the ArrayList the default implementation of IComparer is called, which uses QuickSort to call the IComparable implementation of CompareTo() on each element in the ArrayList.

You are free to create your own implementation of IComparer, which you might want to do if you need control over how the sort is accomplished. For example, in the next example, you will add a second field to Employee, yearsOfSvc. You want to be able to sort the Employee objects in the ArrayList on either field, empID or yearsOfSvc.

To accomplish this, you will create a custom implementation of IComparer, which you will pass to the Sort( ) method of ArrayList. This IComparer class, EmployeeComparer, knows about Employee objects and knows how to sort them.

EmployeeComparer has a property, WhichComparison, of type Employee. EmployeeComparer.ComparisonType:

```
public Employee.EmployeeComparer.ComparisonType
   WhichComparison
{
   get
   {
      return whichComparison;
   }
   set
   {
      whichComparison=value;
   }
}
```

ComparisonType is an enumeration with two values, empID or yearsOfSvc (indicating that you want to sort by employee ID or years of service, respectively):

```
public enum ComparisonType
{
   EmpID,
   Yrs
};
```

Before invoking Sort( ), you will create an instance of EmployeeComparer and set its ComparisionType property:

```
Employee.EmployeeComparer c = Employee.GetComparer( );
c.WhichComparison=Employee.EmployeeComparer.ComparisonType.EmpID;
empArray.Sort(c);
```

When you invoke Sort( ) the ArrayList will call the Compare method on the EmployeeComparer, which in turn will delegate the comparison to the Employee. CompareTo( ) method, passing in its WhichComparison property.

```
public int Compare(object lhs, object rhs)
{
   Employee l = (Employee) lhs;
   Employee r = (Employee) rhs;
   return l.CompareTo(r,WhichComparison);
}
```

The Employee object must implement a custom version of CompareTo( ), which takes the comparison and compares the objects accordingly:

```
   public int CompareTo(
      Employee rhs,
      Employee.EmployeeComparer.ComparisonType which)
{
   switch (which)
   {
      case Employee.EmployeeComparer.ComparisonType.EmpID:
         return this.empID.CompareTo(rhs.empID);
      case Employee.EmployeeComparer.ComparisonType.Yrs:
         return this.yearsOfSvc.CompareTo(rhs.yearsOfSvc);
   }
   return 0;
}
```

The complete source for this example is shown in Example 9-14. The integer array has been removed to simplify the example, and the output of the employee's ToString( ) method enhanced to enable you to see the effects of the sort.

Example 9-14. Sorting an array by employees' IDs and years of service

```
namespace Programming_CSharp
{
   using System;
   using System.Collections;

   // a simple class to store in the array
   public class Employee : IComparable
   {
      public Employee(int empID)
      {
         this.empID = empID;
      }

      public Employee(int empID, int yearsOfSvc)
      {
         this.empID = empID;
         this.yearsOfSvc = yearsOfSvc;
      }

      public override  string ToString()
      {
         return "ID: " + empID.ToString() +
         ". Years of Svc: " + yearsOfSvc.ToString( );
      }

      // static method to get a Comparer object
      public static EmployeeComparer GetComparer( )
      {
         return new Employee.EmployeeComparer( );
      }

      // Comparer delegates back to Employee
      // Employee uses the integer's default
      // CompareTo method
```

Example 9-14. Sorting an array by employees' IDs and years of service (continued)

```
public int CompareTo(Object rhs)
{
    Employee r = (Employee) rhs;
    return this.empID.CompareTo(r.empID);
}


// Special implementation to be called by custom comparer
public int CompareTo(
    Employee rhs,
    Employee.EmployeeComparer.ComparisonType which)
{
    switch (which)
    {
        case Employee.EmployeeComparer.ComparisonType.EmpID:
            return this.empID.CompareTo(rhs.empID);
        case Employee.EmployeeComparer.ComparisonType.Yrs:
            return this.yearsOfSvc.CompareTo(rhs.yearsOfSvc);
    }
    return 0;

}


// nested class which implements IComparer
public class EmployeeComparer : IComparer
{
    // enumeration of comparsion types
    public enum ComparisonType
    {
        EmpID,
        Yrs
    };

    // Tell the Employee objects to compare themselves
    public int Compare(object lhs, object rhs)
    {
        Employee l = (Employee) lhs;
        Employee r = (Employee) rhs;
        return l.CompareTo(r,WhichComparison);
    }

    public Employee.EmployeeComparer.ComparisonType
        WhichComparison
    {
        get
        {
            return whichComparison;
        }
        set
        {
            whichComparison=value;
        }
    }
```

Example 9-14. Sorting an array by employees' IDs and years of service (continued)

```
        // private state variable
        private Employee.EmployeeComparer.ComparisonType
            whichComparison;
    }
    private int empID;
    private int yearsOfSvc = 1;
}
public class Tester
{
    static void Main( )
    {
        ArrayList empArray = new ArrayList( );

        // generate random numbers for
        // both the integers and the
        // employee id's
        Random r = new Random( );

        // populate the array
        for (int i = 0;i<5;i++)
        {
            // add a random employee id
            empArray.Add(
              new Employee(
                r.Next(10)+100,r.Next(20)
              )
            );
        }

        // display all the contents of the Employee array
        for (int i = 0;i<empArray.Count;i++)
        {
            Console.Write("\n{0} ", empArray[i].ToString( ));
        }
        Console.WriteLine("\n");

        // sort and display the employee array
        Employee.EmployeeComparer c = Employee.GetComparer( );
        c.WhichComparison=Employee.EmployeeComparer.ComparisonType.EmpID;
        empArray.Sort(c);
        // display all the contents of the Employee array
        for (int i = 0;i<empArray.Count;i++)
        {
            Console.Write("\n{0} ", empArray[i].ToString( ));
        }
        Console.WriteLine("\n");

        c.WhichComparison=Employee.EmployeeComparer.ComparisonType.Yrs;
        empArray.Sort(c);
        for (int i = 0;i<empArray.Count;i++)
        {
            Console.Write("\n{0} ", empArray[i].ToString( ));
```

Example 9-14. Sorting an array by employees' IDs and years of service (continued)

```
        }
        Console.WriteLine("\n");


    }
  }
}
```

Output:
```
ID: 103. Years of Svc: 11
ID: 108. Years of Svc: 15
ID: 107. Years of Svc: 14
ID: 108. Years of Svc: 5
ID: 102. Years of Svc: 0

ID: 102. Years of Svc: 0
ID: 103. Years of Svc: 11
ID: 107. Years of Svc: 14
ID: 108. Years of Svc: 15
ID: 108. Years of Svc: 5

ID: 102. Years of Svc: 0
ID: 108. Years of Svc: 5
ID: 103. Years of Svc: 11
ID: 107. Years of Svc: 14
ID: 108. Years of Svc: 15
```

The first block of output shows the Employee objects as they are added to the ArrayList. The employee ID values and the years of service are in random order. The second block shows the results of sorting by the employee ID, and the third block shows the results of sorting by years of service.

Queues

A *queue* represents a first-in, first-out (FIFO) collection. The classic analogy is to a line (or queue if you are British) at a ticket window. The first person in line ought to be the first person to come off the line to buy a ticket.

A queue is a good collection to use when you are managing a limited resource. For example, you might want to send messages to a resource that can only handle one message at a time. You would then create a message queue so that you can say to your clients: "Your message is important to us. Messages are handled in the order in which they are received."

The Queue class has a number of member methods and properties, as shown in Table 9-4.

Table 9-4. Queue methods and properties

Method or property	Purpose
Synchronized( )	Public static method that returns a Queue wrapper that is thread-safe.
Count	Public property that gets the number of elements in the Queue.
IsSynchronized	Public property to get a value indicating if the Queue is synchronized.
SyncRoot	Public property that returns an object that can be used to synchronize access to the Queue.
Clear( )	Removes all objects from the Queue.
Clone( )	Creates a shallow copy.
Contains( )	Determines if an element is in the Queue.
CopyTo( )	Copies the Queue elements to an existing one-dimensional array.
Dequeue( )	Removes and returns the object at the beginning of the Queue.
Enqueue( )	Adds an object to the end of the Queue.
GetEnumerator( )	Returns an enumerator for the Queue.
Peek( )	Returns the object at the beginning of the Queue without removing it.
ToArray( )	Copies the elements to a new array.

Add elements to your queue with the Enqueue command and take them off the queue with Dequeue or by using an enumerator. Example 9-15 illustrates.

Example 9-15. Working with a queue

```
namespace Programming_CSharp
{
    using System;
    using System.Collections;

    public class Tester
    {

        static void Main( )
        {
            Queue intQueuee = new Queue( );

            // populate the array
            for (int i = 0;i<5;i++)
            {
                intQueuee.Enqueue(i*5);
            }

            // Display the Queue.
            Console.Write( "intQueuee values:\t" );
            PrintValues( intQueuee );

            // Remove an element from the queue.
            Console.WriteLine(
                "\n(Dequeue)\t{0}", intQueuee.Dequeue( ) );
```

Example 9-15. Working with a queue (continued)

```
        // Display the Queue.
        Console.Write( "intQueuee values:\t" );
        PrintValues( intQueuee );

        // Remove another element from the queue.
        Console.WriteLine(
        "\n(Dequeue)\t{0}", intQueuee.Dequeue() );

        // Display the Queue.
        Console.Write( "intQueuee values:\t" );
        PrintValues( intQueuee );

        // View the first element in the
        // Queue but do not remove.
        Console.WriteLine(
            "\n(Peek)   \t{0}", intQueuee.Peek() );

        // Display the Queue.
        Console.Write( "intQueuee values:\t" );
        PrintValues( intQueuee );

    }

    public static void PrintValues( IEnumerable myCollection )
    {
        IEnumerator myEnumerator =
            myCollection.GetEnumerator();
        while ( myEnumerator.MoveNext() )
            Console.Write( "{0} ",myEnumerator.Current );
        Console.WriteLine();
    }

  }
}
```

Output:
```
intQueuee values:       0 5 10 15 20

(Dequeue)       0
intQueuee values:       5 10 15 20

(Dequeue)       5
intQueuee values:       10 15 20

(Peek)          10
intQueuee values:       10 15 20
```

In this example the ArrayList is replaced by a Queue. I've dispensed with the Employee class to save room, but of course you can Enqueue user-defined objects as well.

The output shows that queuing objects adds them to the Queue, and calls to Dequeue return the object and also remove them from the Queue. The Queue class also provides a Peek( ) method that allows you to see, but not remove, the first element.

Because the Queue class is enumerable, you can pass it to the PrintValues method, which is provided as an IEnumerable interface. The conversion is implicit. In the PrintValues method you call GetEnumerator, which you will remember is the single method of all IEnumerable classes. This returns an IEnumerator, which you then use to enumerate all the objects in the collection.

Stacks

A *stack* is a last-in, first-out (LIFO) collection, like a stack of dishes at a buffet table, or a stack of coins on your desk. Add a dish on top, which is the first dish you take off the stack.

The principal methods for adding to and removing from a stack are Push and Pop( ); Stack also offers a Peek( ) method, very much like Queue. The significant methods and properties for Stack are shown in Table 9-5.

Table 9-5. Stack methods and properties

Method or property	Purpose
Synchronized( )	Public static method that returns a thread-safe Stack wrapper.
Count	Public property that gets the number of elements in the Stack.
IsSynchronized	Public property that gets a value indicating if the Stack is synchronized.
SyncRoot	Public property that returns an object that can be used to synchronize access to the Stack.
Clear( )	Removes all objects from the Stack.
Clone( )	Creates a shallow copy.
Contains( )	Determines if an element is in the Stack.
CopyTo( )	Copies the Stack elements to an existing one-dimensional array.
GetEnumerator( )	Returns an enumerator for the Stack.
Peek( )	Returns the object at the top of the Stack without removing it.
Pop( )	Removes and returns the object at the top of the Stack.
Push( )	Inserts an object at the top of the Stack.
ToArray( )	Copies the elements to a new array.

The ArrayList, Queue, and Stack types contain overloaded CopyTo( ) and ToArray( ) methods for copying their elements to an array. In the case of a Stack, the CopyTo( ) method will copy its elements to an existing one-dimensional array, overwriting the contents of the array beginning at the index you specify. The ToArray( ) method returns a new array with the contents of the stack's elements. Example 9-16 illustrates.

Example 9-16. Working with a Stack

```csharp
namespace Programming_CSharp
{
    using System;
    using System.Collections;

    public class Tester
    {
        static void Main( )
        {
            Stack intStack = new Stack( );

            // populate the array
            for (int i = 0;i<8;i++)
            {
                intStack.Push(i*5);
            }

            // Display the Stack.
            Console.Write( "intStack values:\t" );
            PrintValues( intStack );

            // Remove an element from the stack.
            Console.WriteLine( "\n(Pop)\t{0}",
                intStack.Pop( ) );

            // Display the Stack.
            Console.Write( "intStack values:\t" );
            PrintValues( intStack );

            // Remove another element from the stack.
            Console.WriteLine( "\n(Pop)\t{0}",
                intStack.Pop( ) );

            // Display the Stack.
            Console.Write( "intStack values:\t" );
            PrintValues( intStack );

            // View the first element in the
            // Stack but do not remove.
            Console.WriteLine( "\n(Peek)   \t{0}",
                intStack.Peek( ) );

            // Display the Stack.
            Console.Write( "intStack values:\t" );
            PrintValues( intStack );

            // declare an array object which will
            // hold 12 integers
            Array targetArray=Array.CreateInstance(
                typeof(int), 12  );

            targetArray.SetValue( 100, 0 );
```

Example 9-16. Working with a Stack (continued)

```
        targetArray.SetValue( 200, 1 );
        targetArray.SetValue( 300, 2 );
        targetArray.SetValue( 400, 3 );
        targetArray.SetValue( 500, 4 );
        targetArray.SetValue( 600, 5 );
        targetArray.SetValue( 700, 6 );
        targetArray.SetValue( 800, 7 );
        targetArray.SetValue( 900, 8 );

        // Display the values of the target Array instance.
        Console.WriteLine( "\nTarget array:  " );
        PrintValues( targetArray );

        // Copy the entire source Stack to the
        // target Array instance, starting at index 6.
        intStack.CopyTo( targetArray, 6 );

        // Display the values of the target Array instance.
        Console.WriteLine( "\nTarget array after copy:  " );
        PrintValues( targetArray );

        // Copy the entire source Stack
        // to a new standard array.
        Object[] myArray = intStack.ToArray();

        // Display the values of the new standard array.
        Console.WriteLine( "\nThe new  array:" );
        PrintValues( myArray );
    }

    public static void PrintValues(
        IEnumerable myCollection )
    {
        System.Collections.IEnumerator enumerator =
            myCollection.GetEnumerator();
        while ( enumerator.MoveNext() )
            Console.Write( "{0}  ",enumerator.Current );
        Console.WriteLine();
    }
  }
}
```

Output:
```
intStack values:      35  30  25  20  15  10  5  0

(Pop)   35
intStack values:      30  25  20  15  10  5  0

(Pop)   30
intStack values:      25  20  15  10  5  0

(Peek)          25
```

Example 9-16. Working with a Stack (continued)

```
intStack values:        25  20  15  10  5  0

Target array:
100  200  300  400  500  600  700  800  900  0  0  0

Target array after copy:
100  200  300  400  500  600  25  20  15  10  5  0

The new  array:
25  20  15  10  5  0

25
```

The output reflects that the items pushed onto the stack were popped in reverse order. In fact, the entire stack is stored in reverse order to reflect its LIFO nature.

Example 9-16 uses the `Array` class that serves as the base class for all arrays. The example creates an array of 12 integers by calling the static method of `CreateInstance( )`. This method takes two arguments: a type (in this case, `int`) and a number representing the size of the array.

The array is populated with the `SetValue( )` method which takes two arguments: the object to add and the offset at which to add it.

The effect of `CopyTo( )` can be seen by examining the target array before and after calling `CopyTo( )`. The array elements are overwritten beginning with the index specified (6).

Notice also that the `ToArray( )` method is designed to return an array of objects, and so `myArray` is declared appropriately:

```
Object[] myArray = intStack.ToArray( );
```

Dictionaries

A *dictionary* is a collection that associates a *key* to a *value*. A language dictionary, such as Webster's, associates a word (the key) with its definition (the value).

To see the value of dictionaries, start by imagining that you want to keep a list of the state capitals. One approach might be to put them in an array:

```
string[] stateCapitals = new string[50];
```

The `stateCapitals` array will hold 50 state capitals. Each capital is accessed as an offset into the array. For example, to access the capital for Arkansas, you need to know that Arkansas is the fourth state in alphabetical order:

```
string capitalOfArkansas = stateCapitals[3];
```

It is inconvenient, however, to access state capitals using array notation. After all, if I need the capital for Massachusetts, there is no easy way for me to determine that Massachusetts is the 21st state alphabetically.

It would be far more convenient to store the capital with the state name. A *dictionary* allows you to store a value (in this case, the capital) with a key (in this case, the name of the state).

A .NET Framework dictionary can associate any kind of key (string, integer, object, etc.) with any kind of value (string, integer, object, etc.). Typically, of course, the key is fairly short, the value fairly complex.

The most important attributes of a good dictionary are that it is easy to add values and it is quick to retrieve values. Some dictionaries are faster at adding new values, and others are optimized for retrieval. One example of a dictionary type is the hashtable.

Hashtables

A *hashtable* is a dictionary optimized for fast retrieval. The principal methods and properties of Hashtable are summarized in Table 9-6.

Table 9-6. Hashtable methods and properties

Method or property	Purpose
Synchronized( )	Public static method that returns a Hashtable wrapper that is thread-safe (see Chapter 20).
Count	Public property that gets the number of elements in the Hashtable.
IsReadOnly	Public property that gets a value indicating if the Hashtable is read-only.
IsSynchronized	Public property that gets a value indicating if the Hashtable is synchronized.
Item( )	The indexer for the Hashtable.
Keys	Public property that gets an ICollection containing the keys in the Hashtable. (See also Values, later in this table.)
SyncRoot	Public property that returns an object that can be used to synchronize access to the Hashtable.
Values	Public property that gets an ICollection containing the values in the Hashtable. (See also Keys, earlier in this table.)
Add( )	Adds an entry with a specified Key and Value.
Clear( )	Removes all objects from the Hashtable.
Clone( )	Creates a shallow copy.
Contains( ) ContainsKey( )	Determines whether the Hashtable has a specified key.
ContainsValue( )	Determines whether the Hashtable has a specified value.
CopyTo( )	Copies the Hashtable elements to an existing one-dimensional array.
GetEnumerator( )	Returns an enumerator for the Hashtable.
GetObjectData( )	Implements ISerializable and returns the data needed to serialize the Hashtable.
OnDeserialization( )	Implements ISerializable and raises the deserialization event when the deserialization is complete.
Remove( )	Removes the entry with the specified Key.

In a Hashtable, each value is stored in a "bucket." The bucket is numbered, much like an offset into an array.

Because the key may not be an integer, it must be possible to translate the key (e.g., "Massachusetts") into a bucket number. Each key must provide a GetHashCode() method that will accomplish this magic.

Remember that everything in C# derives from object. The object class provides a virtual method GetHashCode(), which the derived types are free to inherit as is or to override.

A trivial implementation of a GetHashCode() function for a string might simply add up the Unicode values of each character in the string and then use the modulus operator to return a value between 0 and the number of buckets in the Hashtable. It is not necessary to write such a method for the string type, however, as the CLR provides one for you.

When you insert the values (the state capitals) into the Hashtable, the Hashtable calls GetHashCode() on each key provided. This method returns an int, which identifies the bucket into which the state capital is placed.

It is possible, of course, for more than one key to return the same bucket number. This is called a *collision*. There are a number of ways to handle a collision. The most common solution, and the one adopted by the CLR, is simply to have each bucket maintain an ordered list of values.

When you retrieve a value from the Hashtable, you provide a key. Once again the Hashtable calls GetHashCode() on the key and uses the returned int to find the appropriate bucket. If there is only one value, it is returned. If there is more than one value, a binary search of the bucket's contents is performed. Because there are few values, this search is typically very fast.

The key in a Hashtable can be a primitive type, or it can be an instance of a user-defined type (an object). Objects used as keys for a Hashtable must implement GetHashCode() as well as Equals. In most cases, you can simply use the inherited implementation from Object.

IDictionary

Hash tables are dictionaries because they implement the IDictionary interface. IDictionary provides a public property Item. The Item property retrieves a value with the specified key. In C#, the declaration for the Item property is:

```
object this[object key]
{get; set;}
```

The Item property is implemented in C# with the index operator ([]). Thus, you access items in any Dictionary object using the offset syntax, as you would with an array.

Example 9-17 demonstrates adding items to a Hashtable and then retrieving them with the Item property.

Example 9-17. The Item property as offset operators

```
namespace Programming_CSharp
{
    using System;
    using System.Collections;

    public class Tester
    {
        static void Main( )
        {
            // Create and initialize a new Hashtable.
            Hashtable hashTable = new Hashtable( );
            hashTable.Add("000440312", "Jesse Liberty");
```

Example 9-17. The Item property as offset operators (continued)

```
        hashTable.Add("000123933", "Stacey Liberty");
        hashTable.Add("000145938", "John Galt");
        hashTable.Add("000773394", "Ayn Rand");

        // access a particular item
        Console.WriteLine("myHashTable[\"000145938\"]: {0}",
            hashTable["000145938"]);
    }
  }
}
```

Output:
```
hashTable["000145938"]: John Galt
```

Example 9-17 begins by instantiating a new `Hashtable`. We use the simplest constructor accepting the default initial capacity and load factor (see the sidebar, "Load Factor"), the default hash code provider, and the default comparer.

We then add four key/value pairs. In this example, the social security number is tied to the person's full name. (Note that the social security numbers here are intentionally bogus.)

Once the items are added, we access the third item using its key.

The Keys and Values Collections

Dictionary collections provide two additional properties: `Keys` and `Values`. `Keys` retrieves an `ICollection` object with all the keys in the `Hashtable`, as `Values` retrieves an `ICollection` object with all the values. Example 9-18 illustrates.

Example 9-18. Keys and Values collections

```
namespace Programming_CSharp
{
   using System;
   using System.Collections;

   public class Tester
   {
      static void Main()
      {
         // Create and initialize a new Hashtable.
         Hashtable hashTable = new Hashtable();
         hashTable.Add("000440312", "George Washington");
         hashTable.Add("000123933", "Abraham Lincoln");
         hashTable.Add("000145938", "John Galt");
         hashTable.Add("000773394", "Ayn Rand");

         // get the keys from the hashTable
         ICollection keys = hashTable.Keys;
```

Example 9-18. Keys and Values collections (continued)

```
        // get the values
        ICollection values = hashTable.Values;

        // iterate over the keys ICollection
        foreach(string key in keys)
        {
            Console.WriteLine("{0} ", key);
        }

        // iterate over the values collection
        foreach (string val in values)
        {
            Console.WriteLine("{0} ", val);
        }
    }
  }
}
```
Output:
```
000440312
000123933
000773394
000145938
George Washington
Abraham Lincoln
Ayn Rand
John Galt
```

Although the order of the Keys collection is not guaranteed, it *is* guaranteed to be the same order as returned in the Values collection.

IDictionaryEnumerator Interface

IDictionary objects also support the foreach construct by implementing the GetEnumerator method, which returns an IDictionaryEnumerator.

The IDictionaryEnumerator is used to enumerate through any IDictionary object. It provides properties to access both the key and value for each item in the dictionary. Example 9-19 illustrates.

Example 9-19. Using the IDictionaryEnumerator interface
```
namespace Programming_CSharp
{
    using System;
    using System.Collections;

    public class Tester
    {

        static void Main()
        {
```

Example 9-19. Using the IDictionaryEnumerator interface (continued)

```
        // Create and initialize a new Hashtable.
        Hashtable hashTable = new Hashtable( );
        hashTable.Add("000440312", "George Washington");
        hashTable.Add("000123933", "Abraham Lincoln");
        hashTable.Add("000145938", "John Galt");
        hashTable.Add("000773394", "Ayn Rand");

        // Display the properties and values of the Hashtable.
        Console.WriteLine( "hashTable" );
        Console.WriteLine( "  Count:    {0}", hashTable.Count );
        Console.WriteLine( "  Keys and Values:" );
        PrintKeysAndValues( hashTable );
    }

    public static void PrintKeysAndValues( Hashtable table )
    {
        IDictionaryEnumerator enumerator = table.GetEnumerator( );
        while ( enumerator.MoveNext( ) )
           Console.WriteLine( "\t{0}:\t{1}",
              enumerator.Key, enumerator.Value );
        Console.WriteLine( );

    }
  }
}
```

Output:
```
hashTable
  Count:    4
  Keys and Values:
        000440312:      George Washington
        000123933:      Abraham Lincoln
        000773394:      Ayn Rand
        000145938:      John Galt
```

CHAPTER 10

Strings and Regular Expressions

There was a time when people thought of computers exclusively as manipulating numeric values. Early computers were first used to calculate missile trajectories, and programming was taught in the math department of major universities.

Today, most programs are concerned more with strings of characters than with strings of numbers. Typically these strings are used for word processing, document manipulation, and creation of web pages.

C# provides built-in support for a fully functional string type. More importantly, C# treats strings as objects that encapsulate all the manipulation, sorting, and searching methods normally applied to strings of characters.

Complex string manipulation and pattern matching is aided by the use of *regular expressions*. C# combines the power and complexity of regular expression syntax, originally found only in string manipulation languages such as awk and Perl, with a fully object-oriented design.

In this chapter, you will learn to work with the C# string type and the .NET Framework System.String class that it aliases. You will see how to extract substrings, manipulate and concatenate strings, and build new strings with the StringBuilder class. In addition, you will learn how to use the RegEx class to match strings based on complex regular expressions.

Strings

C# treats strings as first-class types that are flexible, powerful, and easy to use. Each string object is an *immutable* sequence of Unicode characters. In other words, methods that appear to change the string actually return a modified copy; the original string remains intact.

When you declare a C# string using the string keyword, you are in fact declaring the object to be of the type System.String, one of the built-in types provided by the .NET

Framework Class Library. A C# string type *is* a System.String type, and we will use the names interchangeably throughout the chapter.

The declaration of the System.String class is:

```
public sealed class String :
    IComparable, ICloneable, IConvertible, IEnumerable
```

This declaration reveals that the class is sealed, meaning that it is not possible to derive from the string class. The class also implements four system interfaces— IComparable, ICloneable, IConvertible, and IEnumerable—which dictate functionality that System.String shares with other classes in the .NET Framework.

As seen in Chapter 9, the IComparable interface is implemented by types whose values can be ordered. Strings, for example, can be alphabetized; any given string can be compared with another string to determine which should come first in an ordered list. IComparable classes implement the CompareTo method. IEnumerable, also discussed in Chapter 9, lets you use the foreach construct to enumerate a string as a collection of chars.

ICloneable objects can create new instances with the same value as the original instance. In this case, it is possible to clone a string to produce a new string with the same values (characters) as the original. ICloneable classes implement the Clone( ) method.

IConvertible classes provide methods to facilitate conversion to other primitive types such as ToInt32( ), ToDouble( ), ToDecimal( ), etc.

Creating Strings

The most common way to create a string is to assign a quoted string of characters, known as a *string literal*, to a user-defined variable of type string:

```
string newString = "This is a string literal";
```

Quoted strings can include *escape characters,* such as "\n" or "\t," which begin with a backslash character (\) and are used to indicate where line breaks or tabs are to appear. Because the backslash is itself used in some command-line syntaxes, such as URLs or directory paths, in a quoted string the backslash must be preceded by another backslash.

Strings can also be created using *verbatim* string literals, which start with the (@) symbol. This tells the String constructor that the string should be used verbatim, even if it spans multiple lines or includes escape characters. In a verbatim string literal, backslashes and the characters that follow them are simply considered additional characters of the string. Thus, the following two definitions are equivalent:

```
string literalOne = "\\\\MySystem\\MyDirectory\\ProgrammingC#.cs";
string verbatimLiteralOne = @"\\MySystem\MyDirectory\ProgrammingC#.cs";
```

In the first line, a nonverbatim string literal is used, and so the backslash characters (\) must be *escaped*. This means it must be preceded by a second backslash character. In the second line, a verbatim literal string is used, so the extra backslash is not needed. A second example illustrates multiline verbatim strings:

```
string literalTwo = "Line One\nLine Two";
string verbatimLiteralTwo = @"Line One
Line Two";
```

Again, these declarations are interchangeable. Which one you use is a matter of convenience and personal style.

The ToString Method

Another common way to create a string is to call the ToString( ) method on an object and assign the result to a string variable. All the built-in types override this method to simplify the task of converting a value (often a numeric value) to a string representation of that value. In the following example, the ToString( ) method of an integer type is called to store its value in a string:

```
int myInteger = 5;
string integerString = myInteger.ToString( );
```

The call to myInteger.ToString( ) returns a String object, which is then assigned to integerString.

The .NET String class provides a wealth of overloaded constructors that support a variety of techniques for assigning string values to string types. Some of these constructors enable you to create a string by passing in a character array or character pointer. Passing in a character array as a parameter to the constructor of the String creates a CLR-compliant new instance of a string. Passing in a character pointer creates a noncompliant, "unsafe" instance.

Manipulating Strings

The string class provides a host of methods for comparing, searching, and manipulating strings, as shown in Table 10-1.

Table 10-1. Methods and fields for the string class

Method or field	Explanation
Empty	Public static field that represents the empty string.
Compare( )	Overloaded public static method that compares two strings.
CompareOrdinal( )	Overloaded public static method that compares two strings without regard to local or culture.
Concat( )	Overloaded public static method that creates a new string from one or more strings.
Copy( )	Public static method that creates a new string by copying another.

Table 10-1. Methods and fields for the string class (continued)

Method or field	Explanation
Equals( )	Overloaded public static and instance methods that determines if two strings have the same value.
Format( )	Overloaded public static method that formats a string using a format specification.
Intern( )	Public static method that returns a reference to the specified instance of a string.
IsInterned( )	Public static method that returns a reference for the string.
Join( )	Overloaded public static method that concatenates a specified string between each element of a string array.
Chars	The string indexer.
Length	The number of characters in the instance.
Clone( )	Returns the string.
CompareTo( )	Compares this string with another.
CopyTo( )	Copies the specified number of characters to an array of Unicode characters.
EndsWith( )	Indicates whether the specified string matches the end of this string.
Equals( )	Determines if two strings have the same value.
Insert( )	Returns a new string with the specified string inserted.
LastIndexOf( )	Reports the index of the last occurrence of a specified character or string within the string.
PadLeft( )	Right-aligns the characters in the string, padding to the left with spaces or a specified character.
PadRight( )	Left-aligns the characters in the string, padding to the right with spaces or a specified character.
Remove( )	Deletes the specified number of characters.
Split( )	Returns the substrings delimited by the specified characters in a string array.
StartsWith( )	Indicates if the string starts with the specified characters.
Substring( )	Retrieves a substring.
ToCharArray( )	Copies the characters from the string to a character array.
ToLower( )	Returns a copy of the string in lowercase.
ToUpper( )	Returns a copy of the string in uppercase.
Trim( )	Removes all occurrences of a set of specified characters from beginning and end of the string.
TrimEnd( )	Behaves like Trim, but only at the end.
TrimStart( )	Behaves like Trim, but only at the start.

Example 10-1 illustrates the use of some of these methods, including Compare( ), Concat( ) (and the overloaded + operator), Copy( ) (and the = operator), Insert( ), EndsWith( ), and IndexOf( ).

Example 10-1. Working with strings

```
namespace Programming_CSharp
{
    using System;
```

Example 10-1. Working with strings (continued)

```csharp
public class StringTester
{
    static void Main( )
    {
        // create some strings to work with
        string s1 = "abcd";
        string s2 = "ABCD";
        string s3 = @"Liberty Associates, Inc.
                provides custom .NET development,
                on-site Training and Consulting";

        int result;  // hold the results of comparisons

        // compare two strings, case sensitive
        result = string.Compare(s1, s2);
        Console.WriteLine(
            "compare s1: {0}, s2: {1}, result: {2}\n",
            s1, s2, result);

        // overloaded compare, takes boolean "ignore case"
        //(true = ignore case)
        result = string.Compare(s1,s2, true);
        Console.WriteLine("compare insensitive\n");
        Console.WriteLine("s4: {0}, s2: {1}, result: {2}\n",
            s1, s2, result);

        // concatenation method
        string s6 = string.Concat(s1,s2);
        Console.WriteLine(
            "s6 concatenated from s1 and s2: {0}", s6);

        // use the overloaded operator
        string s7 = s1 + s2;
        Console.WriteLine(
            "s7 concatenated from s1 + s2: {0}", s7);

        // the string copy method
        string s8 = string.Copy(s7);
        Console.WriteLine(
            "s8 copied from s7: {0}", s8);

        // use the overloaded operator
        string s9 = s8;
        Console.WriteLine("s9 = s8: {0}", s9);

        // three ways to compare.
        Console.WriteLine(
            "\nDoes s9.Equals(s8)?: {0}",
            s9.Equals(s8));
        Console.WriteLine(
            "Does Equals(s9,s8)?: {0}",
            string.Equals(s9,s8));
```

Example 10-1. Working with strings (continued)

```
        Console.WriteLine(
            "Does s9==s8?: {0}", s9 == s8);

        // Two useful properties: the index and the length
        Console.WriteLine(
            "\nString s9 is {0} characters long. ",
            s9.Length);
        Console.WriteLine(
            "The 5th character is {1}\n",
            s9.Length, s9[4]);

        // test whether a string ends with a set of characters
        Console.WriteLine("s3:{0}\nEnds with Training?: {1}\n",
            s3,
            s3.EndsWith("Training") );
        Console.WriteLine(
            "Ends with Consulting?: {0}",
            s3.EndsWith("Consulting"));

        // return the index of the substring
        Console.WriteLine(
            "\nThe first occurrence of Training ");
        Console.WriteLine ("in s3 is {0}\n",
            s3.IndexOf("Training"));

        // insert the word excellent before "training"
        string s10 = s3.Insert(101,"excellent ");
        Console.WriteLine("s10: {0}\n",s10);

        // you can combine the two as follows:
        string s11 = s3.Insert(s3.IndexOf("Training"),
            "excellent ");
        Console.WriteLine("s11: {0}\n",s11);
    }
  }
}
```
Output
```
compare s1: abcd, s2: ABCD, result: -1

compare insensitive

s4: abcd, s2: ABCD, result: 0

s6 concatenated from s1 and s2: abcdABCD
s7 concatenated from s1 + s2: abcdABCD
s8 copied from s7: abcdABCD
s9 = s8: abcdABCD

Does s9.Equals(s8)?: True
Does Equals(s9,s8)?: True
Does s9==s8?: True
```

Example 10-1. Working with strings (continued)

```
String s9 is 8 characters long.
The 5th character is A

s3:Liberty Associates, Inc.
             provides custom .NET development,
             on-site Training and Consulting
Ends with Training?: False

Ends with Consulting?: True

The first occurrence of Training
in s3 is 101

s10: Liberty Associates, Inc.
             provides custom .NET development,
             on-site excellent Training and Consulting

s11: Liberty Associates, Inc.
             provides custom .NET development,
             on-site excellent Training and Consulting
```

Example 10-1 begins by declaring three strings:

```
string s1 = "abcd";
string s2 = "ABCD";
string s3 = @"Liberty Associates, Inc.
      provides custom .NET development,
      on-site Training and Consulting";
```

The first two are string literals, and the third is a verbatim string literal. We begin by comparing s1 to s2. The Compare method is a public static method of string, and it is overloaded. The first overloaded version takes two strings and compares them:

```
// compare two strings, case sensitive
result = string.Compare(s1, s2);
Console.WriteLine("compare s1: {0}, s2: {1}, result: {2}\n",
    s1, s2, result);
```

This is a case-sensitive comparison and returns different values, depending on the results of the comparison:

- A negative integer, if the first string is less than the second string
- 0, if the strings are equal
- A positive integer, if the first string is greater than the second string

In this case, the output properly indicates that s1 is "less than" s2. In Unicode (as in ASCII), a lowercase letter has a smaller value than an uppercase letter:

```
compare s1: abcd, s2: ABCD, result: -1
```

The second comparison uses an overloaded version of Compare that takes a third, Boolean parameter, whose value determines whether case should be ignored in the comparison. If the value of this "ignore case" parameter is true, the comparison is made without regard to case, as in the following:

```
result = string.Compare(s1,s2, true);
Console.WriteLine("compare insensitive\n");
Console.WriteLine("s4: {0}, s2: {1}, result: {2}\n",
    s1, s2, result);
```

 The result is written with two WriteLine statements to keep the lines short enough to print properly in this book.

This time the case is ignored and the result is 0, indicating that the two strings are identical (without regard to case):

```
compare insensitive

s4: abcd, s2: ABCD, result: 0
```

Example 10-1 then concatenates some strings. There are a couple of ways to accomplish this. You can use the Concat( ) method, which is a static public method of string:

```
string s6 = string.Concat(s1,s2);
```

or you can simply use the overloaded concatenation (+) operator:

```
string s7 = s1 + s2;
```

In both cases, the output reflects that the concatenation was successful:

```
s6 concatenated from s1 and s2: abcdABCD
s7 concatenated from s1 + s2: abcdABCD
```

Similarly, creating a new copy of a string can be accomplished in two ways. First, you can use the static Copy method:

```
string s8 = string.Copy(s7);
```

Otherwise, for convenience, you might instead use the overloaded assignment operator (=), which will implicitly make a copy:

```
string s9 = s8;
```

Once again, the output reflects that each method has worked:

```
s8 copied from s7: abcdABCD
s9 = s8: abcdABCD
```

The .NET String class provides three ways to test for the equality of two strings. First, you can use the overloaded Equals( ) method and ask s9 directly whether s8 is of equal value:

```
Console.WriteLine("\nDoes s9.Equals(s8)?: {0}",
    s9.Equals(s8));
```

A second technique is to pass both strings to String's static method Equals( ):

```
Console.WriteLine("Does Equals(s9,s8)?: {0}",
    string.Equals(s9,s8));
```

A final method is to use the overloaded equality operator (==) of String:

```
Console.WriteLine("Does s9==s8?: {0}", s9 == s8);
```

In each of these cases, the returned result is a Boolean value, as shown in the output:

```
Does s9.Equals(s8)?: True
Does Equals(s9,s8)?: True
Does s9==s8?: True
```

The equality operator is the most natural when you have two string objects. However, some languages, such as VB.NET, do not support operator overloading, so be sure to override the Equals instance method as well.

The next several lines in Example 10-1 use the index operator ([ ]) to find a particular character within a string, and use the Length property to return the length of the entire string:

```
Console.WriteLine("\nString s9 is {0} characters long.,
    s9.Length);
Console.WriteLine("The 5th character is {1}\n",
    s9.Length, s9[4]);
```

Here's the output:

```
String s9 is 8 characters long.
The 5th character is A
```

The EndsWith( ) method asks a string whether a substring is found at the end of the string. Thus, you might ask first s3 if it ends with Training (which it does not) and then if it ends with Consulting (which it does):

```
// test whether a string ends with a set of characters
Console.WriteLine("s3:{0}\nEnds with Training?: {1}\n",
    s3, s3.EndsWith("Training") );
Console.WriteLine("Ends with Consulting?: {0}",
    s3.EndsWith("Consulting"));
```

The output reflects that the first test fails and the second succeeds:

```
s3:Liberty Associates, Inc.
                provides custom .NET development,
                on-site Training and Consulting
Ends with Training?: False
Ends with Consulting?: True
```

The IndexOf( ) method locates a substring within our string, and the Insert( ) method inserts a new substring into a copy of the original string.

The following code locates the first occurrence of Training in s3:

```
Console.WriteLine("\nThe first occurrence of Training ");
Console.WriteLine ("in s3 is {0}\n",
    s3.IndexOf("Training"));
```

The output indicates that the offset is 101:

```
The first occurrence of Training
in s3 is 101
```

You can then use that value to insert the word excellent, followed by a space, into that string. Actually the insertion is into a copy of the string returned by the Insert( ) method and assigned to s10:

```
string s10 = s3.Insert(101,"excellent");
Console.WriteLine("s10: {0}\n",s10);
```

Here's the output:

```
s10: Liberty Associates, Inc.
            provides custom .NET development,
            on-site excellent Training and Consulting
```

Finally, you can combine these operations to make a more efficient insertion statement:

```
string s11 = s3.Insert(s3.IndexOf("Training"),"excellent ");
Console.WriteLine("s11: {0}\n",s11);
```

with the identical output:

```
s11: Liberty Associates, Inc.
            provides custom .NET development,
            on-site excellent Training and Consulting
```

Finding Substrings

The String type provides an overloaded Substring method for extracting substrings from within strings. Both versions take an index indicating where to begin the extraction, and one of the two versions takes a second index to indicate where to end the search. The Substring method is illustrated in Example 10-2.

Example 10-2. Using the Substring() method

```
namespace Programming_CSharp
{
   using System;
   using System.Text;

   public class StringTester
   {
      static void Main( )
      {
         // create some strings to work with
         string s1 = "One Two Three Four";

         int ix;

         // get the index of the last space
         ix=s1.LastIndexOf(" ");
```

Example 10-2. Using the Substring() method (continued)

```
        // get the last word.
        string s2 = s1.Substring(ix+1);

        // set s1 to the substring starting at 0
        // and ending at ix (the start of the last word
        // thus s1 has one two three
        s1 = s1.Substring(0,ix);

        // find the last space in s1 (after two)
        ix = s1.LastIndexOf(" ");

        // set s3 to the substring starting at
        // ix, the space after "two" plus one more
        // thus s3 = "three"
        string s3 = s1.Substring(ix+1);

        // reset s1 to the substring starting at 0
        // and ending at ix, thus the string "one two"
        s1 = s1.Substring(0,ix);

        // reset ix to the space between
        // "one" and "two"
        ix = s1.LastIndexOf(" ");

        // set s4 to the substring starting one
        // space after ix, thus the substring "two"
        string s4 = s1.Substring(ix+1);

        // reset s1 to the substring starting at 0
        // and ending at ix, thus "one"
        s1 = s1.Substring(0,ix);

        // set ix to the last space, but there is
        // none so ix now = -1
        ix = s1.LastIndexOf(" ");

        // set s5 to the substring at one past
        // the last space. there was no last space
        // so this sets s5 to the substring starting
        // at zero
        string s5 = s1.Substring(ix+1);

        Console.WriteLine ("s2: {0}\ns3: {1}",s2,s3);
        Console.WriteLine ("s4: {0}\ns5: {1}\n",s4,s5);
        Console.WriteLine ("s1: {0}\n",s1);

    }
  }
}
```

Output:
s2: Four

Example 10-2. Using the Substring() method (continued)

```
s3: Three
s4: Two
s5: One

s1: One
```

Example 10-2 is not an elegant solution to the problem of extracting words from a string, but it is a good first approximation and it illustrates a useful technique. The example begins by creating a string, s1:

```
string s1 = "One Two Three Four";
```

Then ix is assigned the value of the *last* space in the string:

```
ix=s1.LastIndexOf(" ");
```

Then the substring that begins one space later is assigned to the new string, s2:

```
string s2 = s1.Substring(ix+1);
```

This extracts from x1+1 to the end of the line, assigning to s2 the value Four.

The next step is to remove the word Four from s1. You can do this by assigning to s1 the substring of s1, which begins at 0 and ends at ix:

```
s1 = s1.Substring(0,ix);
```

Reassign ix to the last (remaining) space, which points you to the beginning of the word Three, which we then extract into string s3. Continue like this until s4 and s5 are populated s4 and s5. Finally, print the results:

```
s2: Four
s3: Three
s4: Two
s5: One

s1: One
```

This isn't elegant, but it worked and it illustrates the use of Substring. This is not unlike using pointer arithmetic in C++, but without using pointers and unsafe code.

Splitting Strings

A more effective solution to the problem illustrated in Example 10-2 is to use the Split() method of String, whose job is to parse a string into substrings. To use Split(), pass in an array of delimiters (characters that will indicate a split in the words) and the method returns an array of substrings. Example 10-3 illustrates:

Example 10-3. Using the Split() method

```
namespace Programming_CSharp
{
    using System;
    using System.Text;
```

Example 10-3. Using the Split() method (continued)

```
public class StringTester
{
    static void Main( )
    {
        // create some strings to work with
        string s1 = "One,Two,Three Liberty Associates, Inc.";

        // constants for the space and comma characters
        const char Space = ' ';
        const char Comma = ',';

        // array of delimiters to split the sentence with
        char[] delimiters = new char[]
            {
                Space,
                Comma
            };

        string output = "";
        int ctr = 1;

        // split the string and then iterate over the
        // resulting array of strings
        foreach (string subString in s1.Split(delimiters))
        {
            output += ctr++;
            output += ": ";
            output += subString;
            output += "\n";
        }
        Console.WriteLine(output);
    }
}
```

Output:
```
1: One
2: Two
3: Three
4: Liberty
5: Associates
6:
7: Inc.
```

You start by creating a string to parse:

```
string s1 = "One,Two,Three Liberty Associates, Inc.";
```

The delimiters are set to the space and comma characters. You then call split on this string, and pass the results to the foreach loop:

```
foreach (string subString in s1.Split(delimiters))
```

Start by initializing output to an empty string and then build up the output string in four steps. Concatenate the value of ctr. Next add the colon, then the substring returned by split, then the newline. With each concatenation a new copy of the string is made, and all four steps are repeated for each substring found by split. This repeated copying of string is terribly inefficient.

The problem is that the string type is not designed for this kind of operation. What you want is to create a new string by appending a formatted string each time through the loop. The class you need is StringBuilder.

Manipulating Dynamic Strings

The System.Text.StringBuilder class is used for creating and modifying strings. Semantically, it is the encapsulation of a constructor for a String. The important members of StringBuilder are summarized in Table 10-2.

Table 10-2. StringBuilder methods

Method	Explanation
Capacity	Retrieves or assigns the number of characters the StringBuilder is capable of holding.
Chars	The indexer.
Length	Retrieves or assigns the length of the StringBuilder.
MaxCapacity	Retrieves the maximum capacity of the StringBuilder.
Append( )	Overloaded public method that appends a typed object to the end of the current StringBuilder.
AppendFormat( )	Overloaded public method that replaces format specifiers with the formatted value of an object.
EnsureCapacity( )	Ensures the current StringBuilder has a capacity at least as large as the specified value.
Insert( )	Overloaded public method that inserts an object at the specified position.
Remove( )	Removes the specified characters.
Replace( )	Overloaded public method that replaces all instances of specified characters with new characters.

Unlike String, StringBuilder is mutable; when you modify a StringBuilder, you modify the actual string, not a copy. Example 10-4 replaces the String object in Example 10-3 with a StringBuilder object.

Example 10-4. Using a StringBuilder

```
namespace Programming_CSharp
{
    using System;
    using System.Text;

    public class StringTester
    {
```

Example 10-4. Using a StringBuilder (continued)

```csharp
static void Main( )
{
    // create some strings to work with
    string s1 = "One,Two,Three Liberty Associates, Inc.";

    // constants for the space and comma characters
    const char Space = ' ';
    const char Comma = ',';

    // array of delimiters to split the sentence with
    char[] delimiters = new char[]
    {
        Space,
        Comma
    };

    // use a StringBuilder class to build the
    // output string
    StringBuilder output = new StringBuilder( );
    int ctr = 1;

    // split the string and then iterate over the
    // resulting array of strings
    foreach (string subString in s1.Split(delimiters))
    {
        // AppendFormat appends a formatted string
        output.AppendFormat("{0}: {1}\n",ctr++,subString);
    }
    Console.WriteLine(output);
}
}
}
```

Only the last part of the program is modified. Rather than using the concatenation operator to modify the string, use the `AppendFormat` method of `StringBuilder` to append new, formatted strings as you create them. This is much easier and far more efficient. The output is identical:

```
1: One
2: Two
3: Three
4: Liberty
5: Associates
6:
7: Inc.
```

Regular Expressions

Regular expressions are a powerful language for describing and manipulating text. A regular expression is *applied* to a string—that is, to a set of characters. Often that string is an entire text document.

The result of applying a regular expression to a string is either to return a substring, or to return a new string representing a modification of some part of the original string. Remember that strings are immutable and so cannot be changed by the regular expression.

By applying a properly constructed regular expression to the following string:

```
One,Two,Three Liberty Associates, Inc.
```

you can return any or all of its substrings (e.g., Liberty or One), or modified versions of its substrings (e.g., LIBeRtY or OnE). What the regular expression *does* is determined by the syntax of the regular expression itself.

A regular expression consists of two types of characters: *literals* and *metacharacters*. A literal is a character you wish to match in the target string. A metacharacter is a special symbol that acts as a command to the regular expression parser. The parser is the engine responsible for understanding the regular expression. For example, if you create a regular expression:

```
^(From|To|Subject|Date):
```

this will match any substring with the letters "From," "To," "Subject," or "Date," so long as those letters start a new line (^) and end with a colon (:).

The caret (^) in this case indicates to the regular expression parser that the string you're searching for must begin a new line. The letters "From" and "To" are literals, and the metacharacters left and right parentheses ((,)) and vertical bar (|) are all used to group sets of literals and indicate that any of the choices should match. (Note that ^ is a metacharacter as well, used to indicate the start of the line.)

Thus you would read this line:

```
^(From|To|Subject|Date):
```

as follows: "match any string that begins a new line followed by any of the four literal strings From, To, Subject, or Date followed by a colon."

A full explanation of regular expressions is beyond the scope of this book, but all the regular expressions used in the examples are explained. For a complete understanding of regular expressions, I highly recommend *Mastering Regular Expressions* by Jeffrey E. F. Friedl (published by O'Reilly & Associates, Inc.).

Using Regular Expressions: Regex

The .NET Framework provides an object-oriented approach to regular expression matching and replacement.

C#'s regular expressions are based on Perl5 *regexp*, including lazy quantifiers (??, *?, +?, {n,m}?), positive and negative look ahead, and conditional evaluation.

The Base Class Library namespace System.Text.RegularExpressions is the home to all the .NET Framework objects associated with regular expressions. The central class for regular expression support is Regex, which represents an immutable, compiled regular expression. Although instances of Regex can be created, the class also provides a number of useful static methods. The use of Regex is illustrated in Example 10-5.

Example 10-5. Using the Regex class for regular expressions

```
namespace Programming_CSharp
{
    using System;
    using System.Text;
    using System.Text.RegularExpressions;

    public class Tester
    {
        static void Main()
        {
            string s1 =
                "One,Two,Three Liberty Associates, Inc.";
            Regex theRegex = new Regex(" |, |,");
            StringBuilder sBuilder = new StringBuilder();
            int id = 1;

            foreach (string subString in theRegex.Split(s1))
            {
                sBuilder.AppendFormat(
                    "{0}: {1}\n", id++, subString);
            }
            Console.WriteLine("{0}", sBuilder);
```

Example 10-5. Using the Regex class for regular expressions (continued)

```
        }
    }
}
```

Output:
```
1: One
2: Two
3: Three
4: Liberty
5: Associates
6: Inc.
```

Example 10-5 begins by creating a string, s1, that is identical to the string used in Example 10-4.

```
    string s1 = "One,Two,Three Liberty Associates, Inc.";
```

It also creates a regular expression, which will be used to search that string:

```
    Regex theRegex = new Regex(" |,|, ");
```

One of the overloaded constructors for Regex takes a regular expression string as its parameter. This is a bit confusing. In the context of a C# program, which is the regular expression? Is it the text passed in to the constructor, or the Regex object itself? It is true that the text string passed to the constructor is a regular expression in the traditional sense of the term. From an object-oriented C# point of view, however, the argument to the constructor is just a string of characters; it is theRegex that is the regular expression object.

The rest of the program proceeds like the earlier Example 10-4, except that rather than calling Split( ) on string s1, the Split( ) method of Regex is called. Regex. Split( ) acts in much the same way as String.Split( ), returning an array of strings as a result of matching the regular expression pattern within theRegex.

Regex.Split( ) is overloaded. The simplest version is called on an instance of Regex, as shown in Example 10-5. There is also a static version of this method, which takes a string to search and the pattern to search with, as illustrated in Example 10-6.

Example 10-6. Using static Regex.Split()

```
namespace Programming_CSharp
{
    using System;
    using System.Text;
    using System.Text.RegularExpressions;

    public class Tester
    {
        static void Main( )
        {
            string s1 =
```

Example 10-6. Using static Regex.Split() (continued)

```
        "One,Two,Three Liberty Associates, Inc.";
    StringBuilder sBuilder = new StringBuilder();
    int id = 1;
    foreach (string subStr in Regex.Split(s1," |, |,"))
    {
        sBuilder.AppendFormat("{0}: {1}\n", id++, subStr);
    }
    Console.WriteLine("{0}", sBuilder);
        }
    }
}
```

Example 10-6 is identical to Example 10-5, except that the latter example does not instantiate an object of type Regex. Instead, Example 10-6 uses the static version of Split( ), which takes two arguments: a string to search for and a regular expression string that represents the pattern to match.

The instance method of Split( ) is also overloaded with versions that limit the number of times the split will occur and also determine the position within the target string where the search will begin.

Using Regex Match Collections

Two additional classes in the .NET RegularExpressions namespace allow you to search a string repeatedly, and to return the results in a collection. The collection returned is of type MatchCollection, which consists of zero or more Match objects. Two important properties of a Match object are its length and its value, each of which can be read as illustrated in Example 10-7.

Example 10-7. Using MatchCollection and Match

```
namespace Programming_CSharp
{
    using System;
    using System.Text.RegularExpressions;

    class Test
    {
        public static void Main( )
        {
            string string1 = "This is a test string";

            // find any nonwhitespace followed by whitespace
            Regex theReg = new Regex(@"(\S+)\s");

            // get the collection of matches
            MatchCollection theMatches =
                theReg.Matches(string1);
```

Example 10-7. Using MatchCollection and Match (continued)

```
        // iterate through the collection
        foreach (Match theMatch in theMatches)
        {
            Console.WriteLine(
                "theMatch.Length: {0}", theMatch.Length);

            if (theMatch.Length != 0)
            {
                Console.WriteLine("theMatch: {0}",
                    theMatch.ToString( ));
            }
        }
    }
  }
}
```

Output:
```
theMatch.Length: 5
theMatch: This
theMatch.Length: 3
theMatch: is
theMatch.Length: 2
theMatch: a
theMatch.Length: 5
theMatch: test
```

Example 10-7 creates a simple string to search:

```
string string1 = "This is a test string";
```

and a trivial regular expression to search it:

```
Regex theReg = new Regex(@"(\S+)\s");
```

The string \S finds nonwhitespace, and the plus sign indicates one or more. The string \s (note lowercase) indicates whitespace. Thus, together, this string looks for any nonwhitespace characters followed by whitespace.

 Remember the at (@) symbol before the string creates a verbatim string, which avoids the necessity of escaping the backslash (\) character.

The output shows that the first four words were found. The final word was not found because it is not followed by a space. If you insert a space after the word string and before the closing quote marks, this program will find that word as well.

The length property is the length of the captured substring, and is discussed in the section "Using CaptureCollection," later in this chapter.

Using Regex Groups

It is often convenient to group subexpression matches together so that you can parse out pieces of the matching string. For example, you might want to match on IP addresses and group all IP addresses found anywhere within the string.

 IP addresses are used to locate computers on a network, and typically have the form *x.x.x.x*, where *x* is generally any digit between 0 and 255 (such as 192.168.0.1).

The Group class allows you to create groups of matches based on regular expression syntax, and represents the results from a single grouping expression.

A grouping expression names a group and provides a regular expression; any substring matching the regular expression will be added to the group. For example, to create an ip group you might write:

```
@"(?<ip>(\d|\.)+)\s"
```

The Match class derives from Group, and has a collection called "Groups" that contains all the groups your Match finds.

Creation and use of the Groups collection and Group classes is illustrated in Example 10-8.

Example 10-8. Using the Group class

```
namespace Programming_CSharp
{
    using System;
    using System.Text.RegularExpressions;

    class Test
    {
        public static void Main( )
        {
            string string1 = "04:03:27 127.0.0.0 LibertyAssociates.com";

            // group time = one or more digits or colons followed by space
            Regex theReg = new Regex(@"(?<time>(\d|\:)+)\s" +
            // ip address = one or more digits or dots followed by  space
            @"(?<ip>(\d|\.)+)\s" +
            // site = one or more characters
            @"(?<site>\S+)");

            // get the collection of matches
            MatchCollection theMatches = theReg.Matches(string1);
```

Example 10-8. Using the Group class (continued)

```
        // iterate through the collection
        foreach (Match theMatch in theMatches)
        {
            if (theMatch.Length != 0)
            {
                Console.WriteLine("\ntheMatch: {0}",
                    theMatch.ToString());
                Console.WriteLine("time: {0}",
                    theMatch.Groups["time"]);
                Console.WriteLine("ip: {0}",
                    theMatch.Groups["ip"]);
                Console.WriteLine("site: {0}",
                    theMatch.Groups["site"]);
            }
        }
    }
}
```

Again, Example 10-8 begins by creating a string to search:

```
string string1 = "04:03:27 127.0.0.0 LibertyAssociates.com";
```

This string might be one of many recorded in a web server log file or produced as the result of a search of the database. In this simple example, there are three columns: one for the time of the log entry, one for an IP address, and one for the site, each separated by spaces. Of course, in a real example solving a real-life problem, you might need to do more complex searches and choose to use other delimiters and more complex searches.

In Example 10-8, we want to create a single Regex object to search strings of this type and break them into three groups: time, ip address, and site. The regular expression string is fairly simple, so the example is easy to understand (however, keep in mind that in a real search, you would probably only use a part of the source string rather than the entire source string, as shown here:)

```
// group time = one or more digits or colons
// followed by space
Regex theReg = new Regex(@"(?<time>(\d|\:)+)\s" +
// ip address = one or more digits or dots
// followed by  space
@"(?<ip>(\d|\.)+)\s" +
// site = one or more characters
@"(?<site>\S+)");
```

Let's focus on the characters that create the group:

```
(?<time>
```

The parentheses create a group. Everything between the opening parenthesis (just before the question mark) and the closing parenthesis (in this case, after the + sign) is a single unnamed group.

```
(@"(?<time>(\d|\:)+)
```

The string ?<time> names that group time, and the group is associated with the matching text, which is the regular expression (\d|\:)+)\s". This regular expression can be interpreted as "one or more digits or colons followed by a space."

Similarly, the string ?<ip> names the ip group, and ?<site> names the site group. As Example 10-7 does, Example 10-8 asks for a collection of all the matches:

```
MatchCollection theMatches = theReg.Matches(string1);
```

Example 10-8 iterates through the Matches collection, finding each Match object.

If the Length of the Match is greater than 0, a Match was found; it prints the entire match:

```
Console.WriteLine("\ntheMatch: {0}",
    theMatch.ToString());
```

Here's the output:

```
theMatch: 04:03:27 127.0.0.0 LibertyAssociates.com
```

It then gets the "time" group from the Match's Groups collection and prints that value:

```
Console.WriteLine("time: {0}",
    theMatch.Groups["time"]);
```

This produces the output:

```
time: 04:03:27
```

The code then obtains ip and site groups:

```
Console.WriteLine("ip: {0}",
    theMatch.Groups["ip"]);
Console.WriteLine("site: {0}",
    theMatch.Groups["site"]);
```

This produces the output:

```
ip: 127.0.0.0
site: LibertyAssociates.com
```

In Example 10-8, the Matches collection has only one Match. It is possible, however, to match more than one expression within a string. To see this, modify string1 in Example 10-8 to provide several logFile entries instead of one, as follows:

```
string string1 = "04:03:27 127.0.0.0 LibertyAssociates.com " +
"04:03:28 127.0.0.0 foo.com " +
"04:03:29 127.0.0.0 bar.com " ;
```

This creates three matches in the MatchCollection, called theMatches. Here's the resulting output:

```
theMatch: 04:03:27 127.0.0.0 LibertyAssociates.com
time: 04:03:27
ip: 127.0.0.0
site: LibertyAssociates.com
```

```
theMatch: 04:03:28 127.0.0.0 foo.com
time: 04:03:28
ip: 127.0.0.0
site: foo.com

theMatch: 04:03:29 127.0.0.0 bar.com
time: 04:03:29
ip: 127.0.0.0
site: bar.com
```

In this example, theMatches contains three Match objects. Each time through the outer foreach loop we find the next Match in the collection and display its contents:

```
foreach (Match theMatch in theMatches)
```

For each of the Match items found, you can print out the entire match, various groups, or both.

Using CaptureCollection

Each time a Regex object matches a subexpression, a Capture instance is created and added to a CaptureCollection collection. Each capture object represents a single capture. Each group has its own capture collection of the matches for the subexpression associated with the group.

A key property of the Capture object is its length, which is the length of the captured substring. When you ask Match for its length, it is Capture.Length that you retrieve because Match derives from Group, which in turn derives from Capture.

The regular expression inheritance scheme in .NET allows Match to include in its interface the methods and properties of these parent classes. In a sense, a Group *is-a* capture: it is a capture that encapsulates the idea of grouping subexpressions. A Match, in turn, *is-a* Group: it is the encapsulation of all the groups of subexpressions making up the entire match for this regular expression. (See Chapter 5 for more about the *is-a* relationship and other relationships.)

Typically, you will find only a single Capture in a CaptureCollection, but that need not be so. Consider what would happen if you were parsing a string in which the company name might occur in either of two positions. To group these together in a single match, create the ?<company> group in two places in your regular expression pattern:

```
Regex theReg = new Regex(@"(?<time>(\d|\:)+)\s" +
@"(?<company>\S+)\s" +
@"(?<ip>(\d|\.)+)\s" +
@"(?<company>\S+)\s");
```

This regular expression group captures any matching string of characters that follows time, and also any matching string of characters that follows ip. Given this regular expression, you are ready to parse the following string:

```
string string1 = "04:03:27 Jesse 0.0.0.127 Liberty ";
```

The string includes names in both the positions specified. Here is the result:

```
theMatch: 04:03:27 Jesse 0.0.0.127 Liberty
time: 04:03:27
ip: 0.0.0.127
Company: Liberty
```

What happened? Why is the Company group showing Liberty? Where is the first term, which also matched? The answer is that the second term overwrote the first. The group, however, has captured both. Its Captures collection can demonstrate, as illustrated in Example 10-9.

Example 10-9. Examining the capture collection

```
namespace Programming_CSharp
{
    using System;
    using System.Text.RegularExpressions;

    class Test
    {
        public static void Main( )
        {
            // the string to parse
            // note that names appear in both
            // searchable positions
            string string1 =
                "04:03:27 Jesse 0.0.0.127 Liberty ";

            // regular expression which groups company twice
            Regex theReg = new Regex(@"(?<time>(\d|\:)+)\s" +
                @"(?<company>\S+)\s" +
                @"(?<ip>(\d|\.)+)\s" +
                @"(?<company>\S+)\s");

            // get the collection of matches
            MatchCollection theMatches =
                theReg.Matches(string1);

            // iterate through the collection
            foreach (Match theMatch in theMatches)
            {
                if (theMatch.Length != 0)
                {
                    Console.WriteLine("theMatch: {0}",
                        theMatch.ToString( ));
```

Example 10-9. Examining the capture collection (continued)

```
                Console.WriteLine("time: {0}",
                    theMatch.Groups["time"]);
                Console.WriteLine("ip: {0}",
                    theMatch.Groups["ip"]);
                Console.WriteLine("Company: {0}",
                    theMatch.Groups["company"]);

                // iterate over the captures collection
                // in the company group within the
                // groups collection in the match
                foreach (Capture cap in
                    theMatch.Groups["company"].Captures)
                {
                    Console.WriteLine("cap: {0}",cap.ToString( ));
                }
            }
        }
    }
}
```

Output:
```
theMatch: 04:03:27 Jesse 0.0.0.127 Liberty
time: 04:03:27
ip: 0.0.0.127
Company: Liberty
cap: Jesse
cap: Liberty
```

The code in bold iterates through the Captures collection for the Company group.

```
foreach (Capture cap in
    theMatch.Groups["company"].Captures)
```

Let's review how this line is parsed. The compiler begins by finding the collection that it will iterate over. theMatch is an object that has a collection named Groups. The Groups collection has an indexer that takes a string and returns a single Group object. Thus, the following line returns a single Group object:

```
theMatch.Groups["company"]
```

The Group object has a collection named Captures. Thus, the following line returns a Captures collection for the Group stored at Groups["company"] within the theMatch object:

```
theMatch.Groups["company"].Captures
```

The foreach loop iterates over the Captures collection, extracting each element in turn and assigning it to the local variable cap, which is of type Capture. You can see from the output that there are two capture elements: Jesse and Liberty. The second one overwrites the first in the group, and so the displayed value is just Liberty. However, by examining the Captures collection, you can find both values that were captured.

CHAPTER 11

Handling Exceptions

C#, like many object-oriented languages, handles errors and abnormal conditions with *exceptions*. An exception is an object that encapsulates information about an unusual program occurrence.

It is important to distinguish between bugs, errors, and exceptions. A *bug* is a programmer mistake that should be fixed before the code is shipped. Exceptions are not a protection against bugs. Although a bug might cause an exception to be thrown, you should not rely on exceptions to handle your bugs. Rather, you should fix the bug.

An *error* is caused by user action. For example, the user might enter a number where a letter is expected. Once again, an error might cause an exception, but you can prevent that by catching errors with validation code. Whenever possible, errors should be anticipated and prevented.

Even if you remove all bugs and anticipate all user errors, you will still run into predictable but unpreventable problems, such as running out of memory or attempting to open a file that no longer exists. You cannot prevent exceptions, but you can handle them so that they do not bring down your program.

When your program encounters an exceptional circumstance, such as running out of memory, it *throws* (or "raises") an exception. When an exception is thrown, execution of the current function halts and the stack is unwound until an appropriate exception handler is found.

This means that if the currently running function does not handle the exception, the current function will terminate and the calling function will get a chance to handle the exception. If none of the calling functions handles it, the exception will ultimately be handled by the CLR, which will abruptly terminate your program.

An *exception handler* is a block of code designed to handle the exception you've thrown. Exception handlers are implemented as catch statements. Ideally, if the exception is caught and handled, the program can fix the problem and continue.

Even if your program can't continue, by catching the exception you have an opportunity to print a meaningful error message and terminate gracefully.

If there is code in your function that must run regardless of whether an exception is encountered (e.g., to release resources you've allocated), you can place that code in a finally block, where it is certain to run, even in the presence of exceptions.

Throwing and Catching Exceptions

In C#, you can throw only objects of type System.Exception, or objects derived from that type. The CLR System namespace includes a number of exception types that can be used by your program. These exception types include ArgumentNullException, InvalidCastException, and OverflowException, as well as many others.

The throw Statement

To signal an abnormal condition in a C# class, you throw an exception. To do this, use the keyword throw. This line of code creates a new instance of System.Exception and then throws it:

```
throw new System.Exception( );
```

Throwing an exception immediately halts execution while the CLR searches for an exception handler. If an exception handler cannot be found in the current method, the runtime unwinds the stack, popping up through the calling methods until a handler is found. If the runtime returns all the way through Main( ) without finding a handler, it terminates the program. Example 11-1 illustrates.

Example 11-1. Throwing an exception

```
namespace Programming_CSharp
{
    using System;

    public class Test
    {
        public static void Main( )
        {
            Console.WriteLine("Enter Main...");
            Test t = new Test( );
            t.Func1( );
            Console.WriteLine("Exit Main...");

        }

        public void Func1( )
        {
            Console.WriteLine("Enter Func1...");
            Func2( );
            Console.WriteLine("Exit Func1...");
```

Example 11-1. Throwing an exception (continued)

```
        }

        public void Func2()
        {
            Console.WriteLine("Enter Func2...");
            throw new System.Exception();
            Console.WriteLine("Exit Func2...");
        }
    }
}
```

Output:
```
Enter Main...
Enter Func1...
Enter Func2...

Exception occurred: System.Exception: An exception of type
System.Exception was thrown.
   at Programming_CSharp.Test.Func2()
       in ...exceptions01.cs:line 26
   at Programming_CSharp.Test.Func1()
       in ...exceptions01.cs:line 20
   at Programming_CSharp.Test.Main()
       in ...exceptions01.cs:line 12
```

This simple example writes to the console as it enters and exits each method. Main()
creates an instance of type Test and call Func1(). After printing out the Enter Func1
message, Func1() immediately calls Func2(). Func2() prints out the first message and
throws an object of type System.Exception.

Execution immediately stops, and the CLR looks to see if there is a handler in Func2().
There is not, and so the runtime unwinds the stack (never printing the exit statement) to Func1(). Again, there is no handler, and the runtime unwinds the stack back
to Main(). With no exception handler there, the default handler is called, which prints
the error message.

The catch Statement

In C#, an exception handler is called a *catch block* and is created with the catch
keyword.

In Example 11-2, the throw statement is executed within a try block, and a catch
block is used to announce that the error has been handled.

Example 11-2. Catching an exception
```
namespace Programming_CSharp
{
    using System;
```

Example 11-2. Catching an exception (continued)

```
public class Test
{
    public static void Main( )
    {
        Console.WriteLine("Enter Main...");
        Test t = new Test( );
        t.Func1( );
        Console.WriteLine("Exit Main...");

    }

    public void Func1( )
    {
        Console.WriteLine("Enter Func1...");
        Func2( );
        Console.WriteLine("Exit Func1...");
    }

    public void Func2( )
    {
        Console.WriteLine("Enter Func2...");
        try
        {
            Console.WriteLine("Entering try block...");
            throw new System.Exception( );
            Console.WriteLine("Exiting try block...");
        }
        catch
        {
            Console.WriteLine(
                "Exception caught and handled.");
        }
        Console.WriteLine("Exit Func2...");
    }
}
```

Output:
```
Enter Main...
Enter Func1...
Enter Func2...
Entering try block...
Exception caught and handled.
Exit Func2...
Exit Func1...
Exit Main...
```

Example 11-2 is identical to Example 11-1 except that now the program includes a try/catch block. You would typically put the try block around a potentially "dangerous" statement, such as accessing a file, allocating memory, and so forth.

Following the try statement is a generic catch statement. The catch statement in Example 11-2 is generic because you haven't specified what kind of exceptions to catch. In this case, the statement will catch any exceptions that are thrown. Using catch statements to catch specific types of exceptions is discussed later in this chapter.

Taking corrective action

In Example 11-2, the catch statement simply reports that the exception has been caught and handled. In a real-world example, you might take corrective action to fix the problem that caused an exception to be thrown. For example, if the user is trying to open a read-only file, you might invoke a method that allows the user to change the attributes of the file. If the program has run out of memory, you might give the user an opportunity to close other applications. If all else fails, the catch block can print an error message so that the user knows what went wrong.

Unwinding the call stack

Examine the output of Example 11-2 carefully. You see the code enter Main( ), Func1( ), Func2( ), and the try block. You never see it exit the try block, though it does exit Func2( ), Func1( ), and Main( ). What happened?

When the exception is thrown, execution halts immediately and is handed to the catch block. It *never* returns to the original code path. It never gets to the line that prints the exit statement for the try block. The catch block handles the error, and then execution falls through to the code following catch.

Without catch the call stack unwinds, but with catch it does not unwind as a result of the exception. The exception is now handled; there are no more problems and the program continues. This becomes a bit clearer if you move the try/catch blocks up to Func1( ), as shown in Example 11-3.

Example 11-3. Catch in a calling function

```
namespace Programming_CSharp
{
    using System;

    public class Test
    {
        public static void Main()
        {
            Console.WriteLine("Enter Main...");
            Test t = new Test();
            t.Func1();
            Console.WriteLine("Exit Main...");

        }

        public void Func1()
        {
```

Example 11-3. Catch in a calling function (continued)

```
        Console.WriteLine("Enter Func1...");
        try
        {
            Console.WriteLine("Entering try block...");
            Func2();
            Console.WriteLine("Exiting try block...");
        }
        catch
        {
            Console.WriteLine(
                "Exception caught and handled.");
        }

        Console.WriteLine("Exit Func1...");
    }

    public void Func2()
    {
        Console.WriteLine("Enter Func2...");
        throw new System.Exception();
        Console.WriteLine("Exit Func2...");
    }
  }
}
```

Output:
```
Enter Main...
Enter Func1...
Entering try block...
Enter Func2...
Exception caught and handled.
Exit Func1...
Exit Main...
```

This time the exception is not handled in Func2( ); it is handled in Func1( ). When Func2( ) is called, it prints the Enter statement and then throws an exception. Execution halts and the runtime looks for a handler, but there isn't one. The stack unwinds, and the runtime finds a handler in Func1( ). The catch statement is called, and execution resumes immediately following the catch statement, printing the Exit statement for Func1( ) and then for Main( ).

Make sure you are comfortable with why the Exiting Try Block statement and the Exit Func2 statement are not printed. This is a classic case where putting the code into a debugger and then stepping through it can make things very clear.

Creating dedicated catch statements

So far, you've been working only with generic catch statements. You can create dedicated catch statements that handle only some exceptions and not others, based on the type of exception thrown. Example 11-4 illustrates how to specify which exception you'd like to handle.

Example 11-4. Specifying the exception to catch

```
namespace Programming_CSharp
{
    using System;

    public class Test
    {
        public static void Main( )
        {
            Test t = new Test( );
            t.TestFunc( );
        }

        // try to divide two numbers
        // handle possible exceptions
        public void TestFunc( )
        {
            try
            {
                double a = 5;
                double b = 0;
                Console.WriteLine ("{0} / {1} = {2}",
                    a, b, DoDivide(a,b));
            }

            // most derived exception type first
            catch (System.DivideByZeroException)
            {
                Console.WriteLine(
                    "DivideByZeroException caught!");
            }

            catch (System.ArithmeticException)
            {
                Console.WriteLine(
                    "ArithmeticException caught!");
            }

            // generic exception type last
            catch
            {
                Console.WriteLine(
                    "Unknown exception caught");
            }

        }

        // do the division if legal
        public double DoDivide(double a, double b)
```

Example 11-4. Specifying the exception to catch (continued)

```
        {
            if (b == 0)
                throw new System.DivideByZeroException( );
            if (a == 0)
                throw new System.ArithmeticException( );
            return a/b;
        }
    }
}
```

Output:
```
DivideByZeroException caught!
```

In this example, the DoDivide( ) method will not let you divide zero by another number, nor will it let you divide a number by zero. It throws an instance of DivideByZeroException if you try to divide by zero. If you try to divide zero by another number, there is no appropriate exception—dividing zero by another number is a legal mathematical operation and shouldn't throw an exception at all. For the sake of this example, assume you don't want to allow division by zero; you will throw an ArithmeticException.

When the exception is thrown, the runtime examines each exception handler *in order* and matches the first one it can. When you run this with a=5 and b=7, the output is:

```
5 / 7 = 0.7142857142857143
```

As you'd expect, no exception is thrown. However, when you change the value of a to 0, the output is:

```
ArithmeticException caught!
```

The exception is thrown, and the runtime examines the first exception, DivideByZeroException. Because this does not match, it goes on to the next handler, ArithmeticException, which does match.

In a final pass through, suppose you change a to 7 and b to 0. This throws the DivideByZeroException.

You have to be particularly careful with the order of the catch statements, because the DivideByZeroException is derived from ArithmeticException. If you reverse the catch statements, the DivideByZeroException will match the ArithmeticException handler and the exception will never get to the DivideByZeroException handler. In fact, if their order is reversed, it will be impossible for *any* exception to reach the DivideByZeroException handler. The compiler will recognize that the DivideByZeroException handler cannot be reached and will report a compile error!

It is possible to distribute your try/catch statements, catching some specific exceptions in one function and more generic exceptions in higher, calling functions. Your design goals should dictate the exact design.

Assume you have a method A that calls another method B, which in turn calls method C. Method C calls method D, which then calls method E. Method E is deep in your code; methods B and A are higher up. If you anticipate that method E might throw an exception, you should create a try/catch block deep in your code to catch that exception as close as possible to the place where the problem arises. You might also want to create more general exception handlers higher up in the code in case unanticipated exceptions slip by.

The finally Statement

In some instances, throwing an exception and unwinding the stack can create a problem. For example, if you have opened a file or otherwise committed a resource, you might need an opportunity to close the file or flush the buffer.

 In C#, this is less of a problem than in other languages, such as C++, because the garbage collection prevents the exception from causing a memory leak.

In the event, however, that there is some action you must take regardless of whether an exception is thrown, such as closing a file, you have two strategies to choose from. One approach is to enclose the dangerous action in a try block and then to close the file in both the catch and try blocks. However, this is an ugly duplication of code, and it's error prone. C# provides a better alternative in the finally block.

The code in the finally block is guaranteed to be executed regardless of whether an exception is thrown. The TestFunc() method in Example 11-5 simulates opening a file as its first action. The method undertakes some mathematical operations, and the file is closed. It is possible that some time between opening and closing the file an exception will be thrown. If this were to occur, it would be possible for the file to remain open. The developer knows that no matter what happens, at the end of this method the file should be closed, so the file close function call is moved to a finally block, where it will be executed regardless of whether an exception is thrown.

Example 11-5. Using a finally block

```
namespace Programming_CSharp
{
    using System;

    public class Test
    {
```

Example 11-5. Using a finally block (continued)

```
public static void Main()
{
    Test t = new Test();
    t.TestFunc();
}

// try to divide two numbers
// handle possible exceptions
public void TestFunc()
{
    try
    {
        Console.WriteLine("Open file here");
        double a = 5;
        double b = 0;
        Console.WriteLine ("{0} / {1} = {2}",
            a, b, DoDivide(a,b));
        Console.WriteLine (
            "This line may or may not print");
    }

    // most derived exception type first
    catch (System.DivideByZeroException)
    {
        Console.WriteLine(
            "DivideByZeroException caught!");
    }
    catch
    {
        Console.WriteLine("Unknown exception caught");
    }
    finally
    {
        Console.WriteLine ("Close file here.");
    }

}

// do the division if legal
public double DoDivide(double a, double b)
{
    if (b == 0)
        throw new System.DivideByZeroException();
    if (a == 0)
        throw new System.ArithmeticException();
    return a/b;
}
}
}
```

Output:
```
Open file here
```

Example 11-5. Using a finally block (continued)

```
DivideByZeroException caught!
Close file here.
```

Output when b = 12:
```
Open file here
5 / 12 = 0.416666666666667
This line may or may not print
Close file here.
```

In this example, one of the catch blocks has been eliminated to save space and a finally block has been added. Whether or not an exception is thrown, the finally block is executed, and so in both output examples you see the message: Close file here.

 A finally block can be created with or without catch blocks, but a finally block requires a try block to execute. It is an error to exit a finally block with break, continue, return, or goto.

Exception Objects

So far you've been using the exception as a sentinel—that is, the presence of the exception signals the errors—but you haven't touched or examined the Exception object itself. The System.Exception object provides a number of useful methods and properties. The Message property provides information about the exception, such as why it was thrown. The Message property is read-only; the code throwing the exception can set the Message property as an argument to the exception constructor.

The HelpLink property provides a link to the help file associated with the exception. This property is read/write.

The StackTrace property is read-only and is set by the runtime. In Example 11-6, the Exception.HelpLink property is set and retrieved to provide information to the user about the DivideByZeroException. The StackTrace property of the exception is used to provide a stack trace for the error statement. A stack trace displays the *call stack*: the series of method calls that lead to the method in which the exception was thrown.

Example 11-6. Working with an exception object

```
namespace Programming_CSharp
{
    using System;

    public class Test
    {
        public static void Main()
        {
```

Example 11-6. Working with an exception object (continued)

```
        Test t = new Test( );
        t.TestFunc( );
}

// try to divide two numbers
// handle possible exceptions
public void TestFunc( )
{
    try
    {
        Console.WriteLine("Open file here");
        double a = 12;
        double b = 0;
        Console.WriteLine ("{0} / {1} = {2}",
            a, b, DoDivide(a,b));
        Console.WriteLine (
          "This line may or may not print");
    }

    // most derived exception type first
    catch (System.DivideByZeroException e)
    {
        Console.WriteLine(
            "\nDivideByZeroException! Msg: {0}",
            e.Message);
        Console.WriteLine(
            "\nHelpLink: {0}", e.HelpLink);
        Console.WriteLine(
            "\nHere's a stack trace: {0}\n",
            e.StackTrace);
    }
    catch
    {
        Console.WriteLine(
            "Unknown exception caught");
    }
    finally
    {
        Console.WriteLine (
          "Close file here.");
    }

}

// do the division if legal
public double DoDivide(double a, double b)
{
    if (b == 0)
    {
        DivideByZeroException e =
          new DivideByZeroException( );
        e.HelpLink =
```

Example 11-6. Working with an exception object (continued)

```
                "http://www.libertyassociates.com";
            throw e;
        }
        if (a == 0)
            throw new ArithmeticException( );
        return a/b;
    }
}
}
```

Output:
```
Open file here

DivideByZeroException! Msg: Attempted to divide by zero.

HelpLink: http://www.libertyassociates.com

Here's a stack trace:
at Programming_CSharp.Test.DoDivide(Double a, Double b)
 in c:\...exception06.cs:line 56
at Programming_CSharp.Test.TestFunc( )
in...exception06.cs:line 22

Close file here.
```

In the output, the stack trace lists the methods in the reverse order in which they were called; that is, it shows that the error occurred in DoDivide( ), which was called by TestFunc( ). When methods are deeply nested, the stack trace can help you understand the order of method calls.

In this example, rather than simply throwing a DivideByZeroException, you create a new instance of the exception:

```
DivideByZeroException e = new DivideByZeroException( );
```

You do not pass in a custom message, and so the default message will be printed:

```
DivideByZeroException! Msg: Attempted to divide by zero.
```

You can modify this line of code to pass in a default message:

```
new DivideByZeroException(
    "You tried to divide by zero which is not meaningful");
```

In this case, the output message will reflect the custom message:

```
DivideByZeroException! Msg:
You tried to divide by zero which is not
meaningful
```

Before throwing the exception, set the HelpLink property:

```
e.HelpLink = "http://www.libertyassociates.com";
```

When this exception is caught, the program prints the message and the `HelpLink`:

```
catch (System.DivideByZeroException e)
{
    Console.WriteLine("\nDivideByZeroException! Msg: {0}",
        e.Message);
    Console.WriteLine("\nHelpLink: {0}", e.HelpLink);
```

This allows you to provide useful information to the user. In addition, it prints the `StackTrace` by getting the `StackTrace` property of the exception object:

```
Console.WriteLine("\nHere's a stack trace: {0}\n",
    e.StackTrace);
```

The output of this call reflects a full `StackTrace` leading to the moment the exception was thrown:

```
Here's a stack trace:
at Programming_CSharp.Test.DoDivide(Double a, Double b)
 in c:\...exception06.cs:line 56
at Programming_CSharp.Test.TestFunc()
in...exception06.cs:line 22
```

Note that I've shortened the pathnames, so your printout might look a little different.

Custom Exceptions

The intrinsic exception types the CLR provides, coupled with the custom messages shown in the previous example, will often be all you need to provide extensive information to a catch block when an exception is thrown. There will be times, however, when you want to provide more extensive information or need special capabilities in your exception. It is a trivial matter to create your own *custom exception* class; the only restriction is that it must derive (directly or indirectly) from `System.ApplicationException`. Example 11-7 illustrates the creation of a custom exception.

Example 11-7. Creating a custom exception

```
namespace Programming_CSharp
{
    using System;

    public class MyCustomException :
        System.ApplicationException
    {
        public MyCustomException(string message):
            base(message)
        {

        }
    }

    public class Test
    {
```

Example 11-7. Creating a custom exception (continued)

```csharp
public static void Main( )
{
   Test t = new Test( );
   t.TestFunc( );
}

// try to divide two numbers
// handle possible exceptions
public void TestFunc( )
{
   try
   {
      Console.WriteLine("Open file here");
      double a = 0;
      double b = 5;
      Console.WriteLine ("{0} / {1} = {2}",
         a, b, DoDivide(a,b));
      Console.WriteLine (
         "This line may or may not print");
   }

   // most derived exception type first
   catch (System.DivideByZeroException e)
   {
      Console.WriteLine(
         "\nDivideByZeroException! Msg: {0}",
         e.Message);
      Console.WriteLine(
         "\nHelpLink: {0}\n", e.HelpLink);
   }
   catch (MyCustomException e)
   {
      Console.WriteLine(
         "\nMyCustomException! Msg: {0}",
         e.Message);
      Console.WriteLine(
         "\nHelpLink: {0}\n", e.HelpLink);
   }
   catch
   {
      Console.WriteLine(
         "Unknown exception caught");
   }
   finally
   {
      Console.WriteLine ("Close file here.");
   }

}

// do the division if legal
public double DoDivide(double a, double b)
```

Example 11-7. Creating a custom exception (continued)

```
    {
        if (b == 0)
        {
            DivideByZeroException e =
                new DivideByZeroException( );
            e.HelpLink=
                "http://www.libertyassociates.com";
            throw e;
        }
        if (a == 0)
        {
            MyCustomException e =
                new MyCustomException(
                    "Can't have zero divisor");
            e.HelpLink =
            "http://www.libertyassociates.com/NoZeroDivisor.htm";
            throw e;
        }
        return a/b;
    }
  }
}
```

MyCustomException is derived from System.ApplicationException and consists of nothing more than a constructor that takes a string message that it passes to its base class, as described in Chapter 4. In this case, the advantage of creating this custom exception class is that it better reflects the particular design of the Test class, in which it is not legal to have a zero divisor. Using the ArithmeticException rather than a custom exception would work as well, but it might confuse other programmers because a zero divisor wouldn't normally be considered an arithmetic error.

Rethrowing Exceptions

You might want your catch block to take some initial corrective action and then rethrow the exception to an outer try block (in a calling function). It might rethrow the *same* exception, or it might throw a different one. If it throws a different one, it may want to embed the original exception inside the new one so that the calling method can understand the exception history. The InnerException property of the new exception retrieves the original exception.

Because the InnerException is also an exception, it too might have an inner exception. Thus, an entire chain of exceptions can be nested one within the other, much like Ukrainian dolls are contained one within the other. Example 11-8 illustrates.

Example 11-8. Rethrowing and inner exceptions

```
namespace Programming_CSharp
{
```

Example 11-8. Rethrowing and inner exceptions (continued)

```csharp
using System;

public class MyCustomException : System.ApplicationException
{
   public MyCustomException(
      string message,Exception inner):
      base(message,inner)
   {

   }
}

public class Test
{
   public static void Main( )
   {
      Test t = new Test( );
      t.TestFunc( );
   }

   public void TestFunc( )
   {
      try
      {
         DangerousFunc1( );
      }

      // if you catch a custom exception
      // print the exception history
      catch (MyCustomException e)
      {
         Console.WriteLine("\n{0}", e.Message);
         Console.WriteLine(
            "Retrieving exception history...");
         Exception inner =
            e.InnerException;
         while (inner != null)
         {
            Console.WriteLine(
               "{0}",inner.Message);
            inner =
               inner.InnerException;
         }
      }
   }

   public void DangerousFunc1( )
   {
      try
      {
         DangerousFunc2( );
      }
```

Example 11-8. Rethrowing and inner exceptions (continued)

```
        // if you catch any exception here
        // throw a custom exception
        catch(System.Exception e)
        {
            MyCustomException ex =
                new MyCustomException(
                    "E3 - Custom Exception Situation!",e);
            throw ex;
        }
    }

    public void DangerousFunc2()
    {
        try
        {
            DangerousFunc3();
        }

        // if you catch a DivideByZeroException take some
        // corrective action and then throw a general exception
        catch (System.DivideByZeroException e)
        {
            Exception ex =
                new Exception(
                    "E2 - Func2 caught divide by zero",e);
            throw ex;
        }
    }

    public void DangerousFunc3()
    {
        try
        {
            DangerousFunc4();
        }
        catch (System.ArithmeticException)
        {
            throw;
        }

        catch (System.Exception)
        {
            Console.WriteLine(
                "Exception handled here.");
        }
    }

    public void DangerousFunc4()
    {
        throw new DivideByZeroException("E1 - DivideByZero Exception");
```

Example 11-8. Rethrowing and inner exceptions (continued)
```
        }
    }
}
```
Output:
```
E3 - Custom Exception Situation!
Retrieving exception history...
E2 - Func2 caught divide by zero
E1 - DivideByZeroException
```

Because this code has been stripped to the essentials, the output might leave you scratching your head. The best way to see how this code works is to use the debugger to step through it.

Begin by calling DangerousFunc1( ) in a try block:

```
    try
    {
        DangerousFunc1( );
    }
```

DangerousFunc1( ) calls DangerousFunc2( ), which calls DangerousFunc3( ), which in turn calls DangerousFunc4( ). All these calls are in their own try blocks. At the end, DangerousFunc4( ) throws a DivideByZeroException. System.DivideByZeroException normally has its own error message, but you are free to pass in a custom message. Here, to make it easier to identify the sequence of events, the custom message E1 – DivideByZeroException is passed in.

The exception thrown in DangerousFunc4( ) is caught in the catch block in DangerousFunc3( ). The logic in DangerousFunc3( ) is that if any ArithmeticException is caught (such as DivideByZeroException), it takes no action; it just rethrows the exception:

```
    catch (System.ArithmeticException)
    {
        throw;
    }
```

The syntax to rethrow the exact same exception (without modifying it) is just the word throw.

The exception is thus rethrown to DangerousFunc2( ), which catches it, takes some corrective action, and throws a new exception of type Exception. In the constructor to that new exception, DangerousFunc2( ) passes in a custom message (E2 - Func2 caught divide by zero) *and the original exception.* Thus, the original exception (E1) becomes the InnerException for the new exception (E2). DangerousFunc2( ) then throws this new E2 exception to DangerousFunc1( ).

DangerousFunc1( ) catches the exception, does some work, and creates a new exception of type MyCustomException. It passes a new string (E3 - Custom Exception Situation!) to the constructor as well as the exception it just caught (E2). Remember, the exception it just caught is the exception with a DivideByZeroException (E1) as its inner exception. At this point, you have an exception of type MyCustomException (E3), with an inner exception of type Exception (E2), which in turn has an inner exception of type DivideByZeroException (E1). All this is then thrown to the test function, where it is caught.

When the catch function runs, it prints the message:

```
E3 - Custom Exception Situation!
```

and then drills down through the layers of inner exceptions, printing their messages:

```
while (inner != null)
{
    Console.WriteLine("{0}",inner.Message);
    inner = inner.InnerException;
}
```

The output reflects the chain of exceptions thrown and caught:

```
Retrieving exception history...
E2 - Func2 caught divide by zero
E1 - DivideByZero Exception
```

CHAPTER 12

Delegates and Events

When a head of state dies, the president of the United States typically does not have time to attend the funeral personally. Instead, he dispatches a delegate. Often this delegate is the vice president, but sometimes the VP is unavailable and the president must send someone else, such as the secretary of state or even the first lady. He doesn't want to "hardwire" his delegated authority to a single person; he might delegate this responsibility to anyone who is able to execute the correct international protocol.

The president defines in advance what authority will be delegated (attend the funeral), what parameters will be passed (condolences, kind words), and what value he hopes to get back (good will). He then assigns a particular person to that delegated responsibility at "runtime" as the course of his presidency progresses.

In programming, you are often faced with situations where you need to execute a particular action, but you don't know in advance which method, or even which object, you'll want to call upon to execute that action. For example, a button might know that it must notify *some* object when it is pushed, but it might not know which object or objects need to be notified. Rather than wiring the button to a particular object, you will connect the button to a *delegate* and then resolve that delegate to a particular method when the program executes.

In the early, dark, and primitive days of computing, a program would begin execution and then proceed through its steps until it completed. If the user was involved, the interaction was strictly controlled and limited to filling in fields.

Today's Graphical User Interface (GUI) programming model requires a different approach, known as *event-driven programming*. A modern program presents the user interface and waits for the user to take an action. The user might take many different actions, such as choosing among menu selections, pushing buttons, updating text fields, clicking icons, and so forth. Each action causes an event to be raised. Other events can be raised without direct user action, such as events that correspond to timer ticks of the internal clock, email being received, file-copy operations completing, etc.

An event is the encapsulation of the idea that "something happened" to which the program must respond. Events and delegates are tightly coupled concepts because flexible event handling requires that the response to the event be dispatched to the appropriate event handler. An event handler is typically implemented in C# as a delegate.

Delegates are also used as callbacks so that one class can say to another "do this work and when you're done, let me know." This second usage will be covered in detail in Chapter 21. Delegates can also be used to specify methods that will only become known at runtime. This topic is developed in the following sections.

Delegates

In C#, delegates are first-class objects, fully supported by the language. Technically, a delegate is a reference type used to encapsulate a method with a specific signature and return type. You can encapsulate any matching method in that delegate. (In C++ and many other languages, you can accomplish this requirement with function pointers and pointers to member functions. Unlike function pointers, delegates are object-oriented and type-safe.)

A delegate is created with the delegate keyword, followed by a return type and the signature of the methods that can be delegated to it, as in the following:

```
public delegate int WhichIsFirst(object obj1, object obj2);
```

This declaration defines a delegate named WhichIsFirst, which will encapsulate any method that takes two objects as parameters and returns an int.

Once the delegate is defined, you can encapsulate a member method with that delegate by instantiating the delegate, i.e., passing in a method that matches the return type and signature.

Using Delegates to Specify Methods at Runtime

Delegates specify the kinds of methods that can handle events and implement callbacks in your applications. They can also specify static and instance methods that won't be known until runtime.

Suppose, for example, that you want to create a simple container class called a Pair that can hold and sort any two objects passed to it. You can't know in advance what kind of objects a Pair will hold, but by creating methods within those objects to which the sorting task can be delegated, you can delegate responsibility for determining their order to the objects themselves.

Different objects will sort differently; for example, a Pair of counter objects might sort in numeric order, while a Pair of Buttons might sort alphabetically by their name. As the author of the Pair class, you want the objects in the pair to have the responsibility of knowing which should be first and which should be second. To accomplish this, insist that the objects to be stored in the Pair provide a method that tells you how to sort the objects.

Define the method you require by creating a delegate that defines the signature and return type of the method the object (e.g., Button) must provide to allow the Pair to determine which object should be first and which should be second.

The Pair class defines a delegate, WhichIsFirst. The Sort method will take a parameter, an instance of WhichIsFirst. When the Pair needs to know how to order its objects it will invoke the delegate passing in its two objects as parameters. The responsibility for deciding which of the two objects comes first is delegated to the method encapsulated by the delegate.

To test the delegate, create two classes: a Dog class and a Student class. Dogs and Students have little in common, except they both implement methods that can be encapsulated by WhichComesFirst; thus both Dog objects and Student objects are eligible to be held within Pair objects.

In the test program, create a couple of Students and a couple of Dogs, and store them each in a Pair. You will then create delegate objects to encapsulate their respective methods that match the delegate signature and return type, and ask the Pair objects to sort the Dog and Student objects. Let's take this step by step.

Begin by creating a Pair constructor that takes two objects and stashes them away in a private array:

```
public class Pair
{

    // two objects, added in order received
    public Pair(object firstObject, object secondObject)
    {
        thePair[0] = firstObject;
        thePair[1] = secondObject;
    }
    // hold both objects
    private object[]thePair = new object[2];
```

Next, you override ToString( ) to obtain the string value of the two objects:

```
public override string ToString()
{
    return thePair [0].ToString() + ", " + thePair[1].ToString();
}
```

You now have two objects in your Pair and you can print out their values. You're ready to sort them and print the results of the sort. You can't know in advance what kind of objects you will have, so you would like to delegate the responsibility of deciding which object comes first in the sorted Pair to the objects themselves. Thus, you require that each object stored in a Pair implement a method to return which of the two comes first. The method will take two objects (of whatever type) and return an enumerated value: theFirstComesFirst if the first object comes first, and theSecondComesFirst if the second does.

These required methods will be encapsulated by the delegate WhichIsFirst that you define within the Pair class:

```
public delegate comparison
    WhichIsFirst(object obj1, object obj2);
```

The return value is of type comparison, the enumeration.

```
public enum comparison
{
    theFirstComesFirst = 1,
    theSecondComesFirst = 2
}
```

Any static method that takes two objects and returns a comparison can be encapsulated by this delegate at runtime.

You can now define the Sort method for the Pair class:

```
public void Sort(WhichIsFirst theDelegatedFunc)
{
    if (theDelegatedFunc(thePair[0],thePair[1]) ==
        comparison.theSecondComesFirst)
    {
        object temp = thePair[0];
        thePair[0] = thePair[1];
        thePair[1] = temp;
    }
}
```

This method takes a parameter: a delegate of type WhichIsFirst named theDelegatedFunc. The Sort( ) method delegates responsibility for deciding which of the two objects in the Pair comes first to the method encapsulated by that delegate. It invokes the delegated method in the body of the Sort( ) method and examines the return value, which will be one of the two enumerated values of comparsion.

If the value returned is theSecondComesFirst, the objects within the pair are swapped; otherwise no action is taken.

Notice that theDelegatedFunc is the name of the parameter to represent the method encapsulated by the delegate. You can assign any method (with the appropriate return value and signature) to this parameter. It is as if you had a method that took an int as a parameter:

```
int SomeMethod (int myParam){//...}
```

The parameter name is myParam, but you can pass in any int value or variable. Similarly the parameter name in the delegate example is theDelegatedFunc, but you can pass in any method that meets the return value and signature defined by the delegate WhichIsFirst.

Imagine you are sorting students by name. Write a method that returns theFirstComesFirst if the first student's name comes first, and returns theSecondComesFirst if the second student's name does. If you pass in "Amy, Beth," the method returns theFirstComesFirst, and if you pass in "Beth, Amy," it returns theSecondComesFirst. If you get back theSecondComesFirst, the Sort method reverses the items in its array, setting Amy to the first position and Beth to the second.

Now add one more method, ReverseSort, which will put the items into the array in reverse order:

```
public void ReverseSort(WhichIsFirst theDelegatedFunc)
{
    if (theDelegatedFunc(thePair[0], thePair[1]) ==
            comparison.theFirstComesFirst)
    {
        object temp = thePair[0];
        thePair[0] = thePair[1];
        thePair[1] = temp;
    }
}
```

The logic here is identical to the Sort(), except that this method performs the swap if the delegated method says that the first item comes first. Because the delegated function thinks the first item comes first, and this is a reverse sort, the result you want is for the second item to come first. This time if you pass in "Amy, Beth," the delegated function returns theFirstComesFirst (i.e., Amy should come first). However, because this is a *reverse* sort it swaps the values, setting Beth first. This allows you to use the same delegated function as you used with Sort, without forcing the object to support a function that returns the reverse sorted value.

Now all you need are some objects to sort. You'll create two absurdly simple classes: Student and Dog. Assign Student objects a name at creation:

```
public class Student
{
    public Student(string name)
    {
        this.name = name;
    }
}
```

The Student class requires two methods, one to override ToString() and the other to be encapsulated as the delegated method.

Student must override ToString() so that the ToString() method in Pair, which invokes ToString() on the contained objects, will work properly; the implementation does nothing more than return the student's name (which is already a string object):

```
public override string ToString()
{
    return name;
}
```

It must also implement a method to which `Pair.Sort()` can delegate the responsibility of determining which of two objects comes first:

```
return (String.Compare(s1.name, s2.name) < 0 ?
    comparison.theFirstComesFirst :
    comparison.theSecondComesFirst);
```

`String.Compare()` is a .NET Framework method on the `String` class that compares two strings and returns less than zero if the first is smaller, greater than zero if the second is smaller, and zero if they are the same. This method is discussed in some detail in Chapter 10. Notice that the logic here returns theFirstComesFirst only if the first string is smaller; if they are the same or the second is larger, this method returns theSecondComesFirst.

Notice that the `WhichStudentComesFirst()` method takes two objects as parameters and returns a comparison. This qualifies it to be a `Pair.WhichIsFirst` delegated method, whose signature and return value it matches.

The second class is `Dog`. For our purposes, `Dog` objects will be sorted by weight, lighter dogs before heavier. Here's the complete declaration of `Dog`:

```
public class Dog
{
    public Dog(int weight)
    {
        this.weight=weight;
    }

    // dogs are ordered by weight
    public static comparison WhichDogComesFirst(
        Object o1, Object o2)
    {
        Dog d1 = (Dog) o1;
        Dog d2 = (Dog) o2;
        return d1.weight > d2.weight ?
          comparison.theSecondComesFirst :
            comparison.theFirstComesFirst;
    }
    public override string ToString()
    {
        return weight.ToString();
    }
    private int weight;
}
```

Notice that the `Dog` class also overrides `ToString` and implements a static method with the correct signature for the delegate. Notice also that the `Dog` and `Student` delegate methods do not have the same name. They do not need to have the same name, as they will be assigned to the delegate dynamically at runtime.

You can call your delegated method names anything you like, but creating parallel names (e.g., WhichDogComesFirst and WhichStudentComesFirst) makes the code easier to read, understand, and maintain.

Example 12-1 is the complete program, which illustrates how the delegate methods are invoked.

Example 12-1. Working with delegates

```
namespace Programming_CSharp
{
    using System;

    public enum comparison
    {
        theFirstComesFirst = 1,
        theSecondComesFirst = 2
    }

    // a simple collection to hold 2 items
    public class Pair
    {
        // the delegate declaration
        public delegate comparison
            WhichIsFirst(object obj1, object obj2);

        // passed in constructor take two objects,
        // added in order received
        public Pair(
            object firstObject,
            object secondObject)
        {
            thePair[0] = firstObject;
            thePair[1] = secondObject;
        }

        // public method which orders the two objects
        // by whatever criteria the object likes!
        public void Sort(
            WhichIsFirst theDelegatedFunc)
        {
            if (theDelegatedFunc(thePair[0],thePair[1])
                == comparison.theSecondComesFirst)
            {
                object temp = thePair[0];
                thePair[0] = thePair[1];
                thePair[1] = temp;
            }
        }
    }
```

Example 12-1. Working with delegates (continued)

```csharp
    // public method which orders the two objects
    // by the reverse of whatever criteria the object likes!
    public void ReverseSort(
        WhichIsFirst theDelegatedFunc)
    {
        if (theDelegatedFunc(thePair[0],thePair[1]) ==
            comparison.theFirstComesFirst)
        {
            object temp = thePair[0];
            thePair[0] = thePair[1];
            thePair[1] = temp;
        }
    }

    // ask the two objects to give their string value
    public override string ToString()
    {
        return thePair[0].ToString() + ", "
            + thePair[1].ToString();
    }

    // private array to hold the two objects
    private object[] thePair = new object[2];
}

public class Dog
{
    public Dog(int weight)
    {
        this.weight=weight;
    }

    // dogs are ordered by weight
    public static comparison WhichDogComesFirst(
        Object o1, Object o2)
    {
        Dog d1 = (Dog) o1;
        Dog d2 = (Dog) o2;
        return d1.weight > d2.weight ?
            comparison.theSecondComesFirst :
            comparison.theFirstComesFirst;
    }
    public override string ToString()
    {
        return weight.ToString();
    }
    private int weight;
}

public class Student
{
```

Example 12-1. Working with delegates (continued)

```
    public Student(string name)
    {
        this.name = name;
    }

    // students are ordered alphabetically
    public static comparison
        WhichStudentComesFirst(Object o1, Object o2)
    {
        Student s1 = (Student) o1;
        Student s2 = (Student) o2;
        return (String.Compare(s1.name, s2.name) < 0 ?
            comparison.theFirstComesFirst :
            comparison.theSecondComesFirst);
    }

    public override string ToString( )
    {
        return name;
    }
    private string name;
}

public class Test
{
    public static void Main( )
    {
        // create two students and two dogs
        // and add them to Pair objects
        Student Jesse = new Student("Jesse");
        Student Stacey = new Student ("Stacey");
        Dog Milo = new Dog(65);
        Dog Fred = new Dog(12);

        Pair studentPair = new Pair(Jesse,Stacey);
        Pair dogPair = new Pair(Milo, Fred);
        Console.WriteLine("studentPair\t\t\t: {0}",
            studentPair.ToString( ));
        Console.WriteLine("dogPair\t\t\t\t: {0}",
            dogPair.ToString( ));

        // Instantiate  the delegates
        Pair.WhichIsFirst  theStudentDelegate =
            new Pair.WhichIsFirst(
            Student.WhichStudentComesFirst);

        Pair.WhichIsFirst theDogDelegate =
            new Pair.WhichIsFirst(
            Dog.WhichDogComesFirst);

        // sort using the delegates
        studentPair.Sort(theStudentDelegate);
```

Example 12-1. Working with delegates (continued)

```
        Console.WriteLine("After Sort studentPair\t\t: {0}",
            studentPair.ToString( ));
        studentPair.ReverseSort(theStudentDelegate);
        Console.WriteLine("After ReverseSort studentPair\t: {0}",
            studentPair.ToString( ));

        dogPair.Sort(theDogDelegate);
        Console.WriteLine("After Sort dogPair\t\t: {0}",
            dogPair.ToString( ));
        dogPair.ReverseSort(theDogDelegate);
        Console.WriteLine("After ReverseSort dogPair\t: {0}",
            dogPair.ToString( ));
    }
  }
}
```

Output:
```
studentPair                : Jesse, Stacey
dogPair                    : 65, 12
After Sort studentPair     : Jesse, Stacey
After ReverseSort studentPair : Stacey, Jesse
After Sort dogPair         : 12, 65
After ReverseSort dogPair  : 65, 12
```

The Test program creates two Student objects and two Dog objects and then adds
them to Pair containers. The student constructor takes a string for the student's
name and the dog constructor takes an int for the dog's weight.

```
    Student Jesse = new Student("Jesse");
    Student Stacey = new Student ("Stacey");
    Dog Milo = new Dog(65);
    Dog Fred = new Dog(12);

    Pair studentPair = new Pair(Jesse,Stacey);
    Pair dogPair = new Pair(Milo, Fred);
    Console.WriteLine("studentPair\t\t\t: {0}",
        studentPair.ToString( ));
    Console.WriteLine("dogPair\t\t\t\t: {0}",
        dogPair.ToString( ));
```

It then prints the contents of the two Pair containers to see the order of the objects.
The output looks like this:

```
    studentPair        : Jesse, Stacey
    dogPair            : 65, 12
```

As expected, the objects are in the order in which they were added to the Pair containers. We next instantiate two delegate objects:

```
    Pair.WhichIsFirst  theStudentDelegate =
        new Pair.WhichIsFirst(
        Student.WhichStudentComesFirst);
```

```
Pair.WhichIsFirst theDogDelegate =
    new Pair.WhichIsFirst(
    Dog.WhichDogComesFirst);
```

The first delegate, theStudentDelegate, is created by passing in the appropriate static method from the Student class. The second delegate, theDogDelegate, is passed a static method from the Dog class.

The delegates are now objects that can be passed to methods. Pass the delegates first to the Sort method of the Pair object, and then to the ReverseSort method. The results are printed to the console:

```
After Sort studentPair          : Jesse, Stacey
After ReverseSort studentPair    : Stacey, Jesse
After Sort dogPair               : 12, 65
After ReverseSort dogPair        : 65, 12
```

Static Delegates

A disadvantage of Example 12-1 is that it forces the calling class, in this case Test, to instantiate the delegates it needs in order to sort the objects in a Pair. It would be nice to get the delegate from the Student or Dog class. You can do this by giving each class its own static delegate. Thus, you can modify Student to add the following:

```
public static readonly Pair.WhichIsFirst OrderStudents =
    new Pair.WhichIsFirst(Student.WhichStudentComesFirst);
```

This creates a static, readonly delegate named OrderStudents.

 Marking OrderStudents readonly denotes that once this static field is created, it will not be modified.

You can create a similar delegate within Dog:

```
public static readonly Pair.WhichIsFirst OrderDogs =
    new Pair.WhichIsFirst(Dog. WhichDogComesFirst);
```

These are now static fields of their respective classes. Each is prewired to the appropriate method within the class. You can invoke delegates without declaring a local delegate instance. Just pass in the static delegate of the class:

```
studentPair.Sort(Student.OrderStudents);
Console.WriteLine("After Sort studentPair\t\t: {0}",
    studentPair.ToString());
studentPair.ReverseSort(Student.OrderStudents);
Console.WriteLine("After ReverseSort studentPair\t: {0}",
    studentPair.ToString());

dogPair.Sort(Dog.OrderDogs);
Console.WriteLine("After Sort dogPair\t\t: {0}",
    dogPair.ToString());
```

```
    dogPair.ReverseSort(Dog.OrderDogs);
    Console.WriteLine("After ReverseSort dogPair\t: {0}",
        dogPair.ToString());
```

The output from these changes is identical to the previous example.

Delegates as Properties

The problem with static delegates is that they must be instantiated—whether or not they are ever used—as with Student and Dog in the previous example. You can improve these classes by changing the static delegate fields to properties.

For Student, take out the declaration:

```
public static readonly Pair.WhichIsFirst OrderStudents =
    new Pair.WhichIsFirst(Student.WhichStudentComesFirst);
```

and replace it with the following:

```
public static Pair.WhichIsFirst OrderStudents
{
    get
    {
        return new Pair.WhichIsFirst(WhichStudentComesFirst);
    }
}
```

Similarly, replace the Dog static field with:

```
public static Pair.WhichIsFirst OrderDogs
{
    get
    {
        return new Pair.WhichIsFirst(WhichDogComesFirst);
    }
}
```

The assignment of the delegates is unchanged:

```
        studentPair.Sort(Student.OrderStudents);
        dogPair.Sort(Dog.OrderDogs);
```

When the OrderStudent property is accessed, the delegate is created:

```
return new Pair.WhichIsFirst(WhichStudentComesFirst);
```

The key advantage is that the delegate is not created until it is requested. This allows the test class to determine when it needs a delegate but still allows the details of the creation of the delegate to be the responsibility of the Student (or Dog) class.

Setting Order of Execution with Arrays of Delegates

Delegates can help you create a system in which the user can dynamically decide on the order of operations. Suppose you have an image processing system in which an

---

image can be manipulated in a number of well-defined ways, such as blurring, sharpening, rotating, filtering, and so forth. Assume, as well, that the order in which these effects are applied to the image is important. The user wishes to choose from a menu of effects, applying all that he likes, and then telling the image processor to run the effects, one after the other in the order that he has specified.

You can create delegates for each operation and add them to an ordered collection, such as an array, in the order you'd like them to execute. Once all the delegates are created and added to the collection, simply iterate over the array, invoking each delegated method in turn.

Begin by creating a class Image to represent the image that will be processed by the ImageProcessor:

```
public class Image
{
    public Image( )
    {
        Console.WriteLine("An image created");
    }
}
```

You can imagine that this stands in for a *.gif* or *.jpeg* file or other image.

The ImageProcessor then declares a delegate. You can of course define your delegate to return any type and take any parameters you like. For this example you'll define the delegate to encapsulate any method that returns void and takes no arguments:

```
public delegate void DoEffect( );
```

The ImageProcessor then declares a number of methods, each of which processes an image and each of which matches the return type and signature of the delegate:

```
public static void Blur( )
{
    Console.WriteLine("Blurring image");
}

public static void Filter( )
{
    Console.WriteLine("Filtering image");
}

public static void Sharpen( )
{
    Console.WriteLine("Sharpening image");
}

public static void Rotate( )
{
    Console.WriteLine("Rotating image");
}
```

In a production environment these methods would be very complicated, and they'd actually do the work of blurring, filtering, sharpening, and rotating the image.

The ImageProcessor class needs an array to hold the delegates that the user picks, a variable to hold the running total of how many effects are in the array, and of course a variable for the image itself:

```
DoEffect[] arrayOfEffects;
Image image;
int numEffectsRegistered = 0;
```

The ImageProcessor also needs a method to add delegates to the array:

```
public void AddToEffects(DoEffect theEffect)
{
    if (numEffectsRegistered >= 10)
    {
        throw new Exception("Too many members in array");
    }
    arrayOfEffects[numEffectsRegistered++] = theEffect;

}
```

It needs another method to actually call each method in turn:

```
public void ProcessImages()
{
    for (int i = 0;i < numEffectsRegistered;i++)
    {
        arrayOfEffects[i]();
    }
}
```

Finally, you need only declare the static delegates that the client can call, hooking them to the processing methods:

```
public DoEffect BlurEffect = new DoEffect(Blur);
public DoEffect SharpenEffect = new DoEffect(Sharpen);
public DoEffect FilterEffect = new DoEffect(Filter);
public DoEffect RotateEffect = new DoEffect(Rotate);
```

In a production environment in which you might have dozens of effects, you might choose to make these properties rather than static methods. That would save creating the effects unless they are needed, at the cost of making the program slightly more complicated.

The client code would normally have an interactive user-interface component, but you simulate that by choosing the effects, adding them to the array, and then calling ProcessImage, as shown in Example 12-2.

Example 12-2. Using an array of delegates

```csharp
namespace Programming_CSharp
{
    using System;

    // the image which we'll manipulate
    public class Image
    {
        public Image( )
        {
            Console.WriteLine("An image created");
        }
    }

    public class ImageProcessor
    {
        // declare the delegate
        public delegate void DoEffect( );

        // create various static delegates tied to member methods
        public DoEffect BlurEffect =
            new DoEffect(Blur);
        public DoEffect SharpenEffect =
            new DoEffect(Sharpen);
        public DoEffect FilterEffect =
            new DoEffect(Filter);
        public DoEffect RotateEffect =
            new DoEffect(Rotate);

        // the constructor initializes the image and the array
        public ImageProcessor(Image image)
        {
            this.image = image;
            arrayOfEffects = new DoEffect[10];
        }

        // in a production environment we'd use a more
        // flexible collection.
        public void AddToEffects(DoEffect theEffect)
        {
            if (numEffectsRegistered >= 10)
            {
                throw new Exception(
                    "Too many members in array");
            }
            arrayOfEffects[numEffectsRegistered++]
                = theEffect;

        }

        // the image processing methods...
        public static void Blur( )
        {
```

Example 12-2. Using an array of delegates (continued)

```csharp
        Console.WriteLine("Blurring image");
    }

    public static void Filter()
    {
        Console.WriteLine("Filtering image");
    }

    public static void Sharpen()
    {
        Console.WriteLine("Sharpening image");
    }

    public static void Rotate()
    {
        Console.WriteLine("Rotating image");
    }


    public void ProcessImages()
    {
        for (int i = 0;i < numEffectsRegistered;i++)
        {
            arrayOfEffects[i]();
        }
    }

    // private member variables...
    private DoEffect[] arrayOfEffects;
    private Image image;
    private int numEffectsRegistered = 0;

}

// test driver
public class Test
{
    public static void Main()
    {
        Image theImage = new Image();

        // no ui to keep things simple, just pick the
        // methods to invoke, add them in the required
        // order, and then call on the image processor to
        // run them in the order added.
        ImageProcessor theProc =
            new ImageProcessor(theImage);
        theProc.AddToEffects(theProc.BlurEffect);
        theProc.AddToEffects(theProc.FilterEffect);
        theProc.AddToEffects(theProc.RotateEffect);
        theProc.AddToEffects(theProc.SharpenEffect);
```

Example 12-2. Using an array of delegates (continued)

```
        theProc.ProcessImages( );
    }
  }
}
```

Output:
An image created
Blurring image
Filtering image
Rotating image
Sharpening image

In the Test class of Example 12-2, the ImageProcessor is instantiated and effects are added. If the user chooses to blur the image before filtering it, it is a simple matter to add the delegates to the array in the appropriate order. Similarly, any given operation can be repeated as often as the user desires, just by adding more delegates to the collection.

You can imagine displaying the order of operations in a list box that might allow the user to reorder the methods, moving them up and down the list at will. As the operations are reordered, you need only change their sort order in the collection. You might even decide to capture the order of operations to a database and then load them dynamically, instantiating delegates as dictated by the records you've stored in the database.

Delegates provide the flexibility to determine dynamically which methods will be called, in what order, and how often.

Multicasting

At times it is desirable to *multicast*, or call two implementing methods through a single delegate. This becomes particularly important when handling events (discussed later in this chapter).

The goal is to have a single delegate that invokes more than one method. This is different from having a collection of delegates, each of which invokes a single method. In the previous example, the collection was used to order the various delegates. It was possible to add a single delegate to the collection more than once and to use the collection to reorder the delegates to control their order of invocation.

With multicasting, you create a single delegate that will call multiple encapsulated methods. For example, when a button is pressed, you might want to take more than one action. You could implement this by giving the button a collection of delegates, but it is cleaner and easier to create a single multicast delegate.

 You can use multicasting with delegates that return a value (that is, they have a non-void return type). However, you'll only get one return value: the return value of the delegate that was invoked last.

Two delegates can be combined with the addition operator (+). The result is a new multicast delegate that invokes both of the original implementing methods. For example, assuming Writer and Logger are delegates, the following line will combine them and produce a new multicast delegate named myMulticastDelegate:

```
myMulticastDelegate = Writer + Logger;
```

You can add delegates to a multicast delegate using the plus-equals (+=) operator. This operator adds the delegate on the right side of the operator to the multicast delegate on the left. For example, assuming Transmitter and myMulticastDelegate are delegates, the following line adds Transmitter to myMulticastDelegate:

```
myMulticastDelegate += Transmitter;
```

To see how multicast delegates are created and used, let's walk through a complete example. In Example 12-3, you create a class called MyClassWithDelegate, which defines a delegate that takes a string as a parameter and returns void:

```
public delegate void StringDelegate(string s);
```

You then define a class called MyImplementingClass, which has three methods, all of which return void and take a string as a parameter: WriteString, LogString, and TransmitString. The first writes the string to standard output, the second simulates writing to a log file, and the third simulates transmitting the string across the Internet. You instantiate the delegates to invoke the appropriate methods:

```
Writer("String passed to Writer\n");
Logger("String passed to Logger\n");
Transmitter("String passed to Transmitter\n");
```

To see how to combine delegates, create another Delegate instance:

```
MyClassWithDelegate.StringDelegate myMulticastDelegate;
```

Assign to it the result of "adding" two existing delegates:

```
myMulticastDelegate = Writer + Logger;
```

Add an additional delegate to this delegate using the += operator:

```
myMulticastDelegate += Transmitter;
```

Finally, selectively remove delegates using the -= operator:

```
DelegateCollector -= Logger;
```

Example 12-3. Combining delegates

```
namespace Programming_CSharp
{
    using System;

    public class MyClassWithDelegate
    {
        // the delegate declaration
        public delegate void StringDelegate(string s);
```

Example 12-3. Combining delegates (continued)

```
    }

    public class MyImplementingClass
    {
        public static void WriteString(string s)
        {
            Console.WriteLine("Writing string {0}", s);
        }

        public static void LogString(string s)
        {
            Console.WriteLine("Logging string {0}", s);
        }

        public static void TransmitString(string s)
        {
            Console.WriteLine("Transmitting string {0}", s);
        }

    }

    public class Test
    {
        public static void Main( )
        {
            // define three StringDelegate objects
            MyClassWithDelegate.StringDelegate
                Writer, Logger, Transmitter;

            // define another StringDelegate
            // to act as the multicast delegate
            MyClassWithDelegate.StringDelegate
                myMulticastDelegate;

            // Instantiate the first three delegates,
            // passing in methods to encapsulate
            Writer = new MyClassWithDelegate.StringDelegate(
                MyImplementingClass.WriteString);
            Logger = new MyClassWithDelegate.StringDelegate(
                MyImplementingClass.LogString);
            Transmitter =
                new MyClassWithDelegate.StringDelegate(
                MyImplementingClass.TransmitString);

            // Invoke the Writer delegate method
            Writer("String passed to Writer\n");

            // Invoke the Logger delegate method
            Logger("String passed to Logger\n");

            // Invoke the Transmitter delegate method
```

Example 12-3. Combining delegates (continued)

```
        Transmitter("String passed to Transmitter\n");

        // Tell the user you are about to combine
        // two delegates into the multicast delegate
        Console.WriteLine(
            "myMulticastDelegate = Writer + Logger");

        // combine the two delegates, the result is
        // assigned to myMulticast Delegate
        myMulticastDelegate = Writer + Logger;

        // Call the delegated methods, two methods
        // will be invoked
        myMulticastDelegate(
            "First string passed to Collector");

        // Tell the user you are about to add
        // a third delegate to the multicast
        Console.WriteLine(
            "\nmyMulticastDelegate += Transmitter");

        // add the third delegate
        myMulticastDelegate += Transmitter;

        // invoke the three delegated methods
        myMulticastDelegate(
            "Second string passed to Collector");

        // tell the user you are about to remove
        // the logger delegate
        Console.WriteLine(
            "\nmyMulticastDelegate -= Logger");

        // remove the logger delegate
        myMulticastDelegate -= Logger;

        // invoke the two remaining
        // delegated methods
        myMulticastDelegate(
            "Third string passed to Collector");
    }
  }
}
```

Output:
```
Writing string String passed to Writer

Logging string String passed to Logger

Transmitting string String passed to Transmitter

myMulticastDelegate = Writer + Logger
Writing string First string passed to Collector
```

Example 12-3. Combining delegates (continued)

```
Logging string First string passed to Collector

myMulticastDelegate += Transmitter
Writing string Second string passed to Collector
Logging string Second string passed to Collector
Transmitting string Second string passed to Collector

myMulticastDelegate -= Logger
Writing string Third string passed to Collector
Transmitting string Third string passed to Collector
```

In the test portion of Example 12-3, the delegate instances are defined and the first three (Writer, Logger, and Transmitter) are invoked. The fourth delegate, myMulticastDelegate, is then assigned the combination of the first two and it is invoked, causing both delegated methods to be called. The third delegate is added, and when myMulticastDelegate is invoked, all three delegated methods are called. Finally, Logger is removed; when myMulticastDelegate is invoked, only the two remaining methods are called.

The power of multicast delegates is best understood in terms of events, discussed in the next section. When an event such as a button press occurs, an associated multicast delegate can invoke a series of event-handler methods that will respond to the event.

Events

Graphical user interfaces (GUIs), Windows, and web browsers (such as Microsoft), require that programs respond to *events*. An event might be a button push, a menu selection, the completion of a file transfer, and so forth. In short, something happens and you must respond to it. You cannot predict the order in which events will arise. The system is quiescent until the event, and then it springs into action to handle the event.

In a GUI environment, any number of widgets can *raise* an event. For example, when you click a button, it might raise the Click event. When you add to a drop-down list, it might raise a ListChanged event.

Other classes will be interested in responding to these events. How they respond is not of interest to the class raising the event. The button says "I was clicked," and the responding classes react appropriately.

Publishing and Subscribing

In C#, any object can *publish* a set of events to which other classes can *subscribe*. When the publishing class raises an event, all the subscribed classes are notified.

This design implements the Publish/Subscribe (Observer) Pattern described in the seminal work "Design Patterns," by Gamma, et al. (Addison Wesley, 1995). Gamma describes the intent of this pattern, "Define a one-to-many dependency between objects so that when one object changes state, all its dependents are notified and updated automatically."

With this mechanism, your object can say "Here are things I can notify you about," and other classes might sign up, saying "Yes, let me know when that happens." For example, a button might notify any number of interested observers when it is clicked. The button is called the *publisher* because the button publishes the Click event and the other classes are the *subscribers* because they subscribe to the Click event.

Events and Delegates

Events in C# are implemented with delegates. The publishing class defines a delegate that the subscribing classes must implement. When the event is raised, the subscribing class's methods are invoked through the delegate.

A method that handles an event is called an *event handler*. You can declare your event handlers as you would any other delegate.

By convention, event handlers in the .NET Framework return void and take two parameters. The first parameter is the *source* of the event; that is, the publishing object. The second parameter is an object derived from EventArgs. It is recommended that your event handlers follow this design pattern.

EventArgs is the base class for all event data. Other than its constructor, the EventArgs class inherits all its methods from Object, though it does add a public static field empty, which represents an event with no state (to allow for the efficient use of events with no state). The EventArgs derived class contains information about the event.

Events are properties of the class publishing the event. The keyword event controls how the event property is accessed by the subscribing classes. The event keyword is designed to maintain the publish/subscribe idiom.

Suppose you want to create a Clock class that uses events to notify potential subscribers whenever the local time changes value by one second. Call this event OnSecondChange. Declare the event and its event-handler delegate type as follows:

```
[attributes] [modifiers] event type
    member-name
```

For example:

```
public event SecondChangeHandler OnSecondChange;
```

This example has no attributes (attributes are covered in Chapter 18). The modifier can be abstract, new, override, static, virtual, or one of the four access modifiers—in this case, public.

The modifier is followed by the keyword event.

The type is the delegate to which you want to associate the event—in this case, SecondChangeHandler.

The member name is the name of the event, in this case OnSecondChange. It is customary to begin events with the word On.

Altogether, this declaration states that OnSecondChange is an event that is implemented by a delegate of type SecondChangeHandler.

The declaration for the SecondChangeHandler delegate is:

```
public delegate void SecondChangeHandler(
    object clock,
    TimeInfoEventArgs timeInformation
    );
```

This declares the delegate. As stated earlier, by convention an event handler returns void and takes two parameters: the source of the event (in this case clock) and an object derived from EventArgs—in this case, TimeInfoEventArgs. TimeInfoEventArgs is defined as follows:

```
public class TimeInfoEventArgs : EventArgs
{
    public TimeInfoEventArgs(int hour, int minute, int second)
    {
        this.hour = hour;
        this.minute = minute;
        this.second = second;
    }
    public readonly int hour;
    public readonly int minute;
    public readonly int second;
}
```

The TimeInfoEventArgs object will have information about the current hour, minute, and second. It defines a constructor and three public, read-only integer variables.

In addition to a delegate and an event, a Clock has three member variables: hour, minute, and second, as well as a single method, Run( ):

```
public void Run( )
{
    for(;;)
    {
        // sleep 10 milliseconds
        Thread.Sleep(10);

        // get the current time
```

```
        System.DateTime dt = System.DateTime.Now;

        // if the second has changed
        // notify the subscribers
        if (dt.Second != second)
        {
            // create the TimeInfoEventArgs object
            // to pass to the subscriber
            TimeInfoEventArgs timeInformation =
                new TimeInfoEventArgs(dt.Hour,dt.Minute,dt.Second);

            // if anyone has subscribed, notify them
            if (OnSecondChange != null)
            {
                OnSecondChange(this,timeInformation);
            }
        }

        // update the state
        this.second = dt.Second;
        this.minute = dt.Minute;
        this.hour = dt.Hour;

    }
}
```

Run creates an infinite for loop that periodically checks the system time. If the time has changed from the Clock object's current time, it notifies all its subscribers and then updates its own state.

The first step is to sleep for 10 milliseconds:

```
Thread.Sleep(10);
```

This makes use of a static method of the Thread class from the System.Threading namespace, which is covered in some detail in Chapter 20. The call to Sleep() prevents the loop from running so tightly that little else on the computer gets done.

After sleeping for 10 milliseconds, the method checks the current time:

```
System.DateTime dt = System.DateTime.Now;
```

About every 100 times it checks, the second will have incremented. The method notices that change and notifies its subscribers. To do so, it first creates a new TimeInfoEventArgs object:

```
if (dt.Second != second)
{
    // create the TimeInfoEventArgs object
    // to pass to the subscriber
    TimeInfoEventArgs timeInformation =
        new TimeInfoEventArgs(dt.Hour,dt.Minute,dt.Second);
```

It then notifies the subscribers by firing the OnSecondChange event:

```
    // if anyone has subscribed, notify them
    if (OnSecondChange != null)
```

```
        {
            OnSecondChange(this,timeInformation);
        }
    }
```

If an event has no subscribers registered, it will evaluate to null. The test above checks that the value is not null, ensuring that there are subscribers before calling OnSecondChange.

You will remember that OnSecondChange takes two arguments: the source of the event and the object derived from EventArgs. In the snippet, you see that the clock's this reference is passed because the clock is the source of the event. The second parameter is the TimeInfoEventArgs object. timeInformation is created on the line above.

Raising the event will invoke whatever methods have been registered with the Clock class through the delegate. We examine this in a moment.

Once the event is raised, update the state of the Clock class:

```
this.second = dt.Second;
this.minute = dt.Minute;
this.hour = dt.Hour;
```

 Note that no attempt has been made to make this code thread safe. Thread safety and synchronization are discussed in Chapter 20.

All that is left is to create classes that can subscribe to this event. You'll create two. Your first will be the DisplayClock class. The job of DisplayClock is not to keep track of time, but rather to display the current time to the console.

The example simplifies this class down to two methods. The first is a helper method named Subscribe. Subscribe's job is to subscribe to the clock's OnSecondChange event. The second method is the event handler TimeHasChanged:

```
public class DisplayClock
{
    public void Subscribe(Clock theClock)
    {
        theClock.OnSecondChange +=
            new Clock.SecondChangeHandler(TimeHasChanged);
    }

    public void TimeHasChanged(
        object theClock, TimeInfoEventArgs ti)
    {
        Console.WriteLine("Current Time: {0}:{1}:{2}",
            ti.hour.ToString(),
            ti.minute.ToString(),
            ti.second.ToString());
    }
}
```

When the first method, Subscribe, is invoked, it creates a new SecondChangeHandler delegate, passing in its event-handler method TimeHasChanged. It then registers that delegate with the OnSecondChange event of Clock.

Create a second class that will also respond to this event, LogCurrentTime. This class would normally log the event to a file, but for our demonstration purposes, it will log to the standard console:

```
public class LogCurrentTime
{
    public void Subscribe(Clock theClock)
    {
        theClock.OnSecondChange +=
            new Clock.SecondChangeHandler(WriteLogEntry);
    }

    // this method should write to a file
    // we write to the console to see the effect
    // this object keeps no state
    public void WriteLogEntry(
        object theClock, TimeInfoEventArgs ti)
    {
        Console.WriteLine("Logging to file: {0}:{1}:{2}",
            ti.hour.ToString( ),
            ti.minute.ToString( ),
            ti.second.ToString( ));
    }
}
```

Although in this example these two classes are very similar, in a production program any number of disparate classes might subscribe to an event.

Notice that events are added using the += operator. This allows new events to be added to the Clock object's OnSecondChange event without destroying the events already registered. When LogCurrentTime subscribes to the OnSecondChange event, you do not want the event to lose track of the fact that DisplayClock has already subscribed.

All that remains is to create a Clock class and the DisplayClock class, and tell the latter to subscribe to the event. Then create a LogCurrentTime class and tell it to subscribe as well. Finally, tell the Clock to run. All this is shown in Example 12-4.

Example 12-4. Working with events

```
namespace Programming_CSharp
{
    using System;
    using System.Threading;

    // a class to hold the information about the event
    // in this case it will hold only information
```

Example 12-4. Working with events (continued)

```csharp
// available in the clock class, but could hold
// additional state information
public class TimeInfoEventArgs : EventArgs
{
    public TimeInfoEventArgs(int hour, int minute, int second)
    {
        this.hour = hour;
        this.minute = minute;
        this.second = second;
    }
    public readonly int hour;
    public readonly int minute;
    public readonly int second;
}

// our subject -- it is this class that other classes
// will observe. This class publishes one event:
// OnSecondChange. The observers subscribe to that event
public class Clock
{
    // the delegate the subscribers must implement
    public delegate void SecondChangeHandler
        (
        object clock,
        TimeInfoEventArgs timeInformation
        );

    // the event we publish
    public event SecondChangeHandler OnSecondChange;

    // set the clock running
    // it will raise an event for each new second
    public void Run( )
    {
        for(;;)
        {
            // sleep 10 milliseconds
            Thread.Sleep(10);

            // get the current time
            System.DateTime dt = System.DateTime.Now;

            // if the second has changed
            // notify the subscribers
            if (dt.Second != second)
            {
                // create the TimeInfoEventArgs object
                // to pass to the subscriber
                TimeInfoEventArgs timeInformation =
                    new TimeInfoEventArgs(
                        dt.Hour,dt.Minute,dt.Second);
```

Example 12-4. Working with events (continued)

```
                    // if anyone has subscribed, notify them
                    if (OnSecondChange != null)
                    {
                        OnSecondChange(
                            this,timeInformation);
                    }
                }

            // update the state
            this.second = dt.Second;
            this.minute = dt.Minute;
            this.hour = dt.Hour;

        }
    }
    private int hour;
    private int minute;
    private int second;
}

// an observer. DisplayClock subscribes to the
// clock's events. The job of DisplayClock is
// to display the current time
public class DisplayClock
{
    // given a clock, subscribe to
    // its SecondChangeHandler event
    public void Subscribe(Clock theClock)
    {
        theClock.OnSecondChange +=
            new Clock.SecondChangeHandler(TimeHasChanged);
    }

    // the method that implements the
    // delegated functionality
    public void TimeHasChanged(
        object theClock, TimeInfoEventArgs ti)
    {
        Console.WriteLine("Current Time: {0}:{1}:{2}",
            ti.hour.ToString(),
            ti.minute.ToString(),
            ti.second.ToString());
    }
}

// a second subscriber whose job is to write to a file
public class LogCurrentTime
{
    public void Subscribe(Clock theClock)
    {
        theClock.OnSecondChange +=
            new Clock.SecondChangeHandler(WriteLogEntry);
```

Example 12-4. Working with events (continued)

```
        }

        // this method should write to a file
        // we write to the console to see the effect
        // this object keeps no state
        public void WriteLogEntry(
            object theClock, TimeInfoEventArgs ti)
        {
            Console.WriteLine("Logging to file: {0}:{1}:{2}",
                ti.hour.ToString(),
                ti.minute.ToString(),
                ti.second.ToString());
        }
    }

    public class Test
    {
        public static void Main()
        {
            // create a new clock
            Clock theClock = new Clock();

            // create the display and tell it to
            // subscribe to the clock just created
            DisplayClock dc = new DisplayClock();
            dc.Subscribe(theClock);

            // create a Log object and tell it
            // to subscribe to the clock
            LogCurrentTime lct = new LogCurrentTime();
            lct.Subscribe(theClock);

            // Get the clock started
            theClock.Run();
        }
    }
}
```

Output:
```
Current Time: 14:53:56
Logging to file: 14:53:56
Current Time: 14:53:57
Logging to file: 14:53:57
Current Time: 14:53:58
Logging to file: 14:53:58
Current Time: 14:53:59
Logging to file: 14:53:59
Current Time: 14:54:0
Logging to file: 14:54:0
```

The net effect of this code is to create two classes, `DisplayClock` and `LogCurrentTime`. Both of these subscribe to a third class event (`Clock.OnSecondChange`).

Decoupling Publishers from Subscribers

The Clock class could simply print the time rather than raising an event, so why bother with the indirection of using delegates? The advantage of the publish/subscribe idiom is that any number of classes can be notified when an event is raised. The subscribing classes do not need to know how the Clock works, and the Clock does not need to know what they are going to do in response to the event. Similarly, a button can publish an Onclick event, and any number of unrelated objects can subscribe to that event, receiving notification when the button is clicked.

The publisher and the subscribers are decoupled by the delegate. This is highly desirable as it makes for more flexible and robust code. The Clock can change how it detects time without breaking any of the subscribing classes. The subscribing classes can change how they respond to time changes without breaking the Clock. The two classes spin independently of one another, which makes for code that is easier to maintain.

Programming with C#

CHAPTER 13

Building Windows Applications

The previous chapters have used console applications to demonstrate C# and the Common Language Runtime. Although console applications can be implemented simply, it is time to turn your attention to the reason you're learning the C# language in the first place: building Windows and web applications.

In the early days of Windows computing, an application ran on a desktop, in splendid isolation. Over time, developers found it beneficial to spread their applications across a network, with the user interface on one computer and a database on another. This division of responsibilities or partitioning of an application came to be called two-tier or client-server application development. Later three-tier or *n*-tier approaches emerged as developers began to use web servers to host business objects that could handle the database access on behalf of clients.

When the Web first came along, there was a clear distinction between Windows applications and web applications. Windows applications ran on the desktop or a local area network (LAN), and web applications ran on a distant server and were accessed by a browser. This distinction is now being blurred as Windows applications reach out to the Web for services. Many new applications consist of logic running on a client, a database server, and remote third-party computers located on the Web. Traditional desktop applications such as Excel or Outlook are now able to integrate data retrieved through web connections seamlessly, and web applications can distribute some of their processing to client-side components.

The primary remaining distinction between a Windows application and a web application might be this: who owns the user interface? Will your application use a browser to display its user interface, or will the UI be built into the executable running on the desktop?

There are enormous advantages to web applications, starting with the obvious: they can be accessed from any browser that can connect to the server. In addition, updates can be made at the server, without the need to distribute new dynamic link libraries (DLLs) to your customers.

On the other hand, if your application derives no benefit from being on the Web, you might find that you can achieve greater control over the look and feel of your application or that you can achieve better performance by building a desktop application.

.NET offers closely related, but distinguishable, suites of tools for building Windows or web applications. Both are based on forms, with the premise that many applications have user interfaces centered on interacting with the user through forms and controls, such as buttons, list boxes, text, and so forth.

The tools for creating web applications are called Web Forms and are considered in Chapter 15. The tools for creating Windows applications are called Windows Forms and are the subject of this chapter.

 It is my prediction that the distinction between Web Forms and Windows Forms is temporary. There is such obvious similarity between these two approaches that I'd be very surprised if the next version of .NET didn't merge these two tools into one unified development environment.

In the following pages, you will learn how to create a simple Windows Form using either a text editor such as Notepad or the Design tool in Visual Studio .NET. Next you will build a more complex Windows application using Visual Studio, the Windows Forms framework, and a number of C# programming techniques you learned in earlier chapters. The chapter concludes with a brief introduction to Documentation Comments, a new XML-facilitated means to document applications, and an introduction to the deployment of .NET applications.

Creating a Simple Windows Form

A Windows Form is a tool for building a Windows application. The .NET Framework offers extensive support for Windows application development, the centerpiece of which is the Windows Forms framework. Not surprisingly, Windows Forms use the metaphor of a form. This idea was borrowed from the wildly successful Visual Basic (VB) environment and supports Rapid Application Development (RAD). Arguably, C# is the first development environment to marry the RAD tools of Visual Basic with the object-oriented and high-performance characteristics of a C-family language.

Using Notepad

Visual Studio .NET provides a rich set of drag-and-drop tools for working with Windows Forms. It *is* possible to build a Windows application without using the Visual Studio Integrated Development Environment (IDE), but it is far more painful and takes a lot longer.

However, just to prove the point, you'll use Notepad to create a simple Windows Form application that displays text in a window and implements a Cancel button. The application display is shown in Figure 13-1.

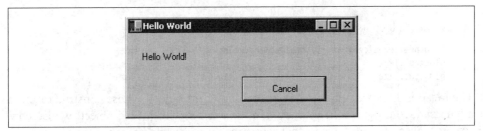

Figure 13-1. The hand-drawn Windows Form

You start by adding a using statement for the Windows Forms namespace:

```
using System.Windows.Forms;
```

The key to creating a Windows Form application is to derive your form from System. Windows.Forms.Form:

```
public class HandDrawnClass : Form
```

The Form object represents any window displayed in your application. You can use the Form class to create standard windows, as well as floating windows, tools, dialog boxes, and so forth. Microsoft apparently chose to call this a form rather than a window to emphasize that most windows now have an interactive component that includes controls for interacting with users.

All the Windows widgets you'll need (labels, buttons, list boxes, etc.) are found within the Windows.Forms namespace. In the IDE, you'll be able to drag and drop these objects onto a designer, but for now you'll declare them right in your program code.

To get started, declare the two widgets you need, a label to hold the Hello World text, and a button to exit the application:

```
private System.Windows.Forms.Label lblOutput;
private System.Windows.Forms.Button btnCancel;
```

You're now ready to instantiate these objects, which is done in the Form's constructor:

```
this.lblOutput = new System.Windows.Forms.Label();
this.btnCancel = new System.Windows.Forms.Button();
```

Next you can set the Form's title text to Hello World:

```
this.Text = "Hello World";
```

 Note that the preceding statements appear in your form's constructor, HandDrawnClass, and so the this keyword refers to the form itself.

Set the label's location, text, and size:

```
lblOutput.Location = new System.Drawing.Point (16, 24);
lblOutput.Text = "Hello World!";
lblOutput.Size = new System.Drawing.Size (216, 24);
```

The location is expressed as a System.Drawing.Point object, whose constructor takes a horizontal and vertical position. The size is set with a Size object, whose constructor takes a pair of integers that represent the width and height of the object.

 The .NET Framework provides the System.Drawing namespace, which encapsulates the Win32 GDI+ graphics functions. Much of the .NET Framework Class Library (FCL) consists of classes that encapsulate Win32 methods as objects.

Next, do the same for the button object, setting its location, size, and text:

```
btnCancel.Location = new System.Drawing.Point (150,200);
btnCancel.Size = new System.Drawing.Size (112, 32);
btnCancel.Text = "&Cancel";
```

The button also needs an event handler. As described in Chapter 12, events (in this case the cancel button-click event) are implemented using delegates. The publishing class (Button) defines a delegate (System.EventHandler) that the subscribing class (your form) must implement.

The delegated method can have any name but must return void and take two parameters: an object (sender) and a SystemEventArgs object, typically named e:

```
protected void btnCancel_Click (
        object sender, System.EventArgs e)
{
   //...
}
```

Register your event-handler method in two steps. First, create a new System.EventHandler delegate, passing in the name of your method as a parameter:

```
new System.EventHandler (this.btnCancel_Click);
```

Then add that delegate to the button's click event-handler list with the += operator.

The following line combines these steps into one:

```
btnCancel.Click +=
    new System.EventHandler (this.btnCancel_Click);
```

Now you must set up the form's dimensions. The form property `AutoScaleBaseSize` sets the base size used at display time to compute the scaling factor for the form. The `ClientSize` property sets the size of the form's client area, which is the size of the form excluding borders and titlebar. (When you use the designer, these values are provided for you interactively.):

```
this.AutoScaleBaseSize = new System.Drawing.Size (5, 13);
this.ClientSize = new System.Drawing.Size (300, 300);
```

Finally, remember to add the widgets to the form:

```
this.Controls.Add (this.btnCancel);
this.Controls.Add (this.lblOutput);
```

Having registered the event handler, you must supply the implementation. For this example, clicking Cancel will exit the application, using the static method `Exit( )` of the `Application` class:

```
protected void btnCancel_Click (
   object sender, System.EventArgs e)
{
    Application.Exit ();
}
```

That's it; you just need an entry point to invoke the constructor on the form:

```
public static void Main( )
{
    Application.Run(new HandDrawnClass( ));
}
```

The complete source is shown in Example 13-1. When you run this application, the window is opened and the text is displayed. Pressing Cancel closes the application.

Example 13-1. Creating a hand-drawn Windows Form

```
using System;
using System.Windows.Forms;

namespace ProgCSharp
{
   public class HandDrawnClass : Form
   {
      // a label to display Hello World
```

Example 13-1. Creating a hand-drawn Windows Form (continued)

```
private System.Windows.Forms.Label
   lblOutput;

// a cancel button
private System.Windows.Forms.Button
   btnCancel;

public HandDrawnClass( )
{
   // create the objects
   this.lblOutput =
      new System.Windows.Forms.Label ( );
   this.btnCancel =
      new System.Windows.Forms.Button ( );

   // set the form's title
   this.Text = "Hello World";

   // set up the output label
   lblOutput.Location =
      new System.Drawing.Point (16, 24);
   lblOutput.Text = "Hello World!";
   lblOutput.Size =
      new System.Drawing.Size (216, 24);

   // set up the cancel button
   btnCancel.Location =
      new System.Drawing.Point (150,200);
   btnCancel.Size =
      new System.Drawing.Size (112, 32);
   btnCancel.Text = "&Cancel";

   // set up the event handler
   btnCancel.Click +=
      new System.EventHandler (this.btnCancel_Click);

   // Add the controls and set the client area
   this.AutoScaleBaseSize =
      new System.Drawing.Size (5, 13);
   this.ClientSize =
      new System.Drawing.Size (300, 300);
   this.Controls.Add (this.btnCancel);
   this.Controls.Add (this.lblOutput);

}

// handle the cancel event
protected void btnCancel_Click (
   object sender, System.EventArgs e)
```

Example 13-1. Creating a hand-drawn Windows Form (continued)

```
    {
        Application.Exit();
    }

    // Run the app
    public static void Main()
    {
        Application.Run(new HandDrawnClass());
    }
  }
}
```

Using the Visual Studio .Net Designer

Although hand coding is always great fun, it is also a lot of work, and the result in the previous example is not as elegant as most programmers would expect. The Visual Studio IDE provides a design tool for Windows Forms that is much easier to use.

To begin work on a new Windows application, first open Visual Studio and choose New Project. In the New Project window, create a new C# Windows application and name it ProgCSharpWindowsForm, as shown in Figure 13-2.

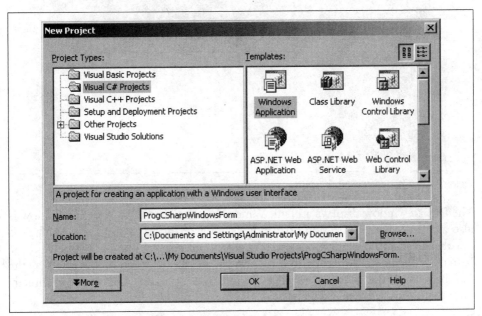

Figure 13-2. Creating a Windows Form application

Visual Studio responds by creating a Windows Form application, and, best of all, putting you into a design environment, as shown in Figure 13-3.

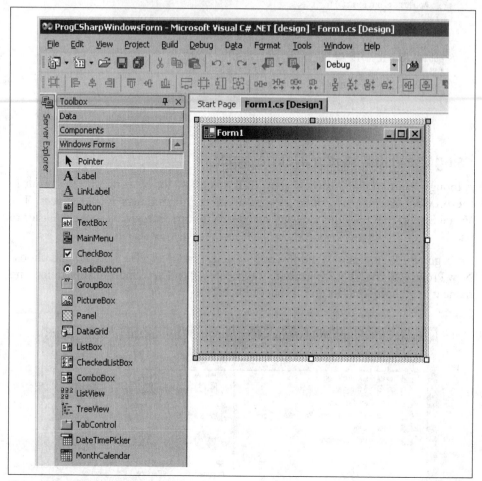

Figure 13-3. The design environment

The Design window displays a blank Windows Form (Form1). A Toolbox window is also available, with a selection of Windows widgets and controls. If the Toolbox is not displayed, try clicking the word "Toolbox," or select View → Toolbox on the Visual Studio menu. You can also use the keyboard shortcut Ctrl-Alt-X to display the Toolbox. With the Toolbox displayed, you can drag a label and a button directly onto the form, as shown in Figure 13-4.

Before proceeding, take a look around. The Toolbox is filled with controls that you can add to your Windows Form application. In the upper-right corner you should see the Solution Explorer, which is a window that displays all the files in your projects. In the lower-right corner is the Properties window, which displays all the

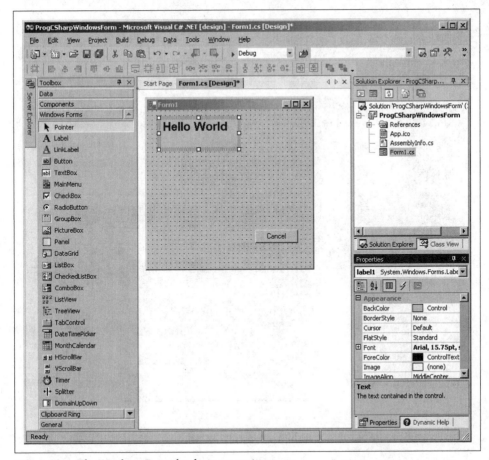

Figure 13-4. The Windows Form development environment

properties of the currently selected item. In Figure 13-4, the label (label1) is selected, and the Properties window displays *its* properties.

You can use the Properties window to set the static properties of the various controls. For example, to add text to label1, you can type the words "Hello World" into the box to the right of its Text property. If you want to change the font for the lettering in the HelloWorld label, click the Font property shown in the lower-right corner of Figure 13-5. (You can provide text in the same way for your button (button1) by selecting it in the Property window and typing the word "Cancel" into its Text property.)

Any one of these steps is much easier than modifying these properties in code (though that is certainly still possible).

Once you have the form laid out the way you want, all that remains is to create an event handler for the Cancel button. Double-clicking the Cancel button will create the event handler, register it, and put you on the *code-behind* page (the page that

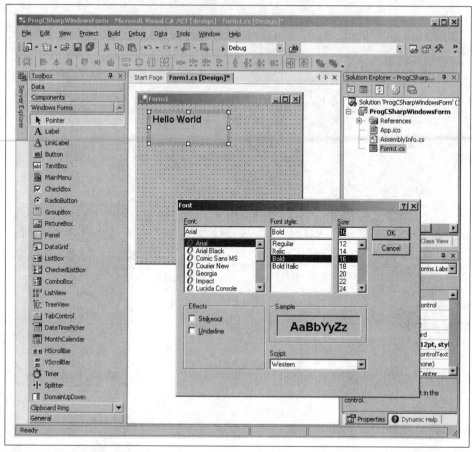

Figure 13-5. Modifying the font

holds the source code for this form), in which you can enter the event-handling logic, as shown in Figure 13-6.

The cursor is already in place; you have only to enter the one line of code:

```
Application.Exit();
```

In the IDE, the cursor flashes, making it very easy to see where the code goes. For most readers, the cursor probably will not flash in this book.

Visual Studio .NET generates all the code necessary to create and initialize the components. The complete source code is shown in Example 13-2, including the one line of code you provided (shown in bold in this example) to handle the Cancel button-click event.

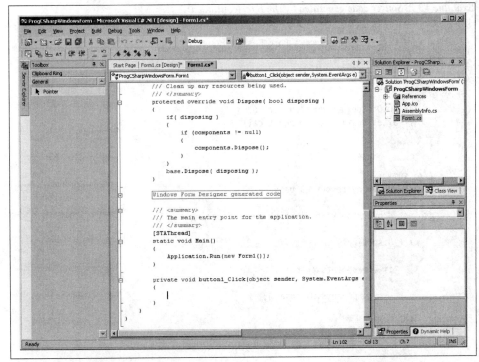

Figure 13-6. After double-clicking the Cancel button

Example 13-2. Source code generated by the IDE

```csharp
using System;
using System.Drawing;
using System.Collections;
using System.ComponentModel;
using System.Windows.Forms;
using System.Data;

namespace ProgCSharpWindowsForm
{
    /// <summary>
    /// Summary description for Form1.
    /// </summary>
    public class Form1 : System.Windows.Forms.Form
    {
        private System.Windows.Forms.Label lblOutput;
        private System.Windows.Forms.Button btnCancel;
        /// <summary>
        /// Required designer variable.
        /// </summary>
        private System.ComponentModel.Container components = null;

        public Form1( )
        {
```

Example 13-2. Source code generated by the IDE (continued)

```
        //
        // Required for Windows Form Designer support
        //
        InitializeComponent( );

        //
        // TODO: Add any constructor code
        // after InitializeComponent call
        //
    }


    /// <summary>
    /// Clean up any resources being used.
    /// </summary>
    protected override void Dispose( bool disposing )
    {
        if( disposing )
        {
            if (components != null)
            {
                components.Dispose( );
            }
        }
        base.Dispose( disposing );
    }


    #region Windows Form Designer generated code
    /// <summary>
    /// Required method for Designer support - do not modify
    /// the contents of this method with the code editor.
    /// </summary>
    private void InitializeComponent( )
    {
        this.lblOutput = new System.Windows.Forms.Label( );
        this.btnCancel = new System.Windows.Forms.Button( );
        this.SuspendLayout( );
        //
        // lblOutput
        //
        this.lblOutput.Font = new System.Drawing.Font("Arial", 15.75F,
            System.Drawing.FontStyle.Bold,
            System.Drawing.GraphicsUnit.Point, ((System.Byte)(0)));
        this.lblOutput.Location = new System.Drawing.Point(24, 16);
        this.lblOutput.Name = "lblOutput";
        this.lblOutput.Size = new System.Drawing.Size(136, 48);
        this.lblOutput.TabIndex = 0;
        this.lblOutput.Text = "Hello World";
        //
        // btnCancel
        //
        this.btnCancel.Location = new System.Drawing.Point(192, 208);
        this.btnCancel.Name = "btnCancel";
```

Example 13-2. Source code generated by the IDE (continued)

```
            this.btnCancel.TabIndex = 1;
            this.btnCancel.Text = "Cancel";
            this.btnCancel.Click += new System.EventHandler(
                this.btnCancel_Click);
            //
            // Form1
            //
            this.AutoScaleBaseSize = new System.Drawing.Size(5, 13);
            this.ClientSize = new System.Drawing.Size(292, 273);
            this.Controls.AddRange(new System.Windows.Forms.Control[] {
                    this.btnCancel, this.lblOutput});
            this.Name = "Form1";
            this.Text = "Form1";
            this.ResumeLayout(false);

        }
        #endregion

        /// <summary>
        /// The main entry point for the application.
        /// </summary>
        [STAThread]
        static void Main( )
        {
            Application.Run(new Form1( ));
        }

        private void btnCancel_Click(object sender, System.EventArgs e)
        {
            Application.Exit( );
        }


    }
}
```

 Some of the code in this listing has been reformatted to fit the printed page.

There is quite a bit of code in this listing that didn't appear in Example 13-1, though most of it is not terribly important. When Visual Studio creates the application, it must add some boilerplate code that is not essential for this simple application.

A careful examination reveals that the essentials are the same, but there are some key differences worth examining. The listing starts with special comment marks:

```
/// <summary>
/// Summary description for Form1.
/// </summary>
```

These marks are used for creating documentation; they are explained in detail later in this chapter.

The form derives from System.Windows.Forms.Form as did our earlier example. The widgets are defined as in the previous example:

```
public class Form1 : System.Windows.Forms.Form
{
    private System.Windows.Forms.Label lblOutput;
    private System.Windows.Forms.Button btnCancel;
```

The designer creates a private container variable for its own use:

```
private System.ComponentModel.Container components = null;
```

In this and in every Windows Form application generated by Visual Studio .NET, the constructor calls a private method, InitializeComponent(). This is used to define and set the properties of all the controls. The properties are set based on the values you've chosen (or on the default values you've left alone) in the designer. The InitializeComponent() method is marked with a comment that you should not modify the contents of this method; making changes to this method might confuse the designer.

This program will behave exactly as your earlier hand-crafted application did.

Creating a Windows Form Application

To see how Windows Forms can be used to create a more realistic Windows application, in this section you'll build a utility named FileCopier that copies all files from a group of directories selected by the user to a single target directory or device, such as a floppy or backup hard drive on the company network. Although you won't implement every possible feature, you can imagine programming this application so that you can mark dozens of files and have them copied to multiple disks, packing them as tightly as possible. You might even extend the application to compress the files. The true goal of this example is for you to exercise many of the C# skills learned in earlier chapters and to explore the Windows.Forms namespace.

For the purposes of this example and to keep the code simple, focus on the user interface and the steps needed to wire up its various controls. The final application UI is shown in Figure 13-7.

The user interface for FileCopier consists of the following controls:

- Labels: Source Files and Target Directory
- Buttons: Clear, Copy, Delete, and Cancel
- An Overwrite if exists checkbox
- A text box displaying the path of the selected target directory
- Two large tree view controls, one for available source directories and one for available target devices and directories

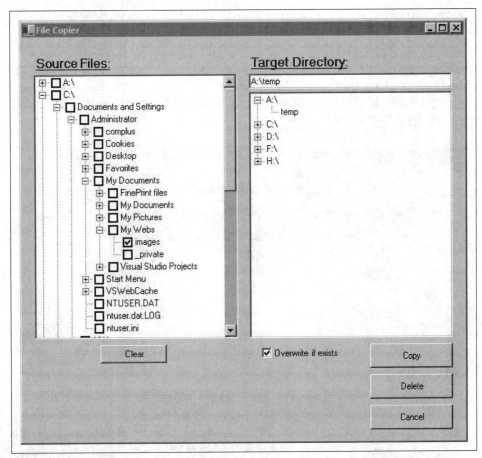

Figure 13-7. The FileCopier user interface

The goal is to allow the user to check files (or entire directories) in the left tree view (source). If the user presses the Copy button, the files checked on the left side will be copied to the Target Directory specified in the right-hand control. If the user presses Delete, the checked files will be deleted.

The rest of this chapter implements a number of FileCopier features in order to demonstrate the fundamental features of Windows Forms.

Creating the Basic UI Form

The first task is to open a new project named FileCopier. The IDE puts you into the Designer, in which you can drag widgets onto the form. You can expand the form to the size you want. Drag, drop, and set the Name properties of labels (lblSource, lblTarget, lblStatus), buttons (btnClear, btnCopy, btnDelete, btnCancel), a checkbox (chkOverwrite), a textbox (txtTargetDir), and tree view controls (tvwSource, tvwTargetDir) from the Toolbox onto your form until it looks more or less like the one shown in Figure 13-8.

You want checkboxes next to the directories and files in the source selection window but not in the target (where only one directory will be chosen). Set the CheckBoxes property on the left TreeView control, tvwSource, to true, and set the property on the right-hand TreeView control, tvwTargetDir, to false. To do so, click each control in turn and adjust the values in the Properties window.

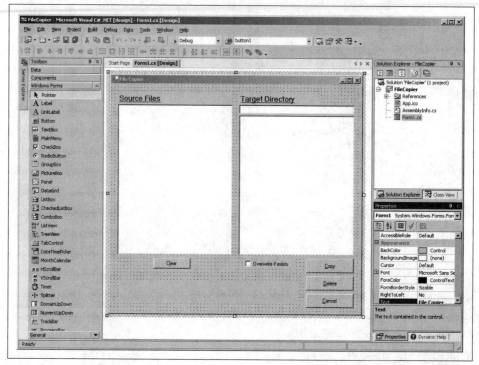

Figure 13-8. Creating the form in the designer

Once this is done, double-click the Cancel button to create its event handler—when you double-click a control, Visual Studio .NET creates an event handler for that object. One particular event is the target event, and Visual Studio .NET opens that event's event handler:

```
protected void btnCancel_Click (object sender, System.EventArgs e)
{
    Application.Exit();
}
```

You can set many different events for the TreeView control. Do so programmatically by clicking the Events button in the Properties window. From there you can create new handlers, just by filling in a new event-handler method name. Visual Studio .NET will register the event handler and open the editor for the code, where it will create the header and put the cursor in an empty method body.

So much for the easy part. Visual Studio .NET will generate code to set up the form and initialize all the controls, but it won't fill the TreeView controls. That you must do by hand.

Populating the TreeView Controls

The two TreeView controls work identically, except that the left control, tvwSource, lists the directories and files, whereas the right control, tvwTargetDir, lists only directories. The CheckBoxes property on tvwSource is set to true, and on tvwTargetDir it is set to false. Also, although tvwSource will allow multiselect, which is the default for TreeView controls, you will enforce single selection for tvwTargetDir.

You'll factor the common code for both TreeView controls into a shared method FillDirectoryTree and pass in the control with a flag indicating whether to get the files. You'll call this method from the Form's constructor, once for each of the two controls:

```
FillDirectoryTree(tvwSource, true);
FillDirectoryTree(tvwTargetDir, false);
```

The FillDirectoryTree implementation names the TreeView parameter tvw. This will represent the source TreeView and the destination TreeView in turn. You'll need some classes from System.IO, so add a using System.IO; statement at the top of Form1.cs. Next, add the method declaration to Form1.cs:

```
private void FillDirectoryTree(TreeView tvw, bool isSource)
```

TreeNode objects

The TreeView control has a property, Nodes, which gets a TreeNodeCollection object. The TreeNodeCollection is a collection of TreeNode objects, each of which represents a node in the tree. Start by emptying that collection:

```
tvw.Nodes.Clear();
```

You are ready to fill the TreeView's Nodes collection by recursing through the directories of all the drives. First, get all the logical drives on the system. To do so, call a static method of the Environment object, GetLogicalDrives(). The Environment class provides information about and access to the current platform environment. You can use the Environment object to get the machine name, OS version, system directory, and so forth, from the computer on which you are running your program.

```
string[] strDrives = Environment.GetLogicalDrives();
```

GetLogicalDrives() returns an array of strings, each of which represents the root directory of one of the logical drives. You will iterate over that collection, adding nodes to the TreeView control as you go.

```
foreach (string rootDirectoryName in strDrives)
{
```

You should process each drive within the foreach loop. You can add these two lines to limit the search to a particular drive (this is good if you have several large drives or some network drives):

```
if (rootDirectoryName != @"C:\")
            continue;
```

The very first thing you need to determine is whether the drive is ready. My hack for that is to get the list of top-level directories from the drive by calling GetDirectories( ) on a DirectoryInfo object I created for the root directory:

```
DirectoryInfo dir = new DirectoryInfo(rootDirectoryName);
dir.GetDirectories( );
```

The DirectoryInfo class exposes instance methods for creating, moving, and enumerating through directories, their files, and their subdirectories. The DirectoryInfo class is covered in detail in Chapter 21.

The GetDirectories( ) method returns a list of directories, but throw this list away. You are calling it here only to generate an exception if the drive is not ready.

Wrap the call in a try block and take no action in the catch block. The effect is that if an exception is thrown, the drive is skipped. Once you know that the drive is ready, create a TreeNode to hold the root directory of the drive and add that node to the TreeView control:

```
TreeNode ndRoot = new TreeNode(rootDirectoryName);
tvw.Nodes.Add(ndRoot);
```

You now want to recurse through the directories, so you call into a new routine, GetSubDirectoryNodes( ), passing in the root node, the name of the root directory, and the flag indicating whether you want files:

```
if (isSource)
{
    GetSubDirectoryNodes(ndRoot, ndRoot.Text, true);
}
else
{
    GetSubDirectoryNodes(ndRoot, ndRoot.Text, false);
}
```

You are probably wondering why you need to pass in ndRoot.Text if you're already passing in ndRoot. Patience; you will see why this is needed when you recurse back into GetSubDirectoryNodes. You are now finished with FillDirectoryTree( ). See Example 13-3 for a complete listing of this method.

Recursing through the subdirectories

GetSubDirectoryNodes( ) begins by once again calling GetDirectories( ), this time stashing away the resulting array of DirectoryInfo objects:

```
private void GetSubDirectoryNodes(
    TreeNode parentNode, string fullName, bool getFileNames)
```

```
{
    DirectoryInfo dir = new DirectoryInfo(fullName);
    DirectoryInfo[] dirSubs = dir.GetDirectories();
```

Notice that the node passed in is named parentNode. The current level of nodes will be considered children to the node passed in. This is how you map the directory structure to the hierarchy of the tree view.

Iterate over each subdirectory, skipping any that are marked Hidden:

```
foreach (DirectoryInfo dirSub in dirSubs)
{
    if ( (dirSub.Attributes &
        FileAttributes.Hidden) != 0 )
    {
        continue;
    }
```

FileAttributes is an enum; other possible values include Archive, Compressed, Directory, Encrypted, Hidden, Normal, ReadOnly, etc.

> The property dirSub.Attributes is the bit pattern of the current attributes of the directory. If you logically AND that value with the bit pattern FileAttributes.Hidden, a bit is set if the file has the hidden attribute; otherwise all the bits are cleared. You can check for any hidden bit by testing whether the resulting int is other than zero.

Create a TreeNode with the directory name and add it to the Nodes collection of the node passed in to the method (parentNode):

```
TreeNode subNode = new TreeNode(dirSub.Name);
parentNode.Nodes.Add(subNode);
```

Now recurse back into the GetSubDirectoryNodes() method, passing in the node you just created as the new parent, the full path as the full name of the parent, and the flag:

```
GetSubDirectoryNodes(subNode,dirSub.FullName,getFileNames);
```

> Notice that the call to the TreeNode constructor uses the Name property of the DirectoryInfo object, while the call to GetSubDirectoryNodes() uses the FullName property. If your directory is c:\WinNT\Media\Sounds, the FullName property will return the full path, while the Name property will return just Sounds. Pass in only the name to the node because that is what you want displayed in the tree view. Pass in the full name with path to the GetSubDirectoryNodes() method so that the method can locate all the subdirectories on the disk. This answers the question asked earlier as to why you need to pass in the root node's name the first time you call this method; what is passed in is not the name of the node, it is the full path to the directory represented by the node!

Getting the files in the directory

Once you've recursed through the subdirectories, it is time to get the files for the directory if the getFileNames flag is true. To do so, call the GetFiles( ) method on the DirectoryInfo object. An array of FileInfo objects is returned:

```
if (getFileNames)
{
    // Get any files for this node.
    FileInfo[] files = dir.GetFiles();
```

The FileInfo class (covered in Chapter 21) provides instance methods for manipulating files.

You can now iterate over this collection, accessing the Name property of the FileInfo object and passing that name to the constructor of a TreeNode, which you then add to the parent node's Nodes collection (thus creating a child node). There is no recursion this time because files do not have subdirectories:

```
foreach (FileInfo file in files)
{
    TreeNode fileNode = new TreeNode(file.Name);
    parentNode.Nodes.Add(fileNode);
}
```

That's all it takes to fill the two tree views. See Example 13-3 for a complete listing of this method.

 If you found any of this confusing, I highly recommend putting the code into your debugger and stepping through the recursion; you can watch the TreeView build its nodes.

Handling TreeView Events

You must handle a number of events in this example. First, the user might click Cancel, Copy, Clear, or Delete. Second, the user might click one of the checkboxes in the left TreeView or one of the nodes in the right TreeView.

Let's consider the clicks on the TreeViews first, as they are the more interesting, and potentially the more challenging.

Clicking the source TreeView

There are two TreeView objects, each with its own event handler. Consider the source TreeView object first. The user checks the files and directories he wants to copy from. Each time the user clicks a file or directory, a number of events are raised. The event you must handle is AfterCheck.

To do so, implement a custom event-handler method you will create and name tvwSource_AfterCheck( ). Visual Studio .NET will wire this to the event handler, or if you are not using the integrated development environment, you must do so yourself.

```
tvwSource.AfterCheck +=
new System.Windows.Forms.TreeViewEventHandler
    (this.tvwSource_AfterCheck);
```

The implementation of AfterCheck( ) delegates the work to a recursable method named SetCheck( ) that you'll also write. To add the AfterCheck event, select the tvwSource control, click the Events icon in the Properties window, then double-click on AfterCheck. This will add the event, wire it up, and place you in the code editor where you can add the body of the method:

```
private void tvwSource_AfterCheck (
object sender, System.Windows.Forms.TreeViewEventArgs e)
{
    SetCheck(e.Node,e.Node.Checked);
}
```

The event handler passes in the sender object and an object of type TreeViewEventArgs. It turns out that you can get the node from this TreeViewEventArgs object (e). Call SetCheck( ), passing in the node and the state of whether the node has been checked.

Each node has a Nodes property, which gets a TreeNodeCollection containing all the subnodes. SetCheck( ) recurses through the current node's Nodes collection, setting each subnode's check mark to match that of the node that was checked. In other words, when you check a directory, all its files and subdirectories are checked, recursively, all the way down.

It's Turtles, All the Way Down

Here's my favorite story on recursion: it happened that a famous Darwinist was telling a story about primitive creation myths. "Some peoples," he said, "believe the world rests on the back of a great turtle. Of course, that raises the question: on what does the turtle rest?"

An elderly woman from the back of the room stood up and said, "Very clever, Sonny, but it's turtles, all the way down."

For each TreeNode in the Nodes collection, check to see if it is a leaf. A node is a leaf if its own Nodes collection has a count of zero. If it is a leaf, set its check property to whatever was passed in as a parameter. If it is not a leaf, recurse.

```
private void SetCheck(TreeNode node, bool check)
{
    // find all the child nodes from this node
    foreach (TreeNode n in node.Nodes)
    {
        n.Checked = check;    // check the node
```

```
        // if this is a node in the tree, recurse
    if (n.Nodes.Count != 0)
    {
        SetCheck(n,check);
    }
    }
}
```

This propagates the check mark (or clears the check mark) down through the entire structure. In this way, the user can indicate that he wants to select all the files in all the subdirectories by clicking a single directory.

Clicking the target TreeView

The event handler for the target TreeView is somewhat trickier. The event itself is AfterSelect. (Remember that the target TreeView does not have checkboxes.) This time, you want to take the one directory chosen and put its full path into the text box at the upper-left corner of the form.

To do so, you must work your way up through the nodes, finding the name of each parent directory and building the full path:

```
private void tvwTargetDir_AfterSelect (
    object sender, System.Windows.Forms.TreeViewEventArgs e)
{

    string theFullPath = GetParentString(e.Node);
```

We'll look at GetParentString( ) in just a moment. Once you have the full path, you must lop off the backslash (if any) on the end and then you can fill the text box:

```
if (theFullPath.EndsWith("\\"))
{
    theFullPath =
        theFullPath.Substring(0,theFullPath.Length-1);
}
txtTargetDir.Text = theFullPath;
```

The GetParentString( ) method takes a node and returns a string with the full path. To do so, it recurses upward through the path, adding the backslash after any node that is not a leaf:

```
private string GetParentString(TreeNode node)
{
    if(node.Parent == null)
    {
        return node.Text;
    }
    else
    {
        return GetParentString(node.Parent) + node.Text +
            (node.Nodes.Count == 0  ? "" : "\\");
    }
}
```

The conditional operator (?) is the only ternary operator in C# (a ternary operator takes three terms). The logic is "test whether node.Nodes.Count is zero; if so return the value before the colon (in this case an empty string). Otherwise return the value after the colon (in this case a backslash)."

The recursion stops when there is no parent; that is, when you hit the root directory.

Handling the Clear button event

Given the SetCheck( ) method developed earlier, handling the Clear button's click event is trivial:

```
protected void btnClear_Click (object sender, System.EventArgs e)
{
    foreach (TreeNode node in tvwSource.Nodes)
    {
        SetCheck(node, false);
    }
}
```

Just call the SetCheck( ) method on the root nodes and tell them to recursively uncheck all their contained nodes.

Implementing the Copy Button Event

Now that you can check the files and pick the target directory, you're ready to handle the Copy button-click event. The very first thing you need to do is to get a list of which files were selected. What you want is an array of FileInfo objects, but you have no idea how many objects will be in the list. That is a perfect job for ArrayList. Delegate responsibility for filling the list to a method called GetFileList( ):

```
private void btnCopy_Click (
        object sender, System.EventArgs e)
{
    ArrayList fileList = GetFileList();
```

Let's pick that method apart before returning to the event handler.

Getting the selected files

Start by instantiating a new ArrayList object to hold the strings representing the names of all the files selected:

```
private ArrayList GetFileList()
{
    ArrayList fileNames = new ArrayList();
```

To get the selected filenames, you can walk through the source TreeView control:

```
foreach (TreeNode theNode in tvwSource.Nodes)
{
```

```
        GetCheckedFiles(theNode, fileNames);
    }
```

To see how this works, step into the GetCheckedFiles( ) method. This method is pretty simple: it examines the node it was handed. If that node has no children (node.Nodes.Count == 0), it is a leaf. If that leaf is checked, get the full path (by calling GetParentString( ) on the node) and add it to the ArrayList passed in as a parameter:

```
private void GetCheckedFiles(TreeNode node, ArrayList fileNames)
{
    if (node.Nodes.Count == 0)
    {
        if (node.Checked)
        {
            string fullPath = GetParentString(node);
            fileNames.Add(fullPath);
        }
    }
```

If the node is *not* a leaf, recurse down the tree, finding the child nodes:

```
    else
    {
        foreach (TreeNode n in node.Nodes)
        {
            GetCheckedFiles(n,fileNames);
        }
    }
}
```

This will return the ArrayList filled with all the filenames. Back in GetFileList( ), use this ArrayList of filenames to create a second ArrayList, this time to hold the actual FileInfo objects:

```
ArrayList fileList = new ArrayList( );
```

Notice that once again you do not tell the ArrayList constructor what kind of object it will hold. This is one of the advantages of a rooted type–system: the collection only needs to know that it has some kind of Object; because all types are derived from Object, the list can hold FileInfo objects as easily as it can hold string objects.

You can now iterate through the filenames in ArrayList, picking out each name and instantiating a FileInfo object with it. You can detect if it is a file or a directory by calling the Exists property, which will return false if the File object you created is actually a directory. If it is a File, you can add it to the new ArrayList:

```
foreach (string fileName in fileNames)
{
    FileInfo file = new FileInfo(fileName);

    if (file.Exists)
    {
        fileList.Add(file);
    }
}
```

Sorting the list of selected files

You want to work your way through the list of selected files in large to small order so that you can pack the target disk as tightly as possible. You must therefore sort the ArrayList. You can call its Sort( ) method, but how will it know how to sort File objects? Remember, the ArrayList has no special knowledge about its contents.

To solve this, you must pass in an IComparer interface. We'll create a class called FileComparer that will implement this interface and that will know how to sort FileInfo objects:

```
public class FileComparer : IComparer
{
```

This class has only one method, Compare( ), which takes two objects as arguments:

```
public int Compare (object f1, object f2)
{
```

The normal approach is to return 1 if the first object (f1) is larger than the second (f2), to return –1 if the opposite is true, and to return 0 if they are equal. In this case, however, you want the list sorted from big to small, so you should reverse the return values.

 Since this is the only use of this compare method, it is reasonable to put this special knowledge that the sort is from big to small right into the compare method itself. The alternative is to sort small to big, and have the calling method reverse the results, as you saw in Example 12-1.

To test the length of the FileInfo object, you must cast the Object parameters to FileInfo objects (which is safe, as you know this method will never receive anything else):

```
FileInfo file1 = (FileInfo) f1;
FileInfo file2 = (FileInfo) f2;
if (file1.Length > file2.Length)
{
    return -1;
}
if (file1.Length < file2.Length)
{
    return 1;
}
return 0;
}
}
```

 In a production program, you might want to test the type of the object and perhaps handle the exception if the object is not of the expected type.

Returning to GetFileList(), you were about to instantiate the IComparer reference and pass it to the Sort() method of fileList:

```
IComparer comparer = (IComparer) new FileComparer();
fileList.Sort(comparer);
```

That done, you can return fileList to the calling method:

```
return fileList;
```

The calling method was btnCopy_Click. Remember you went off to GetFileList() in the first line of the event handler!

```
protected void btnCopy_Click (object sender, System.EventArgs e)
{
    ArrayList fileList = GetFileList();
```

At this point you've returned with a sorted list of File objects, each representing a file selected in the source TreeView.

You can now iterate through the list, copying the files and updating the UI:

```
foreach (FileInfo file in fileList)
{
    try
    {
        lblStatus.Text = "Copying " +
          txtTargetDir.Text + "\\" +
            file.Name + "...";
        Application.DoEvents();

        file.CopyTo(txtTargetDir.Text + "\\" +
            file.Name,chkOverwrite.Checked);
    }

    catch (Exception ex)
    {
        MessageBox.Show(ex.Message);
    }
}
lblStatus.Text = "Done.";
Application.DoEvents();
```

As you go, write the progress to the lblStatus label and call Application.DoEvents() to give the UI an opportunity to redraw. Then call CopyTo() on the file, passing in the target directory obtained from the text field, and a Boolean flag indicating whether the file should be overwritten if it already exists.

You'll notice that the flag you pass in is the value of the chkOverwrite checkbox. The Checked property evaluates true if the checkbox is checked and false if not.

The copy is wrapped in a try block because you can anticipate any number of things going wrong when copying files. For now, handle all exceptions by popping up a dialog box with the error, but you might want to take corrective action in a commercial application.

That's it; you've implemented file copying!

Handling the Delete Button Event

The code to handle the delete event is even simpler. The very first thing you do is ask the user if she is sure she wants to delete the files:

```
protected void btnDelete_Click
(object sender, System.EventArgs e)
{
System.Windows.Forms.DialogResult result =
    MessageBox.Show(
    "Are you quite sure?",              // msg
    "Delete Files",                     // caption
    MessageBoxButtons.OKCancel,         // buttons
    MessageBoxIcon.Exclamation,         // icons
    MessageBoxDefaultButton.Button2);   // default button
```

You can use the `MessageBox` static `Show()` method, passing in the message you want to display, the title "Delete Files" as a string, and flags.

- `MessageBox.OKCancel` asks for two buttons: OK and Cancel.

- `MessageBox.IconExclamation` indicates that you want to display an exclamation mark icon.

- `MessageBox.DefaultButton.Button2` sets the second button (Cancel) as the default choice.

When the user chooses OK or Cancel, the result is passed back as a `System.Windows.Forms.DialogResult` enumerated value. You can test this value to see if the user pressed OK:

```
if (result == System.Windows.Forms.DialogResult.OK)
{
```

If so, you can get the list of `fileNames` and iterate through it, deleting each as you go:

```
ArrayList fileNames = GetFileList();

foreach (FileInfo file in fileNames)
{
    try
    {
        lblStatus.Text = "Deleting " +
            txtTargetDir.Text + "\\" +
            file.Name + "...";
        Application.DoEvents();

        file.Delete();
    }

    catch (Exception ex)
    {
        MessageBox.Show(ex.Message);
    }
}
```

```
        lblStatus.Text = "Done.";
        Application.DoEvents( );
```

This code is identical to the copy code, except that the method that is called on the file is Delete( ).

Example 13-3 provides the commented source code for this example.

 To save space, this example shows only the custom methods and leaves out the declarations of the Windows.Forms objects as well as the boilerplate code produced by Visual Studio .NET. As explained in the preface, you can download the complete source code from my web site, *http://www.LibertyAssociates.com*.

Example 13-3. File copier source code

```
using System;
using System.Drawing;
using System.Collections;
using System.ComponentModel;
using System.Windows.Forms;
using System.Data;
using System.IO;

/// <remarks>
///     File Copier - WinForms demonstration program
///     (c) Copyright 2001 Liberty Associates, Inc.
/// </remarks>
namespace FileCopier
{
    /// <summary>
    /// Form demonstrating Windows Forms implementation
    /// </summary>
    public class Form1 : System.Windows.Forms.Form
    {

        // < declarations of Windows widgets cut here >

        /// <summary>
        /// Required designer variable.
        /// </summary>
        private System.ComponentModel.Container components = null;

        /// <summary>
        ///     internal class which knows how to compare
        ///     two files we want to sort large to small,
        ///     so reverse the normal return values.
        /// </summary>
        public class FileComparer : IComparer
        {
            public int Compare (object f1, object f2)
            {
                FileInfo file1 = (FileInfo) f1;
```

Example 13-3. File copier source code (continued)

```csharp
            FileInfo file2 = (FileInfo) f2;
            if (file1.Length > file2.Length)
            {
                return -1;
            }
            if (file1.Length < file2.Length)
            {
                return 1;
            }
            return 0;
        }
    }

    public Form1( )
    {
        //
        // Required for Windows Form Designer support
        //
        InitializeComponent( );

        // fill the source and target directory trees
        FillDirectoryTree(tvwSource, true);
        FillDirectoryTree(tvwTargetDir, false);
    }

    /// <summary>
    /// Fill the directory tree for either the Source or
    /// Target TreeView.
    /// </summary>
    private void FillDirectoryTree(
      TreeView tvw, bool isSource)
    {

        // Populate tvwSource, the Source TreeView,
        // with the contents of
        // the local hard drive.
        // First clear all the nodes.
        tvw.Nodes.Clear( );

        // Get the logical drives and put them into the
        // root nodes. Fill an array with all the
        // logical drives on the machine.
        string[] strDrives =
            Environment.GetLogicalDrives( );

        // Iterate through the drives, adding them to the tree.
        // Use a try/catch block, so if a drive is not ready,
        // e.g. an empty floppy or CD,
        //    it will not be added to the tree.
        foreach (string rootDirectoryName in strDrives)
        {
            if (rootDirectoryName != @"C:\")
```

Example 13-3. File copier source code (continued)

```
            continue;
        try
        {

            // Fill an array with all the first level
            // subdirectories. If the drive is
            // not ready, this will throw an exception.
            DirectoryInfo dir =
                new DirectoryInfo(rootDirectoryName);
            dir.GetDirectories();

            TreeNode ndRoot = new TreeNode(rootDirectoryName);

            // Add a node for each root directory.
            tvw.Nodes.Add(ndRoot);

            // Add subdirectory nodes.
            // If Treeview is the source,
            // then also get the filenames.
            if (isSource)
            {
                GetSubDirectoryNodes(
                    ndRoot, ndRoot.Text, true);
            }
            else
            {
                GetSubDirectoryNodes(
                    ndRoot, ndRoot.Text, false);
            }
        }
        // Catch any errors such as
        // Drive not ready.
        catch (Exception e)
        {
            MessageBox.Show(e.Message);
        }
    }
} //  close for FillSourceDirectoryTree

/// <summary>
/// Gets all the subdirectories below the
/// passed in directory node.
/// Adds to the directory tree.
/// The parameters passed in are the parent node
/// for this subdirectory,
/// the full path name of this subdirectory,
/// and a Boolean to indicate
/// whether or not to get the files in the subdirectory.
/// </summary>
private void GetSubDirectoryNodes(
    TreeNode parentNode, string fullName, bool getFileNames)
{
```

Example 13-3. File copier source code (continued)

```csharp
            DirectoryInfo dir = new DirectoryInfo(fullName);
            DirectoryInfo[] dirSubs = dir.GetDirectories();

            // Add a child node for each subdirectory.
            foreach (DirectoryInfo dirSub in dirSubs)
            {

                // do not show hidden folders
                if ( (dirSub.Attributes & FileAttributes.Hidden)
                    != 0 )
                {
                    continue;
                }

                /// <summary>
                ///     Each directory contains the full path.
                ///     We need to split it on the backslashes,
                ///     and only use
                ///     the last node in the tree.
                ///     Need to double the backslash since it
                ///     is normally
                ///     an escape character
                /// </summary>
                TreeNode subNode = new TreeNode(dirSub.Name);
                parentNode.Nodes.Add(subNode);

                // Call GetSubDirectoryNodes recursively.
                GetSubDirectoryNodes(
                    subNode,dirSub.FullName,getFileNames);

            }
            if (getFileNames)
            {
                // Get any files for this node.
                FileInfo[] files = dir.GetFiles();

                // After placing the nodes,
                // now place the files in that subdirectory.
                foreach (FileInfo file in files)
                {
                    TreeNode fileNode = new TreeNode(file.Name);
                    parentNode.Nodes.Add(fileNode);
                }
            }
        }


        // < boilerplate code cut here >

        /// <summary>
        /// The main entry point for the application.
        /// </summary>
```

Example 13-3. File copier source code (continued)

```
[STAThread]
static void Main( )
{
    Application.Run(new Form1( ));
}


/// <summary>
///     Create an ordered list of all
///     the selected files, copy to the
///     target directory
/// </summary>
private void btnCopy_Click(object sender,
    System.EventArgs e)
{
    // get the list
    ArrayList fileList = GetFileList( );

    // copy the files
    foreach (FileInfo file in fileList)
    {
        try
        {
            // update the label to show progress
            lblStatus.Text = "Copying " + txtTargetDir.Text +
                "\\" + file.Name + "...";
            Application.DoEvents( );

            // copy the file to its destination location
            file.CopyTo(txtTargetDir.Text + "\\" +
                file.Name,chkOverwrite.Checked);
        }

        catch (Exception ex)
        {
            // you may want to do more than
            // just show the message
            MessageBox.Show(ex.Message);
        }
    }
    lblStatus.Text = "Done.";
    Application.DoEvents( );

}

/// <summary>
///     on cancel, exit
/// </summary>
private void btnCancel_Click(object sender, System.EventArgs e)
{
    Application.Exit( );
}
```

Example 13-3. File copier source code (continued)

```csharp
/// <summary>
///     Tell the root of each tree to uncheck
///     all the nodes below
/// </summary>
private void btnClear_Click(object sender, System.EventArgs e)
{
    // get the top most node for each drive
    // and tell it to clear recursively
    foreach (TreeNode node in tvwSource.Nodes)
    {
        SetCheck(node, false);
    }
}

/// <summary>
///     check that the user does want to delete
///     Make a list and delete each in turn
/// </summary>
private void btnDelete_Click(object sender, System.EventArgs e)
{
    // ask them if they are sure
    System.Windows.Forms.DialogResult result =
        MessageBox.Show(
        "Are you quite sure?",              // msg
        "Delete Files",                     // caption
        MessageBoxButtons.OKCancel,         // buttons
        MessageBoxIcon.Exclamation,         // icons
        MessageBoxDefaultButton.Button2);   // default button

    // if they are sure...
    if (result == System.Windows.Forms.DialogResult.OK)
    {
        // iterate through the list and delete them.
        // get the list of selected files
        ArrayList fileNames = GetFileList();

        foreach (FileInfo file in fileNames)
        {
            try
            {
                // update the label to show progress
                lblStatus.Text = "Deleting " +
                    txtTargetDir.Text + "\\" +
                    file.Name + "...";
                Application.DoEvents();

                // Danger Will Robinson!
                file.Delete();
            }

            catch (Exception ex)
            {
```

Example 13-3. File copier source code (continued)

```
                            // you may want to do more than
                            // just show the message
                            MessageBox.Show(ex.Message);
                        }
                    }
                    lblStatus.Text = "Done.";
                    Application.DoEvents();
        }


    }

    /// <summary>
    ///    Get the full path of the chosen directory
    ///    copy it to txtTargetDir
    /// </summary>
    private void tvwTargetDir_AfterSelect(
        object sender,
        System.Windows.Forms.TreeViewEventArgs e)
    {
        // get the full path for the selected directory
        string theFullPath = GetParentString(e.Node);

        // if it is not a leaf, it will end with a back slash
        // remove the backslash
        if (theFullPath.EndsWith("\\"))
        {
            theFullPath =
                theFullPath.Substring(0,theFullPath.Length-1);
        }
        // insert the path in the text box
        txtTargetDir.Text = theFullPath;
    }

    /// <summary>
    ///    Mark each node below the current
    ///    one with the current value of checked
    /// </summary>
    private void tvwSource_AfterCheck(object sender,
        System.Windows.Forms.TreeViewEventArgs e)
    {
        // Call a recursible method.
        // e.node is the node which was checked by the user.
        // The state of the check mark is already
        // changed by the time you get here.
        // Therefore, we want to pass along
        // the state of e.node.Checked.
        SetCheck(e.Node,e.Node.Checked);
    }

    /// <summary>
    ///    recursively set or clear check marks
    /// </summary>
```

Example 13-3. File copier source code (continued)

```
private void SetCheck(TreeNode node, bool check)
{
    // find all the child nodes from this node
    foreach (TreeNode n in node.Nodes)
    {
        n.Checked = check;    // check the node

        // if this is a node in the tree, recurse
        if (n.Nodes.Count != 0)
        {
            SetCheck(n,check);
        }
    }
}


/// <summary>
///     Given a node and an array list
///     fill the list with the names of
///     all the checked files
/// </summary>
// Fill the ArrayList with the full paths of
// all the files checked
private void GetCheckedFiles(TreeNode node,
    ArrayList fileNames)
{
    // if this is a leaf...
    if (node.Nodes.Count == 0)
    {
        // if the node was checked...
        if (node.Checked)
        {
            // get the full path and add it to the arrayList
            string fullPath = GetParentString(node);
            fileNames.Add(fullPath);
        }
    }
    else  // if this node is not a leaf
    {
        // if this node is not a leaf
        foreach (TreeNode n in node.Nodes)
        {
            GetCheckedFiles(n,fileNames);
        }
    }
}


/// <summary>
///     Given a node, return the
///     full path name
/// </summary>
private string GetParentString(TreeNode node)
{
```

Example 13-3. File copier source code (continued)

```
        // if this is the root node (c:\) return the text
        if(node.Parent == null)
        {
            return node.Text;
        }
        else
        {
            // recurse up and get the path then
            // add this node and a slash
            // if this node is the leaf, don't add the slash
            return GetParentString(node.Parent) + node.Text +
                (node.Nodes.Count == 0  ? "" : "\\");
        }
    }
}


    /// <summary>
    ///     shared by delete and copy
    ///     creates an ordered list of all
    ///     the selected files
    /// </summary>
    private ArrayList GetFileList()
    {
        // create an unsorted array list of the full file names
        ArrayList fileNames = new ArrayList();

        // fill the fileNames ArrayList with the
        // full path of each file to copy
        foreach (TreeNode theNode in tvwSource.Nodes)
        {
            GetCheckedFiles(theNode, fileNames);
        }

        // Create a list to hold the FileInfo objects
        ArrayList fileList = new ArrayList();

        // for each of the file names we have in our unsorted list
        // if the name corresponds to a file (and not a directory)
        // add it to the file list
        foreach (string fileName in fileNames)
        {
            // create a file with the name
            FileInfo file = new FileInfo(fileName);

            // see if it exists on the disk
            // this fails if it was a directory
            if (file.Exists)
            {
                // both the key and the value are the file
                // would it be easier to have an empty value?
                fileList.Add(file);
            }
        }
```

Example 13-3. File copier source code (continued)

```
        // Create an instance of the IComparer interface
        IComparer comparer = (IComparer) new FileComparer( );

        // pass the comparer to the sort method so that the list
        // is sorted by the compare method of comparer.
```

XML Documentation Comments

C# supports a new *Documentation Comment* style, with three slash marks (///). You can see these comments sprinkled throughout Example 13-3. The Visual Studio .NET editor recognizes these comments and helps format them properly.

The C# compiler processes these comments into an XML file. You can create this file by using the /doc command-line switch. For example, you might compile the program in Example 13-3 with this command line:

```
csc Form1.cs /doc:XMLDoc.XML
```

You can accomplish this same operation in Visual Studio .NET by clicking the File-Copier project icon in the Solution Explorer window, selecting View → Property Pages on the Visual Studio menu, and then clicking the Configuration Properties folder. Within the Configuration Properties folder, click the Build property page and type in a name for the XML Documentation File property to specify a name for the XML file you want to produce.

Either approach produces the file XMLDoc.XML with your comments in XML format. An excerpt of the file that will be produced for the FileCopier application of the previous section is shown in Example 13-4.

Example 13-4. The XML output (excerpt) for file copy

```
<?xml version="1.0"?>
<doc>
    <assembly>
        <name>FileCopier</name>
    </assembly>
    <members>
        <member name="T:FileCopier.Form1">
            <summary>
            Form demonstrating Windows Forms implementation
            </summary>
        </member>
        <member name="F:FileCopier.Form1.components">
            <summary>
            Required designer variable.
            </summary>
        </member>
        <member name="F:FileCopier.Form1.tvwTargetDir">
            <summary>
              Tree view of potential target directories
```

Example 13-4. The XML output (excerpt) for file copy (continued)

```
        </summary>
    </member>
    <member name="F:FileCopier.Form1.tvwSource">
        <summary>
            Tree view of source directories
            includes check boxes for checking
            chosen files or directories
        </summary>
    </member>
    <member name="F:FileCopier.Form1.txtTargetDir">
```

The file is quite long, and although it can be read by humans, it is not especially useful in that format. You could, however, write an XSLT file to translate the XML into HTML, or you could read the XML document into a database of documentation.

One of the simplest things to do with the documentation comments in your source code is to allow Visual Studio to generate a Code Comment Web Report. You choose this from the Tools menu (Tools → Build Comment Web Pages. . .), and the IDE does the rest. The result is a set of HTML files that you can view from within the IDE or from a browser, as shown in Figure 13-9.

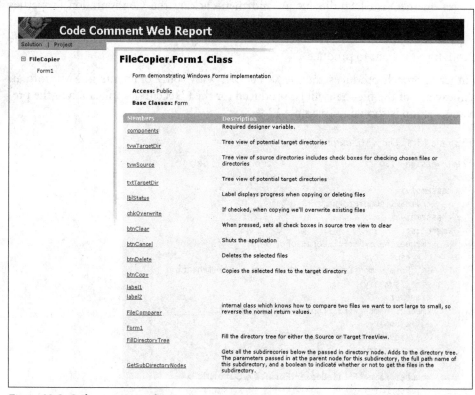

Figure 13-9. Code comment web report

Every member preceded by a documentation comment is included in the XML file via a `<member>` tag added by the compiler, along with a name attribute that identifies the member. You can also make use of predefined tags to increase the richness of the generated documentation. For example, you can add `<see>` comments to reference another member in the class or `<exception>` to document exception classes. A detailed discussion of XML Documentation Comments is beyond the scope of this book, but a complete listing of available tags can be found in the *C# Programmers Reference* that is included with Visual Studio.

Deploying an Application

Now that the application works, how do you deploy it? The good news is that in .NET there is no Registry to fuss with; you could, in fact, just copy the assembly to a new machine.

For example, you can compile the program in Example 13-3 into an assembly named `FileCopier.exe`. You can then copy that file to a new machine and double-click it. Presto! It works. No muss, no fuss.

Deployment Projects

For larger commercial applications, this simple approach might not be enough, sweet as it is. Customers would like you to install the files in the appropriate directories, set up shortcuts, and so forth.

Visual Studio provides extensive help for deployment. The process is to add a `Setup` and `Deployment` project to your application project. For example, assuming you are in the `FileCopier` project, choose Add Project → New Project from the File menu and choose Setup and Deployment Projects. You should see the dialog box shown in Figure 13-10.

You have a variety of choices here. For a Windows project such as this one, your choices include:

Cab Project
Much like a ZIP file, this compresses a number of small files into an easy-to-use (and easy-to-transport) package. This option can be combined with the others.

Merge Module
If you have more than one project that use files in common, this option helps you make intermediate merge modules. You can then integrate these modules into the other deployment projects.

Setup Project
This creates a setup file that automatically installs your files and resources.

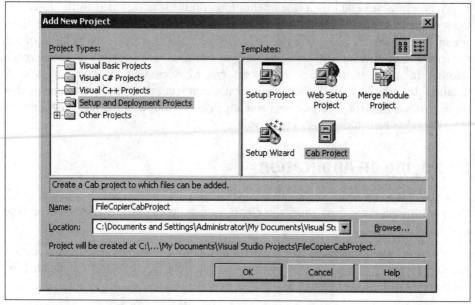

Figure 13-10. The New Project dialog box

Setup Wizard
Helps create one of the other types.

Remote Deploy Wizard
Helps create an installer project that can be deployed automatically.

Web Setup Project
Helps deploy a web-based project.

You would create a Cab Project first if you had many small ancillary files that had to be distributed with your application (for example, if you had *.html* files, *.gif* files, or other resources included with your program).

To see how this works, use the menu choice File → Add Project → New Project and choose and name a Setup and Deployment Project, selecting CAB File. When you name the project (for example, FileCopierCabProject) and click OK, you'll see that the project has been added to your group (as shown in Figure 13-11).

Right-clicking the project brings up a context menu. Choose Add, and you have two choices: Project Output. . . and File. . .. The latter allows you to add *any* arbitrary file to the Cab. The former offers a menu of its own, as shown in Figure 13-12.

Here you can choose to add sets of files to your Cab collection. The Primary output is the target assembly for the selected project. The other files are optional elements of the selected project that you might or might not want to distribute.

Figure 13-11. The Cab project added to your group

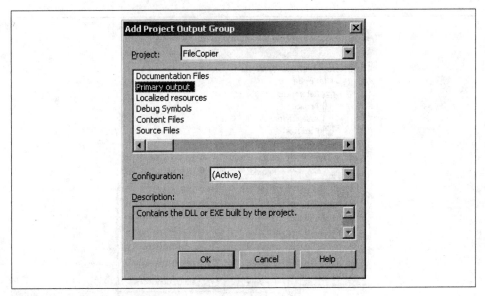

Figure 13-12. Project Output menu

In this case, select Primary Output. The choice is reflected in the Solution Explorer, as shown in Figure 13-13.

You can now build this project, and the result is a *.cab* file (see the Visual Studio Output window to find out where the *.cab* was created). You can examine this file with WinZip, as shown in Figure 13-14. If you do not have WinZip, you can use the *expand* utility (**-D** lists the contents of a *.cab* file):

```
C:\...\FileCopierCabProject\Debug>expand -D FileCopierCabProject.CAB
Microsoft (R) File Expansion Utility  Version 5.1.2600.0
Copyright (C) Microsoft Corp 1990-1999.  All rights reserved.
filecopiercabproject.cab: OSDBF.OSD
filecopiercabproject.cab: FileCopier.exe
2 files total.
```

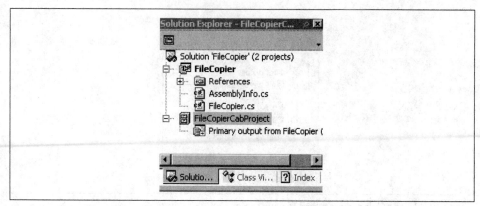

Figure 13-13. The modified project

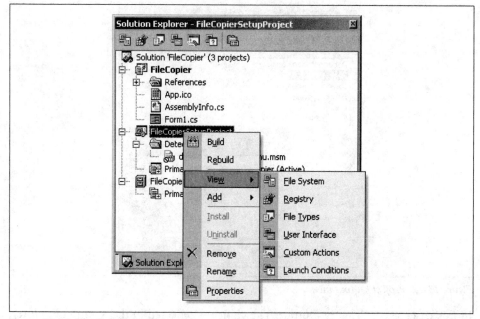

Figure 13-14. The Cab file contents

You see the executable file you expect, along with another file, *Osd8c0.osd* (the name of this file may vary). Opening this file reveals that it is an XML description of the *.cab* file itself, as shown in Example 13-5.

Example 13-5. The .cab file description file

```
<?XML version="1.0" ENCODING='UTF-8'?>
<!DOCTYPE SOFTPKG SYSTEM
"http://www.microsoft.com/standards/osd/osd.dtd">
<?XML::namespace href="http://www.microsoft.com/standards/osd/msicd.dtd"
as="MSICD"?>
```

Example 13-5. The .cab file description file (continued)

```
<SOFTPKG NAME="FileCopierCabProject" VERSION="1,0,0,0">
        <TITLE> FileCopierCabProject </TITLE>
            <MSICD::NATIVECODE>
                <CODE NAME="FileCopier">
                    <IMPLEMENTATION>
                        <CODEBASE FILENAME="FileCopier.exe">
                        </CODEBASE>
                    </IMPLEMENTATION>
                </CODE>
            </MSICD::NATIVECODE>
</SOFTPKG>
```

Setup Project

To create a Setup package, add another project, choosing Setup Project. This project type is very flexible; it allows all of your setup options to be bundled in an MSI installation file.

If you right-click the project and select Add, you see additional options in the pop-up menu. In addition to Project Output and File, you now find Merge Module and Component. As you did with the Cab project, use the Add option to add the Primary output to the Setup Project.

Merge Modules are mix-and-match pieces that can later be added to a full Setup project. Component allows you to add .NET components that your distribution might need but which might not be on the target machine.

The user interface for customizing Setup consists of a split pane whose contents are determined by the View menu. Access the View menu by right-clicking the project itself, as shown in Figure 13-15.

As you make selections from the View menu, the panes in the IDE change to reflect your choices and to offer you options.

For example, if you choose File System, the IDE opens a split-pane viewer, with a directory tree on the left and the details on the right. Clicking the Application Folder shows the file you've already added (the primary output), as shown in Figure 13-16.

You are free to add or delete files. Right-clicking in the detail window brings up a context menu, as shown in Figure 13-17.

You can see there is great flexibility here to add precisely those files you want.

Deployment Locations

The folder into which your files will be loaded (the Application Folder) is determined by the Default Location. The Properties window for the Application Folder describes the Default Location as *[ProgramFilesFolder]\[Manufacturer]\[Product Name]*.

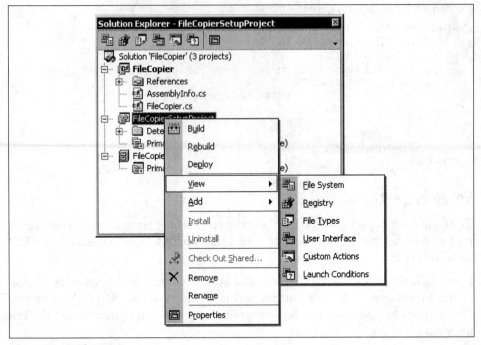

Figure 13-15. The View menu

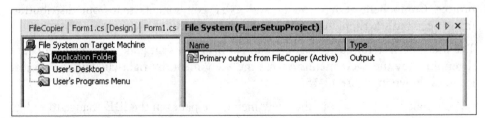

Figure 13-16. The Application Folder

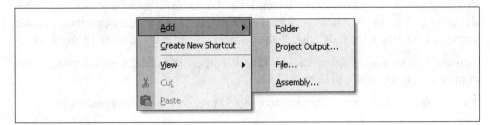

Figure 13-17. Context menu within the File Detail window

ProgramFilesFolder refers to the program files folder on the target machine. The *Manufacturer* and the *Product Name* are properties of the project. If you click the

Project and examine its properties, you see that the IDE has made some good guesses, as shown in Figure 13-18.

Figure 13-18. Setup project properties

You can easily modify these properties. For example, you can modify the property Manufacturer to change the folder in which the product will be stored under Program Files.

Creating a shortcut

If you want the install program to create a shortcut on the user's desktop, you can right-click the Primary Output file in the Application Folder, then create the shortcut and drag it to the user's Desktop, as shown in Figure 13-19.

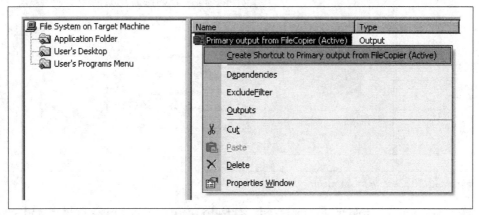

Figure 13-19. Create a shortcut on the user's desktop

Entries in My Documents

You can add items to the *My Documents* folder on the user's machine. First, right-click on *File System on Target Machine*, then choose Add Special Folder → User's Personal Data Folder. You can then place items in the *User's Personal Data Folder*.

Shortcuts in the Start menu

In addition to adding a shortcut to the desktop, you might want to create a folder within the Start → Programs menu. To do so, click the User's Program Menu folder, right-click in the right pane, and choose Add Folder. Within that folder, you can add the Primary Output, either by dragging or by right-clicking and choosing Add.

Adding Special Folders

In addition to the four folders provided for you (Application Folder, User's Desktop, User's Personal Data Folder, User's Program Menu), there are a host of additional options. Right-click the File System On Target Machine folder to get the menu, as shown in Figure 13-20.

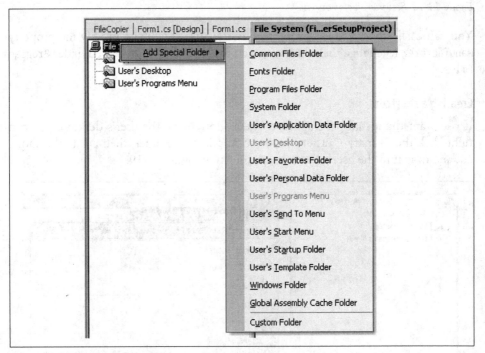

Figure 13-20. Custom folder menu

Here you can add folders for fonts, add items to the user's Favorites Folder, and so forth. Most of these are self-explanatory.

Other View Windows

So far, you've looked only at the File System folders from the original View menu (pictured in Figure 13-15).

Making changes to the Registry

The Registry window (right-click on FileCopierSetupProject, and select Registry from the View menu) allows you to tell Setup to make adjustments to the user's Registry files, as shown in Figure 13-21. Click any folder in this list to edit the associated properties in the Properties window.

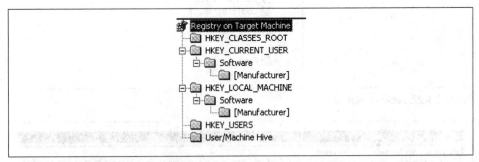

Figure 13-21. Setting up the Registry

 Careful! There is nothing more dangerous than touching the Registry. In most .NET applications this will not be needed because .NET-managed applications do not use the Registry.

Registering file types

The File Types choice on the View menu allows you to associate application-specific file types on the user's machine. You can also set the action to take with these files.

Managing the UI during Setup

The View/User Interface selection lets you take direct control over the text and graphics shown during each step of the Setup process. The workflow of Setup is shown as a tree, as shown in Figure 13-22.

When you click a step in the process, the properties for that form are displayed. For example, clicking the Welcome form under Install/Start displays the properties shown in Figure 13-23.

The properties offer you the opportunity to change the Banner Bitmap and the text displayed in the opening dialog box. You can add dialog boxes that Microsoft provides, or import your own dialog boxes into the process.

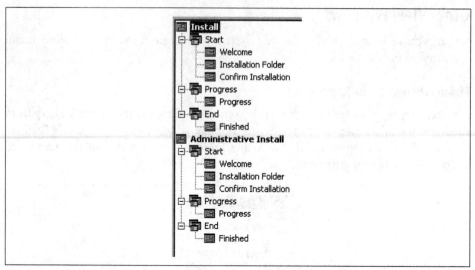

Figure 13-22. Setup workflow

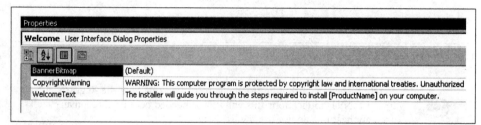

Figure 13-23. The Welcome form

Other View choices

If the workflow does not provide sufficient control, you can choose the Custom Options choice from the View menu. You can also specify Launch conditions for the Setup process itself.

Building the Setup Project

Once you've made all your choices and set all the options, choose Configuration Manager from the Build menu and make sure your Setup Project is included in the current configuration. Next, you can build the Setup project. The result is a single Setup file (*FileCopierSetupProject.msi*) that can be distributed to your customers.

CHAPTER 14

Accessing Data with ADO.NET

Many real-world applications need to interact with a database. The .NET Framework provides a rich set of objects to manage database interaction; these classes are collectively referred to as ADO.NET.

ADO.NET looks very similar to ADO, its predecessor. The key difference is that ADO.NET is a *disconnected* data architecture. In a disconnected architecture, data is retrieved from a database and cached on your local machine. You manipulate the data on your local computer and connect to the database only when you wish to alter records or acquire new data.

There are significant advantages to disconnecting your data architecture from your database. The biggest advantage is that you avoid many of the problems associated with connected data objects that do not scale very well. Database connections are resource-intensive, and it is difficult to have thousands (or hundreds of thousands) of simultaneous continuous connections. A disconnected architecture is resource-frugal.

ADO.NET connects to the database to retrieve data, and connects again to update data when you've made changes. Most applications spend most of their time simply reading through data and displaying it; ADO.NET provides a disconnected subset of the data for your use while reading and displaying.

Disconnected data objects work in a mode similar to that of the Web. All web sessions are disconnected, and state is not preserved between web page requests. A disconnected data architecture makes for a cleaner marriage with the Web.

Relational Databases and SQL

Although one can certainly write an entire book on relational databases, and another on SQL, the essentials of these technologies are not hard to understand. A *database* is a repository of data. A *relational database* organizes your data into tables. Consider the Northwind database provided with Microsoft SQL Server 7, SQL Server 2000, and all versions of Microsoft Access.

Tables, Records, and Columns

The Northwind database describes a fictional company buying and selling food products. The data for Northwind is divided into 13 tables, including Customers, Employees, Orders, Order Details, Products, and so forth.

Every table in a relational database is organized into rows, where each row represents a single record. The rows are organized into columns. All the rows in a table have the same column structure. For example, the Orders table has these columns: OrderID, CustomerID, EmployeeID, OrderDate, etc.

For any given order, you need to know the customer's name, address, contact name, and so forth. You could store that information with each order, but that would be very inefficient. Instead, we use a second table called Customers, in which each row represents a single customer. In the Customers table is a column for the CustomerID. Each customer has a unique ID, and that field is marked as the *primary key* for that table. A primary key is the column or combination of columns that uniquely identifies a record in a given table.

The Orders table uses the CustomerID as a *foreign key*. A foreign key is a column (or combination of columns) that is a primary (or otherwise unique) key from a different table. The Orders table uses the CustomerID (the primary key used in the Customers table) to identify which customer has placed the order. To determine the address for the order, you can use the CustomerID to look up the customer record in the Customers table.

This use of foreign keys is particularly helpful in representing one-to-many or many-to-one relationships between tables. By separating information into tables that are linked by foreign keys, you avoid having to repeat information in records. A single customer, for example, can have multiple orders, but it is inefficient to place the same customer information (name, phone number, credit limit, and so on) in every order record. The process of removing redundant information from your records and shifting it to separate tables is called *normalization*.

Normalization

Normalization not only makes your use of the database more efficient, but also it reduces the likelihood of data corruption. If you kept the customer's name both in the Customers table and also in the Orders table, you would run the risk that a change in one table might not be reflected in the other. Thus, if you changed the customer's address in the Customers table, that change might not be reflected in every row in the Orders table (and a lot of work would be necessary to make sure that it was reflected). By keeping only the CustomerID in Orders, you are free to change the address in Customers, and the change is automatically reflected for each order.

Just as C# programmers want the compiler to catch bugs at compile time rather than at runtime, database programmers want the database to help them avoid data corruption. The compiler helps avoid bugs in C# by enforcing the rules of the language; for example, you can't use a variable you've not defined. SQL Server and other modern relational databases avoid bugs by enforcing constraints that you request. For example, the Customers database marks the CustomerID as a primary key. This creates a primary key constraint in the database, which ensures that each CustomerID is unique. If you were to enter a customer named Liberty Associates, Inc. with the CustomerID of LIBE, and then tried to add Liberty Mutual Funds with a CustomerID of LIBE, the database would reject the second record because of the primary key constraint.

Declarative Referential Integrity

Relational databases use *Declarative Referential Integrity* (DRI) to establish constraints on the relationships among the various tables. For example, you might declare a constraint on the Orders table that dictates that no order can have a CustomerID unless that CustomerID represents a valid record in Customers. This helps avoid two types of mistakes. First, you cannot enter a record with an invalid CustomerID. Second, you cannot delete a Customer record if that CustomerID is used in any order. The integrity of your data and their relationships are thus protected.

SQL

The most popular language for querying and manipulating databases is SQL, usually pronounced "sequel." SQL is a declarative language, as opposed to a procedural language, and it can take a while to get used to working with a declarative language when you are used to languages such as C#.

The heart of SQL is the *query*. A query is a statement that returns a set of records from the database.

For example, you might like to see all the CompanyNames and CustomerIDs of every record in the Customers table in which the customer's address is in London. To do so, write:

```
Select CustomerID, CompanyName from Customers where city = 'London'
```

This returns the following six records as output:

```
CustomerID CompanyName
---------- ----------------------------------------
AROUT      Around the Horn
BSBEV      B's Beverages
CONSH      Consolidated Holdings
EASTC      Eastern Connection
NORTS      North/South
SEVES      Seven Seas Imports
```

SQL is capable of much more powerful queries. For example, suppose the North-winds manager would like to know what products were purchased in July of 1996 by the customer "Vins et alcools Chevalier." This turns out to be somewhat compli-cated. The Order Details table knows the ProductID for all the products in any given order. The Orders table knows which CustomerIDs are associated with an order. The Customers table knows the CustomerID for a customer, and the Products table knows the Product name for the ProductID. How do you tie all this together? Here's the query:

```
select  o.OrderID, productName
from [Order Details] od
join orders o on o.OrderID = od.OrderID
join products p on p.ProductID = od.ProductID
join customers c on o.CustomerID = c.CustomerID
where c.CompanyName = 'Vins et alcools Chevalier'
and orderDate >= '7/1/1996' and orderDate <= '7/31/1996'
```

This asks the database to get the OrderID and the product name from the relevant tables. First, look at Order Details (which we've called od for short), then join that with the Orders table for every record in which the OrderID in the Order Details table is the same as the OrderID in the Orders table.

When you join two tables, you can say either "Get every record that exists in either table" (this is called an *outer join*), or you can say, as I've done here, "Get only those records that exist in both tables" (called an *inner join*). That is, an inner join states to get only the records in Orders that match the records in Order Details by having the same value in the OrderID field (on o.Orderid = od.Orderid).

 SQL joins are inner joins by default. Writing join orders is the same as writing inner join orders.

The SQL statement goes on to ask the database to create an inner join with Products, getting every row in which the ProductID in the Products table is the same as the ProductID in the Order Details table.

Then create an inner join with customers for those rows where the CustomerID is the same in both the Orders table and the Customer table.

Finally, tell the database to constrain the results to only those rows in which the CompanyName is the one you want, and the dates are in July.

The collection of constraints finds only three records that match:

```
OrderID     ProductName
----------- ----------------------------------------
10248       Queso Cabrales
10248       Singaporean Hokkien Fried Mee
10248       Mozzarella di Giovanni
```

This output shows that there was only one order (10248) in which the customer had the right ID and in which the date of the order was July 1996. That order produced three records in the Order Details table, and using the product IDs in these three records, we got the product names from the Products table.

You can use SQL not only for searching for and retrieving data, but also for creating, updating, and deleting tables and generally managing and manipulating both the content and the structure of the database.

For a full explanation of SQL and tips on how to put it to best use, I recommend *Transact SQL Programming*, by Kline, Gould, and Zanevsky (O'Reilly & Associates, 1999).

The ADO.NET Object Model

The ADO.NET object model is rich, but at its heart it is a fairly straightforward set of classes. The most important of these is the DataSet. The DataSet represents a subset of the entire database, cached on your machine without a continuous connection to the database.

Periodically, you'll reconnect the DataSet to its parent database, update the database with changes you've made to the DataSet, and update the DataSet with changes in the database made by other processes.

This is highly efficient, but to be effective the DataSet must be a robust subset of the database, capturing not just a few rows from a single table, but also a set of tables with all the metadata necessary to represent the relationships and constraints of the original database. This is, not surprisingly, what ADO.NET provides.

The DataSet is composed of DataTable objects as well as DataRelation objects. These are accessed as properties of the DataSet object. The Tables property returns a DataTableCollection, which in turn contains all the DataTable objects.

DataTables and DataColumns

The DataTable can be created programmatically or as a result of a query against the database. The DataTable has a number of public properties, including the Columns collection, which returns the DataColumnCollection object, which in turn consists of DataColumn objects. Each DataColumn object represents a column in a table.

DataRelations

In addition to the Tables collection, the DataSet has a Relations property, which returns a DataRelationCollection consisting of DataRelation objects. Each DataRelation represents a relationship between two tables through DataColumn objects. For example, in the Northwind database the Customers table is in a relationship with the Orders table through the CustomerID column.

The nature of the relationship is one-to-many, or parent-to-child. For any given order, there will be exactly one customer, but any given customer might be represented in any number of orders.

Rows

DataTable's Rows collection returns a set of rows for any given table. Use this collection to examine the results of queries against the database, iterating through the rows to examine each record in turn. Programmers experienced with ADO are often confused by the absence of the RecordSet with its moveNext and movePrevious commands. With ADO.NET, you do not iterate through the DataSet; instead, access the table you need, and then you can iterate through the Rows collection, typically with a foreach loop. You'll see this in the first example in this chapter.

Data Adapter

The DataSet is an abstraction of a relational database. ADO.NET uses a DataAdapter as a bridge between the DataSet and the data source, which is the underlying database. DataAdapter provides the Fill() method to retrieve data from the database and populate the DataSet.

DBCommand and DBConnection

The DBConnection object represents a connection to a data source. This connection can be shared among different command objects. The DBCommand object allows you to send a command (typically a SQL statement or a stored procedure) to the database. Often these objects are implicitly created when you create your DataSet, but you can explicitly access these objects, as you'll see in a subsequent example.

The DataAdapter Object

Rather than tie the DataSet object too closely to your database architecture, ADO.NET uses a DataAdapter object to mediate between the DataSet object and the database. This decouples the DataSet from the database and allows a single DataSet to represent more than one database or other data source.

Getting Started with ADO.NET

Enough theory! Let's write some code and see how this works. Working with ADO.NET can be complex, but for many queries, the model is surprisingly simple.

In this example, create a simple Windows Form, with a single list box in it called lbCustomers. Populate this list box with bits of information from the Customers table in the Northwind database.

Begin by creating a DataAdapter object:

```
SqlDataAdapter DataAdapter =
new SqlDataAdapter(
commandString, connectionString);
```

The two parameters are commandString and connectionString. The commandString is the SQL statement that will generate the data you want in your DataSet:

```
string commandString =
    "Select CompanyName, ContactName from Customers";
```

The connectionString is whatever string is needed to connect to the database. In my case, I'm running SQL Server on my development machine where I have left the system administrator (*sa*) password blank (I know, I know, not a good idea. I'll fix it by the time this book is released. Honest.):

```
string connectionString =
    "server=localhost; uid=sa; pwd=; database=northwind";
```

If you do not have SQL Server installed, select *Samples and Quickstart Tutorials* from the Microsoft .NET Framework SDK program group. A web page appears, giving you the option to install the .NET Framework Samples Database, which includes an installation of SQL Server. After you install the samples database, set up the Quick-Starts (this will create the northwind sample database). To use this database, you need this connection string:

```
"server=(local)\\NetSDK; Trusted_Connection=yes; database=northwind"
```

With the DataAdapter in hand, you're ready to create the DataSet and fill it with the data that you obtain from the SQL select statement:

```
DataSet DataSet = new DataSet( );
DataAdapter.Fill(DataSet,"Customers");
```

That's it. You now have a DataSet, and you can query, manipulate, and otherwise manage the data. The DataSet has a collection of tables; you care only about the first one because you've retrieved only a single record:

```
DataTable dataTable = DataSet.Tables[0];
```

You can extract the rows you've retrieved with the SQL statement and add the data to the list box:

```
foreach (DataRow dataRow in dataTable.Rows)
{
    lbCustomers.Items.Add(
        dataRow["CompanyName"] +
        " (" + dataRow["ContactName"] + ")" );
}
```

The list box is filled with the company name and contact name from the table in the database, according to the SQL statement we passed in. Example 14-1 contains the complete source for this example.

Example 14-1. Working with ADO.NET

```csharp
using System;
using System.Drawing;
using System.Collections;
using System.ComponentModel;
using System.Windows.Forms;
using System.Data;
using System.Data.SqlClient;

namespace ProgrammingCSharpWinForm
{

    public class ADOForm1 : System.Windows.Forms.Form
    {
        private System.ComponentModel.Container components;
        private System.Windows.Forms.ListBox lbCustomers;

        public ADOForm1( )
        {
            InitializeComponent( );

            // connect to my local server, northwind db
            string connectionString = "server=(local)\\NetSDK;" +
            "Trusted_Connection=yes; database=northwind";

            // get records from the customers table
            string commandString =
            "Select CompanyName, ContactName from Customers";

            // create the data set command object
            // and the DataSet
            SqlDataAdapter DataAdapter =
            new SqlDataAdapter(
            commandString, connectionString);

            DataSet DataSet = new DataSet( );

            // fill the data set object
            DataAdapter.Fill(DataSet,"Customers");

            // Get the one table from the DataSet
            DataTable dataTable = DataSet.Tables[0];

            // for each row in the table, display the info
            foreach (DataRow dataRow in dataTable.Rows)
            {
                lbCustomers.Items.Add(
                    dataRow["CompanyName"] +
                    " (" + dataRow["ContactName"] + ")" );
            }

        }
```

Example 14-1. Working with ADO.NET (continued)

```
    protected override void Dispose(bool disposing)
    {
        if (disposing)
        {
            if (components == null)
            {
                components.Dispose( );
            }
        }
        base.Dispose(disposing);
    }

    private void InitializeComponent( )
    {
        this.components =
            new System.ComponentModel.Container ( );
        this.lbCustomers = new System.Windows.Forms.ListBox ( );
        lbCustomers.Location = new System.Drawing.Point (48, 24);
        lbCustomers.Size = new System.Drawing.Size (368, 160);
        lbCustomers.TabIndex = 0;
        this.Text = "ADOFrm1";
        this.AutoScaleBaseSize = new System.Drawing.Size (5, 13);
        this.ClientSize = new System.Drawing.Size (464, 273);
        this.Controls.Add (this.lbCustomers);
    }


    public static void Main(string[] args)
    {
        Application.Run(new ADOForm1( ));
    }
  }
}
```

With just a few lines of code, you have extracted a set of data from the database and displayed it in the list box, as shown in Figure 14-1.

The eight lines of code accomplish the following tasks:

- Create the string for the connection:

```
string connectionString = "server=(local)\\NetSDK;" +
"Trusted_Connection=yes; database=northwind";
```

- Create the string for the select statement:

```
string commandString =
"Select CompanyName, ContactName from Customers";
```

- Create the DataAdapter and pass in the selection and connection strings:

```
SqlDataAdapter DataAdapter =
new SqlDataAdapter(
commandString, connectionString);
```

Figure 14-1. Output from Example 14-1

- Create a new DataSet object:

```
DataSet DataSet = new DataSet( );
```

- Fill the DataSet from the Customers table using the DataAdapter:

```
DataAdapter.Fill(DataSet,"Customers");
```

- Extract the DataTable from the DataSet:

```
DataTable dataTable = DataSet.Tables[0];
```

- Use the DataTable to fill the list box:

```
foreach (DataRow dataRow in dataTable.Rows)
{
    lbCustomers.Items.Add(
        dataRow["CompanyName"] +
        " (" + dataRow["ContactName"] + ")" );
}
```

Using OLE DB Managed Providers

The previous example used one of the two managed providers currently available with ADO.NET: the SQL Server Managed Provider and OLE DB Managed Provider. The SQL Server Managed Provider is optimized for SQL Server and is restricted to working with SQL Server databases. The more general solution is the OLE DB Managed Provider, which will connect to any OLE DB provider, including Access.

You can rewrite Example 14-1 to work with the Northwind database using Access rather than SQL Server with just a few small changes. First, you need to change the connection string:

```
string connectionString =
    "provider=Microsoft.JET.OLEDB.4.0; "
    + "data source = c:\\nwind.mdb";
```

This query connects to the Northwind database on C drive. (Your exact path might be different.)

Next, change the DataAdapter object to an ADODataAdapter rather than a Sql-DataAdapter:

```
OleDbDataAdapter DataAdapter =
    new OleDbDataAdapter (commandString, connectionString);
```

Also be sure to add a using statement for the OleDb namespace:

```
using System.Data.OleDb;
```

This design pattern continues throughout the two Managed Providers; for every object whose class name begins with "Sql," there is a corresponding class beginning with "OleDb." Example 14-2 illustrates the complete OLE DB version of Example 14-1.

Example 14-2. Using the ADO Managed Provider

```
using System;
using System.Drawing;
using System.Collections;
using System.ComponentModel;
using System.Windows.Forms;
using System.Data;
using System.Data.OleDb;

namespace ProgrammingCSharpWinForm
{

    public class ADOForm1 : System.Windows.Forms.Form
    {
        private System.ComponentModel.Container components;
        private System.Windows.Forms.ListBox lbCustomers;

        public ADOForm1()
        {
            InitializeComponent();

            // connect to Northwind Access database
            string connectionString =
               "provider=Microsoft.JET.OLEDB.4.0; "
               + "data source = c:\\nwind.mdb";


            // get records from the customers table
            string commandString =
            "Select CompanyName, ContactName from Customers";

            // create the data set command object
            // and the DataSet
```

Example 14-2. Using the ADO Managed Provider (continued)

```
      OleDbDataAdapter DataAdapter =
      new OleDbDataAdapter(
      commandString, connectionString);

      DataSet DataSet = new DataSet( );

      // fill the data set object
      DataAdapter.Fill(DataSet,"Customers");

      // Get the one table from the DataSet
      DataTable dataTable = DataSet.Tables[0];

      // for each row in the table, display the info
      foreach (DataRow dataRow in dataTable.Rows)
      {
         lbCustomers.Items.Add(
            dataRow["CompanyName"] +
            " (" + dataRow["ContactName"] + ")" );
      }

   }

   protected override void Dispose(bool disposing)
   {
      if (disposing)
      {
         if (components == null)
         {
             components.Dispose( );
         }
      }
      base.Dispose(disposing);
   }

   private void InitializeComponent( )
   {
      this.components =
         new System.ComponentModel.Container ( );
      this.lbCustomers = new System.Windows.Forms.ListBox ( );
      lbCustomers.Location = new System.Drawing.Point (48, 24);
      lbCustomers.Size = new System.Drawing.Size (368, 160);
      lbCustomers.TabIndex = 0;
      this.Text = "ADOFrm1";
      this.AutoScaleBaseSize = new System.Drawing.Size (5, 13);
      this.ClientSize = new System.Drawing.Size (464, 273);
      this.Controls.Add (this.lbCustomers);
   }


   public static void Main(string[] args)
   {
```

Example 14-2. Using the ADO Managed Provider (continued)

```
        Application.Run(new ADOForm1( ));
      }
   }
}
```

The output from this is identical to that from the previous example, as shown in Figure 14-2.

Figure 14-2. Using the ADO Managed Provider

The OLE DB Managed Provider is more general than the SQL Managed Provider and can, in fact, be used to connect to SQL Server as well as to any other OLE DB object. Because the SQL Server Provider is optimized for SQL Server, it will be more efficient to use the SQL Server–specific provider when working with SQL Server. In time, any number of specialized managed providers will be available.

Working with Data-Bound Controls

ADO.NET provides good support for "data-bound" objects; that is, objects that can be tied to a particular data set, such as one retrieved from a database by ADO.NET.

A simple example of a data-bound control is the DataGrid control provided with both Windows Forms and Web Forms.

Populating a DataGrid

In its simplest use, a DataGrid is easy to implement. Once again, first create a DataSet and then fill it from the Customers table of the Northwind database, but this time, rather than iterating through the rows of the data set and writing the output to a list box, you can simply bind the Customers table in your data set to a DataGrid control.

To illustrate, alter Example 14-1 by deleting the list box from the form you created in the previous example and replace it with a DataGrid. The default name provided by the Visual Studio design tool is DataGrid1, but let's change it to CustomerDataGrid. After the data set is created and filled, bind the DataGrid through its DataSource property:

```
CustomerDataGrid.DataSource=
    DataSet.Tables["Customers"].DefaultView;
```

Example 14-3 provides the complete source code for this example.

Example 14-3. Using a DataGrid control

```
using System;
using System.Drawing;
using System.Collections;
using System.ComponentModel;
using System.Windows.Forms;
using System.Data;
using System.Data.SqlClient;

namespace ProgrammingCSharpWindows.Form
{

    public class ADOForm3 : System.Windows.Forms.Form
    {
        private System.ComponentModel.Container
            components;
        private System.Windows.Forms.DataGrid
            CustomerDataGrid;

        public ADOForm3( )
        {
            InitializeComponent( );

            // set up connection and command strings
            string connectionString = "server=(local)\\NetSDK;" +
            "Trusted_Connection=yes; database=northwind";
            string commandString =
                "Select CompanyName, ContactName, ContactTitle, "
                + "Phone, Fax from Customers";

            // create a data set and fill it
            SqlDataAdapter DataAdapter =
                new SqlDataAdapter(commandString, connectionString);
            DataSet DataSet = new DataSet( );
            DataAdapter.Fill(DataSet,"Customers");

            // bind the DataSet to the grid
            CustomerDataGrid.DataSource=
                DataSet.Tables["Customers"].DefaultView;
        }

        protected override void Dispose(bool disposing)
        {
```

Example 14-3. Using a DataGrid control (continued)

```
        if (disposing)
        {
            if (components == null)
            {
                components.Dispose( );
            }
        }
        base.Dispose(disposing);
    }

    private void InitializeComponent( )
    {
        this.components =
            new System.ComponentModel.Container ( );
        this.CustomerDataGrid =
            new System.Windows.Forms.DataGrid ( );
        CustomerDataGrid.BeginInit ( );
        CustomerDataGrid.Location =
            new System.Drawing.Point (8, 24);
        CustomerDataGrid.Size =
            new System.Drawing.Size (656, 224);
        CustomerDataGrid.DataMember = "";
        CustomerDataGrid.TabIndex = 0;
        CustomerDataGrid.Navigate +=
            new System.Windows.Forms.NavigateEventHandler
            (this.dataGrid1_Navigate);
        this.Text = "Using the Data Grid";
        this.AutoScaleBaseSize =
            new System.Drawing.Size (5, 13);
        this.ClientSize = new System.Drawing.Size (672, 273);
        this.Controls.Add (this.CustomerDataGrid);
        CustomerDataGrid.EndInit ( );
    }

    protected void dataGrid1_Navigate
        (object sender, System.Windows.Forms.NavigateEventArgs ne)
    {

    }

    public static void Main(string[] args)
    {
        Application.Run(new ADOForm3( ));
    }
  }
}
```

The code is embarrassingly easy to implement and the results are quite impressive, as shown in Figure 14-3. Notice that every field in the record is represented by a column in the DataGrid, and that the titles of the columns are the names of the fields. All of this is the default behavior of the DataGrid.

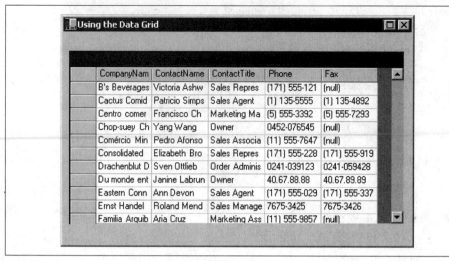

Figure 14-3. Using the DataGrid

Customizing the DataSet

It is possible to control precisely every aspect of creating the DataSet, rather than using the default settings. In the previous examples, when you created the DataSet you passed in a commandString and a connectionString:

```
SqlDataAdapter DataAdapter =
    new SqlDataAdapter(commandString, connectionString);
```

These were assigned internally to a SqlCommand object and a SqlConnection object, respectively. You can instead explicitly create these objects to gain finer control over their properties.

In this next example, you'll give the class four new class members:

```
private System.Data.SqlClient.SqlConnection myConnection;
private System.Data.DataSet myDataSet;
private System.Data.SqlClient.SqlCommand myCommand;
private System.Data.SqlClient.SqlDataAdapter DataAdapter;
```

The connection is created by instantiating a SqlConnection object with the connection string:

```
string connectionString = "server=(local)\\NetSDK;" +
    "Trusted_Connection=yes; database=northwind";
myConnection = new System.Data.Sql.SqlConnection(connectionString);
```

and then it is opened explicitly:

```
myConnection.Open();
```

By hanging on to this connection, you can reuse it (as you'll see in a subsequent example) and you can also use its transaction support if needed.

Next, explicitly create the DataSet object and set one of its properties:

```
myDataSet = new System.Data.DataSet( );
myDataSet.CaseSensitive=true;
```

Setting CaseSensitive to true indicates that string comparisons within DataTable objects are case-sensitive.

Next, explicitly create the SqlCommand object and give that new command object the connection object and the text for the command:

```
myCommand = new System.Data.SqlClient.SqlCommand( )
myCommand.Connection=myConnection;
myCommand.CommandText = "Select * from Customers";
```

Finally, create the SqlDataAdapter object and assign to it the SqlCommand object you just established. Then tell the DataSet how to map the table columns, using the table you're searching, and instruct the SqlDataAdapter to fill the DataSet object:

```
DataAdapter = new System.Data.SqlClient.SqlDataAdapter( );
DataAdapter.SelectCommand= myCommand;
DataAdapter.TableMappings.Add("Table","Customers");
DataAdapter.Fill(myDataSet);
```

That done, you're ready to fill the DataGrid:

```
dataGrid1.DataSource=
    myDataSet.Tables["Customers"].DefaultView;
```

(This time I've used the default name for the DataGrid.)

Example 14-4 provides the complete source code.

Example 14-4. Customizing a Dataset

```
namespace ProgrammingCSharpWindows.Form
{
    using System;
    using System.Drawing;
    using System.Collections;
    using System.ComponentModel;
    using System.Windows.Forms;
    using System.Data;
    using System.Data.SqlClient;

    public class ADOForm1 : System.Windows.Forms.Form
    {
        private System.ComponentModel.Container components;
        private System.Windows.Forms.DataGrid dataGrid1;


        // private System.Data.ADO.ADOConnection myConnection;
        private System.Data.SqlClient.SqlConnection myConnection;
        private System.Data.DataSet myDataSet;
        private System.Data.SqlClient.SqlCommand myCommand;
```

Example 14-4. Customizing a Dataset (continued)

```csharp
    private System.Data.SqlClient.SqlDataAdapter DataAdapter;

    public ADOForm1( )
    {
        InitializeComponent( );

        // create the connection object and open it
        string connectionString = "server=(local)\\NetSDK;" +
            "Trusted_Connection=yes; database=northwind";
        myConnection = new
            System.Data.SqlClient.SqlConnection(connectionString);
        myConnection.Open( );

        // create the DataSet and set a property
        myDataSet = new System.Data.DataSet( );
        myDataSet.CaseSensitive=true;

        // create the SqlCommand  object and assign the
        // connection and the select statement
        myCommand = new System.Data.SqlClient.SqlCommand( );
        myCommand.Connection=myConnection;
        myCommand.CommandText = "Select * from Customers";

        // create the DataAdapter object and pass in the
        // SQL Command object and establish the table mappings
        DataAdapter = new System.Data.SqlClient.SqlDataAdapter( );
        DataAdapter.SelectCommand= myCommand;
        DataAdapter.TableMappings.Add("Table","Customers");

        // Tell the DataAdapter object to fill the DataSet
        DataAdapter.Fill(myDataSet);

        // display it in the grid
        dataGrid1.DataSource=
            myDataSet.Tables["Customers"].DefaultView;
    }

    protected override void Dispose(bool disposing)
    {
        if (disposing)
        {
            if (components == null)
            {
                components.Dispose( );
            }
        }
        base.Dispose(disposing);
    }

    private void InitializeComponent( )
    {
```

Example 14-4. Customizing a Dataset (continued)

```
        this.components = new System.ComponentModel.Container ( );
        this.dataGrid1 = new System.Windows.Forms.DataGrid ( );
        dataGrid1.BeginInit ( );
        dataGrid1.Location = new System.Drawing.Point (24, 32);
        dataGrid1.Size = new System.Drawing.Size (480, 408);
        dataGrid1.DataMember = "";
        dataGrid1.TabIndex = 0;
        this.Text = "Using the Data Grid";
        this.AutoScaleBaseSize = new System.Drawing.Size (5, 13);
        this.ClientSize = new System.Drawing.Size (536, 501);
        this.Controls.Add (this.dataGrid1);
        dataGrid1.EndInit ( );
    }

    public static void Main(string[] args)
    {
        Application.Run(new ADOForm1( ));
    }
  }
}
```

The result of this is shown in Figure 14-4. Now that you have this control, you are in a position to get much fancier in your use of the grid.

Figure 14-4. Taking direct control of the DataGrid

Combining Data Tables

With the work you've done so far, it is easy now to build a grid that reflects the relationship between two or more tables. For example, you might like to examine all the orders that each customer has placed over some period of time.

Relational databases are built on the idea that one table relates to other tables. The relationship between Orders and Customers is that every order includes a CustomerID, which is a *foreign key* in Orders and a *primary key* in Customers. Thus, you have a one-to-many relationship, in which one customer can have many orders, but each order has exactly one customer. You'd like to be able to display this relationship in the grid.

ADO.NET makes this fairly easy, and you can build on the previous example. This time, you want to represent two tables, Customers and Orders, rather than just the Customers table. To do so, you need only a single DataSet object and a single Connection object, but you need two SqlCommand objects and two SqlDataAdapter objects.

After you create the SqlDataAdapter for Customers, just as you did in the previous example, go on to create a second command and adapter for Orders:

```
myCommand2 = new System.Data.SqlClient.SqlCommand( );
DataAdapter2 = new System.Data.SqlClient.SqlDataAdapter( );
myCommand2.Connection = myConnection;
myCommand2.CommandText = "SELECT * FROM Orders";
```

Notice that DataAdapter2 can reuse the same connection as used by the earlier DataAdapter object. The new CommandText is different, of course, because you are searching a different table.

Next, associate the second SqlDataAdapter object with this new command and map its table to Orders. You can then fill the DataSet with the second table:

```
DataAdapter2.SelectCommand = myCommand2;
DataAdapter2.TableMappings.Add ("Table", "Orders");
DataAdapter2.Fill(myDataSet);
```

You now have a single DataSet with two tables. You can display either or both of the tables, but in this example you'll do more. There is a relationship between these tables, and you want to display that relationship. Unfortunately, the DataSet is ignorant of the relationship, unless you explicitly create a DataRelation object and add it to the DataSet.

Start by declaring an object of type DataRelation:

```
System.Data.DataRelation dataRelation;
```

This relation will represent the relationship in the database between Customers.CustomerID and Orders.CustomerID. To model this, you need a pair of DataColumn objects:

```
System.Data.DataColumn dataColumn1;
System.Data.DataColumn dataColumn2;
```

Each DataColumn must be assigned a column in the table within the DataSet:

```
dataColumn1 =
   myDataSet.Tables["Customers"].Columns["CustomerID"];
dataColumn2 =
   myDataSet.Tables["Orders"].Columns["CustomerID"];
```

You're now ready to create the DataRelation object, passing into the constructor the name of the relationship and the two DataColumn objects:

```
dataRelation =
    new System.Data.DataRelation("CustomersToOrders",
    dataColumn1, dataColumn2);
```

You can now add that relation to the DataSet:

```
myDataSet.Relations.Add(dataRelation);
```

Next, create a DataViewManager object that provides a view of the DataSet for the DataGrid, and set the DataGrid.DataSource property to that view:

```
DataViewManager DataSetView =
    myDataSet.DefaultViewManager;
dataGrid1.DataSource = DataSetView;
```

Finally, because the DataGrid now has more than one table, you must tell the grid which table is the "parent" table, or the one table to which many other tables can relate. Do this by setting the DataMember property as shown:

```
dataGrid1.DataMember= "Customers";
```

Example 14-5 provides the complete source for this process.

Example 14-5. Using a DataGrid with two tables

```
using System;
using System.Drawing;
using System.Collections;
using System.ComponentModel;
using System.Windows.Forms;
using System.Data;
namespace ProgrammingCSharpWindows.Form
{
   using System.Data.SqlClient;

   public class ADOForm1 : System.Windows.Forms.Form
   {
      private System.ComponentModel.Container components;
      private System.Windows.Forms.DataGrid dataGrid1;

      // private System.Data.ADO.ADOConnection myConnection;
      private System.Data.SqlClient.SqlConnection myConnection;
      private System.Data.DataSet myDataSet;
      private System.Data.SqlClient.SqlCommand myCommand;
      private System.Data.SqlClient.SqlCommand myCommand2;
```

Example 14-5. Using a DataGrid with two tables (continued)

```
private System.Data.SqlClient.SqlDataAdapter DataAdapter;
private System.Data.SqlClient.SqlDataAdapter DataAdapter2;


public ADOForm1( )
{
    InitializeComponent( );


    // create the connection
    string connectionString = "server=(local)\\NetSDK;" +
        "Trusted_Connection=yes; database=northwind";
    myConnection = new
        System.Data.SqlClient.SqlConnection(connectionString);
    myConnection.Open( );

    // create the data set
    myDataSet = new System.Data.DataSet( );
    myDataSet.CaseSensitive=true;

    // set up the command and DataSet command for the first table
    myCommand = new System.Data.SqlClient.SqlCommand( );
    myCommand.Connection=myConnection;
    myCommand.CommandText = "Select * from Customers";
    DataAdapter = new System.Data.SqlClient.SqlDataAdapter( );
    DataAdapter.SelectCommand= myCommand;
    DataAdapter.TableMappings.Add("Table","Customers");
    DataAdapter.Fill(myDataSet);

    // set up the command and DataSet command for the second table
    myCommand2 = new System.Data.SqlClient.SqlCommand( );
    DataAdapter2 = new System.Data.SqlClient.SqlDataAdapter( );
    myCommand2.Connection = myConnection;
    myCommand2.CommandText = "SELECT * FROM Orders";
    DataAdapter2.SelectCommand = myCommand2;
    DataAdapter2.TableMappings.Add ("Table", "Orders");
    DataAdapter2.Fill(myDataSet);


    // establish the relationship between the tables
    System.Data.DataRelation dataRelation;
    System.Data.DataColumn dataColumn1;
    System.Data.DataColumn dataColumn2;
    dataColumn1 =
        myDataSet.Tables["Customers"].Columns["CustomerID"];
    dataColumn2 =
        myDataSet.Tables["Orders"].Columns["CustomerID"];

    dataRelation =
        new System.Data.DataRelation(
        "CustomersToOrders",
        dataColumn1,
```

Example 14-5. Using a DataGrid with two tables (continued)

```
            dataColumn2);

        // add the relation object to the data set
        myDataSet.Relations.Add(dataRelation);

        // set up the grid's view and member data and display it
        DataViewManager DataSetView =
            myDataSet.DefaultViewManager;
        dataGrid1.DataSource = DataSetView;
        dataGrid1.DataMember= "Customers";
    }

    protected override void Dispose(bool disposing)
    {
        if (disposing)
        {
            if (components == null)
            {
                components.Dispose( );
            }
        }
        base.Dispose(disposing);
    }

    private void InitializeComponent( )
    {
        this.components = new System.ComponentModel.Container ( );
        this.dataGrid1 = new System.Windows.Forms.DataGrid ( );
        dataGrid1.BeginInit ( );
        //@this.TrayHeight = 0;
        //@this.TrayLargeIcon = false;
        //@this.TrayAutoArrange = true;
        dataGrid1.Location = new System.Drawing.Point (24, 32);
        dataGrid1.Size = new System.Drawing.Size (480, 408);
        dataGrid1.DataMember = "";
        dataGrid1.TabIndex = 0;
        this.Text = "Multiple Tables";
        this.AutoScaleBaseSize = new System.Drawing.Size (5, 13);
        this.ClientSize = new System.Drawing.Size (536, 501);
        this.Controls.Add (this.dataGrid1);
        dataGrid1.EndInit ( );
    }


    public static void Main(string[] args)
    {
        Application.Run(new ADOForm1( ));
    }
  }
}
```

The result is impressive. Figure 14-5 shows the grid with one customer chosen. The
CustomersToOrders link is open under customer ID CACTU.

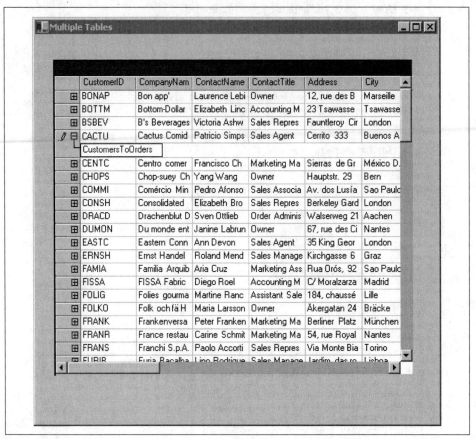

Figure 14-5. All the customers, with a CustomersToOrders link open

Clicking the link opens all the orders for that customer, as shown in Figure 14-6.

Changing Database Records

So far, you've retrieved data from a database, but you haven't manipulated its records in any way. Using ADO.NET, it is of course possible to add records, change an existing record, or delete a record altogether.

In a typical implementation, you might work your way through the following steps:

1. Fill the tables for your DataSet using a stored procedure or SQL.

2. Display the data in various DataTable objects within your DataSet by either binding to a control or looping through the rows in the tables.

3. Change data in individual DataTable objects by adding, modifying, or deleting DataRow objects.

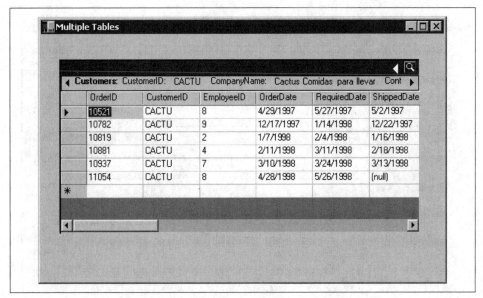

Figure 14-6. All the orders for the chosen customer

4. Invoke the GetChanges( ) method to create a second DataSet that features only the changes to the data.

5. Check for errors in the second newly created DataSet by examining the HasErrors property. If there are errors, check the HasErrors property of each DataTable in the DataSet. If the table has errors, invoke the GetErrors( ) method of the DataTable and get back an array of DataRow objects with errors. On each row you can examine the RowError property for specific information about the error, which you can then resolve.

6. Merge the second Data Set with the first.

7. Call the Update( ) method on the DataAdapter object and pass in the second (changed) DataSet.

8. Invoke the AcceptChanges( ) method on the DataSet, or invoke RejectChanges( ) to cancel the changes.

This process gives you very fine control over the update to your data as well as an opportunity to fix any data that would otherwise cause an error.

In the following example, you'll create a dialog box that displays the contents of the Customer table in Northwinds. The goal is to test updating a record, adding a new record, and deleting a record. As always, I'll keep the code as simple as possible, which means eliminating many of the error-checking and exception-handling routines you might expect in a production program.

Figure 14-7 shows the somewhat crude but useful form I've built to experiment with these features of ADO.NET.

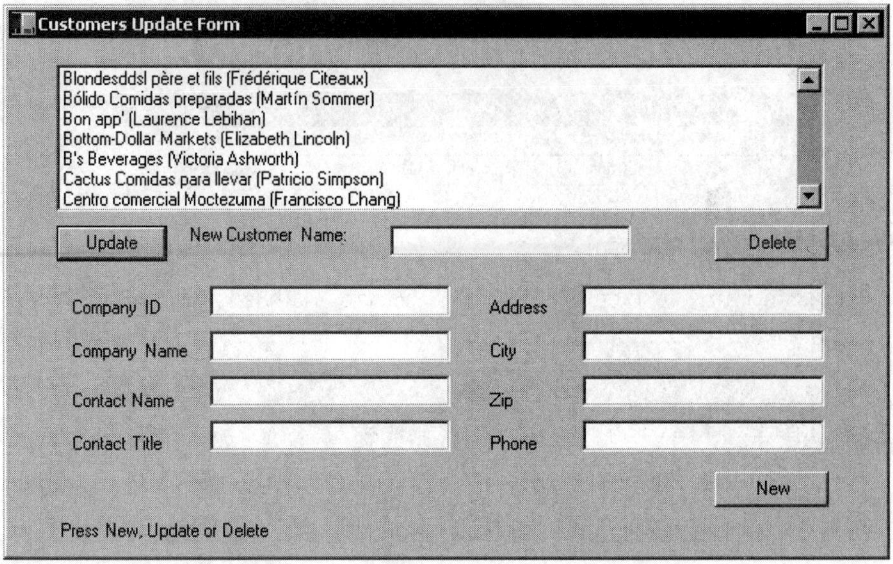

Figure 14-7. The ADO update form

This form consists of a list box (lbCustomers), a button for Update (btnUpdate), an associated text box (txtCustomerName), and a Delete button (btnDelete). There is also a set of eight text fields that are used in conjunction with the New button (btnNew). These text fields represent eight of the fields in the Customers table in the Northwind database. There is also a label (lblMessage) that you can use for writing messages to the user (it currently says Press New, Update, or Delete).

Accessing the Data

First, create the DataAdapter object and the DataSet as private member variables, along with the DataTable:

```
private SqlDataAdapter dataAdapter;
private DataSet dataSet;
private DataTable dataTable;
```

This enables you to refer to these objects from various member methods. Start by creating strings for the connection and the command that will get you the table you need:

```
string connectionString = "server=(local)\\NetSDK;" +
    "Trusted_Connection=yes; database=northwind";
string commandString = "Select * from Customers";
```

These strings are passed as parameters to the SqlDataAdapter constructor:

```
dataAdapter =
    new SqlDataAdapter(commandString, connectionString);
```

A DataAdapter may have four SQL commands associated with it. Right now, we have only one: dataAdapter.SelectCommand. The InitializeCommands() method creates the remaining three: InsertCommand, UpdateCommand, and DeleteCommand. InitializeCommands() uses the AddParms method to associate a column in each SQL command with the columns in the modified rows:

```
private void AddParms(SqlCommand cmd, params string[] cols) {
   // Add each parameter
   foreach (String column in cols) {
     cmd.Parameters.Add(
        "@" + column, SqlDbType.Char, 0, column);
   }
}
```

InitializeCommands() creates each SQL command in turn, using placeholders that correspond to the column argument passed to AddParm( ):

```
private void InitializeCommands( )
{

   // Reuse the SelectCommand's Connection.
   SqlConnection connection =
     (SqlConnection) dataAdapter.SelectCommand.Connection;

   // Create an explicit, reusable insert command
   dataAdapter.InsertCommand = connection.CreateCommand( );
   dataAdapter.InsertCommand.CommandText =
   "Insert into customers " +
      "(CustomerId, CompanyName, ContactName, ContactTitle, " +
      " Address, City, PostalCode, Phone) " +
      "values(@CustomerId, @CompanyName, @ContactName, " +
      "  @ContactTitle, @Address, @City, @PostalCode, @Phone)";
   AddParms(dataAdapter.InsertCommand,
      "CustomerId", "CompanyName", "ContactName", "ContactTitle",
      "Address", "City", "PostalCode", "Phone");

   // Create an explicit update command
   dataAdapter.UpdateCommand = connection.CreateCommand( );
   dataAdapter.UpdateCommand.CommandText = "update Customers " +
      "set CompanyName = @CompanyName where CustomerID = @CustomerId";
   AddParms(dataAdapter.UpdateCommand, "CompanyName", "CustomerID");

   // Create an explicit delete command
   dataAdapter.DeleteCommand = connection.CreateCommand( );
   dataAdapter.DeleteCommand.CommandText =
      "delete from customers where customerID = @CustomerId";
   AddParms(dataAdapter.DeleteCommand, "CustomerID");
}
```

The DataAdapter uses these three commands to modify the table when you invoke Update( ).

Back in the constructor, you can now create the DataSet and fill it with the SqlDataAdapter object you've just created:

```
dataSet = new DataSet( );
dataAdapter.Fill(DataSet,"Customers");
```

Display the table contents by calling the PopulateLB( ) method, which is a private method that fills the list box from the contents of the single table in the DataSet:

```
dataTable = dataSet.Tables[0];
lbCustomers.Items.Clear( );
foreach (DataRow dataRow in dataTable.Rows)
{
    lbCustomers.Items.Add(
        dataRow["CompanyName"] +
        " (" + dataRow["ContactName"] + ")" );
}
```

Updating a Record

The form is now displayed, and you're ready to update a record. Highlight a record and fill in a new customer name in the topmost text field. When you press Update, read the resulting name and put it into the chosen record.

The first task is to get the specific row the user wants to change:

```
DataRow targetRow  = dataTable.Rows[lbCustomers.SelectedIndex];
```

Declare a new object of type DataRow and initialize it with a reference to the specific row in the DataTable's Rows collection that corresponds to the selected item in the list box. Remember that DataTable was declared as a member variable and initialized in the PopulateLB( ) method shown in the previous section.

You can now display the name of the company you're going to update:

```
lblMessage.Text = "Updating " +  targetRow["CompanyName"];
Application.DoEvents( );
```

 The call to the static method DoEvents( ) of the Application class causes the application to process Windows messages and paint the screen with the message. If you were to leave this line out, the current thread would dominate the processor and the messages would not be printed until the button handler completes its work.

Call BeginEdit( ) on the DataRow to put the row into editing mode. This suspends events on the row so that you could, if you chose, edit a number of rows at once without triggering validation rules (there are no validation rules in this example). It is good form to bracket changes on DataRows with calls to BeginEdit( ) and EndEdit( ):

```
targetRow.BeginEdit( );
targetRow["CompanyName"] = txtCustomerName.Text;
targetRow.EndEdit( );
```

The actual edit is to the column CompanyName within the targetRow object, which is set to the text value of the text control txtCustomerName. The net effect is that the CompanyName field in the row is set to whatever the user put into that text box.

Notice that the column you want is indexed within the row by the name of that column. In this case, the name will match the name that is used in the database, but this is not required. When you created the DataSet, you could have used the TableMappings() method to change the names of the columns.

Having edited the column, you are ready to check to make sure there are no errors. First, extract all the changes made to the DataSet (in this case, there will be only one change) using the GetChanges() method, passing in a DataRowState enumeration to indicate that you want only those rows that have been modified. GetChanges() returns a new DataSet object:

```
DataSet dataSetChanged =
    dataSet.GetChanges(DataRowState.Modified);
```

Now you can check for errors. To simplify the code, I've included a flag to indicate that all is OK. If you find any errors, rather than trying to fix them, just set the flag to false and don't make the updates:

```
bool okayFlag = true;
if (dataSetChanged.HasErrors)
{
    okayFlag = false;
    string msg = "Error in row with customer ID ";

    foreach (DataTable theTable in dataSetChanged.Tables)
    {
        if (theTable.HasErrors)
        {
            DataRow[] errorRows = theTable.GetErrors();

            foreach (DataRow theRow in errorRows)
            {
                msg = msg + theRow["CustomerID"];
            }
        }
    }
    lblMessage.Text = msg;
}
```

First test to see whether the new data record set has any errors by checking the HasErrors property. If HasErrors is true, there are errors; set the Boolean okayFlag to false, and then go on to discover where the error lies. To do so, iterate through all the tables in the new database (in this case, there is only one); if a table has errors, you'll get an array of all the rows in that table with errors (shown here as the errorRows array).

Then iterate through the array of rows with errors, handling each in turn. In this case, you just update the message on the dialog box; however, in a production environment you might interact with the user to fix the problem.

If the okayFlag is still true after testing HasErrors, there were no errors and you are ready to update the database:

```
if (okayFlag)
{
    dataAdapter.Update(dataSetChanged,"Customers");
```

This causes the DataAdapter object to create the necessary command text to update the database. Next, update the message:

```
lblMessage.Text = "Updated " + targetRow["CompanyName"];
Application.DoEvents();
```

You now must tell the DataSet to accept the changes and then repopulate the list box from the DataSet:

```
dataSet.AcceptChanges();
PopulateLB();
```

If okayFlag is false, there are errors; in this example, we'd just reject the changes:

```
else
    dataSet.RejectChanges();
```

Deleting a Record

The code for handling the Delete button is even simpler. First, get the target row:

```
DataRow targetRow =
    dataTable.Rows[lbCustomers.SelectedIndex];
```

and form the delete message:

```
string msg = targetRow["CompanyName"] + " deleted. ";
```

You don't want to show the message until the row is deleted, but you need to get it now because after you delete the row it will be too late!

You're now ready to mark the row for deletion:

```
targetRow.Delete();
```

Calling AcceptChanges() on the DataSet causes AcceptChanges() to be called on each table within the DataSet. This in turn causes AcceptChanges() to be called on each row in those tables. Thus the one call to dataSet.AcceptChanges() cascades down through all the contained tables and rows.

Next, you need to call Update() and AcceptChanges(), and then refresh the list box. However, if this operation fails, the row will still be marked for deletion. If you then try to issue a legitimate command, such as an insertion, update, or another deletion, the DataAdapter will try to commit the erroneous deletion again, and the whole batch will fail because of that delete. In order to avert this situation, wrap the remaining operations in a try block and call RejectChanges( ) if they fail:

```
// update the database
try
{
   dataAdapter.Update(dataSet,"Customers");
   dataSet.AcceptChanges( );
   // repopulate the list box without the deleted record
   PopulateLB( );

   // inform the user
   lblMessage.Text = msg;
   Application.DoEvents( );
}
catch (SqlException ex)
{
   dataSet.RejectChanges( );
   MessageBox.Show(ex.Message);
}
```

 Deleting records from the Customers database might cause an exception if the record deleted is constrained by database integrity rules. For example, if a customer has orders in the Orders table, you cannot delete the customer until you delete the orders. To solve this, the following example will create new Customer records that you can then delete at will.

Creating New Records

To create a new record, the user will fill in the fields and press the New button. This will fire the btnNew_Click event, which is tied to the btnNew_Click event handling method:

```
btnNew.Click += new System.EventHandler (this.btnNew_Click);
```

In the event handler, call DataTable.NewRow( ), which asks the table for a new DataRow object:

```
DataRow newRow = dataTable.NewRow( );
```

This is very elegant because the new row that the DataTable produces has all the necessary DataColumns for this table. You can just fill in the columns you care about, taking the text from the user interface (UI):

```
newRow["CustomerID"] = txtCompanyID.Text;
newRow["CompanyName"] = txtCompanyName.Text;
newRow["ContactName"] = txtContactName.Text;
newRow["ContactTitle"] = txtContactTitle.Text;
newRow["Address"] = txtAddress.Text;
```

```
newRow["City"] = txtCity.Text;
newRow["PostalCode"] = txtZip.Text;
newRow["Phone"] = txtPhone.Text;
```

Now that the row is fully populated, just add it back to the table:

```
dataTable.Rows.Add(newRow);
```

The table resides within the DataSet, so all you have to do is tell the DataAdapter
object to update the database with the DataSet and accept the changes:

```
dataAdapter.Update(dataSet,"Customers");
dataSet.AcceptChanges();
```

Next, update the user interface:

```
lblMessage.Text = "Updated!";
Application.DoEvents();
```

You can now repopulate the list box with your new added row and clear the text
fields so that you're ready for another new record:

```
PopulateLB();
ClearFields();
```

ClearFields() is a private method that simply sets all the text fields to empty strings.
That method and the entire program are shown in Example 14-6.

Example 14-6. Updating, deleting, and adding records

```
using System;
using System.Drawing;
using System.Collections;
using System.ComponentModel;
using System.Windows.Forms;
using System.Data;
using System.Data.SqlClient;
namespace ProgrammingCSharpWindows.Form
{
    public class ADOForm1 : System.Windows.Forms.Form
    {
        private System.ComponentModel.Container components;
        private System.Windows.Forms.Label label9;
        private System.Windows.Forms.TextBox txtPhone;
        private System.Windows.Forms.Label label8;
        private System.Windows.Forms.TextBox txtContactTitle;
        private System.Windows.Forms.Label label7;
        private System.Windows.Forms.TextBox txtZip;
        private System.Windows.Forms.Label label6;
        private System.Windows.Forms.TextBox txtCity;
        private System.Windows.Forms.Label label5;
        private System.Windows.Forms.TextBox txtAddress;
        private System.Windows.Forms.Label label4;
        private System.Windows.Forms.TextBox txtContactName;
        private System.Windows.Forms.Label label3;
        private System.Windows.Forms.TextBox txtCompanyName;
```

Example 14-6. Updating, deleting, and adding records (continued)

```
    private System.Windows.Forms.Label label2;
    private System.Windows.Forms.TextBox txtCompanyID;
    private System.Windows.Forms.Label label1;
    private System.Windows.Forms.Button btnNew;
    private System.Windows.Forms.TextBox txtCustomerName;
    private System.Windows.Forms.Button btnUpdate;
    private System.Windows.Forms.Label lblMessage;
    private System.Windows.Forms.Button btnDelete;
    private System.Windows.Forms.ListBox lbCustomers;

    // the DataSet, DataAdapter, and DataTable are members
    // so that we can access them from any member method.
    private SqlDataAdapter dataAdapter;
    private DataSet dataSet;
    private DataTable dataTable;

    public ADOForm1( )
    {
        InitializeComponent( );

        string connectionString = "server=(local)\\NetSDK;" +
          "Trusted_Connection=yes; database=northwind";
        string commandString = "Select * from Customers";
        dataAdapter =
            new SqlDataAdapter(commandString, connectionString);

        InitializeCommands( );

        dataSet = new DataSet( );
        dataAdapter.Fill(dataSet,"Customers");
        PopulateLB( );
    }

    private void AddParms(SqlCommand cmd, params string[] cols) {
      // Add each parameter
      foreach (String column in cols) {
        cmd.Parameters.Add(
          "@" + column, SqlDbType.Char, 0, column);
      }
    }

    private void InitializeCommands( )
    {

        // Reuse the SelectCommand's Connection.
        SqlConnection connection =
          (SqlConnection) dataAdapter.SelectCommand.Connection;

        // Create an explicit, reusable insert command
        dataAdapter.InsertCommand = connection.CreateCommand( );
        dataAdapter.InsertCommand.CommandText =
        "Insert into customers " +
```

Example 14-6. Updating, deleting, and adding records (continued)

```
            "(CustomerId, CompanyName, ContactName, ContactTitle, " +
            " Address, City, PostalCode, Phone) " +
            "values(@CustomerId, @CompanyName, @ContactName, " +
            "  @ContactTitle, @Address, @City, @PostalCode, @Phone)";
        AddParms(dataAdapter.InsertCommand,
          "CustomerId", "CompanyName", "ContactName", "ContactTitle",
          "Address", "City", "PostalCode", "Phone");

        // Create an explicit update command
        dataAdapter.UpdateCommand = connection.CreateCommand( );
        dataAdapter.UpdateCommand.CommandText = "update Customers " +
          "set CompanyName = @CompanyName where CustomerID = @CustomerId";
        AddParms(dataAdapter.UpdateCommand, "CompanyName", "CustomerID");

        // Create an explicit delete command
        dataAdapter.DeleteCommand = connection.CreateCommand( );
        dataAdapter.DeleteCommand.CommandText =
          "delete from customers where customerID = @CustomerId";
        AddParms(dataAdapter.DeleteCommand, "CustomerID");
    }

    // fill the list box with columns from the Customers table
    private void PopulateLB( )
    {
        dataTable = dataSet.Tables[0];
        lbCustomers.Items.Clear( );
        foreach (DataRow dataRow in dataTable.Rows)
        {
            lbCustomers.Items.Add(
                dataRow["CompanyName"] + " (" +
                dataRow["ContactName"] + ")" );
        }

    }

    protected override void Dispose(bool disposing)
    {
        if (disposing)
        {
            if (components == null)
            {
                components.Dispose( );
            }
        }
        base.Dispose(disposing);
    }

    private void InitializeComponent( )
    {
        this.components = new System.ComponentModel.Container ();
        this.txtCustomerName = new System.Windows.Forms.TextBox ();
        this.txtCity = new System.Windows.Forms.TextBox ();
```

Example 14-6. Updating, deleting, and adding records (continued)

```
this.txtCompanyID = new System.Windows.Forms.TextBox ();
this.lblMessage = new System.Windows.Forms.Label ();
this.btnUpdate = new System.Windows.Forms.Button ();
this.txtContactName = new System.Windows.Forms.TextBox ();
this.txtZip = new System.Windows.Forms.TextBox ();
this.btnDelete = new System.Windows.Forms.Button ();
this.txtContactTitle = new System.Windows.Forms.TextBox ();
this.txtAddress = new System.Windows.Forms.TextBox ();
this.txtCompanyName = new System.Windows.Forms.TextBox ();
this.label5 = new System.Windows.Forms.Label ();
this.label6 = new System.Windows.Forms.Label ();
this.label7 = new System.Windows.Forms.Label ();
this.label8 = new System.Windows.Forms.Label ();
this.label9 = new System.Windows.Forms.Label ();
this.label4 = new System.Windows.Forms.Label ();
this.lbCustomers = new System.Windows.Forms.ListBox ();
this.txtPhone = new System.Windows.Forms.TextBox ();
this.btnNew = new System.Windows.Forms.Button ();
this.label1 = new System.Windows.Forms.Label ();
this.label2 = new System.Windows.Forms.Label ();
this.label3 = new System.Windows.Forms.Label ();
//@this.TrayHeight = 0;
//@this.TrayLargeIcon = false;
//@this.TrayAutoArrange = true;
txtCustomerName.Location = new System.Drawing.Point (256, 120);
txtCustomerName.TabIndex = 4;
txtCustomerName.Size = new System.Drawing.Size (160, 20);
txtCity.Location = new System.Drawing.Point (384, 245);
txtCity.TabIndex = 15;
txtCity.Size = new System.Drawing.Size (160, 20);
txtCompanyID.Location = new System.Drawing.Point (136, 216);
txtCompanyID.TabIndex = 7;
txtCompanyID.Size = new System.Drawing.Size (160, 20);
lblMessage.Location = new System.Drawing.Point (32, 368);
lblMessage.Text = "Press New, Update or Delete";
lblMessage.Size = new System.Drawing.Size (416, 48);
lblMessage.TabIndex = 1;
btnUpdate.Location = new System.Drawing.Point (32, 120);
btnUpdate.Size = new System.Drawing.Size (75, 23);
btnUpdate.TabIndex = 0;
btnUpdate.Text = "Update";
btnUpdate.Click +=
    new System.EventHandler (this.btnUpdate_Click);
txtContactName.Location = new System.Drawing.Point (136, 274);
txtContactName.TabIndex = 11;
txtContactName.Size = new System.Drawing.Size (160, 20);
txtZip.Location = new System.Drawing.Point (384, 274);
txtZip.TabIndex = 17;
txtZip.Size = new System.Drawing.Size (160, 20);
btnDelete.Location = new System.Drawing.Point (472, 120);
btnDelete.Size = new System.Drawing.Size (75, 23);
btnDelete.TabIndex = 2;
```

Example 14-6. Updating, deleting, and adding records (continued)

```
btnDelete.Text = "Delete";
btnDelete.Click +=
    new System.EventHandler (this.btnDelete_Click);
txtContactTitle.Location = new System.Drawing.Point (136, 303);
txtContactTitle.TabIndex = 12;
txtContactTitle.Size = new System.Drawing.Size (160, 20);
txtAddress.Location = new System.Drawing.Point (384, 216);
txtAddress.TabIndex = 13;
txtAddress.Size = new System.Drawing.Size (160, 20);
txtCompanyName.Location = new System.Drawing.Point (136, 245);
txtCompanyName.TabIndex = 9;
txtCompanyName.Size = new System.Drawing.Size (160, 20);
label5.Location = new System.Drawing.Point (320, 252);
label5.Text = "City";
label5.Size = new System.Drawing.Size (48, 16);
label5.TabIndex = 14;
label6.Location = new System.Drawing.Point (320, 284);
label6.Text = "Zip";
label6.Size = new System.Drawing.Size (40, 16);
label6.TabIndex = 16;
label7.Location = new System.Drawing.Point (40, 312);
label7.Text = "Contact Title";
label7.Size = new System.Drawing.Size (88, 16);
label7.TabIndex = 28;
label8.Location = new System.Drawing.Point (320, 312);
label8.Text = "Phone";
label8.Size = new System.Drawing.Size (56, 16);
label8.TabIndex = 20;
label9.Location = new System.Drawing.Point (120, 120);
label9.Text = "New Customer Name:";
label9.Size = new System.Drawing.Size (120, 24);
label9.TabIndex = 22;
label4.Location = new System.Drawing.Point (320, 224);
label4.Text = "Address";
label4.Size = new System.Drawing.Size (56, 16);
label4.TabIndex = 26;
lbCustomers.Location = new System.Drawing.Point (32, 16);
lbCustomers.Size = new System.Drawing.Size (512, 95);
lbCustomers.TabIndex = 3;
txtPhone.Location = new System.Drawing.Point (384, 303);
txtPhone.TabIndex = 18;
txtPhone.Size = new System.Drawing.Size (160, 20);
btnNew.Location = new System.Drawing.Point (472, 336);
btnNew.Size = new System.Drawing.Size (75, 23);
btnNew.TabIndex = 25;
btnNew.Text = "New";
btnNew.Click += new System.EventHandler (this.btnNew_Click);
label1.Location = new System.Drawing.Point (40, 224);
label1.Text = "Company ID";
label1.Size = new System.Drawing.Size (88, 16);
label1.TabIndex = 6;
label2.Location = new System.Drawing.Point (40, 252);
```

Example 14-6. Updating, deleting, and adding records (continued)

```
        label2.Text = "Company Name";
        label2.Size = new System.Drawing.Size (88, 16);
        label2.TabIndex = 8;
        label3.Location = new System.Drawing.Point (40, 284);
        label3.Text = "Contact Name";
        label3.Size = new System.Drawing.Size (88, 16);
        label3.TabIndex = 10;
        this.Text = "Customers Update Form";
        this.AutoScaleBaseSize = new System.Drawing.Size (5, 13);
        this.ClientSize = new System.Drawing.Size (584, 421);
        this.Controls.Add (this.label9);
        this.Controls.Add (this.txtPhone);
        this.Controls.Add (this.label8);
        this.Controls.Add (this.txtContactTitle);
        this.Controls.Add (this.label7);
        this.Controls.Add (this.txtZip);
        this.Controls.Add (this.label6);
        this.Controls.Add (this.txtCity);
        this.Controls.Add (this.label5);
        this.Controls.Add (this.txtAddress);
        this.Controls.Add (this.label4);
        this.Controls.Add (this.txtContactName);
        this.Controls.Add (this.label3);
        this.Controls.Add (this.txtCompanyName);
        this.Controls.Add (this.label2);
        this.Controls.Add (this.txtCompanyID);
        this.Controls.Add (this.label1);
        this.Controls.Add (this.btnNew);
        this.Controls.Add (this.txtCustomerName);
        this.Controls.Add (this.btnUpdate);
        this.Controls.Add (this.lblMessage);
        this.Controls.Add (this.btnDelete);
        this.Controls.Add (this.lbCustomers);
    }

    // handle the new button click
    protected void btnNew_Click (object sender, System.EventArgs e)
    {
        // create a new row, populate it
        DataRow newRow = dataTable.NewRow( );
        newRow["CustomerID"]   = txtCompanyID.Text;
        newRow["CompanyName"]  = txtCompanyName.Text;
        newRow["ContactName"]  = txtContactName.Text;
        newRow["ContactTitle"] = txtContactTitle.Text;
        newRow["Address"]      = txtAddress.Text;
        newRow["City"]         = txtCity.Text;
        newRow["PostalCode"]   = txtZip.Text;
        newRow["Phone"]        = txtPhone.Text;

        // add the new row to the table
        dataTable.Rows.Add(newRow);
```

Example 14-6. Updating, deleting, and adding records (continued)

```
        // update the database
        try
        {
          dataAdapter.Update(dataSet,"Customers");
          dataSet.AcceptChanges();

          // inform the user
          lblMessage.Text = "Updated!";
          Application.DoEvents();

          // repopulate the list box
          PopulateLB();
          // clear all the text fields
          ClearFields();
        }
        catch (SqlException ex)
        {
          dataSet.RejectChanges();
          MessageBox.Show(ex.Message);
        }

    }

    // set all the text fields to empty strings
    private void ClearFields()
    {
      txtCompanyID.Text = "";
      txtCompanyName.Text = "";
      txtContactName.Text = "";
      txtContactTitle.Text = "";
      txtAddress.Text = "";
      txtCity.Text = "";
      txtZip.Text = "";
      txtPhone.Text = "";
    }

    // handle the update button click
    protected void btnUpdate_Click (object sender, System.EventArgs e)
    {
      // get the selected row
      DataRow targetRow  = dataTable.Rows[lbCustomers.SelectedIndex];

      // inform the user
      lblMessage.Text = "Updating " +  targetRow["CompanyName"];
      Application.DoEvents();

      // edit the row
      targetRow.BeginEdit();
      targetRow["CompanyName"] = txtCustomerName.Text;
      targetRow.EndEdit();

      // get each row that changed
```

Example 14-6. Updating, deleting, and adding records (continued)

```
        DataSet dataSetChanged =
            dataSet.GetChanges(DataRowState.Modified);

        // test to make sure all the changed rows are without errors
        bool okayFlag = true;
        if (dataSetChanged.HasErrors)
        {
            okayFlag = false;
            string msg = "Error in row with customer ID ";

            // examine each table in the changed DataSet
            foreach (DataTable theTable in dataSetChanged.Tables)
            {
                // if any table has errors, find out which rows
                if (theTable.HasErrors)
                {
                    // get the rows with errors
                    DataRow[] errorRows = theTable.GetErrors();

                    // iterate through the errors and correct
                    // (in our case, just identify)
                    foreach (DataRow theRow in errorRows)
                    {
                        msg = msg + theRow["CustomerID"];
                    }
                }
            }
            lblMessage.Text = msg;
        }
        // if we have no errors
        if (okayFlag)
        {

            // update the database
            dataAdapter.Update(dataSetChanged,"Customers");

            // inform the user
            lblMessage.Text = "Updated " +  targetRow["CompanyName"];
            Application.DoEvents();

            // accept the changes and repopulate the list box
            dataSet.AcceptChanges();
            PopulateLB();
        }
        else  // if we had errors, reject the changes
            dataSet.RejectChanges();
    }


    // handle the delete button click
    protected void btnDelete_Click (object sender, System.EventArgs e)
    {
```

Example 14-6. Updating, deleting, and adding records (continued)

```
    // get the selected row
    DataRow targetRow = dataTable.Rows[lbCustomers.SelectedIndex];

    // prepare message for user
    string msg = targetRow["CompanyName"] + " deleted. ";

    // delete the selected row
    targetRow.Delete( );

    // update the database
    try
    {
      dataAdapter.Update(dataSet,"Customers");
      dataSet.AcceptChanges( );
      // repopulate the list box without the deleted record
      PopulateLB( );

      // inform the user
      lblMessage.Text = msg;
      Application.DoEvents( );
    }
    catch (SqlException ex)
    {
      dataSet.RejectChanges( );
      MessageBox.Show(ex.Message);
    }

  }

  public static void Main(string[] args)
  {
    Application.Run(new ADOForm1( ));
  }
  }
}
```

Figure 14-8 shows the filled-out form just before pressing the New button and Figure 14-9 shows the form immediately after adding the new record.

Note that the new record is appended to the end of the list and the text fields are cleared.

ADO.NET and XML

In this chapter, I have demonstrated the kinds of data access that users have come to expect from ADO and shown how the new ADO.NET data access framework provides such support through its class libraries. I would be remiss, however, if I failed to mention that ADO.NET also provides complete support for XML. Most interesting is its support for presenting the contents of a data set as either a collection of tables, as we have explored in this chapter, or as an XML document.

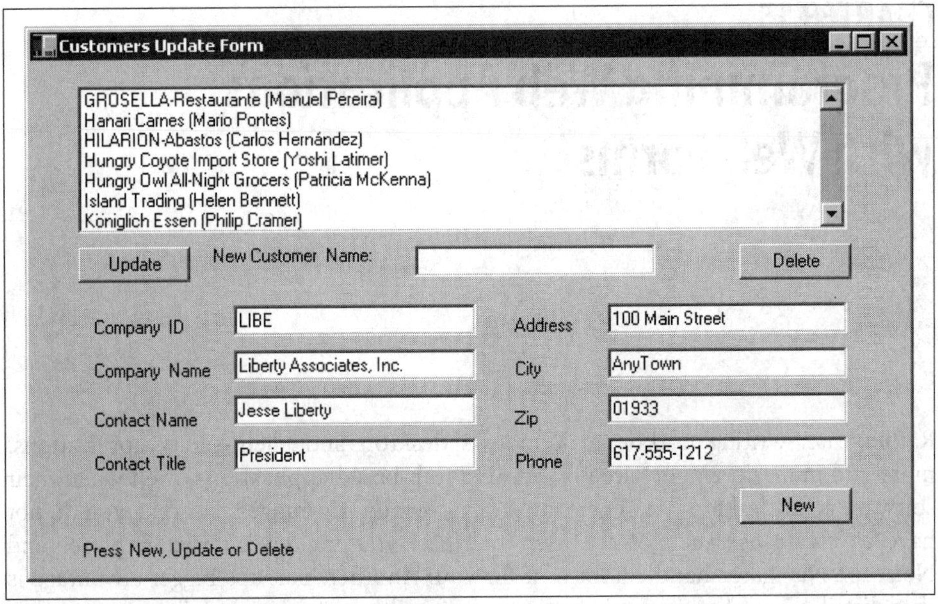

Figure 14-8. Getting ready to add a new record

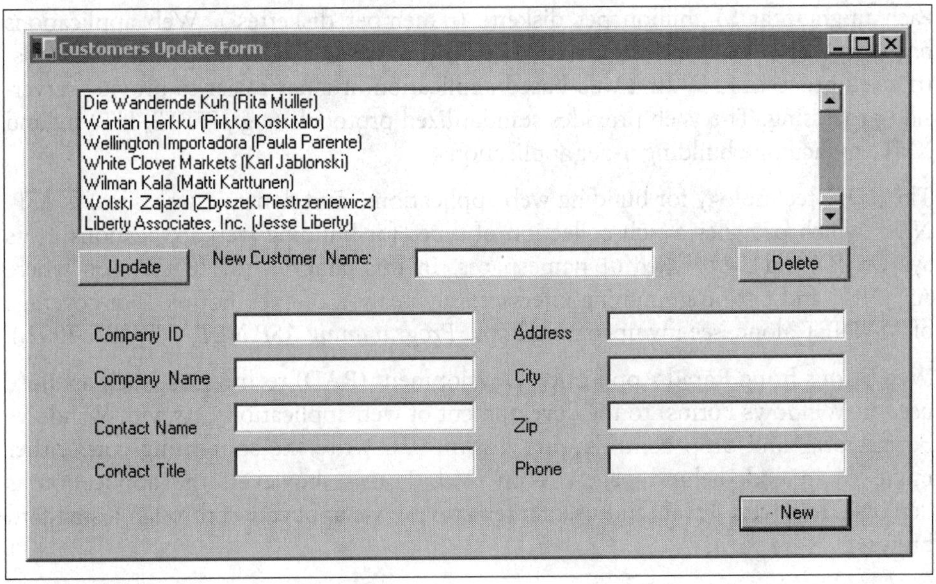

Figure 14-9. After adding the new record

The tight integration of ADO.NET and XML and its applications are beyond the scope of this book, but complete information can be found in the .NET Framework SDK Reference.

CHAPTER 15

Programming Web Applications with Web Forms

Rather than writing traditional Windows desktop and client-server applications, more and more developers are now writing web-based applications, even when their software is for desktop use. There are many obvious advantages. For one, you do not have to create as much of the user interface; you can let Internet Explorer and Netscape Navigator handle a lot of it for you. Another, perhaps bigger advantage is that distribution of revisions is faster, easier, and less expensive. When I worked at an online network that predated the Web, we estimated our cost of distribution for each upgrade at $1 million per diskette (remember diskettes?). Web applications have virtually zero distribution cost. The third advantage of web applications is distributed processing. With a web-based application, it is far easier to provide server-side processing. The Web provides standardized protocols (e.g., HTTP, HTML, and XML) to facilitate building *n*-tier applications.

The .NET technology for building web applications (and dynamic web sites) is ASP. NET, which provides a rich collection of types for building web applications in its System.Web and System.Web.UI namespaces. In this chapter, the focus is on where ASP.NET and C# programming intersect: the creation of Web Forms. (For coverage of ASP.NET alone, see my upcoming book, *Programming ASP.NET*, O'Reilly, 2002.)

Web Forms bring Rapid Application Development (RAD) techniques (such as those used in Windows Forms) to the development of web applications. As with Windows Forms, drag and drop controls onto a form and write the supporting code either inline or in code-behind pages. With Web Forms, however, the application is deployed to a web server, and users interact with the application through a standard browser.

Understanding Web Forms

Web Forms implement a programming model in which web pages are dynamically generated on a web server for delivery to a browser over the Internet. They are, in some ways, the successor to ASP pages, and they marry ASP technology with traditional programming.

With Web Forms, you create an HTML page with static content, and you write C# code to generate dynamic content. The C# code runs on the server, and the data produced is integrated with your static HTML to create the web page. What is sent to the browser is standard HTML.

Web Forms are designed to run on any browser, with the server rendering the correct browser-compliant HTML. You can do the programming for the logic of the Web Form in any .NET language. I will of course use C#, which is arguably the language of choice, though some ASP developers who have used VBScript might opt for VB.NET.

Just as with Windows Forms, you *can* create Web Forms in Notepad (or another editor of your choice) rather than in Visual Studio. Many developers will choose to do so, but Visual Studio makes the process of designing and testing Web Forms *much* easier.

Web Forms divide the user interface into two parts: the visual part or user interface (UI), and the logic that lies behind it. This is very similar to developing Windows Forms as shown in Chapter 14, but with Web Forms the UI page and the code are in separate files.

The UI page is stored in a file with the extension *.aspx*. The logic (code) for that page can be stored in a separate *code-behind* C# source file. When you run the form, the code-behind class file runs and dynamically creates the HTML sent to the client browser. This code makes use of the rich Web Forms types found in the System.Web and System.Web.UI namespaces of the .NET Framework Class Library (FCL).

With Visual Studio, Web Forms programming couldn't be simpler: open a form, drag some controls onto it, and write the code to handle events. Presto! You've written a web application.

On the other hand, even with Visual Studio writing a robust and complete web application can be a daunting task. Web Forms offer a very rich UI; the number and complexity of web controls have greatly multiplied in recent years, and user expectations about the look and feel of web applications have risen accordingly.

In addition, web applications are inherently distributed. Typically, the client will not be in the same building as the server. For most web applications, you must take network latency, bandwidth, and network server performance into account when creating the UI; a round trip from client to host might take a few seconds.

Web Form Events

Web Forms are event-driven. An *event* is an object that encapsulates the idea that "something happened." An event is generated (or *raised*) when the user presses a button, or selects from a list box, or otherwise interacts with the UI. Events can also be generated by the system starting or finishing work. For example, open a file for reading, and the system raises an event when the file has been read into memory.

The method that responds to the event is called the *event handler*. Event handlers are written in C# in the code-behind page and are associated with controls in the HTML page through control attributes.

Event handlers are delegates (see Chapter 12). By convention, ASP.NET event handlers return void and take two parameters. The first parameter represents the object raising the event. The second, called the *event argument*, contains information specific to the event, if any. For most events, the event argument is of type *EventArgs*, which does not expose any properties. For some controls, the event argument might be of a type derived from *EventArgs* that can expose properties specific to that event type.

In web applications, most events are typically handled on the server and, therefore, require a round trip. ASP.NET only supports a limited set of events, such as button clicks and text changes. These are events that the user might expect to cause a significant change, as opposed to Windows events (such as mouse-over) that might happen many times during a single user-driven task.

Postback versus non-postback events

Postback events are those that cause the form to be posted back to the server immediately. These include click type events, such as the Button Click event. In contrast, many events (typically change events) are considered *non-postback* in that the form is not posted back to the server immediately. Instead, these events are cached by the control until the next time that a postback event occurs. You can force controls with non-postback events to behave in a postback manner by setting their `AutoPostBack` property to true.

State

A web application's *State* is the current value of all the controls and variables for the current user in the current session. The Web is inherently a "stateless" environment. This means that every post to the server loses the state from previous posts, unless the developer takes great pains to preserve this session knowledge. ASP.NET, however, provides support for maintaining the state of a user's session.

Whenever a page is posted to the server, it is re-created by the server from scratch before it is returned to the browser. ASP.NET provides a mechanism that automatically maintains state for server controls. Thus, if you provide a list and the user has made a selection, that selection is preserved after the page is posted back to the server and redrawn on the client.

Web Form Life Cycle

Every request for a page made from a web server causes a chain of events at the server. These events, from beginning to end, constitute the *life cycle* of the page and all its components. The life cycle begins with a request for the page, which causes the server to load it. When the request is complete, the page is unloaded. From one end of the life cycle to the other, the goal is to render appropriate HTML output back to the requesting browser. The life cycle of a page is marked by the following events, each of which you can handle yourself or leave to default handling by the ASP.NET server:

Initialize
> Initialize is the first phase in the life cycle for any page or control. It is here that any settings needed for the duration of the incoming request are initialized.

Load ViewState
> The ViewState property of the control is populated. The ViewState information comes from a hidden variable on the control, used to persist the state across round trips to the server. The input string from this hidden variable is parsed by the page framework, and the ViewState property is set. This can be modified via the LoadViewState() method. This allows ASP.NET to manage the state of your control across page loads so that each control is not reset to its default state each time the page is posted.

Process Postback Data
> During this phase, the data sent to the server in the posting is processed. If any of this data results in a requirement to update the ViewState, that update is performed via the LoadPostData() method.

Load
> CreateChildControls() is called, if necessary, to create and initialize server controls in the control tree. State is restored, and the form controls show client-side data. You can modify the load phase by handling the Load event with the OnLoad method.

Send Postback Change Modifications
> If there are any state changes between the current state and the previous state, change events are raised via the RaisePostDataChangedEvent() method.

Handle Postback Events
> The client-side event that caused the postback is handled.

PreRender
> This is the phase just before the output is rendered to the browser. It is essentially your last chance to modify the output prior to rendering using the OnPreRender() method.

Save State
> Near the beginning of the life cycle, the persisted view state was loaded from the hidden variable. Now it is saved back to the hidden variable, persisting as a string object that will complete the round trip to the client. You can override this using the SaveViewState() method.

Render

This is where the output to be sent back to the client browser is generated. You can override it using the Render method. CreateChildControls() is called, if necessary, to create and initialize server controls in the control tree.

Dispose

This is the last phase of the life cycle. It gives you an opportunity to do any final cleanup and release references to any expensive resources, such as database connections. You can modify it using the Dispose() method.

Creating a Web Form

To create the simple Web Form that will be used in the next example, start up Visual Studio .NET and open a New Project named *ProgrammingCSharpWeb*. Select the Visual C# Projects folder (because C# is your language of choice), select ASP.NET Web Application as the project type, and type in its name, *ProgrammingCSharpWeb*. Visual Studio .NET will display *http://localhost/* as the default location, as shown in Figure 15-1.

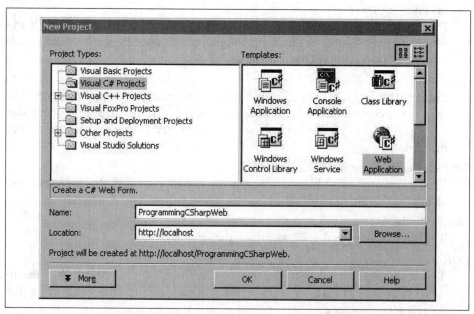

Figure 15-1. Creating a project in the New Project window of Visual Studio .NET

Visual Studio places nearly all the files it creates for the project in a folder within your local machine's default web site—for example, *c:\Inetpub\wwwroot\ProgrammingCSharpWeb*.

In Visual Studio .NET, a *solution* is a set of projects; each project will create a dynamic link library (DLL) or an executable (EXE). All projects are created in the context of a solution, and solutions are managed by *.sln* and *.suo* files.

The solution files and other Visual Studio–specific files are stored in *<drive>\ Documents and Settings\<user name>\My Documents\Visual Studio Projects* (where *<drive>* and *<user name>* are specific to your machine).

You must have IIS and the FrontPage Server extensions installed on your computer to use Web Forms. To configure the FrontPage Server extensions, open the Internet Service Manager and right-click the web site. Select All Tasks → Configure Server Extensions. For further information, please check *http://www.microsoft.com*.

When the application is created, Visual Studio places a number of files in your project. The Web Form itself is stored in a file named *WebForm1.aspx*. This file will contain only HTML. A second, equally important file, *WebForm1.aspx.cs*, stores the C# associated with your form; this is the code-behind file.

Notice that the code-behind file does *not* appear in the Solution Explorer. To see the code-behind (*.cs*) file, you must place the cursor within Visual Studio .NET, right-click the form, and choose "View Code" in the pop-up menu. You can now tab back and forth between the form itself, *WebForm1.aspx,* and the C# code-behind file, *WebForm1.aspx.cs*. When viewing the form, *WebForm1.aspx,* you can choose between Design mode and HTML mode by clicking the tabs at the bottom of the Editor window. Design mode lets you drag controls onto your form; HTML mode allows you to view and edit the HTML code directly.

Let's take a closer look at the *.aspx* and code-behind files that Visual Studio creates. Start by renaming *WebForm1.aspx* to *HelloWeb.aspx*. To do this, close *WebForm1. aspx,* and then right-click its name in the Solution Explorer. Choose Rename and enter the name *HelloWeb.aspx*. After you rename it, open *HelloWeb.aspx* and view the code; you will find that the code-behind file has been renamed as well to *HelloWeb.aspx.cs*.

When you create a new Web Form application, Visual Studio .NET will generate a bit of boilerplate code to get you started, as shown in Example 15-1.

Example 15-1. Wizard-generated code for a Web Form

```
<%@ Page language="c#"
  Codebehind="HelloWeb.aspx.cs"
  AutoEventWireup="false"
  Inherits="ProgrammingCSharpWeb.WebForm1" %>
```

Example 15-1. Wizard-generated code for a Web Form (continued)

```
<!DOCTYPE HTML PUBLIC "-//W3C//DTD HTML 4.0 Transitional//EN" >
<html>
  <head>
    <title>WebForm1</title>
    <meta name="GENERATOR"
      Content="Microsoft Visual Studio 7.0">
    <meta name="CODE_LANGUAGE" Content="C#">
    <meta name="vs_defaultClientScript" content="JavaScript">
    <meta name="vs_targetSchema"
      content="http://schemas.microsoft.com/intellisense/ie5">
  </head>
  <body MS_POSITIONING="GridLayout">

    <form id="Form1" method="post" runat="server">

    </form>

  </body>
</html>
```

What you see is typical boilerplate HTML except for the first line, which contains the following ASP.NET code:

```
<%@ Page language="c#"
  Codebehind="HelloWeb.aspx.cs"
  AutoEventWireup="false"
  Inherits="ProgrammingCSharpWeb.WebForm1" %>
```

The language attribute indicates that the language used on the code-behind page is C#. The Codebehind attribute designates that the filename of that page is *HelloWeb. cs*, and the Inherits attribute indicates that this page derives from WebForm1. WebForm1 is a class declared in *HelloWeb.cs*.

```
public class WebForm1 : System.Web.UI.Page
```

As the C# code makes clear, WebForm1 inherits from System.Web.UI.Page, which is the class that defines the properties, methods, and events common to all server-side pages.

Returning to the HTML view of *HelloWeb.aspx*, you see that a form has been specified in the body of the page using the standard HTML form tag:

```
<form id="Form1" method="post" runat="server">
```

Web Forms assumes that you need at least one form to manage the user interaction, and creates one when you open a project. The attribute runat="server" is the key to the server-side magic. Any tag that includes this attribute is considered a server-side control to be executed by the ASP.NET framework on the server.

Having created an empty Web Form, the first thing you might want to do is add some text to the page. By switching to HTML view, you can add script and HTML directly to the file just as you could with classic ASP. Adding the following line to the body segment of the HTML page will cause it to display a greeting and the current local time:

```
Hello World! It is now <% = DateTime.Now.ToString( ) %>
```

The `<%` and `%>` marks work just as they did in classic ASP, indicating that code falls between them (in this case, C#). The `=` sign immediately following the opening tag causes ASP.NET to display the value, just like a call to `Response.Write( )`. You could just as easily write the line as:

```
Hello World! It is now
<% Response.Write(DateTime.Now.ToString( )); %>
```

Run the page by pressing Ctrl-F5 (or save it and navigate to it in your browser). You should see the string printed to the browser, as in Figure 15-2.

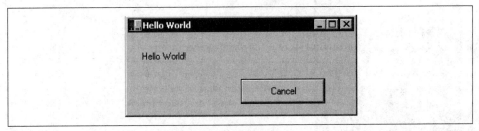

Figure 15-2. Output generated by the HelloWorld.aspx file

Adding Controls

You can add server-side controls to a Web Form in two ways: manually (by writing HTML into the HTML page), or by dragging controls from the toolbox to the Design page. For example, suppose you want to use buttons to let the user choose one of three Shippers provided in the Northwinds database. You could write the following HTML into the `<form>` element in the HTML window:

```
<asp:RadioButton GroupName="Shipper" id="Airborne"
    text = "Airborne Express" Checked="True" runat="server">
</asp:RadioButton>
<asp:RadioButton GroupName="Shipper" id="UPS"
    text = "United Parcel Service" runat="server">
</asp:RadioButton>
<asp:RadioButton GroupName="Shipper" id="Federal"
    text = "Federal Express" runat="server">
</asp:RadioButton>
```

The asp tags declare server-side ASP.NET controls that are replaced with normal HTML when the server processes the page. When you run the application, the browser displays three radio buttons in a button group; pressing one will deselect the others.

You can create the same effect more easily by dragging three buttons from the Visual Studio toolbox onto the Form, as illustrated in Figure 15-3.

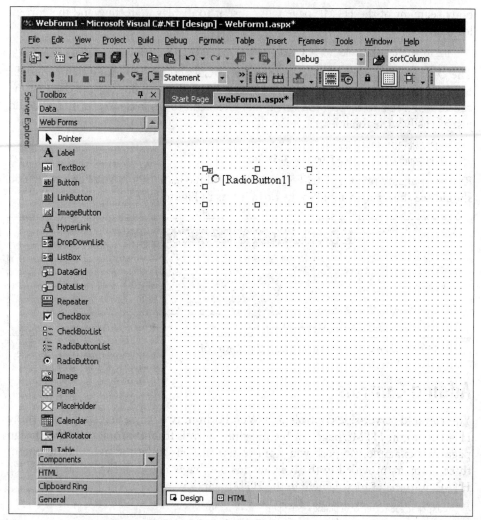

Figure 15-3. Dragging buttons onto the Web Form

You can add controls to a page in one of two modes. The default mode is GridLayout. When you add controls in GridLayout, they are arranged in the browser using absolute positioning (x and y coordinates).

The alternative mode is FlowLayout. With FlowLayout, the controls are added to the form from top to bottom, as in a Microsoft Word document. To change from Grid to Layout or back, change the pageLayout property of the document in Visual Studio .NET.

Web Forms offer two types of server-side controls. The first is server-side HTML controls, also called Web Controls. These are standard HTML controls that you tag with the attribute runat=Server.

The alternative to Web Controls is ASP.NET Server Controls, also called ASP Controls. ASP Controls have been designed to replace the standard HTML controls. ASP Controls provide a more consistent object model and more consistently named attributes. For example, with HTML controls, there are myriad different ways to handle input:

```
<input type = "radio">
<input type="checkbox">
<input type="button">
<input type="text">
<textarea>
```

Each of these behaves differently and takes different attributes. The ASP Controls try to normalize the set of controls, using attributes consistently throughout the ASP control object model. The ASP Controls that correspond to the preceding HTML server-side controls are:

```
<asp:RadioButton>
<asp:CheckBox>
<asp:Button>
<asp:TextBox rows="1">
<asp:TextBox rows="5">
```

The remainder of this chapter focuses on ASP Controls.

Data Binding

Various technologies have offered programmers the opportunity to bind controls to data so that as the data is modified, the controls respond automatically. As Rocky used to say to Bullwinkle, "But that trick never works." Bound controls often provided only limited control over their look and feel, and performance was usually pretty terrible. The ASP.NET designers set out to solve these problems and provide a suite of robust data-bound controls, which simplify display and modification of data, sacrificing neither performance nor control over the UI.

In the previous section, you hardcoded radio buttons onto a form, one for each of three Shippers in the Northwinds database. That can't be the best way to do it; if you change the Shippers in the database, you have to go back and rewire the controls. This section shows how you can create these controls dynamically and then bind them to data in the database.

You might want to create the radio buttons based on data in the database because you can't know at design time what text the buttons will have, or even how many buttons you'll need. To accomplish this, use a RadioButtonList. RadioButtonList is a control that allows you to create radio buttons programatically; you provide the name and values for the buttons, and ASP.NET takes care of the plumbing.

Delete the radio buttons already on the form, and drag and drop a RadioButtonList in their place. Once it is there, you can use the Properties window to rename it to rbl1.

Setting Initial Properties

Web Forms programming is event-based; you write your code to respond to various events. Typically, the events you're responding to are user-initiated. For example, when the user clicks a button, a Button-Click event is generated.

The most important initial event is the Page_Load event, which is fired every time a Web Form is loaded. When the page is loaded, you want to fill the radio buttons with values from the database. For example, if you are creating a purchase form, you might create one radio button for each possible shipping method, such as UPS, FedEx, and so forth. You should therefore put your code into the Page_Load method to create the buttons.

You only want to load these values into the radio buttons the first time the page is loaded. If the user clicks a button or takes another action that sends the page back to the server, you do not want to retrieve the values again when the page is reloaded.

ASP.NET can differentiate the first time the page is displayed from subsequent displays after a client postback of the page to the server. Every Web Form page has the property IsPostBack, which will be true if the page is being loaded in response to a client postback, and false if it is being loaded for the first time.

You can check the value of IsPostBack. If it is false, you know that this is the first time the page is being displayed, and it's therefore time to get the values out of the database:

```
protected void Page_Load(object sender, EventArgs e)
{
    if (!IsPostBack)
    {//... }
}
```

The arguments to the Page_Load method are the normal arguments for events, as discussed in Chapter 12.

Connecting to the Database

The code for making the connection to the database and filling a data set will look very familiar; it is almost identical to what you saw in Chapter 14. There is no difference in creating a data set for Web Forms and creating a data set for Windows Forms.

Start by declaring the member variables you need:

```
private System.Data.SqlClient.SqlConnection myConnection;
private System.Data.DataSet myDataSet;
private System.Data.SqlClient.SqlCommand myCommand;
private System.Data.SqlClient.SqlDataAdapter dataAdapter;
```

As in Chapter 14, use the Structured Query Language (SQL) versions of SqlConnection and dataAdapter. Create the connectionString for the Northwinds database, and use that to instantiate and open the SQLConnection object:

```
string connectionString = "server=(local)\\NetSDK;" +
        "Trusted_Connection=yes; database=northwind";
myConnection =
    new  System.Data.SqlClient.SqlConnection(connectionString);
myConnection.Open( );
```

Create the data set and set it to handle case-sensitive queries:

```
myDataSet = new System.Data.DataSet( );
myDataSet.CaseSensitive=true;
```

Next, create the SqlCommand object and assign it the connection object and the Select statement, which are needed to get the ShipperID and company name identifying each potential shipper. Use the name as the text for the radio button and the ShipperID as the value:

```
myCommand = new System.Data.SqlClient.SqlCommand( );
myCommand.Connection=myConnection;
myCommand.CommandText = "Select ShipperID, CompanyName from Shippers";
```

Now create the dataAdapter object, set its SelectCommand property with your command object, and add the Shippers table to its table mappings:

```
dataAdapter = new System.Data.SqlClient.SqlDataAdapter( );
dataAdapter.SelectCommand= myCommand;
dataAdapter.TableMappings.Add("Table","Shippers");
```

Finally, fill the dataAdapter with the results of the query:

```
dataAdapter.Fill(myDataSet);
```

This is all virtually identical to what you saw in Chapter 14. This time, however, you're going to bind this data to the RadioButtonList you created earlier.

The first step is to set the properties on the RadioButtonList object. The first property of interest tells the RadioButtonList how to flow the radio buttons on the page:

```
rbl1.RepeatLayout =
    System.Web.UI.WebControls.RepeatLayout.Flow;
```

Flow is one of the two possible values in the RepeatLayout enumeration. The other is Table, which displays the radio buttons using a tabular layout. Next you must tell the RadioButtonList which values from the data set are to be used for display (the DataTextField) and which is the value to be returned when selected by the user (the DataValueField):

```
rbl1.DataTextField = "CompanyName";
rbl1.DataValueField = "ShipperID";
```

The final steps are to tell the RadioButtonList which view of the data to use. For this example, use the default view of the Shippers table within the dataset:

```
rbl1.DataSource = myDataSet.Tables["Shippers"].DefaultView;
```

With that done, you're ready to bind the RadioButtonList to the dataset:

```
rbl1.DataBind();
```

Finally, you should ensure that one of the radio buttons is selected, so select the first:

```
rbl1.Items[0].Selected = true;
```

This statement accesses the Items collection within the RadioButtonList, chooses the first item (the first radio button), and sets its Selected property to true.

When you run the program and navigate to the page in your browser, the buttons will be displayed, as shown in Figure 15-4.

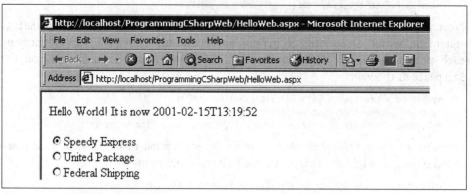

Figure 15-4. RadioButtonList

If you examine the page source, you will not find a RadioButtonList. Instead, standard HTML radio buttons have been created, and each has been given a shared ID. This allows the browser to treat them as a group. Their labels have been created, and each radio button and its label have been wrapped in a <span> tag:

```
<span id="rbl1" style="...">
<input id="rbl1_0" type="radio" name="rbl1"
       value="1" checked="checked" />
<label for="rbl1_0">Speedy Express</label>
<br>
<!-- remaining buttons omitted for brevity -->
</span>
```

This HTML is generated by the server by combining the RadioButtonList you added to your HTML with the processing of the code-behind page. When the page is loaded, the Page_Load() method is called and the data adapter is filled. When you assign the rbl1.DataTextField to CompanyName and the rbl1.DataValueField to shipperID and assign the rbl1.DataSource to the Shipper's table default view, you prepare the radio button list to generate the buttons. When you call DataBind, the radio buttons are created from the data in the data source.

By adding just a few more controls, you can create a complete form with which users can interact. You will do this by adding a more appropriate greeting ("Welcome to

NorthWind"), a text box to accept the name of the user, two new buttons (Order and Cancel), and text that provides feedback to the user. Figure 15-5 shows the finished form.

Figure 15-5. The form

This form will not win any awards for design, but its use will illustrate a number of key points about Web Forms.

 I've never known a developer who didn't think he could design a perfectly fine UI. At the same time, I never knew one who actually could. UI design is one of those skills (such as teaching) that we all think we can do, but only a few very talented folks are good at it. As a developer, I know my limitations; I write the code, someone else lays it out on the page.

Example 15-2 is the complete HTML for the *.aspx* file.

Example 15-2. The .aspx file

```
<%@ Page language="c#"
  Codebehind="HelloWeb.aspx.cs"
  AutoEventWireup="false"
  Inherits="ProgrammingCSharpWeb.WebForm1" %>

<!DOCTYPE HTML PUBLIC "-//W3C//DTD HTML 4.0 Transitional//EN" >
<HTML>
```

Example 15-2. The .aspx file (continued)

```html
<HEAD>
  <title>WebForm1</title>
  <meta name="GENERATOR"
    Content="Microsoft Visual Studio 7.0">
  <meta name="CODE_LANGUAGE" Content="C#">
  <meta name="vs_defaultClientScript"
    content="JavaScript">
  <meta name="vs_targetSchema"
    content="http://schemas.microsoft.com/intellisense/ie5">
</HEAD>

<body MS_POSITIONING="GridLayout">
  <form id="Form1" method="post" runat="server">

    <asp:Label id="Label1"
      style="Z-INDEX: 101; LEFT: 20px; POSITION: absolute; TOP: 28px"
      runat="server">Welcome to NorthWind.</asp:Label>

    <asp:Label id="Label2"
      style="Z-INDEX: 102; LEFT: 20px; POSITION: absolute; TOP: 67px"
      runat="server">Your Name:</asp:Label>

    <asp:Label id="Label3"
      style="Z-INDEX: 103; LEFT: 20px; POSITION: absolute; TOP: 134px"
      runat="server">Shipper:</asp:Label>

    <asp:Label id="lblFeedBack"
      style="Z-INDEX: 104; LEFT: 20px; POSITION: absolute; TOP: 241px"
      runat="server">Please choose the shipper.</asp:Label>

    <asp:Button id="Order"
      style="Z-INDEX: 105; LEFT: 20px; POSITION: absolute; TOP: 197px"
      runat="server" Text="Order"></asp:Button>

    <asp:Button id="Cancel"
      style="Z-INDEX: 106; LEFT: 128px; POSITION: absolute; TOP: 197px"
      runat="server" Text="Cancel"></asp:Button>

    <asp:TextBox id="txtName"
      style="Z-INDEX: 107; LEFT: 128px; POSITION: absolute; TOP: 64px"
      runat="server"></asp:TextBox>

    <asp:RadioButtonList id="rbl1"
      style="Z-INDEX: 108; LEFT: 112px; POSITION: absolute; TOP: 130px"
      runat="server"></asp:RadioButtonList>

  </form>
</body>

</HTML>
```

The <asp:Button> controls will be converted into a standard HTML <input> tag. Again, the advantage of using ASP controls is that they provide a more consistent object model for the programmer and yet they generate standard HTML that every browser can display. Because they are marked with the runat=Server attribute as well as given an id attribute, you can access these buttons programmatically in server-side code if you choose to do so. Example 15-3 is the complete code-behind page to support this HTML.

Example 15-3. The code-behind page supporting the HTML

```
using System;
using System.Collections;
using System.ComponentModel;
using System.Data;
using System.Drawing;
using System.Web;
using System.Web.SessionState;
using System.Web.UI;
using System.Web.UI.WebControls;
using System.Web.UI.HtmlControls;

namespace ProgrammingCSharpWeb
{
    // page constructor
    public class WebForm1 : System.Web.UI.Page
    {
        protected System.Web.UI.WebControls.Label Label1;
        protected System.Web.UI.WebControls.Label Label2;
        protected System.Web.UI.WebControls.Label Label3;
        protected System.Web.UI.WebControls.Label lblFeedBack;
        protected System.Web.UI.WebControls.Button Order;
        protected System.Web.UI.WebControls.Button Cancel;
        protected System.Web.UI.WebControls.TextBox txtName;
        protected System.Web.UI.WebControls.RadioButtonList rbl1;

        private System.Data.SqlClient.SqlConnection myConnection;
        private System.Data.DataSet myDataSet;
        private System.Data.SqlClient.SqlCommand myCommand;
        private System.Data.SqlClient.SqlDataAdapter dataAdapter;


        private void Page_Load(object sender, System.EventArgs e)
        {
            // the first time we load the page, get the data and
            // set the radio buttons
            if (!IsPostBack)
            {
                string connectionString = "server=(local)\\NetSDK;" +
                    "Trusted_Connection=yes; database=northwind";
                myConnection = new System.Data.SqlClient.SqlConnection(
                    connectionString);
                myConnection.Open();
```

Example 15-3. The code-behind page supporting the HTML (continued)

```csharp
        // create the data set and set a property
        myDataSet = new System.Data.DataSet( );
        myDataSet.CaseSensitive=true;

        // create the SqlCommand object and assign the
        // connection and the select statement
        myCommand = new System.Data.SqlClient.SqlCommand( );
        myCommand.Connection=myConnection;
        myCommand.CommandText =
            "Select ShipperID, CompanyName from Shippers";

        // create the dataAdapter object and pass in the
        // SqlCommand object and establish the data mappings
        dataAdapter = new System.Data.SqlClient.SqlDataAdapter( );
        dataAdapter.SelectCommand= myCommand;
        dataAdapter.TableMappings.Add("Table","Shippers");

        // Tell the dataAdapter object to fill the dataSet
        dataAdapter.Fill(myDataSet);

        // set up the properties for the RadioButtonList
        rbl1.RepeatLayout =
            System.Web.UI.WebControls.RepeatLayout.Flow;
        rbl1.DataTextField = "CompanyName";
        rbl1.DataValueField = "ShipperID";

        // set the data source and bind to i
        rbl1.DataSource = myDataSet.Tables["Shippers"].DefaultView;
        rbl1.DataBind( );

        // select the first button
        rbl1.Items[0].Selected = true;
    }
}

#region Web Form Designer generated code
override protected void OnInit(EventArgs e)
{
    //
    // CODEGEN: This call is required by
    //          the ASP.NET Web Form Designer.
    //
    InitializeComponent( );
    base.OnInit(e);
}

/// <summary>
/// Required method for Designer support - do not modify
/// the contents of this method with the code editor.
/// </summary>
private void InitializeComponent( )
{
```

Example 15-3. The code-behind page supporting the HTML (continued)

```
        this.Order.Click += new System.EventHandler(this.Order_Click);
        this.Load += new System.EventHandler(this.Page_Load);

    }
    #endregion

    private void Order_Click(object sender, System.EventArgs e)
    {
        // create the message by getting
        // the values from the controls
        string msg;
        msg = "Thank you " + txtName.Text +". You chose " ;
        // iterate over the radio buttons
        for (int i = 0;i<rbl1.Items.Count;i++)
        {
            // if it is selected, add it to the msg.
            if (rbl1.Items[i].Selected)
            {
                msg = msg + rbl1.Items[i].Text;
                lblFeedBack.Text = msg;
            } // end if selected
        }   // end for loop
    }       // end Order_Click
}           // end class WebForm1
}           // end namespace ProgrammingCSharpWeb
```

Responding to Postback Events

The <asp:button> objects automatically postback when clicked. You need not write any code to handle that event unless you want to do something more than postback to the server. If you take no other action, the page will simply be re-sent to the client.

Normally, when a page is redrawn, each control is redrawn from scratch. The Web is stateless, and if you want to manage the state of a control (e.g., redraw the user's text in the text box), you must do so yourself. In classic ASP, the programmer was responsible for managing this state, but ASP.NET provides some assistance. When the page is posted, a hidden element named ViewState is automatically added to the page:

```
<input type="hidden" name="__VIEWSTATE"
value="YTB6LTI5MTE3ODE1N19hMHpfaHo1ejF4X2Ewel9oejV6NXhfYTB6YTB6YTB6aHpSZXBlYXRMYXlvdX
RfU3lzdGVtLldlYi5VSS5XZWJDb25Ocm9scy5SZXBlYXRMYXlvdXR6VGFibGV4X0RhdGFWYWx1ZUZpZWxkX1N
oaXBwZXXJJRF9EYXRhdGVVceHRGaWVsZF9Db21wYW55TmFtZXhfX3hfYTB6YTB6YXpTcGVlZHkgRVx4cHJlc3Nf
MV94X2F6VW5pdGVkIFBhY2thZ2VfMl94X2F6RmVkZXJhbCBTaGlwcGluZz18zX3hfeF94X3hfX3h4X3hfX3hfX
3hcdDUwX1N5c3RlbS5TdHJpbmc=a15204ed" />
```

This element represents the state of the form (the values are already chosen by the user). When the page is redrawn on the client, ASP.NET uses the view state to return the controls to their previous state.

When the user clicks the Order button, the page is posted and the event handler assigned to that button is invoked:

```
public void Order_Click (object sender, System.EventArgs e)
{
    string msg;
    msg = "Thank you " + txtName.Text +". You chose " ;
    for (int i = 0;i<rbl1.Items.Count;i++)
    {
        if (rbl1.Items[i].Selected)
        {
            msg = msg + rbl1.Items[i].Text;
            lblFeedBack.Text = msg;
        }
    }
}
```

 The easiest way to create the event handler is to double-click the Order button in Design mode in Visual Studio .NET. This will cause Visual Studio to add the event to the InitializeComponent method:

```
Order.Click += new System.EventHandler         (this.Order_
Click);
```

It will also create a skeleton Order_Click event-handler method for you. Alternatively, you can do this all by hand.

This event handler creates a message based on the name you enter and the shipper you choose, and puts that message into the Feedback label. When the form first comes up, it looks like Figure 15-5. If I fill in my name, pick United Parcel Service, and press Order, the form will be submitted and then redisplayed. The result is shown in Figure 15-6.

The form automatically remembers the state of the radio button and text controls (this is what the VIEWSTATE field is for) and that the event handler has been called and run on the server; the label is updated accordingly.

 ASP programmers take note: there is *no* code in the *.aspx* file nor in the *.cs* file to manage the state. Nowhere do you stash away the state of the radio buttons or the text field; all this is managed automatically for you by ASP.NET.

ASP.NET and C#

There is a great deal to learn about ASP.NET, but much of it is language-independent. ASP.NET offers a rich suite of controls and related tools, including tools to validate data, display dates, present advertisements, interact with the user, and so forth. Most of these require no coding whatsoever.

Figure 15-6. Page posted after the user clicks Order

The role of the C# programmer in ASP.NET development is in writing the event handlers that respond to user interaction. Many of the event handlers will either add data to a database or retrieve data and make it available to the controls.

CHAPTER 16
Programming Web Services

.NET Web Services expand on the concept of distributed processing to build components whose methods can be invoked across the Internet. These components can be built in any .NET language, and they communicate using open protocols that are platform-independent.

For example, a stock exchange server might provide a web service method that takes a stock ticker symbol as a parameter and returns a quote. An application might combine that service with another service from a different company that also takes a stock symbol but that returns background data about the company. The application developer can concentrate on adding value to these services, rather than duplicating the same service for his own application.

The list of web services that might be useful to developers and end users seems boundless. A bookstore might provide a web service that takes an ISBN and returns the price and availability of a title. A hotel's web service might take a date range and number of guests and return a reservation. Another web service might take a telephone number and return a name and address. Yet another might provide information about the weather or shuttle launches.

Microsoft has announced a number of commercial .NET services as part of its .NET My Services initiative. Among these are its Passport service for identifying and authenticating users (see *http://www.passport.com*), as well as services for managing storage, notification, appointments, and a host of other applications. These services, as well as the ones you write, can be integrated with your applications just like any other business object.

In such a world, a single application might draw on and stitch together the services of hundreds of small web services distributed all over the world. This takes the Web to an entirely new dimension: not only is information retrieved and exchanged, but also methods are invoked and applications are executed.

SOAP, WSDL, and Discovery

What is needed to make web services possible is a simple, universally accepted protocol for exposing, finding, and invoking web service functions. In 1999, Simple Object Access Protocol (SOAP) was proposed to the World Wide Web Consortium. SOAP has the advantages of being based on XML and of using standard Internet communications protocols.

SOAP is a lightweight, message-based protocol built on XML, HTTP, and SMTP. Two other protocols are desirable, but not required, for a client to use a SOAP-enabled web service: a description of the methods provided by a particular service that can be understood and acted upon by clients, and a description of all such services available at a particular site or URL. The first of these is provided in .NET by the Web Service Description Language (WSDL) protocol, jointly developed by Microsoft, IBM, and others. Two other protocols have been proposed for discovery: UDDI, a joint effort by a number of companies including IBM and Microsoft, and Discovery, a proprietary offering from Microsoft.

WSDL is an XML schema used to describe the available methods—the interface—of a web service. Discovery enables applications to locate and interrogate web service descriptions, a preliminary step for accessing a web service. It is through the discovery process that web service clients learn that a service exists, what its capabilities are, and how to properly interact with it. A Discovery (*.disco*) file provides information to help browsers determine the URLs at any web site at which web services are available. When a server receives a request for a *.disco* file, it generates a list of some or all of the URLs at that site that provide web services.

Server-side Support

The plumbing necessary to discover and invoke web services is integrated into the .NET Framework and provided by classes within the System.Web.Services namespace. Creating a web service requires no special programming on your part; you need only write the implementing code, add the [WebMethod] attribute, and let the server do the rest. You can read about attributes in detail in Chapter 18.

Client-side Support

You make use of a web service by writing client code that acts as though it were communicating directly with the host server by means of a URL. However, in reality, the client interacts with a *proxy*. The job of the proxy is to represent the server on the client machine, to bundle client requests into SOAP messages that are sent on to the server, and to retrieve the responses that contain the result. Proxies and the details of dealing with objects on other machines are covered in detail in Chapter 19.

Building a Web Service

To illustrate the techniques used to implement a web service in C# using the services classes of the .NET Framework, build a simple calculator and then make use of its functions over the Web.

Begin by specifying the web service. To do so, define a class that inherits from System.Web.Services.WebService. The easiest way to create this class is to open Visual Studio and create a new C# Web Service project. The default name that Visual Studio provides is WebService1, but you might want to choose something more appropriate.

Visual Studio .NET creates a skeleton web service and even provides a Web Service example method for you to replace with your own code, as shown in Example 16-1.

Example 16-1. Skeleton web class generated by Visual Studio .NET

```
using System;
using System.Collections;
using System.ComponentModel;
using System.Data;
using System.Diagnostics;
using System.Web;
using System.Web.Services;

namespace WSCalc
{
    /// <summary>
    /// Summary description for Service1.
    /// </summary>
    public class Service1 : System.Web.Services.WebService
    {
        public Service1()
        {
            //CODEGEN: This call is required by
            // the ASP.NET Web Services Designer
            InitializeComponent();
        }

        #region Component Designer generated code

        //Required by the Web Services Designer
        private IContainer components = null;

        /// <summary>
        /// Required method for Designer support - do not modify
        /// the contents of this method with the code editor.
        /// </summary>
        private void InitializeComponent()
        {
        }

        /// <summary>
```

```
        /// Clean up any resources being used.
        /// </summary>
        protected override void Dispose( bool disposing )
        {
            if(disposing && components != null)
            {
                components.Dispose( );
            }
            base.Dispose(disposing);
        }

        #endregion

        // WEB SERVICE EXAMPLE
        // The HelloWorld( ) example service
        // returns the string Hello World
        // To build, uncomment the following lines
        // then save and build the project
        // To test this web service, press F5

//        [WebMethod]
//        public string HelloWorld( )
//        {
//            return "Hello World";
//        }
    }
}
```

Create five methods: Add( ), Sub( ), Mult( ), Div( ), and Pow( ). Each takes two parameters of type double, performs the requested operation, and then returns a value of the same type. For example, here is the code for raising a number to some specified power:

```
public double Pow(double x, double y)
{
    double retVal = x;
    for (int i = 0;i < y-1;i++)
    {
        retVal *= x;
    }
    return retVal;
}
```

To expose each method as a web service, you simply add the [WebMethod] attribute before each method declaration (attributes are discussed in Chapter 18):

```
[WebMethod]
```

You are not required to expose all the methods of your class as web services. You can pick and choose, adding the [WebMethod] attribute only to those methods you want to expose.

That's all you need to do; .NET takes care of the rest.

WSDL and Namespaces

Your web service will use a Web Service Description Language (WSDL) XML document to describe the web-callable end points. Within any WSDL document, an XML namespace must be used to ensure that the end points have unique names. The default XML namespace is *http://tempuri.org*, but you will want to modify this before making your web service publicly available.

You can change the XML namespace by using the WebService attribute:

```
[WebService(Namespace=
    "http://www.LibertyAssociates.com/webServices/")]
```

You can read about attributes in detail in Chapter 18.

Example 16-2 shows the complete source code for the Calculator web service:

Example 16-2. Calculator web service program

```csharp
using System;
using System.Collections;
using System.ComponentModel;
using System.Data;
using System.Diagnostics;
using System.Web;
using System.Web.Services;

namespace WSCalc
{
    [WebService(Namespace="http://www.libertyAssociates.com/webServices/")]
    public class Service1 : System.Web.Services.WebService
    {
        public Service1()
        {
            //CODEGEN: This call is required by the
            //ASP.NET Web Services Designer
            InitializeComponent();
        }

        #region Component Designer generated code

        //Required by the Web Services Designer
        private IContainer components = null;

        /// <summary>
        /// Required method for Designer support - do not modify
        /// the contents of this method with the code editor.
        /// </summary>
        private void InitializeComponent()
        {
        }
```

Example 16-2. Calculator web service program (continued)

```
/// <summary>
/// Clean up any resources being used.
/// </summary>
protected override void Dispose( bool disposing )
{
    if(disposing && components != null)
    {
        components.Dispose( );
    }
    base.Dispose(disposing);
}

#endregion

[WebMethod]
public double Add(double x, double y)
{
    return x+y;
}

[WebMethod]
public double Sub(double x, double y)
{
    return x-y;
}
[WebMethod]
public double Mult(double x, double y)
{
    return x*y;
}
[WebMethod]
public double Div(double x, double y)
{
    return x/y;
}
[WebMethod]
public double Pow(double x, double y)
{
    double retVal = x;
    for (int i = 0;i < y-1;i++)
    {
        retVal *= x;
    }
    return retVal;
}
    }
}
```

When you build this project with Visual Studio .NET, a DLL is created in the appropriate subdirectory of your Internet server (e.g., *c:\InetPub\wwwroot\WSCalc*). A quick check of that directory reveals that a *.vsdisco* file has also been added.

There is nothing magical about using Visual Studio .NET; you can create your server in Notepad if you like. Visual Studio .NET simply saves you the work of creating the directories, creating the *.vsdisco* file, and so forth. Visual Studio .NET is particularly helpful when creating the client files, as you'll see shortly.

Testing Your Web Service

If you open a browser to your web service's URL (or invoke the browser by running the program in Visual Studio .NET), you get an automatically generated, server-side web page that describes the web service, as shown in Figure 16-1. Test pages such as this offer a good way to test your web service. (The next section illuminates the seeming hocus-pocus that produces these pages.)

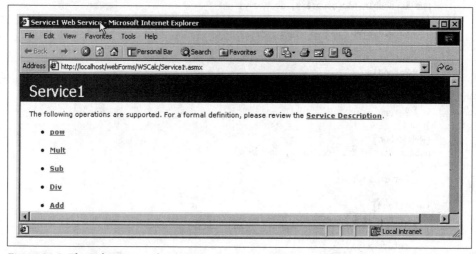

Figure 16-1. The web service web page

Clicking a method brings you to a page that describes the method and allows you to invoke it by typing in parameters and pressing the Invoke button. Figure 16-2 illustrates.

If you type 3 into the first value field and 4 into the second field, you will have asked the web service to raise 3 to the fourth power. The result is an XML page describing the output, as shown in Figure 16-3.

Notice that the URL encodes the parameters of 3 and 4, and the output XML shows the result of 81 (3*3*3*3 = 81).

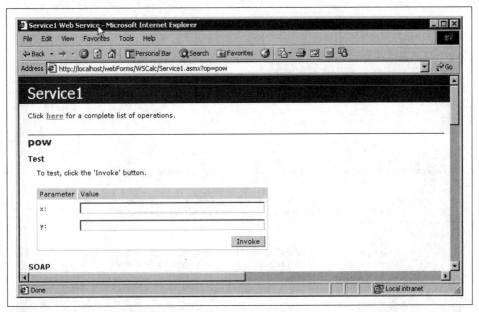

Figure 16-2. Test page for a web service method

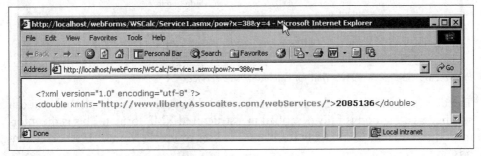

Figure 16-3. XML output for a web service method

Viewing the WSDL Contract

A lot of work is being done for you automatically. HTML pages describing your web service and its methods are generated, and these pages include links to pages in which the methods can be tested. How is this done?

As noted earlier, the web service is described in WSDL. You can see the WSDL document by appending ?WSDL to the web service URL, like this:

```
http://localhost/WSCalc/Service1.asmx?wsdl
```

The browser displays the WSDL document, as shown in Figure 16-4.

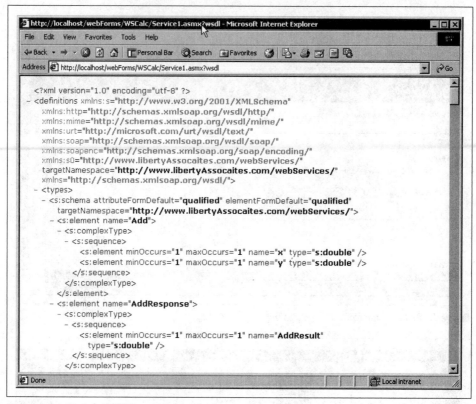

Figure 16-4. Sample WSDL output for calculator web service

The details of the WSDL document are beyond the scope of this book, but you can see that each method is fully described in a structured XML format. This is the information used by SOAP to allow the client browser to invoke your web service methods on the server.

Creating the Proxy

Before you can create a client application to interact with the calculator web service, you must first create a proxy class. Once again, you can do this by hand, but that would be hard work. The folks at Microsoft have provided a tool called wsdl that generates the source code for the proxy based on the information in the WSDL file.

To create the proxy, enter wsdl at the Windows command-line prompt, followed by the path to the WSDL contract. For example, you might enter:

```
wsdl http://localhost/WSCalc/service1.asmx?wsdl
```

The result is the creation of a C# client file named *Service1.cs*, an excerpt of which appears in Example 16-3. You must add the namespace WSCalc because you'll need it when you build your client (the tool does not insert it for you).

Example 16-3. Sample client code to access the calculator web service

```
using System.Xml.Serialization;
using System;
using System.Web.Services.Protocols;
using System.Web.Services;

namespace WSCalc
{
    [System.Web.Services.WebServiceBindingAttribute(
        Name="Service1Soap",
        Namespace="http://www.libertyAssociates.com/webServices/")]
    public class Service1 :
        System.Web.Services.Protocols.SoapHttpClientProtocol
    {

        public Service1( )
        {
            this.Url =
                "http://localhost/WSCalc/service1.asmx";
        }

        [System.Web.Services.Protocols.SoapDocumentMethodAttribute(
            "http://www.libertyAssociates.com/webServices/Add",
            RequestNamespace=
              "http://www.libertyAssociates.com/webServices/",
            ResponseNamespace=
              "http://www.libertyAssociates.com/webServices/",
            Use=System.Web.Services.Description.SoapBindingUse.Literal,
            ParameterStyle=
                System.Web.Services.Protocols.SoapParameterStyle.Wrapped)]
        public System.Double Add(System.Double x, System.Double y)
        {
            object[] results = this.Invoke("Add", new object[] {x,y});
            return ((System.Double)(results[0]));
        }

        public System.IAsyncResult
            BeginAdd(System.Double x, System.Double y,
            System.AsyncCallback callback, object asyncState)
        {
            return this.BeginInvoke("Add", new object[] {x,
                    y}, callback, asyncState);
        }

        public System.Double EndAdd(System.IAsyncResult asyncResult)
        {
            object[] results = this.EndInvoke(asyncResult);
            return ((System.Double)(results[0]));
        }
```

This complex code is produced by the WSDL tool to build the proxy DLL you will need when you build your client. The file uses attributes extensively (see

Chapter 18), but with your working knowledge of C# you can extrapolate at least how some of it works.

The file starts by declaring the Service1 class that derives from the class SoapHttpClientProtocol, which occurs in the namespace called System.Web.Services. Protocols:

```
public class Service1 :
    System.Web.Services.Protocols.SoapHttpClientProtocol
```

The constructor sets the URL property inherited from SoapHttpClientProtocol to the URL of the *.asmx* page you created earlier.

The Add( ) method is declared with a host of attributes that provide the SOAP goo to make the remote invocation work.

The WSDL application has also provided asynchronous support for your methods. For example, for the Add( ) method, it also created BeginAdd( ) and EndAdd( ). This allows you to interact with a web service without performance penalties.

To build the proxy, place the code generated by WSDL into a C# Library project in Visual Studio .NET and then build the project to generate a DLL. Be sure to write down the location of that DLL, as you will need it when you build the client application.

To test the web service, create a very simple C# Console application. The only trick is that in your client code you need to add a reference to the proxy DLL just created. Once that is done, you can instantiate the web service, just like any locally available object:

```
WSCalc.Service1 theWebSvc =
    new WSCalc.Service1( );
```

You can then invoke the Pow( ) method as if it were a method on a locally available object:

```
for (int i = 2;i<10; i++)
    for (int j = 1;j <10;j++)
    {
        Console.WriteLine(
          "{0} to the power of {1} = {2}", i, j,
          theWebSvc.Pow(i, j));
    }
```

This simple loop creates a table of the powers of the numbers 2 through 9, displaying for each the powers 1 through 9. The complete source code and an excerpt of the output is shown in Example 16-4.

Example 16-4. A client program to test the calculator web service

```
using System;

// driver program to test the web service
```

Example 16-4. A client program to test the calculator web service (continued)

```
public class Tester
{
   public static void Main( )
   {
      Tester t = new Tester( );
      t.Run( );
   }

   public void Run( )
   {
      int var1 = 5;
      int var2 = 7;

      // instantiate the web service proxy
      WSCalc.Service1 theWebSvc =
         new WSCalc.Service1( );

      // call the add method
      Console.WriteLine("{0} + {1} = {2}", var1, var2,
         theWebSvc.Add(var1, var2));

      // build a table by repeatedly calling the pow method
      for (int i = 2;i<10; i++)
         for (int j = 1;j <10;j++)
         {
            Console.WriteLine("{0} to the power of {1} = {2}", i, j,
               theWebSvc.Pow(i, j));
         }
   }
}
```

Output (excerpt):
```
5 + 7 = 12
2 to the power of 1 = 2
2 to the power of 2 = 4
2 to the power of 3 = 8
2 to the power of 4 = 16
2 to the power of 5 = 32
2 to the power of 6 = 64
2 to the power of 7 = 128
2 to the power of 8 = 256
2 to the power of 9 = 512
3 to the power of 1 = 3
3 to the power of 2 = 9
3 to the power of 3 = 27
3 to the power of 4 = 81
3 to the power of 5 = 243
3 to the power of 6 = 729
3 to the power of 7 = 2187
3 to the power of 8 = 6561
3 to the power of 9 = 19683
```

Your calculator service is now more available than you might have imagined (depending on your security settings) through the web protocols of HTTP-Get, HTTP-Post, or SOAP. Your client uses the SOAP protocol, but you could certainly create a client that would use HTTP-Get:

```
http://localhost/WSCalc/Service1.asmx/Add?x=23&y=22
```

In fact, if you put that URL into your browser, the browser will respond with the following answer:

```
<?xml version="1.0" encoding="utf-8"?>
<double xmlns="http://www.libertyAssociates.com/webServices/">45</double>
```

The key advantage SOAP has over HTTP-Get and HTTP-Post is that SOAP can support a rich set of datatypes, including all of the C# intrinsic types (int, double, etc.), as well as enums, classes, structs, and ADO.NET DataSets, and arrays of any of these types.

Also, while HTTP-Get and HTTP-Post protocols are restricted to name/value pairs of primitive types and enums, SOAP's rich XML grammar offers a more robust alternative for data exchange.

PART III

The CLR and the .NET Framework

CHAPTER 17

Assemblies and Versioning

The basic unit of .NET programming is the *assembly*. An assembly is a collection of files that appears to the user to be a single dynamic link library (DLL) or executable (EXE). DLLs are collections of classes and methods that are linked into your running program only when they are needed.

Assemblies are the .NET unit of reuse, versioning, security, and deployment. This chapter discusses assemblies in detail, including the architecture and contents of assemblies, private assemblies, and shared assemblies.

In addition to the object code for the application, assemblies contain resources such as *.gif* files, type definitions for each class you define, as well as metadata about the code and data. Metadata is explored in detail in Chapter 18.

PE Files

On disk, assemblies are Portable Executable (PE) files. PE files are not new. The format of a .NET PE file is exactly the same as a normal Windows PE file. PE files are implemented as DLLs or EXEs. Logically (as opposed to physically), assemblies consist of one or more *modules*. Note, however, that an assembly must have exactly one entry point—DLLMain, WinMain, or Main. DLLMain is the entry point for DLLs, WinMain is the entry point for Windows applications, and Main is the entry point for DOS and Console applications.

Modules are created as DLLs and are the constituent pieces of assemblies. Standing alone, modules cannot be executed; they must be combined into assemblies to be useful.

Deploy and reuse the entire contents of an assembly as a unit. Assemblies are loaded on demand and will not be loaded if not needed.

Metadata

Metadata is information stored in the assembly that describes the types and methods of the assembly and provides other useful information about the assembly.

Assemblies are said to be *self-describing* because the metadata fully describes the contents of each module. Metadata is discussed in detail in Chapter 18.

Security Boundary

Assemblies form security boundaries as well as type boundaries. That is, an assembly is the scope boundary for the types it contains, and types cannot cross assemblies. You can, of course, refer to types across assembly boundaries by adding a reference to the required assembly, either in the Integrated Development Environment (IDE) or on the command line, at compile time. What you cannot do is have the definition of a type span two assemblies.

Versioning

Each assembly has a version number, and versions cannot transcend the boundary of the assembly. That is, a version can refer only to the contents of a single assembly. All types and resources within the assembly change versions together.

Manifests

As part of its metadata, every assembly has a *manifest*. This describes what is in the assembly, including identification information (name, version, etc.), a list of the types and resources in the assembly, a map to connect public types with the implementing code, and a list of assemblies referenced by this assembly.

Even the simplest program has a manifest. You can examine that manifest using ILDasm, which is provided as part of your development environment. When you open it in ILDasm, the EXE program created by Example 12-3 looks like Figure 17-1.

Notice the manifest (second line from the top). Double-clicking the manifest opens a Manifest window, as shown in Figure 17-2.

This file serves as a map of the contents of the assembly. You can see in the first line the reference to the mscorlib assembly, which is referenced by this and every .NET application. The mscorlib assembly is the core library assembly for .NET and is available on every .NET platform.

The next assembly line is a reference to the assembly from Example 12-3. You can also see that this assembly consists of a single module. You can ignore the rest of the metadata for now.

Modules in the Manifest

Assemblies can consist of more than one module. In such a case, the manifest includes a hash code identifying each module to ensure that when the program

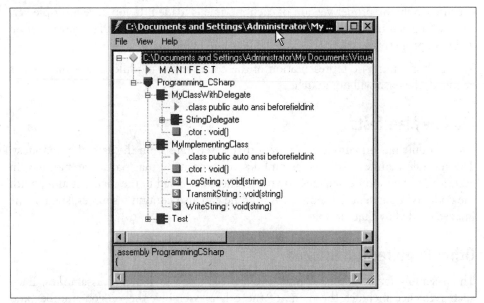

Figure 17-1. ILDasm of Example 12-3

```
MANIFEST                                                              _ □ ×
.assembly extern mscorlib
{
  .publickeytoken = (B7 7A 5C 56 19 34 E0 89 )                    // .z\V.
  .ver 1:0:2411:0
}
.assembly ProgrammingCSharp
{
  .custom instance void [mscorlib]System.Reflection.AssemblyKeyNameAttribute::.
  .custom instance void [mscorlib]System.Reflection.AssemblyKeyFileAttribute::.
  .custom instance void [mscorlib]System.Reflection.AssemblyDelaySignAttribute:
  .custom instance void [mscorlib]System.Reflection.AssemblyTrademarkAttribute:
  .custom instance void [mscorlib]System.Reflection.AssemblyCopyrightAttribute:
  .custom instance void [mscorlib]System.Reflection.AssemblyProductAttribute::.
  .custom instance void [mscorlib]System.Reflection.AssemblyCompanyAttribute::.
  .custom instance void [mscorlib]System.Reflection.AssemblyConfigurationAttrib
  .custom instance void [mscorlib]System.Reflection.AssemblyDescriptionAttribut
  .custom instance void [mscorlib]System.Reflection.AssemblyTitleAttribute::.ct
  // --- The following custom attribute is added automatically, do not uncommen
  //   .custom instance void [mscorlib]System.Diagnostics.DebuggableAttribute::.
  //
  .hash algorithm 0x00008004
  .ver 1:0:535:28584
}
.module ProgrammingCSharp.exe
// MVID: {22DDF4E4-5F73-449B-99D8-99988299F3BB}
.subsystem 0x00000003
.file alignment 512
.corflags 0x00000001
// Image base: 0x03400000
```

Figure 17-2. The Manifest window

executes, only the proper version of each module is loaded. If you have multiple versions of a given module on your machine, the hash code ensures that your program will load properly.

The hash is a numeric representation of the code for the module, and if the code is changed, the hash will not match.

Module Manifests

Each module has a manifest of its own that is separate from the assembly manifest. The module manifest lists the assemblies referenced by that particular module. In addition, if the module declares any types, these are listed in the manifest along with the code to implement the module. A module can also contain resources, such as the images needed by that module.

Other Required Assemblies

The assembly manifest also contains references to other required assemblies. Each such reference includes the name of the other assembly, the version number and required culture, and optionally, the other assembly's originator. The originator is a digital signature for the developer or company that provided the other assembly.

 Culture is an object representing the language and national display characteristics for the person using your program. It is culture that determines, for example, whether dates are in month/date/year format or date/month/year format.

Multi-Module Assemblies

A single-module assembly has a single file that can be an EXE or DLL file. This single module contains all the types and implementations for the application. The assembly manifest is embedded within this module.

A multi-module assembly consists of multiple files (zero or one EXE and zero or more DLL files, though you must have at least one EXE or DLL). The assembly manifest in this case can reside in a standalone file, or it can be embedded in one of the modules. When the assembly is referenced, the runtime loads the file containing the manifest and then loads the required modules as needed.

Benefiting from Multi-Module Assemblies

Multi-module assemblies have advantages for real-world programs, especially if they are developed by multiple developers or are very large.

Imagine that 25 developers are working on a single project. If they were to create a single-module assembly to build and test the application, all 25 programmers would have to check in their latest code simultaneously, and the entire mammoth application would be built. That creates a logistical nightmare.

If they each build their own modules, however, the program can be built with the latest available module from each programmer. This relieves the logistics problems; each module can be checked in when it is ready.

Perhaps more importantly, multiple modules make it easier to deploy and to maintain large programs. Imagine that each of the 25 developers builds a separate module, each in its own DLL. The person responsible for building the application would then create a 26th module with the manifest for the entire assembly. These 26 files can be deployed to the end user. The end user then need only load the one module with the manifest, and he can ignore the other 25. The manifest will identify which of the 25 modules has each method, and the appropriate modules will be loaded as methods are invoked. This will be transparent to the user.

As modules are updated, the programmers need only to send the updated modules (and a module with an updated manifest). Additional modules can be added and existing modules can be deleted; the end user continues to load only the one module with the manifest.

In addition, it is entirely likely that not all 25 modules will need to be loaded into the program. By breaking the program into 25 modules, the loader can load only those parts of the program that are needed. This makes it easy to shunt aside code that is only rarely needed into its own module, which might not be loaded at all in the normal course of events. Although this was the theory behind DLLs all along, .NET accomplishes this without "DLL Hell," a monumental achievement described later in this chapter.

Building a Multi-Module Assembly

To demonstrate the use of multi-module assemblies, the following example creates a couple of very simple modules that you can then combine into a single assembly. The first module is a Fraction class. This simple class will allow you to create and manipulate common fractions. Example 17-1 illustrates.

Example 17-1. The Fraction class

```
namespace ProgCS
{
    using System;

    public class Fraction
    {
        public Fraction(int numerator, int denominator)
        {
            this.numerator = numerator;
            this.denominator = denominator;
```

Example 17-1. The Fraction class (continued)

```
        }

        public Fraction Add(Fraction rhs)
        {
            if (rhs.denominator != this.denominator)
            {
                throw new ArgumentException(
                    "Denominators must match");
            }

            return new Fraction(
                this.numerator + rhs.numerator,
                    this.denominator);
        }

        public override string ToString()
        {
            return numerator + "/" + denominator;
        }

        private int numerator;
        private int denominator;
    }
}
```

Notice that the Fraction class is in the ProgCS namespace. The full name for the class is ProgCS.Fraction.

The Fraction class takes two values in its constructor: a numerator and a denominator. There is also an Add( ) method, which takes a second Fraction and returns the sum, assuming the two share a common denominator. This class is simplistic, but it will demonstrate the functionality necessary for this example.

The second class is the myCalc class, which stands in for a robust calculator. Example 17-2 illustrates.

Example 17-2. The Calculator

```
namespace ProgCS
{
    using System;

    public class myCalc
    {
        public int Add(int val1, int val2)
        {
            return val1 + val2;
        }
        public int Mult(int val1, int val2)
```

Example 17-2. The Calculator (continued)

```
    {
        return val1 * val2;
    }
  }
}
```

Once again, `myCalc` is a very stripped-down class to keep things simple. Notice that `calc` is also in the `ProgCS` namespace.

This is sufficient to create an assembly. Use an *AssemblyInfo.cs* file to add some metadata to the assembly. The use of metadata is covered in Chapter 19.

> You can write your own *AssemblyInfo.cs* file, but the simplest approach is to let Visual Studio generate one for you automatically.

Visual Studio creates single-module assemblies by default. You can create a multi-module resource with the `/addModules` command line. The easiest way to compile and build a multi-module assembly is with a `makefile`, which you can create with Notepad or any text editor.

> If you are unfamiliar with makefiles, don't worry; this is the only example that needs a `makefile`, and that is only to get around the current limitation of Visual Studio creating only single-module assemblies. If necessary, you can just use the `makefile` as offered without fully understanding every line.

Example 17-3 shows the complete `makefile` (which is explained in detail immediately afterward). To run this example, put the `makefile` (with the name 'makefile') in a directory together with a copy of *Calc.cs*, *Fraction.cs*, and *AssemblyInfo.cs*. Start up a .NET command window and `cd` to that directory. Invoke `nmake` without any command switchs. You will find the *SharedAssembly.dll* in the *\bin* subdirectory.

Example 17-3. The complete makefile for a multi-module assembly

```
ASSEMBLY= MySharedAssembly.dll

BIN=.\bin
SRC=.
DEST=.\bin

CSC=csc /nologo /debug+ /d:DEBUG /d:TRACE

MODULETARGET=/t:module
LIBTARGET=/t:library
EXETARGET=/t:exe
```

Example 17-3. The complete makefile for a multi-module assembly (continued)

```
REFERENCES=System.dll

MODULES=$(DEST)\Fraction.dll $(DEST)\Calc.dll
METADATA=$(SRC)\AssemblyInfo.cs

all: $(DEST)\MySharedAssembly.dll

# Assembly metadata placed in same module as manifest
$(DEST)\$(ASSEMBLY): $(METADATA) $(MODULES) $(DEST)
    $(CSC) $(LIBTARGET) /addmodule:$(MODULES: =;) /out:$@ %s

# Add Calc.dll module to this dependency list
$(DEST)\Calc.dll: Calc.cs $(DEST)
    $(CSC) $(MODULETARGET) /r:$(REFERENCES: =;) /out:$@ %s

# Add Fraction
$(DEST)\Fraction.dll: Fraction.cs $(DEST)
    $(CSC) $(MODULETARGET) /r:$(REFERENCES: =;) /out:$@ %s

$(DEST)::
!if !EXISTS($(DEST))
    mkdir $(DEST)
!endif
```

The makefile begins by defining the assembly you want to build:

```
ASSEMBLY= MySharedAssembly.dll
```

It then defines the directories you'll use, putting the output in a bin directory beneath the current directory and retrieving the source code from the current directory:

```
BIN=.\bin
SRC=.
DEST=.\bin
```

Build the assembly as follows:

```
$(DEST)\$(ASSEMBLY): $(METADATA) $(MODULES) $(DEST)
    $(CSC) $(LIBTARGET) /addmodule:$(MODULES: =;) /out:$@ %s
```

This places the assembly (*MySharedAssembly.dll*) in the destination directory (bin). It tells nmake (the program that executes the makefile) that the assembly consists of the metadata and the modules, and it provides the command line required to build the assembly.

The metadata is defined earlier as:

```
METADATA=$(SRC)\AssemblyInfo.cs
```

The modules are defined as the two DLLs:

```
MODULES=$(DEST)\Fraction.dll $(DEST)\Calc.dll
```

The compile line builds the library and adds the modules, putting the output into the assembly file *MySharedAssembly.dll*:

```
$(DEST)\$(ASSEMBLY): $(METADATA) $(MODULES) $(DEST)
    $(CSC) $(LIBTARGET) /addmodule:$(MODULES: =;) /out:$@ %s
```

To accomplish this, nmake needs to know how to make the modules. Start by telling nmake how to create *calc.dll*. You need the *calc.cs* source file for this; tell nmake on the command line to build that DLL:

```
$(DEST)\Calc.dll: Calc.cs $(DEST)
    $(CSC) $(MODULETARGET) /r:$(REFERENCES: =;) /out:$@ %s
```

Then do the same thing for *fraction.dll*:

```
$(DEST)\Fraction.dll: Fraction.cs $(DEST)
    $(CSC) $(MODULETARGET) /r:$(REFERENCES: =;) /out:$@ %s
```

The result of running nmake on this makefile is to create three DLLs: *fraction.dll, calc.dll*, and *MySharedAssembly.dll*. If you open *MySharedAssembly.dll* with ILDasm, you'll find that it consists of nothing but a manifest, as shown in Figure 17-3.

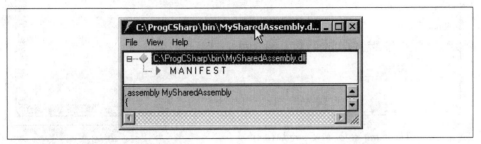

Figure 17-3. MySharedAssembly.dll

If you examine the manifest, you see the metadata for the libraries you created, as shown in Figure 17-4.

You first see an external assembly for the core library (mscorlib), followed by the two modules, ProgCS.Fraction and ProgCS.myCalc.

You now have an assembly that consists of three DLL files: *MySharedAssembly.dll* with the manifest, and *Calc.dll* and *Fraction.dll* with the types and implementation needed.

Testing the assembly

To use these modules, you need to create a driver program that will load in the modules as needed. Example 17-4 illustrates. Save this program as *Test.cs* in the same directory as the other modules.

```
.assembly extern mscorlib
{
  .publickeytoken = (B7 7A 5C 56 19 34 E0 89 )                     // .z\V.4..
  .hash = (8B BB 5A BD 8D A3 12 7D 08 A2 25 D0 48 17 28 4F  // ..Z....}..%.H.(O
           20 57 EA 07 )                                                     // W..
  .ver 1:0:2411:0
}
.assembly MySharedAssembly
{
  // --- The following custom attribute is added automatically, do not uncomment -------
  //   .custom instance void [mscorlib]System.Diagnostics.DebuggableAttribute::.ctor(bool,
  //                                                                    bool) = ( 01 00 01
  .custom instance void [mscorlib]System.Reflection.AssemblyKeyNameAttribute::.ctor(string) = ( 01 00
  .custom instance void [mscorlib]System.Reflection.AssemblyKeyFileAttribute::.ctor(string) = ( 01 00
  .custom instance void [mscorlib]System.Reflection.AssemblyDelaySignAttribute::.ctor(bool) = ( 01 00
  .custom instance void [mscorlib]System.Reflection.AssemblyTrademarkAttribute::.ctor(string) = ( 01 0
  .custom instance void [mscorlib]System.Reflection.AssemblyCopyrightAttribute::.ctor(string) = ( 01 0
  .custom instance void [mscorlib]System.Reflection.AssemblyProductAttribute::.ctor(string) = ( 01 00
  .custom instance void [mscorlib]System.Reflection.AssemblyCompanyAttribute::.ctor(string) = ( 01 00
  .custom instance void [mscorlib]System.Reflection.AssemblyConfigurationAttribute::.ctor(string) = (
  .custom instance void [mscorlib]System.Reflection.AssemblyDescriptionAttribute::.ctor(string) = ( 01
  .custom instance void [mscorlib]System.Reflection.AssemblyTitleAttribute::.ctor(string) = ( 01 00 00
  .hash algorithm 0x00008004
  .ver 1:0:535:29053
}
.file Fraction.dll
    .hash = (DB EB 60 2F E3 2C F3 6B 55 3F 34 0A 50 EE CD 51  // ..`/...kU?4.P..Q
             F4 44 58 C6 )                                                    // .DX.
.file Calc.dll
    .hash = (92 1C 3D AB 27 E2 0D FE 60 62 94 9E 6C 4C 63 03  // ..=.'...`b..lLc.
             5C 4F 1D CD )                                                    // \O..
.class extern public ProgCS.Fraction
{
  .file Fraction.dll
  .class 0x02000002
}
.class extern public ProgCS.myCalc
{
  .file Calc.dll
  .class 0x02000002
}
.module MySharedAssembly.dll
// MVID: {F5D8C740-E1DA-465A-A528-B861CA6E04E8}
.subsystem 0x00000003
.file alignment 512
.corflags 0x00000001
// Image base: 0x03440000
```

Figure 17-4. The manifest for MySharedAssembly

Example 17-4. A module test driver

```
namespace Programming_CSharp
{
    using System;

    public class Test
    {
        // main will not load the shared assembly
        static void Main()
        {
            Test t = new Test();
            t.UseCS();
            t.UseFraction();

        }

        // calling this loads the myCalc assembly
        // and the mySharedAssembly assembly as well
        public void UseCS()
        {
            ProgCS.myCalc calc = new ProgCS.myCalc();
```

Example 17-4. A module test driver (continued)

```
        Console.WriteLine("3+5 = {0}\n3*5 = {1}",
            calc.Add(3,5), calc.Mult(3,5));
    }

    // calling this adds the Fraction assembly
    public void UseFraction()
    {
        ProgCS.Fraction frac1 = new ProgCS.Fraction(3,5);
        ProgCS.Fraction frac2 = new ProgCS.Fraction(1,5);
        ProgCS.Fraction frac3 = frac1.Add(frac2);
        Console.WriteLine("{0} + {1} = {2}",
            frac1, frac2, frac3);
    }
}
}
```

```
Output:
3+5 = 8
3*5 = 15
3/5 + 1/5 = 4/5
```

For the purposes of this demonstration, it is important not to put any code in Main( ) that depends on your modules. You do not want the modules loaded when Main( ) loads, and so no Fraction or Calc objects are placed in Main( ). When you call into UseFraction and UseCalc, you'll be able to see that the modules are individually loaded.

Loading the assembly

An assembly is loaded into its application by the AssemblyResolver through a process called *probing*. The assembly resolver is called by the .NET Framework automatically; you do not call it explicitly. Its job is to resolve the assembly name to an EXE program and load your program.

With a private assembly, the AssemblyResolver looks only in the application load directory and its subdirectories—that is, the directory in which you invoked your application.

 The three DLLs produced earlier must be in the directory in which Example 17-4 executes or in a subdirectory of that directory.

Put a break point on the second line in Main, as shown in Figure 17-5.

Execute to the break point and open the Modules window. Only two modules are loaded, as shown in Figure 17-6.

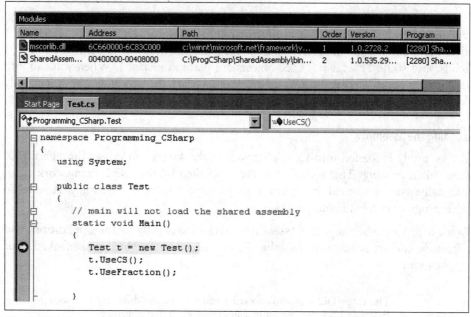

```
Programming_CSharp.Test                                    Main()

namespace Programming_CSharp
{
    using System;

    public class Test
    {
        // main will not load the shared assembly
        static void Main()
        {
            Test t = new Test();
            t.UseCS();
            t.UseFraction();

        }
```

Figure 17-5. A break point in Main()

```
Modules
Name              Address              Path                                          Order   Version          Program
mscorlib.dll      6C660000-6C83C000    c:\winnt\microsoft.net\framework\v...   1       1.0.2728.2       [2280] Sha...
SharedAssem...    00400000-00408000    C:\ProgCSharp\SharedAssembly\bin...     2       1.0.535.29...    [2280] Sha...


Start Page   Test.cs

Programming_CSharp.Test                                    UseCS()

namespace Programming_CSharp
{
    using System;

    public class Test
    {
        // main will not load the shared assembly
        static void Main()
        {
            Test t = new Test();
            t.UseCS();
            t.UseFraction();

        }
```

Figure 17-6. Only two modules loaded

 If you did not develop *Test.cs* as part of a Visual Studio .NET solution, put a call to System.Diagnostics.Debugger.Launch( ) just before the second line in Main. This lets you choose which debugger to use. (Make sure you compile *Test.cs* with the /debug and /r: MySharedAssembly.dll options.)

Step into the first method call and watch the modules window. As soon as you step into UseCS, the AssemblyLoader recognizes that it needs an assembly from *MyShare-dAssembly.Dll*. The DLL is loaded, and from that assembly's manifest the AssemblyLoader finds that it needs *Calc.dll*, which is loaded as well, as shown in Figure 17-7.

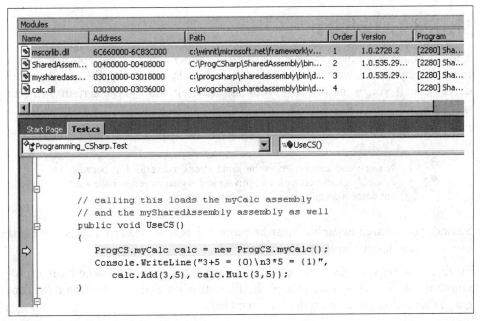

Figure 17-7. Modules loaded on demand

When you step into Fraction, the final DLL is loaded. The advantage of multi-module assemblies is that a module is loaded only when it is needed.

Private Assemblies

Assemblies come in two flavors: *private* and *shared*. Private assemblies are intended to be used by only one application; shared assemblies are intended to be shared among many applications.

All the assemblies you've built so far are private. By default, when you compile a C# application, a private assembly is created. The files for a private assembly are all kept in the same folder (or in a tree of subfolders). This tree of folders is isolated from the rest of the system, as nothing other than the one application depends on it, and you can redeploy this application to another machine just by copying the folder and its subfolders.

A private assembly can have any name you choose. It does not matter if that name clashes with assemblies in another application; the names are local only to a single application.

In the past, DLLs were installed on a machine and an entry was made in the Windows Registry. It was difficult to avoid corrupting the Registry, and reinstalling the program on another machine was nontrivial. With assemblies, all of that goes away. With private assemblies, installing is as simple as copying the files to the appropriate directory. Period.

Shared Assemblies

You can create assemblies that can be shared by other applications. You might want to do this if you have written a generic control or a class that might be used by other developers. If you want to share your assembly, it must meet certain stringent requirements.

First, your assembly must have a *strong name*. Strong names are globally unique.

 No one else can generate the same strong name as you because an assembly generated with one private key is guaranteed to have a different name than any assembly generated with another private key.

Second, your shared assembly must be protected against newer versions trampling over it, and so it must have version control.

Finally, to share your assembly, place it in the *Global Assembly Cache (GAC)* (pronounced GACK). This is an area of the filesystem set aside by the Common Language Runtime (CLR) to hold shared assemblies.

The End of DLL Hell

Assemblies mark the end of DLL Hell. Remember this scenario: you install Application A on your machine, and it loads a number of DLLs into your Windows directory. It works great for months. You then install Application B on your machine, and suddenly, unexpectedly, Application A breaks. Application B is in no way related to Application A. So what happened? It turns out, you later learn, that Application B replaced a DLL that Application A needed, and suddenly Application A begins to stagger about, blind and senseless.

When DLLs were invented, disk space was at a premium and reusing DLLs seemed like a good idea. The theory was that DLLs would be backward-compatible, so automatically upgrading to the new DLL would be painless and safe. As my old boss Pat Johnson used to say, "In theory, theory and practice are the same. But in practice, they never are."

When the new DLL was added to the computer, the old application, which was happily minding its own business in another corner of your machine, suddenly linked to a DLL that was incompatible with its expectations and hey! Presto! It went into the dance of death. This phenomenon led customers to be justifiably leery of installing new software, or even of upgrading existing programs, and it is one of the reasons Windows machines are perceived to be unstable. With assemblies, this entire nightmare goes away.

Versions

Shared assemblies in .NET are uniquely identified by their names and their versions. The GAC allows for "side-by-side" versions in which an older version of an assembly is available alongside a newer version. This allows particular applications to say "give me the newest" or "give me the latest build of Version 2," or even "give me only the version I was built with."

 Side-by-side versioning applies only to items in the GAC. Private assemblies do not need this feature and do not have it.

A version number for an assembly might look like this: 1:0:2204:21 (four numbers, separated by colons). The first two numbers (1:0) are the major and minor version. The third number (2204) is the build, and the fourth (21) is the revision.

When two assemblies have different major or minor numbers, they are considered to be incompatible. When they have different build numbers, they might or might not be compatible, and when they have different revision numbers, they are considered *definitely* compatible with each other.

Revision numbers are intended for bug fixes. If you fix a bug and are prepared to certify that your DLL is fully backward-compatible with the existing version, you should increment the revision. When an application loads an assembly, it specifies the major and minor version that it wants, and the AssemblyResolver finds the highest build and revision numbers.

Strong Names

In order to use a shared assembly, you must meet three requirements:

- You need to be able to specify the exact assembly you want to load. Therefore, you need a globally unique name for the shared assembly.
- You need to ensure that the assembly has not been tampered with. That is, you need a digital signature for the assembly when it is built.
- You need to ensure that the assembly you are loading is the one authored by the actual creator of the assembly. You therefore need to record the identity of the originator.

All these requirements are met by *strong names*. Strong names must be globally unique and use public key encryption to ensure that the assembly hasn't been tampered with and was written by the creator. A strong name is a string of hexadecimal digits and is not meant to be human-readable.

To create a strong name, a public-private key pair is generated for the assembly. A hash is taken of the names and contents of the files in the assembly. The hash is then encrypted with the private key for the assembly and placed in the manifest. This is known as *signing the assembly*. The public key is incorporated into the strong name of the assembly.

Public Key Encryption

Strong names are based on public key encryption technology. The essence of public key encryption is that your data is encoded with a complex mathematical formula that returns two keys. Data encrypted with the first key can only be decrypted with the second. Data encrypted with the second key can only be decrypted with the first.

Distribute your first key as a *public key* that anyone can have. Keep your second key as a *private key* that no one but you can have access to.

The reciprocal relationship between the keys allows anyone to encrypt data with your public key, and then you can decrypt it with your private key. No one else has access to the data once it is encrypted, including the person who encrypted it.

Similarly, you can encrypt data with your private key, and then anyone can decrypt that data with your public key. Although this makes the data freely available, it ensures that only you could have created it. This is called a *digital signature*.

When an application loads the assembly, the CLR uses the public key to decode the hash of the files in the assembly to ensure that they have not been tampered with. This also protects against name clashes.

You can create a strong name with the sn utility:

```
sn -k c:\myStrongName.snk
```

The –k flag indicates that you want a new key pair written to the specified file. You can call the file anything you like. Remember, a strong name is a string of hexadecimal digits and is not meant to be human-readable.

You can associate this strong name with your assembly by using an attribute:

```
using System.Runtime.CompilerServices;
[assembly: AssemblyKeyFile("c:\myStrongName.key")]
```

Attributes are covered in detail in Chapter 18. For now, you can just put this code at the top of your file to associate the strong name you generated with your assembly.

The Global Assembly Cache

Once you've created your strong name and associated it with your assembly, all that remains is to place the assembly in the GAC, which is a reserved system directory. You can do that with the gacutil utility:

```
gacutil /i MySharedAssembly.dll
```

Or you can open your File Explorer and drag your assembly into the GAC. To see the GAC, open the File Explorer and navigate to *%SystemRoot%\assembly*; Explorer turns into a GAC utility.

Building a Shared Assembly

The best way to understand shared assemblies is to build one. Let's return to the earlier multi-module project (see Examples 17-1 through 17-4) and navigate to the directory that contains the files *calc.cs* and *fraction.cs*.

Try this experiment: locate the bin directory for the driver program and make sure that you do not have a local copy of the MySharedAssembly DLL files.

> The referenced assembly (MySharedAssembly) should have its CopyLocal property set to false.

Run the program. It should fail with an exception saying it cannot load the assembly:

```
Unhandled Exception: System.IO.FileNotFoundException: File or assembly name
MySharedAssembly, or one of its dependencies, was not found.
File name: "MySharedAssembly"
    at Programming_CSharp.Test.UseCS( )
    at Programming_CSharp.Test.Main( )
```

Now copy the DLLs into the driver program's directory tree, run it again, and this time you should find that it works fine.

Let's make the MySharedAssembly into a shared assembly. This is done in two steps. First, create a strong name for the assembly, and then you put the assembly into the GAC.

Step 1: Create a strong name

Create a key pair by opening a command window and entering:

```
sn -k keyFile.snk
```

Now open the *AssemblyInfo.cs* file in the project for the *MySharedAssembly.dll* and modify this line:

```
[assembly: AssemblyKeyFile("")]
```

as follows:

```
[assembly: AssemblyKeyFile(".\\keyFile.snk")]
```

This sets the key file for the assembly. Rebuild with the same make file as earlier, and then open the resulting DLL in ILDasm and open the manifest. You should see a public key, as shown in Figure 17-8.

```
.publickey = (00 24 00 00 04 80 00 00 94 00 00 00 06 02 00 00   // .$..............
              00 24 00 00 52 53 41 31 00 04 00 00 01 00 01 00   // .$..RSA1........
              11 13 95 3C 41 19 2B 41 28 29 E8 AF DE 8C A2 04   // ...<A.+A().....
              88 22 BD 4F A9 E1 F5 57 2C 2D E2 43 CF C3 68 4E   // .".O...W,-.C..hN
              F7 C7 72 E8 55 94 85 11 EA 66 30 F6 D4 22 DB 0D   // ..r.U....f0..".
              6E D6 A6 0D 6D 58 28 10 E9 75 D8 BF CC 82 2A EB   // n...mX(..u....*.
              04 19 D5 C1 86 B0 CF D5 CB E6 5C 58 43 08 0D E9   // ..........\XC..
              20 8F 9B DC 29 AC 46 A3 CD 7A 87 3C F8 92 7A 84   //  ...).F..z.<..z.
              E3 47 84 AD 56 73 3E 0D AD 1D C0 A2 FA 15 14 A3   // .G..Vs>.........
              88 17 01 AC F3 A3 7A F8 59 BC 3A 16 CB AB 34 C5 ) // ......z.Y.:..4.
```

Figure 17-8. The originator in the manifest of MySharedAssembly.dll

By adding the strong name, you have signed this assembly (your exact values will be different). You now need to get the strong name from the DLL. To do this, navigate to the directory with the DLL and enter the following at a command prompt:

```
sn -T MySharedAssembly.dll
```

 Note that sn is case-sensitive. Do not write sn -t.

The response should be something like this:

```
Public key token is 01fad8e0f0941a4d
```

This value is an abbreviated version of the assembly's public key, called the *public key token.*

Remove the DLLs from the test program's directory structure and run it again. It should fail again. Although you've given this assembly a strong name, you've not yet registered it in the GAC.

Step 2: Put the shared assembly in the GAC

The next step is to drag the library into the GAC. To do so, open an Explorer window and navigate to the *%SystemRoot%* directory. When you double-click the Assembly subdirectory, Explorer will turn into a GAC viewer.

You can drag and drop into the GAC viewer, or you can invoke this command-line utility:

```
Gacutil /i mySharedAssembly.dll
```

In either case, be sure to check that your assembly was loaded into the GAC, and that the originator value shown in the GAC viewer matches the value you got back from sn:

```
Public key token is 01fad8e0f0941a4d
```

This is illustrated in Figure 17-9.

Global Assembly Name	Type	Version	Culture	Public Key Token
Microsoft.Vsa		7.0.9188.0		b03f5f7f11d50a3a
Microsoft.Vsa		7.0.9174.0		b03f5f7f11d50a3a
Microsoft.Vsa.Vb.CodeDOMProcessor		7.0.0.0		b03f5f7f11d50a3a
msatinterop		1.0.0.0		826aaeb3f85826a0
mscorcfg		1.0.2411.0		b03f5f7f11d50a3a
mscorlib	PreJit	1.0.2411.0		b77a5c561934e089
MySharedAssembly		1.0.535.29377		a5929f0102e0c473

Figure 17-9. The GAC

Once this is done, you have a shared assembly that can be accessed by any client. Refresh the client by building it again and look at its manifest, as shown in Figure 17-10.

```
.assembly extern MySharedAssembly
{
  .publickeytoken = (A5 92 9F 01 02 E0 C4 73 )
  .ver 1:0:535:29377
}
```

Figure 17-10. The manifest

There's MySharedAssembly, listed as an external assembly, and the public key now matches the value shown in the GAC. Very nice, time to try it.

Close ILDasm and compile and run your code. It should work fine, even though there are no DLLs for this library in its immediate path. You have just created and used a shared assembly.

CHAPTER 18

Attributes and Reflection

Throughout this book, I have emphasized that a .NET application contains code, data, and metadata. *Metadata* is information about the data—that is, information about the types, code, assembly, and so forth—stored along with your program. This chapter explores how some of that metadata is created and used.

Attributes are a mechanism for adding metadata, such as compiler instructions and other data about your data, methods, and classes, to the program itself. Attributes are inserted into the metadata and are visible through *ILDasm* and other metadata-reading tools.

Reflection is the process by which a program can read its own metadata. A program is said to reflect on itself, extracting metadata from its assembly and using that metadata either to inform the user or to modify its own behavior.

Attributes

An *attribute* is an object that represents data you want to associate with an element in your program. The element to which you attach an attribute is referred to as the *target* of that attribute. For example, the attribute:

```
[NoIDispatch]
```

is associated with a class or an interface to indicate that the target class should derive from IUnknown rather than IDispatch when exporting to COM. COM interface programming is discussed in detail in Chapter 22.

In Chapter 17, you saw this attribute:

```
[assembly: AssemblyKeyFile("c:\\myStrongName.key")]
```

This inserts metadata into the assembly to designate the program's StrongName.

Intrinsic Attributes

Attributes come in two flavors: *intrinsic* and *custom*. *Intrinsic* attributes are supplied as part of the Common Language Runtime (CLR), and they are integrated into .NET. *Custom* attributes are attributes you create for your own purposes.

Most programmers will use only intrinsic attributes, though custom attributes can be a powerful tool when combined with reflection, described later in this chapter.

Attribute Targets

If you search through the CLR, you'll find a great many attributes. Some attributes are applied to an assembly, others to a class or interface, and some, such as [WebMethod], are applied to class members. These are called the *attribute targets*. Possible attribute targets are detailed in Table 18-1.

Table 18-1. Possible attribute targets

Member name	Usage
All	Applied to any of the following elements: assembly, class, constructor, delegate, enum, event, field, interface, method, module, parameter, property, return value, or struct
Assembly	Applied to the assembly itself
Class	Applied to instances of the class
Constructor	Applied to a given constructor
Delegate	Applied to the delegated method
Enum	Applied to an enumeration
Event	Applied to an event
Field	Applied to a field
Interface	Applied to an interface
Method	Applied to a method
Module	Applied to a single module
Parameter	Applied to a parameter of a method
Property	Applied to a property (both get and set, if implemented)
ReturnValue	Applied to a return value
Struct	Applied to a struct

Applying Attributes

Apply attributes to their targets by placing them in square brackets immediately before the target item. You can combine attributes by stacking one on top of another:

```
[assembly: AssemblyDelaySign(false)]-
[assembly: AssemblyKeyFile(".\\keyFile.snk")]
```

This can also be done by separating the attributes with commas:

```
[assembly: AssemblyDelaySign(false),
   assembly: AssemblyKeyFile(".\\keyFile.snk")]
```

 You must place assembly attributes after all using statements and before any code.

Many intrinsic attributes are used for interoperating with COM, as discussed in detail in Chapter 22. You've already seen use of one attribute ([WebMethod]) in Chapter 16. You'll see other attributes, such as the [Serializable] attribute, used in the discussion of serialization in Chapter 19.

The System.Runtime namespace offers a number of intrinsic attributes, including attributes for assemblies (such as the keyname attribute), for configuration (such as debug to indicate the debug build), and for version attributes.

You can organize the intrinsic attributes by how they are used. The principal intrinsic attributes are those used for COM, those used to modify the Interface Definition Language (IDL) file from within a source-code file, those used by the ATL Server classes, and those used by the Visual C++ compiler.

Perhaps the attribute you are most likely to use in your everyday C# programming (if you are not interacting with COM) is [Serializable]. As you'll see in Chapter 19, all you need to do to ensure that your class can be serialized to disk or to the Internet is add the [Serializable] attribute to the class:

```
[Serializable]
class MySerializableClass
```

The attribute tag is put in square brackets immediately before its target—in this case, the class declaration.

The key fact about intrinsic attributes is that you know when you need them; the task will dictate their use.

Custom Attributes

You are free to create your own custom attributes and use them at runtime as you see fit. Suppose, for example, that your development organization wants to keep track of bug fixes. You already keep a database of all your bugs, but you'd like to tie your bug reports to specific fixes in the code.

You might add comments to your code along the lines of:

```
// Bug 323 fixed by Jesse Liberty 1/1/2005.
```

This would make it easy to see in your source code, but there is no enforced connection to Bug 323 in the database. A custom attribute might be just what you need. You would replace your comment with something like this:

```
[BugFixAttribute(323,"Jesse Liberty","1/1/2005",
Comment="Off by one error")]
```

You could then write a program to read through the metadata to find these bug-fix notations and update the database. The attribute would serve the purposes of a comment, but would also allow you to retrieve the information programmatically through tools you'd create.

Declaring an Attribute

Attributes, like most things in C#, are embodied in classes. To create a custom attribute, derive your new custom attribute class from System.Attribute:

```
public class BugFixAttribute : System.Attribute
```

You need to tell the compiler which kinds of elements this attribute can be used with (the attribute target). Specify this with (what else?) an attribute:

```
[AttributeUsage(AttributeTargets.Class |
    AttributeTargets.Constructor |
    AttributeTargets.Field |
    AttributeTargets.Method |
    AttributeTargets.Property,
    AllowMultiple = true)]
```

AttributeUsage is an attribute applied to attributes: a *meta-attribute*. It provides, if you will, meta-metadata—that is, data about the metadata. For the AttributeUsage attribute constructor, you pass two arguments. The first argument is a set of flags that indicate the target—in this case, the class and its constructor, fields, methods, and properties. The second argument is a flag that indicates whether a given element might receive more than one such attribute. In this example, AllowMultiple is set to true, indicating that class members can have more than one BugFixAttribute assigned.

Naming an Attribute

The new custom attribute in this example is named BugFixAttribute. The convention is to append the word Attribute to your attribute name. The compiler supports this by allowing you to call the attribute with the shorter version of the name. Thus, you can write:

```
[BugFix(123, "Jesse Liberty", "01/01/05", Comment="Off by one")]
```

The compiler will first look for an attribute named BugFix and, if it does not find that, will then look for BugFixAttribute.

Constructing an Attribute

Every attribute must have at least one constructor. Attributes take two types of parameters: *positional* and *named*. In the BugFix example, the programmer's name and the date are positional parameters, and comment is a named parameter. Positional parameters are passed in through the constructor and must be passed in the order declared in the constructor:

```
public BugFixAttribute(int bugID, string programmer,
string date)
{
    this.bugID = bugID;
    this.programmer = programmer;
    this.date = date;
}
```

Named parameters are implemented as properties:

```
public string Comment
{
    get
    {
        return comment;
    }
    set
    {
        comment = value;
    }
}
```

It is common to create read-only properties for the positional parameters:

```
public int BugID
{
    get
    {
        return bugID;
    }
}
```

Using an Attribute

Once you have defined an attribute, you can put it to work by placing it immediately before its target. To test the BugFixAttribute of the preceding example, the following program creates a simple class named MyMath and gives it two functions. Assign BugFixAttributes to the class to record its code-maintenance history:

```
[BugFixAttribute(121,"Jesse Liberty","01/03/05")]
[BugFixAttribute(107,"Jesse Liberty","01/04/05",
    Comment="Fixed off by one errors")]
public class MyMath
```

These attributes will be stored with the metadata. Example 18-1 shows the complete program.

Example 18-1. Working with custom attributes

```
namespace Programming_CSharp
{
   using System;
   using System.Reflection;

   // create custom attribute to be assigned to class members
   [AttributeUsage(AttributeTargets.Class |
      AttributeTargets.Constructor |
      AttributeTargets.Field |
      AttributeTargets.Method |
      AttributeTargets.Property,
      AllowMultiple = true)]
   public class BugFixAttribute : System.Attribute
   {
      // attribute constructor for
      // positional parameters
      public BugFixAttribute
         (int bugID,
         string programmer,
         string date)
      {
         this.bugID = bugID;
         this.programmer = programmer;
         this.date = date;
      }

      // accessor
      public int BugID
      {
         get
         {
            return bugID;
         }
      }

      // property for named parameter
      public string Comment
      {
         get
         {
            return comment;
         }
         set
         {
            comment = value;
```

Example 18-1. Working with custom attributes (continued)

```
        }
    }

    // accessor
    public string Date
    {
        get
        {
            return date;
        }
    }

    // accessor
    public string Programmer
    {
        get
        {
            return programmer;
        }
    }

    // private member data
    private int      bugID;
    private string   comment;
    private string   date;
    private string   programmer;
}


// ********* assign the attributes to the class ********

[BugFixAttribute(121,"Jesse Liberty","01/03/05")]
[BugFixAttribute(107,"Jesse Liberty","01/04/05",
    Comment="Fixed off by one errors")]
public class MyMath
{

    public double DoFunc1(double param1)
    {
        return param1 + DoFunc2(param1);
    }

    public double DoFunc2(double param1)
    {
        return param1 / 3;
    }

}

public class Tester
{
```

Example 18-1. Working with custom attributes (continued)

```
   public static void Main( )
   {
      MyMath mm = new MyMath( );
      Console.WriteLine("Calling DoFunc(7). Result: {0}",
         mm.DoFunc1(7));
   }
  }
}
```

Output:
```
Calling DoFunc(7). Result: 9.3333333333333333
```

As you can see, the attributes had absolutely no impact on the output. In fact, for the moment, you have only my word that the attributes exist at all. A quick look at the metadata using ILDasm does reveal that the attributes are in place, however, as shown in Figure 18-1. You'll see how to get at this metadata and use it in your program in the next section.

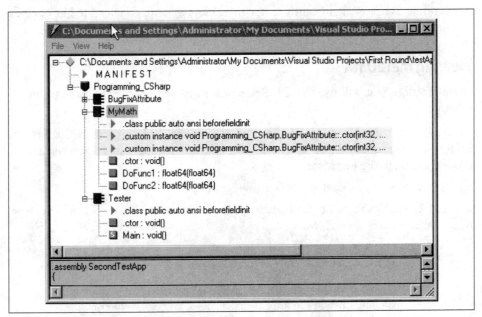

Figure 18-1. The metadata in the assembly

Reflection

For the attributes in the metadata to be useful, you need a way to access them—ideally during runtime. The classes in the Reflection namespace, along with the System.Type and System.TypedReference classes, provide support for examining and interacting with the metadata.

Reflection is generally used for any of four tasks:

Viewing metadata

This might be used by tools and utilities that wish to display metadata.

Performing type discovery

This allows you to examine the types in an assembly and interact with or instantiate those types. This can be useful in creating custom scripts. For example, you might want to allow your users to interact with your program using a script language, such as JavaScript, or a scripting language you create yourself.

Late binding to methods and properties

This allows the programmer to invoke properties and methods on objects dynamically instantiated based on type discovery. This is also known as *dynamic invocation*.

Creating types at runtime (Reflection Emit)

The ultimate use of reflection is to create new types at runtime and then to use those types to perform tasks. You might do this when a custom class, created at runtime, will run significantly faster than more generic code created at compile time. An example is offered later in this chapter.

Viewing MetaData

In this section, you will use the C# Reflection support to read the metadata in the MyMath class.

Start by initializing an object of the type MemberInfo. This object, in the System. Reflection namespace, is provided to discover the attributes of a member and to provide access to the metadata:

```
System.Reflection.MemberInfo inf = typeof(MyMath);
```

Call the typeof operator on the MyMath type, which returns an object of type Type, which derives from MemberInfo.

> The Type class is the root of the reflection classes. Type encapsulates a representation of the type of an object. The Type class is the primary way to access metadata. Type derives from MemberInfo and encapsulates information about the members of a class (e.g., methods, properties, fields, events, etc.).

The next step is to call GetCustomAttributes on this MemberInfo object, passing in the type of the attribute you want to find. You get back an array of objects, each of type BugFixAttribute:

```
object[] attributes;
attributes =
    inf.GetCustomAttributes(typeof(BugFixAttribute),false);
```

You can now iterate through this array, printing out the properties of the BugFixAttribute object. Example 18-2 replaces the Tester class from Example 18-1.

Example 18-2. Using reflection

```
public static void Main( )
{
    MyMath mm = new MyMath( );
    Console.WriteLine("Calling DoFunc(7). Result: {0}",
        mm.DoFunc1(7));

    // get the member information and use it to
    // retrieve the custom attributes
    System.Reflection.MemberInfo inf = typeof(MyMath);
    object[] attributes;
    attributes =
        inf.GetCustomAttributes(
            typeof(BugFixAttribute), false);

    // iterate through the attributes, retrieving the
    // properties
    foreach(Object attribute in attributes)
    {
        BugFixAttribute bfa = (BugFixAttribute) attribute;
        Console.WriteLine("\nBugID: {0}", bfa.BugID);
        Console.WriteLine("Programmer: {0}", bfa.Programmer);
        Console.WriteLine("Date: {0}", bfa.Date);
        Console.WriteLine("Comment: {0}", bfa.Comment);
    }
}
```

Output:
```
Calling DoFunc(7). Result: 9.3333333333333333

BugID: 121
Programmer: Jesse Liberty
Date: 01/03/05
Comment:

BugID: 107
Programmer: Jesse Liberty
Date: 01/04/05
Comment: Fixed off by one errors
```

When you put this replacement code into Example 18-1 and run it, you can see the metadata printed as you'd expect.

Type Discovery

You can use reflection to explore and examine the contents of an assembly. You can find the types associated with a module; the methods, fields, properties, and events associated with a type, as well as the signatures of each of the type's methods; the interfaces supported by the type; and the type's base class.

To start, load an assembly dynamically with the Assembly.Load static method. The Assembly class encapsulates the actual assembly itself, for purposes of reflection. The signature for the Load method is:

```
public static Assembly.Load(AssemblyName)
```

For the next example, pass in the Core Library to the Load method. MsCorLib.dll has the core classes of the .NET Framework:

```
Assembly a = Assembly.Load("Mscorlib.dll");
```

Once the assembly is loaded, you can call GetTypes() to return an array of Type objects. The Type object is the heart of reflection. Type represents type declarations (classes, interfaces, arrays, values, and enumerations):

```
Type[] types = a.GetTypes();
```

The assembly returns an array of types that you can display in a foreach loop, as shown in Example 18-3. Because this listing uses the Type class, you will want to add a using statement for the System.Reflection namespace.

Example 18-3. Reflecting on an assembly

```
namespace Programming_CSharp
{
    using System;
    using System.Reflection;

    public class Tester
    {
        public static void Main( )
        {
            // what is in the assembly
            Assembly a = Assembly.Load("Mscorlib.dll");
            Type[] types = a.GetTypes( );
            foreach(Type t in types)
            {
                    Console.WriteLine("Type is {0}", t);
            }
            Console.WriteLine(
                "{0} types found", types.Length);
        }
    }
}
```

The output from this would fill many pages. Here is a short excerpt:

```
Type is System.TypeCode
Type is System.Security.Util.StringExpressionSet
Type is System.Runtime.InteropServices.COMException
Type is System.Runtime.InteropServices.SEHException
Type is System.Reflection.TargetParameterCountException
```

```
Type is System.Text.UTF7Encoding
Type is System.Text.UTF7Encoding+Decoder
Type is System.Text.UTF7Encoding+Encoder
Type is System.ArgIterator
1426 types found
```

This example obtained an array filled with the types from the Core Library and printed them one by one. The array contained 1,426 entries on my machine.

Reflecting on a Type

You can reflect on a single type in the mscorlib assembly as well. To do so, extract a type from the assembly with the GetType( ) method, as shown in Example 18-4.

Example 18-4. Reflecting on a type

```
namespace Programming_CSharp
{
    using System;
    using System.Reflection;

    public class Tester
    {
        public static void Main( )
        {
            // examine a single object
            Type theType =
                Type.GetType(
                    "System.Reflection.Assembly");
            Console.WriteLine(
                "\nSingle Type is {0}\n", theType);
        }
    }
}
```

Output:
```
Single Type is System.Reflection.Assembly
```

Finding all type members

You can ask the Assembly type for all its members using the GetMembers( ) method of the Type class, which lists all the methods, properties, and fields, as shown in Example 18-5.

Example 18-5. Reflecting on the members of a type

```
namespace Programming_CSharp
{
    using System;
    using System.Reflection;

    public class Tester
```

Example 18-5. Reflecting on the members of a type (continued)

```
{
    public static void Main( )
    {
        // examine a single object
        Type theType =
            Type.GetType(
                "System.Reflection.Assembly");
        Console.WriteLine(
            "\nSingle Type is {0}\n", theType);

        // get all the members
        MemberInfo[] mbrInfoArray =
            theType.GetMembers( );
        foreach (MemberInfo mbrInfo in mbrInfoArray )
        {
            Console.WriteLine("{0} is a {1}",
                mbrInfo, mbrInfo.MemberType);
        }
    }
}
}
```

Once again the output is quite lengthy, but within the output you see fields, methods, constructors, and properties, as shown in this excerpt:

```
Boolean IsDefined(System.Type, Boolean) is a Method
System.Object[] GetCustomAttributes(Boolean) is a Method
System.Object[] GetCustomAttributes(System.Type, Boolean) is a Method
System.Security.Policy.Evidence get_Evidence( ) is a Method
System.String get_Location( ) is a Method
```

Finding type methods

You might want to focus on methods only, excluding the fields, properties, and so forth. To do so, remove the call to GetMembers( ):

```
MemberInfo[] mbrInfoArray =
    theType.GetMembers(BindingFlags.LookupAll);
```

and add a call to GetMethods( ):

```
mbrInfoArray = theType.GetMethods( );
```

The output now is nothing but the methods:

```
Output (excerpt):
Boolean Equals(System.Object) is a Method
System.String ToString( ) is a Method
System.String CreateQualifiedName(
        System.String, System.String) is a Method
Boolean get_GlobalAssemblyCache( ) is a Method
```

Finding particular type members

Finally, to narrow it down even further, you can use the FindMembers method to find particular members of the type. For example, you can narrow your search to methods whose names begin with the letters Get.

To narrow the search, use the FindMembers method, which takes four parameters: MemberTypes, BindingFlags, MemberFilter, and object.

MemberTypes

> A MemberTypes object that indicates the type of the member to search for. These include All, Constructor, Custom, Event, Field, Method, Nestedtype, Property, and TypeInfo. You will also use the MemberTypes.Method to find a method.

BindingFlags

> An enumeration that controls the way searches are conducted by reflection. There are a great many BindingFlag values, including IgnoreCase, Instance, Public, Static, and so forth.

MemberFilter

> A delegate (see Chapter 12) that is used to filter the list of members in the MemberInfo array of objects. The filter you'll use is Type.FilterName, a field of the Type class used for filtering on a name.

Object

> A string value that will be used by the filter. In this case you'll pass in "Get*" to match only those methods that begin with the letters Get.

The complete listing for filtering on these methods is shown in Example 18-6.

Example 18-6. Finding particular members

```
namespace Programming_CSharp
{
    using System;
    using System.Reflection;

    public class Tester
    {
        public static void Main( )
        {
            // examine a single object
            Type theType = Type.GetType(
                "System.Reflection.Assembly");

            // just members which are methods beginning with Get
            MemberInfo[] mbrInfoArray =
                theType.FindMembers(MemberTypes.Method,
                    BindingFlags.Public |
                    BindingFlags.Static |
                    BindingFlags.NonPublic |
```

Example 18-6. Finding particular members (continued)

```
                BindingFlags.Instance |
                BindingFlags.DeclaredOnly,
                Type.FilterName, "Get*");
        foreach (MemberInfo mbrInfo in mbrInfoArray )
        {
            Console.WriteLine("{0} is a {1}",
                mbrInfo, mbrInfo.MemberType);
        }
    }
}
```

Output (excerpt):
```
System.Type[] GetTypes( ) is a Method
System.Type[] GetExportedTypes( ) is a Method
System.Type GetType(System.String, Boolean) is a Method
System.Type GetType(System.String) is a Method
System.Reflection.AssemblyName GetName(Boolean) is a Method
System.Reflection.AssemblyName GetName( ) is a Method
```

Late Binding

Once you have discovered a method, it's possible to invoke it using reflection. For example, you might like to invoke the Cos( ) method of System.Math, which returns the cosine of an angle.

> You could, of course, call Cos( ) in the normal course of your code, but reflection allows you to bind to that method at runtime. This is called *late-binding* and offers the flexibility of choosing at runtime which object you will bind to and invoking it programmatically. This can be useful when creating a custom script to be run by the user or when working with objects that might not be available at compile time. For example, by using late-binding, your program can interact with the spellchecker or other components of a running commercial word processing program such as Microsoft Word.

To invoke Cos( ), you will first get the Type information for the System.Math class:

```
Type theMathType = Type.GetType("System.Math");
```

With that type information, you could dynamically load an instance of a class by using a static method of the Activator class. Since Cos( ) is static, you don't need to construct an instance of System.Math (and you can't, since System.Math has no public constructor).

The Activator class contains four methods, all static, which you can use to create objects locally or remotely, or to obtain references to existing objects. The four methods are CreateComInstanceFrom, CreateInstanceFrom, GetObject, and CreateInstance:

CreateComInstanceFrom
   Used to create instances of COM objects.

CreateInstanceFrom
   Used to create a reference to an object from a particular assembly and type name.

GetObject
   Used when marshaling objects. Marshaling is discussed in detail in Chapter 19.

CreateInstance
   Used to create local or remote instances of an object.

For example:

```
Object theObj = Activator.CreateInstance(someType);
```

Back to the Cos( ) example, you now have one object in hand: a Type object named theMathType, which you created by calling GetType.

Before you can invoke a method on the object, you must get the method you need from the Type object, theMathType. To do so, you'll call GetMethod( ), and you'll pass in the signature of the Cos method.

The signature, you will remember, is the name of the method (Cos) and its parameter types. In the case of Cos( ), there is only one parameter: a double. However, Type.GetMethod takes two parameters. The first represents the name of the method you want, and the second represents the parameters. The name is passed as a string; the parameters are passed as an array of types:

```
MethodInfo CosineInfo =
    theMathType.GetMethod("Cos",paramTypes);
```

Before calling GetMethod, you must prepare the array of types:

```
Type[] paramTypes = new Type[1];
paramTypes[0]= Type.GetType("System.Double");
```

This code declares the array of Type objects and then fills the first element (paramTypes[0]) with a Type representing a double. Obtain the type representing a double by calling the static method Type.GetType( ), and passing in the string "System.Double".

You now have an object of type MethodInfo on which you can invoke the method. To do so, you must pass in the object to invoke the method on and the actual value of the parameters, again in an array. Since this is a static method, pass in theMathType. (If Cos( ) was an instance method, you could use theObj instead of theMathType.)

```
Object[] parameters = new Object[1];
parameters[0] = 45 * (Math.PI/180); // 45 degrees in radians
Object returnVal = CosineInfo.Invoke(theMathType,parameters);
```

Note that you've created two arrays. The first, paramTypes, holds the type of the parameters. The second, parameters, holds the actual value. If the method had taken two arguments, you'd have declared these arrays to hold two values. If the method did not take any values, you still would create the array, but you would give it a size of zero!

```
Type[] paramTypes = new Type[0];
```

Odd as this looks, it is correct.

Example 18-7 illustrates dynamically calling the Cos( ) method.

Example 18-7. Dynamically invoking a method

```
namespace Programming_CSharp
{
    using System;
    using System.Reflection;

    public class Tester
    {
        public static void Main( )
        {
            Type theMathType = Type.GetType("System.Math");
            // Since System.Math has no public constructor, this
            // would throw an exception.
            //Object theObj =
            //    Activator.CreateInstance(theMathType);

            // array with one member
            Type[] paramTypes = new Type[1];
            paramTypes[0]= Type.GetType("System.Double");

            // Get method info for Cos( )
            MethodInfo CosineInfo =
                theMathType.GetMethod("Cos",paramTypes);

            // fill an array with the actual parameters
            Object[] parameters = new Object[1];
            parameters[0] = 45 * (Math.PI/180); // 45 degrees in radians
            Object returnVal =
                CosineInfo.Invoke(theMathType,parameters);
            Console.WriteLine(
                "The cosine of a 45 degree angle {0}",
                returnVal);

        }
    }
}
```

That was a lot of work just to invoke a single method. The power, however, is that you can use reflection to discover an assembly on the user's machine, to query what methods are available, and to invoke one of those members dynamically!

Reflection Emit

So far we've seen reflection used for three purposes: viewing metadata, type discovery, and dynamic invocation. You might use these techniques when building tools (such as a development environment) or when processing scripts. The most powerful use of reflection, however, is with reflection emit.

Reflection emit supports the dynamic creation of new types at runtime. You can define an assembly to run dynamically or to save itself to disk, and you can define modules and new types with methods that you can then invoke.

 The use of dynamic invocation and reflection emit should be considered an advanced topic. Most developers will never have need to use reflection emit. This demonstration is based on an example provided at the Microsoft Author's Summit, Fall 2000.

To understand the power of reflection emit, you must first consider a slightly more complicated example of dynamic invocation.

Problems can have general solutions that are relatively slow and specific solutions that are fast. To keep things manageably simple, consider a DoSum( ) method, which provides the sum of a string of integers from 1...*n*, where *n* will be supplied by the user.

Thus, DoSum(3) is equal to 1+2+3, or 6. DoSum(10) is 55. Writing this in C# is very simple:

```csharp
public int DoSum1(int n)
{
    int result = 0;
    for(int i = 1;i <= n; i++)
    {
        result += i;
    }
    return result;
}
```

The method simply loops, adding the requisite number. If you pass in 3, the method adds 1 + 2 + 3 and returns an answer of 6.

With large numbers, and when run many times, this might be a bit slow. Given the value 20, this method would be considerably faster if you removed the loop:

```csharp
public int DoSum2( )
{
    return 1+2+3+4+5+6+7+8+9+10+11+12+13+14+15+16+17+18+19+20;
}
```

DoSum2 runs more quickly than DoSum1 does. How much more quickly? To find out, you'll need to put a timer on both methods. To do so, use a DateTime object to mark the start time and a TimeSpan object to compute the elapsed time.

For this experiment, you need to create two DoSum( ) methods; the first will use the loop and the second will not. Call each 1,000,000 times. (Computers are very fast, so to see a difference you have to work hard!) Then compare the times. Example 18-8 illustrates the entire test program.

Example 18-8. Comparing loop to brute force

```
namespace Programming_CSharp
{
    using System;
    using System.Diagnostics;
    using System.Threading;

    public class MyMath
    {
        // sum numbers with a loop
        public int DoSum(int n)
        {
            int result = 0;
            for(int i = 1; i <= n; i++)
            {
                result += i;
            }
            return result;
        }

        // brute force by hand
        public int DoSum2( )
        {
            return 1+2+3+4+5+6+7+8+9+10+11
                +12+13+14+15+16+17+18+19+20;
        }

    }

    public class TestDriver
    {
        public static void Main( )
        {

            const int val = 20;   // val to sum

            // 1,000,000 iterations
            const int iterations = 1000000;

            // hold the answer
            int result = 0;

            MyMath m = new MyMath( );
```

Example 18-8. Comparing loop to brute force (continued)

```
        // mark the start time
        DateTime startTime = DateTime.Now;

        // run the experiment
        for (int i = 0;i < iterations;i++)
        {
            result = m.DoSum(val);
        }
        // mark the elapsed time
        TimeSpan elapsed =
            DateTime.Now - startTime;

        // display the results
        Console.WriteLine(
            "Loop: Sum of ({0}) = {1}",
                val, result);
        Console.WriteLine(
            "The elapsed time in milliseconds is: " +
            elapsed.TotalMilliseconds.ToString( ));

        // mark a new start time
        startTime = DateTime.Now;

        // run the experiment
        for (int i = 0;i < iterations;i++)
        {
            result = m.DoSum2( );
        }

        // mark the new elapsed time
        elapsed = DateTime.Now - startTime;

        // display the results
        Console.WriteLine(
            "Brute Force: Sum of ({0}) = {1}",
                val, result);
        Console.WriteLine(
            "The elapsed time in milliseconds is: " +
            elapsed.TotalMilliseconds);
    }
  }
}
```

Output:
```
Loop: Sum of (20) = 210
The elapsed time in milliseconds is: 187.5
Brute Force: Sum of (20) = 210
The elapsed time in milliseconds is: 31.25
```

As you can see, both methods returned the same answer (one million times!), but the brute-force method was six times faster.

Is there a way to avoid the loop and still provide a general solution? In traditional programming, the answer would be no, but with reflection you do have one other option. You can, at runtime, take the value the user wants (20, in this case) and write out to disk a class that implements the brute-force solution. You can then use dynamic invocation to invoke that method.

There are at least three ways to achieve this result, each increasingly elegant. The third, reflection emit, is the best, but a close look at two other techniques is instructive. If you are pressed for time, you might wish to jump ahead to the section entitled "Dynamic Invocation with Reflection Emit," later in this chapter.

Dynamic Invocation with InvokeMember( )

The first approach will be to dynamically create a class named BruteForceSums at runtime. The BruteForceSums class will contain a method, ComputeSum( ), that implements the brute-force approach. You'll write that class to disk, compile it, and then use dynamic invocation to invoke its brute-force method by means of the InvokeMember( ) method of the Type class. The key point is that *BruteForceSums.cs* won't exist until you run the program. You'll create it when you need it and supply its arguments then.

To accomplish this, you'll create a new class named ReflectionTest. The job of the ReflectionTest class is to create the BruteForceSums class, write it to disk, and compile it. ReflectionTest has only two methods: DoSum and GenerateCode.

ReflectionTest.DoSum is a public method that returns the sum, given a value. That is, if you pass in 10, it returns the sum of 1+2+3+4+5+6+7+8+9+10. It does this by creating the BruteForceSums class and delegating the job to its ComputeSum method.

ReflectionTest has two private fields:

```
Type theType = null;
object theClass = null;
```

The first is an object of type Type, which you use to load your class from disk; the second is an object of type object, which you use to dynamically invoke the ComputeSums( ) method of the BruteForceSums class you'll create.

The driver program instantiates an instance of ReflectionTest and calls its DoSum method, passing in the value. For this version of the program, the value is increased to 200.

The DoSum method checks whether theType is null; if it is, the class has not been created yet. DoSum calls the helper method GenerateCode to generate the code for the BruteForceSums class and the class's ComputeSums method. GenerateCode then writes this newly created code to a *.cs* file on disk and runs the compiler to turn it into an assembly on disk. Once this is completed, DoSum can call the method using reflection.

Once the class and method are created, load the assembly from disk and assign the class type information to theType—DoSum can use that to invoke the method dynamically to get the correct answer.

You begin by creating a constant for the value to which you'll sum:

```
const int val = 200;
```

Each time you compute a sum, it will be the sum of the values 1 to 200.

Before you create the dynamic class, you need to go back and re-create MyMath:

```
MyMath m = new MyMath( );
```

Give MyMath a method DoSumLooping, much as you did in the previous example:

```
public int DoSumLooping (int initialVal)
{
    int result = 0;
    for(int i = 1;i <=initialVal;i++)
    {
        result += i;
    }
    return result;
}
```

This serves as a benchmark against which you can compare the performance of the brute-force method.

Now you're ready to create the dynamic class and compare its performance with the looping version. First, instantiate an object of type ReflectionTest and invoke the DoSum( ) method on that object:

```
ReflectionTest t = new ReflectionTest( );
result = t.DoSum(val);
```

ReflectionTest.DoSum checks to see if its Type field, theType, is null. If it is, you haven't yet created and compiled the BruteForceSums class and must do so now:

```
if (theType == null)
{
    GenerateCode(theValue);
}
```

The GenerateCode method takes the value (in this case, 200) as a parameter to know how many values to add.

GenerateCode begins by creating a file on disk. The details of file I/O will be covered in Chapter 21. For now, I'll walk you through this quickly. First, call the static method File.Open, and pass in the filename and a flag indicating that you want to create the file. File.Open returns a Stream object:

```
string fileName = "BruteForceSums";
Stream s = File.Open(fileName + ".cs", FileMode.Create);
```

Once you have the Stream, you can create a StreamWriter so that you can write into that file:

```
StreamWriter wrtr = new StreamWriter(s);
```

You can now use the WriteLine methods of StreamWriter to write lines of text into the file. Begin the new file with a comment:

```
wrtr.WriteLine("// Dynamically created BruteForceSums class");
```

This writes the text:

```
// Dynamically created BruteForceSums class
```

to the file you've just created (*BruteForceSums.cs*). Next, write out the class declaration:

```
string className = "BruteForceSums";
wrtr.WriteLine("class {0}", className);
wrtr.WriteLine("{");
```

Within the braces of the class, create the ComputeSum method:

```
wrtr.WriteLine("\tpublic double ComputeSum( )");
wrtr.WriteLine("\t{");
wrtr.WriteLine("\t// Brute force sum method");
wrtr.WriteLine("\t// For value = {0}", theVal);
```

Now it is time to write out the addition statements. When you are done, you want the file to have this line:

```
return 0+1+2+3+4+5+6+7+8+9...
```

continuing up to value (in this case, 200):

```
wrtr.Write("\treturn 0");
for (int i = 1;i<=theVal;i++)
{
    wrtr.Write("+ {0}",i);
}
```

Notice how this works. What will be written to the file is:

```
\treturn 0+ 1+ 2+ 3+...
```

The initial \t causes the code to be indented in the source file.

When the loop completes, end the return statement with a semicolon and then close the method and the class:

```
wrtr.WriteLine(";");
wrtr.WriteLine("\t}");
wrtr.WriteLine("}");
```

Close the streamWriter and the stream, thus closing the file:

```
wrtr.Close( );
s.Close( );
```

When this runs, the *BruteForceSums.cs* file will be written to disk. It will look like this:

```
// Dynamically created BruteForceSums class
class BruteForceSums
{
    public double ComputeSum( )
    {
    // Brute force sum method
    // For value = 200
    return 0+ 1+ 2+ 3+ 4+ 5+ 6+ 7+ 8+ 9+ 10+
11+ 12+ 13+ 14+ 15+ 16+ 17+ 18+ 19+ 20+ 21+
22+ 23+ 24+ 25+ 26+ 27+ 28+ 29+ 30+ 31+ 32+
33+ 34+ 35+ 36+ 37+ 38+ 39+ 40+ 41+ 42+ 43+
44+ 45+ 46+ 47+ 48+ 49+ 50+ 51+ 52+ 53+ 54+
55+ 56+ 57+ 58+ 59+ 60+ 61+ 62+ 63+ 64+ 65+
66+ 67+ 68+ 69+ 70+ 71+ 72+ 73+ 74+ 75+ 76+
77+ 78+ 79+ 80+ 81+ 82+ 83+ 84+ 85+ 86+ 87+
88+ 89+ 90+ 91+ 92+ 93+ 94+ 95+ 96+ 97+ 98+
99+ 100+ 101+ 102+ 103+ 104+ 105+ 106+ 107+
108+ 109+ 110+ 111+ 112+ 113+ 114+ 115+ 116+
117+ 118+ 119+ 120+ 121+ 122+ 123+ 124+ 125+
126+ 127+ 128+ 129+ 130+ 131+ 132+ 133+ 134+
135+ 136+ 137+ 138+ 139+ 140+ 141+ 142+ 143+
144+ 145+ 146+ 147+ 148+ 149+ 150+ 151+ 152+
153+ 154+ 155+ 156+ 157+ 158+ 159+ 160+ 161+
162+ 163+ 164+ 165+ 166+ 167+ 168+ 169+ 170+
171+ 172+ 173+ 174+ 175+ 176+ 177+ 178+ 179+
180+ 181+ 182+ 183+ 184+ 185+ 186+ 187+ 188+
189+ 190+ 191+ 192+ 193+ 194+ 195+ 196+ 197+
198+ 199+ 200;
    }
}
```

This accomplishes the goal of dynamically creating a class with a method that finds the sum through brute force.

The only remaining task is to build the file and then use the method. To build the file, you must start a new process (processes are explained in some detail in Chapter 20). The best way to launch this process is with a ProcessStartInfo structure that will hold the command line. Instantiate a ProcessStartInfo and set its filename to *cmd.exe*:

```
ProcessStartInfo psi = new ProcessStartInfo( );
  psi.FileName = "cmd.exe";
```

You need to pass in the string you want to invoke at the command line. The ProcessStartInfo.Arguments property specifies the command-line arguments to use when starting the program. The command-line argument to the *cmd.exe* program will be */c* to tell *cmd.exe* to exit after it executes the command, and then the command for *cmd.exe*. The command for *cmd.exe* is the command-line compiler:

```
string compileString = "/c {0}csc /optimize+ ";
compileString += " /target:library ";
compileString += "{1}.cs > compile.out";
```

The string compileString will invoke the C# compiler (*csc*), telling it to optimize the code (after all, you're doing this to gain performance) and to build a dynamic link library (DLL) file (*/target:library*). Redirect the output of the compile to a file named *compile.out* so that you can examine it if there are errors.

Combine compileString with the filename, using the static method Format of the string class, and assign the combined string to psi.Arguments. The first placeholder, {0}, holds the location of the compiler (*%SystemRoot%\Microsoft.NET\Framework\ <version>*), and the second placeholder, {1}, holds the source code filename:

```
string frameworkDir =
    RuntimeEnvironment.GetRuntimeDirectory( );
psi.Arguments = String.Format(compileString, frameworkDir, fileName);
```

The effect of all this is to set the Arguments property of the ProcessStartInfo object psi to:

```
/c csc /optimize+ /target:library
BruteForceSums.cs > compile.out
```

Before invoking *cmd.exe,* set the WindowStyle property of psi to Minimized so that when the command executes, the window does not flicker onto and then off of the user's display:

```
psi.WindowStyle = ProcessWindowStyle.Minimized;
```

You are now ready to start the *cmd.exe* process—wait until it finishes before proceeding with the rest of the GenerateCode method:

```
Process proc = Process.Start(psi);
proc.WaitForExit( );
```

Once the process is done, you can get the assembly; from the assembly, you can get the class you've created. Finally, you can ask that class for its type and assign that to your theType member variable:

```
Assembly a = Assembly.LoadFrom(fileName + ".dll");
theClass = a.CreateInstance(className);
theType = a.GetType(className);
```

You can now delete the *.cs* file you generated:

```
File.Delete(fileName + ".cs");
```

You've now filled theType, and you're ready to return to DoSum to invoke the ComputeSum method dynamically. The Type object has a method InvokeMember( ), which can be used to invoke a member of the class described by the Type object. The InvokeMember method is overloaded; the version you'll use takes five arguments:

```
public object InvokeMember(
    string name,
    BindingFlags invokeAttr,
    Binder binder,
    object target,
    object[] args
);
```

name

The name of the method you wish to invoke.

invokeAttr

A bit mask of BindingFlags that specify how the search of the object is conducted. In this case, you'll use the InvokeMethod flag OR'd with the Default flag. These are the standard flags for invoking a method dynamically.

binder

Used to assist in type conversions. By passing in null, you'll specify that you want the default binder.

target

The object on which you'll invoke the method. In this case, you'll pass in theClass, which is the class you just created from the assembly you just built.

args

An array of arguments to pass to the method you're invoking.

The complete invocation of InvokeMember looks like this:

```
object[] arguments = new object[0];
object retVal =
    theType.InvokeMember("ComputeSum",
    BindingFlags.Default |
    BindingFlags.InvokeMethod,
    null,
    theClass,
    arguments);
return (double) retVal;
```

The result of invoking this method is assigned to the local variable retVal, which is then returned, as a double, to the driver program. The complete listing is shown in Example 18-9.

Example 18-9. Dynamic invocation with Type and InvokeMethod()

```
namespace Programming_CSharp
{
    using System;
    using System.Diagnostics;
    using System.IO;
    using System.Reflection;
    using System.Runtime.InteropServices; // provides RuntimeEnvironment

    // used to benchmark the looping approach
    public class MyMath
    {
        // sum numbers with a loop
        public int DoSumLooping(int initialVal)
        {
            int result = 0;
            for(int i = 1;i <=initialVal;i++)
            {
```

Example 18-9. Dynamic invocation with Type and InvokeMethod( ) (continued)

```
            result += i;
        }
        return result;
    }
}

// responsible for creating the BruteForceSums
// class and compiling it and invoking the
// DoSums method dynamically
public class ReflectionTest
{
    // the public method called by the driver
    public double DoSum(int theValue)
    {
        // if you don't have a reference
        // to the dynamically created class
        // create it
        if (theType == null)
        {
            GenerateCode(theValue);
        }

        // with the reference to the dynamically
        // created class you can invoke the method
        object[] arguments = new object[0];
        object retVal =
            theType.InvokeMember("ComputeSum",
            BindingFlags.Default |
            BindingFlags.InvokeMethod,
            null,
            theClass,
            arguments);
        return (double) retVal;
    }

    // generate the code and compile it
    private void GenerateCode(int theVal)
    {
        // open the file for writing
        string fileName = "BruteForceSums";
        Stream s =
            File.Open(fileName + ".cs", FileMode.Create);
        StreamWriter wrtr = new StreamWriter(s);
        wrtr.WriteLine(
            "// Dynamically created BruteForceSums class");

        // create the class
        string className = "BruteForceSums";
        wrtr.WriteLine("class {0}", className);
        wrtr.WriteLine("{");

        // create the method
```

Example 18-9. Dynamic invocation with Type and InvokeMethod() (continued)

```
        wrtr.WriteLine("\tpublic double ComputeSum( )");
        wrtr.WriteLine("\t{");
        wrtr.WriteLine("\t// Brute force sum method");
        wrtr.WriteLine("\t// For value = {0}", theVal);

        // write the brute force additions
        wrtr.Write("\treturn 0");
        for (int i = 1;i<=theVal;i++)
        {
            wrtr.Write("+ {0}",i);
        }
        wrtr.WriteLine(";");      // finish method
        wrtr.WriteLine("\t}");     // end method
        wrtr.WriteLine("}");      // end class

        // close the writer and the stream
        wrtr.Close( );
        s.Close( );

        // Build the file
        ProcessStartInfo psi =
            new ProcessStartInfo( );
        psi.FileName = "cmd.exe";

        string compileString = "/c {0}csc /optimize+ ";
        compileString += "/target:library ";
        compileString += "{1}.cs > compile.out";

        string frameworkDir =
            RuntimeEnvironment.GetRuntimeDirectory( );
        psi.Arguments =
            String.Format(compileString, frameworkDir, fileName);
        psi.WindowStyle = ProcessWindowStyle.Minimized;

        Process proc = Process.Start(psi);
        proc.WaitForExit(2000);

        // Open the file, and get a
        // pointer to the method info
        Assembly a =
            Assembly.LoadFrom(fileName + ".dll");
        theClass = a.CreateInstance(className);
        theType = a.GetType(className);
        // File.Delete(fileName + ".cs");  // clean up
    }
    Type theType = null;
    object theClass = null;
}

public class TestDriver
{
    public static void Main( )
```

Example 18-9. Dynamic invocation with Type and InvokeMethod( ) (continued)

```
    {
        const int val = 200;   // 1..200
        const int iterations = 100000;
        double result = 0;

        // run the benchmark
        MyMath m = new MyMath( );
        DateTime startTime = DateTime.Now;
        for (int i = 0;i < iterations;i++)
        {
            result = m.DoSumLooping(val);
        }
        TimeSpan elapsed =
            DateTime.Now - startTime;
        Console.WriteLine(
            "Sum of ({0}) = {1}",val, result);
        Console.WriteLine(
            "Looping. Elapsed milliseconds: " +
            elapsed.TotalMilliseconds +
            " for {0} iterations", iterations);

        // run our reflection alternative
        ReflectionTest t = new ReflectionTest( );

        startTime = DateTime.Now;
        for (int i = 0;i < iterations;i++)
        {
            result = t.DoSum(val);
        }

        elapsed = DateTime.Now - startTime;
        Console.WriteLine(
            "Sum of ({0}) = {1}",val, result);
        Console.WriteLine(
            "Brute Force. Elapsed milliseconds: " +
            elapsed.TotalMilliseconds +
            " for {0} iterations", iterations);
    }
  }
}
```

Output:
```
Sum of (200) = 20100
Looping. Elapsed milliseconds:
78.125 for 100000 iterations
Sum of (200) = 20100
Brute Force. Elapsed milliseconds:
3843.75 for 100000 iterations
```

Notice that the dynamically invoked method is *far* slower than the loop. This is not a surprise; writing the file to disk, compiling it, reading it from disk, and invoking the method all bring significant overhead. You accomplished your goal, but it was a pyrrhic victory.

Dynamic Invocation with Interfaces

It turns out that dynamic invocation is particularly slow. You want to maintain the general approach of writing the class at runtime and compiling it on the fly. But rather than using dynamic invocation, you'd just like to call the method. One way to speed things up is to use an interface to call the ComputeSums( ) method directly.

To accomplish this, you need to change ReflectionTest.DoSum( ) from:

```
public double DoSum(int theValue)
{
    if (theType == null)
    {
        GenerateCode(theValue);
    }
    object[] arguments = new object[0];
    object retVal =
        theType.InvokeMember("ComputeSum",
        BindingFlags.Default | BindingFlags.InvokeMethod,
        null,
        theFunction,
        arguments);
    return (double) retVal;
}
```

to the following:

```
public double DoSum(int theValue)
{
    if (theComputer == null)
    {
        GenerateCode(theValue);
    }
    return (theComputer.ComputeSum( ));
}
```

In this example, theComputer is an interface to an object of type BruteForceSums. It must be an interface and not an object because when you compile this program, theComputer won't yet exist; you'll create it dynamically.

Remove the declarations for thetype and theClass and replace them with:

```
IComputer theComputer = null;
```

This declares theComputer to be an IComputer interface. At the top of your program, declare the interface:

```
public interface IComputer
{
    double ComputeSum( );
}
```

When you create the BruteForceSum class, you must make it implement IComputer:

```
wrtr.WriteLine(
"class {0} : Programming_CSharp.IComputer ",
className);
```

Save your program in a project file named Reflection, and modify compileString in GenerateCode as follows:

```
string compileString = "/c csc /optimize+ ";
compileString += "/r:\"Reflection.exe\" ";
compileString += "/target:library ";
compileString += "{0}.cs > compile.out";
```

The compile string will need to reference the ReflectionTest program itself (*Reflection.exe*) so that the dynamically called compiler will know where to find the declaration of IComputer.

After you build the assembly, you will no longer assign the instance to theClass and then get the type for theType, as these variables are gone. Instead, you will assign the instance to the interface IComputer:

```
theComputer = (IComputer) a.CreateInstance(className);
```

Use the interface to invoke the method directly in DoSum:

```
return (theComputer.ComputeSum( ));
```

Example 18-10 is the complete source code.

Example 18-10. Dynamic invocation with interfaces

```
namespace Programming_CSharp
{
   using System;
   using System.Diagnostics;
   using System.IO;
   using System.Reflection;
   using System.Runtime.InteropServices; // provides RuntimeEnvironment

   // used to benchmark the looping approach
   public class MyMath
   {
      // sum numbers with a loop
      public int DoSumLooping(int initialVal)
      {
         int result = 0;
         for(int i = 1;i <=initialVal;i++)
         {
            result += i;
         }
         return result;
      }
   }

   public interface IComputer
```

Example 18-10. Dynamic invocation with interfaces (continued)

```csharp
{
    double ComputeSum( );
}

// responsible for creating the BruteForceSums
// class and compiling it and invoking the
// DoSums method dynamically
public class ReflectionTest
{
    // the public method called by the driver
    public double DoSum(int theValue)
    {
        if (theComputer == null)
        {
            GenerateCode(theValue);
        }
        return (theComputer.ComputeSum( ));
    }

    // generate the code and compile it
    private void GenerateCode(int theVal)
    {
        // open the file for writing
        string fileName = "BruteForceSums";
        Stream s =
            File.Open(fileName + ".cs", FileMode.Create);
            StreamWriter wrtr = new StreamWriter(s);
            wrtr.WriteLine(
            "// Dynamically created BruteForceSums class");

        // create the class
        string className = "BruteForceSums";
        wrtr.WriteLine(
            "class {0} : Programming_CSharp.IComputer ",
            className);
        wrtr.WriteLine("{");

        // create the method
        wrtr.WriteLine("\tpublic double ComputeSum( )");
        wrtr.WriteLine("\t{");
        wrtr.WriteLine("\t// Brute force sum method");
        wrtr.WriteLine("\t// For value = {0}", theVal);

        // write the brute force additions
        wrtr.Write("\treturn 0");
        for (int i = 1;i<=theVal;i++)
        {
            wrtr.Write("+ {0}",i);
        }
        wrtr.WriteLine(";");      // finish method
        wrtr.WriteLine("\t}");     // end method
        wrtr.WriteLine("}");      // end class
```

Example 18-10. Dynamic invocation with interfaces (continued)

```
        // close the writer and the stream
        wrtr.Close( );
        s.Close( );

        // Build the file
        ProcessStartInfo psi =
            new ProcessStartInfo( );
        psi.FileName = "cmd.exe";

        string compileString = "/c {0}csc /optimize+ ";
        compileString += "/r:\"Reflection.exe\" ";
        compileString += "/target:library ";
        compileString += "{1}.cs > compile.out";

        string frameworkDir =
            RuntimeEnvironment.GetRuntimeDirectory( );
        psi.Arguments =
            String.Format(compileString, frameworkDir, fileName);
        psi.WindowStyle = ProcessWindowStyle.Minimized;

        Process proc = Process.Start(psi);
        proc.WaitForExit( );    // wait at most 2 seconds

        // Open the file, and get a
        // pointer to the method info
        Assembly a =
            Assembly.LoadFrom(fileName + ".dll");
        theComputer = (IComputer) a.CreateInstance(className);
        File.Delete(fileName + ".cs");  // clean up
    }
    IComputer theComputer = null;
}

public class TestDriver
{
    public static void Main( )
    {
        const int val = 200;  // 1..200
        const int iterations = 1000000;
        double result = 0;

        // run the benchmark
        MyMath m = new MyMath( );
        DateTime startTime = DateTime.Now;
        for (int i = 0;i < iterations;i++)
        {
            result = m.DoSumLooping(val);
        }
        TimeSpan elapsed =
            DateTime.Now - startTime;
        Console.WriteLine(
            "Sum of ({0}) = {1}",val, result);
```

Example 18-10. Dynamic invocation with interfaces (continued)

```
        Console.WriteLine(
            "Looping. Elapsed milliseconds: " +
            elapsed.TotalMilliseconds +
            " for {0} iterations", iterations);

        // run our reflection alternative
        ReflectionTest t = new ReflectionTest();

        startTime = DateTime.Now;
        for (int i = 0;i < iterations;i++)
        {
            result = t.DoSum(val);
        }

        elapsed = DateTime.Now - startTime;
        Console.WriteLine(
            "Sum of ({0}) = {1}",val, result);
        Console.WriteLine(
            "Brute Force. Elapsed milliseconds: " +
            elapsed.TotalMilliseconds  +
            " for {0} iterations", iterations);
    }
  }
}
```

Output:
```
Sum of (200) = 20100
Looping. Elapsed milliseconds:
951.368 for 1000000 iterations
Sum of (200) = 20100
Brute Force. Elapsed milliseconds:
530.7632 for 1000000 iterations
```

This output is much more satisfying; our dynamically created brute-force method now runs twice as fast as the loop does. But you can do a lot better than that by using reflection emit.

Dynamic Invocation with Reflection Emit

So far you've created an assembly on the fly by writing its source code to disk and then compiling that source code. You then dynamically invoked the method you wanted to use from that assembly, which was compiled on disk. That brings a lot of overhead, and what have you accomplished? When you're done with writing the file to disk, you have source code you can compile; when you're done compiling, you have IL (Intermediate Language) op codes on disk that you can ask the .NET Framework to run.

Reflection emit allows you to skip a few steps and just "emit" the op codes directly. This is writing assembly code directly from your C# program and then invoking the result. It just doesn't get any cooler than that.

You start much as you did in the previous examples. Create a constant for the number to add to (200) and the number of iterations (1,000,000). You then re-create the myMath class as a benchmark.

Once again you have a ReflectionTest class, and once again you call DoSum, passing in the value:

```
ReflectionTest t = new ReflectionTest( );
result = t.DoSum(val);
```

DoSum itself is virtually unchanged:

```
public double DoSum(int theValue)
{
   if (theComputer == null)
   {
      GenerateCode(theValue);
   }

   // call the method through the interface
   return (theComputer.ComputeSum( ));
}
```

As you can see, you will use an interface again, but this time you are not going to write a file to disk.

GenerateCode is quite different now. You no longer write the file to disk and compile it; instead you call the helper method EmitAssembly and get back an assembly. You then create an instance from that assembly and cast that instance to your interface.

```
public void GenerateCode(int theValue)
{
   Assembly theAssembly = EmitAssembly(theValue);
   theComputer = (IComputer)
      theAssembly.CreateInstance("BruteForceSums");
}
```

As you might have guessed, the magic is stashed away in the EmitAssembly method:

```
private Assembly EmitAssembly(int theValue)
```

The value you pass in is the sum you want to compute. To see the power of reflection emit, you'll increase that value from 200 to 2,000.

The first thing to do in EmitAssembly is to create an object of type AssemblyName and give that AssemblyName object the name "DoSumAssembly":

```
AssemblyName assemblyName = new AssemblyName( );
assemblyName.Name = "DoSumAssembly";
```

An AssemblyName is an object that fully describes an assembly's unique identity. As discussed in Chapter 13, an assembly's identity consists of a simple name (DoSumAssembly), a version number, a cryptographic key pair, and a supported culture.

With this object in hand, you can create a new AssemblyBuilder object. To do so, call DefineDynamicAssembly on the current domain, which is done by calling the static GetDomain( ) method of the Thread object. Domains are discussed in detail in Chapter 19.

The parameters to the GetDomain( ) method are the AssemblyName object you just created and an AssemblyBuilderAccess enumeration value (one of Run, RunandSave, or Save). You'll use Run in this case to indicate that the assembly can be run but not saved:

```
AssemblyBuilder newAssembly =
    Thread.GetDomain( ).DefineDynamicAssembly(assemblyName,
        AssemblyBuilderAccess.Run);
```

With this newly created AssemblyBuilder object, you are ready to create a ModuleBuilder object. The job of the ModuleBuilder, not surprisingly, is to build a module dynamically. Modules are discussed in Chapter 17. Call the Define-DynamicModule method, passing in the name of the method you want to create:

```
ModuleBuilder newModule =
newAssembly.DefineDynamicModule("Sum");
```

Now, given that module, you can define a public class and get back a TypeBuilder object. TypeBuilder is the root class used to control the dynamic creation of classes. With a TypeBuilder object, you can define classes and add methods and fields:

```
TypeBuilder myType =
newModule.DefineType("BruteForceSums", TypeAttributes.Public);
```

You are now ready to mark the new class as implementing the IComputer interface:

```
myType.AddInterfaceImplementation(typeof(IComputer));
```

You're almost ready to create the ComputeSum method, but first you must set up the array of parameters. Because you have no parameters at all, create an array of zero length:

```
Type[] paramTypes = new Type[0];
```

Then create a Type object to hold the return type for your method:

```
Type returnType = typeof(int);
```

You're ready to create the method. The DefineMethod( ) method of TypeBuilder will both create the method and return an object of type MethodBuilder, which you will use to generate the IL code:

```
MethodBuilder simpleMethod =
myType.DefineMethod("ComputeSum",
            MethodAttributes.Public |
            MethodAttributes.Virtual,
            returnType,
            paramTypes);
```

Pass in the name of the method, the flags you want (public and virtual), the return type (int), and the paramTypes (the zero length array).

Then use the MethodBuilder object you created to get an ILGenerator object:

```
ILGenerator generator = simpleMethod.GetILGenerator();
```

With your precious ILGenerator object in hand, you are ready to emit the op codes. These are the very op codes that the C# compiler would have created. (In fact, the best way to get the op codes is to write a small C# program, compile it, and then examine the op codes in ILDasm!)

First emit the value 0 to the stack. Then loop through the number values you want to add (1 through 200), adding each to the stack in turn, adding the previous sum to the new number, and leaving the result on the stack:

```
generator.Emit(OpCodes.Ldc_I4, 0);
for (int i = 1; i <= theValue;i++)
{
    generator.Emit(OpCodes.Ldc_I4, i);
    generator.Emit(OpCodes.Add);
}
```

The value that remains on the stack is the sum you want, so you'll return it:

```
generator.Emit(OpCodes.Ret);
```

You're ready now to create a MethodInfo object that will describe the method:

```
MethodInfo computeSumInfo =
    typeof(IComputer).GetMethod("ComputeSum");
```

Now you must specify the implementation that will implement the method. Call DefineMethodOverride on the TypeBuilder object you created earlier, passing in the MethodBuilder you created along with the MethodInfo object you just created:

```
myType.DefineMethodOverride(simpleMethod, computeSumInfo);
```

You're just about done; create the class and return the assembly:

```
myType.CreateType();
return newAssembly;
```

OK, I didn't say it was easy, but it is really cool, and the resulting code runs very fast. The normal loop runs 1,000,000 iterations in 11.5 seconds, but the emitted code runs in .4 second! A full 3,000% faster. Example 18-11 is the full source code.

Example 18-11. Dynamic invocation with reflection emit

```
namespace Programming_CSharp
{
    using System;
    using System.Diagnostics;
    using System.IO;
    using System.Reflection;
    using System.Reflection.Emit;
```

Example 18-11. Dynamic invocation with reflection emit (continued)

```
using System.Threading;

// used to benchmark the looping approach
public class MyMath
{
    // sum numbers with a loop
    public int DoSumLooping(int initialVal)
    {
        int result = 0;
        for(int i = 1;i <=initialVal;i++)
        {
            result += i;
        }
        return result;
    }
}

// declare the interface
public interface IComputer
{
    int ComputeSum( );
}

public class ReflectionTest
{
    // the private method which emits the assembly
    // using op codes
    private Assembly EmitAssembly(int theValue)
    {
        // Create an assembly name
        AssemblyName assemblyName =
            new AssemblyName( );
        assemblyName.Name = "DoSumAssembly";

        // Create a new assembly with one module
        AssemblyBuilder newAssembly =
            Thread.GetDomain( ).DefineDynamicAssembly(
            assemblyName, AssemblyBuilderAccess.Run);
        ModuleBuilder newModule =
            newAssembly.DefineDynamicModule("Sum");

        // Define a public class named "BruteForceSums "
        // in the assembly.
        TypeBuilder myType =
            newModule.DefineType(
            "BruteForceSums", TypeAttributes.Public);

        // Mark the class as implementing IComputer.
        myType.AddInterfaceImplementation(
            typeof(IComputer));

        // Define a method on the type to call. Pass an
```

Example 18-11. Dynamic invocation with reflection emit (continued)

```
        // array that defines the types of the parameters,
        // the type of the return type, the name of the
        // method, and the method attributes.
        Type[] paramTypes = new Type[0];
        Type returnType = typeof(int);
        MethodBuilder simpleMethod =
            myType.DefineMethod(
            "ComputeSum",
            MethodAttributes.Public |
            MethodAttributes.Virtual,
            returnType,
            paramTypes);

        // Get an ILGenerator. This is used
        // to emit the IL that you want.
        ILGenerator generator =
            simpleMethod.GetILGenerator( );

        // Emit the IL that you'd get if you
        // compiled the code example
        // and then ran ILDasm on the output.

        // Push zero onto the stack. For each 'i'
        // less than 'theValue',
        // push 'i' onto the stack as a constant
        // add the two values at the top of the stack.
        // The sum is left on the stack.
        generator.Emit(OpCodes.Ldc_I4, 0);
        for (int i = 1; i <= theValue;i++)
        {
            generator.Emit(OpCodes.Ldc_I4, i);
            generator.Emit(OpCodes.Add);

        }

        // return the value
        generator.Emit(OpCodes.Ret);

        //Encapsulate information about the method and
        //provide access to the method's metadata
        MethodInfo computeSumInfo =
            typeof(IComputer).GetMethod("ComputeSum");

        // specify the method implementation.
        // Pass in the MethodBuilder that was returned
        // by calling DefineMethod and the methodInfo
        // just created
        myType.DefineMethodOverride(simpleMethod, computeSumInfo);

        // Create the type.
        myType.CreateType( );
        return newAssembly;
```

Example 18-11. Dynamic invocation with reflection emit (continued)

```
    }

    // check if the interface is null
    // if so, call Setup.
    public double DoSum(int theValue)
    {
        if (theComputer == null)
        {
            GenerateCode(theValue);
        }

        // call the method through the interface
        return (theComputer.ComputeSum( ));
    }

    // emit the assembly, create an instance
    // and get the interface
    public void GenerateCode(int theValue)
    {
        Assembly theAssembly = EmitAssembly(theValue);
        theComputer = (IComputer)
            theAssembly.CreateInstance("BruteForceSums");
    }

    // private member data
    IComputer theComputer = null;

}

public class TestDriver
{
    public static void Main( )
    {
        const int val = 2000;   // Note 2,000

        // 1 million iterations!
        const int iterations = 1000000;
        double result = 0;

        // run the benchmark
        MyMath m = new MyMath( );
        DateTime startTime = DateTime.Now;
        for (int i = 0;i < iterations;i++)
        {
            result = m.DoSumLooping(val);
        }
        TimeSpan elapsed =
            DateTime.Now - startTime;
        Console.WriteLine(
            "Sum of ({0}) = {1}",val, result);
        Console.WriteLine(
            "Looping. Elapsed milliseconds: " +
```

Example 18-11. Dynamic invocation with reflection emit (continued)

```
            elapsed.TotalMilliseconds +
            " for {0} iterations", iterations);

        // run our reflection alternative
        ReflectionTest t = new ReflectionTest( );

        startTime = DateTime.Now;
        for (int i = 0;i < iterations;i++)
        {
            result = t.DoSum(val);
        }

        elapsed = DateTime.Now - startTime;
        Console.WriteLine(
            "Sum of ({0}) = {1}",val, result);
        Console.WriteLine(
            "Brute Force. Elapsed milliseconds: " +
            elapsed.TotalMilliseconds  +
            " for {0} iterations", iterations);
        }
    }
}
```

Output:
```
Sum of (2000) = 2001000
Looping. Elapsed milliseconds:
11468.75 for 1000000 iterations
Sum of (2000) = 2001000
Brute Force. Elapsed milliseconds:
406.25 for 1000000 iterations
```

Reflection emit is a powerful technique for emitting op codes. Although today's compilers are very fast and today's machines have lots of memory and processing speed, it is comforting to know that when you must, you can get right down to the virtual metal.

CHAPTER 19

Marshaling and Remoting

The days of integrated programs all running in a single process on a single machine are, if not dead, at least seriously wounded. Today's programs consist of complex components running in multiple processes, often across the network. The Web has facilitated distributed applications in a way that was unthinkable even a few years ago, and the trend is toward distribution of responsibility.

A second trend is toward centralizing business logic on large servers. Although these trends appear to be contradictory, in fact they are synergistic: business objects are being centralized while the user interface and even some middleware are being distributed.

The net effect is that objects need to be able to talk with one another at a distance. Objects running on a server handling the web user interface need to be able to interact with business objects living on centralized servers at corporate headquarters.

The process of moving an object across a boundary is called *remoting*. Boundaries exist at various levels of abstraction in your program. The most obvious boundary is between objects running on different machines.

The process of preparing an object to be remoted is called *marshaling*. On a single machine, objects might need to be marshaled across context, app domain, or process boundaries.

A *process* is essentially a running application. If an object in your word processor wants to interact with an object in your spreadsheet, they must communicate across process boundaries.

Processes are divided into *application domains* (often called "app domains"); these in turn are divided into various *contexts*. App domains act like lightweight processes, and contexts create boundaries that objects with similar rules can be contained within. At times, objects will be marshaled across both context and app domain boundaries, as well as across process and machine boundaries. (Processes, app domains, and contexts are all explained in greater detail later in this chapter.)

When an object is remoted, it appears to be sent through the wire from one computer to another, much like Captain Kirk being teleported down to the surface of a planet some miles below the orbiting USS Enterprise.

In Star Trek, Kirk was actually sent to the planet, but in the .NET edition it is all an illusion. If you are standing on the surface of the planet, you might think you are seeing and talking with the real Kirk, but you are not talking to Kirk at all; you are talking to a proxy, or a simulation whose job is to take your message and beam it up to the Enterprise where it is relayed to the real Kirk. Between you and Kirk there are also a number of "sinks."

A *sink* is an object whose job is to enforce policy. For example, if Kirk tries to tell you something that might influence the development of your civilization, the prime-directive sink might disallow the transmission.

When the real Kirk responds, he passes his response through various sinks until it gets to the proxy and the proxy tells you. It seems to you as though Kirk is really there, but he's actually sitting on the bridge, yelling at Scotty that he needs more power.

The actual transmission of your message is done by a *channel*. The channel's job is to know how to move the message from the Enterprise to the planet. The channel works with a *formatter*. The formatter makes sure the message is in the right format. Perhaps you speak only Vulcan, and the poor Captain does not. The formatter can translate your message into Federation Standard, and translate Kirk's response from Federation Standard back to Vulcan. You appear to be talking with one another, but the formatter is silently facilitating the communication.

This chapter demonstrates how your objects can be marshaled across various boundaries, and how proxies and stubs can create the illusion that your object has been squeezed through the network cable to a machine across the office or around the world. In addition, this chapter explains the role of formatters, channels, and sinks, and how to apply these concepts to your programming.

Application Domains

A *process* is, essentially, a running application. Each .NET application runs in its own process. If you have Word, Excel, and Visual Studio open, you have three processes running. If you open another copy of Word, another process starts up. Each process is subdivided into one or more *application domains* (or *app domains*). An app domain acts like a process but uses fewer resources.

App domains can be independently started and halted; they are secure, lightweight, and versatile. An app domain can provide fault tolerance; if you start an object in a second app domain and it crashes, it will bring down the app domain but not your entire program. You can imagine that web servers might use app domains for running users' code; if the code has a problem, the web server can maintain operations.

An app domain is encapsulated by an instance of the AppDomain class, which offers a number of methods and properties. A few of the most important are listed in Table 19-1.

Table 19-1. Methods and properties of the AppDomain class

Method or property	Details
CurrentDomain	Public static property that returns the current application domain for the current thread
CreateDomain( )	Overloaded public static method that creates a new application domain
GetCurrentThreadID( )	Public static method that returns the current thread identifier
Unload( )	Public static method that removes the specified app domain
FriendlyName	Public property that returns the friendly name for this app domain
DefineDynamicAssembly( )	Overloaded public method that defines a dynamic assembly in the current app domain
ExecuteAssembly( )	Public method that executes the designated assembly
GetData( )	Public method that gets the value stored in the current application domain given a key
Load( )	Public method that loads an assembly into the current app domain
SetAppDomainPolicy( )	Public method that sets the security policy for the current app domain
SetData( )	Public method that puts data into the specified app domain property

App domains also support a variety of events—including AssemblyLoad, AssemblyResolve, ProcessExit, and ResourceResolve—that are fired as assemblies are found, loaded, run, and unloaded.

Every process has an initial app domain, and can have additional app domains as you create them. Each app domain exists in exactly one process. Until now, all the programs in this book have been in a single app domain: the default app domain. Each process has its own default app domain. In many, perhaps in most of the programs you write, the default app domain will be all that you'll need.

However, there are times when a single domain is insufficient. You might create a second app domain if you need to run a library written by another programmer. Perhaps you don't trust that the library, and want to isolate it in its own domain so that if a method in the library crashes the program, only the isolated domain will be affected. If you were the author of Internet Information Server (IIS, Microsoft's web hosting software), you might spin up a new app domain for each plug-in application or each virtual directory you host. This would provide fault tolerance, so that if one web application crashed, it would not bring down the web server.

It is also possible that the other library might require a different security environment; creating a second app domain allows the two security environments to coexist. Each app domain has its own security, and the app domain serves as a security boundary.

App domains are not threads and should be distinguished from threads. A thread exists in one app domain at a time, and a thread can access (and report) which app domain it is executing in. App domains are used to isolate applications; within an app domain there might be multiple threads operating at any given moment (see Chapter 20).

To see how app domains work, let's set up an example. Suppose you wish your program to instantiate a Shape class, but in a second app domain.

 There is no good reason for this Shape class to be put in a second app domain, except to illustrate how these techniques work. It is possible, however, that more complex objects might need a second app domain to provide a different security environment. Further, if you are creating classes that might engage in risky behavior, you might like the protection of starting them in a second app domain.

Normally, you'd load the Shape class from a separate assembly, but to keep this example simple, you'll just put the definition of the Shape class into the same source file as all the other code in this example (see Chapter 17). Further, in a production environment, you might run the Shape class methods in a separate thread, but for simplicity, you'll ignore threading for now. (Threading is covered in detail in Chapter 20) By sidestepping these ancillary issues, you can keep the example straightforward and focus on the details of creating and using application domains and marshaling objects across app domain boundaries.

Creating and Using App Domains

Create a new app domain by calling the static method CreateDomain() on the AppDomain class:

```
AppDomain ad2 =
    AppDomain.CreateDomain("Shape Domain");
```

This creates a new app domain with the *friendly name* Shape Domain. The friendly name is a convenience to the programmer; it is a way to interact with the domain programmatically without knowing the internal representation of the domain. You can check the friendly name of the domain you're working in with the property System.AppDomain.CurrentDomain.FriendlyName.

Once you have instantiated an AppDomain object, you can create instances of classes, interfaces, and so forth using its CreateInstance() method. Here's the signature:

```
public ObjectHandle CreateInstance(
    string assemblyName,
    string typeName,
    bool ignoreCase,
    BindingFlags bindingAttr,
    Binder binder,
    object[] args,
```

```
    CultureInfo culture,
    object[] activationAttributes,
    Evidence securityAttributes
);
```

And here's how to use it:

```
ObjectHandle oh = ad2.CreateInstance(
"ProgCSharp",                              // the assembly name
"ProgCSharp.Shape",                        // the type name with namespace
false,                                     // ignore case
System.Reflection.BindingFlags.CreateInstance, // flag
null,                                      // binder
new object[] {3, 5},                       // args
null,                                      // culture
null,                                      // activation attributes
null );                                    // security attributes
```

The first parameter (ProgCSharp) is the name of the assembly, and the second (ProgCSharp.Shape) is the name of the class. The class name must be fully qualified by namespaces.

A *binder* is an object that enables dynamic binding of an assembly at runtime. Its job is to allow you to pass in information about the object you want to create, to create that object for you, and to bind your reference to that object. In the vast majority of cases, including this example, you'll use the default binder, which is accomplished by passing in null.

It is possible, of course, to write your own binder, which might, for example, check your ID against special permissions in a database and reroute the binding to a different object, based on your identity or your privileges.

> *Binding* typically refers to attaching an object name to an object. *Dynamic binding* refers to the ability to make that attachment when the program is running, as opposed to when it is compiled. In this example, the Shape object is bound to the instance variable at runtime, through the app domain's CreateInstance( ) method.

Binding flags help the binder fine-tune its behavior at binding time. In this example, use the BindingFlags enumeration value CreateInstance. The default binder normally only looks at public classes for binding, but you can add flags to have it look at private classes if you have the right permissions.

When you bind an assembly at runtime, do not specify the assembly to load at compile time; rather, determine which assembly you want programmatically, and bind your variable to that assembly when the program is running.

The constructor you're calling takes two integers, which must be put into an object array (new object[] {3, 5}). You can send null for the culture because you'll use the default (en) culture and won't specify activation attributes or security attributes.

You get back an *object handle*, which is a type that is used to pass an object (in a wrapped state) between multiple app domains without loading the metadata for the wrapped object in each object through which the ObjectHandle travels. You can get the actual object itself by calling Unwrap( ) on the object handle, and casting the resulting object to the actual type—in this case, Shape.

The CreateInstance( ) method provides an opportunity to create the object in a new app domain. If you were to create the object with new, it would be created in the current app domain.

Marshaling Across App Domain Boundaries

You've created a Shape object in the Shape domain, but you're accessing it through a Shape object in the original domain. To access the shape object in another domain, you must *marshal* the object across the domain boundary.

Marshaling is the process of preparing an object to move across a boundary; once again, like Captain Kirk teleporting to the planet's surface. Marshaling is accomplished in two ways: *by value* or *by reference*. When an object is marshaled by value, a copy is made. It is as if I called you on the phone and asked you to send me your calculator, and you called up the hardware store and had them send me one that is identical to yours. I can use the copy just as I would the original, but entering numbers on my copy has no effect on your original.

Marshaling by reference is almost like sending me your own calculator. Here's how it works. You do not actually give me the original, but instead keep it in your house. You do send me a proxy. The proxy is very smart: when I press a button on my proxy calculator, it sends a signal to your original calculator, and the number appears over there. Pressing buttons on the proxy looks and feels to me just like I reached through the telephone wire between us and touched your original calculator.

Understanding marshaling with proxies

The Captain Kirk and hardware analogies are fine as far as analogies go, but what actually happens when you marshal by reference? The Common Language Runtime (CLR) provides your calling object with a *transparent proxy* (TP).

The job of the TP is to take everything known about your method call (the return value, the parameters, etc.) off of the stack and stuff it into an object that implements the IMessage interface. That IMessage is passed to a RealProxy object.

RealProxy is an abstract base class from which all proxies derive. You can implement your own real proxy, or any of the other objects in this process except for the transparent proxy. The default real proxy will hand the IMessage to a series of *sink* objects.

Any number of sinks can be used depending on the number of policies you wish to enforce, but the last sink in a chain will put the IMessage into a Channel. Channels are split into client-side and server-side channels, and their job is to move the message across the boundary. Channels are responsible for understanding the transport protocol. The actual format of a message as it moves across the boundary is managed by a *formatter*. The .NET Framework provides two formatters: a Simple Object Access Protocol (SOAP) formatter, which is the default for HTTP channels, and a Binary formatter, which is the default for TCP/IP channels. You are free to create your own formatters and, if you are truly a glutton for punishment, your own channels.

Once a message is passed across a boundary, it is received by the server-side channel and formatter, which reconstitute the IMessage and pass it to one or more sinks on the server side. The final sink in a sink chain is the StackBuilder, whose job is to take the IMessage and turn it back into a stack frame so that it appears to be a function call to the server.

Specifying the marshaling method

To illustrate the distinction between marshaling by value and marshaling by reference, in the next example you'll tell the Shape object to marshal by reference but give it a member variable of type Point, which you'll specify as marshal by value.

Note that each time you create an object that might be used across a boundary, you must choose how it will be marshaled. Normally, objects cannot be marshaled at all; you must take action to indicate that an object can be marshaled, either by value or by reference.

The easiest way to make an object marshal by value is to mark it with the Serializable attribute:

```
[Serializable]
public class Point
```

When an object is serialized, its internal state is written out to a stream, either for marshaling or for storage. The details of serialization are covered in Chapter 21.

The easiest way to make an object marshal by reference is to derive its class from MarshalByRefObject:

```
public class Shape : MarshalByRefObject
```

The Shape class will have just one member variable, upperLeft. This variable will be a Point object, which will hold the coordinates of the upper-left corner of the shape.

The constructor for Shape will initialize its Point member:

```
public Shape(int upperLeftX, int upperLeftY)
{
    Console.WriteLine( "[{0}] Event{1}",
        System.AppDomain.CurrentDomain.FriendlyName,
        "Shape constructor");
    upperLeft = new Point(upperLeftX, upperLeftY);
}
```

Provide Shape with a method for displaying its position:

```
public void ShowUpperLeft( )
{
    Console.WriteLine( "[{0}] Upper left: {1},{2}",
        System.AppDomain.CurrentDomain.FriendlyName,
        upperLeft.X, upperLeft.Y);
}
```

Also provide a second method for returning its upperLeft member variable:

```
public Point GetUpperLeft( )
{
    return upperLeft;
}
```

The Point class is very simple as well. It has a constructor that initializes its two member variables and accessors to get their value.

Once you create the Shape, ask it for its coordinates:

```
s1.ShowUpperLeft( );     // ask the object to display
```

Then ask it to return its upperLeft coordinate as a Point object that you'll change:

```
Point localPoint = s1.GetUpperLeft( );

localPoint.X = 500;
localPoint.Y = 600;
```

Ask that Point to print its coordinates, and then ask the Shape to print *its* coordinates. So, will the change to the local Point object be reflected in the Shape? That will depend on how the Point object is marshaled. If it is marshaled by value, the localPoint object will be a copy, and the Shape object will be unaffected by changing the localPoint variables' values. If, on the other hand, you change the Point object to marshal by reference, you'll have a proxy to the actual upperLeft variable, and changing that *will* change the Shape. Example 19-1 illustrates. Make sure you build Example 19-1 in a project named ProgCSharp. When Main() instantiates the Shape object, the method is looking for *ProgCSharp.exe*.

Example 19-1. Marshaling across app domain boundaries

```
using System;
using System.Runtime.Remoting;

using System.Reflection;

namespace ProgCSharp
{


    // for marshal by reference comment out
    // the attribute and uncomment the base class
    [Serializable]
    public class Point  // : MarshalByRefObject
```

Example 19-1. Marshaling across app domain boundaries (continued)

```csharp
{
    public Point (int x, int y)
    {
        Console.WriteLine( "[{0}] {1}",
            System.AppDomain.CurrentDomain.FriendlyName,
            "Point constructor");

        this.x = x;
        this.y = y;
    }


    public int X
    {
        get
        {
            Console.WriteLine( "[{0}] {1}",
                System.AppDomain.CurrentDomain.FriendlyName,
                "Point x.get");

            return this.x;
        }

        set
        {
            Console.WriteLine( "[{0}] {1}",
                System.AppDomain.CurrentDomain.FriendlyName,
                "Point x.set");
            this.x = value;
        }
    }

    public int Y
    {
        get
        {
            Console.WriteLine( "[{0}] {1}",
                System.AppDomain.CurrentDomain.FriendlyName,
                "Point y.get");
            return this.y;
        }

        set
        {
            Console.WriteLine( "[{0}] {1}",
                System.AppDomain.CurrentDomain.FriendlyName,
                "Point y.set");
            this.y = value;
        }
    }

    private int x;
```

Example 19-1. Marshaling across app domain boundaries (continued)

```
    private int y;
}

// the shape class marshals by reference
public class Shape : MarshalByRefObject
{
    public Shape(int upperLeftX, int upperLeftY)
    {
        Console.WriteLine( "[{0}] {1}",
            System.AppDomain.CurrentDomain.FriendlyName,
            "Shape constructor");

        upperLeft = new Point(upperLeftX, upperLeftY);
    }
    public Point GetUpperLeft()
    {
        return upperLeft;
    }

    public void ShowUpperLeft()
    {
        Console.WriteLine( "[{0}] Upper left: {1},{2}",
            System.AppDomain.CurrentDomain.FriendlyName,
            upperLeft.X, upperLeft.Y);
    }

    private Point upperLeft;
}
public class Tester
{
    public static void Main()
    {

        Console.WriteLine( "[{0}] {1}",
            System.AppDomain.CurrentDomain.FriendlyName,
            "Entered Main");

        // create the new app domain
        AppDomain ad2 =
            AppDomain.CreateDomain("Shape Domain");

        //  Assembly a = Assembly.LoadFrom("ProgCSharp.exe");
        //  Object theShape = a.CreateInstance("Shape");
        // instantiate a Shape object
        ObjectHandle oh = ad2.CreateInstance(
            "ProgCSharp",
            "ProgCSharp.Shape", false,
            System.Reflection.BindingFlags.CreateInstance,
            null, new object[] {3, 5},
            null, null, null );

        Shape s1 = (Shape) oh.Unwrap();
```

Example 19-1. Marshaling across app domain boundaries (continued)

```
        s1.ShowUpperLeft( );      // ask the object to display

        // get a local copy? proxy?
        Point localPoint = s1.GetUpperLeft( );

        // assign new values
        localPoint.X = 500;
        localPoint.Y = 600;

        // display the value of the local Point object
        Console.WriteLine( "[{0}] localPoint: {1}, {2}",
            System.AppDomain.CurrentDomain.FriendlyName,
            localPoint.X, localPoint.Y);

        s1.ShowUpperLeft( );      // show the value once more
    }
  }
}
```

Output:
```
[Programming CSharp.exe] Entered Main
[Shape Domain] Shape constructor
[Shape Domain] Point constructor
[Shape Domain] Point x.get
[Shape Domain] Point y.get
[Shape Domain] Upper left: 3,5
[Programming CSharp.exe] Point x.set
[Programming CSharp.exe] Point y.set
[Programming CSharp.exe] Point x.get
[Programming CSharp.exe] Point y.get
[Programming CSharp.exe] localPoint: 500, 600
[Shape Domain] Point x.get
[Shape Domain] Point y.get
[Shape Domain] Upper left: 3,5
```

Read through the code, or better yet, put it in your debugger and step through it. The output reveals that the Shape and Point constructors run in the Shape domain, as does the access of the values of the Point object in the Shape.

The property is set in the original app domain, setting the local copy of the Point object to 500 and 600. Because Point is marshaled by value, however, you are setting a *copy* of the Point object. When you ask the Shape to display its upperLeft member variable, it is unchanged.

To complete the experiment, comment out the attribute at the top of the Point declaration and uncomment the base class:

```
// [serializable]
public class Point    : MarshalByRefObject
```

Now run the program again. The output is quite different:

```
[Programming CSharp.exe] Entered Main
[Shape Domain] Shape constructor
```

```
[Shape Domain] Point constructor
[Shape Domain] Point x.get
[Shape Domain] Point y.get
[Shape Domain] Upper left: 3,5
[Shape Domain] Point x.set
[Shape Domain] Point y.set
[Shape Domain] Point x.get
[Shape Domain] Point y.get
[Programming CSharp.exe] localPoint: 500, 600
[Shape Domain] Point x.get
[Shape Domain] Point y.get
[Shape Domain] Upper left: 500,600
```

This time you get a proxy for the Point object and the properties are set through the proxy on the original Point member variable. Thus, the changes are reflected within the Shape itself.

Context

App domains themselves are subdivided into *contexts*. Contexts can be thought of as boundaries within which objects share usage rules. These usage rules include synchronization transactions (see Chapter 20), and so forth.

Context-Bound and Context-Agile Objects

Objects are either *context-bound* or they are *context-agile*. If they are context-bound, they exist in a context, and to interact with them the message must be marshaled. If they are context-agile, they act within the context of the calling object; that is, their methods execute in the context of the object that invokes the method and so marshaling is not required.

Suppose you have an object A that interacts with the database and so is marked to support transactions. This creates a context. All method calls on A occur within the context of the protection afforded by the transaction. Object A can decide to roll back the transaction, and all actions taken since the last commit are undone.

Suppose that you have another object, B, which is context-agile. Now suppose that object A passes a database reference to object B and then calls methods on B. Perhaps A and B are in a call-back relationship, in which B will do some work and then call A back with the results. Because B is context-agile, B's method operates in the context of the calling object; thus it will be afforded the transaction protection of object A. The changes B makes to the database will be undone if A rolls back the transaction, because B's methods execute within the context of the caller. So far, so good.

Should B be context-agile or context-bound? In the case examined so far, B worked fine being agile. Suppose one more class exists: C. C does not have transactions, and it calls a method on B that changes the database. Now A tries to roll back, but unfortunately, the work B did for C was in C's context and thus was not afforded the support of transactions. Uh-oh: that work can't be undone.

If B was marked context-bound, when A created it, B would have inherited A's context. In that case, when C invoked a method on B it would have to be marshaled across the context boundary, but then when B executed the method it would have been in the context of A's transaction. Much better.

This would work if B were context-bound but without attributes. B of course could have its own context attributes, and these might force B to be in a different context from A. For example, B might have a transaction attribute marked RequiresNew. In this case, when B is created it gets a new context, and thus cannot be in A's context. Thus, when A rolled back, B's work could not be undone. You might mark B with the RequiresNew enumeration value because B is an audit function. When A takes an action on the database it informs B, which updates an audit trail. You do not want B's work undone when A undoes its transaction. You want B to be in its own transaction context, rolling back only its own mistakes, not A's.

An object thus has three choices. The first option is to be context-agile. A context-agile object operates in the context of its caller. Option two is to be context-bound (accomplished by deriving from ContextBoundObject but have no attributes, and thus operate in the context of the creator. Option three is to be context-bound with context attributes, and thus operate only in the context that matches the attributes.

Which you decide upon depends on how your object will be used. If your object is a simple calculator that cannot possibly need synchronization or transactions or any context support, it is more efficient to be context-agile. If your object should use the context of the object that creates it, you should make that object context-bound with no attributes. Finally, if your object has its own context requirements, you should give it the appropriate attributes.

Marshaling Across Context Boundaries

No proxy is needed when accessing context-agile objects within a single app domain. When an object in one context accesses a context-bound object in a second context, it does so through a proxy, and at that time the two context policies are enforced. It is in this sense that a context creates a boundary; the policy is enforced at the boundary between contexts.

For example, when you mark a context-bound object with the System.EnterpriseServices.Synchronization attribute, you indicate that you want the system to manage synchronization for that object. All objects outside that context must pass through the context boundary to touch one of the objects, and at that time the policy of synchronization will be applied.

Strictly speaking, marking two classes with the Synchronization attribute does not guarantee that they will end up in the same context. Each attribute gets to vote on whether it is happy with the current context at activation. If two objects are marked for synchronization but one is pooled, they will be forced into different contexts.

Objects are marshaled differently across context boundaries, depending on how they are created:

- Typical objects are not marshaled at all; within app domains they are context-agile.

- Objects marked with the Serializable attribute are marshaled by value across app domains and are context-agile.

- Objects that derive from MarshalByRefObject are marshaled by reference across app domains and are context-agile.

- Objects derived from ContextBoundObject are marshaled by reference across app domains as well as by reference across context boundaries.

Remoting

In addition to being marshaled across context and app domain boundaries, objects can be marshaled across process boundaries, and even across machine boundaries. When an object is marshaled, either by value or by proxy, across a process or machine boundary, it is said to be *remoted*.

Understanding Server Object Types

There are two types of server objects supported for remoting in .NET: *well-known* and *client-activated*. The communication with well-known objects is established each time a message is sent by the client. There is no permanent connection with a well-known object, as there is with client-activated objects.

Well-known objects come in two varieties: *singleton* and *single-call*. With a well-known singleton object, all messages for the object, from all clients, are dispatched to a single object running on the server. The object is created when the server is started and is there to provide service to any client that can reach it. Well-known objects must have a parameterless constructor.

With a well-known single-call object, each new message from a client is handled by a new object. This is highly advantageous on server farms, where a series of messages from a given client might be handled in turn by different machines depending on load balancing.

Client-activated objects are typically used by programmers who are creating dedicated servers, which provide services to a client they are also writing. In this scenario, the client and the server create a connection, and they maintain that connection until the needs of the client are fulfilled.

Specifying a Server with an Interface

The best way to understand remoting is to walk through an example. Here, build a simple four-function calculator class, like the one used in an earlier discussion on web services (see Chapter 16), that implements the interface shown in Example 19-2.

Example 19-2. The Calculator interface

```
namespace Programming_CSharp
{
    using System;

    public interface ICalc
    {
        double Add(double x, double y);
        double Sub(double x, double y);
        double Mult(double x, double y);
        double Div(double x, double y);
    }
}
```

Save this in a file named *ICalc.cs* and compile it into a file named *ICalc.dll*. To create and compile the source file in Visual Studio, create a new project of type C# Class Library, enter the interface definition in the Edit window, and then select Build → Build on the Visual Studio menu bar. Alternatively, if you have entered the source code using Notepad, you can compile the file at the command line by entering:

```
csc /t:library ICalc.cs
```

There are tremendous advantages to implementing a server through an interface. If you implement the calculator as a class, the client must link to that class in order to declare instances on the client. This greatly diminishes the advantages of remoting because changes to the server require the class definition to be updated on the client. In other words, the client and server would be tightly coupled. Interfaces help decouple the two objects; in fact, you can later update that implementation on the server, and as long as the server still fulfills the contract implied by the interface, the client need not change at all.

Building a Server

To build the server used in this example, create *CalcServer.cs* in a new project of type C# Console Application (be sure to include a reference to *ICalc.dll*) and then compile it by selecting Build → Build on the Visual Studio menu bar. Or, you can enter the code in Notepad, save it to a file named *CalcServer.cs*, and enter the following at the command-line prompt:

```
csc /t:exe /r:ICalc.dll CalcServer.cs
```

The Calculator class implements ICalc. It derives from MarshalByRefObject so that it will deliver a proxy of the calculator to the client application:

```
public class Calculator : MarshalByRefObject, ICalc
```

The implementation consists of little more than a constructor and simple methods to implement the four functions.

In this example, you'll put the logic for the server into the Main( ) method of *CalcServer.cs*.

Your first task is to create a channel. Use HTTP as the transport because it is simple and you don't need a sustained TCP/IP connection. You can use the HTTPChannel type provided by .NET:

```
HTTPChannel chan = new HTTPChannel(65100);
```

Notice that you register the channel on TCP/IP port 65100 (see the discussion of port numbers in Chapter 21).

Next, register the channel with the CLR ChannelServices using the static method RegisterChannel:

```
ChannelServices.RegisterChannel(chan);
```

This step informs .NET that you will be providing HTTP services on port 65100, much as IIS does on port 80. Because you've registered an HTTP channel and not provided your own formatter, your method calls will use the SOAP formatter by default.

Now you are ready to ask the RemotingConfiguration class to register your well-known object. You must pass in the type of the object you want to register, along with an *endpoint*. An *endpoint* is a name that RemotingConfiguration will associate with your type. It completes the address. If the IP address identifies the machine and the port identifies the channel, the endpoint identifies the actual application that will be providing the service. To get the type of the object, you can call the static method GetType( ) of the Type class, which returns a Type object. Pass in the full name of the object whose type you want:

```
Type calcType =
   Type.GetType("Programming_CSharp.Calculator");
```

Also pass in the enumerated type that indicates whether you are registering a SingleCall or Singleton:

```
RemotingConfiguration.RegisterWellKnownServiceType
   ( calcType, "theEndPoint",WellKnownObjectMode.Singleton );
```

The call to RegisterWellKnownServiceType does not put one byte on the wire. It simply uses reflection to build a proxy for your object.

Now you're ready to rock and roll. Example 19-3 provides the entire source code for the server.

Example 19-3. The Calculator server

```
using System;
using System.Runtime.Remoting;
using System.Runtime.Remoting.Channels;
using System.Runtime.Remoting.Channels.Http;

namespace Programming_CSharp
{
```

Example 19-3. The Calculator server (continued)

```csharp
// implement the calculator class
public class Calculator : MarshalByRefObject, ICalc
{
    public Calculator( )
    {
        Console.WriteLine("Calculator constructor");
    }

    // implement the four functions
    public double Add(double x, double y)
    {
        Console.WriteLine("Add {0} + {1}", x, y);
        return x+y;
    }
    public double Sub(double x, double y)
    {
        Console.WriteLine("Sub {0} - {1}", x, y);
        return x-y;
    }
    public double Mult(double x, double y)
    {
        Console.WriteLine("Mult {0} * {1}", x, y);
        return x*y;
    }
    public double Div(double x, double y)
    {
        Console.WriteLine("Div {0} / {1}", x, y);
        return x/y;
    }
}

public class ServerTest
{
    public static void Main( )
    {
        // create a channel and register it
        HttpChannel chan = new HttpChannel(65100);
        ChannelServices.RegisterChannel(chan);

        Type calcType =
            Type.GetType("Programming_CSharp.Calculator");

        // register our well-known type and tell the server
        // to connect the type to the endpoint "theEndPoint"
        RemotingConfiguration.RegisterWellKnownServiceType
            ( calcType,
              "theEndPoint",
                WellKnownObjectMode.Singleton );

        //  "They also serve who only stand and wait."); (Milton)
        Console.WriteLine("Press [enter] to exit...");
```

Example 19-3. The Calculator server (continued)

```
        Console.ReadLine( );
    }
  }
}
```

When you run this program, it prints its self-deprecating message:

```
    Press [enter] to exit...
```

and then waits for a client to ask for service.

Building the Client

The client must also register a channel, but because you are not listening on that channel, you can use channel 0:

```
    HTTPChannel chan = new HTTPChannel(0);
    ChannelServices.RegisterChannel(chan);
```

The client now need only connect through the remoting services, passing a Type object representing the type of the object it needs (in our case, the ICalc interface) and the URI (Uniform Resource Identifier) of the implementing class:

```
    MarshalByRefObject obj =
        RemotingServices.Connect
            (typeof(Programming_CSharp.ICalc),
            "http://localhost:65100/theEndPoint");
```

In this case the server is assumed to be running on your local machine, so the URI is *http://localhost*, followed by the port for the server (65100), followed in turn by the endpoint you declared in the server (theEndPoint).

The remoting service should return an object representing the interface you've requested. You can then cast that object to the interface and begin using it. Because remoting cannot be guaranteed (the network might be down, the host machine may not be available, and so forth), you should wrap the usage in a try block:

```
    try
    {
        Programming_CSharp.ICalc calc =
            obj as Programming_CSharp.ICalc;

        double sum = calc.Add(3,4);
```

You now have a proxy of the Calculator operating on the server, but usable on the client, across the process boundary and, if you like, across the machine boundary. Example 19-4 shows the entire client (to compile it, you must include a reference to *ICalc.dll* as you did with *CalcServer.cs*).

Example 19-4. The remoting Calculator client

```
namespace Programming_CSharp
{
```

Example 19-4. The remoting Calculator client (continued)

```
using System;
using System.Runtime.Remoting;
using System.Runtime.Remoting.Channels;
using System.Runtime.Remoting.Channels.Http;

public class CalcClient
{
    public static void Main( )
    {

        int[] myIntArray = new int[3];

        Console.WriteLine("Watson, come here I need you...");

        // create an Http channel and register it
        // uses port 0 to indicate won't be listening
        HttpChannel chan = new HttpChannel(0);
        ChannelServices.RegisterChannel(chan);

        // get my object from across the http channel
        MarshalByRefObject obj =
         (MarshalByRefObject) RemotingServices.Connect
           (typeof(Programming_CSharp.ICalc),
            "http://localhost:65100/theEndPoint");

        try
        {
            // cast the object to our interface
            Programming_CSharp.ICalc calc =
                obj as Programming_CSharp.ICalc;

            // use the interface to call methods
            double sum = calc.Add(3.0,4.0);
            double difference = calc.Sub(3,4);
            double product = calc.Mult(3,4);
            double quotient = calc.Div(3,4);

            // print the results
            Console.WriteLine("3+4 = {0}", sum);
            Console.WriteLine("3-4 = {0}", difference);
            Console.WriteLine("3*4 = {0}", product);
            Console.WriteLine("3/4 = {0}", quotient);
        }
        catch( System.Exception ex )
        {
            Console.WriteLine("Exception caught: ");
            Console.WriteLine(ex.Message);
        }
    }
}
```

Example 19-4. The remoting Calculator client (continued)

Output on client::
```
Watson, come here I need you...
3+4 = 7
3-4 = -1
3*4 = 12
3/4 = 0.75
```

Output on server:
```
Calculator constructor
Press [enter] to exit...
Add 3 + 4
Sub 3 - 4
Mult 3 * 4
Div 3 / 4
```

The server starts up and waits for the user to press Enter to signal that it can shut down. The client starts and displays a message to the console. The client then calls each of the four operations. You see the server printing its message as each method is called, and then the results are printed on the client.

It is as simple as that; you now have code running on the server and providing services to your client.

Using SingleCall

To see the difference that SingleCall makes versus Singleton, change one line in the server's Main( ) method. Here's the existing code:

```
RemotingServices. RegisterWellKnownServiceType
    ( "CalcServerApp","Programming_CSharp.Calculator",
        "theEndPoint",WellKnownObjectMode.Singleton );
```

Change the object to SingleCall:

```
RemotingServices. RegisterWellKnownServiceType
    ( "CalcServerApp","Programming_CSharp.Calculator",
        "theEndPoint",WellKnownObjectMode.SingleCall );
```

The output reflects that a new object is created to handle each request:

```
Calculator constructor
Press [enter] to exit...
Calculator constructor
Add 3 + 4
Calculator constructor
Sub 3 - 4
Calculator constructor
Mult 3 * 4
Calculator constructor
Div 3 / 4
```

Understanding RegisterWellKnownServiceType

When you called the `RegisterWellKnownServiceType()` method on the server, what actually happened? Remember that you created a `Type` object for the `Calculator` class:

```
Type.GetType("Programming_CSharp.Calculator");
```

You then called `RegisterWellKnownServiceType()`, passing in that `Type` object along with the endpoint and the `Singleton` enumeration. This signals the CLR to instantiate your `Calculator` and then to associate it with an endpoint.

To do that work yourself, you would need to modify Example 19-3, changing `Main()` to instantiate a `Calculator` and then passing that `Calculator` to the `Marshal()` method of `RemotingServices` with the endpoint to which you want to associate that instance of `Calculator`. The modified `Main()` is shown in Example 19-5 and, as you can see, its output is identical to that of Example 19-3.

Example 19-5. Manually instantiating and associating Calculator with an endpoint

```
public static void Main()
{
    // create a channel and register it
    HttpChannel chan = new HttpChannel(65100);
    ChannelServices.RegisterChannel(chan);


    // make your own instance and call Marshal directly
    Calculator calculator = new Calculator();
    RemotingServices.Marshal(calculator,"theEndPoint");

    //  "They also serve who only stand and wait."); (Milton)
    Console.WriteLine("Press [enter] to exit...");
    Console.ReadLine();
}
```

The net effect is that you have instantiated a calculator object, and associated a proxy for remoting with the endpoint you've specified.

Understanding Endpoints

What is going on when you register this endpoint? Clearly, the server is associating that endpoint with the object you've created. When the client connects, that endpoint is used as an index into a table so that the server can provide a proxy to the correct object (in this case, the Calculator).

If you don't provide an endpoint for the client to talk to, you can instead write all the information about your calculator object to a file and physically give that file to your client. For example, you could send it to your buddy by email, and he could load it on his local computer.

The client can deserialize the object and reconstitute a proxy, which it can then use to access the calculator on your server! (The following example was suggested to me by Mike Woodring of DevelopMentor, who uses a similar example to drive home the idea that the endpoint is simply a convenience for accessing a marshaled object remotely.)

To see how you can invoke an object without a known endpoint, modify the Main( ) method of Example 19-3 once again. This time, rather than calling Marshal( ) with an endpoint, just pass in the object:

```
ObjRef objRef = RemotingServices.Marshal(calculator)
```

Marshal( ) returns an ObjRef object. An ObjRef object stores all the information required to activate and communicate with a remote object. When you do supply an endpoint, the server creates a table that associates the endpoint with an objRef so that the server can create the proxy when a client asks for it. ObjRef contains all the information needed by the client to build a proxy, and objRef itself is serializable.

Open a file stream for writing to a new file and create a new SOAP formatter. You can serialize your ObjRef to that file by invoking the Serialize( ) method on the formatter, passing in the file stream and the ObjRef you got back from Marshal. Presto! You have all the information you need to create a proxy to your object written out to a disk file. The complete replacement for Main( ) is shown in Example 19-6. You will also need to add two using statements to *CalcServer.cs*:

```
using System.IO;
using System.Runtime.Serialization.Formatters.Soap;
```

Example 19-6. Marshaling an object without a well-known endpoint

```
public static void Main( )
{
    // create a channel and register it
    HttpChannel chan = new HttpChannel(65100);
    ChannelServices.RegisterChannel(chan);
    // make your own instance and call Marshal directly
    Calculator calculator = new Calculator( );

    ObjRef objRef = RemotingServices.Marshal(calculator);

    FileStream fileStream =
        new FileStream("calculatorSoap.txt",FileMode.Create);

    SoapFormatter soapFormatter = new SoapFormatter( );

    soapFormatter.Serialize(fileStream,objRef);
    fileStream.Close( );

    //  "They also serve who only stand and wait."); (Milton)
    Console.WriteLine(
```

```
        "Exported to CalculatorSoap.txt. Press ENTER to exit...");
        Console.ReadLine();
}
```

When you run the server, it writes the file *calculatorSoap.txt* to the disk. The server then waits for the client to connect. It might have a long wait.

You can take that file to your client and reconstitute it on the client machine. To do so, again create a channel and register it. This time, however, open a fileStream on the file you just copied from the server:

```
FileStream fileStream =
        new FileStream ("calculatorSoap.txt", FileMode.Open);
```

Then instantiate a SoapFormatter and call Deserialize( ) on the formatter, passing in the filename and getting back an ICalc:

```
SoapFormatter soapFormatter =
    new SoapFormatter ();
try
{
    ICalc calc=
        (ICalc) soapFormatter.Deserialize (fileStream);
```

You are now free to invoke methods on the server through that ICalc, which act as a proxy to the calculator object running on the server that you described in the *calculatorSoap.txt* file. The complete replacement for the client's Main method is shown in Example 19-7. You also need to add two using statements to this example:

```
using System.IO;
using System.Runtime.Serialization.Formatters.Soap;
```

Example 19-7. Replacement of Main( ) from Example 19-4 (the client)

```
public static void Main( )
{

    int[] myIntArray = new int[3];

    Console.WriteLine("Watson, come here I need you...");

    // create an Http channel and register it
    // uses port 0 to indicate you won't be listening
    HttpChannel chan = new HttpChannel(0);
    ChannelServices.RegisterChannel(chan);

    FileStream fileStream =
        new FileStream ("calculatorSoap.txt", FileMode.Open);
    SoapFormatter soapFormatter =
        new SoapFormatter ();

    try
    {
```

```
ICalc calc=
    (ICalc) soapFormatter.Deserialize (fileStream);

// use the interface to call methods
double sum = calc.Add(3.0,4.0);
double difference = calc.Sub(3,4);
double product = calc.Mult(3,4);
double quotient = calc.Div(3,4);

// print the results
Console.WriteLine("3+4 = {0}", sum);
Console.WriteLine("3-4 = {0}", difference);
Console.WriteLine("3*4 = {0}", product);
Console.WriteLine("3/4 = {0}", quotient);
}
catch( System.Exception ex )
{
    Console.WriteLine("Exception caught: ");
    Console.WriteLine(ex.Message);
}
}
```

When the client starts up, the file is read from the disk and the proxy is unmarshaled. This is the mirror operation to marshaling and serializing the object on the server. Once you have unmarshaled the proxy, you are able to invoke the methods on the calculator object running on the server.

CHAPTER 20

Threads and Synchronization

Threads are relatively lightweight processes responsible for multitasking within a single application. The System.Threading namespace provides a wealth of classes and interfaces to manage multithreaded programming. The majority of programmers might never need to manage threads explicitly, however, because the Common Language Runtime (CLR) abstracts much of the threading support into classes that greatly simplify most threading tasks. For example, in Chapter 21, you will see how to create multithreaded reading and writing streams without resorting to managing the threads yourself.

The first part of this chapter shows you how to create, manage, and kill threads. Even if you don't create your own threads explicitly, you'll want to ensure that your code can handle multiple threads if it's run in a multithreading environment. This concern is especially important if you are creating components that might be used by other programmers in a program that supports multithreading. It is particularly significant to web services developers. Although web services (covered in Chapter 16) have many attributes of desktop applications, they are run on the server, generally lack a user interface, and force the developer to think about server-side issues such as efficiency and multithreading.

The second part of this chapter focuses on synchronization. When you have a limited resource, you may need to restrict access to that resource to one thread at a time. A classic analogy is to a restroom on an airplane. You want to allow access to the restroom for only one person at a time. This is done by putting a lock on the door. When passengers want to use the restroom, they try the door handle; if it is locked, they either go away and do something else, or they wait patiently in line with others who want access to the resource. When the resource becomes free, one person is taken off the line and given the resource, which is then locked again.

At times, various threads might want to access a resource in your program, such as a file. It might be important to ensure that only one thread has access to your resource at a time, and so you will lock the resource, allow a thread access, and then unlock the resource. Programming locks can be fairly sophisticated, ensuring a fair distribution of resources.

Threads

Threads are typically created when you want a program to do two things at once. For example, assume you are calculating *pi* (3.141592653589...) to the 10 billionth place. The processor will happily begin computing this, but nothing will write to the user interface while it is working. Because computing *pi* to the 10 billionth place will take a few million years, you might like the processor to provide an update as it goes. In addition, you might want to provide a Stop button so that the user can cancel the operation at any time. To allow the program to handle the click on the Stop button, you will need a second thread of execution.

 An apartment is a logical container within a process, and is used for objects that share the same thread-access requirements. Objects in an apartment can all receive method calls from any object in any thread in the apartment. The .NET Framework does not use apartments, and managed objects (objects created within the CLR) are responsible for thread safety. The only exception to this is when managed code talks to COM. COM interoperability is discussed in Chapter 22.

Another common place to use threading is when you must wait for an event, such as user input, a read from a file, or receipt of data over the network. Freeing the processor to turn its attention to another task while you wait (such as computing another 10,000 values of *pi*) is a good idea, and it makes your program appear to run more quickly.

On the flip side, note that in some circumstances, threading can actually slow you down. Assume that in addition to calculating *pi*, you also want to calculate the Fibonnacci series (1,1,2,3,5,8,13,21...). If you have a multiprocessor machine, this will run faster if each computation is in its own thread. If you have a single-processor machine (as most users do), computing these values in multiple threads will certainly run *slower* than computing one and then the other in a single thread, because the processor must switch back and forth between the two threads. This incurs some overhead.

Starting Threads

The simplest way to create a thread is to create a new instance of the Thread class. The Thread constructor takes a single argument: a delegate type. The CLR provides the ThreadStart delegate class specifically for this purpose, which points to a method you designate. This allows you to construct a thread and to say to it "when you start, run this method." The ThreadStart delegate declaration is:

```
public delegate void ThreadStart();
```

As you can see, the method you attach to this delegate must take no parameters and must return void. Thus, you might create a new thread like this:

```
Thread myThread = new Thread( new ThreadStart(myFunc) );
```

myFunc must be a method that takes no parameters and returns void.

For example, you might create two worker threads, one that counts up from zero:

```
public void Incrementer()
{
    for (int i =0;i<10;i++)
    {
        Console.WriteLine("Incrementer: {0}", i);
    }
}
```

and one that counts down from 10:

```
public void Decrementer()
{
    for (int i = 10;i>=0;i--)
    {
        Console.WriteLine("Decrementer: {0}", i);
    }
}
```

To run these in threads, create two new threads, each initialized with a ThreadStart delegate. These in turn would be initialized to the respective member functions:

```
Thread t1 = new Thread( new ThreadStart(Incrementer) );
Thread t2 = new Thread( new ThreadStart(Decrementer) );
```

Instantiating these threads does not start them running. To do so you must call the Start method on the Thread object itself:

```
t1.Start();
t2.Start();
```

 If you don't take further action, the thread will stop when the function returns. You'll see how to stop a thread before the function ends later in this chapter.

Example 20-1 is the full program and its output. You will need to add a using statement for System.Threading to make the compiler aware of the Thread class. Notice the output, where you can see the processor switching from t1 to t2.

Example 20-1. Using threads

```
namespace Programming_CSharp
{
    using System;
    using System.Threading;

    class Tester
    {
        static void Main()
        {
            // make an instance of this class
```

Example 20-1. Using threads (continued)

```
        Tester t = new Tester();

        // run outside static Main
        t.DoTest();

    }

    public void DoTest()
    {
        // create a thread for the Incrementer
        // pass in a ThreadStart delegate
        // with the address of Incrementer
        Thread t1 =
            new Thread(
                new ThreadStart(Incrementer) );

        // create a thread for the Decrementer
        // pass in a ThreadStart delegate
        // with the address of Decrementer
        Thread t2 =
            new Thread(
                new ThreadStart(Decrementer) );

        // start the threads
        t1.Start();
        t2.Start();
    }

    // demo function, counts up to 1K
    public void Incrementer()
    {
        for (int i =0;i<1000;i++)
        {
            Console.WriteLine(
                "Incrementer: {0}", i);
        }
    }

    // demo function, counts down from 1k
    public void Decrementer()
    {
        for (int i = 1000;i>=0;i--)
        {
            Console.WriteLine(
                "Decrementer: {0}", i);
        }
    }
}
}
```

Output:
```
Incrementer: 102
Incrementer: 103
```

Example 20-1. Using threads (continued)

```
Incrementer: 104
Incrementer: 105
Incrementer: 106
Decrementer: 1000
Decrementer: 999
Decrementer: 998
Decrementer: 997
```

The processor allows the first thread to run long enough to count up to 106. Then, the second thread kicks in, counting down from 1000 for a while. Then the first thread is allowed to run. When I run this with larger numbers, I notice that each thread is allowed to run for about 100 numbers before switching. The actual amount of time devoted to any given thread is handled by the thread scheduler and will depend on many factors, such as the processor speed, demands on the processor from other programs, and so forth.

Joining Threads

When you tell a thread to stop processing and wait until a second thread completes its work, you are said to be joining the first thread to the second. It is as if you tied the tip of the first thread on to the tail of the second—hence "joining" them.

To join thread 1 (t1) onto thread 2 (t2), write:

```
t2.Join();
```

If this statement is executed in a method in thread t1, t1 will halt and wait until t2 completes and exits. For example, we might ask the thread in which Main() executes to wait for all our other threads to end before it writes its concluding message. In this next code snippet, assume you've created a collection of threads named myThreads. Iterate over the collection, joining the current thread to each thread in the collection in turn:

```
foreach (Thread myThread in myThreads)
{
    myThread.Join();
}

Console.WriteLine("All my threads are done.");
```

The final message All my threads are done will not be printed until all the threads have ended. In a production environment, you might start up a series of threads to accomplish some task (e.g., printing, updating the display, etc.) and not want to continue the main thread of execution until the worker threads are completed.

Suspending Threads

At times, you want to suspend your thread for a short while. You might, for example, like your clock thread to suspend for about a second in between testing the system time. This lets you display the new time about once a second without devoting hundreds of millions of machine cycles to the effort.

The Thread class offers a public static method, Sleep, for just this purpose. The method is overloaded; one version takes an int, the other a timeSpan object. Each represents the number of milliseconds you want the thread suspended for, expressed either as an int (e.g., 2000 = 2000 milliseconds or two seconds) or as a timeSpan.

Although timeSpan objects can measure *ticks* (100 nanoseconds), the Sleep() method's granularity is in milliseconds (1,000,000 nanoseconds).

To cause your thread to sleep for one second, you can invoke the static method of Thread, Sleep, which suspends the thread in which it is invoked:

```
Thread.Sleep(1000);
```

At times, you'll tell your thread to sleep for only one millisecond. You might do this to signal to the thread scheduler that you'd like your thread to yield to another thread, even if the thread scheduler might otherwise give your thread a bit more time.

If you modify Example 20-1 to add a Thread.Sleep(1) statement after each WriteLine, the output changes significantly:

```
for (int i =0;i<1000;i++)
{
    Console.WriteLine(
        "Incrementer: {0}", i);
    Thread.Sleep(1);
}
```

This small change is sufficient to give each thread an opportunity to run once the other thread prints one value. The output reflects this change:

```
Incrementer: 0
Incrementer: 1
Decrementer: 1000
Incrementer: 2
Decrementer: 999
Incrementer: 3
Decrementer: 998
Incrementer: 4
Decrementer: 997
Incrementer: 5
Decrementer: 996
Incrementer: 6
Decrementer: 995
```

Killing Threads

Typically, threads die after running their course. You can, however, ask a thread to kill itself by calling its Abort() method. This causes a ThreadAbortException

exception to be thrown, which the thread can catch, and thus provides the thread with an opportunity to clean up any resources it might have allocated.

```
catch (ThreadAbortException)
{
    Console.WriteLine("[{0}] Aborted! Cleaning up...",
        Thread.CurrentThread.Name);
}
```

The thread ought to treat the ThreadAbortException exception as a signal that it is time to exit, and as quickly as possible. You don't so much kill a thread as politely request that it commit suicide.

You might wish to kill a thread in reaction to an event, such as the user pressing the Cancel button. The event handler for the Cancel button might be in thread T1, and the event it is canceling might be in thread T2. In your event handler, you can call Abort on T1:

```
T1.Abort();
```

An exception will be raised in T1's currently running method that T1 can catch. This gives T1 the opportunity to free its resources and then exit gracefully.

In Example 20-2, three threads are created and stored in an array of Thread objects. Before the Threads are started, the IsBackground property is set to true. Each thread is then started and named (e.g., Thread1, Thread2, etc.). A message is displayed indicating that the thread is started, and then the main thread sleeps for 50 milliseconds before starting up the next thread.

After all three threads are started and another 50 milliseconds have passed, the first thread is aborted by calling Abort( ). The main thread then joins all three of the running threads. The effect of this is that the main thread will not resume until all the other threads have completed. When they do complete, the main thread prints a message: All my threads are done. The complete source is displayed in Example 20-2.

Example 20-2. Interrupting a thread

```
namespace Programming_CSharp
{
    using System;
    using System.Threading;

    class Tester
    {
        static void Main()
        {
            // make an instance of this class
            Tester t = new Tester();

            // run outside static Main
            t.DoTest();
```

Example 20-2. Interrupting a thread (continued)

```csharp
    }

    public void DoTest( )
    {
        // create an array of unnamed threads
        Thread[] myThreads =
            {
                new Thread( new ThreadStart(Decrementer) ),
                new Thread( new ThreadStart(Incrementer) ),
                new Thread( new ThreadStart(Incrementer) )
            };

        // start each thread
        int ctr = 1;
        foreach (Thread myThread in myThreads)
        {
            myThread.IsBackground=true;
            myThread.Start( );
            myThread.Name = "Thread" + ctr.ToString( );
            ctr++;
            Console.WriteLine("Started thread {0}", myThread.Name);
            Thread.Sleep(50);
        }

        // having started the threads
        // tell thread 1 to abort
        myThreads[1].Abort( );

        // wait for all threads to end before continuing
        foreach (Thread myThread in myThreads)
        {
            myThread.Join( );
        }

        // after all threads end, print a message
        Console.WriteLine("All my threads are done.");
    }

    // demo function, counts down from 1k
    public void Decrementer( )
    {
        try
        {
            for (int i = 1000;i>=0;i--)
            {
                Console.WriteLine(
                    "Thread {0}. Decrementer: {1}",
                    Thread.CurrentThread.Name,
                    i);
                Thread.Sleep(1);
            }
        }
```

Example 20-2. Interrupting a thread (continued)

```
        catch (ThreadAbortException)
        {
            Console.WriteLine(
                "Thread {0} aborted! Cleaning up...",
                Thread.CurrentThread.Name);
        }
        finally
        {
            Console.WriteLine(
                "Thread {0} Exiting. ",
                Thread.CurrentThread.Name);
        }
    }


    // demo function, counts up to 1K
    public void Incrementer()
    {
        try
        {
            for (int i =0;i<1000;i++)
            {
                Console.WriteLine(
                    "Thread {0}. Incrementer: {1}",
                    Thread.CurrentThread.Name,
                    i);
                Thread.Sleep(1);
            }
        }
        catch (ThreadAbortException)
        {
            Console.WriteLine(
                "Thread {0} aborted! Cleaning up...",
                Thread.CurrentThread.Name);
        }
        finally
        {
            Console.WriteLine(
                "Thread {0} Exiting. ",
                Thread.CurrentThread.Name);
        }
    }
}
```

Output (excerpt):
```
Started thread Thread1
Thread Thread1. Decrementer: 1000
Thread Thread1. Decrementer: 999
Thread Thread1. Decrementer: 998
Started thread Thread2
Thread Thread1. Decrementer: 997
Thread Thread2. Incrementer: 0
```

Example 20-2. Interrupting a thread (continued)

```
Thread Thread1. Decrementer: 996
Thread Thread2. Incrementer: 1
Thread Thread1. Decrementer: 995
Thread Thread2. Incrementer: 2
Thread Thread1. Decrementer: 994
Thread Thread2. Incrementer: 3
Started thread Thread3
Thread Thread1. Decrementer: 993
Thread Thread2. Incrementer: 4
Thread Thread2. Incrementer: 5
Thread Thread1. Decrementer: 992
Thread Thread2. Incrementer: 6
Thread Thread1. Decrementer: 991
Thread Thread3. Incrementer: 0
Thread Thread2. Incrementer: 7
Thread Thread1. Decrementer: 990
Thread Thread3. Incrementer: 1
Thread Thread2 aborted! Cleaning up...
Thread Thread2 Exiting.
Thread Thread1. Decrementer: 989
Thread Thread3. Incrementer: 2
Thread Thread1. Decrementer: 988
Thread Thread3. Incrementer: 3
Thread Thread1. Decrementer: 987
Thread Thread3. Incrementer: 4
Thread Thread1. Decrementer: 986
Thread Thread3. Incrementer: 5
// ...
Thread Thread1. Decrementer: 1
Thread Thread3. Incrementer: 997
Thread Thread1. Decrementer: 0
Thread Thread3. Incrementer: 998
Thread Thread1 Exiting.
Thread Thread3. Incrementer: 999
Thread Thread3 Exiting.
All my threads are done.
```

You see the first thread start and decrement from 1000 to 998. The second thread starts, and the two threads are interleaved for a while until the third thread starts. After a short while, however, Thread2 reports that it has been aborted, and then it reports that it is exiting. The two remaining threads continue until they are done. They then exit naturally, and the main thread, which was joined on all three, resumes to print its exit message.

Synchronization

At times, you might want to control access to a resource, such as an object's properties or methods, so that only one thread at a time can modify or use that resource. Your object is similar to the airplane restroom discussed earlier, and the various threads are like the people waiting in line. Synchronization is provided by a lock on the object, which prevents a second thread from barging in on your object until the first thread is finished with it.

In this section you examine three synchronization mechanisms provided by the CLR: the Interlock class, the C# lock statement, and the Monitor class. But first, you need to simulate a shared resource, such as a file or printer, with a simple integer variable: counter. Rather than opening the file or accessing the printer, you'll increment counter from each of two threads.

To start, declare the member variable and initialize it to 0:

```
int counter = 0;
```

Modify the Incrementer method to increment the counter member variable:

```
public void Incrementer( )
{
    try
    {
        while (counter < 1000)
        {
            int temp = counter;
            temp++; // increment

            // simulate some work in this method
            Thread.Sleep(1);

            // assign the Incremented value
            // to the counter variable
            // and display the results
            counter = temp;
            Console.WriteLine(
                "Thread {0}. Incrementer: {1}",
                Thread.CurrentThread.Name,
                counter);
        }
    }
}
```

The idea here is to simulate the work that might be done with a controlled resource. Just as we might open a file, manipulate its contents, and then close it, here we read the value of counter into a temporary variable, increment the temporary variable, sleep for one millisecond to simulate work, and then assign the incremented value back to counter.

The problem is that your first thread will read the value of counter (0) and assign that to a temporary variable. It will then increment the temporary variable. While it is doing its work, the second thread will read the value of counter (still 0) and assign that value to a temporary variable. The first thread finishes its work, then assigns the temporary value (1) back to counter and displays it. The second thread does the same. What is printed is 1,1. In the next go around, the same thing happens. Rather than having the two threads count 1,2,3,4, we see 1,1,2,2,3,3. Example 20-3 shows the complete source code and output for this example.

Example 20-3. Simulating a shared resource

```
namespace Programming_CSharp
{
   using System;
   using System.Threading;

   class Tester
   {
      private int counter = 0;

      static void Main()
      {
         // make an instance of this class
         Tester t = new Tester();

         // run outside static Main
         t.DoTest();
      }

      public void DoTest()
      {
         Thread t1 = new Thread( new ThreadStart(Incrementer) );
         t1.IsBackground=true;
         t1.Name = "ThreadOne";
         t1.Start();
         Console.WriteLine("Started thread {0}",
            t1.Name);

         Thread t2 = new Thread( new ThreadStart(Incrementer) );
         t2.IsBackground=true;
         t2.Name = "ThreadTwo";
         t2.Start();
         Console.WriteLine("Started thread {0}",
            t2.Name);
         t1.Join();
         t2.Join();

         // after all threads end, print a message
         Console.WriteLine("All my threads are done.");
      }

      // demo function, counts up to 1K
      public void Incrementer()
      {
         try
         {
            while (counter < 1000)
            {
               int temp = counter;
               temp++; // increment

               // simulate some work in this method
               Thread.Sleep(1);
```

Example 20-3. Simulating a shared resource (continued)

```
                    // assign the decremented value
                    // and display the results
                    counter = temp;
                    Console.WriteLine(
                        "Thread {0}. Incrementer: {1}",
                        Thread.CurrentThread.Name,
                        counter);
                }
            }
            catch (ThreadInterruptedException)
            {
                Console.WriteLine(
                    "Thread {0} interrupted! Cleaning up...",
                    Thread.CurrentThread.Name);
            }
            finally
            {
                Console.WriteLine(
                    "Thread {0} Exiting. ",
                    Thread.CurrentThread.Name);
            }
        }
    }
}
```

Output:
```
Started thread ThreadOne
Started thread ThreadTwo
Thread ThreadOne. Incrementer: 1
Thread ThreadOne. Incrementer: 2
Thread ThreadOne. Incrementer: 3
Thread ThreadTwo. Incrementer: 3
Thread ThreadTwo. Incrementer: 4
Thread ThreadOne. Incrementer: 4
Thread ThreadTwo. Incrementer: 5
Thread ThreadOne. Incrementer: 5
Thread ThreadTwo. Incrementer: 6
Thread ThreadOne. Incrementer: 6
```

Assume your two threads are accessing a database record rather than reading a member variable. For example, your code might be part of an inventory system for a book retailer. A customer asks if *Programming C#* is available. The first thread reads the value and finds that there is one book on hand. The customer wants to buy the book, so the thread proceeds to gather credit card information and validate the customer's address.

While this is happening, a second thread asks if this wonderful book is still available. The first thread has not yet updated the record, so one book still shows as available. The second thread begins the purchase process. Meanwhile, the first thread finishes and decrements the counter to zero. The second thread, blissfully unaware of the activity of the first, also sets the value back to zero. Unfortunately, you have now sold the same copy of the book twice.

As noted earlier, you need to synchronize access to the counter object (or to the database record, file, printer, etc.).

Using Interlocked

The CLR provides a number of synchronization mechanisms. These include the common synchronization tools such as critical sections (called *Locks* in .NET), as well as more sophisticated tools such as a Monitor class. Each is discussed later in this chapter.

Incrementing and decrementing a value is such a common programming pattern, and one which so often needs synchronization protection, that C# offers a special class, Interlocked, just for this purpose. Interlocked has two methods, Increment and Decrement, which not only increment or decrement a value, but also do so under synchronization control.

Modify the Incrementer method from Example 20-3 as follows:

```
public void Incrementer( )
{
    try
    {
        while (counter < 1000)
        {
            Interlocked.Increment(ref counter);

            // simulate some work in this method
            Thread.Sleep(1);

            // assign the decremented value
            // and display the results
            Console.WriteLine(
                "Thread {0}. Incrementer: {1}",
                Thread.CurrentThread.Name,
                counter);
        }
    }
}
```

The catch and finally blocks and the remainder of the program are unchanged from the previous example.

Interlocked.Increment( ) expects a single parameter: a reference to an int. Because int values are passed by value, use the ref keyword, as described in Chapter 4.

The Increment( ) method is overloaded and can take a reference to a long, rather than to an int, if that is more convenient.

Once this change is made, access to the counter member is synchronized, and the output is what we'd expect.

```
Output (excerpts):
Started thread ThreadOne
Started thread ThreadTwo
Thread ThreadOne. Incrementer: 1
Thread ThreadTwo. Incrementer: 2
Thread ThreadOne. Incrementer: 3
Thread ThreadTwo. Incrementer: 4
Thread ThreadOne. Incrementer: 5
Thread ThreadTwo. Incrementer: 6
Thread ThreadOne. Incrementer: 7
Thread ThreadTwo. Incrementer: 8
Thread ThreadOne. Incrementer: 9
Thread ThreadTwo. Incrementer: 10
Thread ThreadOne. Incrementer: 11
Thread ThreadTwo. Incrementer: 12
Thread ThreadOne. Incrementer: 13
Thread ThreadTwo. Incrementer: 14
Thread ThreadOne. Incrementer: 15
Thread ThreadTwo. Incrementer: 16
Thread ThreadOne. Incrementer: 17
Thread ThreadTwo. Incrementer: 18
Thread ThreadOne. Incrementer: 19
Thread ThreadTwo. Incrementer: 20
```

Using Locks

Although the Interlocked object is fine if you want to increment or decrement a value, there will be times when you want to control access to other objects as well. What is needed is a more general synchronization mechanism. This is provided by the .NET Lock object.

A lock marks a critical section of your code, providing synchronization to an object you designate while the lock is in effect. The syntax of using a Lock is to request a lock on an object and then to execute a statement or block of statements. The lock is removed at the end of the statement block.

C# provides direct support for locks through the lock keyword. Pass in a reference object and follow the keyword with a statement block:

```
lock(expression) statement-block
```

For example, you can modify Incrementer once again to use a lock statement, as follows:

```
public void Incrementer()
{
    try
    {
        while (counter < 1000)
        {
            lock (this)
            {
                int temp = counter;
                temp ++;
                Thread.Sleep(1);
                counter = temp;
            }

            // assign the decremented value
            // and display the results
            Console.WriteLine(
                "Thread {0}. Incrementer: {1}",
                Thread.CurrentThread.Name,
                counter);
        }
    }
}
```

The catch and finally blocks and the remainder of the program are unchanged from the previous example.

The output from this code is identical to that produced using Interlocked.

Using Monitors

The objects used so far will be sufficient for most needs. For the most sophisticated control over resources, you might want to use a *monitor*. A monitor lets you decide when to enter and exit the synchronization, and it lets you wait for another area of your code to become free.

A monitor acts as a smart lock on a resource. When you want to begin synchronization, call the Enter() method of the monitor, passing in the object you want to lock:

```
Monitor.Enter(this);
```

If the monitor is unavailable, the object protected by the monitor is in use. You can do other work while you wait for the monitor to become available and then try again. You can also explicitly choose to Wait(), suspending your thread until the moment the monitor is free. Wait() helps you control thread ordering.

For example, suppose you are downloading and printing an article from the Web. For efficiency, you'd like to print in a background thread, but you want to ensure that at least 10 pages have downloaded before you begin.

Your printing thread will wait until the get-file thread signals that enough of the file has been read. You don't want to Join the get-file thread because the file might be hundreds of pages. You don't want to wait until it has completely finished downloading, but you do want to ensure that at least 10 pages have been read before your print thread begins. The Wait( ) method is just the ticket.

To simulate this, rewrite Tester and add back the decrementer method. Your incrementer will count up to 10. The decrementer method will count down to zero. It turns out you don't want to start decrementing unless the value of counter is at least 5.

In decrementer, call Enter on the monitor. Then check the value of counter, and if it is less than 5, call Wait on the monitor:

```
if (counter < 5)
{
    Monitor.Wait(this);
}
```

This call to Wait( ) frees the monitor, but signals the CLR that you want the monitor back the next time it is free. Waiting threads will be notified of a chance to run again if the active thread calls Pulse( ):

```
Monitor.Pulse(this);
```

Pulse( ) signals the CLR that there has been a change in state that might free a thread that is waiting. The CLR will keep track of the fact that the earlier thread asked to wait, and threads will be guaranteed access in the order in which the waits were requested. ("Your wait is important to us and will be handled in the order received.")

When a thread is finished with the monitor, it can mark the end of its controlled area of code with a call to Exit( ):

```
Monitor.Exit(this);
```

Example 20-4 continues the simulation, providing synchronized access to a counter variable using a Monitor.

Example 20-4. Using a Monitor object

```
namespace Programming_CSharp
{
    using System;
    using System.Threading;

    class Tester
    {
        static void Main( )
        {
            // make an instance of this class
            Tester t = new Tester( );
```

Example 20-4. Using a Monitor object (continued)

```
        // run outside static Main
        t.DoTest( );
    }

    public void DoTest( )
    {
        // create an array of unnamed threads
        Thread[] myThreads =
            {
                new Thread( new ThreadStart(Decrementer) ),
                new Thread( new ThreadStart(Incrementer) )
            };

        // start each thread
        int ctr = 1;
        foreach (Thread myThread in myThreads)
        {
            myThread.IsBackground=true;
            myThread.Start( );
            myThread.Name = "Thread" + ctr.ToString( );
            ctr++;
            Console.WriteLine("Started thread {0}", myThread.Name);
            Thread.Sleep(50);
        }

        // wait for all threads to end before continuing
        foreach (Thread myThread in myThreads)
        {
            myThread.Join( );
        }

        // after all threads end, print a message
        Console.WriteLine("All my threads are done.");
    }

    void Decrementer( )
    {
        try
        {
            // synchronize this area of code
            Monitor.Enter(this);

            // if counter is not yet 10
            // then free the monitor to other waiting
            // threads, but wait in line for your turn
            if (counter < 10)
            {
                Console.WriteLine(
                    "[{0}] In Decrementer. Counter: {1}. Gotta Wait!",
                    Thread.CurrentThread.Name, counter);
                Monitor.Wait(this);
            }
```

Example 20-4. Using a Monitor object (continued)

```
        while (counter >0)
        {
            long temp = counter;
            temp--;
            Thread.Sleep(1);
            counter = temp;
            Console.WriteLine(
                "[{0}] In Decrementer. Counter: {1}. ",
                Thread.CurrentThread.Name, counter);


        }
    }
    finally
    {
        Monitor.Exit(this);
    }
}

void Incrementer( )
{
    try
    {
        Monitor.Enter(this);
        while (counter < 10)
        {
            long temp = counter;
            temp++;
            Thread.Sleep(1);
            counter = temp;
            Console.WriteLine(
                "[{0}] In Incrementer. Counter: {1}",
                Thread.CurrentThread.Name, counter);
        }

        // I'm done incrementing for now, let another
        // thread have the Monitor
        Monitor.Pulse(this);
    }
    finally
    {
        Console.WriteLine("[{0}] Exiting...",
            Thread.CurrentThread.Name);
        Monitor.Exit(this);
    }
}
    private long counter = 0;
    }
}
```

Output:
```
Started thread Thread1
[Thread1] In Decrementer. Counter: 0. Gotta Wait!
```

Example 20-4. Using a Monitor object (continued)

```
Started thread Thread2
[Thread2] In Incrementer. Counter: 1
[Thread2] In Incrementer. Counter: 2
[Thread2] In Incrementer. Counter: 3
[Thread2] In Incrementer. Counter: 4
[Thread2] In Incrementer. Counter: 5
[Thread2] In Incrementer. Counter: 6
[Thread2] In Incrementer. Counter: 7
[Thread2] In Incrementer. Counter: 8
[Thread2] In Incrementer. Counter: 9
[Thread2] In Incrementer. Counter: 10
[Thread2] Exiting...
[Thread1] In Decrementer. Counter: 9.
[Thread1] In Decrementer. Counter: 8.
[Thread1] In Decrementer. Counter: 7.
[Thread1] In Decrementer. Counter: 6.
[Thread1] In Decrementer. Counter: 5.
[Thread1] In Decrementer. Counter: 4.
[Thread1] In Decrementer. Counter: 3.
[Thread1] In Decrementer. Counter: 2.
[Thread1] In Decrementer. Counter: 1.
[Thread1] In Decrementer. Counter: 0.
All my threads are done.
```

In this example, decrementer is started first. In the output you see Thread1 (the decrementer) start up and then realize that it has to wait. You then see Thread2 start up. Only when Thread2 pulses does Thread1 begin its work.

Try some experiments with this code. First, comment out the call to Pulse( ). You'll find that Thread1 never resumes. Without Pulse( ) there is no signal to the waiting threads.

As a second experiment, rewrite Incrementer to pulse and exit the monitor after each increment:

```
void Incrementer( )
{
    try
    {
        while (counter < 10)
        {
         Monitor.Enter(this);
          long temp = counter;
           temp++;
           Thread.Sleep(1);
           counter = temp;
           Console.WriteLine(
               "[{0}] In Incrementer. Counter: {1}",
               Thread.CurrentThread.Name, counter);
           Monitor.Pulse(this);
           Monitor.Exit(this);
        }
```

Rewrite Decrementer as well, changing the if statement to a while statement and knocking down the value from 10 to 5:

```
//if (counter < 10)
while (counter < 5)
```

The net effect of these two changes is to cause Thread2, the Incrementer, to pulse the Decrementer after each increment. While the value is smaller than five, the Decrementer must continue to wait; once the value goes over five, the Decrementer runs to completion. When it is done, the Incrementer thread can run again. The output is shown here:

```
[Thread2] In Incrementer. Counter: 2
[Thread1] In Decrementer. Counter: 2. Gotta Wait!
[Thread2] In Incrementer. Counter: 3
[Thread1] In Decrementer. Counter: 3. Gotta Wait!
[Thread2] In Incrementer. Counter: 4
[Thread1] In Decrementer. Counter: 4. Gotta Wait!
[Thread2] In Incrementer. Counter: 5
[Thread1] In Decrementer. Counter: 4.
[Thread1] In Decrementer. Counter: 3.
[Thread1] In Decrementer. Counter: 2.
[Thread1] In Decrementer. Counter: 1.
[Thread1] In Decrementer. Counter: 0.
[Thread2] In Incrementer. Counter: 1
[Thread2] In Incrementer. Counter: 2
[Thread2] In Incrementer. Counter: 3
[Thread2] In Incrementer. Counter: 4
[Thread2] In Incrementer. Counter: 5
[Thread2] In Incrementer. Counter: 6
[Thread2] In Incrementer. Counter: 7
[Thread2] In Incrementer. Counter: 8
[Thread2] In Incrementer. Counter: 9
[Thread2] In Incrementer. Counter: 10
```

Race Conditions and Deadlocks

The .NET library provides sufficient thread support that you will rarely find yourself: creating your own threads and managing synchronization manually.

Thread synchronization can be tricky, especially in complex programs. If you do decide to create your own threads, you must confront and solve all the traditional problems of thread synchronization, such as race conditions and deadlock.

Race Conditions

A *race condition* exists when the success of your program depends on the uncontrolled order of completion of two independent threads.

Suppose, for example, that you have two threads—one is responsible for opening a file and the other is responsible for writing to the file. It is important that you control the second thread so that it's assured that the first thread has opened the file. If not, under some conditions the first thread will open the file, and the second thread will work fine; under other unpredictable conditions, the first thread won't finish opening the file before the second thread tries to write to it, and you'll throw an exception (or worse, your program will simply seize up and die). This is a race condition, and race conditions can be very difficult to debug.

You cannot leave these two threads to operate independently; you must ensure that Thread1 will have completed before Thread2 begins. To accomplish this, you might Join( ) Thread2 on Thread1. As an alternative, you can use a Monitor and Wait( ) for the appropriate conditions before resuming Thread2.

Deadlock

When you wait for a resource to become free, you are at risk of *deadlock*, also called a *deadly embrace*. In a deadlock, two or more threads are waiting for each other, and neither can become free.

Suppose you have two threads, ThreadA and ThreadB. ThreadA locks down an Employee object and then tries to get a lock on a row in the database. It turns out that ThreadB already has that row locked, so ThreadA waits.

Unfortunately, ThreadB can't update the row until it locks down the Employee object, which is already locked down by ThreadA. Neither thread can proceed, and neither thread will unlock its own resource. They are waiting for each other in a deadly embrace.

As described, the deadlock is fairly easy to spot—and to correct. In a program running many threads, deadlock can be very difficult to diagnose, let alone solve. One guideline is to get all the locks you need or to release all the locks you have. That is, as soon as ThreadA realizes that it can't lock the Row, it should release its lock on the Employee object. Similarly, when ThreadB can't lock the Employee, it should release the Row. A second important guideline is to lock as small a section of code as possible and to hold the lock as briefly as possible.

CHAPTER 21

Streams

For many applications, data is held in memory and accessed as if it were a three-dimensional solid; when you need to access a variable or an object, use its name—and, presto, it is available to you. When you want to move your data into or out of a file, across the network, or over the Internet, however, your data must be *streamed*. In a *stream*, packets of data flow one after the other, much like bubbles in a stream of water.

The endpoint of a stream is a backing store. The backing store provides a source for the stream, like a lake provides a source for a river. Typically, the backing store is a file, but it is also possible for the backing store to be a network or web connection.

Files and directories are abstracted by classes in the .NET Framework. These classes provide methods and properties for creating, naming, manipulating, and deleting files and directories on your disk.

The .NET Framework provides both buffered and unbuffered streams, as well as classes for asynchronous I/O. With asynchronous I/O you can instruct the .NET classes to read your file; while they are busy getting the bits off the disk your program can be working on other tasks. The asynchronous I/O tasks notify you when their work is done. The asynchronous classes are sufficiently powerful and robust that you might be able to avoid creating threads explicitly (see Chapter 20).

Streaming into and out of files is no different than streaming across the network, and the second part of this chapter will describe streaming using both TCP/IP and web protocols.

To create a stream of data, your object must be *serialized*, or written to the stream as a series of bits. You have already encountered serialization in Chapter 19. The .NET Frameworks provide extensive support for serialization, and the final part of this chapter walk you through the details of taking control of the serialization of your object.

Files and Directories

Before looking at how you can get data into and out of files, let's start by examining the support provided for file and directory manipulation.

The classes you need are in the System.IO namespace. These include the File class, which represents a file on disk, and the Directory class, which represents a directory (known in Windows as a *folder*).

Working with Directories

The Directory class exposes static methods for creating, moving, and exploring directories. All the methods of the Directory class are static, and therefore you can call them all without having an instance of the class.

The DirectoryInfo class is a similar class but one which has nothing but instance members (i.e., no static members at all). DirectoryInfo derives from FileSystemInfo, which in turn derives from MarshalByRefObject. The FileSystemInfo class has a number of properties and methods that provide information about a file or directory.

Table 21-1 lists the principal methods of the Directory class, and Table 21-2 lists the principal methods of the DirectoryInfo class, including important properties and methods inherited from FileSystemInfo.

Table 21-1. Principal methods of the Directory class

Method	Use
CreateDirectory( )	Creates all directories and subdirectories specified by its path parameter.
Delete( )	Deletes the directory and deletes all its contents.
Exists( )	Returns a Boolean value, which is true if the path provided as a parameter leads to an existing directory.
GetCreationTime( ) SetCreationTime( )	Returns and sets the creation date and time of the directory.
GetCurrentDirectory( ) SetCurrentDirectory( )	Returns and sets the current directory.
GetDirectories( )	Gets an array of subdirectories.
GetDirectoryRoot( )	Returns the root of the specified path.
GetFiles( )	Returns an array of strings with the filenames for the files in the specified directory.
GetLastAccessTime( ) SetLastAccessTime( )	Returns and sets the last time the specified directory was accessed.
GetLastWriteTime( ) SetLastWriteTime( )	Returns and sets the last time the specified directory was written to.
GetLogicalDrives( )	Returns the names of all the logical drives in the form <drive1>:\.
GetParent( )	Returns the parent directory for the specified path.
Move( )	Moves a directory and its contents to a specified path.

Table 21-2. Principal methods and properties of the DirectoryInfo class

Method or property	Use
Attributes	Inherits from `FileSystemInfo`; gets or sets the attributes of the current file.
CreationTime	Inherits from `FileSystemInfo`; gets or sets the creation time of the current file.
Exists	Public property Boolean value, which is `true` if the directory exists.
Extension	Public property inherited from `FileSystemInfo`; i.e., the file extension.
FullName	Public property inherited from `FileSystemInfo`; i.e., the full path of the file or directory.
LastAccessTime	Public property inherited from `FileSystemInfo`; gets or sets the last access time.
LastWriteTime	Public property inherited from `FileSystemInfo`; gets or sets the time when the current file or directory was last written to.
Name	Public property name of this instance of `DirectoryInfo`.
Parent	Public property parent directory of the specified directory.
Root	Public property root portion of the path.
Create()	Public method that creates a directory.
CreateSubdirectory()	Public method that creates a subdirectory on the specified path.
Delete()	Public method that deletes a `DirectoryInfo` and its contents from the path.
GetDirectories()	Public method that returns a `DirectoryInfo` array with subdirectories.
GetFiles()	Public method that returns a list of files in the directory.
GetFileSystemInfos()	Public method that retrieves an array of `FileSystemInfo` objects.
MoveTo()	Public method that moves a `DirectoryInfo` and its contents to a new path.
Refresh()	Public method inherited from `FileSystemInfo`; refreshes the state of the object.

Creating a DirectoryInfo Object

To explore a directory hierarchy, you need to instantiate a `DirectoryInfo` object. The `DirectoryInfo` class provides methods for getting not just the names of contained files and directories, but also `FileInfo` and `DirectoryInfo` objects, allowing you to dive into the hierarchical structure, extracting subdirectories and exploring these recursively.

Instantiate a `DirectoryInfo` object with the name of the directory you want to explore:

```
string path = Environment.GetEnvironmentVariable("SystemRoot");
DirectoryInfo dir = new DirectoryInfo(path);
```

Remember that the @ sign before a string creates a verbatim string literal in which it is not necessary to escape characters such as the backslash. This is covered in Chapter 10.

You can ask that DirectoryInfo object for information about itself, including its name, full path, attributes, the time it was last accessed, and so forth. To explore the subdirectory hierarchy, ask the current directory for its list of subdirectories.

```
DirectoryInfo[] directories = dir.GetDirectories();
```

This returns an array of DirectoryInfo objects, each of which represents a directory. You can then recurse into the same method, passing in each DirectoryInfo object in turn:

```
foreach (DirectoryInfo newDir in directories)
{
    dirCounter++;
    ExploreDirectory(newDir);
}
```

The dirCounter static int member variable keeps track of how many subdirectories have been found altogether. To make the display more interesting, add a second static int member variable indentLevel that will be incremented each time you recurse into a subdirectory, and decremented when you pop out. This will allow you to display the subdirectories indented under the parent directories. The complete listing is shown in Example 21-1.

Example 21-1. Recursing through subdirectories

```
namespace Programming_CSharp
{
    using System;
    using System.IO;

    class Tester
    {
        public static void Main()
        {
            Tester t = new Tester();

            // choose the initial subdirectory
            string theDirectory =
                Environment.GetEnvironmentVariable("SystemRoot");

            // call the method to explore the directory,
            // displaying its access date and all
            // subdirectories
            DirectoryInfo dir = new DirectoryInfo(theDirectory);

            t.ExploreDirectory(dir);

            // completed. print the statistics
            Console.WriteLine(
                "\n\n{0} directories found.\n",
                dirCounter);
        }
```

Example 21-1. Recursing through subdirectories (continued)

```csharp
        // Set it running with a directoryInfo object
        // for each directory it finds, it will call
        // itself recursively
        private void ExploreDirectory(DirectoryInfo dir)
        {
            indentLevel++;  // push a directory level

            // create indentation for subdirectories
            for (int i = 0; i < indentLevel; i++)
                Console.Write("  "); // two spaces per level

            // print the directory and the time last accessed
            Console.WriteLine("[{0}] {1} [{2}]\n",
                indentLevel, dir.Name, dir.LastAccessTime);

            // get all the directories in the current directory
            // and call this method recursively on each
            DirectoryInfo[] directories = dir.GetDirectories();
            foreach (DirectoryInfo newDir in directories)
            {
                dirCounter++;  // increment the counter
                ExploreDirectory(newDir);
            }
            indentLevel--; // pop a directory level
        }

        // static member variables to keep track of totals
        // and indentation level
        static int dirCounter = 1;
        static int indentLevel  = -1; // so first push = 0
    }
}
```

Output (excerpt):

```
    [2] logiscan [5/1/2001 3:06:41 PM]

    [2] miitwain [5/1/2001 3:06:41 PM]

  [1] Web [5/1/2001 3:06:41 PM]

    [2] printers [5/1/2001 3:06:41 PM]

      [3] images [5/1/2001 3:06:41 PM]

    [2] Wallpaper [5/1/2001 3:06:41 PM]

363 directories found.
```

The program begins by identifying a directory (*%SystemRoot%*, usually *C:\WinNT* or *C:\Windows*) and creating a DirectoryInfo object for that directory. It then calls

ExploreDirectory, passing in that DirectoryInfo object. ExploreDirectory displays information about the directory, and then retrieves all the subdirectories.

The list of all the subdirectories of the current directory is obtained by calling GetDirectories. This returns an array of DirectoryInfo objects. ExploreDirectory is the recursive method; each DirectoryInfo object is passed into ExploreDirectory in turn. The effect is to push recursively into each subdirectory, and then pop back out to explore sister directories until all the subdirectories of *%SystemRoot%* are displayed. When ExploreDirectory finally returns, the calling method prints a summary.

Working with Files

The DirectoryInfo object can also return a collection of all the files in each subdirectory found. The GetFiles() method returns an array of FileInfo objects, each of which describes a file in that directory. The FileInfo and File objects relate to one another, much as DirectoryInfo and Directory do. Like the methods of Directory, all the File methods are static; like DirectoryInfo, all the methods of FileInfo are instance methods.

Table 21-3 lists the principal methods of the File class, and Table 21-4 lists the important members of the FileInfo class.

Table 21-3. Principal public static methods of the File class

Method	Use
AppendText()	Creates a StreamWriter that appends text to the specified file.
Copy()	Copies an existing file to a new file.
Create()	Creates a file in the specified path.
CreateText()	Creates a StreamWriter that writes a new text file to the specified file.
Delete()	Deletes the specified file.
Exists()	Returns true if the specified file exists.
GetAttributes() SetAttributes()	Gets and sets the FileAttributes of the specified file.
GetCreationTime() SetCreationtime()	Returns and sets the creation date and time of the file.
GetLastAccessTime() SetLastAccessTime()	Returns and sets the last time the specified file was accessed.
GetLastWriteTime() SetLastWriteTime()	Returns and sets the last time the specified file was written to.
Move()	Moves a file to a new location; can be used to rename a file.
OpenRead()	Public static method that opens a FileStream on the file.
OpenWrite()	Creates a read/write Stream on the specified path.

Table 21-4. Methods and properties of the FileInfo class

Method or property	Use
Attributes( )	Inherits from FileSystemInfo; gets or sets the attributes of the current file.
CreationTime	Inherits from FileSystemInfo; gets or sets the creation time of the current file.
Directory	Public property that gets an instance of the parent directory.
Exists	Public property Boolean value, which is true if the directory exists.
Extension	Public property inherited from FileSystemInfo; i.e., the file extension.
FullName	Public property inherited from FileSystemInfo; i.e., the full path of the file or directory.
LastAccessTime	Public property inherited from FileSystemInfo; gets or sets the last access time.
LastWriteTime	Public property inherited from FileSystemInfo; gets or sets the time when the current file or directory was last written to.
Length	Public property that gets the size of the current file.
Name	Public property Name of this DirectoryInfo instance.
AppendText( )	Public method that creates a StreamWriter that appends text to a file.
CopyTo( )	Public method that copies an existing file to a new file.
Create( )	Public method that creates a new file.
Delete( )	Public method that permanently deletes a file.
MoveTo( )	Public method to move a file to a new location; can be used to rename a file.
Open( )	Public method that opens a file with various read/write and sharing privileges.
OpenRead( )	Public method that creates a read-only FileStream.
OpenText( )	Public method that creates a StreamReader that reads from an existing text file.
OpenWrite( )	Public method that creates a write-only FileStream.

Example 21-2 modifies Example 21-1, adding code to get a FileInfo object for each file in each subdirectory. That object is used to display the name of the file, along with its length and the date and time it was last accessed.

Example 21-2. Exploring files and subdirectories

```
namespace Programming_CSharp
{
   using System;
   using System.IO;

   class Tester
   {
      public static void Main( )
      {
         Tester t = new Tester( );
```

Example 21-2. Exploring files and subdirectories (continued)

```
        // choose the initial subdirectory
        string theDirectory =
            Environment.GetEnvironmentVariable("SystemRoot");

        // call the method to explore the directory,
        // displaying its access date and all
        // subdirectories
        DirectoryInfo dir = new DirectoryInfo(theDirectory);

        t.ExploreDirectory(dir);

        // completed. print the statistics
        Console.WriteLine(
            "\n\n{0} files in {1}  directories found.\n",
            fileCounter,dirCounter);
    }

    // Set it running with a directoryInfo object
    // for each directory it finds, it will call
    // itself recursively
    private void ExploreDirectory(DirectoryInfo dir)
    {
        indentLevel++;  // push a directory level

        // create indentation for subdirectories
        for (int i = 0; i < indentLevel; i++)
            Console.Write("  "); // two spaces per level

        // print the directory and the time last accessed
        Console.WriteLine("[{0}] {1} [{2}]\n",
            indentLevel, dir.Name, dir.LastAccessTime);

        // get all the files in the directory and
        // print their name, last access time, and size
        FileInfo[] filesInDir = dir.GetFiles();
        foreach (FileInfo file in filesInDir)
        {
            // indent once extra to put files
            // under their directory
            for (int i = 0; i < indentLevel+1; i++)
                Console.Write("  "); // two spaces per level

            Console.WriteLine("{0} [{1}] Size: {2} bytes",
                file.Name,
                file.LastWriteTime,
                file.Length);
            fileCounter++;
        }

        // get all the directories in the current directory
        // and call this method recursively on each
        DirectoryInfo[] directories = dir.GetDirectories();
```

Example 21-2. Exploring files and subdirectories (continued)

```
        foreach (DirectoryInfo newDir in directories)
        {
            dirCounter++;  // increment the counter
            ExploreDirectory(newDir);
        }
        indentLevel--; // pop a directory level
    }

    // static member variables to keep track of totals
    // and indentation level
    static int dirCounter = 1;
    static int indentLevel  = -1; // so first push = 0
    static int fileCounter = 0;
    }
}
```

Output (excerpt):
```
[0] WinNT [5/1/2001 3:34:01 PM]

  Active Setup Log.txt [4/20/2001 10:42:22 AM] Size: 10620 bytes
  actsetup.log [4/20/2001 12:05:02 PM] Size: 8717 bytes
  Blue Lace 16.bmp [12/6/1999 4:00:00 PM] Size: 1272 bytes
    [2] Wallpaper [5/1/2001 3:14:32 PM]
      Boiling Point.jpg [4/20/2001 8:30:24 AM] Size: 28871 bytes
      Chateau.jpg [4/20/2001 8:30:24 AM] Size: 70605 bytes
      Windows 2000.jpg [4/20/2001 8:30:24 AM] Size: 129831 bytes

8590 files in 363  directories found.
```

The example is initialized with the name of the *%SystemRoot%* directory. It prints information about all the files in that directory and then recursively explores all the subdirectories and all their subdirectories (your output might differ). This can take quite a while to run because the *%SystemRoot%* directory tree is rather large (363 subdirectories on my machine, as shown in the output).

Modifying Files

As you can see from Tables 21-3 and 21-4, it is possible to use the FileInfo class to create, copy, rename, and delete files. The next example will create a new subdirectory, copy files in, rename some, delete others, and then delete the entire directory.

 To set up these examples, create a \test directory and copy the media directory from WinNT or Windows into the test directory. Do not work on files in the system root directly; when working with system files you want to be extraordinarily careful.

The first step is to create a DirectoryInfo object for the test directory:

```
string theDirectory = @"c:\test\media";
DirectoryInfo dir = new DirectoryInfo(theDirectory);
```

Next, create a subdirectory within the test directory by calling `CreateSubDirectory` on the `DirectoryInfo` object. You get back a new `DirectoryInfo` object, representing the newly created subdirectory:

```
string newDirectory = "newTest";
DirectoryInfo newSubDir =
    dir.CreateSubdirectory(newDirectory);
```

You can now iterate over the test and copy files to the newly created subdirectory:

```
FileInfo[] filesInDir = dir.GetFiles();
foreach (FileInfo file in filesInDir)
{
    string fullName = newSubDir.FullName +
        "\\" + file.Name;
    file.CopyTo(fullName);
    Console.WriteLine("{0} copied to newTest",
        file.FullName);
}
```

Notice the syntax of the `CopyTo` method. This is a method of the `FileInfo` object. Pass in the full path of the new file, including its full name and extension.

Once you've copied the files, you can get a list of the files in the new subdirectory and work with them directly:

```
filesInDir = newSubDir.GetFiles();
foreach (FileInfo file in filesInDir)
{
```

Create a simple integer variable named counter and use it to rename every other file:

```
if (counter++ %2 == 0)
{
    file.MoveTo(fullName + ".bak");
    Console.WriteLine("{0} renamed to {1}",
        fullName,file.FullName);
}
```

You rename a file by "moving" it to the same directory but with a new name. You can, of course, move a file to a new directory with its original name, or you can move and rename at the same time.

Rename every other file, and delete the ones you don't rename:

```
file.Delete();
Console.WriteLine("{0} deleted.",
    fullName);
```

Once you're done manipulating the files, you can clean up by deleting the entire subdirectory:

```
newSubDir.Delete(true);
```

The Boolean parameter determines whether this is a recursive delete. If you pass in false, and if this directory has subdirectories with files in it, it throws an exception.

Example 21-3 lists the source code for the complete program. Be careful when running this; when it is done, the subdirectory is gone. To see the renaming and deletions, either put a breakpoint on the last line or remove the last line.

Example 21-3. Creating a subdirectory and manipulating files

```
namespace Programming_CSharp
{
    using System;
    using System.IO;

    class Tester
    {
        public static void Main( )
        {
            // make an instance and run it
            Tester t = new Tester( );
            string theDirectory = @"c:\test\media";
            DirectoryInfo dir = new DirectoryInfo(theDirectory);
            t.ExploreDirectory(dir);
        }

        // Set it running with a directory name
        private void ExploreDirectory(DirectoryInfo dir)
        {

            // make a new subdirectory
            string newDirectory = "newTest";
            DirectoryInfo newSubDir =
                dir.CreateSubdirectory(newDirectory);

            // get all the files in the directory and
            // copy them to the new directory
            FileInfo[] filesInDir = dir.GetFiles( );
            foreach (FileInfo file in filesInDir)
            {
                string fullName = newSubDir.FullName +
                    "\\" + file.Name;
                file.CopyTo(fullName);
                Console.WriteLine("{0} copied to newTest",
                    file.FullName);
            }

            // get a collection of the files copied in
            filesInDir = newSubDir.GetFiles( );

            // delete some and rename others
            int counter = 0;
            foreach (FileInfo file in filesInDir)
            {
                string fullName = file.FullName;

                if (counter++ %2 == 0)
```

Example 21-3. Creating a subdirectory and manipulating files (continued)

```
                {
                    file.MoveTo(fullName + ".bak");
                    Console.WriteLine("{0} renamed to {1}",
                        fullName,file.FullName);
                }
                else
                {
                    file.Delete( );
                    Console.WriteLine("{0} deleted.",
                        fullName);
                }
            }

            newSubDir.Delete(true); // delete the subdirectory
        }
    }
}
```

Output (excerpts):
```
c:\test\media\Bach's Brandenburg Concerto No. 3.RMI
        copied to newTest
c:\test\media\Beethoven's 5th Symphony.RMI copied to newTest
c:\test\media\Beethoven's Fur Elise.RMI copied to newTest
c:\test\media\canyon.mid copied to newTest
c:\test\media\newTest\Bach's Brandenburg Concerto
        No. 3.RMI renamed to
c:\test\media\newTest\Bach's Brandenburg Concerto
        No. 3.RMI.bak
c:\test\media\newTest\Beethoven's 5th Symphony.RMI deleted.
c:\test\media\newTest\Beethoven's Fur Elise.RMI renamed to
c:\test\media\newTest\Beethoven's Fur Elise.RMI.bak
c:\test\media\newTest\canyon.mid deleted.
```

Reading and Writing Data

Reading and writing data is accomplished with the Stream class. Remember streams? This is a chapter about streams.[*]

Stream supports synchronous and asynchronous reads and writes. The .NET Framework provides a number of classes derived from Stream, including FileStream, MemoryStream, and NetworkStream. In addition, there is a BufferedStream class, which provides buffered I/O and which can be used in conjunction with any of the other stream classes. The principal classes involved with I/O are summarized in Table 21-5.

---

[*] With a tip of the hat to Arlo Guthrie.

Table 21-5. Principle I/O classes of the .NET Framework

Class	Use
Stream	Abstract class that supports reading and writing bytes.
BinaryReader/BinaryWriter	Read and write encoded strings and primitive datatypes to and from streams.
File, FileInfo, Directory, DirectoryInfo	Provide implementations for the abstract FileSystemInfo classes, including creating, moving, renaming, and deleting files and directories.
FileStream	For reading to and from File objects; supports random access to files. Opens files synchronously by default; supports asynchronous file access.
TextReader, TextWriter, StringReader, StringWriter	TextReader and TextWriter are abstract classes designed for Unicode character I/O. StringReader and StringWriter write to and from strings, allowing your input and output to be either a stream or a string.
BufferedStream	A stream that adds buffering to another stream such as a Network-Stream. Note that FileStream has buffering built in. Buffered-Streams can improve performance of the stream to which they are attached.
MemoryStream	A nonbuffered stream whose encapsulated data is directly accessible in memory. A MemoryStream has no backing store, and is most useful as a temporary buffer.
NetworkStream	A stream over a network connection.

Binary Files

This section starts by using the basic Stream class to perform a binary read of a file. The term *binary read* is used to distinguish from a *text read*. If you don't know for certain that a file is just text, it is safest to treat it as a stream of bytes, known as a *binary* file.

The Stream class is chock-a-block with methods, but the most important are Read( ), Write( ), BeginRead( ), BeginWrite( ), and Flush( ). All of these are covered in the next few sections.

To perform a binary read, begin by creating a pair of Stream objects, one for reading and one for writing.

```
Stream inputStream = File.OpenRead(
    @"C:\test\source\test1.cs");

Stream outputStream = File.OpenWrite(
    @"C:\test\source\test1.bak");
```

To open the files to read and write, use the static OpenRead( ) and OpenWrite( ) methods of the File class. The static overload of these methods takes the path for the file as an argument, as shown previously.

Binary reads work by reading into a buffer. A buffer is just an array of bytes that will hold the data read by the Read( ) method.

Pass in the buffer, the offset in the buffer at which to begin storing the data read in, and the number of bytes to read. InputStream.Read reads bytes from the backing store into the buffer and returns the total number of bytes read.

It continues reading until no more bytes remain.

```
while ( (bytesRead =
    inputStream.Read(buffer,0,SIZE_BUFF)) > 0 )
{
    outputStream.Write(buffer,0,bytesRead);
}
```

Each buffer-full of bytes is written to the output file. The arguments to Write are the buffer from which to read, the offset into that buffer at which to start reading, and the number of bytes to write. Notice that you write the same number of bytes as you just read.

Example 21-4 provides the complete listing.

Example 21-4. Implementing a binary read and write to a file

```
namespace Programming_CSharp
{
    using System;
    using System.IO;

    class Tester
    {
        const int SizeBuff = 1024;

        public static void Main( )
        {
            // make an instance and run it
            Tester t = new Tester( );
            t.Run( );
        }

        // Set it running with a directory name
        private void Run( )
        {
            // the file to read from
            Stream inputStream = File.OpenRead(
                @"C:\test\source\test1.cs");

            // the file to write to
            Stream outputStream = File.OpenWrite(
                @"C:\test\source\test1.bak");

            // create a buffer to hold the bytes
            byte[] buffer = new Byte[SizeBuff];
            int bytesRead;

            // while the read method returns bytes
            // keep writing them to the output stream
```

Example 21-4. Implementing a binary read and write to a file (continued)

```
        while ( (bytesRead =
            inputStream.Read(buffer,0,SizeBuff)) > 0 )
        {
            outputStream.Write(buffer,0,bytesRead);
        }

        // tidy up before exiting
        inputStream.Close( );
        outputStream.Close( );
    }
  }
}
```

The result of running this program is that a copy of the input file (*test1.cs*) is made in the same directory and named *test1.bak*.

Buffered Streams

In the previous example, you created a buffer to read into. When you called Read, a buffer-full was read from disk. It might be, however, that the operating system can be much more efficient if it reads a larger (or smaller) number of bytes at once.

A *buffered stream* object allows the operating system to create its own internal buffer, and read bytes to and from the backing store in whatever increments it thinks is most efficient. It will still fill your buffer in the increments you dictate, but your buffer is filled from the in-memory buffer, not from the backing store. The net effect is that the input and output are more efficient and thus faster.

A BufferedStream object is composed around an existing Stream object that you already have created. To use a BufferedStream, start by creating a normal stream class as you did in Example 21-4:

```
Stream inputStream = File.OpenRead(
    @"C:\test\source\folder3.cs");

Stream outputStream = File.OpenWrite(
    @"C:\test\source\folder3.bak");
```

Once you have the normal stream, pass that stream object to the buffered stream's constructor:

```
BufferedStream bufferedInput =
    new BufferedStream(inputStream);

BufferedStream bufferedOutput =
    new BufferedStream(outputStream);
```

You can then use the BufferedStream as a normal stream, calling Read( ) and Write( ) just as you did before. The operating system handles the buffering:

```
while ( (bytesRead =
    bufferedInput.Read(buffer,0,SIZE_BUFF)) > 0 )
```

```
        {
            bufferedOutput.Write(buffer,0,bytesRead);
        }
```

The only change is that you must remember to flush the buffer when you want to ensure that the data is written out to the file:

```
        bufferedOutput.Flush();
```

This essentially tells the operating system to take the entire contents of the in-memory buffer and write it out to disk.

Example 21-5 provides the complete listing.

Example 21-5. Implementing buffered I/O

```
namespace Programming_CSharp
{
    using System;
    using System.IO;

    class Tester
    {
        const int SizeBuff = 1024;

        public static void Main()
        {
            // make an instance and run it
            Tester t = new Tester();
            t.Run();
        }

        // Set it running with a directory name
        private void Run()
        {
            // create binary streams
            Stream inputStream = File.OpenRead(
                @"C:\test\source\folder3.cs");

            Stream outputStream = File.OpenWrite(
                @"C:\test\source\folder3.bak");

            // add buffered streams on top of the
            // binary streams
            BufferedStream bufferedInput =
                new BufferedStream(inputStream);

            BufferedStream bufferedOutput =
                new BufferedStream(outputStream);
            byte[] buffer = new Byte[SizeBuff];
            int bytesRead;

            while ( (bytesRead =
```

Example 21-5. Implementing buffered I/O (continued)

```
        bufferedInput.Read(buffer,0,SizeBuff)) > 0 )
    {
        bufferedOutput.Write(buffer,0,bytesRead);
    }

    bufferedOutput.Flush( );
    bufferedInput.Close( );
    bufferedOutput.Close( );

    }
  }
}
```

With larger files, this example should run more quickly than Example 21-4 did.

Working with Text Files

If you know that the file you are reading (and writing) contains nothing but text, you might want to use the StreamReader and StreamWriter classes. These classes are designed to make manipulation of text easier. For example, they support the ReadLine( ) and WriteLine( ) methods that read and write a line of text at a time. You've used WriteLine( ) with the Console object.

To create a StreamReader instance, start by creating a FileInfo object and then call the OpenText( ) method on that object:

```
FileInfotheSourceFile =
    new FileInfo (@"C:\test\source\test1.cs");

StreamReader stream = theSourceFile.OpenText( );
```

OpenText( ) returns a StreamReader for the file. With the StreamReader in hand, you can now read the file, line by line:

```
do
{
    text = stream.ReadLine( );
} while (text != null);
```

ReadLine( ) reads a line at a time until it reaches the end of the file. The StreamReader will return null at the end of the file.

To create the StreamWriter class, call the StreamWriter constructor, passing in the full name of the file you want to write to:

```
StreamWriter writer = new
StreamWriter(@"C:\test\source\folder3.bak",false);
```

The second parameter is the Boolean argument append. If the file already exists, true will cause the new data to be appended to the end of the file, and false will cause the file to be overwritten. In this case, pass in false, overwriting the file if it exists.

You can now create a loop to write out the contents of each line of the old file into the new file, and while you're at it, to print the line to the console as well:

```
do
{
    text = reader.ReadLine( );
    writer.WriteLine(text);
    Console.WriteLine(text);
} while (text != null);
```

Example 21-6 provides the complete source code.

Example 21-6. Reading and writing to a text file

```
namespace Programming_CSharp
{
    using System;
    using System.IO;

    class Tester
    {
        public static void Main( )
        {
            // make an instance and run it
            Tester t = new Tester( );
            t.Run( );
        }

        // Set it running with a directory name
        private void Run( )
        {
            // open a file
            FileInfo theSourceFile = new FileInfo(
                @"C:\test\source\test.cs");

            // create a text reader for that file
            StreamReader reader = theSourceFile.OpenText( );

            // create a text writer to the new file
            StreamWriter writer = new StreamWriter(
                @"C:\test\source\test.bak",false);

            // create a text variable to hold each line
            string text;

            // walk the file and read every line
            // writing both to the console
            // and to the file
            do
            {
                text = reader.ReadLine( );
                writer.WriteLine(text);
                Console.WriteLine(text);
            } while (text != null);
```

Example 21-6. Reading and writing to a text file (continued)

```
        // tidy up
        reader.Close( );
        writer.Close( );
      }
    }
}
```

When this program is run, the contents of the original file are written both to the screen and to the new file. Notice the syntax for writing to the console:

```
    Console.WriteLine(text);
```

This syntax is nearly identical to that used to write to the file:

```
    writer.WriteLine(text);
```

The key difference is that the WriteLine( ) method of Console is static, while the WriteLine( ) method of StreamWriter, which is inherited from TextWriter, is an instance method, and thus must be called on an object rather than on the class itself.

Asynchronous I/O

All the programs you've looked at so far perform *synchronous I/O*, meaning that while your program is reading or writing, all other activity is stopped. It can take a long time (relatively speaking) to read data to or from the backing store, especially if the backing store is a slow disk or (horrors!) a slow network.

With large files, or when reading or writing across the network, you'll want *asynchronous I/O*, which allows you to begin a read and then turn your attention to other matters while the Common Language Runtime (CLR) fulfills your request. The .NET Framework provides asynchronous I/O through the BeginRead( ) and BeginWrite( ) methods of Stream.

The sequence is to call BeginRead( ) on your file and then to go on to other, unrelated work while the read progresses in another thread. When the read completes, you are notified via a callback method. You can then process the data that was read, kick off another read, and then go back to your other work.

In addition to the three parameters you've used in the binary read (the buffer, the offset, and how many bytes to read), BeginRead( ) asks for a *delegate* and a *state object*.

The delegate is an optional callback method, which, if provided, is called when the data is read. The state object is also optional. In this example, pass in null for the state object. The state of the object is kept in the member variables of the test class.

You are free to put any object you like in the state parameter, and you can retrieve it when you are called back. Typically (as you might guess from the name), you stash away state values that you'll need on retrieval. The state parameter can be used by the developer to hold the state of the call (paused, pending, running, etc.).

In this example, create the buffer and the Stream object as private member variables of the class:

```
public class AsynchIOTester
{
    private Stream inputStream;
    private byte[] buffer;
    const int BufferSize = 256;
```

In addition, create your delegate as a private member of the class:

```
private AsyncCallback myCallBack; // delegated method
```

The delegate is declared to be of type AsyncCallback, which is what the BeginRead( ) method of Stream expects.

An AsyncCallBack delegate is declared in the System namespace as follows:

```
public delegate void AsyncCallback (IAsyncResult ar);
```

Thus this delegate can be associated with any method that returns void, and that takes an IAsyncResult interface as a parameter. The CLR will pass in the IAsyncResult interface object at runtime when the method is called. You only have to declare the method:

```
void OnCompletedRead(IAsyncResult asyncResult)
```

and then hook up the delegate in the constructor:

```
AsynchIOTester( )
{
    //...
    myCallBack = new AsyncCallback(this.OnCompletedRead);
}
```

Here's how it works, step by step. In Main( ), create an instance of the class and tell it to run:

```
public static void Main( )
{
    AsynchIOTester theApp = new AsynchIOTester( );
    theApp.Run( );
}
```

The call to new invokes the constructor. In the constructor, open a file and get a Stream object back. Then allocate space in the buffer and hook up the callback mechanism:

```
AsynchIOTester( )
{
    inputStream = File.OpenRead(@"C:\test\source\AskTim.txt");
    buffer = new byte[BufferSize];
    myCallBack = new AsyncCallback(this.OnCompletedRead);
}
```

This example needs a large text file. I've copied a column written by Tim O'Reilly ("Ask Tim"), from *http://www.oreilly.com*, into a text file named *AskTim.txt*. I placed that in a subdirectory I created named *test\ source* on my C: drive. You can use any text file in any subdirectory.

In the Run( ) method, call BeginRead( ), which will cause an asynchronous read of the file:

```
inputStream.BeginRead(
    buffer,                 // where to put the results
    0,                      // offset
    buffer.Length,          // BufferSize
    myCallBack,             // call back delegate
    null);                  // local state object
```

Then go on to do other work. In this case, simulate useful work by counting up to 500,000, displaying your progress every 1,000:

```
for (long i = 0; i < 500000; i++)
{
    if (i%1000 == 0)
    {
        Console.WriteLine("i: {0}", i);
    }
}
```

When the read completes, the CLR will call your callback method:

```
void OnCompletedRead(IAsyncResult asyncResult)
{
```

The first thing to do when notified that the read has completed is find out how many bytes were actually read. Do so by calling the EndRead( ) method of the Stream object, passing in the IAsyncResult interface object passed in by the CLR:

```
int bytesRead = inputStream.EndRead(asyncResult);
```

EndRead( ) returns the number of bytes read. If the number is greater than zero, you'll convert the buffer into a string and write it to the console, and then call BeginRead( ) again, for another asynchronous read:

```
if (bytesRead > 0)
{
    String s =
    Encoding.ASCII.GetString (buffer, 0, bytesRead);
    Console.WriteLine(s);
    inputStream.BeginRead(
    buffer, 0, buffer.Length,
    myCallBack, null);
}
```

The effect is that you can do other work while the reads are taking place, but you can handle the read data (in this case, by outputting it to the console) each time a buffer-full is ready. Example 21-7 provides the complete program.

Example 21-7. Implementing asynchronous I/O

```
namespace Programming_CSharp
{
    using System;
    using System.IO;
    using System.Threading;
    using System.Text;

    public class AsynchIOTester
    {
        private Stream inputStream;

        // delegated method
        private AsyncCallback myCallBack;

        // buffer to hold the read data
        private byte[] buffer;

        // the size of the buffer
        const int BufferSize = 256;

        // constructor
        AsynchIOTester()
        {
            // open the input stream
            inputStream =
                File.OpenRead(
                @"C:\test\source\AskTim.txt");

            // allocate a buffer
            buffer = new byte[BufferSize];

            // assign the call back
            myCallBack =
                new AsyncCallback(this.OnCompletedRead);
        }

        public static void Main()
        {
            // create an instance of AsynchIOTester
            // which invokes the constructor
            AsynchIOTester theApp =
                new AsynchIOTester();

            // call the instance method
            theApp.Run();
        }
```

Example 21-7. Implementing asynchronous I/O (continued)

```
      void Run( )
      {
         inputStream.BeginRead(
            buffer,             // holds the results
            0,                  // offset
            buffer.Length,      // (BufferSize)
            myCallBack,         // call back delegate
            null);              // local state object

         // do some work while data is read
         for (long i = 0; i < 500000; i++)
         {
            if (i%1000 == 0)
            {
               Console.WriteLine("i: {0}", i);
            }
         }

      }

      // call back method
      void OnCompletedRead(IAsyncResult asyncResult)
      {
         int bytesRead =
            inputStream.EndRead(asyncResult);

         // if we got bytes, make them a string
         // and display them, then start up again.
         // Otherwise, we're done.
         if (bytesRead > 0)
         {
            String s =
               Encoding.ASCII.GetString(buffer, 0, bytesRead);
            Console.WriteLine(s);
            inputStream.BeginRead(
               buffer, 0, buffer.Length, myCallBack, null);
         }
      }
   }
}
```

Output (excerpt)
```
i: 47000
i: 48000
i: 49000
Date: January 2001
From: Dave Heisler
To: Ask Tim
Subject: Questions About O'Reilly
Dear Tim,
I've been a programmer for about ten years. I had heard of
O'Reilly books,then...
Dave,
```

Example 21-7. Implementing asynchronous I/O (continued)

```
You might be amazed at how many requests for help with
school projects I get;
i: 50000
i: 51000
i: 52000
```

The output reveals that the program is working on the two threads concurrently. The reads are done in the background while the other thread is counting and printing out every thousand. As the reads complete, they are printed to the console, and then you go back to counting. (I've shortened the listings to illustrate the output.)

In a real-world application, you might process user requests or compute values while the asynchronous I/O is busy retrieving or storing to a file or a database.

Network I/O

Writing to a remote object on the Internet is not very different from writing to a file on your local machine. You might want to do this if your program needs to store its data to a file on a machine on your network, or if you were creating a program that displayed information on a monitor connected to another computer on your network.

Network I/O is based on the use of streams created with sockets. Sockets are very useful for client/server applications, peer to peer (P2P), and when making remote procedure calls.

A socket is an object that represents an endpoint for communication between processes communicating across a network. Sockets can work with various protocols, including UDP and TCP/IP. In this section, we create a TCP/IP connection between a server and a client. TCP/IP is a connection-based protocol for network communication. Connection-based means that with TCP/IP, once a connection is made, the two processes can talk with one another as if they were connected by a direct phone line.

 Although TCP/IP is designed to talk across a network, you can simulate network communication by running the two processes on the same machine.

It is possible for more than one application on a given computer to be talking to various clients all at the same time (e.g., you might be running a web server, an FTP server, and a program that provides calculation support). Therefore, each application must have a unique ID so that the client can indicate which application it is looking for. That ID is known as a *port*. Think of the IP address as a phone number and the port as an extension.

The server instantiates a socket and tells that socket to listen for connections on a specific port. The constructor for the socket has one parameter: an int representing the port on which that socket should listen.

 Client applications connect to a specific IP address. For example, Yahoo's IP address is 216.115.108.245. Clients must also connect to a specific port. All web browsers connect to port 80 by default. Port numbers range from 0 to 65,535 (i.e., 2^{16}); however, some numbers are reserved.

Ports are divided into the following ranges:

- 0–1023: well-known ports
- 1024–49151: registered ports
- 49152–65535: dynamic and/or private ports

For a list of all the well-known and registered ports, look at *http://www.iana.org/assignments/port-numbers*.

If you are running your program on a network with a firewall, talk to your network administrator about which ports are closed.

Once the socket is created, call Start( ) on it, which tells the socket to begin accepting network connections. When the server is ready to start responding to calls from clients, call AcceptSocket( ). The thread in which you've called AcceptSocket( ) blocks (waiting sadly by the phone, wringing its virtual hands, hoping for a call).

You can imagine creating the world's simplest socket. It waits patiently for a client to call. When it gets a call, it interacts with that client to the exclusion of all other clients. The next few clients to call will connect, but they will automatically be put on hold. While they are listening to the music and being told their call is important and will be handled in the order received, they will block in their own threads. Once the backlog (hold) queue fills, subsequent callers will get the equivalent of a busy signal. They must hang up and wait for our simple socket to finish with its current client. This model works fine for servers that take only one or two requests a week, but it doesn't scale well for real-world applications. Most servers need to handle thousands, even tens of thousands of connections a minute!

To handle a high volume of connections, applications use asynchronous I/O to accept a call and return a new socket with the connection to the client. The original socket then returns to listening, waiting for the next client. This way your application can handle many calls; each time a call is accepted a new socket is created.

The client is unaware of this sleight of hand in which a new socket is created. As far as the client is concerned, he has connected with the socket at the IP address and port he requested. Note that the new socket establishes a persistent connection with the client. This is quite different from UDP, which uses a connectionless protocol. With TCP/IP, once the connection is made, the client and server know how to talk with each other without having to re-address each packet.

The Socket class itself is fairly simple. It knows how to be an end point, but it doesn't know how to accept a call and create a TCP/IP connection. This is actually done by the TcpListener class. The TcpListener class builds upon the Socket class to provide high-level TCP/IP services.

Creating a Network Streaming Server

To create a network server for TCP/IP streaming, start by creating a TcpListener object to listen to the TCP/IP port you've chosen. I've arbitrarily chosen port 65000 from the available port IDs:

```
TcpListener tcpListener = new TcpListener(65000);
```

Once the TcpListener object is constructed, you can ask it to start listening:

```
tcpListener.Start();
```

Now wait for a client to request a connection:

```
Socket socketForClient = tcpListener.AcceptSocket();
```

The AcceptSocket method of the TcpListener object returns a Socket object which represents a *Berkeley socket interface* and which is bound to a specific end point. AcceptSocket( ) is a synchronous method that will not return until it receives a connection request.

 Because the model is widely accepted by computer vendors, *Berkeley sockets* simplify the task of porting existing socket-based source code from both Windows and Unix environments.

If the socket is connected, you're ready to send the file to the client:

```
if (socketForClient.Connected)
{
```

Create a NetworkStream class, passing the socket into the constructor:

```
NetworkStream networkStream = new NetworkStream(socketForClient);
```

Then create a StreamWriter object much as you did before, except this time not on a file, but rather on the NetworkStream you just created:

```
System.IO.StreamWriter streamWriter = new System.IO.StreamWriter(networkStream);
```

When you write to this stream, the stream is sent over the network to the client. Example 21-8 shows the entire server. (I've stripped this server down to its bare essentials. With a production server, you almost certainly would run the request processing code in a thread, and you'd want to enclose the logic in try blocks to handle network problems.)

Example 21-8. Implementing a network streaming server

```
using System;
using System.Net.Sockets;

public class NetworkIOServer
{

    public static void Main( )
    {
        NetworkIOServer app =
            new NetworkIOServer( );
        app.Run( );
    }

    private void Run( )
    {
        // create a new TcpListener and start it up
        // listening on port 65000
        TcpListener tcpListener = new TcpListener(65000);
        tcpListener.Start( );

        // keep listening until you send the file
        for (;;)
        {
            // if a client connects, accept the connection
            // and return a new socket named socketForClient
            // while tcpListener keeps listening
            Socket socketForClient =
                tcpListener.AcceptSocket( );
            if (socketForClient.Connected)
            {
                Console.WriteLine("Client connected");

                // call the helper method to send the file
                SendFileToClient(socketForClient);

                Console.WriteLine(
                    "Disconnecting from client...");

                // clean up and go home
                socketForClient.Close( );
                Console.WriteLine("Exiting...");
                break;
            }
        }
    }

    // helper method to send the file
    private void SendFileToClient(
        Socket socketForClient )
    {
```

Example 21-8. Implementing a network streaming server (continued)

```
        // create a network stream and a stream writer
        // on that network stream
        NetworkStream networkStream =
            new NetworkStream(socketForClient);
        System.IO.StreamWriter streamWriter =
            new System.IO.StreamWriter(networkStream);

        // create a stream reader for the file
        System.IO.StreamReader streamReader =
            new System.IO.StreamReader(
                @"C:\test\source\myTest.txt");

        string theString;

        // iterate through the file, sending it
        // line-by-line to the client
        do
        {
            theString = streamReader.ReadLine( );

            if( theString != null )
            {
                Console.WriteLine(
                    "Sending {0}", theString);
                streamWriter.WriteLine(theString);
                streamWriter.Flush( );
            }
        }
        while( theString != null );

        // tidy up
        streamReader.Close( );
        networkStream.Close( );
        streamWriter.Close( );
    }
}
```

Creating a Streaming Network Client

The client instantiates a TcpClient class, which represents a TCP/IP client connection to a host:

```
TcpClient socketForServer;
socketForServer = new TcpClient("localHost", 65000);
```

With this TcpClient, you can create a NetworkStream, and on that stream you can create a StreamReader:

```
NetworkStream networkStream = socketForServer.GetStream( );
System.IO.StreamReader streamReader =
    new System.IO.StreamReader(networkStream);
```

Now read the stream as long as there is data on it, outputting the results to the console:

```
do
{
    outputString = streamReader.ReadLine( );

    if( outputString != null )
    {
        Console.WriteLine(outputString);
    }
}
while( outputString != null );
```

Example 21-9 is the complete client.

Example 21-9. Implementing a network streaming client

```
using System;
using System.Net.Sockets;

public class Client
{

    static public void Main( string[] Args )
    {

        // create a TcpClient to talk to the server
        TcpClient socketForServer;

        try
        {
            socketForServer =
                new TcpClient("localHost", 65000);
        }
        catch
        {
            Console.WriteLine(
                "Failed to connect to server at {0}:65000",
                    "localhost");
            return;
        }

        // create the Network Stream and the Stream Reader object
        NetworkStream networkStream =
                socketForServer.GetStream( );
        System.IO.StreamReader streamReader =
            new System.IO.StreamReader(networkStream);

        try
        {
            string outputString;
```

Example 21-9. Implementing a network streaming client (continued)

```
        // read the data from the host and display it
        do
        {
            outputString = streamReader.ReadLine( );

            if( outputString != null )
            {
                Console.WriteLine(outputString);
            }
        }
        while( outputString != null );
    }
    catch
    {
        Console.WriteLine(
            "Exception reading from Server");
    }

    // tidy up
    networkStream.Close( );
    }
}
```

To test this, I created a simple test file named *myText.txt*:

```
This is line one
This is line two
This is line three
This is line four
```

Here is the output from the server and the client:

Output (Server):
```
Client connected
Sending This is line one
Sending This is line two
Sending This is line three
Sending This is line four
Disconnecting from client...
Exiting...
```

Output (Client):
```
This is line one
This is line two
This is line three
This is line four
Press any key to continue
```

 If you are testing this on a single machine, run the client and server in separate command windows or individual instances of the development environment. You will want to start the server first or the client will fail, saying it could not connect.

Handling Multiple Connections

As mentioned earlier, this example does not scale well. Each client demands the entire attention of the server. A server is needed that can accept the connection and then pass the connection to overlapped I/O, providing the same asynchronous solution that you used earlier for reading from a file.

To manage this, create a new server, AsynchNetworkServer, which will nest within it a new class, ClientHandler. When your AsynchNetworkServer receives a client connection, it will instantiate a ClientHandler and pass the socket to that ClientHandler instance.

The ClientHandler constructor will create a copy of the socket and a buffer and will open a new NetworkStream on that socket. It will then use overlapped I/O to asynchronously read and write to that socket. For this demonstration, it will simply echo whatever text the client sends back to the client and also to the console.

To create the asynchronous I/O, ClientHandler will define two delegate methods, OnReadComplete( ) and OnWriteComplete( ), that will manage the overlapped I/O of the strings sent by the client.

The body of the Run( ) method for the server is very similar to what you saw in Example 21-8. First, create a listener and then call Start( ). Then create a forever loop and call AcceptSocket( ). Once the socket is connected, rather than handling the connection, create a new ClientHandler and call StartRead( ) on that object.

The complete source for the server is shown in Example 21-10.

Example 21-10. Implementing an asynchronous network streaming server

```
using System;
using System.Net.Sockets;


public class AsynchNetworkServer
{

   class ClientHandler
   {
      public ClientHandler( Socket socketForClient )
      {
         socket = socketForClient;
         buffer = new byte[256];
         networkStream =
            new NetworkStream(socketForClient);

         callbackRead =
            new AsyncCallback(this.OnReadComplete);

         callbackWrite =
            new AsyncCallback(this.OnWriteComplete);
```

```
    }

    // begin reading the string from the client
    public void StartRead( )
    {
        networkStream.BeginRead(
            buffer, 0, buffer.Length,
            callbackRead, null);
    }

    // when called back by the read, display the string
    // and echo it back to the client
    private void OnReadComplete( IAsyncResult ar )
    {
        int bytesRead = networkStream.EndRead(ar);

        if( bytesRead > 0 )
        {
            string s =
                System.Text.Encoding.ASCII.GetString(
                    buffer, 0, bytesRead);
            Console.Write(
                "Received {0} bytes from client: {1}",
                    bytesRead, s );
            networkStream.BeginWrite(
                buffer, 0, bytesRead, callbackWrite, null);
        }
        else
        {
            Console.WriteLine( "Read connection dropped");
            networkStream.Close( );
            socket.Close( );
            networkStream = null;
            socket = null;
        }
    }

    // after writing the string, print a message and resume reading
    private void OnWriteComplete( IAsyncResult ar )
    {
        networkStream.EndWrite(ar);
        Console.WriteLine( "Write complete");
        networkStream.BeginRead(
            buffer, 0, buffer.Length,
            callbackRead, null);
    }

    private byte[]         buffer;
    private Socket         socket;
    private NetworkStream  networkStream;
    private AsyncCallback  callbackRead;
    private AsyncCallback  callbackWrite;
```

```
    }

    public static void Main( )
    {
        AsynchNetworkServer app =
            new AsynchNetworkServer( );
        app.Run( );
    }

    private void Run( )
    {
        // create a new TcpListener and start it up
        // listening on port 65000
        TcpListener tcpListener = new TcpListener(65000);
        tcpListener.Start( );

        // keep listening until you send the file
        for (;;)
        {
            // if a client connects, accept the connection
            // and return a new socket named socketForClient
            // while tcpListener keeps listening
            Socket socketForClient =
                tcpListener.AcceptSocket( );
            if (socketForClient.Connected)
            {
                Console.WriteLine("Client connected");
                ClientHandler handler =
                    new ClientHandler(socketForClient);
                handler.StartRead( );
            }
        }
    }
}
```

The server starts up and listens to port 65000. If a client connects, the server will instantiate a ClientHandler that will manage the I/O with the client while the server listens for the next client.

> In this example, write the string received from the client to the console in OnReadComplete( ) and OnWriteComplete( ). Writing to the console can block your thread until the write completes. In a production program, you do not want to take any blocking action in these methods because you are using a pooled thread. If you block in OnReadComplete( ) or OnWriteComplete( ), you may cause more threads to be added to the thread pool, which is inefficient and will harm performance and scalability.

The client code is very simple. The client creates a `tcpSocket` for the port on which the server will listen (65000) and creates a `NetworkStream` object for that socket. It then writes a message to that stream and flushes the buffer. The client creates a `StreamReader` to read on that stream and writes whatever it receives to the console. The complete source for the client is shown in Example 21-11.

Example 21-11. Implementing a client for asynchronous network I/O

```csharp
using System;
using System.Net.Sockets;
using System.Threading;
using System.Runtime.Serialization.Formatters.Binary;

public class AsynchNetworkClient
{

    static public int Main( )
    {

        AsynchNetworkClient client =
            new AsynchNetworkClient( );
        return client.Run( );
    }

    AsynchNetworkClient( )
    {
        string serverName = "localhost";
        Console.WriteLine("Connecting to {0}", serverName);
        TcpClient tcpSocket = new TcpClient(serverName, 65000);
        streamToServer = tcpSocket.GetStream( );
    }

    private int Run( )
    {
        string message = "Hello Programming C#";
        Console.WriteLine(
            "Sending {0} to server.", message);

        // create a streamWriter and use it to
        // write a string to the server
        System.IO.StreamWriter writer =
            new System.IO.StreamWriter(streamToServer);
        writer.WriteLine(message);
        writer.Flush( );

        // Read response
        System.IO.StreamReader reader =
            new System.IO.StreamReader(streamToServer);
        string strResponse = reader.ReadLine( );
        Console.WriteLine("Received: {0}", strResponse);
        streamToServer.Close( );
        return 0;
```

Example 21-11. Implementing a client for asynchronous network I/O (continued)

```
    }

    private NetworkStream    streamToServer;
}
```

Server Output:
```
Client connected
Received 22 bytes from client: Hello Programming C#
Write complete
Read connection dropped
```

Client Output:
```
Connecting to localhost
Sending Hello Programming C# to server.
Received: Hello Programming C#
```

In this example, the network server does not block while it is handling client connections, but rather it delegates the management of those connections to instances of ClientHandler. Clients should not experience a delay waiting for the server to handle their connections.

Aysnchronous Network File Streaming

You can now combine the skills learned for asynchronous file reads with asynchronous network streaming to produce a program that serves a file to a client on demand.

Your server will begin with an asynchronous read on the socket, waiting to get a filename from the client. Once you have the filename, you can kick off an asynchronous read of that file on the server. As each buffer-full of the file becomes available, you can begin an asynchronous write back to the client. When the asynchronous write to the client finishes, you can kick off another read of the file; in this way you ping-pong back and forth, filling the buffer from the file and writing the buffer out to the client. The client need do nothing but read the stream from the server. In the next example the client will write the contents of the file to the console, but you could easily begin an asynchronous write to a new file on the client, thereby creating a network-based file copy program.

The structure of the server is not unlike that shown in Example 21-10. Once again you will create a ClientHandler class, but this time add an AsyncCallBack named myFileCallBack, which you initialize in the constructor along with the callbacks for the network read and write.

```
    myFileCallBack =
        new AsyncCallback(this.OnFileCompletedRead);

    callbackRead =
```

```
      new AsyncCallback(this.OnReadComplete);

  callbackWrite =
      new AsyncCallback(this.OnWriteComplete);
```

The Run( ) function of the outer class, now named AsynchNetworkFileServer, is unchanged. Once again you create and start the TcpListener class as well as create a forever loop in which you call AcceptSocket( ). If you have a socket, instantiate the ClientHandler and call StartRead( ). As in the previous example, StartRead( ) kicks off a BeginRead( ), passing in the buffer and the delegate to OnReadComplete.

When the read from the network stream completes, your delegated method OnReadComplete( ) is called and it retrieves the filename from the buffer. If text is returned, OnReadComplete( ) retrieves a string from the buffer using the static System. Text.Encoding.ASCII.GetString( ) method:

```
if( bytesRead > 0 )
{
    string fileName =
        System.Text.Encoding.ASCII.GetString(
        buffer, 0, bytesRead);
```

You now have a filename; with that you can open a stream to the file and use the exact same asynchronous file read used in Example 21-7.

```
inputStream =
    File.OpenRead(fileName);

inputStream.BeginRead(
    buffer,             // holds the results
    0,                  // offset
    buffer.Length,      // Buffer Size
    myFileCallBack,     // call back delegate
    null);              // local state object
```

This read of the file has its own callback that will be invoked when the input stream has read a buffer-full from the file on the server disk drive.

 As noted earlier, you normally would not want to take any action in an overlapped I/O method that might block the thread for any appreciable time. The call to open the file and begin reading it would normally be pushed off to a helper thread, instead of doing this work in OnReadComplete( ). It has been simplified for this example to avoid distracting from the issues at hand.

When the buffer is full, OnFileCompletedRead( ) is called, which checks to see if any bytes were read from the file. If so, it begins an asynchronous write to the network:

```
if (bytesRead > 0)
{
    // write it out to the client
    networkStream.BeginWrite(
        buffer, 0, bytesRead, callbackWrite, null);
}
```

If `OnFileCompletedRead` was called and no bytes were read, this signifies that the entire file has been sent. The server reacts by closing the `NetworkStream` and socket, thus letting the client know that the transaction is complete:

```
networkStream.Close();
socket.Close();
networkStream = null;
socket = null;
```

When the network write completes, the `OnWriteComplete()` method is called, and this kicks off another read from the file:

```
private void OnWriteComplete( IAsyncResult ar )
{
    networkStream.EndWrite(ar);
    Console.WriteLine( "Write complete");

    inputStream.BeginRead(
        buffer,               // holds the results
        0,                    // offset
        buffer.Length,        // (BufferSize)
        myFileCallBack,        // call back delegate
        null);                // local state object

}
```

The cycle begins again with another read of the file, and the cycle continues until the file has been completely read and transmitted to the client. The client code simply writes a filename to the network stream to kick off the file read:

```
string message = @"C:\test\source\AskTim.txt";
System.IO.StreamWriter writer =
    new System.IO.StreamWriter(streamToServer);
writer.Write(message);
writer.Flush();
```

The client then begins a loop, reading from the network stream until no bytes are sent by the server. When the server is done, the network stream is closed. Start by initializing a Boolean value to `false` and creating a buffer to hold the bytes sent by the server:

```
bool fQuit = false;
while (!fQuit)
{
    char[] buffer = new char[BufferSize];
```

You are now ready to create a new `StreamReader` from the `NetworkStream` member variable `streamToServer`:

```
System.IO.StreamReader reader =
    new System.IO.StreamReader(streamToServer);
```

The call to `Read()` takes three parameters: the buffer, the offset at which to begin reading, and the size of the buffer:

```
int bytesRead = reader.Read(buffer,0, BufferSize);
```

Check to see if the Read( ) returned any bytes; if not you are done and you can set the Boolean value fQuit to true, causing the loop to terminate:

```
if (bytesRead == 0)
    fQuit = true;
```

If you did receive bytes, you can write them to the console, or write them to a file, or do whatever it is you will do with the values sent from the server:

```
        else
        {
            string theString = new String(buffer);
            Console.WriteLine(theString);
        }
    }
}
```

Once you break out of the loop, close the NetworkStream.

```
        streamToServer.Close( );
```

The complete annotated source for the server is shown in Example 21-12, with the client following in Example 21-13.

Example 21-12. Implementing an asynchronous network file server

```
using System;
using System.Net.Sockets;
using System.Text;
using System.IO;

// get a file name from the client
// open the file and send the
// contents from the server to the client
public class AsynchNetworkFileServer
{

    class ClientHandler
    {
        // constructor
        public ClientHandler(
            Socket socketForClient )
        {
            // initialize member variable
            socket = socketForClient;

            // initialize buffer to hold
            // contents of file
            buffer = new byte[256];

            // create the network stream
            networkStream =
                new NetworkStream(socketForClient);

            // set the file callback for reading
            // the file
```

```
        myFileCallBack =
            new AsyncCallback(this.OnFileCompletedRead);

        // set the callback for reading from the
        // network stream
        callbackRead =
            new AsyncCallback(this.OnReadComplete);

        // set the callback for writing to the
        // network stream
        callbackWrite =
            new AsyncCallback(this.OnWriteComplete);
    }

    // begin reading the string from the client
    public void StartRead( )
    {
        // read from the network
        // get a filename
        networkStream.BeginRead(
            buffer, 0, buffer.Length,
            callbackRead, null);
    }

    // when called back by the read, display the string
    // and echo it back to the client
    private void OnReadComplete( IAsyncResult ar )
    {
        int bytesRead = networkStream.EndRead(ar);

        // if you got a string
        if( bytesRead > 0 )
        {
            // turn the string to a file name
            string fileName =
                System.Text.Encoding.ASCII.GetString(
                buffer, 0, bytesRead);

            // update the console
            Console.Write(
                "Opening file {0}", fileName);

            // open the file input stream
            inputStream =
                File.OpenRead(fileName);

            // begin reading the file
            inputStream.BeginRead(
                buffer,             // holds the results
                0,                  // offset
                buffer.Length,      // BufferSize
                myFileCallBack,     // call back delegate
```

Example 21-12. Implementing an asynchronous network file server (continued)

```
                null);              // local state object

        }
        else
        {
            Console.WriteLine( "Read connection dropped");
            networkStream.Close( );
            socket.Close( );
            networkStream = null;
            socket = null;
        }
    }

    // when you have a buffer-full of the file
    void OnFileCompletedRead(IAsyncResult asyncResult)
    {
        int bytesRead =
            inputStream.EndRead(asyncResult);

        // if you read some file
        if (bytesRead > 0)
        {
            // write it out to the client
            networkStream.BeginWrite(
                buffer, 0, bytesRead, callbackWrite, null);
        }
        else
        {
            Console.WriteLine("Finished.");
            networkStream.Close( );
            socket.Close( );
            networkStream = null;
            socket = null;
        }
    }

    // after writing the string, get more of the file
    private void OnWriteComplete( IAsyncResult ar )
    {
        networkStream.EndWrite(ar);
        Console.WriteLine( "Write complete");

        // begin reading more of the file
        inputStream.BeginRead(
            buffer,            // holds the results
            0,                 // offset
            buffer.Length,     // (BufferSize)
            myFileCallBack,     // call back delegate
            null);             // local state object

    }
```

```
        private const int      BufferSize = 256;
        private byte[]         buffer;
        private Socket         socket;
        private NetworkStream  networkStream;
        private Stream         inputStream;
        private AsyncCallback  callbackRead;
        private AsyncCallback  callbackWrite;
        private AsyncCallback  myFileCallBack;


    }



    public static void Main( )
    {
        AsynchNetworkFileServer app =
            new AsynchNetworkFileServer( );
        app.Run( );
    }

    private void Run( )
    {
        // create a new TcpListener and start it up
        // listening on port 65000
        TcpListener tcpListener = new TcpListener(65000);
        tcpListener.Start( );

        // keep listening until you send the file
        for (;;)
        {
            // if a client connects, accept the connection
            // and return a new socket named socketForClient
            // while tcpListener keeps listening
            Socket socketForClient =
                tcpListener.AcceptSocket( );
            if (socketForClient.Connected)
            {
                Console.WriteLine("Client connected");
                ClientHandler handler =
                    new ClientHandler(socketForClient);
                handler.StartRead( );
            }
        }
    }
}
```

Example 21-13. Implementing a client for an asynchronous network file server

```
using System;
using System.Net.Sockets;
using System.Threading;
```

Example 21-13. Implementing a client for an asynchronous network file server (continued)

```
using System.Text;

public class AsynchNetworkClient
{

    static public int Main( )
    {

        AsynchNetworkClient client =
            new AsynchNetworkClient( );
        return client.Run( );
    }

    AsynchNetworkClient( )
    {
        string serverName = "localhost";
        Console.WriteLine("Connecting to {0}", serverName);
        TcpClient tcpSocket = new TcpClient(serverName, 65000);
        streamToServer = tcpSocket.GetStream( );
    }

    private int Run( )
    {
        string message = @"C:\test\source\AskTim.txt";
        Console.Write(
            "Sending {0} to server.", message);

        // create a streamWriter and use it to
        // write a string to the server
        System.IO.StreamWriter writer =
            new System.IO.StreamWriter(streamToServer);
        writer.Write(message);
        writer.Flush( );

        bool fQuit = false;

        // while there is data coming
        // from the server, keep reading
        while (!fQuit)
        {
            // buffer to hold the response
            char[] buffer = new char[BufferSize];

            // Read response
            System.IO.StreamReader reader =
                new System.IO.StreamReader(streamToServer);

            // see how many bytes are
            // retrieved to the buffer
            int bytesRead =
                reader.Read(buffer,0,BufferSize);
            if (bytesRead == 0)  // none? quite
```

Example 21-13. Implementing a client for an asynchronous network file server (continued)

```
            fQuit = true;
        else                    // got some?
        {
            // display it as a string
            string theString = new String(buffer);
            Console.WriteLine(theString);
        }
    }
    streamToServer.Close( ); // tidy up
    return 0;

    }

    private const int BufferSize = 256;
    private NetworkStream    streamToServer;
}
```

By combining the asynchronous file read with the asynchronous network read, you have created a scalable application that can handle requests from a number of clients.

Web Streams

Rather than reading from a stream provided by a custom server, you can just as easily read from any web page on the Internet.

A WebRequest is an object that requests a Uniform Resource Identifier (URI) such as the URL for a web page. You can use a WebRequest object to create a WebResponse object that will encapsulate the object pointed to by the URI. That is, you can call GetResponse( ) on your WebRequest object to get the actual object (e.g., a web page) pointed to by the URI. What is returned is encapsulated in a WebResponse object. You can then ask that WebResponse object for a Stream object by calling GetResponseStream( ). GetResponseStream( ) returns a stream that encapsulates the contents of the web object (e.g., a stream with the web page).

The next example retrieves the contents of a web page as a stream. To get a web page, you'll want to use HttpWebRequest. HttpWebRequest derives from WebRequest and provides additional support for interacting with the HTTP protocol.

To create the HttpWebRequest, cast the WebRequest returned from the static Create( ) method of the WebRequestFactory:

```
HttpWebRequest webRequest =
    (HttpWebRequest) WebRequest.Create
    ("http://www.libertyassociates.com/book_edit.htm");
```

Create( ) is a static method of WebRequest. When you pass in a URI, an instance of HTTPWebRequest is created.

The method is overloaded on the type of the parameter. It returns different derived types depending on what is passed in. For example, if you pass in a URI, an object of type HttpWebRequest is created. The return type, however, is WebRequest, and so you must cast the returned value to HttpWebRequest.

Creating the HTTPWebRequest establishes a connection to a page on my web site. What you get back from the host is encapsulated in an HttpWebResponse object, which is an HTTP protocol–specific subclass of the more general WebResponse class:

```
HttpWebResponse webResponse =
    (HttpWebResponse) webRequest.GetResponse( );
```

You can now open a StreamReader on that page by calling the GetResponseStream( ) method of the WebResponse object:

```
StreamReader streamReader = new StreamReader(
    webResponse.GetResponseStream( ), Encoding.ASCII);
```

You can read from that stream exactly as you read from the network stream. Example 21-14 shows the complete listing.

Example 21-14. Reading a web page as an HTML stream

```
using System;
using System.Net;
using System.Net.Sockets;
using System.IO;
using System.Text;

public class Client
{
    static public void Main( string[] Args )
    {

        // create a webRequest for a particular page
        HttpWebRequest webRequest =
            (HttpWebRequest) WebRequest.Create
            ("http://www.libertyassociates.com/book_edit.htm");

        // ask the web request for a webResponse encapsulating
        // that page
        HttpWebResponse webResponse =
            (HttpWebResponse) webRequest.GetResponse( );

        // get the streamReader from the response
        StreamReader streamReader = new StreamReader(
            webResponse.GetResponseStream( ), Encoding.ASCII);

        try
        {
```

Example 21-14. Reading a web page as an HTML stream (continued)

```
        string outputString;
        outputString = streamReader.ReadToEnd( );
        Console.WriteLine(outputString);
    }
    catch
    {
        Console.WriteLine("Exception reading from web page");
    }
    streamReader.Close( );

    }
}
```

Output (excerpt):
```
<!DOCTYPE HTML PUBLIC "-//IETF//DTD HTML//EN">
<html>

<head>
<title>Books &amp; Resources</title>
</head>

<body bgcolor="#ffffff" vlink="#808080"
alink="#800000" topmargin="0" leftmargin
="0">
<table border="0" cellpadding="0" cellspacing="0" width="454" bgcolor="#ffffff">

  <tr>
&quot;More
        than just about any other writer, Jesse Liberty
        is brilliant at communicating what it's really
        like to work on a programming project.&quot;
        </font></b><font face="times new roman, times,
        serif" size="3"><b>
  </b> Barnes &amp; Noble</font></i><font size="3"><br>
```

The output shows that what is sent through the stream is the HTML of the page you requested. You might use this capability for *screen scraping*; reading a page from a site into a buffer and then extracting the information you need.

 All examples of screen scraping in this book assume that you are reading a site for which you have copyright permission.

Serialization

When an object is streamed to disk, its various member data must be *serialized*—that is, written out to the stream as a series of bytes. The object will also be serialized when stored in a database or when marshaled across a context, app domain, process, or machine boundary.

The CLR provides support for serializing an *object-graph*—an object and all the member data of that object. As noted in Chapter 19, by default, types are not serialized. To serialize an object, you must explicitly mark it with the [Serializable] attribute.

In either case, the CLR will do the work of serializing your object for you. Because the CLR knows how to serialize all the primitive types, if your object consists of nothing but primitive types (all your member data consists of integers, longs, strings, etc.), you're all set. If your object consists of other user-defined types (classes), you must ensure that these types are also serializable. The CLR will try to serialize each object contained by your object (and all their contained objects as well), but these objects themselves must either be primitive types or they must be serializable.

This was also evident in Chapter 19 when you marshaled a Shape object that contained a Point object as member data. The Point object in turn consisted of primitive data. In order to serialize (and thus marshal) the Shape object, its constituent member, the Point object, also had to be marked as serializable.

When an object is marshaled, either by value or by reference, it must be serialized. The difference is only whether a copy is made or a proxy is provided to the client. Objects marked with the [Serializable] attribute are marshaled by value; those that derive from MarshalByRefObject are marshaled by reference, but both are serialized. See Chapter 19 for more information.

Using a Formatter

When data is serialized, it will eventually be read; either by the same program or by a different program running on another machine. In any case, the code reading the data will expect that data to be in a particular format. Most of the time in a .NET application, the expected format will either be native binary format or Simple Object Access Protocol (SOAP).

SOAP is a simple, lightweight XML-based protocol for exchanging information across the Web. SOAP is highly modular and very extensible. It also leverages existing Internet technologies, such as HTTP and SMTP.

When data is serialized, the format of the serialization is determined by the *formatter* you apply. In Chapter 19, you used formatters with channels when communicating with a remote object. Formatter classes implement the interface IFormatter; you are also free to create your own formatter, though very few programmers will ever need or want to! The CLR provides both a SoapFormatter for Internet serialization and a BinaryFormatter that is useful for fast local storage.

You can instantiate these objects with their default constructors:

```
BinaryFormatter binaryFormatter =
    New BinaryFormatter();
```

Once you have an instance of a formatter, you can invoke its Serialize() method, passing in a stream and an object to serialize. You'll see how this is done in the next example.

Working with Serialization

To see serialization at work, you need a sample class that you can serialize and then deserialize. You can start by creating a class named SumOf. SumOf has three member variables:

```
private int startNumber = 1;
private int endNumber;
private int[] theSums;
```

The member array theSums represents the value of the sums of all the numbers from startNumber through endNumber. Thus, if startNumber is 1 and endNumber is 10, the array will have the values:

```
1,3,6,10,15,21,28,36,45,55
```

Each value is the sum of the previous value plus the next in the series. Thus if the series is 1,2,3,4, the first value in theSums will be 1. The second value is the previous value (1) plus the next in the series (2); thus, theSums[1] will hold the value 3. Likewise, the third value is the previous value (3) plus the next in the series—theSums[2] is 6. Finally, the fourth value in theSums is the previous value (6) plus the next in the series (4), for a value of 10.

The constructor for the SumOf object takes two integers: the starting number and the ending number. It assigns these to the local values and then calls a helper function to compute the contents of the array:

```
public SumOf(int start, int end)
{
    startNumber = start;
    endNumber = end;
    ComputeSums();
```

The ComputeSums helper function fills in the contents of the array by computing the sums in the series from startNumber through endNumber:

```
private void ComputeSums()
{
    int count = endNumber - startNumber + 1;
    theSums = new int[count];
    theSums[0] = startNumber;
    for (int i=1,j=startNumber + 1;i<count;i++,j++)
    {
```

```
        theSums[i] =  j + theSums[i-1];
    }
}
```

You can display the contents of the array at any time by using a foreach loop:

```
private void DisplaySums( )
{
    foreach(int i in theSums)
    {
        Console.WriteLine("{0}, ",i);
    }
}
```

Serializing the object

Now, mark the class as eligible for serialization with the [Serializable] attribute:

```
[Serializable]
class SumOf
```

To invoke serialization, you first need a file stream object into which you'll serialize the SumOf object:

```
FileStream fileStream =
    new FileStream("DoSum.out",FileMode.Create);
```

You are now ready to call the formatter's Serialize( ) method, passing in the stream and the object to serialize. Because this will be done in a method of SumOf, you can pass in the this object, which points to the current object:

```
binaryFormatter.Serialize(fileStream,this);
```

This will serialize the SumOf object to disk.

Deserializing the object

To reconstitute the object, open the file and ask a binary formatter to DeSerialize it:

```
public static SumOf DeSerialize( )
{
    FileStream fileStream =
        new FileStream("DoSum.out",FileMode.Open);
    BinaryFormatter binaryFormatter =
        new BinaryFormatter( );
    return (SumOf) binaryFormatter.Deserialize(fileStream);
    fileStream.Close( );

}
```

To make sure all this works, first instantiate a new object of type SumOf and tell it to serialize itself. Then create a new instance of type SumOf by calling the static deserializer and asking it to display its values:

```
public static void Main( )
{
    Console.WriteLine("Creating first one with new...");
```

```
        SumOf app = new SumOf(1,10);

        Console.WriteLine(
            "Creating second one with deserialize...");
        SumOf newInstance = SumOf.DeSerialize();
        newInstance.DisplaySums();
    }
```

Example 21-15 provides the complete source code to illustrate serialization and deserialization.

Example 21-15. Serializing and deserializing an object

```
namespace Programming_CSharp
{
    using System;
    using System.IO;
    using System.Runtime.Serialization;
    using System.Runtime.Serialization.Formatters.Binary;

    [Serializable]
    class SumOf
    {

        public static void Main()
        {
            Console.WriteLine("Creating first one with new...");
            SumOf app = new SumOf(1,10);

            Console.WriteLine("Creating second one with deserialize...");
            SumOf newInstance = SumOf.DeSerialize();
            newInstance.DisplaySums();
        }

        public SumOf(int start, int end)
        {
            startNumber = start;
            endNumber = end;
            ComputeSums();
            DisplaySums();
            Serialize();
        }

        private void ComputeSums()
        {
            int count = endNumber - startNumber + 1;
            theSums = new int[count];
            theSums[0] = startNumber;
            for (int i=1,j=startNumber + 1;i<count;i++,j++)
            {
                theSums[i] =  j + theSums[i-1];

            }
        }
```

Example 21-15. Serializing and deserializing an object (continued)

```
    private void DisplaySums()
    {
        foreach(int i in theSums)
        {
            Console.WriteLine("{0}, ",i);
        }
    }

    private void Serialize()
    {
        Console.Write("Serializing...");
        // create a file stream to write the file
        FileStream fileStream =
            new FileStream("DoSum.out",FileMode.Create);
        // use the CLR binary formatter
        BinaryFormatter binaryFormatter =
            new BinaryFormatter();
        // serialize to disk
        binaryFormatter.Serialize(fileStream,this);
        Console.WriteLine("...completed");
        fileStream.Close();
    }

    public static SumOf DeSerialize()
    {
        FileStream fileStream =
            new FileStream("DoSum.out",FileMode.Open);
        BinaryFormatter binaryFormatter =
            new BinaryFormatter();
        return (SumOf) binaryFormatter.Deserialize(fileStream);
        fileStream.Close();

    }
    private int startNumber = 1;
    private int endNumber;
    private int[] theSums;
    }
}
```

Output:
```
Creating first one with new...
1,
3,
6,
10,
15,
21,
28,
36,
45,
55,
Serializing......completed
```

Example 21-15. Serializing and deserializing an object (continued)

```
Creating second one with deserialize...
1,
3,
6,
10,
15,
21,
28,
36,
45,
55,
```

The output shows that the object was created, displayed, and then serialized. The object was then deserialized and output again, with no loss of data.

Handling Transient Data

In some ways, the approach to serialization demonstrated in Example 21-15 is very wasteful. Because you can compute the contents of the array given its starting and ending numbers, there really is no reason to store its elements to disk. Although the operation might be inexpensive with a small array, it could become costly with a very large one.

You can tell the serializer not to serialize some data by marking it with the [NonSerialized] attribute:

```
[NonSerialized] private int[] theSums;
```

If you don't serialize the array, however, the object you create will not be correct when you deserialize it. The array will be empty. Remember, when you deserialize the object, you simply read it up from its serialized form; no methods are run.

To fix the object before you return it to the caller, implement the IDe-serializationCallback interface:

```
[Serializable]
class SumOf : IDeserializationCallback
```

Also implement the one method of this interface: OnDeserialization( ). The CLR promises that if you implement this interface, your class's OnDeserialization( ) method will be called when the entire object graph has been deserialized. This is just what you want; the CLR will reconstitute what you've serialized, and then you have the opportunity to fix up the parts that were not serialized.

This implementation can be very simple; just ask the object to recompute the series:

```
public virtual void OnDeserialization (Object sender)
{
    ComputeSums( );
}
```

This is a classic space/time trade-off; by not serializing the array you make deserialization somewhat slower (because you must take the time to recompute the array), and you make the file somewhat smaller. To see if not serializing the array had any effect, I ran the program with the digits 1 to 5,000. Before setting [NonSerialized] on the array, the serialized file was 20K. After setting [NonSerialized], the file was 1K. Not bad. Example 21-16 shows the source code using the digits 1 to 5 as input (to simplify the output).

Example 21-16. Working with a nonserialized object

```
namespace Programming_CSharp
{
    using System;
    using System.IO;
    using System.Runtime.Serialization;
    using System.Runtime.Serialization.Formatters.Binary;

    [Serializable]
    class SumOf : IDeserializationCallback
    {
        public static void Main( )
        {
            Console.WriteLine("Creating first one with new...");
            SumOf app = new SumOf(1,5);

            Console.WriteLine("Creating second one with deserialize...");
            SumOf newInstance = SumOf.DeSerialize( );
            newInstance.DisplaySums( );
        }

        public SumOf(int start, int end)
        {
            startNumber = start;
            endNumber = end;
            ComputeSums( );
            DisplaySums( );
            Serialize( );
        }

        private void ComputeSums( )
        {
            int count = endNumber - startNumber + 1;
            theSums = new int[count];
            theSums[0] = startNumber;
            for (int i=1,j=startNumber + 1;i<count;i++,j++)
            {
                theSums[i] =  j + theSums[i-1];

            }
        }
```

Example 21-16. Working with a nonserialized object (continued)

```
    private void DisplaySums( )
    {
        foreach(int i in theSums)
        {
            Console.WriteLine("{0}, ",i);
        }
    }

    private void Serialize( )
    {
        Console.Write("Serializing...");
        // create a file stream to write the file
        FileStream fileStream =
            new FileStream("DoSum.out",FileMode.Create);
        // use the CLR binary formatter
        BinaryFormatter binaryFormatter =
            new BinaryFormatter( );
        // serialize to disk
        binaryFormatter.Serialize(fileStream,this);
        Console.WriteLine("...completed");
        fileStream.Close( );
    }

    public static SumOf DeSerialize( )
    {
        FileStream fileStream =
            new FileStream("DoSum.out",FileMode.Open);
        BinaryFormatter binaryFormatter =
            new BinaryFormatter( );
        return (SumOf) binaryFormatter.Deserialize(fileStream);
        fileStream.Close( );

    }

    // fix up the nonserialized data
    public virtual void OnDeserialization
        (Object sender)
    {
        ComputeSums( );
    }

    private int startNumber = 1;
    private int endNumber;
    [NonSerialized] private int[] theSums;
    }
}
```

Output:
```
Creating first one with new...
1,
3,
6,
```

Example 21-16. Working with a nonserialized object (continued)

```
10,
15,
Serializing......completed
Creating second one with deserialize...
1,
3,
6,
10,
15,
```

You can see in the output that the data was successfully serialized to disk and then reconstituted by deserialization. The trade-off of disk storage space versus time does not make a lot of sense with five values, but it makes a great deal of sense with five million values.

So far you've streamed your data to disk for storage and across the network for easy communication with distant programs. There is one other time you might create a stream: to store permanent configuration and status data on a per-user basis. For this purpose, the .NET Frameworks offer *isolated storage*.

Isolated Storage

The .NET CLR provides isolated storage to allow the application developer to store data on a *per-user* basis. Isolated storage provides much of the functionality of traditional Windows *.ini* files or the more recent HKEY_CURRENT_USER key in the Windows Registry.

Applications save data to a unique *data compartment* associated with the application. The CLR implements the data compartment with a *data store*, which is typically a directory on the filesystem.

Administrators are free to limit how much isolated storage individual applications can use. They can also use security so that less trusted code cannot call more highly trusted code to write to isolated storage.

What is important about isolated storage is that the CLR provides a standard place to store your application's data, but it does not impose (or support) any particular layout or syntax for that data. In short, you can store anything you like in isolated storage.

Typically, you will store text, often in the form of name-value pairs. Isolated storage is a good mechanism for saving user configuration information such as login name, the position of various windows and widgets, and other application-specific, user-specific information. The data is stored in a separate file for each user, but the files can be isolated even further by distinguishing among different aspects of the identity of the code (by assembly or by originating application domain).

Using isolated storage is fairly straightforward. To write to isolated storage, create an instance of an IsolatedStorageFileStream, which you initialize with a filename and a file mode (create, append, etc.):

```
IsolatedStorageFileStream configFile =
    new IsolatedStorageFileStream
    ("Tester.cfg",FileMode.Create);
```

Then create a StreamWriter on that file:

```
StreamWriter writer =
    new StreamWriter(configFile);
```

Then write to that stream as you would to any other. Example 21-17 illustrates.

Example 21-17. Writing to isolated storage

```
namespace Programming_CSharp
{
    using System;
    using System.IO;
    using System.IO.IsolatedStorage;

    public class Tester
    {
        public static void Main( )
        {
            Tester app = new Tester( );
            app.Run( );
        }

        private void Run( )
        {
            // create the configuration file stream
            IsolatedStorageFileStream configFile =
                new IsolatedStorageFileStream
                ("Tester.cfg",FileMode.Create);

            // create a writer to write to the stream
            StreamWriter writer =
                new StreamWriter(configFile);

            // write some data to the config. file
            String output;
            System.DateTime currentTime = System.DateTime.Now;
            output = "Last access: " + currentTime.ToString( );
            writer.WriteLine(output);
            output = "Last position = 27,35";
            writer.WriteLine(output);

            // flush the buffer and clean up
            writer.Flush( );
            writer.Close( );
            configFile.Close( );
```

Example 21-17. Writing to isolated storage (continued)

```
        }
    }
}
```

After running this code, search your hard disk for *Tester.cfg*. On my machine, this file is found in:

```
c:\Documents and Settings\Administrator\ApplicationData\
Microsoft\COMPlus\IsolatedStorage\0.4\
Url.wj4zpd5ni41dynqxx1uz0x0aoaraftc\
Url.wj4zpd5ni41dynqxx1uz0ix0aoaraftc\files
```

You can read this file with Notepad if what you've written is just text:

```
Last access: 5/2/2001 10:00:57 AM
Last position = 27,35
```

Or, you can access this data programmatically. To do so, reopen the file:

```
IsolatedStorageFileStream configFile =
    new IsolatedStorageFileStream
    ("Tester.cfg",FileMode.Open);
```

Create a StreamReader object:

```
StreamReader reader =
    new StreamReader(configFile);
```

Use the standard stream idiom to read through the file:

```
string theEntry;
do
{
    theEntry = reader.ReadLine( );
    Console.WriteLine(theEntry);
} while (theEntry != null);
Console.WriteLine(theEntry);
```

Isolated storage is scoped by assembly (so, if you shut down your program and start it later, you can read the configuration file you created). Example 21-18 provides the method needed to read the file. Replace the Run( ) method in the previous example, recompile it, and run it (but don't change its name, or it won't be able to access the isolated storage you created previously):

Example 21-18. Reading from isolated storage

```
        private void Run( )
        {
            // open the configuration file stream
            IsolatedStorageFileStream configFile =
                new IsolatedStorageFileStream
                ("Tester.cfg",FileMode.Open);

            // create a standard stream reader
            StreamReader reader =
```

Example 21-18. Reading from isolated storage (continued)

```
        new StreamReader(configFile);

        // read through the file and display
        string theEntry;
        do
        {
            theEntry = reader.ReadLine( );
            Console.WriteLine(theEntry);
        } while (theEntry != null);

        reader.Close( );
        configFile.Close( );
    }
```

Output:
```
Last access: 5/2/2001 10:00:57 AM
Last position = 27,35
```

Programming .NET and COM

Programmers love a clean slate. Although it would be nice if we could throw away all the code we've ever written and start over, this typically isn't a viable option for most companies. Over the past decade, many development organizations have made a substantial investment in developing and purchasing COM components and ActiveX controls. If .NET is to be a viable platform, these legacy components must be usable from within .NET applications, and to a lesser degree, .NET components must be callable from COM.

This chapter describes the support .NET provides for importing ActiveX controls and COM components into your application, for exposing .NET classes to COM-based applications, and for making direct calls to Win32 APIs. You will also learn about C# pointers and keywords for accessing memory directly, a technique that may be crucial in some applications.

Importing ActiveX Controls

ActiveX controls are COM components typically dropped into a form, which might or might not have a user interface. When Microsoft developed the OCX standard, which allowed developers to build ActiveX controls in Visual Basic and use them with C++ (and vice versa), the ActiveX control revolution began. Over the past few years, thousands of such controls have been developed, sold, and used. They are small, easy to work with, and an effective example of binary reuse.

Importing ActiveX controls into .NET is surprisingly easy, considering that the COM binary standard and the .NET binary standard are not compatible. Visual Studio .NET is able to import ActiveX controls. Microsoft has also developed a command-line utility, AxImp, which will create the assemblies necessary for the control to be used in a .NET application.

Creating an ActiveX Control

To demonstrate the ability to use classic ActiveX controls in a .NET application, first develop a simple four-function calculator as an ActiveX control and then invoke that ActiveX control from within a C# application. Build the control in VB6, and test it in a VB6 application. If you don't have VB6 or don't want to bother creating the control, you can download the control from my web site (*http://www.LibertyAssociates.com*).

Once the control is working in the standard Windows environment, you'll copy it to your .NET development environment, register it, and import it into a Windows Forms application.

To create the control, open VB6 and choose ActiveX Control as the new project type. Make the project form as small as possible, because this control will not have a user interface. Right-click UserControl1 and choose Properties. Rename it Calculator in the Properties window. Click the Project in the project explorer, and in the Properties window, rename it to CalcControl. Immediately save the project and name both the file and the project CalcControl, as shown in Figure 22-1.

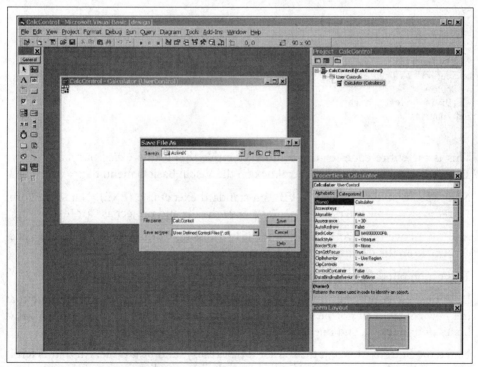

Figure 22-1. Creating a VB ActiveX control

Now you can add the four calculator functions by right-clicking the CalcControl form, selecting View Code from the pop-up menu, and typing in the VB code shown in Example 22-1.

Example 22-1. Implementing the CalcControl ActiveX control

```
Public Function _
Add(left As Double, right As Double) _
As Double
    Add = left + right
End Function

Public Function _
Subtract(left As Double, right As Double) _
As Double
    Subtract = left - right
End Function

Public Function _
Multiply(left As Double, right As Double) _
As Double
    Multiply = left * right
End Function

Public Function _
Divide(left As Double, right As Double) _
As Double
    Divide = left / right
End Function
```

This is the entire code for the control. Compile this to the *CalcControl.ocx* file by choosing File → Make CalcControl.ocx on the Visual Basic 6 menu bar.

Next open a second project in VB as a standard executable (EXE). Name the form TestForm and name the project CalcTest. Save the file and project as CalcTest.

Add the ActiveX control as a component by pressing Control-T and choosing Calc-Control from the Controls tab, as shown in Figure 22-2.

This action puts a new control on the toolbox, as shown circled in Figure 22-3.

Drag the new control on to the form TestForm and name it CalcControl. Note that the new control will not be visible; this control has no user interface. Add two text boxes, four buttons, and one label, as shown in Figure 22-4.

Name the buttons btnAdd, btnSubtract, btnMultiply, and btnDivide. All that is left is for you to implement methods for handling the button click events of the calculator

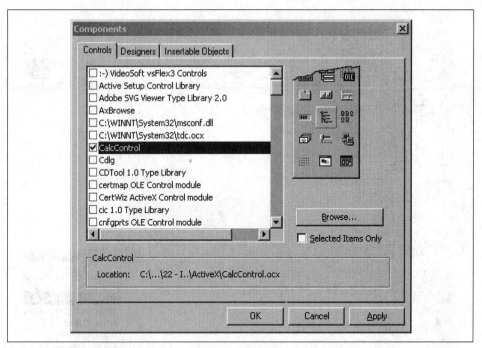

Figure 22-2. Adding the CalcControl to the VB6 toolbox

Figure 22-3. Locating CalcControl in the Visual Basic 6 toolbox

buttons. Each time a button is clicked, you want to get the values in the two text boxes, cast them to double (as required by CalcControl) using the VB6 CDbl function, invoke a CalcControl function, and print the result in the label control. Example 22-2 provides the complete source code.

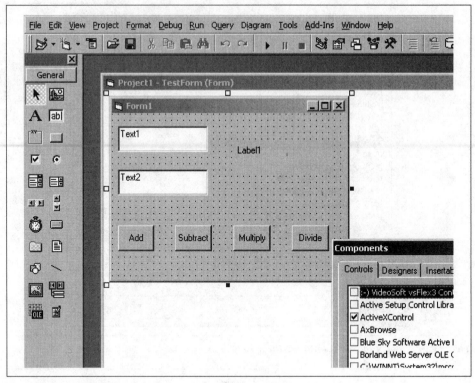

Figure 22-4. Building the TestForm user interface

Example 22-2. Using the CalcControl ActiveX control in a VB program (TestForm)

```
Private Sub btnAdd_Click( )
    Label1.Caption = _
        calcControl.Add(CDbl(Text1.Text), _
            CDbl(Text2.Text))
End Sub

Private Sub btnDivide_Click( )
    Label1.Caption = _
        calcControl.Divide(CDbl(Text1.Text), _
            CDbl(Text2.Text))
End Sub

Private Sub btnMultiply_Click( )
    Label1.Caption = _
        calcControl.Multiply(CDbl(Text1.Text), _
            CDbl(Text2.Text))
End Sub

Private Sub btnSubtract_Click( )
    Label1.Caption = _
```

Example 22-2. Using the CalcControl ActiveX control in a VB program (TestForm) (continued)

```
    calcControl.Subtract(CDbl(Text1.Text), _
        CDbl(Text2.Text))
End Sub
```

Figure 22-5 shows the result of running the `CalcTest` program, typing in two numbers and clicking the Multiply button.

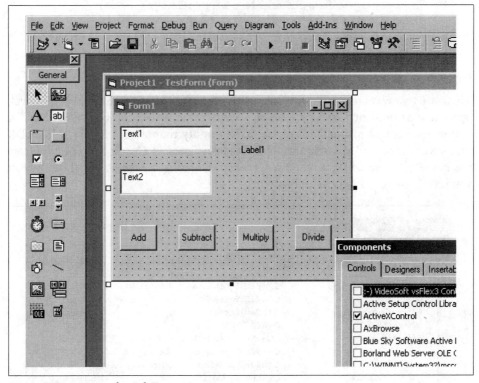

Figure 22-5. Running the CalcTest program

Importing a Control in .NET

Now that you've shown that the CalcControl ActiveX control is working, you can copy the *CalcControl.ocx* file to your .NET development environment. Once you have copied it, register the *CalcControl.ocx* file using `Regsvr32`. You're now ready to build a test program in .NET to use the calculator:

```
    Regsvr32 CalcControl.ocx
```

To get started, create a Visual C# Windows Form project in Visual Studio .NET (see Chapter 13), name the project `InteropTest`, and design a form (such as the TestForm form you created in VB in the preceding section) by dragging and dropping controls onto it. Name the form TestForm. A complete sample form is shown in Figure 22-6.

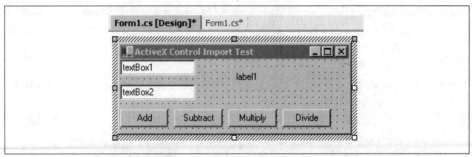

Figure 22-6. Building a Windows Form to test the CalcControl ActiveX control

Importing a control

There are two ways to import an ActiveX control into the Visual Studio .NET development environment. You can use the Visual Studio .NET tools themselves, or import the control manually using the *aximp* utility that ships with the .NET SDK Framework. To use Visual Studio .NET, choose Tools → Customize Toolbox from the menu. On the COM Components tab find the CalcControl.Calculator object you just registered, as shown in Figure 22-7.

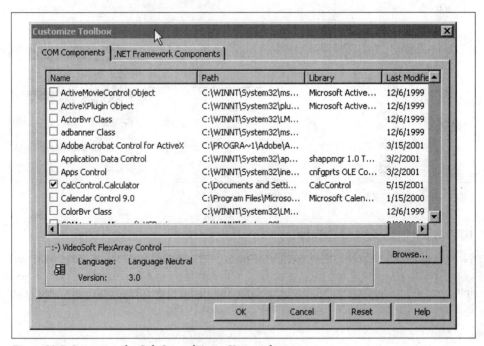

Figure 22-7. Importing the CalcControl ActiveX control

Because CalcControl is registered on your .NET machine, the Visual Studio .NET Customize Toolbox is able to find it. When you select the control from this dialog box, it is imported into your application; Visual Studio takes care of the details. Alternatively, you can open a command box and import the control manually using the *aximp.exe* utility, as shown in Figure 22-8.

Figure 22-8. Running aximp

aximp.exe takes one argument, the ActiveX control you want to import (*CalcControl.dll*). It produces three files:

AxCalcControl.dll
    A .NET Windows control

CalcControl.dll
    A proxy .NET class library

AxCalcControl.pdb
    A debug file

Adding a control to the Visual Studio toolbox

Once this is done, you can return to the Customize Toolbox window, but this time select .NET Framework Components. You can now browse to the location at which the .NET Windows control *AxCalcControl.dll* was generated and import that file into the toolbox, as shown in Figure 22-9.

Once imported, the control appears on the toolbox menu, as shown in Figure 22-10. Note that the control may appear at the bottom of the toolbox.

Now you can drag this control onto your Windows Form and make use of its functions, just as you did in the VB6 example.

Add event handlers for each of the four buttons. The event handlers will delegate their work to the ActiveX control you wrote in VB6 and imported into .NET.

The source for the event handlers is shown in Example 22-3.

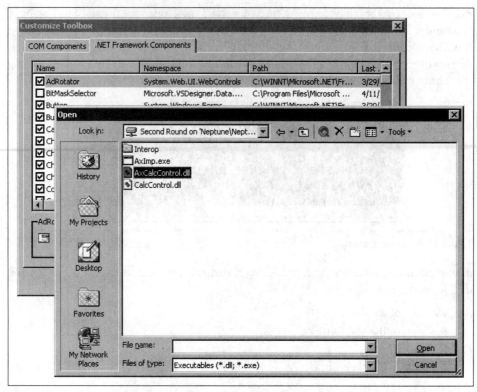

Figure 22-9. Browsing for the imported control

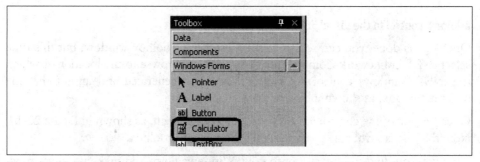

Figure 22-10. Viewing the AxCalcControl calculator after importing it into the toolbox

Example 22-3. Implementing event handlers for the test Windows Form

```
private void btnAdd_Click(object sender, System.EventArgs e)
{
    double left = double.Parse(textBox1.Text);
    double right = double.Parse(textBox2.Text);
    label1.Text = axCalculator1.Add( ref left, ref right).ToString( );
}
```

Example 22-3. Implementing event handlers for the test Windows Form (continued)

```
private void btnDivide_Click(object sender, System.EventArgs e)
{
    double left = double.Parse(textBox1.Text);
    double right = double.Parse(textBox2.Text);
    label1.Text = axCalculator1.Divide(ref left, ref right).ToString( );
}

private void btnMultiply_Click(object sender, System.EventArgs e)
{
    double left = double.Parse(textBox1.Text);
    double right = double.Parse(textBox2.Text);
    label1.Text = axCalculator1.Multiply(ref left, ref right).ToString( );
}

private void btnSubtract_Click(object sender, System.EventArgs e)
{
    double left = double.Parse(textBox1.Text);
    double right = double.Parse(textBox2.Text);
    label1.Text = axCalculator1.Subtract(ref left, ref right).ToString( );
}
```

Each implementing method obtains the values in the text fields, converts them to double using the static method double.Parse( ), and passes those values to the calculator's methods. The results are cast back to a string and inserted in the label, as shown in Figure 22-11.

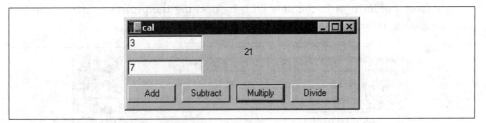

Figure 22-11. Running the imported ActiveX Control in a Windows Form

Importing COM Components

Importing ActiveX controls turns out to be fairly straightforward. Many of the COM components that companies develop are not ActiveX controls, however; they are standard COM dynamic link library (DLL) files. To see how to use these with .NET, return to VB6 and create a COM business object that will act exactly as the component from the previous section did.

The first step is to create a new ActiveX DLL project. This is how VB6 creates standard COM DLLs. Name the class ComCalc and name the project ComCalculator. Save the file and project. Copy the methods from Example 22-4 into the code window.

Example 22-4. Implementing the methods for ComCalc

```
Public Function _
Add(left As Double, right As Double) _
As Double
    Add = left + right
End Function

Public Function _
Subtract(left As Double, right As Double) _
As Double
    Subtract = left - right
End Function

Public Function _
Multiply(left As Double, right As Double) _
As Double
    Multiply = left * right
End Function

Public Function _
Divide(left As Double, right As Double) _
As Double
    Divide = left / right
End Function
```

Build the DLL by using the menu sequence File → Make ComCalculator.dll. You can test this by returning to your earlier test program and removing the Calculator control from the form. Add the new DLL by opening the project reference window and navigating to the ComCalculator, as shown in Figure 22-12.

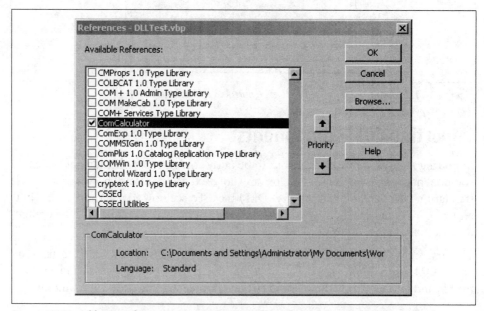

Figure 22-12. Adding a reference to ComCalculator.dll

Coding the COMTestForm program

The code to exercise the COM component is very similar to the earlier example. This time, however, you instantiate a ComCalc object and call its methods, as shown in Example 22-5.

Example 22-5. The driver program for ComCalc.dll

```
Private Sub btnAdd_Click( )
    Dim theCalc As New ComCalc
    Label1.Caption = _
        theCalc.Add(CDbl(Text1.Text), _
            CDbl(Text2.Text))
End Sub

Private Sub btnDivide_Click( )
    Dim theCalc As New ComCalc
    Label1.Caption = _
        theCalc.Divide(CDbl(Text1.Text), _
            CDbl(Text2.Text))
End Sub

Private Sub btnMultiply_Click( )
    Dim theCalc As New ComCalc
    Label1.Caption = _
        theCalc.Multiply(CDbl(Text1.Text), _
            CDbl(Text2.Text))
End Sub

Private Sub btnSubtract_Click( )
    Dim theCalc As New ComCalc
    Label1.Caption = _
        theCalc.Subtract(CDbl(Text1.Text), _
            CDbl(Text2.Text))
End Sub
```

Importing the COM .DLL to .NET

Now that you have a working ComCalc DLL, you can import it to .NET. Before you can import it, however, you must choose between *early* and *late binding*. When the client calls a method on the server, the address of the server's method in memory must be resolved. That process is called *binding*.

With *early binding*, the resolution of the address of a method on the server occurs when the client project is compiled and metadata is added to the client .NET module. With *late binding*, the resolution does not happen until runtime, when COM explores the server to see if it supports the method.

Early binding has many advantages. The most significant is performance. Early-bound methods are invoked far more quickly than late-bound methods. For the compiler to perform early binding, it must interrogate the server's type library. For the compiler to interrogate the server's type library, it must first be imported into .NET.

Importing the Type Library

The VB6-created COM DLL has a type library within it, but the format of a COM type library cannot be used by a .NET application. To solve this problem, you must import the COM type library into an assembly. Once again, you have two ways of doing this. You can allow the Integrated Development Environment (IDE) to import the class by registering the component, as shown in the following section, or you can import the type library manually by using the standalone program *TlbImp.exe*.

TlbImp.exe will produce a proxy assembly with a manifest within it. This proxy assembly is called a *Runtime Class Wrapper* (RCW). The .NET client will use the RCW to bind to the methods in the COM object, as shown in the following section.

Importing Manually

Start by copying the *ComCalculator.DLL* file to your .NET environment and registering it with Regsvr32. Then you're ready to import the COM object into .NET, by running *TlbImp.exe*. The syntax is to enter the name of the COM component, followed by an optional name for the filename produced, as shown in Figure 22-13.

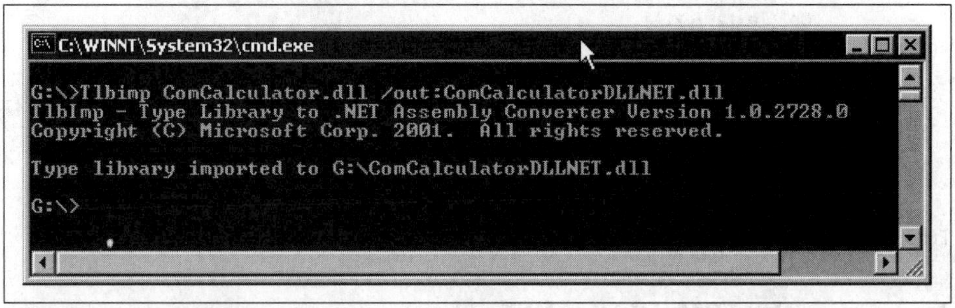

Figure 22-13. Running TlbImp.exe

Creating a Test Program

Now it's time to create a driver program to test the COM object, which you'll name COMDllTest.

If you decided not to import the library manually, you import it through the IDE. To do so, select the COM tab on the Add Reference dialog and select the registered COM object, as shown in Figure 22-14.

This will invoke *TlbImp* for you and will copy the resulting RCW to:

    C:/Documents and Settings/Administrator/Application Data/Microsoft/VisualStudio/RCW

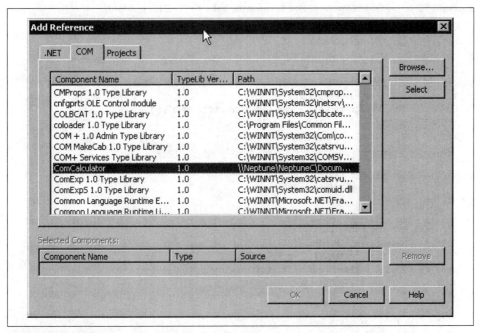

Figure 22-14. Adding a reference to ComCalculator

You'll have to be careful, however, because the DLL it produces has the same name as the COM DLL.

If you do use *TlbImp.exe*, you can add the reference from the Projects tab. Browse to the directory in which *ComCalculatorDLLNET.dll* was created, and add it to the references.

In either case, you can now create the user interface, which is, again, similar to that used for testing the ActiveX control, as shown in Figure 22-15.

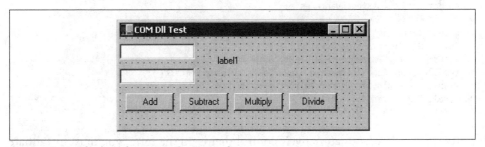

Figure 22-15. The form for testing the COM object

All that is left is to wire up the event handlers for the four buttons, as shown in Example 22-6.

Example 22-6. Implementing event handlers for the VB 6 COM DLL test form

```
private void btnAdd_Click(
    object sender, System.EventArgs e)
{
    Double left, right, result;
    left = Double.Parse(textBox1.Text);
    right = Double.Parse(textBox2.Text);
    ComCalculator.ComCalc theCalc = new ComCalculator.ComCalc();
    result = theCalc.Add(ref left, ref right);
    label1.Text = result.ToString();
}

private void btnSubtract_Click(
    object sender, System.EventArgs e)
{
    Double left, right, result;
    left = Double.Parse(textBox1.Text);
    right = Double.Parse(textBox2.Text);
    ComCalculator.ComCalc theCalc = new ComCalculator.ComCalc();
    result = theCalc.Subtract(ref left, ref right);
    label1.Text = result.ToString();

}

private void btnMultiply_Click(
    object sender, System.EventArgs e)
{
    Double left, right, result;
    left = Double.Parse(textBox1.Text);
    right = Double.Parse(textBox2.Text);
    ComCalculator.ComCalc theCalc = new ComCalculator.ComCalc();
    result = theCalc.Multiply(ref left, ref right);
    label1.Text = result.ToString();
}

private void btnDivide_Click(
    object sender, System.EventArgs e)
{
    Double left, right, result;
    left = Double.Parse(textBox1.Text);
    right = Double.Parse(textBox2.Text);
    ComCalculator.ComCalc theCalc = new ComCalculator.ComCalc();
    result = theCalc.Divide(ref left, ref right);
    label1.Text = result.ToString();
}
```

Rather than referring to an ActiveX control that is on the form, you must instantiate the ComCalculator.ComCalc object. The COM object is then available for use as if it had been created in a .NET assembly, and the running program works as expected, as shown in Figure 22-16.

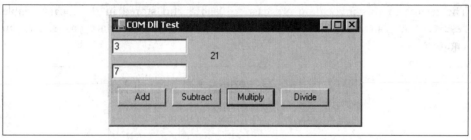

Figure 22-16. The test driver program in action

Using Late Binding and Reflection

If you do not have a type library file for your third-party COM object, you must use late binding with reflection. In Chapter 18, you saw how to invoke methods dynamically in .NET assemblies; the process with COM objects is not terribly different.

To see how to do this, start with the application shown in Example 22-6, but remove the reference to the imported library. The four button handlers must now be rewritten. You can no longer instantiate a ComCalculator.Calc object, so instead you must invoke its methods dynamically.

Just as you saw in Chapter 18, you begin by creating a Type object to hold information about the ComCalc type.

```
Type comCalcType;
comCalcType = Type.GetTypeFromProgID("ComCalculator.ComCalc");
```

The call to GetTypeFromProgID instructs the .NET Framework to open the registered COM DLL and retrieve the necessary type information for the specified object. This is the equivalent to calling GetType, as you did in Chapter 18:

```
Type theMathType = Type.GetType("System.Math");
```

You can now proceed exactly as you would if you were invoking this method on a class described in a .NET assembly. Start by calling CreateInstance to get back an instance of the ComCalc object:

```
object comCalcObject = Activator.CreateInstance(comCalcType);
```

Next create an array to hold the arguments, and then invoke the method using InvokeMember, passing in the method you want to invoke as a string, a binder flag, a null binder, the object returned by CreateInstance, and the input argument array:

```
object[] inputArguments = {left, right };
result = (Double) comCalcType.InvokeMember(
    "Subtract",                     // the method to invoke
    BindingFlags.InvokeMethod,      // how to bind
    null,                           // binder
    comCalcObject,                  // the COM object
    inputArguments);                // the method arguments
```

The results of this invocation are cast to Double and stored in the local variable result. You can then display this result in the user interface, as shown in Figure 22-17.

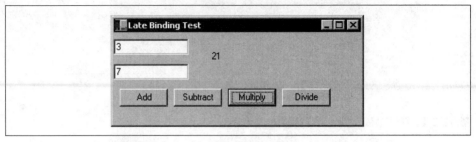

Figure 22-17. Late-binding test

Because all four event handlers must replicate this work, differing only in the method they call, you'll factor the common code to a private helper method named Invoke, as shown in Example 22-7. You also need to add a using statement for System. Reflection in the source code.

Example 22-7. Late binding of COM objects

```
private void btnAdd_Click(
    object sender, System.EventArgs e)
{
    Invoke("Add");
}

private void btnSubtract_Click(
    object sender, System.EventArgs e)
{
    Invoke("Subtract");
}

private void btnMultiply_Click(
    object sender, System.EventArgs e)
{
    Invoke("Multiply");
}

private void btnDivide_Click(
    object sender, System.EventArgs e)
{
    Invoke("Divide");
}


private void Invoke(string whichMethod)
{
    Double left, right, result;
    left = Double.Parse(textBox1.Text);
```

Example 22-7. Late binding of COM objects (continued)

```
    right = Double.Parse(textBox2.Text);

    // create a Type object to hold type information
    Type comCalcType;

    // an array for the arguments
    object[] inputArguments =
        {left, right };

    // get the type info from the COM object
    comCalcType =
        Type.GetTypeFromProgID(
            "ComCalculator.ComCalc");

    // create an instance
    object comCalcObject =
        Activator.CreateInstance(comCalcType);

    // invoke the method dynamically and
    // cast the result to double
    result = (Double) comCalcType.InvokeMember(
        whichMethod,                    // the method to invoke
        BindingFlags.InvokeMethod,      // how to bind
        null,                           // binder
        comCalcObject,                  // the COM object
        inputArguments);                // the method arguments

    label1.Text = result.ToString( );
}
```

Exporting .NET Components

You can export your .NET class for use with existing COM components, although this is an unusual requirement. The Regasm tool will register the metadata from your component in the system registry.

Invoke Regasm with the name of the DLL, which must be installed in the GAC (see Chapter 17). For example:

```
    Regasm myAssembly.dll
```

This will export your component's metadata to the Registry. For example, you can create a new C# DLL project in which you re-create your four-function calculator, as shown in Example 22-8.

Example 22-8. The four-function calculator in a DLL

```
using System;
using System.Reflection;

[assembly: AssemblyKeyFile("test.key")]
```

Example 22-8. The four-function calculator in a DLL (continued)

```
namespace Programming_CSharp
{
    public class Calculator
    {
        public Calculator( )
        {

        }
        public Double Add (Double left, Double right)
        {
            return left + right;
        }
        public Double Subtract (Double left, Double right)
        {
            return left - right;
        }
        public Double Multiply (Double left, Double right)
        {
            return left * right;
        }
        public Double Divide (Double left, Double right)
        {
            return left / right;
        }
    }
}
```

Save this to a file named *Calculator.cs* in a project named `ProgrammingCSharpDLL`. Create a key, compile the program, add it to the GAC, and register it with:

```
sn -k test.key
csc /t:library /out:ProgrammingCSharpDLL.cs Calculator.cs
gacutil /i ProgrammingCSharpDLL.dll
Regasm ProgrammingCSharpDLL.dll
```

A quick check of the Registry shows that a PROGID was created for the DLL, as shown in Figure 22-18.

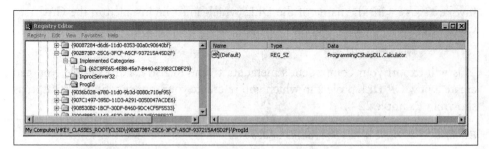

Figure 22-18. The Registry after registering the DLL

You can now invoke the four-function calculator as a COM object using standard VBScript. For example, you can create a tiny Windows script host file, as shown in Example 22-9.

Example 22-9. Invoking the Calculator COM object with a Windows scripting host file

```
dim calc
dim msg
dim result
set calc = CreateObject("Programming_CSharp.Calculator")
result = calc.Multiply(7,3)
msg = "7 * 3 =" & result & "."
Call MsgBox(msg)
```

When this is run, a dialog box pops up to verify that the object was created and invoked, as shown in Figure 22-19.

Figure 22-19. Late binding via COM

Creating a Type Library

If you wish to use early binding with your .NET DLL, you need to create a type library. You can do so with the TlbExp (Type Library Export) utility, by writing:

```
TlbExp ProgrammingCSharpDLL.dll /out:Calc.tlb
```

The result is a type library that you can browse and view in the OLE/COM object viewer within Visual Studio, as shown in Figure 22-20.

With this type library in hand, you can import the calculator class into any COM environment.

P/Invoke

It is possible, though generally undesirable, to invoke unmanaged code from within C#. The .NET *platform invoke facility* (P/Invoke) was originally intended only to provide access to the Windows API, but you can use it to expose functions in any DLL.

To see how this works, let's revisit Example 21-3 from Chapter 21. You will recall that you used the Stream class to rename files by invoking the MoveTo( ) method:

```
file.MoveTo(fullName + ".bak");
```

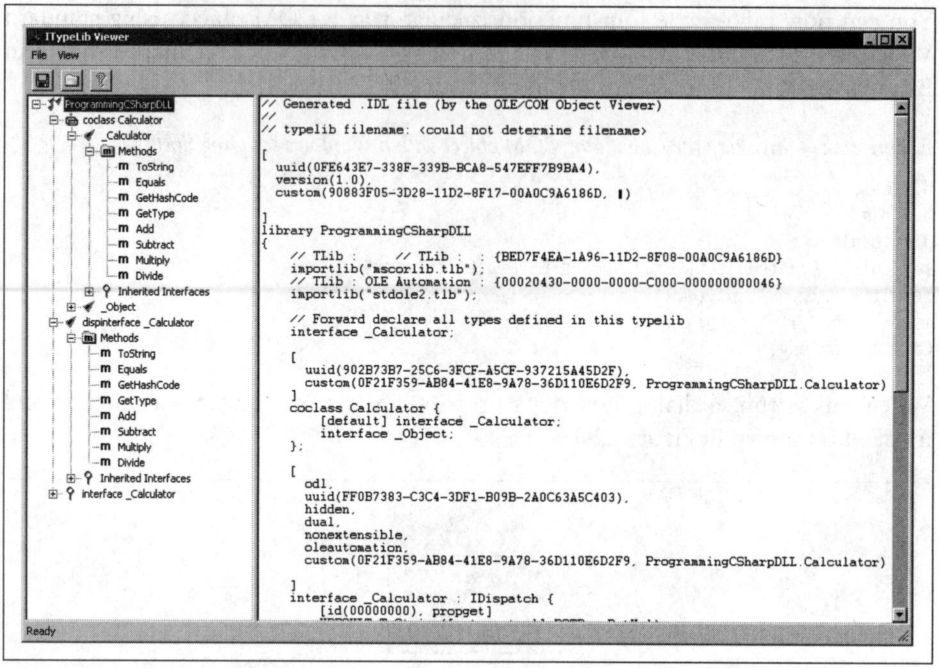

Figure 22-20. Viewing the type library contents

You can accomplish the same thing by using Windows' *kernel32.dll* and invoking the MoveFiles method. To do so, you need to declare the method as a static extern and use the DllImport attribute:

```
[DllImport("kernel32.dll", EntryPoint="MoveFile",
    ExactSpelling=false, CharSet=CharSet.Unicode,
    SetLastError=true)]
static extern bool MoveFile(
    string sourceFile, string destinationFile);
```

The DllImportAttribute class is used to indicate that an unmanaged method will be invoked through P/Invoke.

The parameters are:

EntryPoint

Indicates the name of the DLL entry point (the method) to call.

ExactSpelling

Setting this to false allows matching of the entry point name without case sensitivity.

CharSet

Indicates how the string arguments to the method should be marshaled.

SetLastError

Setting this to true allows you to call GetLastError to check if an error occurred when invoking this method.

The rest of the code is virtually unchanged, except for the invocation of the MoveFile( ) method itself. Notice that MoveFile( ) is declared to be a static method of the class, so use static method semantics:

```
Tester.MoveFile(file.FullName,file.FullName + ".bak");
```

Pass in the original filename and the new name and the file is moved, just as it was when calling file.MoveTo( ). In this example, there is no advantage—and actually considerable disadvantage—to using P/Invoke. You have left managed code, and the result is not object-oriented. P/Invoke really only makes sense when you absolutely, positively need to invoke a method for which there is no reasonable substitute within managed code. Example 22-10 shows the complete source code for using P/Invoke to move the files.

Example 22-10. Using P/Invoke to call a Win32 API method

```
namespace Programming_CSharp
{
    using System;
    using System.IO;
    using System.Runtime.InteropServices;

    class Tester
    {

        // declare the WinAPI method you wish to P/Invoke
        [DllImport("kernel32.dll", EntryPoint="MoveFile",
            ExactSpelling=false, CharSet=CharSet.Unicode,
            SetLastError=true)]
        static extern bool MoveFile(
            string sourceFile, string destinationFile);

        public static void Main( )
        {
            // make an instance and run it
            Tester t = new Tester( );
            string theDirectory = @"c:\test\media";
            DirectoryInfo dir =
                new DirectoryInfo(theDirectory);
            t.ExploreDirectory(dir);
        }

        // Set it running with a directory name
        private void ExploreDirectory(DirectoryInfo dir)
        {

            // make a new subdirectory
            string newDirectory = "newTest";
            DirectoryInfo newSubDir =
                dir.CreateSubdirectory(newDirectory);

            // get all the files in the directory and
```

Example 22-10. Using P/Invoke to call a Win32 API method (continued)

```
        // copy them to the new directory
        FileInfo[] filesInDir = dir.GetFiles();
        foreach (FileInfo file in filesInDir)
        {
            string fullName = newSubDir.FullName +
                "\\" + file.Name;
            file.CopyTo(fullName);
            Console.WriteLine("{0} copied to newTest",
                file.FullName);
        }

        // get a collection of the files copied in
        filesInDir = newSubDir.GetFiles();

        // delete some and rename others
        int counter = 0;
        foreach (FileInfo file in filesInDir)
        {
            string fullName = file.FullName;

            if (counter++ %2 == 0)
            {
                // P/Invoke the Win API
                Tester.MoveFile(fullName, fullName + ".bak");

                Console.WriteLine("{0} renamed to {1}",
                    fullName,file.FullName);
            }
            else
            {
                file.Delete();
                Console.WriteLine("{0} deleted.",
                    fullName);
            }
        }
        // delete the subdirectory
        newSubDir.Delete(true);
    }
  }
}
Output (excerpt):
c:\test\media\newTest\recycle.wav renamed to
    c:\test\media\newTest\recycle.wav
c:\test\media\newTest\ringin.wav renamed to
   c:\test\media\newTest\ringin.wav
```

Pointers

Until now you've seen no code using C/C++ style pointers. Only here, in the final paragraphs of the final pages of the book, does this topic arise, even though pointers are central to the C family of languages. In C#, pointers are relegated to unusual and advanced programming; typically they are used only when interoperating with COM.

C# supports the usual C pointer operators, listed in Table 22-1.

Table 22-1. C# pointer operators

Operator	Meaning
&	The *address-of* operator returns a pointer to the address of a value.
*	The *dereference* operator returns the value at the address of a pointer.
->	The *member access* operator is used to access the members of a type.

The use of pointers is almost never required, and is nearly always discouraged. When you do use pointers, you must mark your code with the C# unsafe modifier. The code is marked unsafe because you can manipulate memory locations directly with pointers. This is a feat that is otherwise impossible within a C# program. In unsafe code you can directly access memory, perform conversions between pointers and integral types, take the address of variables, and so forth. In exchange, you give up garbage collection and protection against uninitialized variables, dangling pointers, and accessing memory beyond the bounds of an array. In essence, unsafe code creates an island of C++ code within your otherwise safe C# application.

As an example of when this might be useful, read a file to the console by invoking two Win32 API calls: CreateFile and ReadFile. ReadFile takes, as its second parameter, a pointer to a buffer. The declaration of the two imported methods is not unlike those shown in Example 22-11.

Example 22-11. Declaring Win32 API methods for import into a C# program

```
[DllImport("kernel32", SetLastError=true)]
static extern unsafe int CreateFile(
    string filename,
    uint desiredAccess,
    uint shareMode,
    uint attributes,
    uint creationDisposition,
    uint flagsAndAttributes,
    uint templateFile);

[DllImport("kernel32", SetLastError=true)]
static extern unsafe bool ReadFile(
    int hFile,
    void* lpBuffer,
    int nBytesToRead,
    int* nBytesRead,
    int overlapped);
```

You will create a new class `APIFileReader` whose constructor will invoke the `CreateFile( )` method. The constructor takes a filename as a parameter, and passes that filename to the `CreateFile( )` method:

```
public APIFileReader(string filename)
{
    fileHandle = CreateFile(
        filename,        // filename
        GenericRead,     // desiredAccess
        UseDefault,      // shareMode
        UseDefault,      // attributes
        OpenExisting,    // creationDisposition
        UseDefault,      // flagsAndAttributes
        UseDefault);     // templateFile
}
```

The `APIFileReader` class implements only one other method, `Read( )`, which invokes `ReadFile( )`. It passes in the file handle created in the class constructor, along with a pointer into a buffer, a count of bytes to retrieve, and a reference to a variable that will hold the number of bytes read. It is the pointer to the buffer that is of interest to us here. To use this API call you must use a pointer.

Because you will access it with a pointer, the buffer needs to be *pinned* in memory; the .NET Framework cannot be allowed to move the buffer during garbage collection. To accomplish this, use the C# fixed keyword. Fixed allows you to get a pointer to the memory used by the buffer, and also to mark that instance so that the garbage collector won't move it.

The block of statements following the fixed keyword creates a scope, within which the memory will be pinned. At the end of the fixed block the instance will be marked so that it can be moved. This is known as *declarative pinning*:

```
public unsafe int Read(byte[] buffer, int index, int count)
{
    int bytesRead = 0;
    fixed (byte* bytePointer = buffer)
    {
        ReadFile(
            fileHandle,
            bytePointer +      index,
            count,
            &bytesRead, 0);
    }
    return bytesRead;
}
```

Notice that the method must be marked with the unsafe keyword. This allows you to create pointers and creates an unsafe context. To compile this you must use the */unsafe* compiler option.

The test program instantiates the `APIFileReader` and an `ASCIIEncoding` object. It passes the filename to the constructor of the `APIFileReader` and then creates a loop to repeatedly fill its buffer by calling the Read( ) method, which invokes the ReadFile API call. An array of bytes is returned, which is converted to a string using the ASCII-EncodingObjects's GetString( ) method. That string is passed to the Console.Write( ) method, to be displayed on the console. The complete source is shown in Example 22-12.

Example 22-12. Using pointers in a C# program

```
using System;
using System.Runtime.InteropServices;
using System.Text;

class APIFileReader
{
    [DllImport("kernel32", SetLastError=true)]
    static extern unsafe int CreateFile(
        string filename,
        uint desiredAccess,
        uint shareMode,
        uint attributes,
        uint creationDisposition,
        uint flagsAndAttributes,
        uint templateFile);

    [DllImport("kernel32", SetLastError=true)]
    static extern unsafe bool ReadFile(
        int hFile,
        void* lpBuffer,
        int nBytesToRead,
        int* nBytesRead,
        int overlapped);

    // constructor opens an existing file
    // and sets the file handle member
    public APIFileReader(string filename)
    {
        fileHandle = CreateFile(
            filename,       // filename
            GenericRead,    // desiredAccess
            UseDefault,     // shareMode
            UseDefault,     // attributes
            OpenExisting,   // creationDisposition
            UseDefault,     // flagsAndAttributes
            UseDefault);    // templateFile
    }

    public unsafe int Read(byte[] buffer, int index, int count)
    {
        int bytesRead = 0;
        fixed (byte* bytePointer = buffer)
        {
            ReadFile(
                fileHandle,             // hfile
```

Example 22-12. Using pointers in a C# program (continued)

```
                bytePointer + index,    // lpBuffer
                count,                  // nBytesToRead
                &bytesRead,             // nBytesRead
                0);                     // overlapped
    }
    return bytesRead;
}

    const uint GenericRead = 0x80000000;
    const uint OpenExisting = 3;
    const uint UseDefault = 0;
    int fileHandle;
}

class Test
{
    public static void Main( )
    {
        // create an instance of the APIFileReader,
        // pass in the name of an existing file
        APIFileReader fileReader =
          new APIFileReader("myTestFile.txt");

        // create a buffer and an ASCII coder
        const int BuffSize = 128;
        byte[] buffer = new byte[BuffSize];
        ASCIIEncoding asciiEncoder = new ASCIIEncoding( );

        // read the file into the buffer and display to console
        while (fileReader.Read(buffer, 0, BuffSize) != 0)
        {
            Console.Write("{0}", asciiEncoder.GetString(buffer));
        }
    }
}
```

The key section of code is shown in bold, where you create a pointer to the buffer and fix that buffer in memory using the fixed keyword. You need to use a pointer here because the API call demands it, though you've seen in Chapter 21 that all this can be done without the API call at all.

C# Keywords

abstract
A class modifier that specifies that the class must be derived from to be instantiated.

ListGlossTerm
A binary operator type that casts the left operand to the type specified by the right operand and that returns `null` rather than throwing an exception if the cast fails.

base
A variable with the same meaning as `this`, except it accesses a base class implementation of a member.

bool
A logical datatype that can be `true` or `false`.

break
A jump statement that exits a loop or `switch` statement block.

byte
A one-byte unsigned integral datatype.

case
A selection statement that defines a particular choice in a `switch` statement.

catch
The part of a `try` statement that catches exceptions of a specific type defined in the `catch` clause.

char
A two-byte Unicode character datatype.

checked
A statement or operator that enforces arithmetic bounds checking on an expression or statement block.

class
An extendable reference type that combines data and functionality into one unit.

const
A modifier for a local variable or field declaration that indicates the value is a constant. A `const` is evaluated at compile time and can only be a predefined type.

continue
A jump statement that skips the remaining statements in a statement block and continues to the next iteration in a loop.

decimal
A 16-byte precise decimal datatype.

default
A marker in a `switch` statement specifying the action to take when no `case` statements match the `switch` expression.

delegate
A type for defining a method signature so that delegate instances can hold and invoke a method or list of methods that match its signature.

do
A loop statement to iterate a statement block until an expression at the end of the loop evaluates to `false`.

double
An eight-byte floating-point datatype.

else
A conditional statement that defines the action to take when a preceding `if` expression evaluates to `false`.

enum

A value type that defines a group of named numeric constants.

event

A member modifier for a delegate field or property that indicates only the += and –= methods of the delegate can be accessed.

explicit

An operator that defines an explicit conversion.

extern

A method modifier that indicates the method is implemented with unmanaged code.

false

A Boolean literal.

finally

The part of a try statement that is always executed when control leaves the scope of the try block.

fixed

A statement to pin down a reference type so that the garbage collector won't move it during pointer arithmetic operations.

float

A four-byte floating-point datatype.

for

A loop statement that combines an initialization statement, stopping condition, and iterative statement into one statement.

foreach

A loop statement that iterates over collections that implement IEnumerable.

get

The name of the accessor that returns the value of a property.

goto

A jump statement that jumps to a label within the same method and same scope as the jump point.

if

A conditional statement that executes its statement block if its expression evaluates to true.

implicit

An operator that defines an implicit conversion.

in

The operator between a type and an IEnumerable in a foreach statement.

int

A four-byte signed integral datatype.

interface

A contract that specifies the members a class or struct can implement to receive generic services for that type.

internal

An access modifier that indicates a type or type member is accessible only to other types in the same assembly.

is

A relational operator that evaluates to true if the left operand's type matches, is derived from, or implements the type specified by the right operand.

lock

A statement that acquires a lock on a reference-type object to help multiple threads cooperate.

long

An eight-byte signed integral datatype.

namespace

Maps a set of types to a common name.

new

An operator that calls a constructor on a type, allocating a new object on the heap if the type is a reference type, or initializing the object if the type is a value type. The keyword is overloaded to hide an inherited member.

null

A reference-type literal that indicates no object is referenced.

object

The type all other types derive from.

operator

A method modifier that overloads operators.

out

A parameter modifier that specifies the parameter is passed by reference and must be assigned by the method being called.

override

A method modifier that indicates that a method of a class overrides a virtual method of a class or interface.

params

A parameter modifier that specifies that the last parameter of a method can accept multiple parameters of the same type.

private

An access modifier that indicates that only the containing type can access the member.

protected

An access modifier that indicates that only the containing type or derived types can access the member.

public

An access modifier that indicates that a type or type member is accessible to all other types.

readonly

A field modifier specifying that a field can be assigned only once, in either its declaration or its containing type's constructor.

ref

A parameter modifier that specifies that the parameter is passed by reference and is assigned before being passed to the method.

return

A jump statement that exits a method, specifying a return value when the method is nonvoid.

sbyte

A one-byte signed integral datatype.

sealed

A class modifier that indicates a class cannot be derived from.

set

The name of the accessor that sets the value of a property.

short

A two-byte signed integral datatype.

sizeof

An operator that returns the size in bytes of a struct.

stackalloc

An operator that returns a pointer to a specified number of value types allocated on the stack.

static

A type member modifier that indicates that the member applies to the type rather than an instance of the type.

string

A predefined reference type that represents an immutable sequence of Unicode characters.

struct

A value type that combines data and functionality in one unit.

switch

A selection statement that allows a selection of choices to be made based on the value of a predefined type.

this

A variable that references the current instance of a class or struct.

throw

A jump statement that throws an exception when an abnormal condition has occurred.

true

A Boolean literal.

try

A statement that provides a way to handle an exception or a premature exit in a statement block.

typeof

An operator that returns the type of an object as a System.Type object.

uint

A four-byte unsigned integral datatype.

ulong

An eight-byte unsigned integral datatype.

unchecked

A statement or operator that prevents arithmetic bounds from checking on an expression.

unsafe
> A method modifier or statement that permits pointer arithmetic to be performed within a particular block.

ushort
> A two-byte unsigned integral datatype.

using
> Specifies that types in a particular namespace can be referred to without requiring their fully qualified type names. The using statement defines a scope. At the end of the scope, the object is disposed.

value
> The name of the implicit variable set by the set accessor of a property.

virtual
> A class method modifier that indicates that a method can be overridden by a derived class.

void
> A keyword used in place of a type for methods that don't have a return value.

volatile
> Indicates that a field may be modified by the operating system or another thread.

while
> A loop statement to iterate a statement block until an expression at the start of each iteration evaluates to false.

Index

Symbols

++ (increment) operator, 56
{ } (braces), 47
    array elements, initializing, 167
    classes, defining, 64
    properties and behaviors, defining, 10
( ) (parentheses), 232
    methods, using, 11
[ ] (square brackets)
    declaring arrays, 162
    for indexing, 179, 213
        in strings, 225
    jagged arrays and, 172
&& (and) operator, 54
%= (assignment) operator, 52, 56
&= (assignment) operator, 56
*= (assignment) operator, 56
+= (assignment) operator, 52, 56
-= (assignment) operator, 52, 56
<<= (assignment) operator, 56
= (assignment) operator, 33, 49, 224
    precedence of, 55
>>= (assignment) operator, 56
^= (assignment) operator, 56
|= (assignment) operator, 56
\ (backslashes), using escape characters, 26, 218
: (colon), 232
    calling base class constructors, 100
" (double quotes), using escape characters, 26
== (equal to) relational operator, 37, 53, 119

conversion operators and, 123
    precedence of, 56
    strings, manipulating, 225
> (greater than) relational operator, 37, 53, 119
    precedence of, 56
< (less than) relational operator, 37, 53, 119
    precedence of, 56
& (logical AND) operator, 56
    as an address-of C++ operator, 605
^ (logical XOR) operator, 56
-> (member access) operator, 605
. (member access) operator, 13
    writing text to the monitor, 12
% (modulus) operator, 46
    precedence of, 56
    returning remainders, 50
* (multiplication) operator, 49
    as a dereference operator, 605
    operator precedence of, 55
!= (not equal) operator, 53, 56, 119
! (not) operator, 54
    precedence of, 56
*= operator, 52
+= operator, 288
    delegates, adding to multicast delegates with, 280
<< operator, 56
<= operator, 119
>= operator, 53, 119
>> operator, 56
~ operator, 56
|| (or) operator, 54

We'd like to hear your suggestions for improving our indexes. Send email to *index@oreilly.com*.

C

Property attribute target, 439
protected access modifier, 66, 611
proxies, 405
   creating, 412–416
public access modifier, 66, 101
public keys, 434
   tokens, 436
public keyword, 64
public properties
   AppDomain class, 481
   Arraylist, 194
   FileInfo class and, 531
   Hashtable, 211
   Queue, 205
   stacks, 207
   System.Array, 162
public static fields, for string class, 219
public static methods, 205
   ArrayList, 194
   Hashtable, 211
   stacks, 207
   System.Array, 162
   threads, suspending, 508
publishers, 283
   buttons, creating, 298
   decoupling from subscribers, 292
Pulse( ) method, using monitors, 519
Push( ) method, 207
   adding to or removing from stacks, 207

Q

query statement in SQL, 345
queues, 204–207

R

\r (carriage return escape character), 27
race conditions, synchronizing threads, 523
RAD (Rapid Application Development), 296, 384
RaisePostDataChangedEvent( ) method, 387
Rank property, 162
Rapid Application Development (RAD), 296, 384
RCW (Runtime Class Wrapper), 594
Read( ) method, 607
   binary files and, 537
   implementing an interface, 134
      explicit, 151
      overriding, 147–151
ReadFile( ) method, 605

ReadLine( ) method, working with text
   files, 541
ReadOnly( ) method, 194
readonly delegates, 273
readonly field modifiers, 93, 611
records for databases, 344, 366–382
   creating, 373–382
   deleting, 372
   updating, 370–372
rectangular arrays, 169–172
ref modifier, 611
reference types, 24, 71
   default values of, 69
   stacks and heaps, using, 25
ReferenceEquals( ) method, 111
reflection, 438, 445–478
   emit (see reflection emit)
   late binding and, 597–599
reflection emit, 455–478
   dynamic invocation, with, 471–478
Refresh( ) method, 527
Regasm tool, exporting .NET
   components, 599
regex, 233–235
   groups, 237–240
   match collections, using, 235
regexp, 233
#region preprocessor, 61
RegisterWellKnownServiceType( )
   method, 499
Registry window in Visual Studio .NET,
   making changes to, 341
regular expressions, 231–242
   regex, using, 233–235
RegularExpressions namespace, 235
RejectChanges( ) method, 367
relational databases, 343–347
relational operators, 53
Remote Deploy Wizard in Visual Studio
   .NET, 334
remoting, 479, 492–502
   server object types, 492
RemotingConfiguration class, 494
Remove( ) method
   ArrayList methods and, 194
   Hashtable methods and, 211
   string class and, 220
   StringBuilder methods and, 230
RemoveAt( ) method, 194
RemoveRange( ) method, 194
Repeat( ) method, 194
Replace( ) method, 230

Reset( ) method, 189
ResourceResolve event, 481
return statement, 36, 43, 611
ReturnValue attribute target, 439
Reverse( ) method, 162, 194
Root property, 527
Rows collection, 348
Run( ) method, 285, 560
    asynchronous I/O and, 545
Runtime Class Wrapper (RCW), 594

S

SaveViewState( ) method, 387
sbyte integral type, 24, 611
screen scraping, 569
sealed classes, 95, 110, 611
sealed structs, 128
security boundaries, 420
semicolons (;)
    abstract classes and, 107
    ending statements with, 35
Serializable attribute, 492
serialization, 569–578
    formatters, using, 570–575
    objects, creating a stream of data, 525
    working with, 571–575
servers
    building, 493–496
    interfaces, specifying, 492
    network streaming, creating, 550–552
    object types, 492
server-side support, 405
set( ) method, indexing, 179
set accessor, 93
set keyword, 611
SetAppDomainPolicy( ) method, 481
SetAttributes( ) method, 530
SetCreationTime( ) method, 526, 530
SetCurrentDirectory( ) method, 526
SetData( ) method, 481
SetLastAccessTime( ) method, 526, 530
SetLastError parameter, 602
SetLastWriteTime( ) method, 526, 530
SetRange( ) method, 194
Setup Project in Visual Studio .NET, 333,
    337
    building, 342
Setup Wizard in Visual Studio .NET, 334
SetValue( ) method, 162
Shape class, 485
shared assemblies, 431–437
    building, 435

DLL Hell and, 432
    versions, 433
short integral type, 611
short type, 24, 26
Side-by-side versioning, 433
signatures (digital), 434
signatures of methods, 87
signing the assembly, 434
Simple Object Access Protocol (SOAP), 405,
    485, 570
single quotes ('), using escape characters, 26
SingleCall, 498
single-call objects, 492
single-module assembly, 422
singleton objects, 492
sinks, 480
    marshaling with proxies, 484
sizeof operator, 611
    precedence of, 56
slash marks (//), using for comments, 11
    XML documentation, 331
Sleep public static method, 508
.sln files, 389
SOAP (Simple Object Access Protocol), 405,
    485, 570
SoapFormatter, 570
sockets, 548
    multiple connections, handling, 555
Solution Explorer in Visual Studio
    .NET, 335
Sort( ) method, 106, 162, 194
    copy button, implementing events, 320
    delegates and, 265
    IComparable, implementing, 197
    IComparer, implementing, 199
spaces (whitespace), 34
specialization of classes and objects, 95
Split( ) method, 220, 234
splitting strings, 228–230
SQL Server 2000, 4
SQL (Structured Query Language), 6, 395
    Managed Provider, 355
    relational databases and, 343–347
square brackets ([ ])
    declaring arrays, 162
    for indexing, 179, 213
        in strings, 225
    jagged arrays and, 172
Stack( ) method, adding or removing from
    stacks, 207
stackalloc operator, 611
    precedence of, 56

T

\t (horizontal tab escape character), 27, 51
tables, 344, 361–366
tabs (whitespace), 34
target object, 463
targets (attribute), 439
TcpClient class, 552
TCP/IP connections, 548
   streaming network client, creating, 552
ternary (?:) operator, 56
Tester class, 128
text editors, compiling programs with, 15
text files, working with, 541–543
text read, 537
TextReader class, 537
TextWriter class, 537
this keyword, 74, 611
Thread class, 286, 504
ThreadAbortException exception, 509
threads, 503–524
   creating, 504–507
   deadlocks, 523
   joining, 507
   killing, 508–512
   race conditions, 523
   suspending, 507
   synchronizing, 512–523
      Interlocked class, using, 516
      locks, using, 517
      monitors, using, 518–523
throw statement, 36, 244, 611
TlbImp.exe, importing the type library, 594
ToArray( ) method, 195, 205, 207
ToCharArray( ) method, 220
tokens (public key), 436
ToLower( ) method, 220
Toolbox window in Visual Studio .NET, 302
   Basic UI form, creating, 310
ToString( ) method, 111, 124, 219
   accessing array elements, 165
   delegates and, 265, 267
   structs, creating, 129
ToUpper( ) method, 220
TP (transparent proxy), 484
transient data, handling, 575–578
transparent proxy (TP), 484
TreeView controls, 311–314
   clear button event, handling, 317
   handling, 314–317
Trim( ) method, 220

TrimEnd( ) method, 220
TrimStart( ) method, 220
TrimToSize( ) method, 195
true keyword, 611
true values, 25, 44
   relational operators and, 53
try statement, 611
Turbo Pascal, 7
(T)x operator, 56
Type class, 494
type discovery, 446, 447
typeof (type retrieval) operator, 446, 611
   precedence of, 56
types, 9–15, 23–27
   creating new, 65
   libraries, 594, 601
   reflecting on, 446, 449–451

U

UI (user interface), 385
   design tools, 12
   forms, 309
      managing during Setup process, 341
uint integral type, 24, 611
ulong integral type, 25, 611
UML (Unified Modeling Language), 96
unboxing types, 112
unchecked (arithmetic check off)
      operator, 611
   precedence of, 56
unconditional branching statements, 35
Unicode characters, using char type, 26
Unified Modeling Language (UML), 96
Uniform Resource Identifier (URI), 567
Unload( ) method, 481
unsafe modifier, 612
URI (Uniform Resource Identifier), 496, 567
user interface (UI), 385
   design tools, 12
   forms, 309
      managing during Setup process, 341
user_defined types, 23
ushort type, 24, 26, 612
using keyword, 14, 81, 612
   identifiers, defining with, 59
using System statement, 14

V

\v (vertical tab escape character), 27
value keyword, 612

About the Author

Jesse Liberty is the author of a dozen books, including *Programming ASP.NET* from O'Reilly. Jesse is the president of Liberty Associates, Inc. (*http://www.LibertyAssociates.com*), where he provides .NET training, contract programming, and consulting. He is a former Vice President of electronic delivery for Citibank, and a former Distinguished Software Engineer and architect for AT&T, Ziff Davis, Xerox, and PBS.

Colophon

Our look is the result of reader comments, our own experimentation, and feedback from distribution channels. Distinctive covers complement our distinctive approach to technical topics, breathing personality and life into potentially dry subjects.

The animal on the cover of *Programming C#*, Second Edition is an African crowned crane. This tall, skinny bird wanders the marshes and grasslands of west and east Africa (the Western and Eastern African crowned cranes, *Balearica pavonina pavonina* and *Balearica regulorum gibbericeps*, respectively).

Adult birds stand about three feet tall and weigh six to nine pounds. Inside their long necks is a five-foot long windpipe—part of which is coiled inside their breastbone—giving voice to loud calls that can carry for miles. They live for about 22 years, spending most of their waking hours looking for the various plants, small animals, and insects they like to eat. (One crowned crane food-finding technique, perfected during the 38 to 54 million years these birds have existed, is to stamp their feet as they walk, flushing out tasty bugs.) They are the only type of crane to perch in trees, which they do at night when sleeping.

Social and talkative, African crowned cranes group together in pairs or families, and the smaller groups band together in flocks of more than 100 birds. Their elaborate mating dance has served as a model for some of the dances of local people.

Mary Brady was the production editor and proofreader for *Programming C#*, Second Edition. Claire Cloutier and Colleen Gorman provided quality control. Joe Wizda wrote the index.

Ellie Volckhausen designed the cover of this book, based on a series design by Edie Freedman. The cover image is an original engraving from the 19th century. Emma Colby produced the cover layout with QuarkXPress 4.1, using Adobe's ITC Garamond font.

David Futato designed the interior layout. Neil Walls prepared the files in FrameMaker 5.5.6 using tools created by Mike Sierra. The text font is Linotype Birka; the heading font is Adobe Myriad Condensed; and the code font is LucasFont's TheSans Mono Condensed. The illustrations that appear in the book were produced by Robert Romano and Jessamyn Read using Macromedia FreeHand 9 and Adobe Photoshop 6. The tip and warning icons were drawn by Christopher Bing. This colophon was written by Leanne Soymelez.